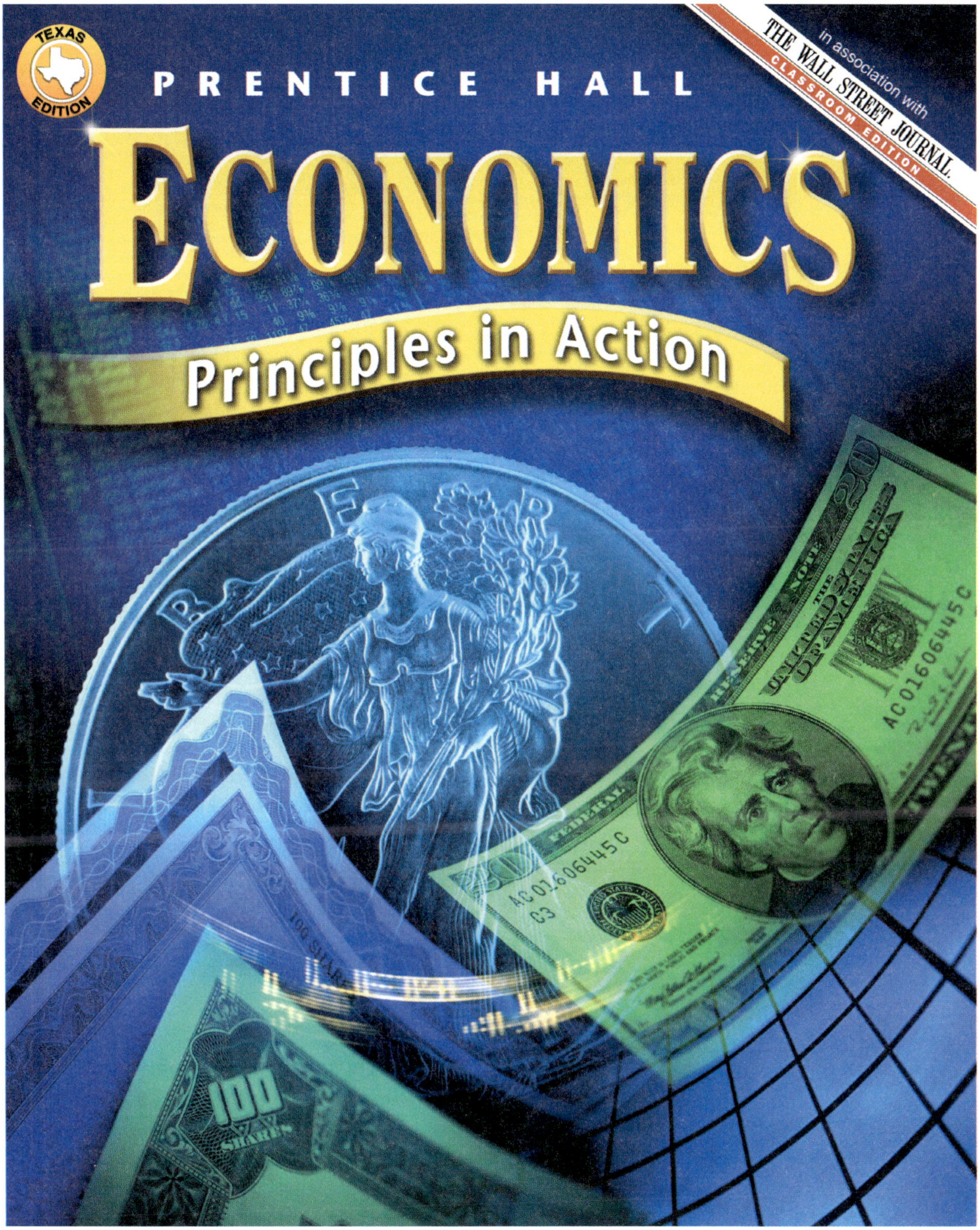

PRENTICE HALL

ECONOMICS
Principles in Action

in association with
THE WALL STREET JOURNAL
CLASSROOM EDITION

TEXAS EDITION

Arthur O'Sullivan • Steven M. Sheffrin

PEARSON
Prentice
Hall

Needham, Massachusetts
Upper Saddle River, New Jersey
Glenview, Illinois

About the Authors

Arthur O'Sullivan, Ph.D

Arthur O'Sullivan is a professor of economics at Lewis and Clark College in Portland, Oregon. After receiving his B.S. degree in economics at the University of Oregon, he spent two years in the Peace Corps, working with city planners in the Philippines. He received his Ph.D. degree in economics from Princeton University in 1981 and has taught at the University of California, Davis, and Oregon State University. He recently accepted an endowed professorship at Lewis and Clark College, where he teaches microeconomics and urban economics.

Steven M. Sheffrin, Ph.D

Steven M. Sheffrin is dean of the division of social sciences and professor of economics at the University of California, Davis. He received his B.A. from Wesleyan University and Ph.D. in economics from the Massachusetts Institute of Technology. He has been a visiting professor at Princeton University, Oxford University, and the London School of Economics and served as a financial economist with the Office of Tax Analysis of the United States Department of the Treasury. Professor Sheffrin is the author of numerous books and articles in the fields of macroeconomics, public finance, and international economics.

Texas Program Consultant

Sharon Pope has devoted her career to advancing social studies education in the state of Texas. A graduate of Rice University, with a master's degree from the University of St. Thomas, Sharon taught in both Spring Branch and Cypress Fairbanks districts, was a social studies supervisor in Spring Branch ISD, and served as president of TSSSA. She has worked with the authors, as well as with the members of the Texas Advisory Board (listed on facing page), to ensure that this book meets the needs of Texas educators.

THE WALL STREET JOURNAL.
CLASSROOM EDITION

The Wall Street Journal Classroom Edition is a supplemental educational program published since 1991 by Dow Jones and Company, publisher of *The Wall Street Journal.* The program is designed to improve the economic and business literacy of America's secondary-school students. The centerpiece of the program is a full-color student newspaper, published monthly from September to May. Regular features focus on business, economics, careers, entrepreneurship, technology, personal finance, and global interdependence. Articles are drawn directly from the pages of the daily *Wall Street Journal.*

PEARSON
Prentice
Hall

7 8 9 10   VO63   11
ISBN 0-13-063459-X

Program Reviewers

Academic Consultants

Jean Caldwell,
  Professor Emeritus
Department of Economics
University of Central
  Oklahoma
Edmond, Oklahoma

Adhip Chaudhuri
Department of Economics
Georgetown University
Washington, D.C.

W. Michael Cox
Senior Vice President and
  Chief Economist
Federal Reserve Bank of
  Dallas
Dallas, Texas

Suzanne Allen Gulledge
Associate Director
School of Education
University of North Carolina
Chapel Hill, North Carolina

Douglas Kinnear
Department of Economics
Colorado State University
Fort Collins, Colorado

Bonnie T. Meszaros
Center for Economic
  Education and
  Entrepreneurship
University of Delaware
Newark, Delaware

David Ramsour
President, Texas Council on
  Economic Education
Houston, Texas

Robert Smith
Director of Special Projects
Texas Council on Economic
  Education
Houston, Texas

Patricia D. Taylor
Senior Instructor
Colorado State University
Fort Collins, Colorado

Texas Advisory Board

Odette Alexander
Texas History, 8th Grade
  U.S. History
Fort Bend, ISD
Houston, Texas

John Arevalo
AP U.S. History, World
  History
Harlandale ISD
San Antonio, Texas

Betty Barringer
Texas History, 8th Grade
  U.S. History
Dallas, ISD
Dallas, Texas

Rebecca A. Corley
Texas History, World
  Geography
Lubbock ISD
Lubbock, Texas

Evaliza Fuentes
8th Grade U.S. History
Brownsville ISD
Brownsville, Texas

Taddie Hamilton
Economics, American
  Government
Hurst-Euless-Bedford ISD
Euless, Texas

Sherry Henderson
World Geography
Spring Branch ISD
Houston, Texas

Mary Lee Karl
6th Grade Social Studies
El Paso ISD
El Paso, Texas

Dr. James Kracht
Professor, Dept. of Geography
Associate Dean, College of
  Education
Texas A & M University
College Station, Texas

Marilyn Kretzer
8th Grade, High School
  U.S. History
Houston ISD
Houston, Texas

Lotty Repp-Casillas
American Government, U.S.
  History
Dallas ISD
Dallas, Texas

General Scott
World History, U.S. History
Houston ISD
Houston, Texas

Kelly Taylor
American Government, U.S.
  History
North East ISD
San Antonio, Texas

Mick West
K-12 Social Studies
  Supervisor
McAllen ISD
McAllen, Texas

Bruce Wright
American Government
Liberty ISD
Liberty, Texas

Teacher Reviewers

John Beacom
Redwood High School
Visalia, California

DiAnn Fernandez
Pasadena ISD
Houston, Texas

Linda Tate Hudson
Central High School Magnet
  Career Academy
Louisville, Kentucky

Dan Richardson
East Troy Community Schools
East Troy, Wisconsin

Stuart Rubin
Bellmore-Merrick C.H.S.D.
Bellmore, New York

Denny Schillings
Homewood-Flossmoor
  High School
Flossmoor, Illinois

John T. Wende
Bowie High School
Austin, Texas

Content Area Reading Specialist

Dr. Lois E. Huffman
North Carolina State
  University
Raleigh, North Carolina

Block Scheduling Consultants

Sharon Dragon
Nimitz High School
Houston, Texas

Barbara Slater Stern
Assistant Professor
James Madison University
Harrisonburg, Virginia

Internet Reviewer

Vincent M. Seeley
Greenville High School
Greenville, New York

Personal Finance Handbook Reviewers

Rosella Bannister
Jump$tart Coalition
  for Personal Financial
  Literacy
Washington, D.C.

John E. Clow,
  Professor Emeritus
Economics and Business
  Dept.
State University of
  New York at Oneonta
Oneonta, New York

Curriculum and Assessment Specialist

Jan Moberley
Dallas, Texas

Program Advisors

Pat Easterbrook
Social Studies Consultant
Cary, North Carolina

Michal Howden
Social Studies Consultant
Zionsville, Indiana

Kathy Lewis
Social Studies Consultant
Fort Worth, Texas

Rick Moulden
Social Studies Consultant
Federal Way, Washington

Joe Wieczorek
Social Studies Consultant
Baltimore, Maryland

Contents

iv

Unit 3 Business and Labor 182

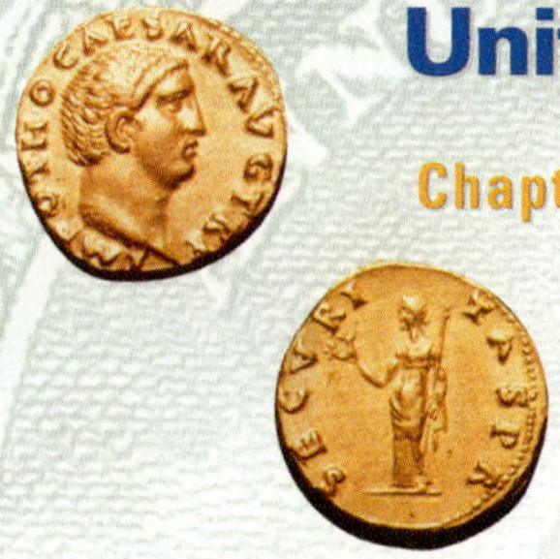

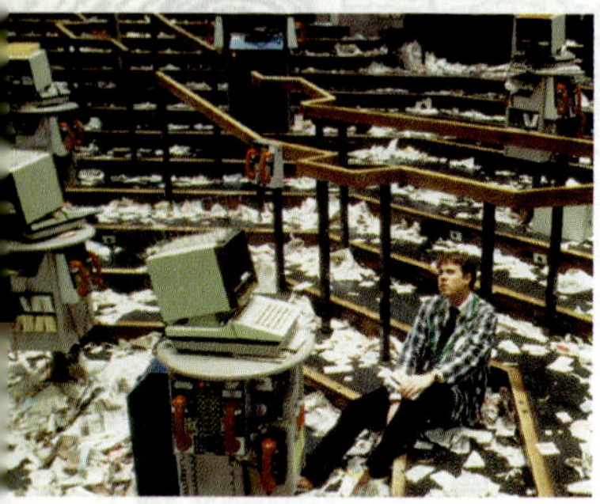

Unit 7 The Global Economy 438

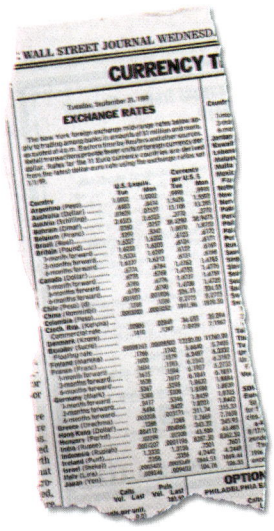

Reference Section

Special Features

Skills for LIFE
Step-by-step lessons to learn and practice important skills

Real-life Case Study
Case Studies show how economic concepts apply to everyday life

Economic Profiles
Biographies of influential and successful economists and entrepreneurs

THE WALL STREET JOURNAL.

CLASSROOM EDITION

In the News

Brief news items from *The Wall Street Journal Classroom Edition* illustrate economic principles in action

DEBATING CURRENT ISSUES

Excerpts from *Wall Street Journal Classroom Edition* articles provide background for classroom debates on important economic issues

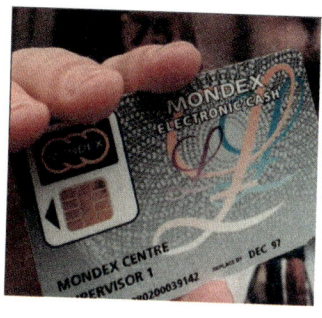

Economics Simulation

Hands-on experiments to help you understand key economic concepts

Global Connections

Explore economic principles at work in today's changing global economy

Graphs, Charts, and Tables

More than 250 graphs, charts, and tables to help you visualize key economic concepts

Chapter 1

Chapter 2

Chapter 3

Chapter 4

Graphs, Charts, and Tables (continued)

Graphs, Charts, and Tables (continued)

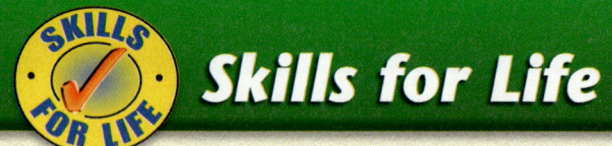

Skills for Life

What are the keys to social studies success?

In every social studies course, you will need to know how to use the following 20 core skills. Building these skills year by year will make you a stronger student.

Read through this list of skills and their definitions. Which ones do you know well? Which ones do you need to strengthen? Beside each definition, the page where you can find help in developing that skill is listed.

Skill	Definition	Example
GEOGRAPHIC LITERACY		
1. Using the Cartographer's Tools	The ability to use the • compass rose to find directions and relative location. • scale to estimate distance. • latitude and longitude grid to determine exact location. • key, or legend, to understand map symbols and colors.	p. 476
2. Using Special-Purpose Maps	The ability to analyze and interpret maps of • natural features, such as elevation and climate. • features made by people, such as land use, roads, countries, population density, and battles.	p. 455
VISUAL ANALYZING		
3. Analyzing Graphic Data	The ability to read and interpret numeric information represented in • bar graphs. • line graphs. • circle graphs.	p. 12
4. Analyzing Images	The ability to identify and interpret symbols, tone, and message in • paintings and drawings. • photos. • posters and political cartoons.	p. 155
CRITICAL THINKING AND READING		
5. Identifying Main Ideas/ Summarizing	Identifying the main idea is the ability to distinguish the general idea of a passage from its supporting details. Summarizing is the ability to combine main ideas into an overview.	p. 434
6. Sequencing	The ability to organize items in order according to time, size, or priority.	p. 45
7. Identifying Cause and Effect/ Making Predictions	Identifying cause and effect is the ability to understand how an action or event leads to a result. Making predictions is the ability to use cause-and-effect understanding to determine the likely outcome of subsequent events or actions.	p. 132

Skill	Definition	Example
8. Drawing Inferences and Conclusions	Drawing inferences is the ability to determine the necessary consequences of an assumption: if this is true, that must be true. Drawing conclusions is the ability to analyze several inferences to make a reasoned judgment.	p. 21
9. Making Valid Generalizations	The ability to apply conclusions from specific circumstances to larger circumstances while maintaining accuracy.	p. 235
10. Distinguishing Fact and Opinion	The ability to separate those statements that can be proven to be true from those that reflect a personal viewpoint.	p. 364
11. Comparing and Contrasting	The ability to identify how different ideas, objects, historical figures, or situations are alike and/or different.	p. 207
12. Analyzing Primary Sources	The ability to evaluate a firsthand account for accuracy, tone, viewpoint, and frame of reference.	p. 61
13. Recognizing Bias and Propaganda	The ability to identify a stated or unstated viewpoint or slant that is designed to promote one set of beliefs over another.	p. 419
14. Identifying Frame of Reference and Point of View	The ability to identify an opinion expressed in writing or visual art and to understand the influences that shaped the writer's or artist's position.	p. 477
15. Decision Making	The ability to state a question clearly, identify and evaluate possible choices, and select the option that seems to produce the best outcome.	p. 264
16. Problem Solving	The ability to state a problem clearly, identify possible solutions, determine the likely outcome of each, select an option, and then evaluate its effectiveness.	p. 18

COMMUNICATIONS

Skill	Definition	Example
17. Using Reliable Information	The ability to locate and apply information for a variety of purposes that has been evaluated for its accuracy, age, authority, and bias.	p. 194
18. Transferring Information From One Medium to Another	The ability to translate numerical or visual information into text and to translate written information into graphs, tables, or diagrams.	p. 448
19. Synthesizing Information	The ability to analyze and combine information from several sources to draw conclusions and/or to create a new presentation of information.	p. 47
20. Supporting a Position	The ability to present evidence or reasoning that defends a given opinion or statement.	p. 180–181

UNIT 1

Introduction to Economics

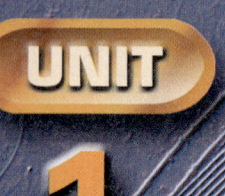

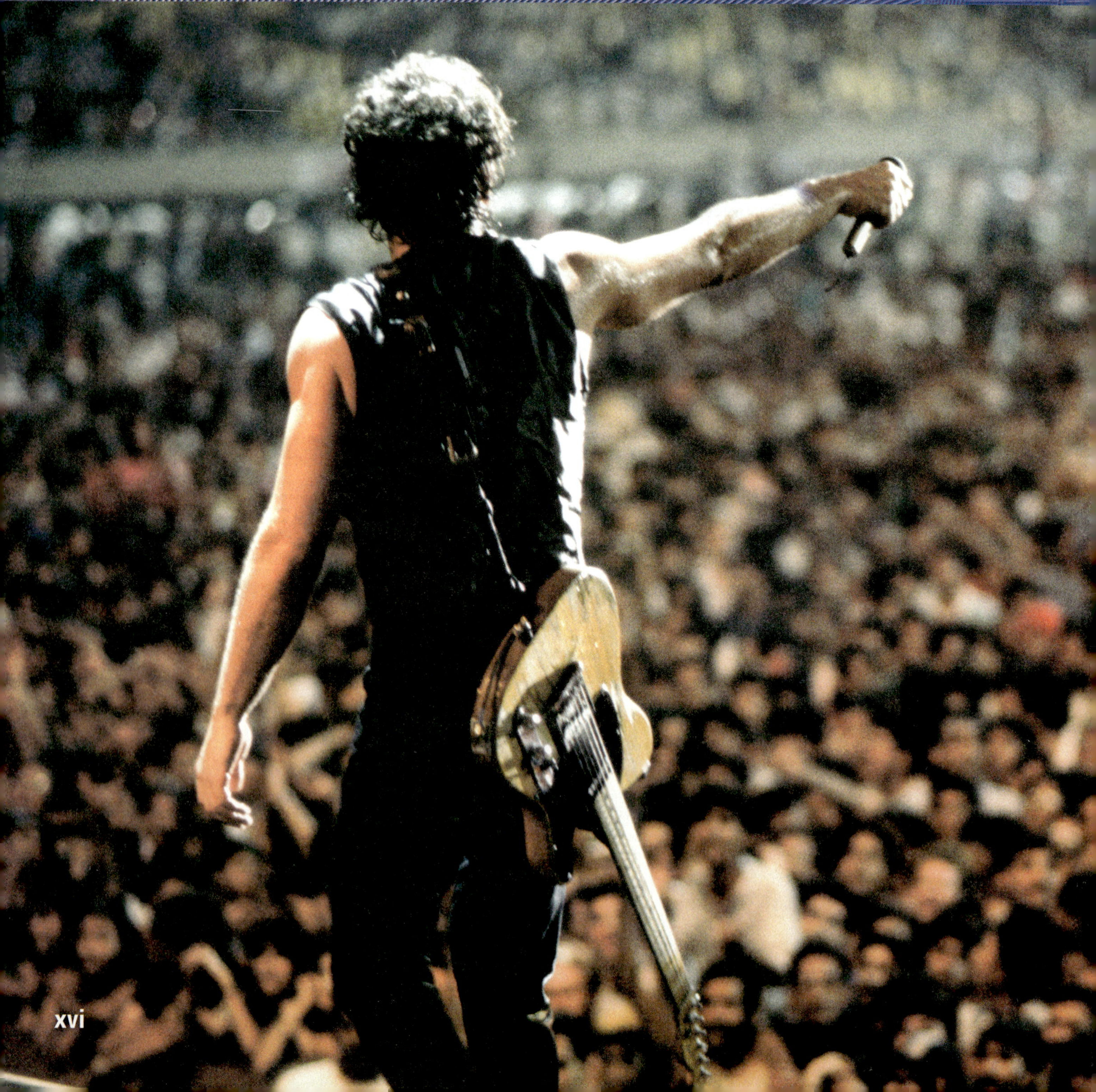

You have to *make a decision . . .*

Your favorite band is giving a concert in town, and you really want to go! The tickets are expensive though, and there are so many things you could do with that money. You could buy a concert ticket or . . .

- Use the money to see five movies
- Use the money to buy the band's new CD plus a pair of jeans
- Save the money for your vacation

The choice you will make is rooted in economics. At its core, economics is the study of how people choose to use their limited resources. In this unit you'll read more about the tools that economics offers to help you make decisions as a buyer, seller, worker, and citizen.

Focus Activity

When you hear the word *economics,* what are the first ten words that you think of? Compare your list with those of your classmates. Do the words on your lists fall into any obvious categories?

Chapter 1 What Is Economics?

Which CD to buy? How many hours to study? Which movie to see? If you're like most people, you constantly face decisions because you don't have enough time and money to do everything. At its most basic level, economics is the study of how people make choices when they face a limited supply of resources. In this chapter you will begin your study of economics by investigating two basic economic ideas: scarcity and trade-offs.

Economics Journal

Quickly jot down three decisions you made within the last 24 hours. For each decision, list two choices you decided against when you made the decision.

Keep It Current

Items marked with this logo are periodically updated on the Internet. Keep up-to-date with what's in the news. To get current information that answers the question "What is economics?" go to **www.phschool.com**

Scarcity and the Factors of Production

Preview

Objectives

After studying this section you will be able to:

1. **Explain** why scarcity and choice are basic problems of economics.
2. **Identify** land, labor, and capital as the three factors of production, and identify the two types of capital.
3. **Explain** the role of entrepreneurs.
4. **Explain** why economists say all resources are scarce.

Section Focus

People, businesses, and governments must choose among limited or scarce resources. Economics describes how people seek to satisfy their needs and wants by choosing among many alternatives.

Key Terms

need
want
economics
goods
services
scarcity
shortage
factors of production

land
labor
capital
physical capital
human capital
entrepreneur

As you begin your study of economics, consider three scenes: In the first scene, members of a household work together to do the laundry, purchase groceries, make meals, earn money, decide how to spend their money, and decide who gets to hold the TV remote.

In the second scene, the leaders of a large corporation sit at a table for their monthly meeting. They discuss whether to add a new product to their product line and advertising options on television and the Internet.

In the third scene, senators in the United States Congress gather to debate the important issues of the day: How can we ensure that people are well fed and have access to health care? What limits should the government place on businesses and international trade? Who gets to control the Internet? Economists look at the decisions made in each of these scenes and study those decisions in greater detail.

Scarcity and Choice

The study of economics begins with the idea that people cannot have everything they **need** and **want**. A need is something like air, food, or shelter that is necessary for survival. A want is an item that we desire but that is not essential to survival. Because people cannot have everything they need or want, they must consider their options and decide which choice will fill their needs best.

To look at the world economically, we can focus on the decisions that people make. You, for example, have to decide what to do with your time—go to a movie or study for a test. Businesses have to decide how many people to employ and how much to produce. A city government may have to decide whether to spend its budget to build a school or a park.

Economics is the study of how people seek to satisfy their needs and wants by making choices. Because people act individually, in groups (such as businesses), and through governments, economists study each of these groups. But why must people make such choices? The reason is scarcity.

Scarcity

Living in a relatively wealthy country, many Americans may find it hard to understand the idea of scarcity. Store shelves brim with goods. **Goods** are physical objects such as shoes and shirts. We have access to countless services. **Services** are actions or activities that one person performs for another. Haircuts, dental checkups, and tutoring are

need *something like air, food, or shelter that is necessary for survival*

want *an item that we desire but that is not essential to survival*

economics *the study of how people seek to satisfy their needs and wants by making choices*

goods *physical objects such as clothes or shoes*

services *actions or activities that one person performs for another*

scarcity *limited quantities of resources to meet unlimited wants*

shortage *a situation in which a good or service is unavailable*

factors of production *land, labor, and capital; the three groups of resources that are used to make all goods and services*

land *natural resources that are used to make goods and services*

labor *the effort that people devote to a task for which they are paid*

capital *any human-made resource that is used to create other goods and services*

physical capital *all human-made goods that are used to produce other goods and services; tools and buildings*

all services. Indeed, we see ads everywhere urging us to purchase goods and services. Yet scarcity exists in all places, at all times.

Defining Scarcity

All of the goods and services we produce are scarce. **Scarcity** implies limited quantities of resources to meet unlimited wants. While one person might be able to buy hundreds of basketballs or pencils or pianos, no one can have an endless supply of everything. Sooner or later, a limit is always reached. At its core, economics is about solving the problem of scarcity.

Scarcity Versus Shortages

Scarcity is not the same as a **shortage**. A shortage occurs when producers will not or cannot offer goods or services at the current prices. Shortages can be temporary or long-term. During the holiday season, a customer may see an empty shelf on Tuesday, but return on Friday to find that same shelf filled to overflowing. Wars and droughts can also create shortages that last for many years.

Scarcity, in contrast, always exists because our needs and wants are always greater than our resource supply. Goods and services are scarce because they are all made from resources that are scarce.

Land

Economists call the resources that are used to make all goods and services the **factors of production**, or factor resources. The factors of production are land, labor, and capital.

Economists use the term **land** to refer to all natural resources used to produce goods and services. Natural resources are materials found in nature. They include fertile land for farming and products that are in or on the land, such as coal, water, and forests.

Labor

Another factor of production is **labor**. Labor is the effort that a person devotes to a task for which that person is paid. Labor includes the medical aid provided by a doctor and the tightening of a clamp by an assembly line worker. It is an artist's creation of a painting or the repair of a television.

Capital

Capital is any human-made resource that is used to produce other goods and services. The two categories of capital are physical capital and human capital.

Physical Capital

Human-made objects used to create other goods and services are called **physical capital**. (The term *capital goods* is a synonym for *physical capital*.) Physical capital includes buildings and tools. A shoe factory building and all of the sewing machines and other specialized machinery for making shoes make up part of the shoe company's physical capital.

Physical capital is an important factor of production because it can save people and companies a great deal of time and money. A building is physical capital because it helps workers do their work by providing protection and space. Similarly, tools such as tractors, conveyor belts, and pencils are physical capital because they, too, help workers produce a good or a service.

When we create or buy physical capital to accomplish a job, we usually become more productive. Suppose that your family of 6

▲ While people's needs and wants are unlimited, the resources available to meet those wants are limited, or scarce. **Which scarce resources were used to produce the fruits and vegetables shown here?**

Figure 1.1 The Factors of Production

Land
All of the natural resources that are used to produce goods and services

Labor
Any effort a person devotes to a task for which that person is paid

Capital
Any human-made resource that is used to create other goods and services

Entrepreneur
A person who assembles the factors of production to create new goods and services

Goods and Services

BUILDING KEY CONCEPTS

Land, labor, and capital, also known as the factors of production, are the "inputs," or resources, used to create all goods and services.
Entrepreneurs What role do entrepreneurs play in producing goods and services?

---

people washes dishes by hand every day after every meal—breakfast, lunch, and dinner—for a total of 21 meals per week. It takes 30 minutes per meal for 2 family members working together to scrape, stack, wash, rinse, dry, and put away the dishes. That's 21 hours per week that could have been spent on other more productive activities.

Now, suppose that your family decides to buy a dishwasher that costs $400. Using the dishwasher, it will take 15 minutes for a single family member to clean up after each meal. At this rate, it will take the entire family only $5\frac{1}{4}$ hours per week to handle this chore. The benefits that your family reaps from the free time will cover the cost of the new dishwasher, which provides the typical benefits of physical capital:

1. Extra time Your family no longer has to spend 21 hours per week doing the dishes. Instead, the family gains $15\frac{3}{4}$ hours each week to use for other activities.

2. More knowledge By learning how to wash the dishes by machine, family members learn more about using household appliances in general. They can apply that knowledge to the use of other labor-saving devices, such as washing machines, dryers, and microwaves.

3. More productivity Because family members now have extra time and extra knowledge, they can use their resources and labor to do additional chores or other activities that are beneficial to the family.

Human Capital

In addition to producing physical capital, people can invest in themselves. **Human capital** is the knowledge and skills a worker gains through education and experience.

An economy requires both physical and human capital to produce goods and services. Doctors use stethoscopes and their medical school training to provide their services. Assembly-line workers use equipment and skills acquired through training and practice to produce goods.

human capital *the skills and knowledge gained by a worker through education and experience*

entrepreneur
ambitious leader who combines land, labor, and capital to create and market new goods and services

Entrepreneurs

If land, labor, and capital are the essential ingredients for creating all goods and services, who pulls these resources together? The answer is entrepreneurs. **Entrepreneurs** are ambitious leaders who decide how to combine land, labor, and capital resources to create new goods and services. They are the individuals who take risks to develop original ideas, start businesses, create new industries, and fuel economic growth.

You need not be Bill Gates of Microsoft or Henry Ford to be considered an entrepreneur. An individual who opens a corner food store and transforms it into a 10-store supermarket chain is an entrepreneur.

Scarce Resources

Economists say that all goods and services are scarce because the land, labor, and capital used to create them are scarce. Consider French fries. A typical portion of French fries started as a potato in a field in Idaho. Seven and one-half gallons of water irrigated the half-foot plot where the potato grew. Nurtured with fertilizers and protected by pesticides, the potato was harvested, processed, frozen, and then transported to Seattle. In Seattle, it was fried in corn oil from Nebraska, sprinkled with salt from Louisiana, and eaten in a restaurant.

All of the economic resources, or factors of production, that were used to create the French fries are scarce. First, the quantity of the land and water available for growing potatoes is limited. Second, the labor available to grow the crop and to process and transport the potatoes is limited by the size, time, age, and energy of a population. Finally, because land and labor are limited, the amount of physical capital available to create the French fries, such as farm equipment, is also limited.

While we have been talking about French fries, we could easily have been talking about a pair of blue jeans or a new space shuttle. No matter what good or service we were to look at, we would discover that the supplies of land, labor, and capital used to produce it are scarce, and that each resource has many alternative uses.

Section 1 Assessment

Key Terms and Main Ideas

1. What is the difference between a **good** and a **service?**
2. Why is the idea of **scarcity** a starting point for thinking economically?
3. How is **scarcity** different from **shortages?**
4. Describe the three **factors of production**.
5. What special advantages does **physical capital** offer?
6. What role do **entrepreneurs** play in the economy?

Applying Economic Concepts

7. *Critical Thinking* Why might an economist look at hundreds of cars moving along an assembly line and say, "There is an example of scarcity"?

8. *Decision Making* Which factor of production is represented by each of the following? **(a)** an office building **(b)** an assembly line worker **(c)** a tree used to make paper **(d)** unused soil **(e)** an artist **(f)** a student

9. *Try This* Leaving class today, you decide to start an economics tutoring business. Your first step is to get the two categories of capital. Next you need to obtain the other factors of production. Specifically, what do you need in terms of land, labor, and capital?

10. *Critical Thinking* Do you agree or disagree with the following statement? *Creating capital is like depositing money in a savings account. You save now in order to have more in the future.*

Take It to the NET

Read about the patents of some potential entrepreneurs, and then write or draw a summary of one of the patent ideas. Use the links provided in the Social Studies area at the following Web site for help in completing this activity. **www.phschool.com**

Profile

Gary Becker (b. 1930)

Nobel Prize-winning economist Gary Becker looks at daily life and sees economics at work in all we do. Becker even sees marriage as an economic decision that many people make based on opportunity costs. To understand how Becker arrived at this intriguing conclusion, you have to look at how he came to see the world.

Economics and Social Issues

Like many high school seniors, Becker knew what he was good at—mathematics—but wanted some practical way to apply it. Leaving his small Pennsylvania hometown, Becker went to Princeton University and decided to pursue economics. But he lost interest in the subject because it didn't "deal with important social problems."

Becker briefly considered a degree in sociology, but found the subject "too difficult." Later, as a graduate student at the University of Chicago, he realized that economics could indeed help answer social questions. His first book, based on his studies at Chicago, was an economic analysis of racial discrimination.

"It started me down the path of applying economics to social issues," states Becker, "a path that I have continued to follow." In 1992, that path led to the Nobel Prize in economics, which Becker received for using economic analysis to study a wide range of human behavior. "Economy is the art of making the most of life," he says.

Economics and Personal Decisions

Becker maintains that economics guides even life's most personal decisions. He sees the process of dating as part of a "marriage market." Most people do not marry the first prospect they meet, he notes. The opportunity cost of such a marriage would be high because better prospects are likely to exist. Instead, people try to search for better prospects.

Considering Costs and Benefits

An extended search for a mate, however, consumes time, effort, and other resources. It involves expenditures on personal appearance, in social situations, for education, and for other things that help attract a mate. A person decides to marry, Becker says, when the cost of searching exceeds the possible benefits of finding a better mate.

People measure the benefits of a potential spouse by criteria such as job, appearance, education, and family, Becker says, and they try to judge other traits by these factors. For example, the probability that a person is honest and good-natured may be judged by looking at the person's family. Intelligence is gauged by the person's education. Becker maintains that this process causes people to marry on the basis of imperfect information. Not until later do they truly learn about their partner's personality and compatibility, qualities that take longer to assess.

CHECK FOR UNDERSTANDING

1. Source Reading Interpret the following passage from an article by Becker that appeared in *BusinessWeek:* "Human capital is as much a part of the wealth of nations as are factories, housing, machinery, and other physical capital."

2. Critical Thinking How does what you've read in this introductory chapter on economics support or conflict with Becker's idea that "economy is the art of making the most of life"?

3. Decision Making Do you agree or disagree with Becker's idea that economics guides even life's most personal decisions? Support your position with two or three examples of your own.

Preview

Objectives

After studying this section you will be able to:

1. **Describe** why every decision involves trade-offs.

2. **Explain** the concept of opportunity cost.

3. **Explain** how people make decisions by thinking at the margin.

Section Focus

All human decisions involve trade-offs. The next best alternative to any choice is called an opportunity cost. Decision-making grids can make it easier to identify the trade-offs and opportunity cost of a decision.

Key Terms

trade-off
guns or butter
opportunity cost
thinking at the margin

trade-off *an alternative that we sacrifice when we make a decision*

guns or butter *a phrase that refers to the trade-offs that nations face when choosing whether to produce more or less military or consumer goods*

Several years ago, a few hotels in Washington, D.C., offered a special service to their guests. A popular art exhibit was in town, but the only way to get tickets was to wait in line for several hours. Many of the hotel's guests were unable or unwilling to do this. Instead, the hotels hired people to stand in line to purchase the $5 tickets. The hotels then sold the tickets to guests for $50 apiece. These guests spent money rather than time in order to get their exhibit tickets. Similarly, when we decide on one alternative, we gain one thing but lose something else.

Trade-Offs

Economists point out that all individuals, businesses, and large groups of people—even governments—make decisions that involve **trade-offs**. Trade-offs are all the alternatives that we give up whenever we choose one course of action over another.

Individuals and Trade-Offs

Every decision we make involves trade-offs. For example, if you choose to spend more time at work, you give up watching a movie or going to a baseball game. Choosing to play soccer might prevent you from working on the yearbook or having a part-time job.

Businesses and Trade-Offs

The decisions that businesspeople make about how to use land, labor, and capital resources also create trade-offs. Farmers who plant broccoli cannot use the same land at the same time to grow cauliflower. A manufacturer who decides to use all her equipment to build chairs eliminates the possibility of building tables or desks at that same time.

Society and Trade-Offs

Countries also make decisions that involve trade-offs. Economists simplify their explanations of the trade-offs countries face by using the example of **guns or butter.** In short, a country that decides to produce more military goods ("guns") has fewer resources to devote to consumer goods ("butter") and vice versa. (Remember, resources are limited!) The steel used to make a tank is no longer available for building the dairy equipment needed to make butter.

What are some of the trade-offs of buying a car? ▼

Because decisions are not always as clear-cut as the one in this cartoon, economists encourage us to consider the trade-offs and opportunity cost of a decision before we make it.

Defining Opportunity Cost

Whenever individuals, businesses, or governments decide on a course of action, they face many trade-offs. One alternative, though, is usually more desirable than all the others. The most desirable alternative given up as the result of a decision is called the **opportunity cost**.

If a family buys a computer, family members cannot use the same money to pay for their second choice, going on a trip. The trip, then, is the opportunity cost of buying the computer. The farmer who chose to grow broccoli instead of cauliflower experienced the opportunity cost of planting cauliflower. If a government decides to produce more "guns," then having less "butter" is the opportunity cost.

Similarly, every ordinary decision that we make every day involves an opportunity cost. For each of the following choices, which alternative would you choose?

- Sleep late or wake up early for a ski trip?
- Sleep late or wake up early to eat your breakfast?
- Sleep late or wake up early to study for a test?

Most likely, you did not choose "sleep late" for all three decisions. Your decision depended on the specific opportunity cost—whatever you were willing to sacrifice.

Using a Decision-Making Grid

At times, a decision's opportunity cost may be unclear or complicated. Using a decision-making grid like the one in Figure 1.2 can help you determine whether you are willing

to accept the opportunity cost of a choice you are about to make. In this particular grid, Karen is trying to decide whether to sleep late or get up early to study for a test. Karen likes to sleep. Getting up early is tough. However, getting up early to study would probably improve her test score.

Karen knows that she is choosing between her two top alternatives: sleeping late and waking up early to study. Because of scarcity, she cannot do both. The time can only be occupied in one way.

To help her decide, Karen lists the benefits of each alternative on the grid. Waking up early to study will probably result in a better grade. Also, she will receive teacher and parental approval and experience the personal satisfaction that comes with doing well on a test. However, she knows she would enjoy sleeping later and that the extra sleep would give her more energy during the day.

opportunity cost *the most desirable alternative given up as the result of a decision*

Global Connections

Global Trade-Offs The same decision made in two different countries can have vastly different opportunity costs. Malaysia bought two warships in 1992, paying a price equal to the cost of providing safe drinking water for the 5 million Malaysians lacking it. In other words, the opportunity cost of the warships was safe drinking water for 5 million people. The opportunity cost of building warships in wealthier countries is not nearly so high. However, there are still costs to consider. In the United States, the number of people employed by the military decreased dramatically following the end of the cold war. In response, the Pentagon developed a new program, "Troops to Teachers," to help former soldiers get jobs teaching in schools. The switch from army duty to teaching reminds us that the opportunity cost of a soldier may be a teacher and vice versa. **Why does the opportunity cost of a decision vary from one situation to another?**

Figure 1.2 Karen's Decision-Making Grid

	Alternatives	
	Sleep late	**Wake up early to study**
Benefits	• Enjoy more sleep • Have more energy during the day	• Better grade on test • Teacher and parental approval • Personal satisfaction
Decision	Sleep late	Wake up early to study for test
Opportunity cost	Extra study time	Extra sleep time
Benefits forgone	• Better grade on test • Teacher and parental approval • Personal satisfaction	• Enjoy more sleep • Have more energy during the day

Using a decision-making grid can help us see what we gain and lose when we have to choose between alternatives.

Opportunity Cost What benefits will Karen forgo if she chooses to sleep later?

---

thinking at the margin
deciding whether to do or use one additional unit of some resource

Making the Decision

Karen is a practical person. After considering the opportunity cost, she decides that waking up early to study offers the most desirable benefits. She is willing to accept the opportunity cost: extra sleep time. She knows that she is giving up the benefits of sleeping late, namely the pleasure of more sleep and the extra energy it provides.

Karen might have made a different decision when choosing between sleeping and breakfast or sleeping and getting up early to study on a Saturday. With each new situation, the opportunity costs and benefits change.

We always face an opportunity cost, though. When we select one alternative, we have to sacrifice at least one alternative and forgo its benefits. By recognizing what we are sacrificing, we can decide whether the decision is worth it. An economist might say, "Choosing is refusing."

Thinking at the Margin

When economists look at decisions, they point out one more characteristic in addition to opportunity cost. Many decisions involve adding one unit or subtracting one unit, such as one minute or one dollar. From an economist's point of view, when you decide how much more or less to do, you are **thinking at the margin**.

To understand what it means to think at the margin, you might picture a piece of paper with a line drawn down the left side. That line separates the space used for writing from extra space on the paper. You could use some of that extra space or you could leave it blank. Similarly, thinking at the margin means you are thinking about using one additional unit.

Making a Decision at the Margin

When deciding whether or not to study, Karen used the "all or nothing" approach as shown in Figure 1.2. She was either going to wake up early to study or sleep late and not study at all that morning.

In reality, Karen could have decided from among several options rather than just two. She could have decided to get up one, two, or three hours earlier to study or to sleep instead. She could have made her decision by looking specifically at how many extra hours to study that morning. Making a decision about each extra hour would mean that she was thinking at the margin.

To make a decision at the margin, Karen should look at the opportunity cost of each extra hour of studying and compare it to the benefit. In Figure 1.3, we can see that one hour of studying means an opportunity cost of an hour of sleep and a benefit of probably passing the test with a C. Two hours of studying "cost" two hours of sleep and perhaps getting a B. Three hours of studying mean sacrificing three hours of sleep and probably getting only a slightly higher grade of B+.

What should Karen decide? At three hours, the cost is no longer worth the benefit to Karen because her grade will improve only slightly. Thus, Karen decides to awaken two hours earlier.

Cost and Benefit at the Margin

Comparing opportunity costs and benefits at the margin enabled Karen to decide how many hours to study. Likewise, such a comparison could help someone decide how much money to spend on a car, how many hours to work, and how much time to spend watching television. Employers think at the margin when they decide how many extra workers to hire. Legislators think at the margin when deciding if a government program should include more or less of a particular benefit.

Deciding by thinking at the margin is just like making any other decision. Decision makers just have to compare the opportunity costs and the benefits—what they will sacrifice and what they will gain. Once the opportunity cost outweighs the benefits, then no more units should be added.

Figure 1.3 Decision Making at the Margin

Options	Benefit	Opportunity cost
1st hour of extra study time	Grade of C on test	One hour of sleep
2nd hour of extra study time	Grade of B on test	2 hours of sleep
3rd hour of extra study time	Grade of B+ on test	3 hours of sleep

This person has to decide how many extra hours to study. By comparing the opportunity cost to the benefit of each extra hour, she can decide how much is the right amount. **Opportunity Cost At what point is this person paying an added cost with little extra benefit?**

Section 2 Assessment

Key Terms and Main Ideas

1. Present three examples that illustrate how all decisions involve **trade-offs**.

2. Why must the **opportunity cost** of a decision always be something desirable?

3. How do economists use the phrase **"guns or butter"**?

4. What does it mean to **"think at the margin"**?

Applying Economic Concepts

5. *Problem Solving* Suppose that you can save $50 by buying your car in a different city. If the trip requires only $10 in gasoline, is the trip worthwhile? Why or why not?

6. *Decision Making* Determine an opportunity cost for each of the following. **(a)** eating pizza **(b)** going to see a movie on a Tuesday **(c)** going to see a movie on a Saturday **(d)** watching television

7. *Try This* Create a decision-making grid like the one in Figure 1.2 to defend a decision you will make today.

8. *Critical Thinking* Decide whether to work 2, 4, or 6 hours at an after-school job by comparing the opportunity cost and benefit of each alternative.

9. *Decision Making* Which factors would an employer consider if he or she were trying to decide whether to hire an additional worker?

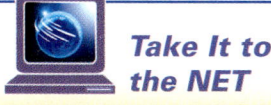

Take It to the NET Brainstorm a list of the trade-offs of **(a)** continuing your education beyond high school and **(b)** not continuing your education beyond high school. Use the links provided in the Social Studies area at the following Web site for help in completing this activity.
www.phschool.com

Interpreting Line Graphs

Line graphs easily and clearly present a large quantity of statistical data. Economists use line graphs to illustrate patterns or trends over time and to explain the relationship between two or more variables. A variable is a factor with a value that can change. Use the following steps to read and interpret the line graph below.

1. **Identify the type of information presented on the graph.** Before you can begin to interpret the information on a graph, you must identify specifically what is being shown. The graph title and the axes' labels indicate the meanings of the points and lines on the graph. Answer the following questions. (**a**) What do the numbers on the horizontal axis (across) represent? (**b**) What do the numbers on the vertical axis (up and down) represent? (**c**) What relationship does the line graph describe?

2. **Read the data shown on the graph. Study the graph's axes carefully.** Before studying the overall patterns, look carefully at specific points on the graph.

Answer the following questions. (**a**) What is the maximum number of points per game that can be shown on the graph? (**b**) How many hours a week did Player B practice? (**c**) How many points per game did Player E average?

3. **Study the data shown on the graph to look for relationships or draw conclusions about a topic.** Use the graph below to draw conclusions about the relationship between time spent practicing and the number of points scored per game. What could you conclude from the information on the line graph about the relationship between practice and points per game?

Additional Practice

Note that the points on the graph do not form a perfectly straight line. For example, Player D did not score as many points per game as Player C, although Player D practiced more hours each week. Why might this be so? What does this information say about the conclusions we can draw from line graphs?

Hours of Practice vs. Points Scored

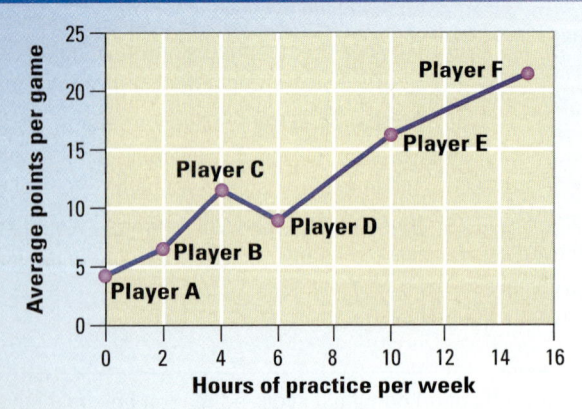

12

Section 3

Production Possibilities Curves

Preview

Objectives

After studying this section you will be able to:

1. **Interpret** a production possibilities curve.
2. **Demonstrate** how production possibilities curves show efficiency, growth, and cost.
3. **Understand** that a country's production possibilities depend on its available resources and technology.

Section Focus

Decisions about which goods and services to produce affect each of us every day. Production possibilities graphs can help us examine the opportunity cost of these decisions.

Key Terms

production
    possibilities curve
production
    possibilities frontier
efficiency
underutilization
cost
law of increasing costs

As the United States entered World War II in 1941, it faced an urgent task: create the weapons and equipment needed to win the war or face defeat. Government agencies took the lead in switching the output of America's factories, farms, and mines from the production of consumer products to the production of military products.

Whether at war or not, individuals must choose what to produce. In 1999, farmers in the United States grew over 2 million tons of watermelons. Could they have produced more? If they had, what would have been the opportunity cost?

Production Possibilities

Economists often use graphs to analyze the choices and trade-offs that people make. Why? Because graphs help us see how one value relates to another value. A **production possibilities curve**, or graph, shows alternative ways to use an economy's resources. The axes of the graph can show categories of goods and services, such as farm goods and factory goods or capital goods and consumer goods. The axes can also display any pair of specific goods or services, such as hats on one axis and shoes on the other.

production possibilities curve *a graph that shows alternative ways to use an economy's resources*

◀ During World War II, consumer goods were in short supply as the nation shifted resources to increase production of planes, ships, artillery, and ammunition. Ration coupons (far left) were used to ensure that civilians got a fair share of consumer goods.

"We feel he's either going to be an artist or an economist."

▲ Why do economists use graphs?

production possibilities frontier *the line on a production possibilities graph that shows the maximum possible output*

Capeland, could produce 15 million pairs of shoes if it used all of its resources to produce only shoes.

The horizontal axis represents watermelons. Graph B indicates that Capeland could produce 21 million tons of watermelons if that's the only product it chose to produce. So Capeland can produce a maximum of:

15 million pairs of shoes
OR
21 million tons of watermelons

A third, more likely, alternative appears in Figure 1.5. The citizens of Capeland could also produce both shoes and watermelons, and this range of choices appears in the table and graph in that figure. It shows six different ways that Capelanders could use their resources to produce watermelons and shoes. Using the made-up data from the table, we can plot points on the graph and then connect them to draw the line shown in Figure 1.5. This line that we can draw, called the **production possibilities frontier**, shows combinations of the production of both shoes and watermelons. Any spot on

Drawing a Production Possibilities Curve

To draw a production possibilities curve, an economist begins by deciding which goods or services to examine; for example, farm goods and factory goods. In this example shoes and watermelons become the values shown on the two axes of the graph. If the vertical axis in Graphs A and B in Figure 1.4 represents shoes, Graph A indicates that this fictional country,

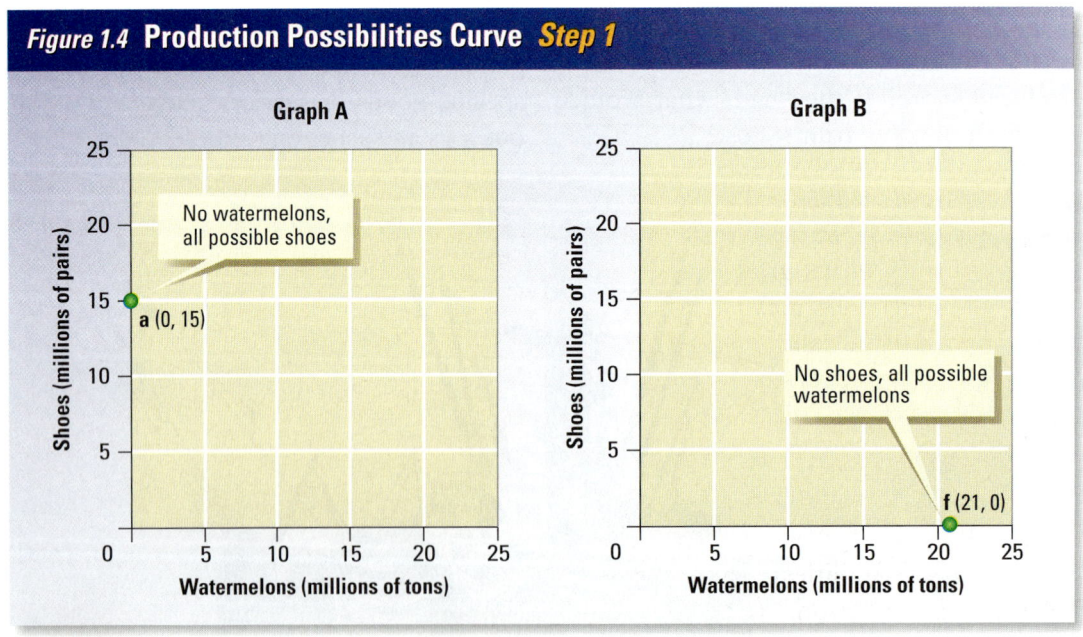

Figure 1.4 Production Possibilities Curve *Step 1*

Graph A

No watermelons, all possible shoes

a (0, 15)

Shoes (millions of pairs)

Watermelons (millions of tons)

Graph B

No shoes, all possible watermelons

f (21, 0)

Shoes (millions of pairs)

Watermelons (millions of tons)

BUILDING KEY CONCEPTS

You can begin to build a production possibilities curve by plotting two of the production choices on a grid. Graph A reflects a decision to produce 15 million pairs of shoes. Graph B reflects a decision to produce 21 million tons of watermelons.

Opportunity Cost What is the opportunity cost of the decision shown in Graph A?

Figure 1.5 Production Possibilities Curve *Step 2*

Watermelons (millions of tons)	Shoes (millions of pairs)
0	15
8	14
14	12
18	9
20	5
21	0

Shoes (millions of pairs)

a (0,15)
b (8,14)
c (14,12)
d (18,9)
e (20,5)
f (21,0)

A production possibilities frontier

Watermelons (millions of tons)

The table above shows six different combinations of watermelon and shoes that Capeland could produce using all of its factor resources. Each combination of numbers in the table is drawn as a point on the graph. Connecting the points forms a line known as the production possibilities frontier.

Opportunity Cost What is the opportunity cost of choosing to produce the combination of goods shown at point c instead of that shown at point d?

that line represents a point at which Capeland is using all of its resources to produce a maximum combination of those two products.

Trade-Offs

Each point in Figure 1.5 reflects a trade-off. Near the top of the curve (points a and b), shoe factories produce more shoes, but farms grow fewer watermelons. Moving down the curve, farms grow more watermelons, but factories make fewer shoes. Why? Because land, labor, and capital are scarce. Using the factors of production to make one product means that fewer resources are left to make something else.

Efficiency, Growth, and Cost

Production possibilities graphs tell us important information. They can show how efficient an economy is, whether an economy has grown or shrunk, and the opportunity cost of a decision to produce more of one good or service.

Efficiency

A production possibilities frontier represents an economy working at its most efficient level of production. **Efficiency** means using resources in such a way as to maximize the production or output of goods and services. However, sometimes economies operate inefficiently. For example, what would happen if some farmers and factory workers were laid off? The farms and factories where they worked would produce fewer goods. This trade-off is represented by drawing a point inside the production possibilities frontier.

Any point inside the line indicates an **underutilization** of resources. Underutilization means using fewer resources than the economy is capable of using. Point g in Figure 1.6 shows that Capeland is harvesting 5 million tons of watermelons and manufacturing 8 million pairs of shoes—much less than the maximum possible production.

efficiency *using resources in such a way as to maximize the production of goods and services*

underutilization *using fewer resources than an economy is capable of using*

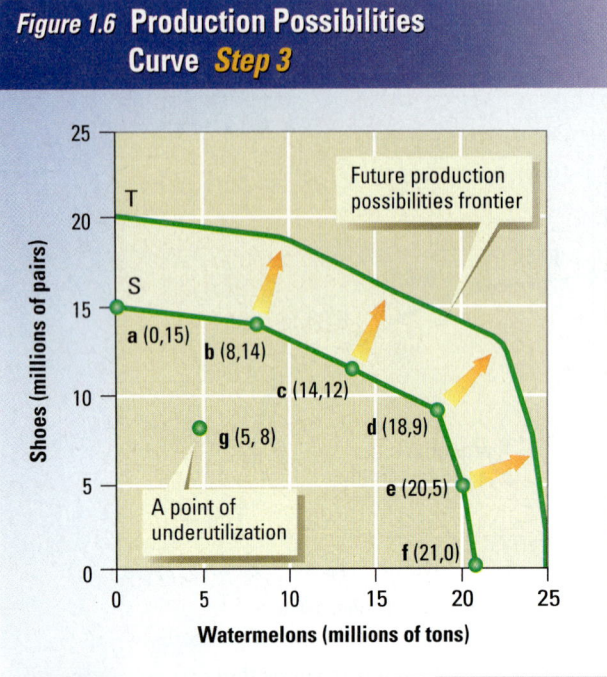

Figure 1.6 Production Possibilities Curve **Step 3**

Future production possibilities frontier

T

S

a (0,15)

b (8,14)

c (14,12)

g (5, 8)

d (18,9)

A point of underutilization

e (20,5)

f (21,0)

Shoes (millions of pairs)

Watermelons (millions of tons)

At point g on this graph, not all factor resources are being used, and the output of farm and factory goods is less than what is possible. Line S represents the economy's current production possibilities. Line T represents future production possibilities if more land, labor, or capital resources become available. **Investment** How does a society benefit when it invests money in the development of new technologies?

cost *to an economist, the alternative that is given up because of a decision*

Growth

A production possibilities curve reflects the country's current production possibilities as if the country's resources were frozen in time. In the real world, however, the quantity of resources a country has is constantly changing. If the quantity or quality of available land, labor, or capital changes, then the production possibilities curve will move. For example, if immigrants pour into a country, then more labor becomes available. In this way, the maximum amount of goods the nation can produce increases. Likewise, new inventions can change existing technology and allow workers to produce more goods and services at lower

costs. When an economy grows, economists say that the entire production possibilities curve has "shifted to the right." Line T in Figure 1.6 shows such a shift.

By contrast, when a country's production capacity decreases, the curve shifts to the left. A decrease could occur, for example, when a country goes to war and loses part of its land as a result. Likewise, if a country's population ages, or becomes less healthy or less educated, the supply of labor and human capital would decrease, and the curve would shift to the left.

Cost

Speaking economically, note that cost is not necessarily money. Rather, to an economist, **cost** is the alternative we give up when we choose one option over the other. This statement should sound familiar. To an economist, cost always means *opportunity cost*. We can use production possibilities graphs to see the opportunity cost involved in a decision.

Looking at the table in Figure 1.5, we can see that the cost of moving from producing no watermelons to producing 8 million tons of watermelons is 1 million pairs of shoes. In other words, we had to sacrifice 1 million pairs of shoes to produce 8 million tons of watermelons. In the same way, if we decide to produce 14 million tons of watermelons—an increase of only 6 million tons—it costs 2 million pairs of shoes. In the first step, those 8 million tons of watermelons cost 1 million pairs of shoes. In the second step, an increase of only 6 million tons of watermelons cost an additional 2 million pairs of shoes. This amounts to 3 million pairs of shoes for 14 million tons of watermelons.

Everyone would agree that switching from shoes to watermelons costs something. An economist looking at Capeland's economy would say that the switch has *increasing* costs. Each time we grow more watermelons, the sacrifice in terms of shoes increases. Finally, at the bottom of the table, it costs an *additional* 5 million pairs of shoes to increase watermelon production by only 1 million tons.

Figure 1.7   The Law of Increasing Costs

STEP 1

Initially, resources are used efficiently to make a balance of watermelons and shoes.

Shoe factories

The most suitable land for farming is used to grow watermelons.

STEP 2

A decision is made to grow more watermelons. Less suitable resources are shifted to farm production. Farm production increases. Shoe production decreases.

Land with rocky soil is now used to grow watermelons.

STEP 3

A decision is made to grow even more watermelons, and more resources are shifted to farm production. Because the added land is less productive, a greater amount of it must be cultivated. Farm output increases. Shoe output decreases by an even greater amount.

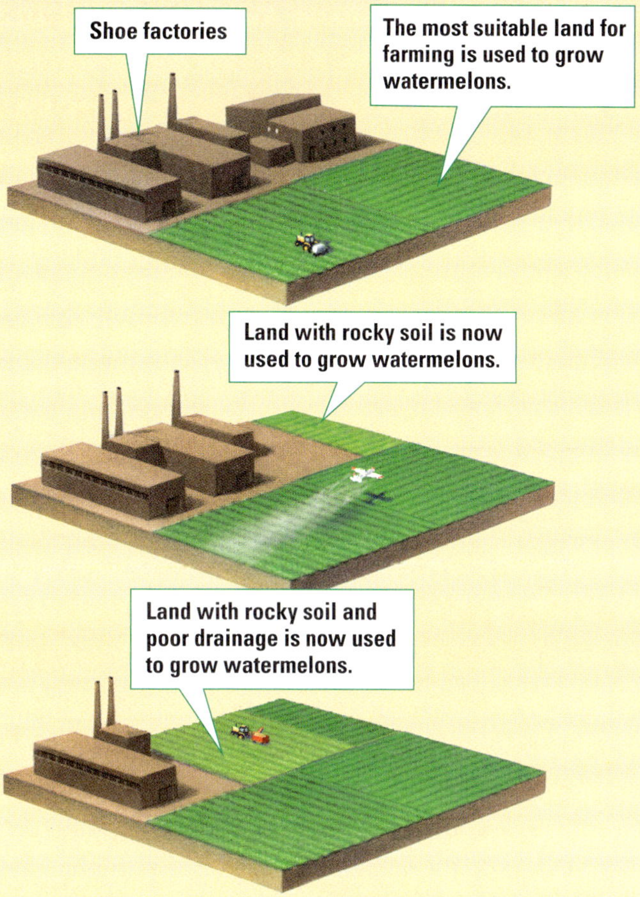

Land with rocky soil and poor drainage is now used to grow watermelons.

BUILDING KEY CONCEPTS

The law of increasing costs states that as production shifts from one item to another, in this case from shoes to watermelons, more and more resources are necessary to increase production of the second item, in this case, watermelons.
Opportunity Cost **According to this diagram, what is the cost of increasing watermelon production?**

Economists explain these increasingly expensive trade-offs with the **law of increasing costs**. This law states that as production switches from one item to another (for example, from shoes to watermelons), more and more resources are necessary to increase production of the second item (watermelons). Therefore, the opportunity cost increases.

Why does the cost increase? In this example it is because some resources are better suited for use in farming, while others are more appropriate for manufacturing. Moving resources from factory to farm production means that farmers must use resources that are not as suitable for farming. For example, say that at first this economy used its most fertile land for growing watermelons. After the best land was used up, farmers had to use poorer land that could produce less per acre than the fertile land could. To increase output on the poorer land, farmers had to use more land and other resources.

The law of increasing costs explains why production possibilities frontiers, such as the one in Figure 1.5, usually curve. As we move along the curve, we trade off more and more to get less and less additional output.

law of increasing costs
law that states that as we shift factors of production from making one good or service to another, the cost of producing the second item increases

The United States and Western Europe are the heaviest computer-using regions of the world.

Opportunity Cost
What opportunity cost might a poorer country face if it chose to purchase or produce more computers?

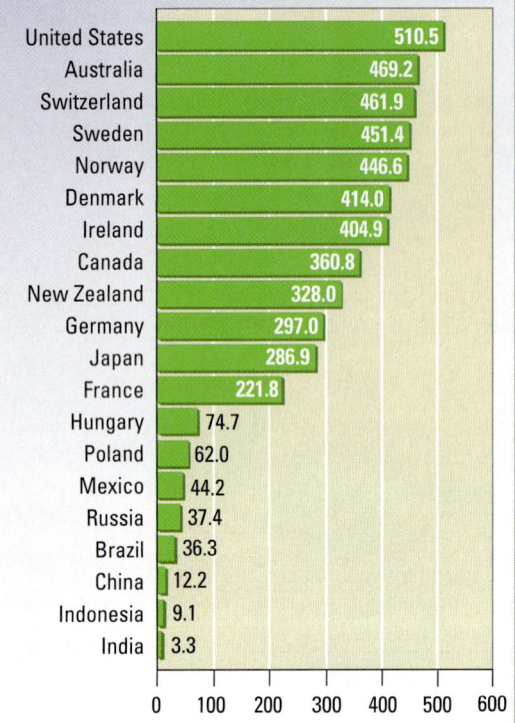

Figure 1.8 **Personal Computers per 1,000 People, 1999**

Country	Personal Computers per 1,000 People
United States	510.5
Australia	469.2
Switzerland	461.9
Sweden	451.4
Norway	446.6
Denmark	414.0
Ireland	404.9
Canada	360.8
New Zealand	328.0
Germany	297.0
Japan	286.9
France	221.8
Hungary	74.7
Poland	62.0
Mexico	44.2
Russia	37.4
Brazil	36.3
China	12.2
Indonesia	9.1
India	3.3

Source: World Bank, 2001 World Development Indicators

Resources and Technology

When economists collect data to create production possibility curves, they must first determine which goods and services a country can produce, given its current resources. A country's resources include its land and natural resources, its work force, and its physical and human capital. Both human and physical capital reflect a vital ingredient—technology. At any time, countries have different ways to produce shoes or watermelons or any of the thousands of products in the world. Each production method uses different technology, or know-how, to create products. So economists also must assess each country's level of technological know-how: whether Capeland makes shoes and plants watermelons by hand or whether they have machines to help. A country's production possibilities depend on both its technological level and the resources it has available.

Section 3 Assessment

Key Terms and Main Ideas

1. How is **underutilization** depicted on a production possibilities frontier?

2. How does a **production possibilities curve** illustrate how efficient an economy is?

3. How does a production possibilities curve illustrate **opportunity cost**?

Applying Economic Concepts

4. *Using the Databank* Turn to the charts showing the number of farms and the average size of farms on page 535. If the number of farms has decreased since 1950, does this mean that the production possibilities for farm output have also decreased? Why or why not?

5. *Problem Solving* How would you illustrate the impact of each of the following events on a production possibilities curve for factory goods and farm goods? **(a)** the computer is invented **(b)** 1 million farm workers remain unemployed for six months **(c)** a drought

6. *Critical Thinking* Describe a specific event that would make each of the following happen to a production possibilities curve. **(a)** a point moves down and to the left **(b)** the frontier shifts to the right

7. *Decision Making* Assume that graphs A and B below each represent a production trade-off made by a society for its economy. Write a brief description of each society. Include specific examples of what the society is producing.

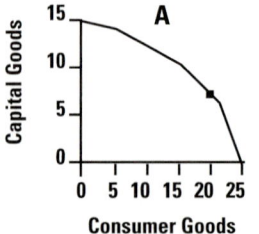

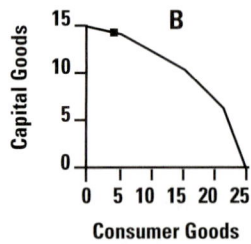

Take It to the NET

Changes in technology have had a great impact on the economy of the United States. Read about technological inventions and describe the impact of one or more on the nation's production possibilities frontier. Use the links provided in the Social Studies area at the following Web site for help in completing this activity. **www.phschool.com**

Safety at Any Cost?

When you buy a car, you face trade-offs: Do you buy the new subcompact that may not have enough room for your gear or the larger used sedan that needs a paint job? The features that make a car safer may also involve trade-offs. Economists urge consumers to consider the trade-offs and opportunity costs of each of their purchase decisions. Most of these opportunity costs fall into one of three categories: cost and convenience, size, and personal freedom.

Safety Devices Versus Cost and Convenience Over 40,000 people are killed every year in crashes on our roads. Safety features like antilock brakes and dual-side air bags may save lives, but they also make cars more expensive. Some features like seatbelts are sometimes seen as an inconvenience, so consumers do not always use them. Manufactures would like to produce safe cars, but they must sell them at a price that buyers are willing to pay. Safety features are defeated if travelers ignore or disable them.

▲ Safety devices save lives but also involve some opportunity costs.

Size Versus Pollution Heavier cars are generally safer cars—they tend to hold up better when there is an accident and provide passengers with more protection. SUVs have become increasingly popular because they are heavy and taller, giving the driver a better view of the road. On the other hand, they are also more expensive to buy and more costly to run because they have lower fuel efficiency.

Burning extra fuel also means increasing auto emissions. The U.S. currently generates more greenhouse gas emissions than any other country in the world, and the amount is growing. Also, "gas guzzlers" increase our dependence on foreign oil.

Safety Laws Versus Personal Freedom Many states have struggled with laws requiring the use of seatbelts in cars, carseats for infants and young children, or helmets for motorcyclists. There is considerable evidence that these safety precautions reduce the severity of injury if there is an accident. However, laws requiring people to use seatbelts or helmets also restrict individual freedom, so there is a trade-off between a national interest in keeping people safe and a personal interest in being able to make your own life choices.

Applying Economic Ideas

1. Suppose you are buying a car. How would the trade-offs discussed above affect your decision?

2. The table at the right shows the specific costs of various optional auto safety devices. On what basis would you decide which, if any, of these safety options to buy?

The Costs of Auto Safety

Cost of vehicle: $10,000

Safety feature	Cost
Antilock brakes	$400.00
Side impact air bags	$350.00
Traction control	$1,200.00

Cost of vehicle: $14,205

Safety feature	Cost
Antilock brakes	$645.00
Side impact air bags	$295.00
Traction control	n/a

Cost of vehicle: $19,175

Safety feature	Cost
Antilock brakes	$600.00
Side impact air bags	$390.00
Traction control	$600.00

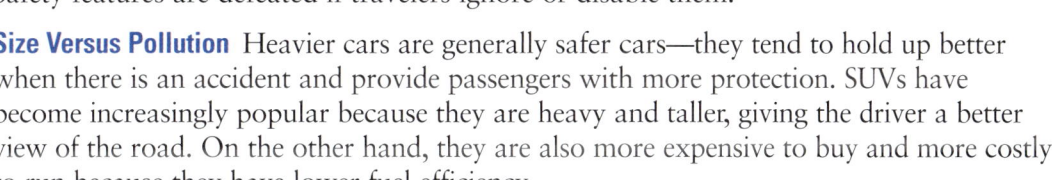

Chapter 1 Assessment

Chapter Summary

A summary of major ideas in Chapter 1 appears below. See also the **Guide to the Essentials of Economics**, which provides additional review and test practice of key concepts in Chapter 1.

Section 1 Scarcity and the Factors of Production (pp. 3–6)

Economics is the study of how people seek to satisfy their needs and wants by making choices. People, businesses, and governments must make choices because all resources are scarce. **Scarcity** means limited quantities of resources to meet unlimited needs or desires. Economists call the resources that are used to make all goods and services the factors of production. The three factors of production are land, labor, and capital. Entrepreneurs are leaders who combine the three factors of production to create new goods and services.

Section 2 Opportunity Cost (pp. 8–11)

Every decision involves **trade-offs.** Trade-offs are all the alternatives that we give up when we choose one course of action over another. The most desirable alternative given up as the result of a decision is called the **opportunity cost.** If a decision involves choosing one more or one fewer unit of an input, economists say we are **thinking at the margin.** Employers think at the margin to decide how many workers to hire.

Section 3 Production Possibilities Curves (pp. 13–18)

Economists draw curves or graphs in order to help them analyze the choices and trade-offs people make. A **production possibilities curve** shows the alternative ways in which an economy's resources can be used. The **production possibilities frontier** is the line or curve on the graph that represents the maximum amount that an economy can produce. Points inside the frontier reflect an **underutilization** of resources. If the amount of available land, labor, or capital increases, the entire curve can shift to the right. The **law of increasing costs** states that as production shifts from one item to a second item, more and more resources are necessary to increase production of the second item.

Key Terms

Complete each sentence by choosing the correct answer from the list of terms below. You will not use all of the terms.

capital	opportunity cost
entrepreneur	scarcity
goods	trade-offs
"guns or butter"	underutilization
land	economics

1. Economists define _____ as "limited quantities to meet unlimited wants."
2. All decisions involve _____ because we must give up some alternatives when we choose a certain course of action.
3. The term _____ refers to all natural resources that are used to produce goods and services.
4. Economists use the phrase _____ to describe the trade-offs a country is forced to make when choosing between military and consumer production.
5. A(n) _____ is the most important sacrifice that results from making a decision.
6. A person who starts a new business or develops an original idea is known as a(n) _____.
7. _____ of resources occurs when an economy uses fewer resources than it is capable of expending.

Using Graphic Organizers

8. On a separate sheet of paper, copy the tree map below to help you organize information about the factors of production. Complete the tree map by writing descriptions and examples for each of the headings shown.

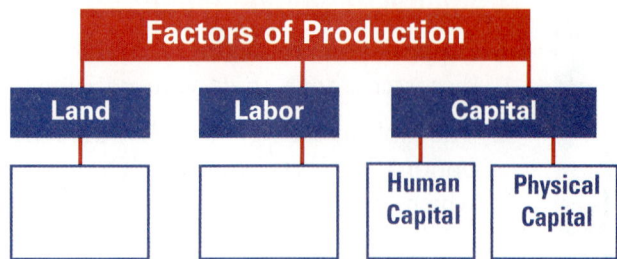

Reviewing Main Ideas

9. Using examples of land, labor, and capital, explain why economists believe that all goods and services are scarce.

10. Explain how each of the following people would talk about scarcity and trade-offs. (a) the President of the United States (b) the leader of a developing nation (c) a U.S. citizen whose income is in the top one percent (d) a U.S. citizen whose income is in the bottom 5 percent

11. What three important pieces of information can we learn by reading a production possibilities graph?

12. Explain the law of increasing costs.

Critical Thinking

13. **Testing Conclusions** Review the typical benefits of physical capital described in Section 1. Give specific examples of how the first railroads in the United States created or did not create the benefits of physical capital.

14. **Predicting Consequences** Describe three services that the government provides to its citizens. Identify some of the opportunity costs of providing each of those services.

15. **Drawing Conclusions** Some economists consider entrepreneurship to be a fourth factor of production in addition to land, labor, and capital. Other economists consider entrepreneurship to be a special category of labor. Which group of economists do you agree with? Why?

Problem-Solving Activity

16. Suppose that you lent $100 to a friend, and he or she paid you back one year later. What was the cost of lending your friend this money?

Economics Journal

Essay Writing Review your Economics Journal entry for Chapter 1. Write a brief essay describing the opportunity cost for each of the three decisions that you noted in your journal.

Skills for Life

Interpreting Line Graphs Review the steps shown on page 12; then answer the following questions about the line graph shown below.

17. What relationship does the line graph describe?

18. What is the average annual income of men with 16 years of education?

19. How many years of schooling result in an average annual income of $60,000 for women?

20. What could you conclude from the line graph about the relationship between income and education?

21. Use this graph to practice thinking at the margin. Suppose you have just completed grade 12. If you spend one more year in school, by how much will your lifetime income increase (assuming you work until age 65)?

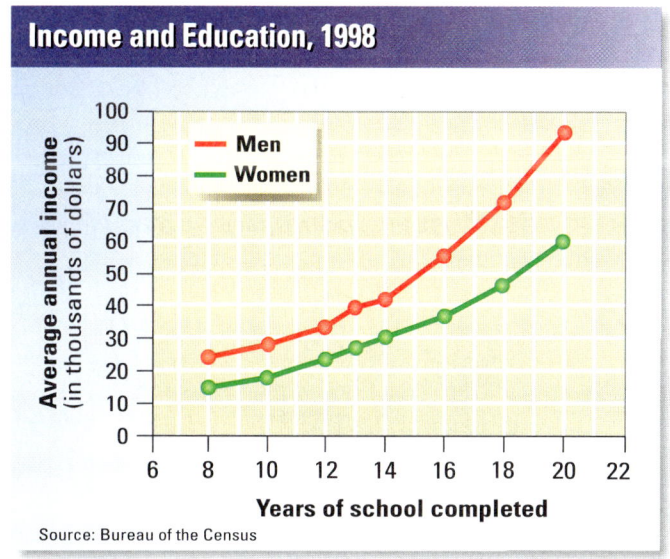

Income and Education, 1998

Average annual income (in thousands of dollars)

Men
Women

Years of school completed

Source: Bureau of the Census

Take It to the NET

Chapter 1 Self-Test As a final review activity, take the Economics Chapter 1 Self-Test in the Social Studies area at the Web site listed below and receive immediate feedback on your answers. The test consists of 20 multiple-choice questions designed to test your understanding of the chapter content.
www.phschool.com

A system is a way of doing something. The trains, tracks, platforms, routes, and schedules of a subway system move people around a city. Our education system teaches us reading, writing, and arithmetic. Economic systems enable societies to produce and distribute goods and services.

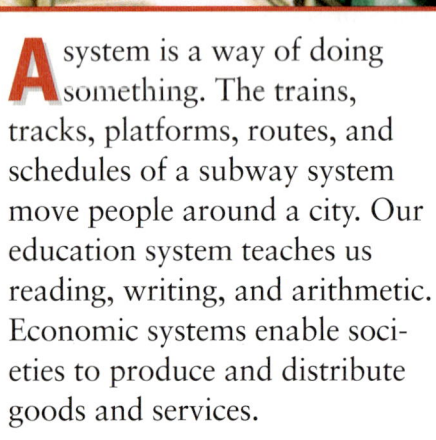

Economics Journal

Make a list of all the different systems you used yesterday. How would your day have been different without these systems?

Keep It Current

Items marked with this logo are periodically updated on the Internet. Keep up-to-date with what's in the news. To get current information on economic systems go to
www.phschool.com

Preview

Objectives

After studying this section you will be able to:

1. **Identify** the three key economic questions of what to produce, how to produce, and who consumes what is produced.
2. **Analyze** the societal values that determine how a country answers the three economic questions.
3. **Explain** the characteristics of traditional, command, and market economies and describe the societal values that influence them.

Section Focus

All societies must answer three key economic questions about the production and consumption of goods and services. How a society answers these questions depends on how much it values different economic goals. Four different economic systems have developed in response to these three questions.

Key Terms

economic system
factor payments
patriotism
safety net
standard of living
traditional economy
market economy
centrally planned economy
command economy
mixed economy

In Chapter 1, you read about the economic concept of scarcity—that we cannot have all that we want or need. Indeed, in some places in the world, people cannot even meet their basic needs for food, clothing, and shelter because their resources are too scarce. Scarcity forces societies and nations to answer some hard economic questions. Different economic systems have evolved in response to the problem of scarcity. An **economic system** is the method used by a society to produce and distribute goods and services. Which economic system a society employs depends on that society's goals and values.

Three Key Economic Questions

Because economic resources are limited, every society must answer three key economic questions:

- What goods and services should be produced?
- How should these goods and services be produced?
- Who consumes these goods and services?

What Goods and Services Should Be Produced?

Individuals in every society must decide what to produce in order to satisfy society's needs and wants. In today's complex societies, it is often difficult to distinguish between needs and wants. While it may be obvious that we need food and shelter, modern societies face additional important considerations. How much of our resources should we devote to national defense, education, public health and welfare, or consumer goods? Which consumer goods should we produce?

Recall the guns-and-butter trade-off described in Chapter 1. Because of our limited resources, each production decision that a society makes comes at an opportunity cost.

How Should Goods and Services Be Produced?

The next question we face is how to use our resources to produce goods and services. For example, should we produce electricity with oil, solar power, or nuclear power? Should teachers have classes of 20 students or 50 students? Should we produce food on large corporate farms or on small family farms?

economic system *the method used by a society to produce and distribute goods and services*

Today, capital—not labor—dominates the answer to how wheat is produced.

Opportunity Cost Identify the opportunity costs of each method of farming.

Figure 2.1 Combining Factor Resources

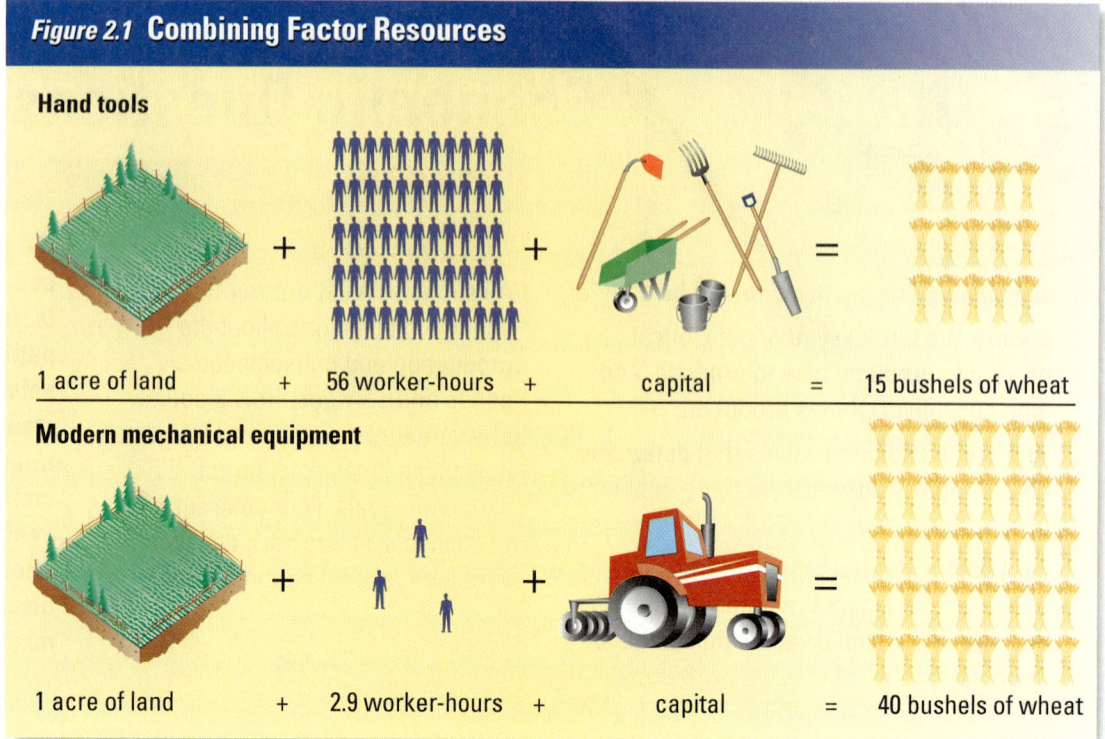

Hand tools

1 acre of land   +   56 worker-hours   +   capital   =   15 bushels of wheat

Modern mechanical equipment

1 acre of land   +   2.9 worker-hours   +   capital   =   40 bushels of wheat

---

factor payments *the income people receive for supplying factors of production, such as land, labor, or capital*

Although there are countless ways to create all of the things we want and need, all require land, labor, and capital. These factors of production can be combined in different ways. For example, examine the chart above (Figure 2.1). Before the introduction of modern farming equipment, a typical combination of resources for producing 15 bushels of wheat was 56 hours of labor, 1 acre of land, and simple hand tools. With today's mechanical farming equipment, farming is much more efficient. Forty bushels of wheat can be harvested from one acre of land with just 2.9 worker-hours of labor.

Who Consumes Goods and Services?

By the end of the 1990s, the top 25 goods manufacturers in the United States were launching an average of 13 new products every day. Retail stores, which 50 years ago typically carried about 3,000 items, now offered about 30,000 different products. American farms produce 315 million metric tons of wheat, rice, and corn and maintain about 180 million head of livestock. Despite this staggering output, quantities are not unlimited.

How does this abundance get divided up? Who gets to drive a new luxury car and who can only afford a subway pass? Who attends a concert and who stays home? Who eats a well-balanced diet and who eats nothing but hot dogs for every meal? Who gets access to a good education? Societies must decide how to distribute the available goods and services.

The answer to the question of distribution is determined by how societies choose to distribute income. **Factor payments** are the income people receive for supplying factors of production—land, labor, capital, or entrepreneurship. Landowners receive rent, workers receive wages, and those who lend money to build factories or buy machinery receive payments called interest. Entrepreneurs earn profits if their enterprises succeed.

How much should we pay the owners of the factors of production? How do we decide how much a particular piece of land is worth, how much teachers should earn versus how much doctors should earn, or what the interest rate should be?

The question of who gets to consume which goods and services lies at the very heart of the differences between economic systems today. Each society answers the question of distribution based on its unique combination of social values and goals.

Economic Goals and Societal Values

Different societies answer the three economic questions based on the importance they attach to various economic goals. Figure 2.2 lists some general economic goals that most economic systems try to address. Bear in mind that societies pursue each of these goals, to some degree, at the expense of the others.

Economic Efficiency

Because resources are always scarce—that is, they always involve an opportunity cost—most societies try to maximize what they can get for the resources they have to work with. If a society can accurately assess what to produce, it increases its economic efficiency. A manufacturer would be wasting resources producing record albums if people prefer to buy CDs. Knowing the best way to produce a product cuts waste, too. Of course, in the end, products need to reach consumers. An economy that can't deliver goods isn't efficient.

Economic Freedom

Most of us value the opportunity to make our own choices. How do you feel about laws that keep you from earning an income? What about laws that forbid you to make certain purchases or possess certain items? The economic systems of different nations allow different degrees of economic freedoms. In general, however, people all over the world face limitations on economic freedom.

In the United States, the economic freedoms that we as Americans enjoy are an important reason for our patriotism. **Patriotism** is the love of one's country—the passion that inspires a person to serve his or her country, either in defending it from invasion or protecting its rights and maintaining its laws and institutions. The freedoms that allow any American who so chooses to become an entrepreneur, for example, are continuing sources of pride and patriotism.

Economic Security and Predictability

Most people don't like uncertainty. We want to know that we can get milk and bread every time we go to the grocery store, or that the gas pumps will be full when we

patriotism *the love of one's country; the passion that inspires a person to serve his or her country*

This family (left) will need to rebuild their home after a devastating hurricane.
Government Which economic goal could help them recover from the storm?

Figure 2.2 Economic Goals

Economic efficiency	Making the most of resources
Economic freedom	Freedom from government intervention in the production and distribution of goods and services
Economic security and predictability	Assurance that goods and services will be available, payments will be made on time, and a safety net will protect individuals in times of economic disaster
Economic equity	Fair distribution of wealth
Economic growth and innovation	Innovation leads to economic growth, and economic growth leads to a higher standard of living.
Other goals	Societies pursue additional goals, such as environmental protection.

go to gas up our cars. We want to feel confident that we will get our paychecks every payday. Ideally, economic systems reassure people that goods and services will be available when they need them and that they can count on receiving expected payments on time.

We also want the security of knowing that help is available if we are elderly, poor, unemployed, or facing some other potential economic disadvantage. Most people feel that the government should provide some kind of **safety net**, or set of government programs that protect people experiencing unfavorable economic conditions. These include injuries, layoffs, natural disasters, or severe shortages. Many countries also provide some sort of base income for retired persons to ensure that older people can support themselves after retirement.

Economic Equity

Each society must decide the best way to divide its economic pie. What constitutes a fair share? Should everyone get the same, or should one's consumption depend on how much one produces? How much should society provide for those who are unable or unwilling to produce?

Many people believe in equal pay for equal work, but society does not value all jobs equally. Most lawyers earn more than most nurses. Most computer programmers

earn more than most truck drivers. Not everyone is able to work. How should we provide for the ill and infirm?

Economic Growth and Innovation

A nation's economy must grow for a nation to improve its **standard of living,** or level of economic prosperity. This is especially true if a country's population is growing. The economy also must grow to provide new jobs and income for people.

Innovation plays a huge role in economic growth. Think of the changes brought about by the shift from nomadism to agriculture, from the agricultural age to the industrial age, from the industrial age to the information age. Innovations in technology increase the efficiency of production and usher in new goods and services. In your lifetime, you are witnessing innovations in computer and networking technology that are changing the ways people work, shop, conduct business, locate information, and communicate.

Additional Goals

A society may value goals in addition to those described above. Environmental protection, full employment, universal medical care, and other important concerns may be among a nation's chief economic goals.

All nations must prioritize their economic goals, or arrange them in order of importance. No matter how a nation prioritizes its goals, one fact remains: achieving any economic goal comes only with some kind of economic trade-off.

Economies and Values

Four different economic systems have developed to address the three key economic questions. Each system reflects a different prioritization of economic goals. It also reflects the values of the societies in which these systems are present.

Traditional Economies

A **traditional economy** relies on habit, custom, or ritual to decide what to

▼ The traditional economy of Guatemala's Quiché Maya includes regular market days.

produce, how to produce it, and to whom to distribute it. There is little room for innovation or change. The traditional economic system revolves around the family. Work tends to be divided along gender lines. Boys tend to take up the occupations of their fathers, while girls follow in the footsteps of their mothers.

Traditional economies are usually communities that tend to stay relatively small and close. Often these societies work to support entire groups, rather than just themselves or their immediate families. Agricultural and hunting practices usually lie at the very heart of the people's lives, laws, and religious beliefs.

Societies with traditional economies have few mechanisms in place to deal effectively with the effects of environmental disaster, such as a flood or drought. They also tend to remain stagnant, resisting change at both the individual and community level. They may be slow to adopt new technology or radical new ideas. They may not have access to goods you see every day at the grocery store. In most cases, these communities lack modern conveniences and have a low standard of living.

Market Economies

In a **market economy,** economic decisions are made by individuals and are based on exchange, or trade. The choices made by individuals determine what gets made and how, as well as who consumes the goods and services produced. Market economies are also called free markets, or capitalism. You will read about the free market in detail in Section 2.

Command Economies

In a **centrally planned economy,** the central government alone decides how to answer all three key economic questions. Centrally planned economies are sometimes called **command economies,** because a central authority is in command of the economy. Section 3 discusses the theories behind centrally planned economies.

Mixed Economies

Most modern economies are **mixed economies**—market-based economic systems in which government plays a limited role. Section 4 describes the reasons for mixed economies and the various ways government is involved in such economies.

market economy
economic system in which decisions on production and consumption of goods and services are based on voluntary exchange in markets

centrally planned economy *economic system in which the central government makes all decisions on the production and consumption of goods and services*

command economy *economic system in which a central authority is in command of the economy; a centrally planned economy*

mixed economy *market-based economic system with limited government involvement*

Section 1 Assessment

Key Terms and Main Ideas

1. What is an **economic system**?

2. How do a **traditional economy,** a **market economy,** a **command economy,** and a **mixed economy** differ?

3. Why aren't all people paid the same amount in **factor payments** for the resources they provide? Provide your own example of two unequal factor payments.

4. Why do governments provide **safety nets** for their citizens?

5. Give at least one example of a traditional, a command, and a market economic system.

Applying Economic Concepts

6. *Using the Databank* Examine the graph "Government Spending, by Category" on page 543. Based on the information in the graph, identify what you think are some economic goals of the United States.

7. *Critical Thinking* Create a chart in which you list the societal values of each of the four economic systems described in the section.

8. *Try This* You and your friends decide to earn money by washing cars. How are the three economic questions answered in this market?

Take It to the NET

Companies answer the three basic economic questions all the time. A company's "mission statement" usually contains the answers to most of these questions. Find a company you already are familiar with, and then identify its mission statement and how it does or does not answer the three basic questions. Use the links provided in the Social Studies area at the following Web site for help in completing this activity. **www.phschool.com**

The Free Market

Preview

Objectives

After studying this section you will be able to:

1. **Explain** why markets exist.
2. **Analyze** a circular flow model of a free market economy.
3. **Understand** the self-regulating nature of the marketplace.
4. **Identify** the advantages of a free market economy.

Section Focus

Markets exist so that people can exchange what they have for what they want. A free market is a self-regulating economic system directed by individuals acting in their own self-interest.

Key Terms

market
specialization
household
firm
factor market
profit
product market

self-interest
incentive
competition
invisible hand
consumer
  sovereignty

---

market *an arrangement that allows buyers and sellers to exchange things*

What do a farmers' market, a sporting goods store, the New York Stock Exchange, and the sign you posted on your community bulletin board advertising baby-sitting services have in common? All are examples of markets. A **market** is an arrangement that allows buyers and sellers to exchange things.

Why Markets Exist

Markets exist because no one is self-sufficient. In other words, none of us produces all we require to satisfy our needs and wants. You probably didn't grow the plants to make the fibers to weave the cloth to make the shirt you're wearing. Instead, you purchased your shirt at a store, which is an example of a market. Markets allow us to exchange the things we have for the things we want.

Specialization

Instead of being self-sufficient, each of us produces just one or a few products. A nurse specializes in caring for the sick. A

► This Thai spice stand, Brazilian stock exchange, and Indian barber shop (left to right) are all examples of markets.

marine mechanic specializes in repairing machinery aboard sea craft. A baker specializes in making breads, cakes, and cookies. **Specialization** is the concentration of the productive efforts of individuals and firms on a limited number of activities.

Specialization makes us more efficient. It is much easier to learn one task or a few tasks very well than to learn them all.

Buying and Selling

Because each of us specializes in producing just a few products, we need markets to sell what we have and to buy what we want. The typical person earns an income (specializing at a particular job) and uses this income to buy the products that he or she wants to consume. If each person were self-sufficient, producing everything he or she wanted to consume, there would be no need for markets.

Free Market Economy

Economic systems that are based on voluntary exchanges in markets are called free market economies. In a free market economy, individuals and businesses use markets to exchange money and products.

In a free market system, individuals and privately owned businesses own the factors of production, make what they want, and buy what they want. In other words, in a free market system, individuals answer the three key economic questions of what to produce, how to produce it, and who consumes that which is produced. As you might guess, a free market economy functions best in an environment of decentralized decision-making such as enjoyed in the United States.

We can represent a free market economy in a special kind of drawing called a circular flow diagram, or model. A circular flow diagram shows at a glance how individuals and businesses exchange money, resources, and products in the marketplace. Figure 2.3 shows a circular flow diagram of a free market economy. The inner ring of the diagram represents the flow of resources and products. The outer ring represents the flow of money.

Households and Firms

The players in the free market economy are households and firms. A **household** is a person or group of people living in the same residence. Households own the factors of production—land, labor, and capital. Households are also the consumers of goods and services.

A business, or **firm,** is an organization that uses resources to produce a product, which it then sells. Firms transform "inputs," or factors of production, into "outputs," or products.

Factor Market

As you can see from the lower half of the circular flow diagram in Figure 2.3, firms purchase factors of production from households. This arena of exchange is called the **factor market**. Firms purchase or rent land (natural resources). They hire workers, paying them wages or salaries for their labor. They also borrow money from households to purchase capital, paying households interest or profits in return. **Profit** is the financial gain made in a transaction.

Product Market

Take a close look at the top half of the circular flow diagram in

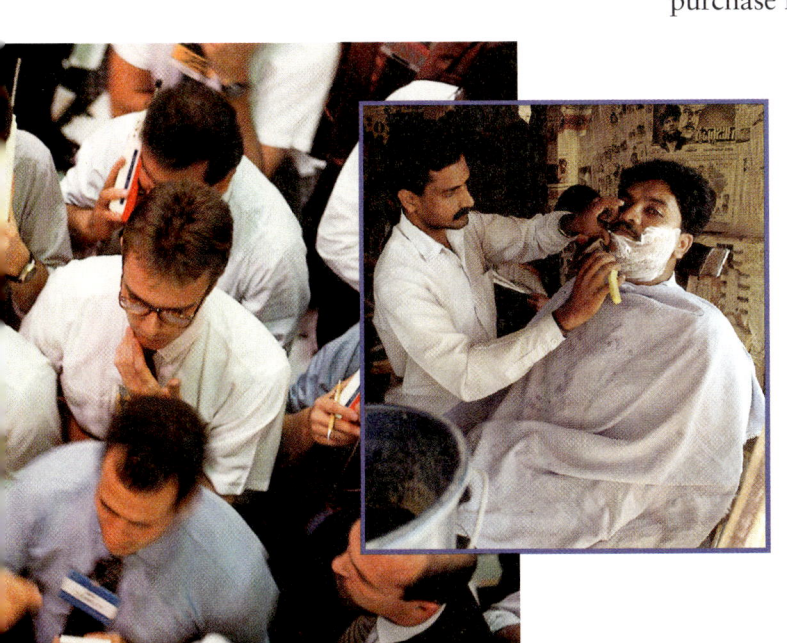

specialization *the concentration of the productive efforts of individuals and firms on a limited number of activities*

household *a person or group of people living in the same residence*

firm *an organization that uses resources to produce a product, which it then sells*

factor market *market in which firms purchase the factors of production from households*

profit *the financial gain made in a transaction*

A circular flow model shows the interactions between households and businesses in the free market.

Economic Systems
What is exchanged in the factor market? In the product market?

Figure 2.3 Circular Flow Model of a Market Economy

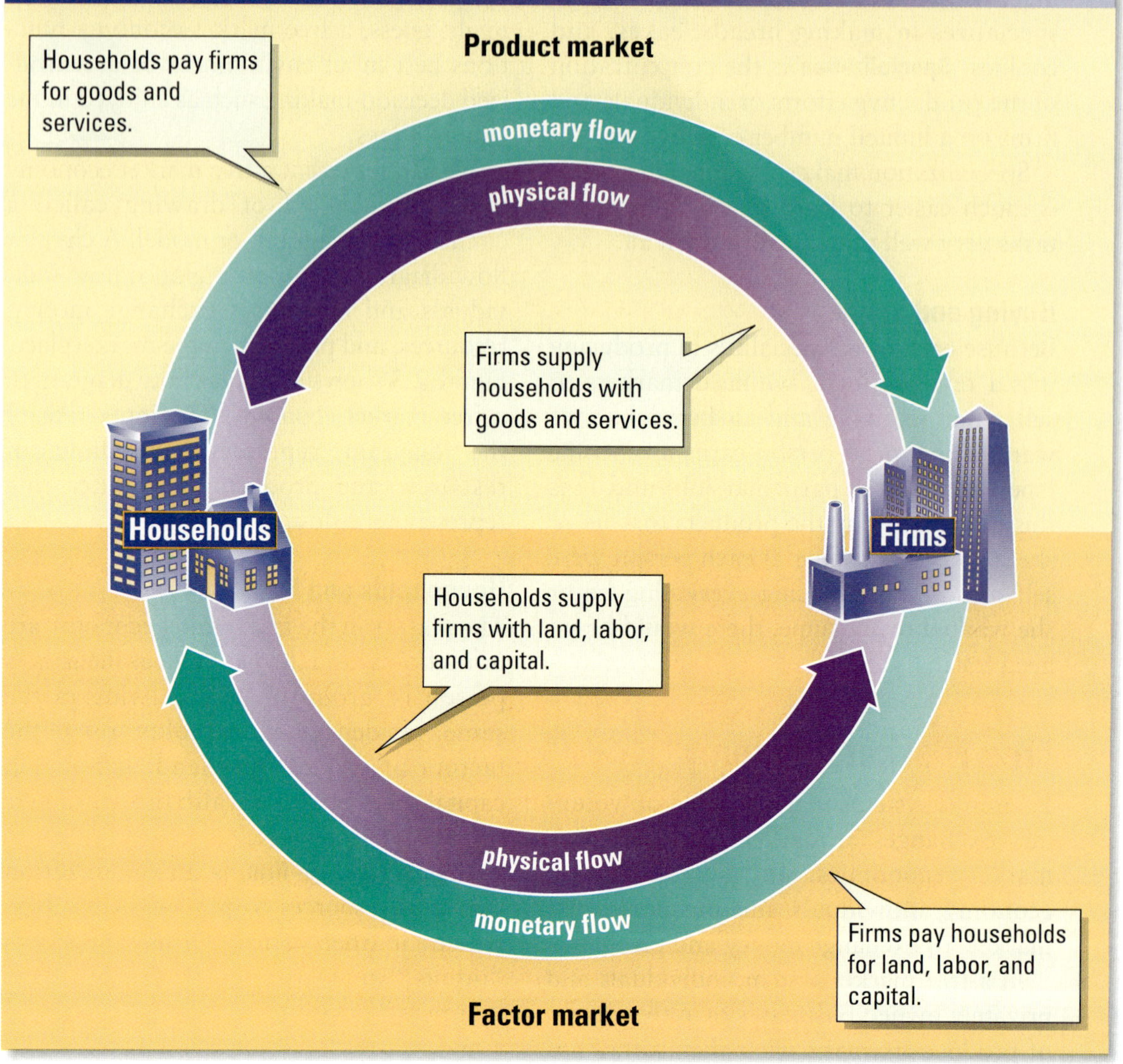

Product market

Households pay firms for goods and services.

monetary flow

physical flow

Firms supply households with goods and services.

Households

Firms

Households supply firms with land, labor, and capital.

physical flow

monetary flow

Firms pay households for land, labor, and capital.

Factor market

---

product market
the market in which households purchase the goods and services that firms produce

Figure 2.3. You can see that the goods and services that firms produce are purchased by households in the **product market**.

If you follow the rings of the diagram, you will see that households purchase the products made by firms with the money they received from firms in the factor market. The flow between the factor market and the product market is truly circular.

The Self-Regulating Nature of the Marketplace

How is it that firms and households cooperate to give each other what they want—factor resources, in the case of firms, and products, in the case of households? As anyone knows who has tried out for the track team, a part in a play, or has applied for a job or to a college, we live in a competitive society. According to Adam Smith, it is, in fact, competition and our own self-interest that keep the marketplace functioning.

Self-Interest

Adam Smith was a Scottish social philosopher who, in 1776, published a book titled *The Wealth of Nations*, in which he described how the market functions. Smith observed that an economy is made up of countless individual transactions. In each transaction, the buyer and seller consider only their **self-interest**, or their own personal gain. Self-interest, in other words, is the motivating force in the free market.

Competition

Consumers (households), in pursuit of their self-interest, have the incentive to look for lower prices. An **incentive** is the hope of reward or the fear of punishment that encourages a person to behave in a certain way. Adam Smith observed that people respond predictably to both positive and negative incentives. As for consumers, we can predict that they will respond to the positive incentive of lower prices. This makes sense, because spending less money on a good lowers the opportunity cost of the purchase.

Firms, meanwhile, seek to make greater profits by increasing sales. Let's take, for example, a shirt manufacturer. The manufacturer produces and sells polka-dotted shirts and striped shirts. The striped shirts are far outselling the polka-dotted shirts. The manufacturer has the incentive—from more potential sales and profits—to produce more striped shirts. Other manufacturers, observing consumers' desire for striped shirts, also have the incentive to sell striped shirts. With all these manufacturers in the market, consumers have all the striped shirts they want.

Manufacturers also have a second incentive—to make the most profit in selling striped shirts. What keeps manufacturers' pursuit of profit from causing prices to

skyrocket? If one manufacturer begins charging $30.00 for a striped shirt, another manufacturer can come along and sell striped shirts for $25.00. If the first manufacturer wants to sell any more striped shirts, he or she had better drop the selling price. Consumers, pursuing their self-interest, will buy the lower-priced shirt. Economists call this struggle among producers for the dollars of consumers **competition**. While self-interest is the motivating force behind the free market, competition is the regulating force.

The Invisible Hand

Self-interest and competition work together to regulate the marketplace. Self-interest spurs consumers to purchase certain goods

"Son, your mother and I have decided to let the free market take care of you."

▲ How could the free market take care of this young man?

self-interest one's own personal gain

incentive an expectation that encourages people to behave in a certain way

competition the struggle among producers for the dollars of consumers

◄ Competing businesses scream for the attention of consumers.

and services and firms to produce them. Competition causes more production and moderates firms' quests for higher prices. The overall result is that consumers get the products they want at prices that closely reflect the cost of producing them. All of this happens without any central plan or direction. Adam Smith called this phenomenon "the **invisible hand** of the marketplace."

Advantages of the Free Market

Competition and the pursuit of self-interest serve the public interest. The free market, on its own, meets many economic goals.

invisible hand *term economists use to describe the self-regulating nature of the marketplace*

consumer sovereignty *the power of consumers to decide what gets produced*

1. *Economic efficiency* Because it is self-regulating, a free market economy responds efficiently to rapidly changing conditions. Producers make only what consumers want, when they want it, and generally at prices they are willing to pay.
2. *Economic freedom* Free market economies have the highest degree of economic freedom of any system. This includes the freedom of workers to work where they want, of firms to produce what they want, and of individuals to consume what they want.
3. *Economic growth* Because competition encourages innovation, free markets encourage growth. Entrepreneurs are always seeking profitable opportunities, contributing new ideas and innovations.
4. *Additional goals* Free markets offer a wider variety of goods and services than any other system, because producers have incentives to meet consumers' desires. Consumers, in essence, decide what gets produced. This is called **consumer sovereignty**.

Despite its advantages, no pure market economy exists on any meaningful scale. The same features that make free markets attractive also represent the weaknesses of the free market. The goals of economic equity and economic security are difficult to achieve in a pure market system. In Section 4, you will read about how the free market system has been modified by various nations in order to better meet the entire array of economic goals.

Section 2 Assessment

Key Terms and Main Ideas

1. How does **specialization** make us more efficient?
2. What is the difference between the **factor market** and the **product market**?
3. What is **profit**?
4. What are the roles of **households** and **firms** in a market economy?
5. How does **competition** among firms benefit consumers?
6. Explain what Adam Smith meant by "the **invisible hand** of the marketplace."
7. What is the connection between **incentives** and **consumer sovereignty** in a free market economy?

Applying Economic Concepts

8. *Critical Thinking* Why is economic equity difficult to achieve in a free market economy?

9. *Try This* You will need a stack of paper and two staplers. You and a friend create "fold-its" by folding each sheet of paper in thirds and stapling both ends. How many fold-its can you make in two minutes? Next, try specializing: one of you folds while the other staples. Now how many fold-its can you make in two minutes?

10. *Critical Thinking* Provide at least three real-world examples to illustrate the circular flow model of a market economy.

Take It to the NET

A high degree of economic freedom is a characteristic of a free market system. Which countries exhibit the most economic freedom? Where are most of these countries located? Use the links provided in the Social Studies area at the following Web site for help in completing this activity. **www.phschool.com**

Profile

Economist

Entrepreneur

Adam Smith (1723–1790)

One of the first people to offer an explanation of how a market economy works was the Scottish philosopher Adam Smith. Beginning in his early twenties, Smith enjoyed a long career teaching at universities in Scotland. Although more than a little absent-minded, Smith was adored by his students and respected by his fellow professors. More importantly, his ideas won him fame and influence across Britain.

The Wealth of Nations

Today, we most remember Adam Smith for the theories expressed in his book *The Wealth of Nations*. Published in 1776, *The Wealth of Nations* still stands as an authoritative description of how a market system can flourish.

In the book, Smith identifies land, labor, and capital as the factors of production that generate a nation's wealth. When the production of goods is divided into many steps, and workers specialize in only one step, productivity increases. Higher productivity increases the overall wealth of the nation.

Laissez Faire

Adam Smith also called for restricting the role of government in the economy. Smith insisted that government must leave individuals as free as possible to pursue their own interests if a market economy is to run smoothly. This policy is known as *laissez faire*, which means "let them do (as they please)." In Smith's view, individuals left alone to try to better themselves will produce a multiplication of riches: more jobs and more goods and services.

The Invisible Hand and Self-Interest

Adam Smith also noticed that businesses could provide the goods and services that consumers needed without the help of a central plan telling them what to do. How do they do it? Smith gave credit to an invisible hand.

In Smith's view, the invisible hand guides a nation's resources to their most productive use. One of the invisible hand's tools is self-interest. Individuals, each pursuing what is best for him or her, make decisions that ultimately benefit the nation.

For example, consumers can satisfy their self-interest by buying goods. Business people satisfy their self-interest by making the goods consumers want and selling them for a profit. As sales increase, businesses can raise prices. At this point the invisible hand takes over. Another person sees the profits and starts a competing business, charging a slightly lower price. Other businesses must follow if they want to keep their customers, and balance is restored to the market.

CHECK FOR UNDERSTANDING

1. Source Reading Rewrite the following passage from *The Wealth of Nations* in your own words: "It is not from the benevolence [kindness] of the butcher, the brewer, or the baker that we expect our dinner, but from their regard to their own interest."

2. Critical Thinking What are the forces that together comprise the invisible hand?

3. Learn More Conduct further research and describe the similarities between two 1776 publications: *The Wealth of Nations* and the Declaration of Independence.

Preview

Objectives

After studying this section you will be able to:

1. **Describe** how a centrally planned economy is organized.
2. **Analyze** the centrally planned economy of the former Soviet Union.
3. **Identify** the problems of a centrally planned economy.

Section Focus

In a centrally planned, or command economy, the central government controls the economy. Central planning has limitations and disadvantages not found in market economies.

Key Terms

socialism
communism
authoritarian
collective
heavy industry

Centrally planned economies operate in direct contrast to free market systems. Centrally planned economies oppose private property, free market pricing, competition, and consumer choice.

How Is a Centrally Planned Economy Organized?

In a centrally planned economy, the central government, rather than individual producers and consumers in markets, answers the key economic questions of production and consumption. A central bureaucracy makes all the decisions about what items to produce, how to produce them, and who gets them. After collecting information, bureaucrats tell each firm what and how much to produce. It is up to the bureaucrats to ensure that each firm has enough raw materials and workers to meet its production goals.

Government Control of Factor Resources and Production

In a centrally planned economy, the government owns both land and capital. In a sense it owns labor, too, by controlling

▶ Government posters in Cuba (left) and Cambodia (right) try to inspire worker productivity in these centrally planned economies.

where individuals work and what wages they are paid. The government decides what to produce, how much to produce, and how much to charge. Each year, it directs workers to produce a certain number of trucks, so many yards of cotton fabric, a certain amount of glass, and so on. Farmers are told what to plant, how to plant, and where to send their crops. The free market forces of self-interest and competition are absent from the system.

For example, let's follow the decision-making process for the production of military uniforms and a consumer product—sweaters.

1. The top planners decide that more military uniforms than sweaters will be made. They send this decision to the materials committee.
2. Knowing how much cotton is available, the materials committee decides how many sweaters and how many military uniforms will be made. They send their decision to the cotton makers, the button makers, and the elastic makers.
3. The cotton, the buttons, and the elastic arrive at sweater factories and uniform factories where they are manufactured into sweaters and uniforms.

As you can see, decisions on what to produce and how much to produce are not determined by consumers. Chances are that many citizens living under this economy would still need new sweaters. This lack of consumer voice in production and distribution shows that under centrally planned economies, consumers do not have consumer sovereignty.

Socialism and Communism

The words most often associated with centrally planned economies are *socialism* and *communism*. They are often used interchangeably, but we need to make a distinction between the two terms.

Socialism is a social and political philosophy based on the belief that democratic means should be used to distribute wealth evenly throughout a society. Real equality, socialists argue, can only exist when

▲ How would you describe production in this Romanian factory?

political equality is coupled with economic equality. Economic equality is possible only if the public controls the centers of economic power. Although socialist nations may be democracies, socialism requires a high degree of central planning to achieve economic equality.

In socialist countries the government often owns major industries, such as utilities. Socialism, as you will see in Section 4, exists to varying degrees in different nations throughout the world.

Communism is a political system that arose out of the philosophy of socialism. **Communism** is characterized by a centrally planned economy with all economic and political power resting in the hands of the central government.

Unlike socialists, however, communists believed that a socialist society can only come about after a violent revolution. While socialist economies can still allow for democracy, communist governments are **authoritarian**. Authoritarian governments exact strict obedience from their citizens and do not allow individuals freedom of judgment and action. Throughout history, communist nations have been dominated by a single political

socialism *a social and political philosophy based on the belief that democratic means should be used to evenly distribute wealth throughout a society*

communism *a political system characterized by a centrally planned economy with all economic and political power resting in the hands of the central government*

authoritarian *requiring strict obedience to an authority, such as a dictator*

▶ Karl Marx (left) and Friedrich Engels (center) introduced their socialist philosophy in *The Communist Manifesto* in 1848. The term *communist* was adopted by the Bolsheviks who, led by Vladimir Lenin (right), took control of Russia in 1917.

collective *large farm leased from the state to groups of peasant farmers*

party or dictator. The former Soviet Union was a communist nation that provides us with a good case study of how a centrally planned economy works—and doesn't work.

The Former Soviet Union

The Soviet Union arose out of a pair of revolutions in Russia in 1917. In March, imperial rule in Russia came to an end when Czar Nicholas II was forced from the throne. A provisional republican government was set up, but by November it, too, was toppled. It was taken over by the Bolsheviks, revolutionary socialists led by Vladimir Lenin. Once in power, they renamed themselves communists, instituted a reign of terror, and murdered the former czar and his wife and children. Under the control of the Communist party, central planning was introduced during the 1920s and continued to operate until the breakup of the Soviet Union in 1991.

Soviet planners were most concerned with building national power and prestige in the international community. As a result, they allocated the best land, labor, and capital to the armed forces, space program, and production of capital goods such as farm equipment and factories. The committees that ran the system were responsible for deciding the quantity, production process, and distribution of 24 million different goods and services.

▶ How would you describe the farming techniques shown in this photo of a Soviet collective?

Soviet Agriculture

In the Soviet Union, the central government created large state-owned farms and collectives for most of the country's agricultural production. On state-run farms, the state provided farmers with all equipment, seed, and fertilizer. Farmers worked for daily wages set by economic planners.

Collectives were large farms leased from the state to groups of peasant farmers. Farmers managed operation of the collectives, though they still were required to produce what the government instructed them to. Farmers either received a share of what they produced or income from its sale.

Agricultural workers were guaranteed employment and income, and the govern-

ment established quotas and distribution. Under such a system, individuals had few incentives to produce more or better crops. While Russia had been a major exporter of wheat until 1913, before long the Soviet Union could not keep its own people fed. Soviet agriculture bore much of the opportunity cost of Soviet central planning decisions.

Soviet Industry

Soviet factories also were state-owned. Planners favored the defense industry, the space program, and **heavy industry**. (Heavy industry requires a large capital investment to produce items used in other industries. Chemical, steel, and heavy machinery manufacturing are heavy industries.) The makers of consumer goods and services paid the opportunity cost of this concentration of resources. They were stuck with leftover, lower-quality resources with which to create their products.

Like agriculture, industry was characterized by a lack of incentives. Jobs were guaranteed, and wages were set by the government. Once a production quota was met, there was no reason to produce more goods. Workers had little incentive to work harder or to innovate. In fact, it was illegal for workers to exhibit entrepreneurial behavior.

▲ Shifting from communism to a free market economy has been a difficult transition. Consumers often waited hours in long lines only to discover nearly empty store shelves.

Soviet Consumers

Consumers, too, experienced the opportunity cost of central planners' decisions. Consumer goods were scarce and usually of poor quality. Manufacturers had the incentive to focus on quantity, not quality. For example, a manufacturer assigned to produce a certain number of suits could loosely stitch the buttons and forget the buttonholes and mismatch coats and trousers. Still, the state store had to accept delivery of the suits. Consumers would be left with no alternatives.

Consumers often had difficulty getting goods, too. They wasted countless hours waiting in line to purchase goods and services. Luxuries such as meat were made affordable by government price setting, but they were rarely available. Housing shortages forced people to live in crowded and poorly constructed apartments. Because of the long waiting list for apartments, it was not unusual to find a family living in just two rooms.

heavy industry *industry that requires a large capital investment and that produces items used in other industries*

THE WALL STREET JOURNAL.
CLASSROOM EDITION

In the News When Alexander Lukashenko became president of Belarus in 1994, the former Soviet republic retreated to a **centrally planned economy**. As this excerpt from a Wall Street Journal Classroom Edition *article shows, entrepreneurship was discouraged.*

City authorities in Minsk "threw the book at Patio Pizza's pasta. Inspectors from the Public Nutrition Department, or Obshepit, decreed the restaurant's menu wasn't in keeping with the official Belarussian cookbook, a 200-page tome designed to guarantee that national dishes are prepared exactly the same way throughout Minsk. For this and [various] other violations, including unauthorized ice levels in [drinks], the city closed the restaurant."

▲ Statues of Lenin were toppled after the collapse of communism in the Soviet Union in 1991.

Problems of Centrally Planned Economies

Central planning can be used to jumpstart selected industries and guarantee jobs and income. The other side of the coin, however, is poor quality, serious shortages of non-priority goods and services, and diminishing production.

In theory, centrally planned economies can work effectively toward explicitly stated goals. For example, in 1928, Soviet leader Joseph Stalin instituted the first of several five-year plans to boost production. While a disaster in terms of agriculture, Stalin had some success in increasing output in heavy industries.

Perhaps the greatest disadvantage of centrally planned economies is that their performance almost always falls far short of the ideals upon which the system is built. In addition, such systems generally cannot meet consumers' needs or wants. Since the government owns all production factors, workers lack any incentive to work hard. These systems also do not reward innovation, actively discouraging any kind of change. The large, expensive bureaucracy necessary to make the thousands of production and distribution decisions to run the economy lacks the flexibility to adjust to consumer demands. Decisions become overly complicated. Finally, command economies sacrifice individual freedoms in order to pursue societal goals.

Many areas of the world, especially less developed countries, have experimented with centrally planned economies, but most of these experiments have failed. Instead, most of these nations have moved toward mixed economies over the past twenty years. In the next section, you will read about today's mixed economies.

Section 3 Assessment

Key Terms and Main Ideas

1. How do **socialism** and **communism** differ?
2. What characterizes an **authoritarian** government?
3. Why did Soviet **collectives** offer little incentive to farmers?
4. In the Soviet Union, what was the opportunity cost of the emphasis on **heavy industry**?

Applying Economic Concepts

5. *Critical Thinking* Why do centrally planned economies have difficulty meeting consumer needs?
6. *Decision Making* Which of the following economic goals are difficult to achieve in a centrally planned economy? **(a)** economic efficiency **(b)** economic security and predictability **(c)** economic equity **(d)** economic growth and innovation

Take It to the NET

Russia, the dominant republic of the former Soviet Union, is now an example of a nation trying to make the transition from a centrally planned economy to a market economy. Identify and describe at least two actions taken to create a freer economy there. How well are these reforms working? Use the links provided in the Social Studies area at the following Web site for help in completing this activity. **www.phschool.com**

Russia in Crisis

In 1991, when the Communist system in Russia collapsed, many Russians rejoiced at the prospect of living under a freer political and economic system. Many specifically looked forward to living in a Western-style free market economy.

During the next decade, Russians experienced an economic crisis. Although economists had predicted that switching to a free enterprise system would be difficult, few predicted how traumatic it would be.

Corruption The confusion caused by the sudden upheaval of both the political and economic systems opened the door for crime and corruption on an enormous scale. Some businessmen and politicians took advantage of the nation's inexperience with a market economy and abused their power by robbing the nation's assets.

Financial Problems Russia's gross domestic product has shrunk nearly every year since the collapse of the Soviet Union. The nation has had to devalue its currency and postpone making payments on the loans it received from Western nations.

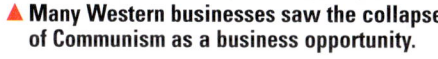
▲ Many Western businesses saw the collapse of Communism as a business opportunity.

Hardest hit of all have been Russia's citizens. Some 40 million people live below the poverty line—defined as about $30 a month. They have suffered through severe food shortages, and many workers have gone months without being paid.

Success Stories Although Russia's problems have been severe, it is possible for a nation to make the transition successfully. Poland, for example, has done so. In the years since the collapse of the Communist regime, Poland has become one of Europe's fastest-growing economies. Poland encourages small start-up companies and refuses to subsidize insolvent firms. Russia, on the other hand, actively discourages start-ups by requiring licensing and imposing other regulations. In Russia, insolvent businesses can still stay afloat because of the elaborate system of bartering among suppliers. This discourages Russian businesses from becoming more efficient.

It is now obvious that Russia's problems in making the transition were seriously underestimated. As this painful process continues, Russians continue to ask whether the nation will have the staying power to overcome these problems and make a free market economy a reality.

Applying Economic Ideas

1. What problems has Russia experienced in switching from a state-controlled to a free market economy?
2. Why might Western nations be willing to make loans to troubled Russia?

Modern Economies

Objectives

After studying this section you will be able to:

1. **Explain** the rise of mixed economic systems.
2. **Interpret** a circular flow model of a mixed economy.
3. **Compare** the mixed economies of various nations along a continuum between centrally planned and free market systems.
4. **Understand** the role of free enterprise in the economy of the United States.

Section Focus

It is doubtful that any nation can exist successfully under a pure centrally planned economy or a pure market economy. Most modern economies mix features of both systems. The economy of the United States is based on the principles of the free market.

Key Terms

laissez faire
private property
free enterprise
continuum
transition
privatize

You cannot find today any economic system that relies exclusively on central planning or the individual initiative of the free market. Instead, most economies are a mixture of economic systems. Most contemporary mixed economies blend the market with government intervention, or involvement, in the marketplace.

The Rise of Mixed Economies

No single economic system has all the answers. Centrally planned economies are cumbersome, do not adequately meet consumer needs, and limit freedom. Traditional economies have little potential for growth or change. Even market economies, with all their advantages, have certain drawbacks.

The Limits of Laissez Faire

Adam Smith and other early free market philosophers believed that, left to its own devices, the free market system would provide the greatest benefit for consumers and raise the standard of living. They

▶ **Most public parks rely on government dollars for support.**

preached **laissez faire**, the doctrine that government generally should not intervene in the marketplace. (See the Profile of Adam Smith on page 33.) Even Smith acknowledged, however, the need for a certain limited degree of government intervention in the economy.

As market economies have evolved since Smith's time, government intervention has become greater because some needs and wants of modern society are difficult to answer in the marketplace. In addition, people's preferences for redistribution have changed.

Some needs that markets could meet fall to governments so that all members of society can participate. Education is one example. Other needs that could fall into this category are health care and mass transit.

Governments create laws protecting property rights and enforcing contracts. There would be little incentive to develop new products without property rights or patent laws (laws that give the inventor of a new product the exclusive right to sell it for a certain period of time). Without laws insisting on competition, many people fear that some firms would dominate others in their industry and be able to charge consumers any price.

You will recall from your study of American history that the 5th and 14th amendments to the Constitution declare that no person may be deprived of "Life, liberty, or property, without due process of law." The 5th Amendment also says that "just compensation" must be paid to owners when private property is taken for public use. **Private property** is property that is owned by individuals or companies, not by the government or the people as a whole. The Framers of the Constitution ensured that the United States government would protect this fundamental right.

Balancing Control and Freedom

A society must assess its values and prioritize its economic goals. Some goals are

◀ These kindergarten students in this school lunch program are enjoying a benefit of government intervention.

better met by the open market and others are better met by government action. In addition, societies must evaluate the opportunity cost of pursuing each goal.

Each nation decides what it is willing to give up to meet its goals. What are you willing to give up? Are you willing to pay taxes to fund the army? To give money to people without jobs? To give all people an education? To subsidize farms? Should the government establish job-safety guidelines or a minimum wage?

laissez faire *the doctrine that states that government generally should not intervene in the marketplace*

private property *property owned by individuals or companies, not by the government or the people as a whole*

Global Connections

Sweden's Mixed Economy Sweden's mixed economy has mixed benefits for the Swedish people. The Swedish government redistributes more than half of Sweden's wealth through social benefit programs. When a child is born, his or her parents are entitled to a combined 450 days of parental leave, with three quarters of their base salary paid by the government. Swedish patients never pay more than 1,300 Swedish kronor (about $170) per year for prescriptions. If you were a teen in Sweden, your new braces would be free. Employers are required to give employees a minimum of 30 days vacation. The trade-off for these benefits is the second-highest tax burden of any industrialized country. Swedes pay around 56 percent of their incomes in taxes, compared to only 32 percent in the United States. **How would you describe the level of government involvement in Sweden's economy?**

This circular flow model shows how government typically interacts with households and businesses in the marketplace.

Economic Systems Explain how government actions affect the circular flow model in a mixed economy.

Figure 2.4 Circular Flow Model of a Mixed Economy

Product market

monetary flow

physical flow

taxes

government purchases

Households — expenditures — Government — expenditures — Firms

government-owned factors

taxes

physical flow

monetary flow

Factor market

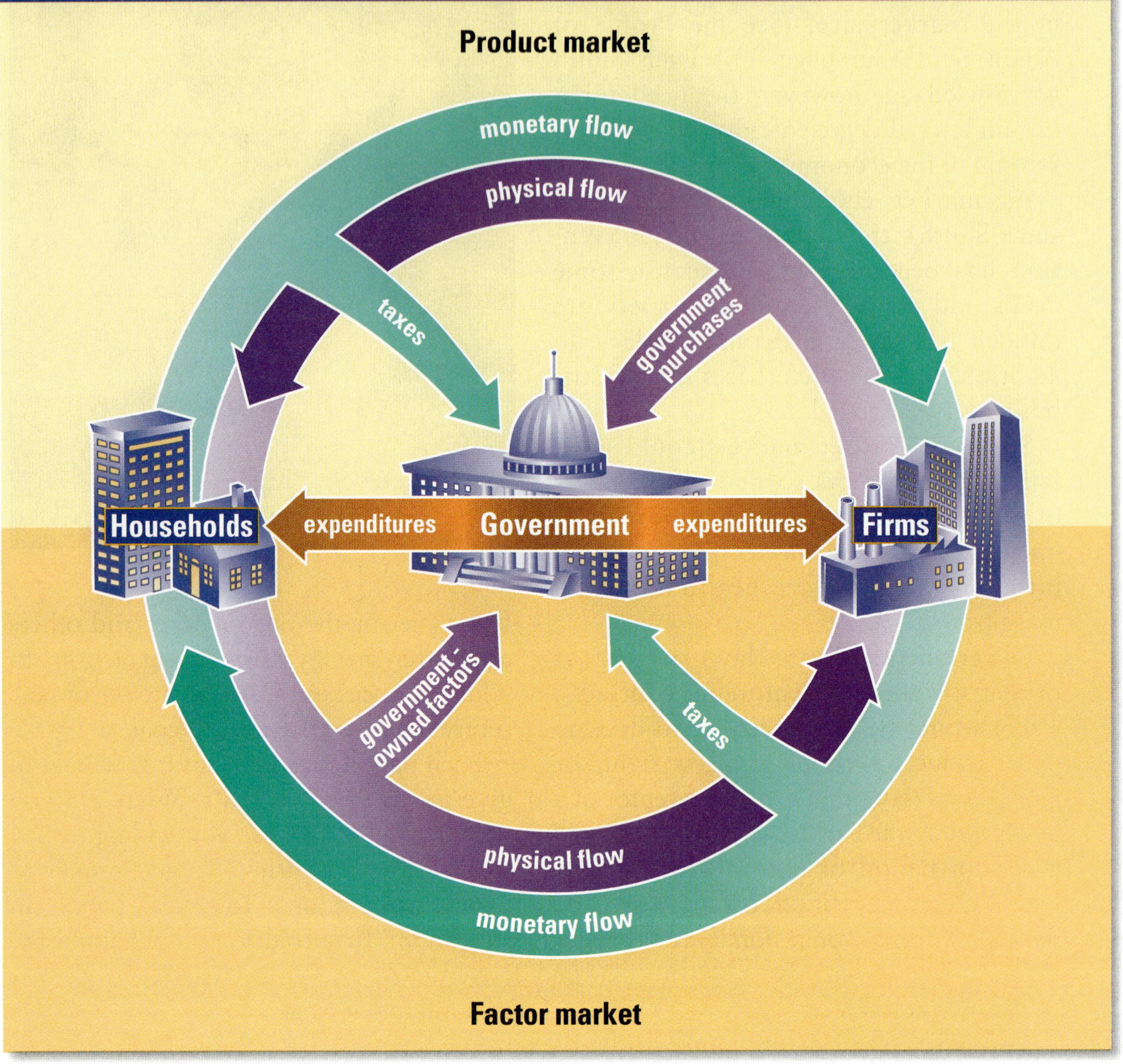

A Circular Flow Model of a Mixed Economy

To illustrate the structure of most modern economies accurately, we need to add government to our picture of the circular flow of economic activity. Figure 2.4 illustrates the government's role in the marketplace in a mixed economy. The government can enter the circular flow of economic activity in many ways.

Government in the Factor Market

Just like businesses, the government purchases land, labor, and capital from households in the factor market. For example, the United States government pays 2.8 million employees $9.7 billion a year for their labor.

Government in the Product Market

Governments purchase goods and services in the product market. They need buildings and office supplies, telephones, computers, and fax machines, for example.

Governments also provide certain goods and services through the factor resources that they combine. The federal, state, and local governments in the United States, for example, provide 4 million miles of roads.

Transferring Money

As you can see from the outer ring of Figure 2.4, governments collect taxes from both households and businesses. Governments then transfer the money they collect to businesses and individuals for a variety of reasons ranging from worker disability to the survival of an industry. The greatest expenditure of the United States government is Social Security.

Comparing Mixed Economies

The foundation of the United States economy is the free market. An economic system characterized by private or corporate ownership of capital goods is called **free enterprise**. In a free enterprise system investments are determined in a free market by private decision rather than by state control. Figure 2.5 below shows a continuum of mixed economies. A **continuum** is a range with no clear divisions. On one end of the scale is the centrally planned economy. On the opposite end is the free market economy.

Mixed Economies Where Government Intervention Dominates

Reflecting an economy almost totally dominated by the government, North Korea occupies one end of the scale.

Government owns all the property and all economic output. State-owned industries produce 95 percent of North Korea's goods. Almost all imports are banned, and production of goods and services by foreign companies is forbidden.

In China, where the economy is dominated by government, one quarter of all enterprises are at least partly owned by individuals. China, like many nations that have relied heavily on central planning in the past, is in **transition,** a period of change in which an economy moves away from central planning toward a market-based system. To make the transition, state firms must be **privatized,** or sold to individuals, and then allowed to compete with one another in the marketplace. As you will read in Chapter 18, economic transition is a difficult, and often painful, process.

Mixed Economies Where the Market System Dominates

At the other end of the scale, with one of the world's freest markets, is Hong Kong. Hong Kong, once administered by Great Britain, is now a special administrative region of China. It continues, at the beginning of the twenty-

> **FAST FACT**
>
> In competition with foreign fast-food restaurant chains, Chinese entrepreneur Shen Qing started his own restaurant chain—the Baked Pig Face restaurants. The seasoned pigs' heads, served in a modern setting, are wildly popular. Mr. Shen benefits by receiving profits, and consumers benefit by being able to choose a traditional Chinese dish over Western-style fast food.

free enterprise *an economic system characterized by private or corporate ownership of capital goods; investments that are determined by private decision rather than by state control; and determined in a free market*

continuum *a range with no clear divisions*

transition *period of change in which an economy moves away from a centrally planned economy toward a market-based system*

privatize *to sell state-run firms to individuals*

Figure 2.5 Continuum of Mixed Economies

Centrally planned ⟶ **Free market**

Iran		South Africa	France		United Kingdom	Hong Kong
North Korea	China	Botswana			Canada	Singapore
Cuba	Russia	Greece	Peru		United States	

Source: *1999 Index of Economic Freedom*, Bryan T. Johnson, Kim R. Holmes, and Melanie Kirkpatrick

The degree of government intervention in the marketplace varies among nations.
Economic Systems How would you explain China's position on this continuum? Why is Hong Kong, technically part of China, so far to the right on this diagram?

► What type of economic system do you see reflected in this busy mall?

foreign trade. Banks in Hong Kong operate independently of the government, and foreign-owned banks have nearly all the same rights as domestic ones.

The United States Economy

The United States has a free enterprise economy. Still, the government intervenes to keep order, provide vital services, and to promote the general welfare. Some people argue for more government services, while others say that the government already intervenes too much in the economy. Nevertheless, the United States enjoys a high level of economic freedom.

United States law protects private property. The marketplace operates with a low level of government regulation. Foreign investment is encouraged. So, too, is free trade, although the United States does protect some domestic industries and does retaliate against trade restrictions imposed by other nations. The banking industry operates under relatively few restrictions, and foreign-owned banks have few additional restrictions. In the next chapter, you will read in detail about the government and the free enterprise economy of the United States.

first century, largely under the free economic system it enjoyed under British rule.

In Hong Kong, the private sector rules. The government protects private property and rarely interferes in the free market, aside from establishing wage and price controls on rent and some public services. It is highly receptive to foreign investment and imposes virtually no barriers on

Section 4 Assessment

Key Terms and Main Ideas

1. What is **laissez faire**?
2. Why have some nations begun a **transition** to **free enterprise**?
3. Why are nations with centrally planned economies sometimes slow to succeed when they **privatize** industry?
4. Compare the U.S. free enterprise system with other economic systems you have read about in this chapter.

Applying Economic Concepts

5. *Critical Thinking* What benefits might citizens of a centrally planned economy derive from a move toward a market-based system?

6. *Try This* Survey newspapers and magazines to find articles describing life in different economic systems. Construct a bulletin board of the continuum of economies in Fig. 2.5. Place each article on the appropriate location on the continuum.

 **Take It to the NET**

Identify four agencies or organizations in the United States government that play a direct role in the nation's economy. Write down each agency's name and purpose. What are the advantages and disadvantages of this government intervention in the marketplace? Use the links provided in the Social Studies area at the following Web site for help in completing this activity. **www.phschool.com**

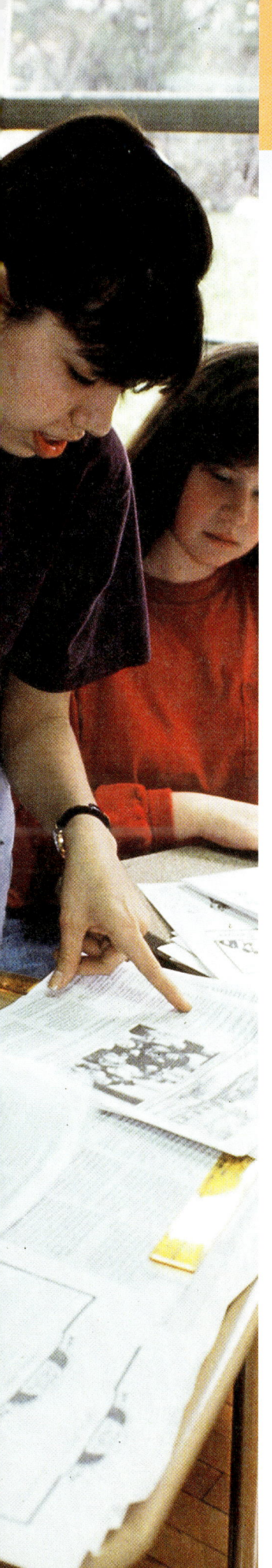

Building Flowcharts

A flowchart is a visual guide to a process that breaks the process down into individual steps. Arrows often indicate the order and relationships among the steps. In economics, flowcharts help people visualize the ways goods are produced, how money flows through the economy, and how decisions can affect many people. Use the following steps to analyze the flowchart below.

1. **Identify the steps of the process.** Read the labels in the boxes to familiarize yourself with the process of writing an article. **(a)** What does Laura do after she interviews people for the article? **(b)** What are the two choices for step one of the process?

2. **Analyze the relationships among steps.** A flowchart shows a series of actions and decisions. **(a)** According to this particular chart, who can make a decision that directly affects the flow? **(b)** Why does the path split into two new paths after Laura submits the article to her editor?

3. **Predict possible future developments.** New arrows and steps can be added anywhere along the flowchart, not just at the ends. Picture how different decisions and actions might change the look of Laura's flowchart. **(a)** Where else might the flowchart split into two new paths? **(b)** Give an example of a new step that could be added to start a new path.

Laura hears about a story that would make a good article.

Laura's editor assigns her a story to research for an article.

Laura interviews several students.

Laura writes an article and submits it to her editor.

Laura's editor decides not to print the article in the next issue.

Laura's editor revises the article and includes it in the next issue.

Laura's article appears in the newspaper that week.

Additional Practice

Construct a flowchart to show the steps that you could take to offer a new product for sale in your small food store.

Chapter 2 Assessment

Chapter Summary

A summary of the major ideas in Chapter 2 appears below. See also the **Guide to the Essentials of Economics,** which provides additional review and test practice of key concepts in Chapter 2.

Section 1 Answering the Three Economic Questions (pp. 23–27)

The three basic economic questions societies ask are (1) What goods and services should be produced? (2) How should these goods and services be produced? and (3) Who consumes these goods and services? An **economic system** is the way a society decides to answer these three economic questions. There are four general types of economic systems: **traditional economies, market economies, centrally planned** (or **command**) **economies,** and **mixed economies.**

Section 2 The Free Market (pp. 28–32)

A free market is a self-regulating economic system powered by individuals acting in their own **self-interest.** In a free market economy, the factors of production are privately owned, and individuals decide how to answer the three economic questions.

Section 3 Centrally Planned Economies (pp. 34–38)

In a **centrally planned economy** the central government controls the factors of production and answers the three basic economic questions for all of society. Two systems often mentioned when centrally planned economies are discussed are **socialism** and **communism.**

Section 4 Modern Economies (pp. 40–44)

Most of the economic systems in the world today are mixed economies. These systems use a combination of government involvement and free markets. Throughout the world there are different levels of government intervention in mixed economies.

Key Terms

Match the following terms with the definitions listed below. You will not use all of the terms.

competition	laissez faire
socialism	privatize
mixed economy	consumer
self-interest	sovereignty
command economy	market economy

1. System that combines the free market with some government intervention
2. One's own personal gain
3. The doctrine that states that government generally should not intervene in the marketplace
4. System in which the central government makes all decisions on the production and consumption of goods and services
5. The struggle among producers for the dollars of consumers
6. System in which decisions on production and consumption of goods and services are based entirely on exchange, or trade

Using Graphic Organizers

7. On a separate sheet of paper, copy the web map below showing the advantages and values of a mixed economy. Complete the web map with examples from your knowledge or experience.

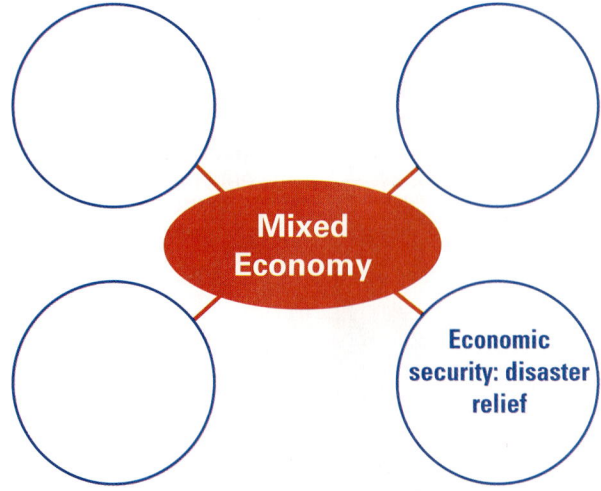

Mixed Economy

Economic security: disaster relief

Reviewing Main Ideas

8. Think of a business in your local area. Describe its operation in terms of factor markets and product markets.

9. Explain how a factory assembly line is an example of specialization.

10. Why are there no pure free market economies in the world?

11. Compare the circular flow diagrams of a free market and a mixed economy. Describe how they differ, and why.

Critical Thinking

12. Synthesizing Information Suppose that your household is its own society. How are the three key economic questions answered?

13. Predicting Consequences Think of three ways your life would change if the United States began using a pure free market system or a pure centrally planned system instead of the free enterprise system.

14. Analyzing Information Review the advantages and disadvantages of both free market economies and centrally planned economies. Assess the way each system values economic freedom and economic equity.

Problem-Solving Activity

15. Suppose that you are opening a new music store in your town. What resources would you need from the factor market? What would you offer in the product market? How would the government affect your business?

Skills for Life

Building Flowcharts Review the steps on page 45; then answer the following questions using the flowchart below.

16. What does Megan do to try to make extra money this weekend?

17. Why does the flowchart split into two paths after Megan sets up her stand?

18. What step does Megan take if the neighbors like her cookies?

19. If the neighbors do not like cookies, where could a step or steps be added so Megan could succeed next time?

20. Organize a flowchart for yourself depicting a goal that you did not achieve. (**a**) Take a close look at the steps you took. (**b**) What errors did you make? (**c**) Decide which steps you can change so you can succeed in the future.

Economics Journal

Organizing Ideas Review your personal list of systems. Rewrite your list in two columns. In one column, list the systems that are more influenced by central planning. In the other column, list the ones that are more influenced by the free market. Add to each list other systems you use on a regular basis.

Take It to the NET

Chapter 2 Self-Test As a final review activity, take the Economics Chapter 2 Self-Test in the Social Studies area at the Web site listed below, and receive immediate feedback on your answers. The test consists of 20 multiple-choice questions designed to test your understanding of the chapter content.
www.phschool.com

Economics Simulation

Designing an Economic System

Most people live and work within an established economic system. Sometimes government economic policy decisions bring gradual shifts or changes to an established system. For example, in the United States during the Great Depression, many new federal programs—notably Social Security—changed the role of government in the American economy. Occasionally, a revolution overthrows an established economic system and puts in place a new one, as you read in Chapter 2.

What if you could design an economic system from scratch? Suppose that you are part of a group of people who have inherited an uninhabited island. As the first settlers on this island, one of your tasks will be to establish an economic system.

Materials

Notebook paper

Box or paper bag

Preparing the Simulation

In this simulation, your group will play the role of an island's first settlers. Your goal is to plan an economic system. Each group has members who represent the major economic systems—free market and centrally planned economies. As the founders of a new community, you may choose either of those systems or you may take elements from different systems and create a new one.

Step 1: The teacher or several student volunteers should prepare one slip of paper for each student in the class, as follows:

One half labeled **"Free Market Economy (Capitalist, Democratic)"**

One half labeled **"Centrally Planned Economy (Socialist, Authoritarian)"**

Step 2: Place the slips in a box or paper bag. Form groups of six to eight people,

▲ **Will services such as postal delivery be provided by the government or by private companies?**

representing Island A, Island B, Island C, and so on. When the groups are set, each member should draw one of the labeled slips of paper, which will determine the economic system that member argues for in the discussion.

Be aware that the groups will probably not be evenly balanced between both economies. (If any group has representatives of only one system, redo the drawing.)

Step 3: Review the basics of the economic system that you represent. You will be advocating this system, so play your role as if this is the system you grew up in and are most familiar with.

48

Conducting the Simulation

This simulation will consist of four phases. Each group will identify and discuss its options, reach an agreement, and present its plan to the class.

Presentation of Options: Within your group, determine the options for your island economy. Delegates for each of the economic systems represented in the group should present the benefits of their systems in a persuasive manner.

Discussion: After the benefits of both systems have been explained, each group should debate the benefits and drawbacks of each economic system. You may want to make a decision-making grid to see the trade-offs.

Negotiation: Then your group should decide whether you wish to accept one of the systems as a whole or create a new system using elements of both systems.

You should answer these questions:
a) Who decides how resources will be allocated?
b) Who owns the factors of production?
c) Who determines what goods and services will be produced?
d) Who determines prices?
e) How is income distributed?
f) Must all members contribute equally?
g) What social benefits does the system supply?
h) What is the role of government in the economy?
Create a chart like the one on this page to summarize the structure of your island's economy.

Class Presentation: Each group should choose a speaker to present the system to the class. After each presentation, class members may ask questions about the system, so the spokesperson should be ready to defend the group's decisions.

Summary of Island Economic System

Feature of Economic System	How Defined in Island Economy
Role of Government	
Ownership of Land and Capital	
Decision Makers for Production and Pricing	
Income Distribution	
Social Benefits	

Simulation Analysis

After listening to each group's speaker present the group's conclusions, answer the following questions:

1. Did the systems your class created closely resemble the systems of any specific countries? If so, which ones?
2. How much did the roles of group members influence the economic decisions you made?
3. What was the most problematic issue for each group?
4. **Making Comparisons** How does living in a free market economy affect your view of another economic system?

Chapter 3 American Free Enterprise

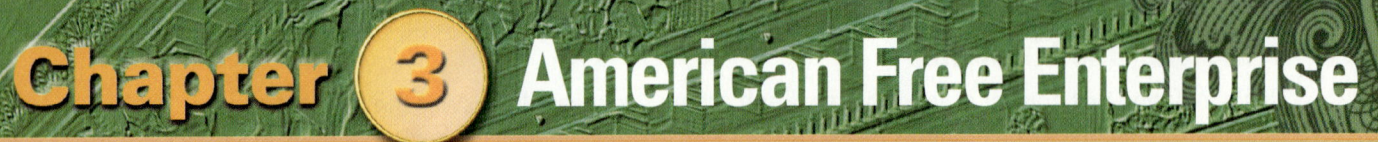

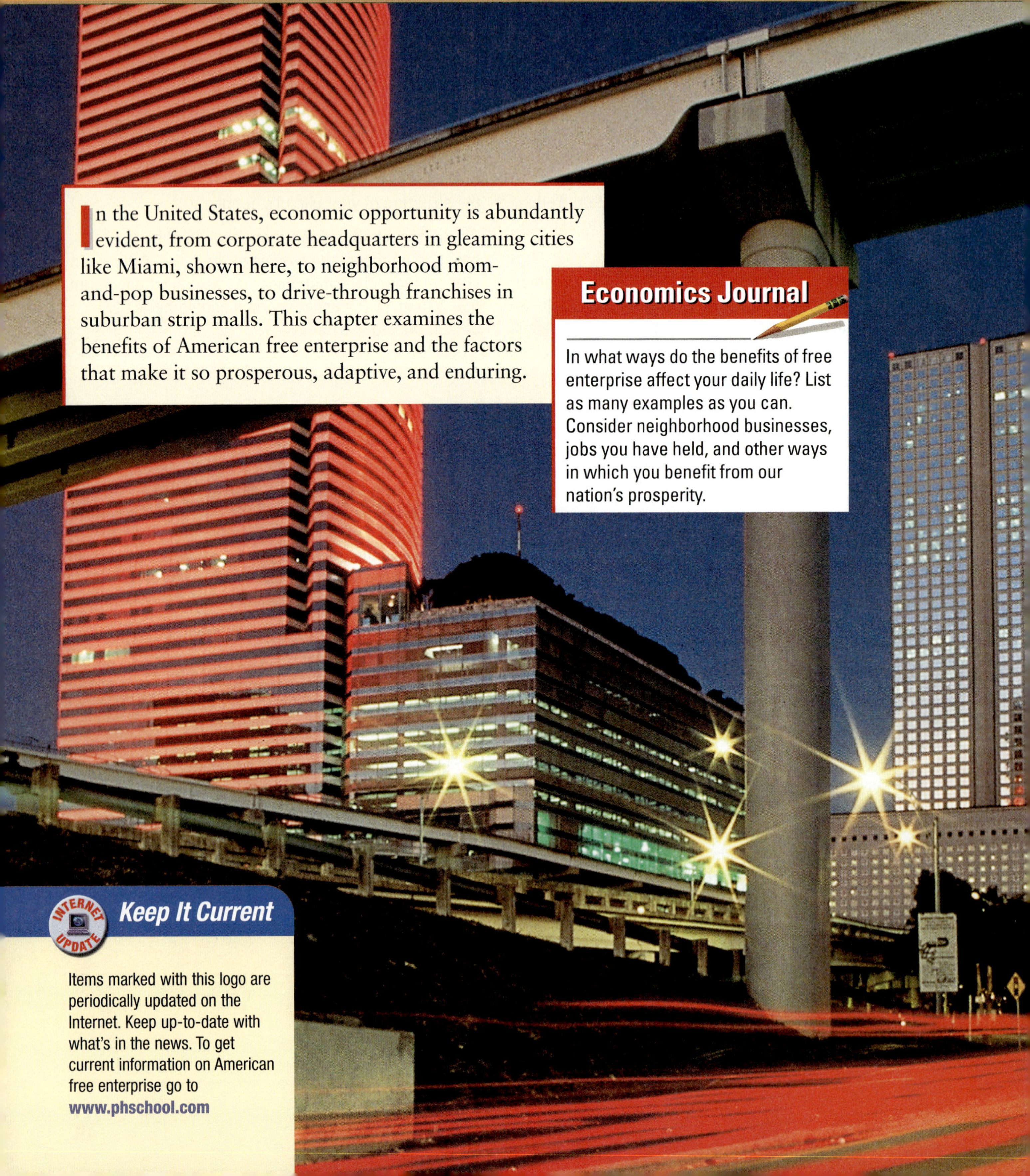

In the United States, economic opportunity is abundantly evident, from corporate headquarters in gleaming cities like Miami, shown here, to neighborhood mom-and-pop businesses, to drive-through franchises in suburban strip malls. This chapter examines the benefits of American free enterprise and the factors that make it so prosperous, adaptive, and enduring.

Economics Journal

In what ways do the benefits of free enterprise affect your daily life? List as many examples as you can. Consider neighborhood businesses, jobs you have held, and other ways in which you benefit from our nation's prosperity.

Keep It Current

Items marked with this logo are periodically updated on the Internet. Keep up-to-date with what's in the news. To get current information on American free enterprise go to **www.phschool.com**

Benefits of Free Enterprise

Objectives

After studying this section you will be able to:

1. **Describe** the tradition of free enterprise in the United States and the constitutional protections that underlie it.
2. **Explain** the basic principles of the U.S. free enterprise system.
3. **Identify** the role of the consumer in the U.S. free enterprise system.
4. **Describe** the role of the government in the U.S. free enterprise system.

Section Focus

American free enterprise is based on the principles of profit motive, voluntary exchange, private property rights, competition, and freedom for producers and consumers. The U.S. Constitution supports the free enterprise system by guaranteeing private property rights, the right to make contracts, and freedom from unfair taxation.

Key Terms

profit motive
open opportunity
private property rights
free contract
voluntary exchange
competition
interest group
public disclosure laws
public interest

Some of the most famous Americans have not been politicians, sports figures, or actors. Do you recognize names like John D. Rockefeller, founder of Standard Oil of New Jersey, or Andrew Carnegie, who started Carnegie Steel Company, or Bill Gates, the founder of Microsoft? Each of these people started with an idea and through persistence, vision, and effort built that idea into a huge business success. They made themselves into the richest people of their time, helped fuel the economy, and contributed vast sums of money to programs and charities for the public good.

A Tradition of Free Enterprise

Today there are over 18 million unincorporated businesses in America, including about 3 million minority-owned businesses. Many of these were started by a single entrepreneur or a small group of friends or family members hoping to earn a living and, perhaps, become successful or even wealthy.

For centuries, people have considered America to be a "land of opportunity"—a place where anyone from any background could achieve success through hard work.

Although immigrants no longer expect to find streets paved with gold, this country does offer special opportunities that have allowed business people to be so successful and have contributed to our overall economic prosperity.

Why has America been such an economic success? Certainly the open land, natural resources, and uninterrupted flow of immigrants with different backgrounds and experiences all contribute. But a key factor has also been the American tradition of free enterprise—the social and political commitment to giving people the freedom

▼ How does this photo represent the American free enterprise system?

Figure 3.1 Features of American Free Enterprise

Economic Freedom *In the United States, individuals have the right to choose their occupations and to work wherever they can find jobs. Businesses can make their own decisions on whom to hire, what to produce, how much to produce, and how much to charge for their products and services. The government generally does not interfere in these decisions.*

Competition *Producers have the right to engage in rivalries to gain business. Competing producers have an incentive to create new and better products. This gives consumers more economic choices.*

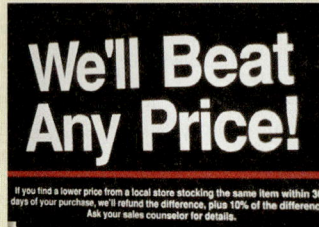

Private Property *Individuals and businesses have the right to buy and sell as much property as they want. Property owners may prohibit others from using their property.*

Contracts *Individuals and businesses have the right to make agreements to buy and sell goods. Such contracts may be written or oral. They are legally binding.*

Self-Interest *Consumers and producers may make decisions on the basis of their own benefit. Their decisions do not have to benefit or please the government or other consumers and producers.*

Voluntary Exchange *Consumers and producers may freely buy and sell goods when the opportunity costs of such exchanges are worthwhile. In a voluntary exchange, both parties expect to gain from the transaction.*

Profit Motive *American free enterprise is driven by the desire for profit, the gain that occurs during financial dealings. Profit is a powerful incentive that leads entrepreneurs and businesses to accept the risk of business failure.*

BUILDING KEY CONCEPTS

Free enterprise in America is founded on ideas so basic to our culture that we tend to take them for granted. **Government** **Choose one of these features and give an example from your own daily life.**

and flexibility to try out their business ideas and compete in the marketplace.

Constitutional Protections

The Bill of Rights to the United States Constitution guarantees certain individual freedoms, such as freedom of speech and freedom of religion. The Constitution also guarantees important rights that allow people to engage in business activities.

Property Rights

The most important of these is the constitutional recognition of property rights. In many other countries, even in modern times, the king or other ruler has had the power to take people's property for his own use. Early American statesmen wanted to protect against this, so they included property as a protected right under the Fifth Amendment. It is a right just as important as the other individual rights. The Fifth Amendment states that no person shall

> *"be deprived of life, liberty, or property, without due process of law; nor shall private property be taken for public use, without just compensation."*

Since the Fifth Amendment applies only to actions by the federal government, the Fourteenth Amendment, ratified in 1868, also includes a due process clause extending the same limitation to the state governments. These due process clauses prevent the government from taking property away from an individual except when there is a public reason—and even then the government must pay the person the fair value of the property that has been taken. These rights apply to corporations as well, so businesses get the same protection from government seizure that individuals enjoy.

Taxation

The Constitution also contains the basic rules for the ways in which the government can tax individuals and businesses. Congress can only tax in the ways the Constitution allows. Article I gives Congress the power to levy taxes, but Sections 2 and 9 require that direct taxes be apportioned according to population so that everyone will pay the same amount. The Sixteenth Amendment, ratified in 1913, first gave Congress the clear right to set taxes based on income.

Finally, the Constitution guarantees people and businesses the right to make binding contracts. Article I, Section 10 prohibits the states from passing any "Law impairing the Obligation of Contracts." This means that individuals or businesses cannot use the political process to get excused from their contracts. No legislature can pass a law changing the terms of someone's business agreement.

Basic Principles of Free Enterprise

Our free enterprise economy has several key characteristics. These include profit motive, open opportunity, legal equality, private property rights, free contract, voluntary exchange, and competition.

Profit Motive

The American economy rests on a recognition of the importance of the **profit motive**—the force that encourages people and organizations to improve their material well-being. Under other economic systems, the government may control business activities, deciding what companies will be formed and how they will be run. In a free enterprise system, business owners and managers make these choices themselves, operating in ways they believe will maximize their profits. This approach forces management to exercise financial discipline because it makes people economically responsible for their own success or failure. It rewards innovation by letting creative companies grow, and it improves productivity by allowing more efficient companies to make more money.

Open Opportunity

The United States economy also benefits from a strong tradition of **open opportunity,** the concept that everyone can compete in the marketplace. We accept that different people and different companies will have different economic outcomes, depending on their success in the marketplace. This allows economic mobility up or down: no matter how much money you start out with, you can end up wealthier or poorer depending on how well your business performs.

Economic Rights

We also have a commitment to **legal equality**—by giving everyone the same legal rights, we allow everyone to compete in the economic marketplace. Countries that restrict the legal rights of women or minorities lose the productive potential of a large portion of their society. Legal equality maximizes a country's use of its human capital.

Another essential component of the American free enterprise system are **private property rights,** the concept that people have the right and privilege to control their possessions as they wish. The free enterprise system allows people to make their own decisions about their own property.

The right of **free contract** allows people to decide what agreements they want to enter into. The right of **voluntary exchange** allows people to decide what and when they want to buy and sell, rather than forcing them to buy or sell at particular times or at specific prices. Because of all these rights, we have extensive **competition,** the rivalry among sellers to attract customers while lowering costs. Competition provides consumers with a larger variety of goods, most of which are sold at reasonable prices.

The Role of the Consumer

A fundamental purpose of the free enterprise system is to give consumers the freedom to make their own economic choices. Consumers make their desires known through their economic dealings with producers. When consumers buy

profit motive *the force that encourages people and organizations to improve their material well-being*

open opportunity *the concept that everyone can compete in the marketplace*

legal equality *the concept of giving everyone the same legal rights*

private property rights *the concept that people have the right and privilege to control their possessions as they wish*

free contract *the concept that people may decide what agreements they want to enter into*

voluntary exchange *the concept that people may decide what and when they want to buy and sell*

competition *the rivalry among sellers to attract customers while lowering costs*

▲ From what aspects of the free enterprise system are these students benefiting?

interest group *a private organization that tries to persuade public officials to act or vote according to group members' interests*

public disclosure laws *laws requiring companies to provide full information about their products*

public interest *the concerns of the public as a whole*

products, they signal to producers what to produce and how much to make.

Consumers can also make their wishes known by joining an **interest group**, which is a private organization that tries to persuade public officials to act or vote according to the interests of the group's members. Interest groups have formed around many economic issues, such as taxation, aid for farmers, and land use.

The Role of the Government

We expect the government to carry out its constitutional responsibilities to protect property rights, contracts, and other business activities in our free enterprise system. Even though such protections are not spelled out in the Constitution, Americans have also come to expect protection from problems that affect us all, such as air pollution or unsafe food.

 **Global Connections**

New Business in Russia Starting a new business in Russia is no easy task. The average new business applicant has to deal with 20 to 30 agencies and needs from 50 to as many as 90 approved registration forms. In addition, many businesses have to pay bribes to government officials for start-up licenses. Because the Russian economy is unreliable, banks are reluctant to lend to new businesses. Taxes are often unpredictable and can be very high. There are a vast number of different taxes that apply to almost every aspect of business life, and filling out the tax forms can be time consuming and expensive. As a final roadblock, a few large companies often control virtually an entire industry, making it difficult for new businesses to break in.

Information and Free Enterprise

In a free market system, consumer buying habits determine what goods get produced. But consumers will not be able to make informed choices if they cannot get basic information about the products they are buying. In other words, educated consumers will make the free market system work more efficiently. Because of this, one of the government's important roles in the economy is to make sure that producers provide consumers with information.

Consumers use government information to protect themselves from dangerous products and fraudulent claims. **Public disclosure laws** require companies to give consumers important information about their products. Often this information will be attached to the product when it is offered for sale in stores. You may have seen fuel efficiency labels on new cars, or energy efficiency tags on refrigerators or air conditioners. Using this information, consumers can evaluate some important aspects of the products they are considering buying.

Protecting Health, Safety, and Well-Being

Federal and state agencies regulate industries whose goods and services affect the well-being of the public. (See Figure 3.2.) Although the government does not get directly involved in running private businesses, it does impose various restrictions.

Businesses must follow certain environmental protection rules. Gas stations, for example, must dispose of used motor oil properly and ensure that gas tanks cannot leak into surrounding soil. Both individuals and businesses are subject to local zoning laws. These laws may forbid homeowners from running businesses out of their homes.

In addition, until the mid-1900s, manufacturers of cars, food, medicine, and other products affecting people's health and well-being were largely unregulated. Starting in the 1960s, however, the federal government and many states became actively involved in economic matters of **public interest,** the concerns of the public as a whole.

A key part of this new government activity was consumer protection. To this end the government sets manufacturing standards, requires that drugs be safe and effective, and supervises the sanitary conditions in which foods are produced. Labels on consumer packages must include information about safe operation of equipment or expiration dates for perishables.

Negative Effects of Regulation

Government regulation, however, can have negative effects on both businesses and consumers. During the 1960s and 1970s, popular demand for government protection of consumers and of the environment resulted in the creation of new governmental agencies and regulations. Businesses pointed out that the rules were costly to implement, cutting into profits, slowing growth, and forcing them to charge unnecessarily high prices. Highly regulated industries, such as the airlines and telephone companies, pointed out that government rules and regulations stifled competition, resulting in prices that were arbitrarily high. The growth in government oversight of industry also raised government spending.

In the 1980s and 1990s, public pressure for leaner, less costly government resulted in budget cuts that curtailed some government regulation of industry. President George W.

Figure 3.2 Major Federal Regulatory Agencies

Agency and Date Created	Role
1906 Food and Drug Administration (FDA)	Sets and enforces standards for food, drugs, and cosmetic products
1914 Federal Trade Commission (FTC)	Enacts and enforces antitrust laws to protect consumers
1934 Federal Communications Commission (FCC)	Regulates interstate and international communications by radio, television, wire, satellite, and cable
1958 Federal Aviation Administration (FAA)	Regulates civil aviation, air-traffic and piloting standards, and air commerce
1964 Equal Employment Opportunity Commission (EEOC)	Promotes equal job opportunity through enforcement of civil rights laws, education, and other programs
1970 Environmental Protection Agency (EPA)	Enacts policies to protect human health and the natural environment
1970 Occupational Safety and Health Administration (OSHA)	Enacts policies to save lives, prevent injuries, and protect the health of workers
1972 Consumer Product Safety Commission (CPSC)	Enacts policies for reducing risks of harm from consumer products
1974 Nuclear Regulatory Commission (NRC)	Regulates civilian use of nuclear products

This table shows a few of the many federal regulatory agencies. **Government Might the free market fulfill the mission of any of these agencies? Give an example.**

Bush's administration promised to be more sensitive to the economic considerations raised by businesses.

Section 1 Assessment

Key Terms and Main Ideas

1. Explain the importance of the following terms in the U.S. free enterprise system: **(a) profit motive, (b) voluntary exchange, (c) private property rights**, and **(d) competition**.

2. What constitutional guarantees underlie the American free enterprise system?

3. Explain at least three benefits of the free enterprise system.

Applying Economic Concepts

4. *Critical Thinking* What are some opportunity costs of a greater government role in the economy?

5. *Decision Making* Explain how the decisions you make as a consumer influence the economy.

6. *Critical Thinking* What is the impact of economic concepts in the U.S. Constitution on contemporary economic issues and policies? Use specific examples from the chapter to support your conclusions.

Take It to the NET Read more about the restrictions that the government places on the use of business and individual property. Then identify three examples and evaluate their costs and benefits to businesses and individuals. Use the links provided in the Social Studies area at the following Web site for help in completing this activity. **www.phschool.com**

Profile

Alice Rivlin (b. 1931)

During the 1994 congressional election campaign, debate raged about how to reduce government spending. Clinton-appointed economist Alice Rivlin recommended controversial cuts in government programs. When the Republicans, who had called for tax cuts instead, gained many seats in the election, the president's political advisors urged that Rivlin be fired.

Principles and Politics

Such controversy was nothing new for Alice Rivlin, who by 1994 had already built a long and distinguished career in Washington. Rivlin's opinions about the role of government in the nation's economy had gained her a reputation as a tough, nonpolitical economic analyst. "I am a fanatical, card-carrying middle-of-the-roader," Rivlin has stated. A former director of the Congressional Budget Office agreed. "She is someone who's called the shots straight," he said.

A Career in Public Service

As a teenager, Alice Rivlin wanted to be a diplomat. After taking an economics course in college, however, she decided on that field instead. Rivlin's talent for analyzing government policy emerged in 1957, when she worked at the Brookings Institution, a Washington "think tank" that researches social issues. In the 1960s, she helped plan President Johnson's "Great Society," a series of government programs aimed at reducing poverty.

In 1975, Rivlin became the first head of the Congressional Budget Office, a federal agency created to help Congress better understand government spending issues. When Bill Clinton became president in 1993, he called Rivlin to serve as Director of the Office of Management and Budget (OMB). In 1996, Clinton appointed her to the Federal Reserve Board, where she served until 1999. Today, Rivlin is chair of the Center on Urban and Metropolitan Policy at the Brookings Institution.

Rethinking Government's Role

Rivlin shuns both direct federal spending and tax policy as ways to stimulate economic growth. Instead, she prefers programs that increase overall productivity. Rivlin also argues that spending on technology, transportation, communications, and education is a better approach to growth than cutting taxes.

Rivlin also questions, in general, the federal government's role in the business sector. She argues that programs to aid business should be at the state level, where a better grasp of specific needs exists. Rivlin favors federal involvement only in areas such as environmental protection, whose effects can be felt across state lines.

CHECK FOR UNDERSTANDING

1. Source Reading In her call for program cuts to reduce government spending, Alice Rivlin wrote: "Everyone looks for ways of accomplishing ambitious goals without effort—lose weight without dieting, learn French while you sleep." Explain what she meant.

2. Critical Thinking Would Alice Rivlin be more likely to favor tax breaks to encourage companies to hire unemployed workers or creating a new government-funded training program to teach workers useful job skills? Explain your answer.

3. Decision Making Do you agree or disagree with Rivlin's opinion that lowering taxes does not effectively raise living standards?

Section 2

Promoting Growth and Stability

Preview

Objectives

After studying this section you will be able to:

1. **Explain** how the government tracks and seeks to influence business cycles.
2. **Analyze** how the government promotes economic strength.
3. **Analyze** the effect of technology on productivity.

Section Focus

The government attempts to stabilize business cycles, aids the growth of the economy, and encourages technological innovation.

Key Terms

macroeconomics
microeconomics
gross domestic product (GDP)
business cycle
work ethic
technology

America's economy is big—very big. It consists of roughly 104 million households of about 273 million people who work at some 139 million jobs and earn more than $8 trillion a year. They make savings deposits of $28 billion or so in about 71,000 banks. They buy close to 880,000 homes and 3.3 million cars a year.

In Washington, armies of economists use the latest computer and other technologies to try to predict whether this massive economy will grow or shrink. Economic policymakers pull in the reins when the economy bolts at breakneck speed, and attempt to kick start it when it gets slow and unproductive.

Tracking Business Cycles

In this section we'll examine how the United States government affects macroeconomic trends. **Macroeconomics** is the study of the behavior and decision making of entire economies. This branch of economics examines major trends for the economy as a whole. **Microeconomics,** in contrast, is the study of the economic behavior and decision making of small units, such as individuals, families, and businesses. (*Macro* means "large," while *micro* means "small.")

One way economists measure economic well-being is by calculating the nation's

gross domestic product (GDP), the total value of all final goods and services produced in an economy. Economists follow the country's GDP and other key statistics to predict business cycles. A **business cycle** is a period of macroeconomic expansion followed by a period of contraction, or decline. These economic cycles are major fluctuations, unlike the day-to-day ups and downs of the stock market. We are always at some point in the business cycle. Cycles may last less than a year or continue for many years.

Free enterprise systems are subject to business cycles because economic decisions about factors such as prices, production, and consumption are made by individuals and businesses acting in their own self-interest. In America's free enterprise system, the government plays a role in attempting to prevent wild swings in economic behavior.

Where we are in a given business cycle affects our lives every day. If the economy doesn't create enough jobs, high school graduates have trouble finding work. If prices rise, but incomes don't, our ability to buy what we need declines.

Promoting Economic Strength

Because the market is vulnerable to business cycles, the government creates

---

macroeconomics *the study of the behavior and decision making of entire economies*

microeconomics *the study of the economic behavior and decision making of small units, such as individuals, families, and businesses*

gross domestic product (GDP) *the total value of all final goods and services produced in a particular economy*

business cycle *a period of macro-economic expansion followed by a period of contraction*

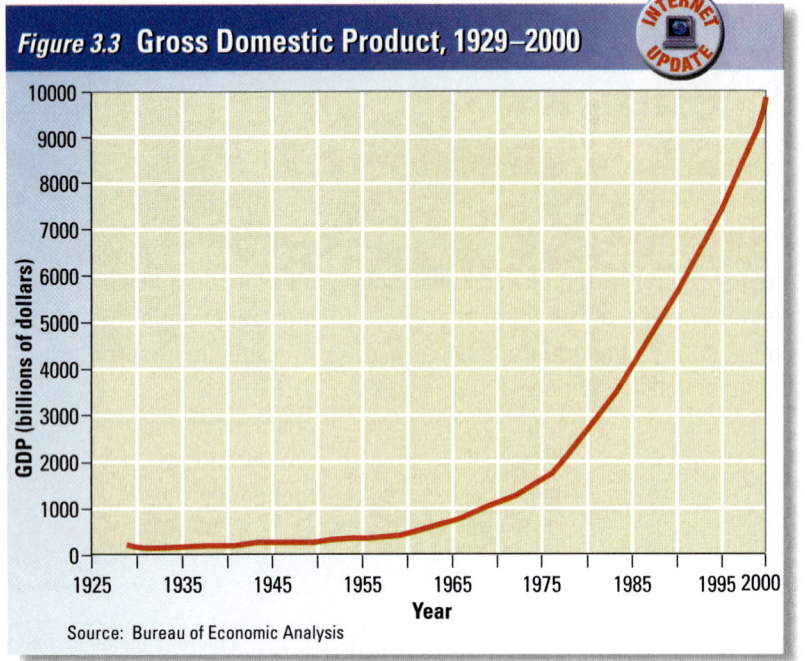

Figure 3.3 Gross Domestic Product, 1929–2000

GDP (billions of dollars) vs. Year

Source: Bureau of Economic Analysis

U.S. economic growth soared in the 1990s.

Economic Systems How does the growth of GDP reflect the strengths of the free enterprise system?

BUILDING KEY CONCEPTS

Stability

Another macroeconomic task that the government pursues is keeping the economy stable and secure. Stability gives consumers, producers, and investors confidence in the economy and in our financial institutions, promoting economic freedom and growth.

One indicator of economic stability is general price levels. The government's aim is to help prevent sudden, drastic shifts in prices. A surge in overall prices puts a strain on consumers, especially people on fixed incomes. When prices sink, producers and consumers feel the pain. A jump in the price of milk, for example, is hard on families with children, while a plunge in milk prices hurts dairy farmers. In either direction, major fluctuations in price levels can cause a macroeconomic chain reaction that policymakers seek to avoid.

Another sign of economic stability is the health of the nation's financial institutions. None of us wants to go to the bank and find it boarded up and empty. When we make a bank deposit or a stock purchase, we want to know that our money will be protected from fraud or mismanagement and shielded from the damaging effects of sudden economic downturns.

To provide such assurances, the federal government monitors and regulates American banks and other financial institutions. It produces hundreds of regulations, and it has the power to enforce them.

Federal banking regulations protect bank deposits and retirees' pensions. Federal regulators investigate fraud and manage interest rates and the flow of money through the economy. You'll learn more about these functions in later chapters.

Economic Citizenship

Achieving macroeconomic growth and stability is not easy. Through the way it spends money and influences other macroeconomic factors such as interest rates, the government helps to compensate for the typical swings of the business cycle in our economy.

public policies that aim to stabilize the economy. Policymakers pursue three main outcomes as they seek to stabilize the economy: high employment, steady growth, and stable prices.

Employment

One aim of federal economic policy is to provide jobs for everyone who is able to work. In the United States, many economists consider an unemployment rate of between 4 percent and 6 percent to be desirable. In the last half of the twentieth century, the jobless rate ranged between 3 percent and 11 percent.

Growth

Part of the American Dream has always been for each generation to enjoy a higher standard of living than that of previous generations. For each generation to do better, the economy must grow to provide additional goods and services to succeeding generations. GDP is a measure of such growth.

▲ The inventions of a single man, Thomas Edison (right), brought a technological revolution to the United States and launched a new era of economic growth. Following that tradition of technological innovation, Charlie Matykiewicz (left) displays his automatic dog washer, a prize winner at the 1997 Invention Convention in Philadelphia.

Do you expect your generation to have a higher standard of living than that of past generations? As a voter, your elective choices will help guide government economic policy. That's why it's more important than ever for American citizens to understand the macroeconomic processes that shape our futures.

Technology and Productivity

The American economy maintains a far higher standard of living, in terms of GDP, than most of the world. You've read that one way to preserve that high standard is by increasing productivity—shifting the production possibilities frontier outward. How do we do that? One way is through the American **work ethic,** a commitment to the value of work and purposeful activity. Another way to increase productivity is through improved technology.

Technological Progress

Technology is the process used to produce a good or service. Improvements in technology allow an economy to produce more output from the same or a smaller quantity of inputs, or resources. Technological progress allows the United States economy to operate more efficiently and productively, increasing GDP and giving U.S. businesses a competitive advantage in the world.

American history is full of innovations that improved productivity. Thomas Edison's invention of the light bulb in 1879 made possible a longer workday. From weaving looms to tractors to computers, machines have allowed us to generate more goods in a shorter amount of time with fewer raw materials.

In addition, although innovation makes some production processes and workers out-of-date, or obsolete, these resources can be used in other ways. For example, old indus-

work ethic *a commitment to the value of work and purposeful activity*

technology *the process used to produce a good or service*

trial buildings can be converted into stores or apartments. Old machines can be recycled and used to produce new machines.

The Government's Role

Inventions are the engine of the free enterprise system. They help us to build "more-better-faster," thus giving consumers more economic choices. Recognizing the need for innovation to maintain America's technological advantage, the government provides incentives for innovation.

Federal agencies fund scores of research and development projects at universities. The Morrill Acts of 1862 and 1890 created so-called land-grant colleges that received federal land and money to pursue the study of "agriculture and the mechanical arts." Land-grant schools from the Massachusetts Institute of Technology to Texas A&M University have been powerhouses of innovation.

The government's own research institutions also produce a steady stream of new technologies that make their way into the marketplace. Probably the best-known example of such an institution is the National Aeronautics and Space Administration (NASA). Technology created by NASA to blast humans into space and to explore distant planets has produced amazing "spinoffs," products with commercial uses. NASA spinoffs include everything from a muscle stimulator for people with paralysis to a scanner that allows firefighters to see "invisible flames" given off by alcohol or hydrogen fires.

The government also plays a role in innovation by offering inventors the possibility of making huge profits in the free market. It does so by granting patents and copyrights.

A U.S. patent gives the inventor of a new product the exclusive right to produce and sell it for 20 years. A copyright grants an author exclusive rights to publish and sell his or her creative works.

The Framers of the Constitution foresaw the economic need to create incentives for innovation. Congressional authority to issue patents and copyrights is stated in Article 1, Section 8 of the Constitution. It gives Congress the power to "promote the progress of science and useful arts, by securing for limited times to authors and inventors the exclusive right to their respective writings and discoveries."

Section 2 Assessment

Key Terms and Main Ideas

1. Compare **macroeconomics** with **microeconomics**, and give an example of each.

2. How does **gross domestic product (GDP)** provide a means to analyze economic growth?

3. What does GDP tell economists about **business cycles?**

4. Give one example of a new **technology** that has resulted in greater productivity for the United States.

5. (a) How do patents and copyrights promote innovation? (b) How does innovation help the economy?

6. Describe and analyze how economic stability is measured.

Applying Economic Concepts

7. *Decision Making* Are the macroeconomic goals of employment, growth, and stability best met by the public sector or by the private sector? Explain.

8. *Critical Thinking* Explain how scientific discoveries and technological innovations create the need for rules and regulations to protect individuals and businesses.

Take It to the NET At NASA's *Spinoff* site, find and describe two examples of products with commercial uses generated by NASA. Use the links provided in the Social Studies area at the following Web site for help in completing this activity. **www.phschool.com**

Analyzing Primary Sources

A primary source is information produced during or soon after an event, usually by a participant or observer. Although primary sources can convey a strong sense of an event or historical period, they may be inaccurate or biased. For that reason, you must analyze primary sources critically. Read the passage below, written during the early 1930s, and then practice analyzing primary sources by following these steps.

1. **Identify the document.** Read the passage for tone and authorship. (**a**) What sort of document is this? (**b**) Who is the author? How can you tell?

2. **Interpret the contents of the document.** Compare the details of this document to what you already know about the Great Depression. (**a**) How did the family live before the Depression?

(**b**) How did the Depression affect the family?

3. **Analyze the document.** Read critically to determine the importance of the selection. (**a**) What do you think the purpose of the story was when it was published in 1934? (**b**) Is this story consistent with the economic statistics below?

A Boy Tramp Tells of the "Big Trouble"

But we got along swell before the big trouble came even if there were seven of us kids. I shined shoes in a barber shop. Jim carried papers. And Marie took care of Mrs. Rolph's kids. Mother always did some sewing for the neighbors. We had a Chevvie and a radio and a piano. I even started to high school mornings, the year the big trouble came...

Dad got sick as usual but we never thought anything of it. When he comes to go back to work he can't get a job, and everybody all of a sudden-like seems to be hard up. I cut the price of shines to a nickel, but it didn't help much...

Mrs. Rolph's husband got a cut and she cans Marie. Jim had to quit the paper route because he lost all his cash customers, and the others never paid. Nobody wanted Mother to sew anything.

Source: Thomas Minehan, *Boy and Girl Tramps of America,* (New York: Holt, Rinehart & Winston, Inc., 1934).

Additional Practice

Find a primary source document that concerns unemployment in a different period of the history of the United States. What similarities and differences do you notice?

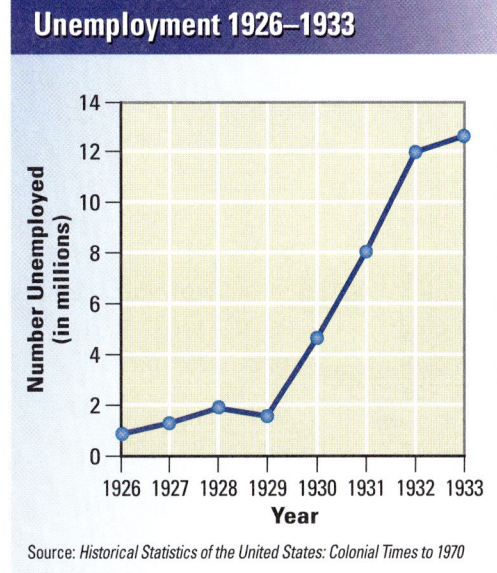

Unemployment 1926–1933

Number Unemployed (in millions) vs. Year

Source: *Historical Statistics of the United States: Colonial Times to 1970*

Preview

Objectives

After studying this section you will be able to:

1. **Identify** examples of public goods.
2. **Analyze** market failures.
3. **Evaluate** how the government allocates some resources by managing externalities.

Section Focus

The government sometimes steps in to provide a shared good or resource when it would be impractical for consumers to pay individually.

Key Terms

public good
public sector
private sector
free rider
market failure
externality

What if the government decided to leave the business of road-building up to private citizens? If you wanted a road in front of your house, you'd have to pay a contractor to build it. Or more likely, you and your neighbors could chip in and hire someone to build you a small network of streets.

What problems might arise in this scenario? For one thing, if groups of individuals pooled their money to build a road or a freeway, who would they allow to use it? Would drivers have to constantly stop and pay the owners of each road they drove on? How would individuals living in sparsely populated areas come up with enough money to build the roads they needed?

Public Goods

Roads are one of many examples in which the government provides a **public good,** a shared good or service for which it would be inefficient or impractical (1) to make consumers pay individually and (2) to exclude nonpayers. Dams are another example of public goods.

Let's look at the first feature, making consumers pay individually: How would you like to receive a bill in your mailbox for your share of launching a space shuttle or cleaning Mount Rushmore? To simplify the funding of government projects in the public interest, the government collects taxes.

What about the second feature of a public good, excluding nonpayers? As a society, we believe that certain facilities or services should be available to all. Besides, excluding nonpayers from highways would be a nightmare.

Most goods are public simply because a private provider could not charge those who benefit or exclude nonpayers from benefiting. For example, in 1872, Congress created the nation's first national park, Yellowstone. The national park system ensured that the natural resources Americans value would be protected.

If a park were privately owned, the owner could charge an admission fee. Yet some benefits generated by the park, such as the preservation of wildlife, would be enjoyed by nonpayers as well as payers. The owner could neither charge people for that public benefit nor exclude them from it.

Public goods have other characteristics: Any number of consumers can use them without reducing the benefits to any single consumer. For the most part, increasing the number of consumers does not increase the cost of providing the public good. So if you're driving on a highway and eight other drivers come along, they do not significantly reduce the road's benefits to

public good a shared good or service for which it would be impractical to make consumers pay individually and to exclude nonpayers

▲ Identify the public goods shown in these photos.

you or increase the government's cost of providing it.

Costs and Benefits

As you read in Section 1, the federal government steps in to act in the public interest whenever it determines that the benefits of a policy outweigh the drawbacks. In road construction, the advantages are obvious. The drawback is the economic freedom we give up, since none of us individually gets to decide what roads will be built, and where. Still, in this example the advantages of public road construction outweigh the drawback. In other cases, weighing benefits against costs is more complicated and open to debate.

Cost is critical in determining whether something gets produced as a public good. When a good or service is public,

1. the benefit to each individual is less than the cost that each would have to pay if it were provided privately, and

2. the total benefits to society are greater than the total cost.

In such circumstances, the market would not provide the good; the government would have to, or else it wouldn't get done.

Study carefully Figure 3.4 on the next page. Does the dam-building project meet the two criteria for a public good?

Public goods are financed by the **public sector,** the part of the economy that involves the transactions of the government. The **private sector,** the part of the economy that involves transactions of individuals and businesses, would have little incentive to produce public goods.

Free-Rider Problem

A phenomenon associated with public goods is called the "free-rider problem." A **free rider** is someone who would not choose to pay for a certain good or service, but would get the benefits of it anyway if it were provided as a public good.

Would you voluntarily contribute, say, $3,500 to buy army helmets—your portion of America's military cost this year? Perhaps not. Yet when the government provides a system of national defense, you benefit, whether you pay or not.

Try another example: Everyone on your street wants fire protection except one penny-pinching neighbor, who says it's not worth the money. Do you want him to have fire protection anyway? Yes. If his

public sector *the part of the economy that involves the transactions of the government*

private sector *the part of the economy that involves the transactions of individuals and businesses*

free rider *someone who would not choose to pay for a certain good or service, but who would get the benefits of it anyway if it were provided as a public good*

market failure *a situation in which the market does not distribute resources efficiently*

house catches fire, yours could ignite as well. So local taxes pay for firefighting services for all property in a given area, because all residents are better off if the government provides this service.

Returning to the example of roads, you might not be willing to pay for a new freeway in your area. But if it is built, you would use it. You would be a free rider.

Free riders consume what they do not pay for. The free-rider problem suggests that if the government stopped collecting taxes and relied on voluntary contributions, many public services would have to be eliminated.

Market Failures

Free riders are examples of **market failure,** a situation in which the market, on its own, does not distribute resources efficiently. To understand market failure, recall how a successful free market operates: Choices made by individuals determine what goods get made, how they get made, and who consumes the goods. Profit incentives attract producers, who, because of competition, provide goods and services that consumers need at a price they can afford.

In the road-building scenario, are these features of a free market present? No. If a company did build a road, it could charge a high price for tolls because it would have no competition. Also, companies would not choose to build roads in sparsely populated areas because profit incentives in those areas might be non-existing. This way of getting roads built would be highly impractical.

In this scenario, the criteria for a properly functioning market system do not exist. That's why economists consider this situation a market failure.

Note that public ownership can sometimes produce negative externalities, however. Some public lands, for example, might be more usefully managed if owned privately.

This diagram shows the process that determines whether a public good will be generated.
Opportunity Costs If the farmers also wanted irrigation ditches built to carry the lake water to their fields, would the ditches be built as a public good? Explain.

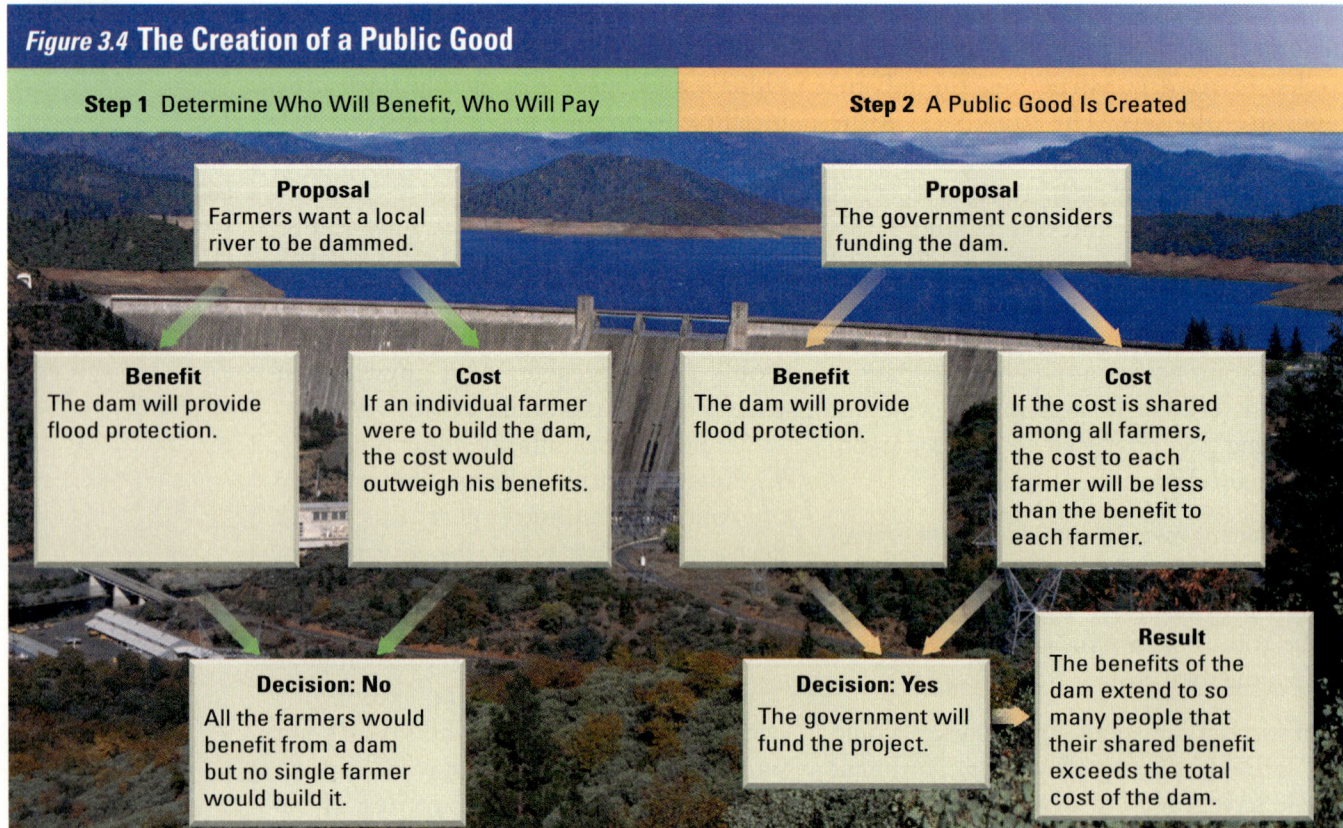

Figure 3.4 The Creation of a Public Good

Step 1 Determine Who Will Benefit, Who Will Pay

Proposal
Farmers want a local river to be dammed.

Benefit
The dam will provide flood protection.

Cost
If an individual farmer were to build the dam, the cost would outweigh his benefits.

Decision: No
All the farmers would benefit from a dam but no single farmer would build it.

Step 2 A Public Good Is Created

Proposal
The government considers funding the dam.

Benefit
The dam will provide flood protection.

Cost
If the cost is shared among all farmers, the cost to each farmer will be less than the benefit to each farmer.

Decision: Yes
The government will fund the project.

Result
The benefits of the dam extend to so many people that their shared benefit exceeds the total cost of the dam.

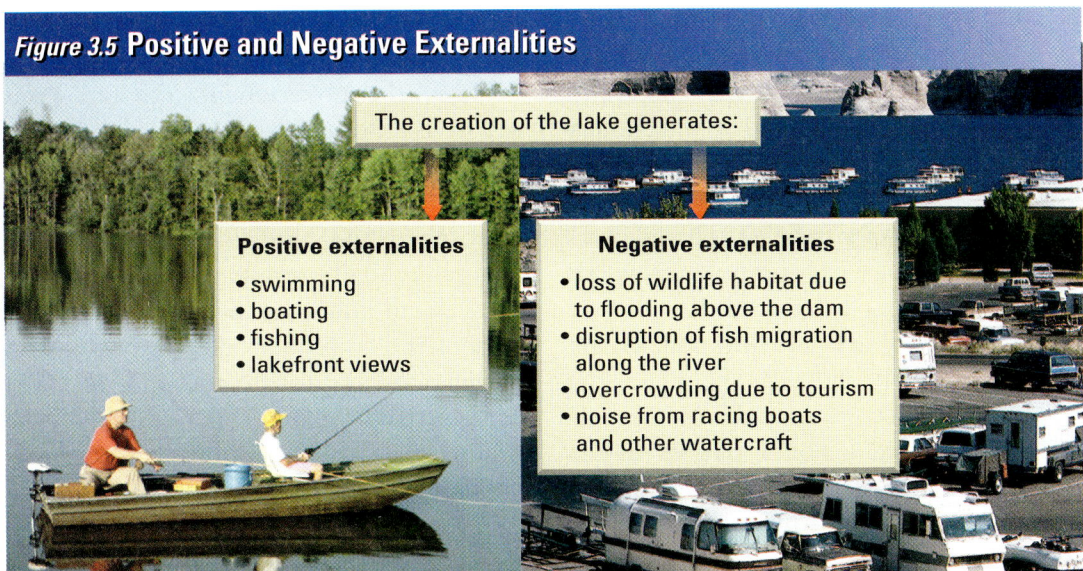

Figure 3.5 Positive and Negative Externalities

The creation of the lake generates:

Positive externalities
- swimming
- boating
- fishing
- lakefront views

Negative externalities
- loss of wildlife habitat due to flooding above the dam
- disruption of fish migration along the river
- overcrowding due to tourism
- noise from racing boats and other watercraft

BUILDING KEY CONCEPTS

Construction of a new dam creates dozens of externalities, positive and negative, depending on your point of view. **Public Policy** **What groups of people might feel the greatest economic impact from the new dam?**

Externalities

All of the previous examples involve side effects of some sort. They illustrate what economists call externalities. An **externality** is an economic side effect of a good or service that generates benefits or costs to someone other than the person deciding how much to produce or consume. Externalities can be positive or negative, as follows.

Positive Externalities

We've said that public goods generate benefits to many people, not just those who pay for the goods. Such beneficial side effects are called *positive externalities*.

The private sector can create positive externalities, too. In fact, many experts believe that the private sector generates positive externalities more efficiently than the public sector can, and at less cost to taxpayers. For instance:

- Dynamo Computers hires underprivileged teenagers and trains them to be computer programmers. Those workers are then available to be hired by other companies, who benefit from the workers' skills without having paid for them.
- Mrs. Garland buys an old house that is an eyesore in the neighborhood. She

paints the house, cuts the grass, and plants flowers. Her neighbors were not involved in her economic decision. But they receive benefits from it, such as higher property values and a better view.

Whether private or public, positive externalities cause part of the benefit of a good to be gained by someone who did not purchase it. In the 1990s, several endangered species, including the bald eagle and the peregrine falcon, were saved from extinction. Protection of species critical to our ecosystem benefits us all.

Negative Externalities

Of course, some decisions to produce goods and services generate unintended costs, called *negative externalities*. Negative externalities cause part of the cost of producing a good or service to be paid for by someone other than the producer. For example:

- The Enchanted Forest Paper Mill dumps chemical wastes into a nearby river, making it unsafe for swimming. The downstream city of Tidyville is forced to install special equipment at its water-treatment plant to clean up the mess. If the treatment cost is $20 per ton of paper

externality *an economic side effect of a good or service that generates benefits or costs to someone other than the person deciding how much to produce or consume*

produced, and the mill's production cost is $100 (the cost of all the materials, labor, and machinery required to produce it), the full, or social, cost of a ton of paper is $120. The community, not the polluter, winds up paying that $20.

• Your next-door neighbor, Mr. Fogler, takes up the accordion and holds Friday night polka parties in his backyard. Unfortunately, you hate polka music.

Government's Goals

When externalities are present, we have a market failure, because the costs or benefits of a good or service are not assigned properly. Understanding externalities helps us see how the government functions in the American economy.

First, the government encourages the creation of positive externalities. Education, for example, benefits students, yet society as a whole also benefits from an educated population. This is because educated workers are generally more productive.

Next, the government aims to limit negative externalities, such as acid rain. Pollutants from coal-burning power plants and auto emissions can drift high into the atmosphere and come down in the form of acid rain, which causes ecological damage. Why is acid rain a negative externality? It is part of the cost of producing power and driving cars, but for decades that cost was being imposed upon people other than the producers of this pollution. The cost was damaged trees, lakes, and wildlife.

To help address this negative externality, the federal government now requires all new cars to have an expensive antipollution device called a catalytic converter. In addition, the Environmental Protection Agency offers incentives to power-plant operators to put "scrubbers" on their smokestacks to cut emissions. These actions transfer the costs of pollution back to its producers.

See the Fast Fact on this page for an explanation of pollution permits. These are another way to help eliminate this negative externality.

Section 3 Assessment

Key Terms and Main Ideas

1. Explain this sentence: Most **public goods** generate positive **externalities.**

2. Why is a **free rider** a type of **market failure?**

3. What is the difference between the **public sector** and the **private sector?** Give examples of each.

Applying Economic Concepts

4. *Critical Thinking* How does the government attempt to encourage positive externalities and limit negative externalities? Give two examples of each.

5. *Critical Thinking* Is the criminal justice system (police and the courts) a public good? Explain.

6. *Decision Making* A city has a shortage of parking spaces near downtown businesses. Should the city build a new parking garage or leave it to the private sector? Explain your reasoning.

7. *Problem Solving* Explain why this statement is true or false: *Government steps in to allocate resources efficiently so that the country is operating on its production possibilities curve instead of under it.*

Take It to the NET

The United States has abundant natural resources. Managing them is a huge task. Find three ways in which the federal government tries to ensure that our natural resources are best used. Use the links provided in the Social Studies area at the following Web site for help in completing this activity. **www.phschool.com**

Providing a Safety Net

Objectives

After studying this section you will be able to:

1. **Summarize** the U.S. political debate on ways to fight poverty.
2. **Describe** the main programs through which the government redistributes income.

Section Focus

Sometimes the United States government has to step in to create programs to aid poor, disabled, and elderly people.

Key Terms

poverty threshold
welfare
cash transfers
in-kind benefits

Prosperity is a hazy memory in East St. Louis. Tumble-down buildings and weed-covered lots scar the urban landscape. Poverty and unemployment are constant companions in this Illinois city of 40,000 or so residents.

The city hugs the banks of the Mississippi River across from its prosperous big brother, St. Louis, Missouri, a city of more than 330,000 people. At one time, both cities profited from their locations on the busy river. But in the 1970s the firms of East St. Louis packed up and fled, having found better business opportunities elsewhere. With few businesses to tax and a jobless population, the city edged toward bankruptcy, unable to provide even the most basic services, like garbage collection and police and fire protection. At the end of the twentieth century, while much of the United States enjoyed economic growth, East St. Louis struggled merely to exist.

The Poverty Problem

While the free market has proven better at generating wealth than has any other economic system, that wealth is spread unevenly throughout society. This leaves some people below the **poverty threshold,** an income level below that which is needed to support families or households. The poverty threshold is a relative figure determined by the federal government and adjusted periodically. In 2000, the poverty threshold for a single parent under age 65, with one child, was $11,869. For a four-person family with two children, it was $17,463. In East St. Louis, the majority of families live below the poverty line. The median household income is a little over $12,000 a year.

The Government's Role

The opportunities that the free market offers can lift the working poor into the middle class. Yet, in poor areas from East St. Louis to rural Appalachia to south-central Los

poverty threshold
an income level below that which is needed to support families or households

▲ **Members of the East St. Louis Action Research Project, founded in 1990, help rehabilitate an economically depressed neighborhood.**

welfare *government aid to the poor*

Angeles, economic opportunities are limited because of factors such as a lack of local jobs and few educational opportunities.

As a society, we recognize some responsibilities to the very young, the very old, the sick, the poor, and the disabled. For these people, the government tries to provide a safety net. Various federal, state, and local government programs help to raise people's standard of living, their level of economic well-being as measured by the ability to purchase the goods and services they need and want.

Yet, in a society that prefers limited government activity in the economy, poverty poses tough questions: What can the government do to combat poverty? What should it do? Is government regulation the best way to help the poor?

The Welfare System

Since the 1930s, the main government effort to ease poverty has been to collect taxes from individuals and redistribute some of those funds in the form of welfare. **Welfare** is a general term that refers to government aid for the poor. It includes many types of redistribution programs.

The nation's welfare system began under President Franklin Delano Roosevelt,

following the Great Depression. Welfare spending increased considerably in the 1960s under President Lyndon B. Johnson's "War on Poverty."

Welfare payments soared in the 1970s and 1980s. In the 1990s, critics of welfare voiced increasing concern about people becoming dependent on welfare and being unable or unwilling to get off it. Some also pointed out that income redistribution discourages productivity, thus actually aggravating poverty. In 1996, Congress made sweeping changes in the welfare system.

Redistribution Programs

Income data are gathered by the U.S. Bureau of the Census, an agency within the Labor Department. The Census Bureau conducts monthly surveys of households to track key economic data. Using the data, the Census Bureau estimates how many people are living in poverty.

Chapter 13 will treat the causes of poverty in detail. In the meantime, here is an overview of the major types of redistribution programs through which the federal government helps the poor and the elderly.

Figure 3.6 **A Century of Federal Programs to Help Those in Need**

1932 Roosevelt's New Deal begins

1935 Congress creates Social Security, Aid to Dependent Children (ADC), and unemployment compensation

1948 Truman's Fair Deal begins

1910　　**1920**　　**1930**　　**1940**　　**1950**

1916 Kern-McGillicuddy Act establishes workers' compensation for federal employees

1933 Federal Emergency Relief Administration (FERA) founded

1950 Social Security extended to 10.5 million more recipients; ADC becomes AFDC (Aid to Families with Dependent Children)

Cash Transfers

State and federal governments provide **cash transfers,** direct payments of money to poor, disabled, and retired people. The following programs distribute direct cash transfers:

1. *Temporary Assistance for Needy Families (TANF)* This program grew out of the 1990s debate about how to ease poverty while decreasing government payments to the poor. TANF replaced the earlier welfare program, Aid to Families with Dependent Children (AFDC). Critics of AFDC said that the program made people dependent on welfare and did not encourage recipients to take responsibility for their lives.

   Launched in 1996 as part of comprehensive welfare reform, TANF discontinues direct federal welfare payments to recipients. Instead, federal money goes to the states, which design and run their own welfare programs. States must adhere to federal rules that create work incentives and establish a lifetime limit for benefits. The reform aims to move people from welfare dependence to the work force.

2. *Social Security* The Social Security program was created in 1935, during the depths of the Great Depression, when many of the elderly lost their life savings and had no income. Social Security provides direct cash transfers of retirement income to the elderly and living expenses to the disabled. The program collects payroll taxes from current workers and redistributes that money to current recipients.

3. *Unemployment insurance* Another cash transfer is the unemployment insurance program, which is funded jointly by federal and state governments. Unemployment compensation provides money to eligible workers who have lost their jobs. Workers must show that they have made efforts to get work during each week that they receive benefits.

4. *Workers' compensation* This program provides a cash transfer of state funds to workers injured on the job. Most employers must pay workers' compensation insurance to cover any future claims their employees might make. This insurance has become more and more expensive as medical expenses and the number of reported on-the-job injuries have increased.

cash transfers *direct payments of money to eligible poor people*

1965 Medical Care Act creates Medicare (for retirees and the disabled) and Medicaid (for the poor)

1974 Food Stamp program extended nationwide

1960   **1970**   **1980**   **1990**   **2000**

1964 Johnson's Great Society program expands welfare with new programs such as Head Start preschool education

A New Beginning

1996 AFDC changed to Temporary Assistance for Needy Families (TANF)

In-Kind Benefits

The government also provides poor people with **in-kind benefits,** goods and services provided for free or at greatly reduced prices. The most common in-kind benefits include food giveaways, food stamps, subsidized housing, and legal aid.

Medical Benefits

Another social service that the U.S. government provides is health insurance for the elderly, the disabled, and the poor. Medicare covers Americans over age 65 as well as the disabled. Medicaid covers some poor people who are unemployed or not covered by their employer's insurance plans. Administered under the Social Security program, Medicare and Medicaid are enormously expensive programs. We will examine them further in Chapter 14.

Education

Federal, state, and local governments all provide educational opportunities to the poor. The federal government funds programs from preschool to college. State and local programs aid students with learning disabilities.

Education programs add to the nation's human capital and labor productivity. As you saw in Chapter 1, improved education and technology can make an entire economy more productive by shifting the production possibilities frontier outward.

Faith-Based Initiatives

In 2001, President George W. Bush announced an initiative to rely on non-governmental support for people in need. His administration "will look first to faith-based organizations, charities, and community groups that have shown the ability to save and change lives."

The President believes that religious organizations have frequently been among the most successful groups delivering social services. These groups not only spend money to solve problems, but also provide a special compassion. He therefore proposed as a next step in welfare reform that faith-based organizations be allowed to compete for federal funds. Under the Bush plan, all public service organizations—including religious ones—will be eligible to receive public funding for charitable activities.

Mr. Bush established an Office of Faith-Based and Community Initiatives to help faith-based groups work more effectively with the federal government. He also encouraged the states to create state offices of faith-based action.

in-kind benefits *goods and services provided for free or at greatly reduced prices*

Section 4 Assessment

Key Terms and Main Ideas

1. How does **welfare** attempt to raise poor people's standard of living?

2. Why does poverty exist in a free market economy?

3. What is the difference between **cash transfers** and **in-kind benefits?**

4. How is Social Security an example of income redistribution?

Applying Economic Concepts

5. ***Math Practice*** Assume that the poverty threshold is $8,480 for an individual and $11,235 for a two-person household. Based on a 40-hour work week, how much would you need to earn per hour in order to be above the poverty threshold for **(a)** an individual and **(b)** a two-person household?

6. ***Critical Thinking*** An old adage states, "Give a person a fish, feed him for a day; teach a person how to fish, feed him for a lifetime." Do any of the government programs in this section reflect this saying? Explain your answer.

Take It to the NET Research and make a plan for getting good quality, affordable health care for an elderly American. Use the links provided in the Social Studies area at the following Web site for help in completing this activity. **www.phschool.com**

Government and the Interstate Highway System

The United States did not always have a good network of roads. In the 19th century, when horse-drawn vehicles were the most common form of transportation, almost all roads were unpaved. Many of them became rutted and uneven, making travel difficult, slow, and uncomfortable. The push to build a network of smoother roads began in the 1880s—through the efforts of a bicycle club.

Early Efforts In 1886, a bicycling craze was sweeping the nation. Many American cyclists belonged to the League of American Wheelmen, an organization that wanted smoother roads for cycling. This club was the first to convince Congress to consider building a national highway system. As motor vehicles later became more common, automobile manufacturers, road builders, and gasoline companies took up the crusade for better roads.

▲ President Dwight Eisenhower signed the Federal Aid-Highway Act on June 29, 1956.

State Highways By the early 1900s, Congress began to provide funding to the states to build highways. Each state, however, focused on building highways within its own borders with its own numbering and sign systems—and the highways did not always connect at state borders. Travelers leaving one state often had to drive over slower roads and streets before connecting up with the next highway.

Federal Highways In 1921, the Federal Highway Act got the U.S. government directly involved in highway construction by setting up a system of major highways that connected from state to state, so that drivers could travel between states without ever having to leave a high-speed highway. The government then created a simple system of numbering and marking these interstate highways, to make navigating the system easy. In 1956, the Federal Aid-Highway Act authorized the construction of 41,000 miles of highways to tie the nation together, creating the interstate highway system we know today.

Today, America's interstate highway system is one of the most important features of the country's infrastructure. It allows people and goods to travel quickly from one part of the country to another, reducing transportation costs and speeding up commerce.

Applying Economic Ideas

1. Why was it inefficient to leave highway construction to individual states?

2. Why do you think it took Congress so long to authorize funds for highway construction?

Chapter Summary

A summary of major ideas in Chapter 3 appears below. See also the **Guide to the Essentials of Economics,** which provides additional review and test practice of key concepts in Chapter 3.

Section 1 Benefits of Free Enterprise (pp. 51–55)

The benefits of the American free enterprise system are the result of the basic principles of **profit motive, voluntary exchange, private property rights,** and **competition.** These benefits include individual freedom for consumers and producers and a wide variety of goods. To protect economic freedoms, the government intervenes in matters of **public interest.** Federal agencies monitor and regulate certain types of businesses. **Public disclosure laws** provide critical information to consumers.

Section 2 Promoting Growth and Stability (pp. 57–60)

Macroeconomics concerns the behavior of whole economies, while **microeconomics** concerns the behavior of smaller economic units, such as households. When necessary, the government takes action to influence macroeconomic **business cycles.** It aids the growth of the economy, as measured by **GDP.** It encourages the creation of new **technologies** by giving patents and copyrights to entrepreneurs.

Section 3 Providing Public Goods (pp. 62–66)

The government provides **public goods,** such as roads, when it would be impractical for individuals to pay for them. Providing public goods produces positive and negative **externalities.**

Section 4 Providing a Safety Net (pp. 67–70)

The government uses tax money to raise the standard of living of people in **poverty.** The nation's welfare system includes programs that distribute various benefits, including **cash transfers, in-kind payments,** and medical benefits.

Key Terms

Choose the italicized word in parentheses that best completes each sentence.

1. Acid rain is an example of a(n) *(externality/free rider).*
2. The tradition of *(private property/open opportunity)* allows everyone to compete in the free market.
3. The right of *(free contract/voluntary exchange)* allows people to decide what agreements they want to enter into.
4. Someone who benefits from a good without paying for it is an example of a *(free rider/public good).*
5. Food stamps are an example of a/an *(cash transfer/in-kind payment).*
6. We can use figures on *(gross domestic product/public goods)* to measure economic growth.
7. Study of the behavior of the entire U.S. economy is an example of *(macroeconomics/microeconomics).*

Using Graphic Organizers

8. On a separate sheet of paper, copy the tree map below to help you organize information about the American free enterprise system. Complete the tree map by writing descriptions and examples for each of the headings shown. You may add branches to the tree.

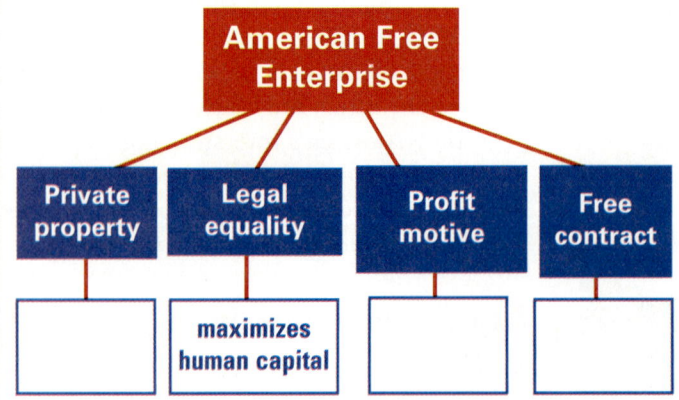

Reviewing Main Ideas

9. **(a)** How does the government support free enterprise and protect public interest? **(b)** Describe and evaluate the government rules and regulations described in this chapter.

10. Explain the basic principles of free enterprise in your own words.

11. Why does the U.S. government track and influence business cycles?

12. Explain why each of the following is either a cash transfer or an in-kind payment. **(a)** unemployment insurance **(b)** Social Security **(c)** food stamps

Critical Thinking

13. **Drawing Inferences** Choose one of the federal agencies mentioned in Section 1, and explain how it acts to limit negative externalities.

14. **Synthesizing Information** Based on your reading of the chapter, write a paragraph in which you describe and analyze the economic rights of businesses.

15. **Predicting Consequences** How might the invention of a new, powerful fuel source for cars and trucks affect the country's production possibilities frontier? How might the new fuel affect GDP?

Problem-Solving Activity

16. Suppose that there is a three-person city. The three residents are considering having a fireworks display. Gabriela is willing to contribute $100 toward the display, while Jerome is willing to pay $80, and Katelyn is willing to pay $60. The fireworks display costs $120. **(a)** Will any single citizen alone be willing to pay for the fireworks? **(b)** What recommendation can you make to this city that will benefit all three citizens?

Economics Journal

Brainstorming Reread your Economics Journal entry for Chapter 3. Of the benefits of free enterprise that you listed, which are most important to you and your family?

Skills for Life

Analyzing Primary Sources Review the steps shown on page 61; then read the primary source below and answer the following questions.

17. What course of action is President Johnson suggesting in this speech?

18. In your own words, state three economic reasons Johnson uses to support his argument.

19. For what type of assignment might you use this primary source quotation? Explain.

> The war on poverty is not a struggle simply to support people, to make them dependent on the generosity of others. It is a struggle to give people a chance.... We do this, first of all, because it is right that we should.... We do it also because helping some will increase the prosperity of all. Our fight against poverty will be an investment in the most valuable of our resources—the skills and strength of our people. And in the future, as in the past, this investment will return its cost many fold to our entire economy.
>
> If we can raise the annual earnings of 10 million among the poor by only $1,000 we will have added $14 billion a year to our national output. In addition we can make important reductions in public assistance payments which now cost us $4 billion a year, and in the large costs of fighting crime and delinquency, disease and hunger....
>
> This is only part of the story. Our history has proved that each time we broaden the base of abundance, giving more people the chance to produce and consume, we create new industry, higher production, increased earnings and better income for all.
>
> —President Lyndon B. Johnson,
> *Public Papers of the Presidents of the United States,* 1965

Take It to the NET

Chapter 3 Self-Test As a final review activity, take the Economics Chapter 3 Self-Test in the Social Studies area at the Web site listed below, and receive immediate feedback on your answers. The test consists of 20 multiple-choice questions designed to test your understanding of the chapter content. **www.phschool.com**

DEBATING CURRENT ISSUES: *Toxic-Waste Cleanup*

◆ Rail yards are among the country's most serious pollution problems, largely because of hazardous chemicals that have leaked or been spilled or dumped over the years. The following excerpts from "Union Pacific Faces a Foe It Can't Easily Steamroller," by Marc Lifsher, Staff Reporter of *The Wall Street Journal,* describe a bitter standoff in the historic rail town of Sacramento, California.

YES — *Should Polluters Determine the Extent of Toxic-Waste Cleanup?*

UNION PACIFIC CORP. finds itself up against a foe that possesses an extraordinary amount of political firepower: the Neighborhoods Working Group. The organization is spearheaded by folks from Sacramento's upscale Curtis Park area, which counts among its residents an impressive line-up of legislative staffers, high-priced private attorneys, and scientific experts.

At issue are plans to redevelop a former rail yard here. The 60-plus-acre tract is now a weed-strewn urban wilderness separating Curtis Park and an even ritzier residential section, Land Park. Though both Union Pacific and neighborhood activists welcome development of this so-called brownfield site, the two sides are at odds over what exactly should be built and where.

These differences—while couched in planning jargon about "densities" and "mixed uses"—boil down to an argument over toxic waste and its removal.

Union Pacific insists its goal is to see a high-quality development get put in place on the site—but one that pencils out financially. So it is promising to clean up half the rail yard for "unrestricted" uses, such as the building of homes and parks. But it wants to remove only some of the toxic material from the other half—a step that could conceivably save it millions of dollars.

The reduced cleanup, Union Pacific officials contend, would still allow for safe construction of supermarkets, small office complexes, and apartments or condominiums. Such "restricted" uses, they say, would ensure that people have no contact with any potentially harmful substances in the soil because the dangerous spots would be paved over. What's more, property sold in the restricted zone would likely be saddled with deed covenants prohibiting any potentially perilous activities, such as digging into the ground.

"The last thing the railroad or the city or the Department of Toxic Substances Control wants to do is to subject the residents to health and safety hazards," says Rick Gooch, director of special properties for Union Pacific in San Francisco. "We will take all precautions necessary."

How clean is clean enough? The extent to which toxic-waste sites are cleaned up is a point of controversy in many communities.

NO

Should Polluters Determine the Extent of Toxic-Waste Cleanup?

THE CURTIS PARK NEIGHBORS don't trust the railroad to clean up sufficient amounts of lead, arsenic, and petroleum that have been mixed into the soil since the old Western Pacific Railroad opened a steam-locomotive maintenance shop in 1910. And they worry the successor, Union Pacific, with the aid of state regulators, is trying to push through a mitigation plan that could threaten the health of future residents. Arsenic and lead are both poisonous. Arsenic is a carcinogen, and high concentrations of lead in the body can cause mental, digestive, and muscular problems.

The state Department of Toxic Substances Control has approved the railroad's "Final Remedial Action Plan." This, as much as anything, is what has inflamed the Curtis Park activists. Not only do they believe the plan is unsafe, but they also say it effectively foists a huge amount of commercial development on the area.

And this isn't what they want. In fact, the group is urging the Sacramento City Council to guarantee that 44 acres of the rail yard are completely cleaned up for residential housing and 22 acres are cleaned up enough for open space, "neighborhood-friendly" commercial use and community-college expansion—not just stores and office buildings. The council has the final say on any redevelopment project.

Politically connected neighbors say they aren't buying any assurances from the railroad and the state that, if the city eventually adopts a plan that calls for more unrestricted construction, additional toxic cleanup would be completed. Thus the activists—backed by the City Council—have enlisted Sen. Deborah Ortiz, a Sacramento Democrat, to introduce legislation that would prevent state regulators from issuing any final cleanup certification until after the city has signed off on the effort.

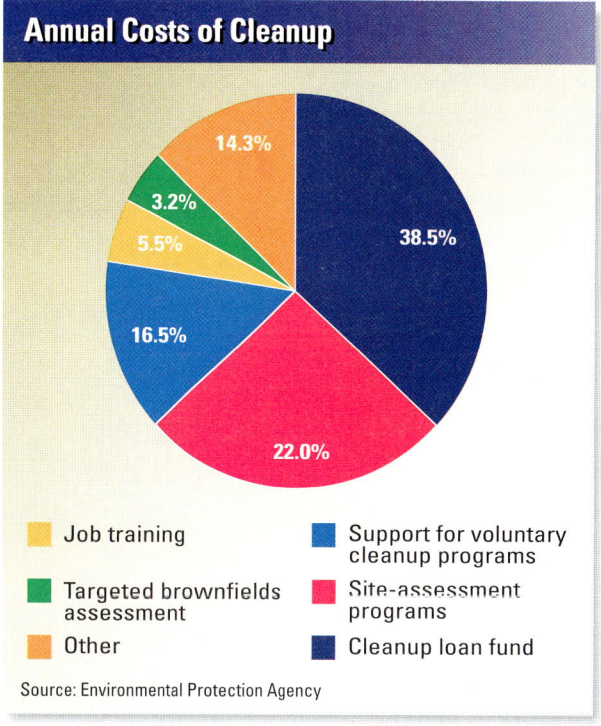

Annual Costs of Cleanup

- 38.5%
- 22.0%
- 16.5%
- 5.5%
- 3.2%
- 14.3%

- Job training
- Targeted brownfields assessment
- Other
- Support for voluntary cleanup programs
- Site-assessment programs
- Cleanup loan fund

Source: Environmental Protection Agency

For fiscal year 1999, Congress appropriated $91 million to the Environmental Protection Agency for the brownfields program, which reclaims contaminated industrial sites to protect human health and the environment.

DEBATING THE ISSUE

1. On what issues in this controversy do Union Pacific and residents of Curtis Park agree? On what issues do they disagree?

2. What would residents say are the disadvantages (costs) of Union Pacific's plan? What would Union Pacific say are the costs of the community's demands?

3. **Critical Thinking** Why should Union Pacific pay for all the cleanup, when it did not cause all the pollution in the rail yard?

4. **Reading Graphs** What percentage of brownfields appropriations went for training people to clean up these sites?

 Take It to the Net Visit **www.phschool.com** for additional resources relating to this debate.

UNIT

2

How Markets Work

76

Today is the Super Bowl . . .

Your favorite team is playing, the stadium is right across town, and you really want to go!

- How many other people are trying to get tickets?
- How many tickets are available?
- What determines the price of the tickets?
- From whom are you going to buy your ticket? Is there more than one ticket outlet?

Answers to all of these questions are based on the laws of supply and demand—two of the most important tools of economic analysis. In this unit you will study supply and demand to see how the prices of goods and services are affected by all sorts of changes in the economy, including higher incomes, technological innovation, and changes in consumer preferences.

Focus Activity

Brainstorm a list of goods that have either a limited supply or are in great demand. What generalizations can you make about the prices of these items? Compare your list with those of your classmates.

Andre couldn't wait to get the hit film on the shelves of the video store he managed. He cleared ten shelves by the front door for display boxes. Every copy was rented that Friday for $3.99. Six weeks later, only one third of the videos were rented on a Friday night. Andre cut the price to $3.00 for a two-night rental. Three years later, Andre moved the one remaining copy to the back corner of the store. Customers could take it home for a week for only 99 cents.

Each of Andre's decisions was shaped by the needs and wishes of his customers. Economists use the term *demand* to describe the ability and desire of consumers to buy a good. Paired with supply, demand forms one of the building blocks of the marketplace.

Economics Journal

Quickly list the last five goods or services you purchased and how much you spent on each. What led you to buy each one?

Keep It Current

Items marked with this logo are periodically updated on the Internet. Keep up-to-date with what's in the news. To get current information on the topic of demand, go to
www.phschool.com

Understanding Demand

Objectives

After studying this section you will be able to:

1. **Explain** the law of demand.
2. **Understand** how the substitution effect and the income effect influence decisions.
3. **Create** a demand schedule for an individual and a market.
4. **Interpret** a demand graph using demand schedules.

Section Focus

According to the law of demand, people buy less of a good when its price rises. Demand schedules and demand curves illustrate how people and markets react to different prices.

Key Terms

demand
law of demand
substitution effect
income effect
demand schedule
market demand
  schedule
demand curve

In Chapter 2, you read about *economic systems,* which are different ways of answering the three economic questions of *what to produce, how much to produce,* and *who gets what.* In the United States, most goods are allocated through a market system. In a market system, the interaction of buyers and sellers determines the prices of most goods as well as what quantity of a good will be produced. Buyers demand goods, sellers supply those goods, and the interactions between the two groups lead to an agreement on the price and the quantity traded.

Demand is the desire to own something and the ability to pay for it. We will look at the demand side of markets in this chapter. In the next chapter we will look at the actions of sellers, which economists call the supply side. In Chapter 6, we will look at supply and demand together and study how they interact to establish the prices that we pay for most goods.

The Law of Demand

Anyone who has ever spent money will easily understand the **law of demand.** The law of demand says that when a good's price is lower, consumers will buy more of it. When the price is higher, consumers will buy less of it. All of us act out this law of

demand in our everyday purchasing decisions. Whether your income is $10 or $10 million, the price of a good will strongly influence your decision to buy.

Ask yourself this question: Would you buy a slice of pizza for lunch if it cost $1? Many of us would, and some of us might

demand *the desire to own something and the ability to pay for it*

law of demand *consumers buy more of a good when its price decreases and less when its price increases*

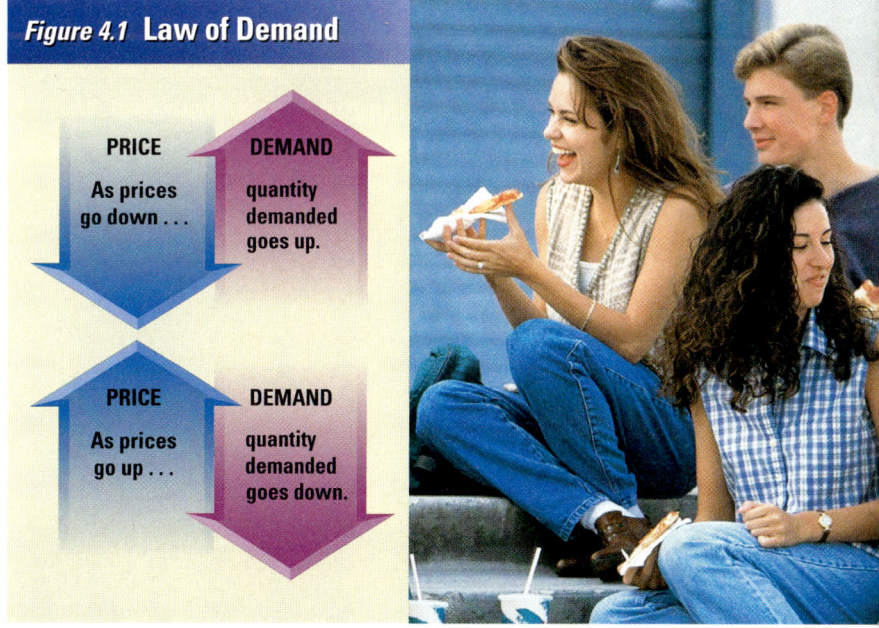

Figure 4.1 Law of Demand

PRICE — As prices go down . . .

DEMAND — quantity demanded goes up.

PRICE — As prices go up . . .

DEMAND — quantity demanded goes down.

If the price of pizza rises, people will buy fewer slices.

Incentives What does the law of demand say about lower prices?

substitution effect *when consumers react to an increase in a good's price by consuming less of that good and more of other goods*

income effect *the change in consumption resulting from a change in real income*

even buy more than one slice. But would you buy the same slice of pizza if it cost $2? Fewer of us would buy it at that price. Even real pizza lovers might reduce their consumption from 3 or 4 slices to just 1 or 2. How many of us would buy a slice for $10? Probably very few. As the price of pizza gets higher and higher, fewer of us are willing to buy it. That is the law of demand in action.

The law of demand is the result of not one pattern of behavior, but of two separate patterns that overlap. These two behavior patterns are the **substitution effect** and the **income effect**. The substitution effect and income effect describe two different ways that a consumer can change his or her spending patterns. Together, they explain why an increase in price decreases the quantity purchased. Figure 4.2 describes how the substitution effect and the income effect can change a consumer's buying habits.

The Substitution Effect

When the price of pizza rises, pizza becomes more expensive compared to other foods, such as tacos and salads. So, as the price of a slice of pizza rises, consumers become more and more likely to buy one of those alternatives as a substitute for pizza. This causes a drop in the amount of pizza demanded. For example, instead of eating pizza for lunch on Mondays and Fridays, a student could eat pizza on Mondays and a bagel on Fridays. This change in spending is known as the substitution effect. The substitution effect takes place when a consumer reacts to a rise in the price of one good by consuming less of that good and more of a substitute good.

The substitution effect can also apply to a drop in prices. If the price of pizza drops, pizza becomes cheaper compared to other alternatives. Consumers will now substitute pizza for tacos, salads, and other lunch choices, causing the quantity of pizza demanded to rise.

The Income Effect

Rising prices have another effect that we have all felt. They make us feel poorer. When the price of movie tickets, shoes, or pizza increases, your limited budget just won't buy as much as it used to. It feels as if you have less money. You can no longer afford to buy the same combination of goods, and you must cut back your purchases of some goods. If you buy fewer slices of pizza without increasing your purchases of other foods, that is the income effect.

One important fact to remember is that economists measure consumption in the amount of a good that is bought, not the amount of money spent to buy it. Although you are spending more on pizza, you are consuming fewer slices, so your consumption has gone down. If the price rises from $1 a slice to $2 a slice, you may decide to pay extra and order your usual lunch, but you certainly would not choose to buy more slices than before. Although people spend more of their money on pizza, when

Figure 4.2 Building the Law of Demand

	Price of A increases		Price of A decreases	
	Consumption of A	Consumption of other goods	Consumption of A	Consumption of other goods
Income effect	↓	↓	↑	↑
Substitution effect	↓	↑	↑	↓
Combined effect	↓	↑	↑	↑

Both the substitution effect and the income effect lead consumers to buy less of good A when it becomes more expensive. However, the income effect leads consumers to spend less on other goods so they can afford good A, while the substitution effect encourages consumers to replace expensive good A with other, less expensive substitutes.

Supply and Demand Explain in your own words how an increase in the price of A affects consumption of other goods.

◀ Today, a bicycle might cost $100, and most people purchase only one. If bikes still cost $8.95, as they did in 1902, you might buy two or more and spend the rest on other goods. This is the income effect in action.

the price goes up, the quantity demanded goes down. In this sense, the income effect leads to the law of demand.

Remember, too, that the income effect also operates when the price is lowered. If the price of pizza falls, all of a sudden you feel wealthier. If as a result you buy more pizza, that's the income effect.

A Demand Schedule

The law of demand explains how the price of any item affects the quantity demanded of that item. Before we look at the relationship between price and quantity demanded for a specific good, we need to look more closely at how economists use the word *demand*.

Understanding Demand

To have demand for a good, you must be willing and able to buy it at the specified price. This means that you want the good,

and you can afford to buy it. You may desperately want a new car, a laptop computer, or a trip to Alaska, but if you can't truly afford any of these goods, then you do not demand them. You might demand compact discs, though, if at the current price you have enough money and want to buy some.

A **demand schedule** is a table that lists the quantity of a good that a person will purchase at each price in a market. For example, the table on the left in Figure 4.3 illustrates individual "demand for pizza." The schedule shows specific quantities that a student named Ashley is willing and able to purchase at specific prices. For example, at a price of $2.00, Ashley's "quantity demanded" of pizza is two slices per day.

Market Demand Schedules

If you owned a store, knowing the demand schedule of one customer might not be very helpful. You would want to know how

demand schedule *a table that lists the quantity of a good a person will buy at each different price*

Figure 4.3 Demand Schedules

Individual Demand Schedule		Market Demand Schedule	
Price of a slice of pizza	Quantity demanded per day	Price of a slice of pizza	Quantity demanded per day
$.50	5	$.50	300
$1.00	4	$1.00	250
$1.50	3	$1.50	200
$2.00	2	$2.00	150
$2.50	1	$2.50	100
$3.00	0	$3.00	50

Demand schedules show that demand for a good falls as the price rises.

Supply and Demand How does the market demand for pizza change when the price falls from $2.50 to $1.00 a slice? Be specific.

▲ **A sale can encourage consumers to buy more.**

market demand schedule *a table that lists the quantity of a good all consumers in a market will buy at each different price*

demand curve *a graphic representation of a demand schedule*

Ashley's demand curve shows the number of slices of pizza she is willing and able to buy at each price.

Supply and Demand
How many slices of pizza does she demand when the price is $1.50?

customers as a whole would react to price changes. When you add up the demand schedules of every buyer in the market, you can create a market demand schedule. A **market demand schedule** shows the quantities demanded at each price by all consumers in the market. A market demand schedule for pizza would allow a restaurant owner to predict the total sales of pizza at several different prices.

The owner of a pizzeria could create a market demand schedule for pizza slices by surveying his or her customers and then adding up the quantities demanded by all individual consumers at each price. The

resulting market demand schedule will look like Ashley's demand schedule, but the quantities will be larger, as shown in Figure 4.3.

Note that the market demand schedule on the right in Figure 4.3 contains the same prices as Ashley's individual demand schedule, since those are the possible prices that may be charged by the pizzeria. The schedule also exhibits the law of demand. At higher prices the quantity demanded is lower. The only difference between the two demand schedules is that the market schedule lists larger quantities demanded. This is the case, since now we are talking about the purchase decisions of *all* potential consumers in the market.

The Demand Graph

What if you took the numbers in Ashley's demand schedule in Figure 4.3 and plotted them on a graph? The result would be a **demand curve**. A demand curve is a graphic representation of a demand schedule.

How do economists create a demand curve? When they transfer numbers from a demand schedule to a graph, they always label the vertical axis with the lowest possible prices at the bottom and the highest at the top. Likewise, they always label the quantities demanded on the horizontal axis with the lowest possible quantity at the left and the highest possible quantity at the right. As Figure 4.4 shows, each pair of price and quantity-demanded numbers on the schedule is plotted as a point on the graph. Connecting the points creates a demand curve.

Reading a Demand Curve

Note two facts about the graph shown in Figure 4.4. First, the graph shows only the relationship between the price of this good and the quantity that Ashley will purchase. It assumes that all other factors that would affect Ashley's demand for pizza—like the price of other goods, her income, and the quality of the pizza—are held constant.

Second, the demand curve on the graph slopes downward to the right. If you follow the curve with your finger from the top left

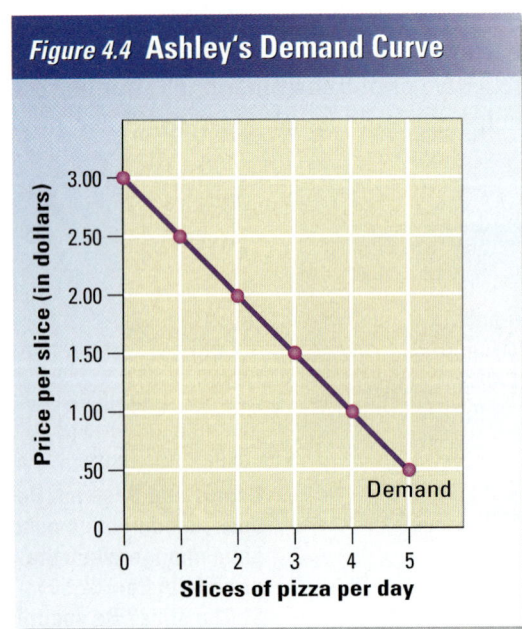

Figure 4.4 Ashley's Demand Curve

to the bottom right, you will notice that as price decreases, the quantity demanded increases. This is just another way of stating the law of demand, which states that higher prices will always lead to lower quantities demanded. All demand schedules and curves reflect the law of demand.

The demand curve in Figure 4.4 shows Ashley's demand for slices of pizza. A market demand curve shows the quantities demanded by all consumers at the same prices. Thus, in Figure 4.5, the prices listed on the vertical axis are identical to those in Ashley's demand curve. The quantities listed on the horizontal axis are much larger, corresponding to those in the market demand schedule in Figure 4.3.

Figure 4.5 **Market Demand Curve**

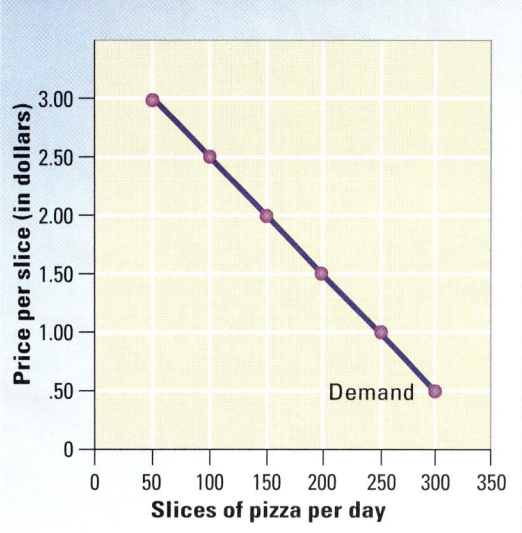

The market demand curve illustrates demand for pizza in an entire market.

Supply and Demand **How is the market demand curve similar to Ashley's demand curve?**

Limits of a Demand Curve
The market demand curve can be used to predict how people will change their buying habits when the price of a good rises or falls. For example, if the price of pizza is $1.50 a slice, the pizzeria will sell 200 slices a day.

This market demand curve is only accurate for one very specific set of market conditions. If a nearby factory were to close, so that fewer people were in the area at lunchtime, the pizzeria would sell less pizza even if the price stayed the same. In the next section, you will read about how demand curves can shift because of changes in factors other than price.

Section 1 Assessment

Key Terms and Main Ideas
1. Define and give an example of the **income effect**.
2. What are three characteristics of a **demand curve?**

Applying Economic Concepts
3. *Critical Thinking* Explain why the law of demand can apply only in a free market economy.
4. *Try This* Create an individual demand schedule like the one in Figure 4.3 for your demand for CDs. Fill in six different prices for CDs. Assume that you have a part-time job that pays $80 a week. How many CDs would you buy at each of the six different prices? Compare your demand schedule to those of your classmates.

5. *Critical Thinking* Some economists believe that there are goods that do not obey the law of demand, because the demand for them would actually drop if their price fell. One example is a top-of-the-line luxury car. Why do you think prospective buyers might feel differently about these goods?

6. *Math Practice* Use the market demand schedule below to draw a demand curve for miniature golf.

Cost to Play a Game	Games Played per Month
$1.50	350
$2.00	250
$3.00	140
$4.00	80

Take It to the NET Demand affects our everyday lives. Find a recent article online that is on the topic of demand. Use the links provided in the Social Studies area at the following Web site for help in completing this activity. **www.phschool.com**

Analyzing Tables

Economists use tables as a way to organize data and illustrate trends. The table below presents the results of a hypothetical survey of 100 high school seniors from across the country and 100 of their parents. Both groups were asked if they would be willing to pay $5 for a ticket to a movie on opening night, for a meal at a fine restaurant, or for an asthma inhaler (assuming they suffered from asthma). Next, they were asked if they would pay $10 for each of these goods, and next, if they would pay $30. The table below lists the number in each group that answered "yes" at each price.

1. **Determine the kinds of information shown in the table.** The title of the table and the labels for each vertical column and horizontal row tell you exactly what information is presented. (**a**) What is the title of the table? (**b**) What does the first column of data specifically describe?

2. **Read the information in the table.** Note that each dollar value has two sets of data, one for students, and the other for parents. Answer the following questions. (**a**) How many students were willing to pay $30 for the meal? (**b**) How many parents? (**c**) Which item were nearly all members of both groups unwilling to buy for $30?

3. **Study the table to find relationships among the data and draw conclusions.** You can use the data in this table to compare the demand for different goods at one price level, or to see how demand for one good changes as the price increases or decreases. (**a**) Which good saw the sharpest drop in demand when its price rose from $5 to $30? (**b**) Which good saw little change in demand when its price rose? Why might this be? (**c**) How did demand change for students when the price of a meal went up? (**d**) Name two conclusions you can draw about the differences between the patterns of demand of the students and their parents.

Additional Practice

Draw a new chart reflecting the data that you might expect to gather if you repeated this survey with different goods, such as a weekly bus pass, a concert ticket, and a best-selling novel.

Demand for Selected Goods						
Goods	**$5**		**$10**		**$30**	
	Students	Parents	Students	Parents	Students	Parents
Movie ticket	70	67	11	35	1	0
Asthma medicine	91	94	86	88	79	85
Restaurant meal	94	96	62	80	13	37

Shifts of the Demand Curve

Objectives

After studying this section you will be able to:

1. **Understand** the difference between a change in quantity demanded and a shift in the demand curve.
2. **Identify** the determinants that create changes in demand and that can cause a shift in the demand curve.
3. **Explain** how the change in the price of one good can affect demand for a related good.

Section Focus

Several factors can change the demand for a good at any price. A change in demand causes the entire demand curve to shift to the left or right.

Key Terms

ceteris paribus
normal good
inferior good
complements
substitutes

The market demand schedule for pizza in Figure 4.3 would appear to give the pizzeria owner all the information she needs to set the prices for her menu. All she has to do is look at the list, pick the price and quantity combination that will earn her the highest profit, and start baking.

Other factors, however, might have an effect. What would happen if the day after she printed a menu, the government announced that tomato sauce had a natural chemical that strengthened the immune system? Demand for pizza at all prices would climb.

When we counted the number of pizza slices that would sell as the price went up or down, we assumed that nothing besides the price of pizza would change. Economists refer to this assumption as **ceteris paribus**, the Latin phrase for "all other things held constant." The demand schedule took only changes in price into account. It did not take the news reports into account, or any one of thousands of other factors that change from day to day. In this section, you will learn how economists consider the impact of these other changes on the demand for goods like pizza.

Changes in Demand

A demand curve is accurate only as long as there are no changes other than price that could affect the consumer's decision. In other words, a demand curve is accurate only as long as the *ceteris paribus* assumption is true. When the price changes, we move along the curve to a different quantity demanded. For example, in the graph of Ashley's demand for slices of pizza, an increase in the price from $1.00 per slice to $1.50 will make Ashley's quantity demanded fall from four slices to three slices per day. This movement along the demand curve is referred to as a

ceteris paribus a Latin phrase that means "all other things held constant"

▼ **A sudden winter storm can increase the demand for snow shovels.**

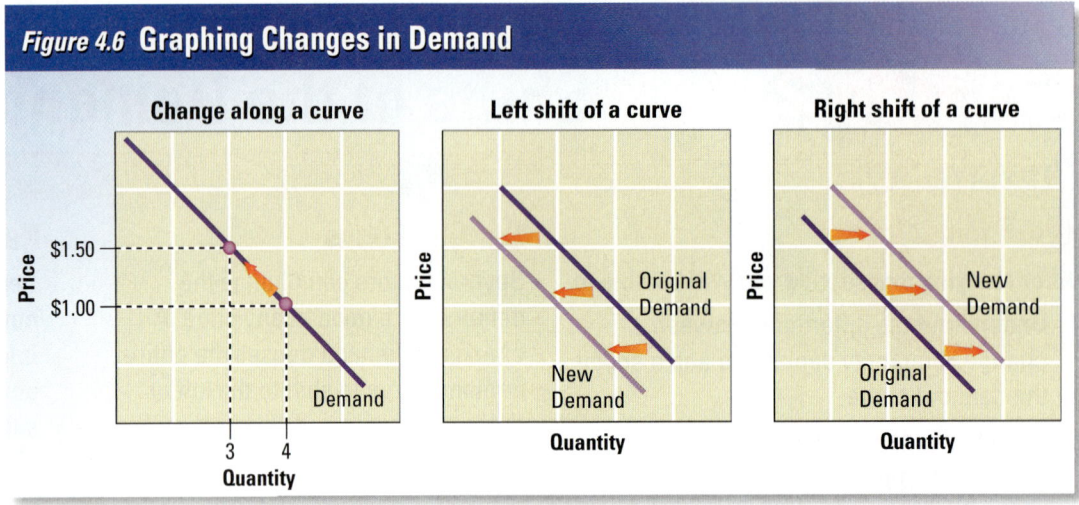

Figure 4.6 Graphing Changes in Demand

Change along a curve

Left shift of a curve

Right shift of a curve

A change in quantity demanded caused by a change in price is shown as a movement along *a demand curve. The curve does not shift. When factors other than price cause demand to fall, the demand curve shifts to the left. An increase in demand appears as a shift to the right.* **Supply and Demand** **If the price of a book rose by $1.00, how would you represent the change on one of these graphs?**

normal good *a good that consumers demand more of when their incomes increase*

decrease in the quantity demanded. By the same reasoning, a decrease in the price of pizza would lead to an *increase* in the quantity demanded.

When we drop the *ceteris paribus* rule and allow other factors to change, we no longer move along the demand curve. Instead, the entire demand curve shifts. A shift in the demand curve means that at

every price, consumers buy a different quantity than before. This shift of the entire curve is what economists refer to as a *change in demand.*

Suppose, for example, that Ashley's town is hit by a heat wave, and Ashley no longer feels as hungry for pizza. She will demand fewer slices at every price. The middle graph in Figure 4.6 shows her original demand curve and her new demand curve, adjusted for hot weather.

What Causes a Shift?

As you have read, a change in the price of a good does not cause the demand curve to shift. The effects of changes in price are already built into the demand curve. However, several other factors can cause demand for a good to change. These changes can lead to a change in demand rather than simply a change in the quantity demanded.

Income

A consumer's income affects his or her demand for most goods. Most items that we purchase are **normal goods,** goods that consumers demand more of when their incomes increase. In other words, an increase

▶ Used paperback books are often inferior goods. When consumers can afford new, clean books, they will buy fewer old paperbacks.

in Ashley's income from $50 per week to $75 per week will cause her to buy more of a normal good at every price level. If we were to draw a new demand schedule for Ashley, it would show a greater demand for slices of pizza at every price. Plotting the new schedule on a graph would produce a curve to the right of Ashley's original curve. For each of the prices on the vertical axis, the quantity demanded would be greater. This shift to the right of the curve is called an *increase in demand*. A fall in income would cause the demand curve to shift left. This shift is called a *decrease in demand*.

There are also other goods called **inferior goods**. They are called inferior goods because an increase in income causes demand for these goods to fall. Inferior goods are goods that you would buy in smaller quantities, or not at all, if your income were to rise and you could afford something better. Possible examples of inferior goods include macaroni and cheese, generic cereals, and used cars.

Consumer Expectations

Our expectations about the future can affect our demand for certain goods today. Suppose that you have had your eye on a new bicycle for several months. One day you walk in the store to look at the bike, and the salesperson mentions that the store will be raising the price in one week. Now that you expect a higher price in the near future, you are more likely to buy the bike today. In other words, the expectation of a higher price in the future has caused your immediate demand to increase.

If, on the other hand, the salesperson were to tell you that the bike will be on sale next week, your immediate demand for the bicycle would fall to zero. You would rather wait until next week to buy the bike at a lower price.

The current demand for a good is positively related to its expected future price. If you expect the price to rise, your current demand will rise, which means you will buy the good sooner. If you expect the price to drop, your current demand will fall and you will wait for the lower price.

Population

Changes in the size of the population will also affect the demand for most products. For example, a growing population needs to be housed and fed. Therefore, a rise in population will increase demand for houses, food, and many other goods and services.

Population trends can have a particularly strong effect on certain goods. For example, when American soldiers returned from World War II in the mid- to late 1940s, record numbers of them married and started families. This trend led to the "baby boom," a jump in the birthrate from the mid-1940s through 1964. Initially, the baby boom led to higher demand for baby clothes, baby food, and books on baby care. In the 1950s and 1960s, towns had to build thousands of new schools. Later, universities opened new class-rooms, dormitories, and even whole new campuses to make room for the flood of new students. The baby boomers have now begun to retire. Over the next few decades the market will face rising demand for the goods and services that are desired by senior citizens, including medical care, recreational vehicles, and homes in the Sunbelt.

Consumer Tastes and Advertising

Who can explain why bell-bottom blue jeans were everywhere one year and rarely seen the next? Is it the result of clever advertising campaigns, social trends, the influence of television shows, or some combination of these factors? Although economists cannot always isolate the reasons why some fads begin, advertising and publicity often play an important role.

Changes in tastes and preferences cannot be explained by changes in income or population or worries about future price increases. Advertising is considered a factor

inferior good *a good that consumers demand less of when their incomes increase*

▲ **When New York City announced that the price of a subway token would rise 25 cents, commuters rushed to buy tokens at the old price. To prevent this, the city introduced a new token (bottom) to replace the older token commuters had bought. Expectations of higher prices had affected demand.**

▲ Ski boots and skis are two goods that are complements.

complements *two goods that are bought and used together*

substitutes *goods used in place of one another*

that shifts demand curves because it plays an important role in many trends. Companies spend money on advertising because they hope that it will increase the demand for the goods they sell. Considering the growing sums of money spent on advertising in the United States each year, companies must feel that this investment is paying off.

Prices of Related Goods

The demand curve for one good can be affected by a change in the demand for another good. There are two types of related goods that interact this way: complements and substitutes.

- **Complements** are two goods that are bought and used together.

- **Substitutes** are goods used in place of one another.

When we consider the demand for skis, ski boots are considered a complement. An increase in the price of ski boots will cause people to buy fewer boots. Because skis are useless without boots, the demand for skis will fall at all prices—after all, why buy new skis if you can't afford the ski boots you need to ski safely?

Now consider the effect on the demand for skis when the price of snowboards rises. Snowboards are a substitute for skis, because consumers will often buy one or the other, but not both. A rise in the price of snowboards will cause people to buy fewer snowboards, and therefore people will buy *more* pairs of new skis at every price. Likewise, a fall in the price of snowboards will lead consumers to buy fewer skis at all price levels.

Section 2 Assessment

Key Terms and Main Ideas

1. What is an example of something you consider an **inferior good**?
2. What is one good that can be considered a **complement** for another?
3. What are two goods that can be considered **substitutes**?
4. How does the *ceteris paribus* assumption affect a demand curve?

Applying Economic Concepts

5. *Using the Databank* According to the law of demand and the chart of median house prices on page 540, how do you think demand for houses changed between 1994 and 1998? Explain.
6. *Critical Thinking* What is the difference between a shift along a demand curve and a shift of a demand curve?

7. *Decision Making* Decide whether each of these events would cause a change in *demand* or only a change in the *quantity demanded* of the good in parentheses, and explain why. **(a)** A computer manufacturer lowers its prices. (computers) **(b)** A volleyball maker convinces high schools to fund varsity volleyball teams. (volleyballs) **(c)** A freeze ruins the orange crop, and orange juice prices rise. (apple juice)

8. *Math Practice* Use the following demand schedule to draw a demand curve. Then find and label a combination of output and price that could result from: **(a)** an increase in the quantity demanded, **(b)** an increase in demand, and **(c)** a decrease in demand.

Price	Quantity Demanded
$1.00	250
$2.00	200
$3.00	150
$4.00	100
$5.00	50

Take It to the NET

Many inferior goods are not inferior in their performance. Recently, people have begun to debate the role of generic medication in health care. Write a brief summary of the generic drug debate. Use the links provided in the Social Studies area at the following Web site for help in completing this activity. **www.phschool.com**

Profile

MARY KAY ASH (1915–2001)

Mary Kay Ash combined hard work, dedication, good business insights, and a strong moral philosophy to create a large, successful company. Mary Kay Cosmetics is now the largest direct seller of skin care products in the United States.

From Modest Beginnings

Mary Kay Ash started out selling child psychology books door-to-door in Texas in the late 1930s and worked her way up to higher positions at other direct sales companies. In 1963, she thought it would be useful to write a book telling women how to succeed in the business world, which at that time was almost totally controlled by men.

Ash made a list of the good features of the companies she had worked for. She made another list of things that could have been done better. By the time she finished the lists, she realized that she had come up with her own idea for starting a company. She took her life savings of $5,000 and started Mary Kay Cosmetics.

Opportunities for Women

Ash's idea was to build a company that would provide an unlimited opportunity for women through sales of high quality products to achieve personal and financial success. She adopted the Golden Rule as her business philosophy, and she encouraged her employees to lead a balanced life as expressed in her personal motto of "God first, family second, career third."

Today Mary Kay Cosmetics, Inc., headquartered in Dallas, has a strong mission statement:

"Mary Kay's mission is to enrich women's lives. We will do this in tangible ways, by offering quality products to consumers, financial opportunities to our independent sales force, and fulfilling careers to our employees. We will also reach out to the heart and spirit of women, enabling personal growth and fulfillment for the women whose lives we touch. We will carry out our mission in a spirit of caring, living the positive values on which our Company was built."

Charitable Commitments

Mary Kay Ash was a strong supporter of charitable activities. After her husband Mel died of cancer in the 1980s, she began funding research on cancers affecting women. She created the Mary Kay Ash Charitable Foundation, which has donated more than 3 million dollars to support women's cancer research studies. Recently the Foundation expanded its scope to help address the worldwide problem of violence against women. The Foundation has made grants to shelters for abused women throughout the country and supports efforts to raise public awareness.

CHECK FOR UNDERSTANDING

1. Source Reading One of Ash's sayings was "People fail forward to success." Explain what she meant in your own words. How might an employer implement this philosophy in the workplace?

2. Critical Thinking Reread Mary Kay's mission statement. What societal values does it reflect?

3. Learn More Use the Internet to learn more about women entrepreneurs. Then write your own economic profile based on your findings.

Elasticity of Demand

Objectives

After studying this section you will be able to:

1. **Explain** how to calculate elasticity of demand.
2. **Identify** factors that affect elasticity.
3. **Explain** how firms use elasticity and revenue to make decisions.

Section Focus

Elasticity of demand describes how consumers will react to a change in the price of a good. Their reaction depends on the original price of the good and the way that good is used by consumers.

Key Terms

elasticity of demand
inelastic
elastic
unitary elastic
total revenue

---

elasticity of demand
a measure of how consumers react to a change in price

inelastic *describes demand that is not very sensitive to a change in price*

elastic *describes demand that is very sensitive to a change in price*

Are there some goods that you would always find money to buy, even if the price were to rise drastically? Are there other goods that you would cut back on, or even stop buying altogether, if the price were to rise just slightly?

Economists describe the way that consumers respond to price changes as **elasticity of demand**. Elasticity of demand dictates how drastically buyers will cut back or increase their demand for a good when the price rises or falls, respectively. Your demand for a good that you will keep buying despite a price increase is **inelastic,** or relatively unresponsive to price changes. In the second example, in which you buy much less of a good after a small price increase, your demand is **elastic**. A consumer with highly elastic demand for a good is very responsive to price changes.

Calculating Elasticity

To compute elasticity of demand, take the percentage change in the demand of a good, and divide this number by the percentage change in the price of the good. You can find the equation for elasticity in Figure 4.7 on page 92. The law of demand implies that the result will always be negative. This is because an increase in the price of a good will always decrease the quantity demanded, and a decrease in the price of a good will always increase the quantity demanded. For the sake of simplicity, economists drop the negative sign.

Price Range

The elasticity of demand for a good varies at every price level. Demand for a good can be highly elastic at one price and inelastic at a different price. For example, demand

LEMINADE
$25.00

"After taxes, operating expenses and profits to stockholders, I'm lucky if I see a nickel of it!"

▲ Misspelling "lemonade" might not be this entrepreneur's only mistake. How many people will buy lemonade if the price rises to $25.00 a glass?

for a glossy magazine will be inelastic when the price rises 50 percent from 20 cents to 30 cents. The price is still very low, and people will buy almost as many copies as they did before. However, when the price increases 50 percent from $4.00 to $6.00, demand will be much more elastic. Many readers will refuse to pay $2.00 more for the magazine. Yet in percentage terms, the change in the magazine's price is exactly the same as when the price rose from 20 cents to 30 cents.

Values of Elasticity

We have been using the terms *inelastic* and *elastic* to describe consumers' responses to price changes. These terms have precise mathematical definitions. If the elasticity of demand for a good at a certain price is *less* than 1, we describe demand as inelastic. If the elasticity is *greater* than one, demand is elastic. If elasticity is exactly equal to 1, we describe demand as **unitary elastic**.

When elasticity of demand is unitary, the percentage change in quantity demanded is exactly equal to the percentage change in the price. Suppose the elasticity of demand for a magazine at $2 is unitary. When the price of the magazine rises by 50 percent to $3, the newsstand will sell exactly half as many copies as before.

Think back to Ashley's demand schedule for pizza in Section 1. Ashley's demand schedule shows that if the price per slice were to rise from $1.00 to $1.50, her quantity demanded would fall from 4 slices to 3 slices per day. The change in price from $1.00 to $1.50 is a 50 percent increase. The change in quantity demanded from 4 to 3 slices is a 25 percent decrease. Dividing the 25 percent decrease in quantity demanded by the 50 percent increase in price gives us an elasticity of demand of 0.5.

Since Ashley's elasticity of demand at prices of $1.00 to $1.50 is less than 1, we say that Ashley's demand for pizza is inelastic. In other words, a price increase has a relatively small effect on the number of slices of pizza she buys.

Suppose that we survey another customer and find that, when the price of pizza rises by 40 percent, this person's quantity demanded falls by 60 percent. The change in the quantity demanded of 60 percent is divided by the change in price of 40 percent, equaling an elasticity of demand of 1.5 (60 percent/40 percent = 1.5). Since this result is greater than 1, this customer's demand is elastic. In other words, this customer is very sensitive to changes in the price of pizza.

Factors Affecting Elasticity

Why is the demand for some goods so much less elastic than for other goods? Rephrase the question and ask yourself, "What is essential to me? What goods must I have, even if the price rises greatly?" The goods you list might have some traits that set them apart from other goods and make your demand for those goods less elastic. Several different factors can affect a person's elasticity of demand for a specific good.

Availability of Substitutes

If there are few substitutes for a good, then even when its price rises greatly, you might still buy it. You feel you have no good alternatives. For example, if your favorite musical group plans to give a concert, and you want to attend, there really is no substitute for a ticket. You could go to a concert to hear some other band, but that would not be as good. You've got to have

unitary elastic
describes demand whose elasticity is exactly equal to 1

Global Connections

Elasticity in the Kitchen Cooking varies from country to country, and so does **elasticity of demand** for certain foods. If the price of a gallon of milk or a pound of ground beef doubled in the United States, consumers might demand intervention by the government. Do you think this would happen if the price rise affected onions and potatoes? These two vegetables are essential to Indian cooking, and when floods ruined crops in India, their prices more than doubled. In November 1998, angry citizens voted the ruling party out of office in several states in part because of the high price of onions.

Figure 4.7 **Elasticity of Demand**

Elasticity is determined using the following formula:

$$\text{Elasticity} = \frac{\text{Percentage change in quantity demanded}}{\text{Percentage change in price}}$$

To find the percentage change in quantity demanded or price, use the following formula: Subtract the new number from the original number, and divide the result by the original number. Ignore any negative signs, and multiply by 100 to convert this number to a percentage:

$$\text{Percentage change} = \frac{\text{Original number} - \text{New number}}{\text{Original number}} \times 100$$

Example 1: Elastic Demand

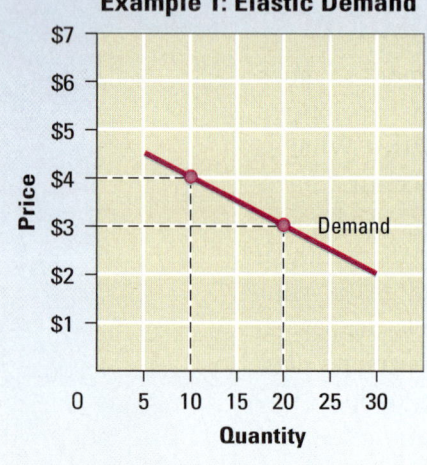

If demand is elastic, a small change in price leads to a relatively large change in the quantity demanded. Follow this demand curve from left to right.

The price decreases from $4 to $3, a decrease of 25 percent.

$$\frac{\$4 - \$3}{\$4} \times 100 = 25$$

The quantity demanded increases from 10 to 20. This is an increase of 100 percent.

$$\frac{10 - 20}{10} \times 100 = 100$$

Elasticity of demand is equal to 4.0. Elasticity is greater than 1, so demand is elastic. In this example, a small decrease in price caused a large increase in the quantity demanded.

$$\frac{100\%}{25\%} = 4.0$$

Example 2: Inelastic Demand

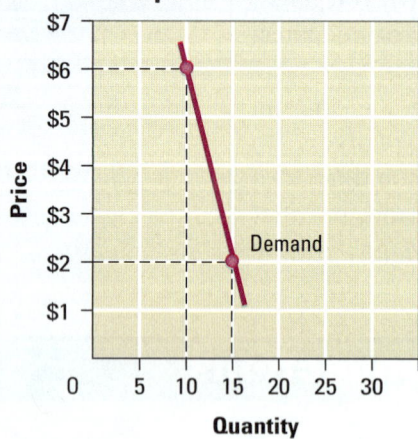

If demand is inelastic, consumers are not very responsive to changes in price. A decrease in price will lead to only a small change in quantity demanded, or perhaps no change at all. Follow this demand curve from left to right as the price decreases sharply from $6 to $2.

The price decreases from $6 to $2, a decrease of about 67 percent.

$$\frac{\$6 - \$2}{\$6} \times 100 \approx 67$$

The quantity demanded increases from 10 to 15, an increase of 50 percent.

$$\frac{10 - 15}{10} \times 100 = 50$$

Elasticity of demand is about 0.75. The elasticity is less than 1, so demand for this good is inelastic. The increase in quantity demanded is small compared to the decrease in price.

$$\frac{50\%}{67\%} \approx 0.75$$

Unitary elastic demand is a special case. When demand is unitary elastic, an increase (or decrease) in price will be met by an equal percentage decrease (or increase) in quantity demanded. Elasticity of demand is exactly 1.

Elasticity of demand describes how strongly consumers will react to a change in price.
Supply and Demand **If a good's elasticity of demand is 0.2, how will consumers react to an increase in price?**

tickets for this concert, and nothing else will do. Under these circumstances, a moderate change in price is not going to change your mind. Your demand is inelastic.

Similarly, demand for life-saving medicine is usually inelastic. For many prescription drugs, the only possible substitute is to try an unproven treatment. For this reason, people with an illness will continue to buy as much needed medicine as they can afford, even when the price goes up.

If the lack of substitutes can make demand inelastic, a wide choice of substitute goods can make demand elastic. The demand for a particular brand of apple juice is probably elastic because people can choose from dozens of good substitutes if the price of their preferred brand rises.

Relative Importance

A second factor in determining a good's elasticity of demand is how much of your budget you spend on the good. If you already spend a large share of your income on a good, a price increase will force you to make some tough choices. Unless you want to cut back drastically on the other goods in your budget, you must reduce consumption of that good by a significant amount to keep your budget under control. The higher the jump in price, the more you will have to adjust your purchases.

If you currently spend half of your budget on clothes, then even a modest increase in the cost of clothing will probably cause a large reduction in the quantity you purchase. In other words, your demand will be elastic.

However, if the price of shoelaces doubled, would you cut back on your shoelace purchases? Probably not. You may not even notice the difference. Even if you spend twice as much on shoelaces, they will still account for only a tiny part of your overall budget. Your demand for shoelaces is inelastic.

Necessities Versus Luxuries

The third factor in determining a good's elasticity varies a great deal from person to person, but it is nonetheless important. Whether a person considers a good to be a necessity or a luxury has a great impact on the good's elasticity of demand for that person. A necessity is a good people will always buy, even when the price increases. Parents often regard milk as a necessity. They will buy it at any reasonable price. If the price of a gallon of milk rises from $2.49 to $4.49, they will still buy as much milk as their children need to stay healthy. Their demand for milk is inelastic.

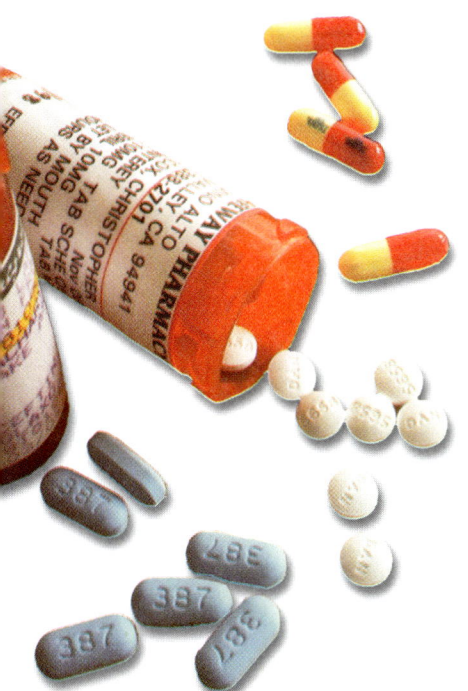

▲ Demand for some prescription drugs is relatively inelastic because the patient has few alternatives. Demand for any one of these drinks would be much more elastic because a consumer can easily find a less expensive choice.

▲ Many people consider lobster a luxury and can easily cut it out of their budget.

The same parents may regard steak as a luxury. When the price of steak increases by a little bit, say 20 percent, parents may cut their monthly purchases of steak by more than 20 percent, or skip steak altogether. Steak is a luxury, and consumers can easily reduce the quantity they consume. Because it is easy to reduce the quantity of luxuries demanded, demand is elastic.

Change over Time

When a price changes, consumers often need time to change their shopping habits. Consumers do not always react quickly to a price increase because it takes time to find substitutes. Because they cannot respond quickly to price changes, their demand is inelastic in the short term. Demand sometimes becomes more elastic over time, however, because people can eventually find substitutes that allow large adjustments to what they buy.

Consider the example of gasoline. When a person purchases a vehicle, he or she might choose a large vehicle that requires a greater volume of gasoline per mile to run. This same person might work at a job many miles away from home and shop at a supermarket that is far from both work and home. These factors determine how much gasoline this person demands, and none can be changed easily.

In the early 1970s, several oil-rich countries cut their oil exports to the United States, and gasoline prices rose quickly. In the short run, there was very little that people could do to reduce their consumption of gasoline. They still needed to drive to school and work. At first, drivers were more likely to pay more for the same amount of gasoline than they were to buy fuel-efficient cars or move closer to their schools and workplaces.

However, because gas prices stayed high for a considerable period of time, some people eventually switched to more fuel-efficient cars. Others formed car pools, walked or rode bicycles, and used public transportation. In the long run, people reduced their consumption of gasoline by finding substitutes. Demand for gasoline, inelastic in the short term, is more elastic in the long term.

As another example, consider what happened to gasoline prices from the early 1980s through the 1990s. Adjusting for inflation, the price of a gallon of gas fell

Think small.

▲ When gas prices rose in the 1970s, auto manufacturers advertised how little fuel their cars used. Gas prices were low in the 1990s, so new advertising emphasized strength and size, even though those cars used more gasoline.

considerably from its highs in the 1970s. In addition, gasoline prices remained low for many years. At first, people continued to seek out fuel-efficient cars. Over time, however, many Americans switched back to larger vehicles that get fewer miles to the gallon. Because the price of gas remained low, people gradually adjusted their habits to use more and more gasoline. Just as demand for gasoline responded slowly to an increase in price, it also responded slowly to a decrease in price.

Elasticity and Revenue

Elasticity is important to the study of economics because elasticity helps us measure how consumers respond to price changes for different products. Elasticity is also an important tool for business planners like the pizzeria owner described in Sections 1 and 2. The elasticity of demand determines how a change in prices will affect a firm's total revenue or income.

Computing a Firm's Total Revenue

A company's **total revenue** is defined as the amount of money the company receives by selling its goods. This is determined by two factors: the price of the goods and the quantity sold. If a pizzeria sells 125 slices of pizza per day at $2.00 per slice, total revenue would be $250 per day.

Total Revenue and Elastic Demand

The law of demand tells us that an increase in price will decrease the quantity demanded. When a good has an elastic demand, raising the price of each unit sold by 20 percent will decrease the quantity sold by a larger percentage, say 50 percent. The quantity sold will drop enough to actually *reduce* the firm's total revenue. Figure 4.8, drawn from the demand curve for the pizzeria, shows how this can happen. An increase in price from $2.50 to $3.00, or 20 percent, decreases the quantity sold from 100 to 50, or 50 percent. As a result, total revenue drops from $250 to $150.

Figure 4.8 Revenue Table

Price of a slice of pizza	Quantity demanded per day	Total revenue
$ .50	300	$150
$1.00	250	$250
$1.50	200	$300
$2.00	150	$300
$2.50	100	$250
$3.00	50	$150

Setting prices too high or too low can hurt revenue.
Markets and Prices When the price doubles from $.50 to $1.00, is demand elastic, unitary elastic, or inelastic?

The same process can also work in reverse. If the firm were to reduce the price by a certain percentage, the quantity demanded could rise by an even greater percentage. In this case, total revenues could rise.

It may surprise you that a firm could lose revenue by raising the price of its goods. But if the pizzeria started selling pizza at $10 a slice, it would not stay in business very long. Remember that elastic demand comes from one or more of these factors:

1. availability of substitute goods
2. a limited budget that does not allow price changes
3. the perception of the good as a luxury item

If these conditions are present, then the demand for the good is elastic, and a firm may find that a price increase reduces its total revenue.

Total Revenue and Inelastic Demand

Remember that if demand is inelastic, consumers' demand is not very responsive to price changes. Thus, if the firm raises its price by 25 percent, the quantity demanded will fall, but by less than 25 percent. The firm will have greater total revenues. In other words, the higher price makes up for the firm's lower sales, and the firm brings in more money.

total revenue *the total amount of money a firm receives by selling goods or services*

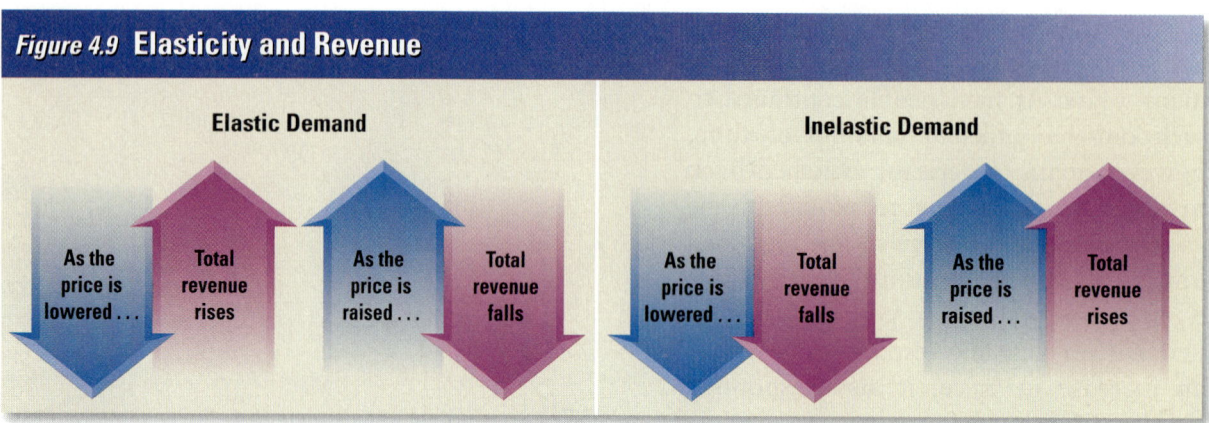

Figure 4.9 **Elasticity and Revenue**

Elastic Demand

As the price is lowered . . . Total revenue rises

As the price is raised . . . Total revenue falls

Inelastic Demand

As the price is lowered . . . Total revenue falls

As the price is raised . . . Total revenue rises

Elasticity of demand determines the effect of a price change on total revenues.
Markets and Prices Why will revenue fall if a firm raises the price of a good whose demand is elastic?

On the other hand, a decrease in price will lead to an increase in the quantity demanded if demand is inelastic. However, demand will not rise as much, in percentage terms, as the price fell, and the firm's total revenue will decrease.

Elasticity and Pricing Policies

Because of these relationships, a firm needs to know whether the demand for its product is elastic or inelastic at a given price. This knowledge helps the firm make pricing decisions that lead to the greatest revenue. If a firm knows that the demand for its product is elastic at the current price, it knows that an increase in price would reduce total revenues. On the other hand, if a firm knows that the demand for its product is inelastic at its current price, it knows that an increase in price will increase total revenue. In the next chapter, you will read more about the choices producers make to reach an ideal level of revenue.

Section 3 Assessment

Key Terms and Main Ideas

1. Explain **elasticity of demand** in your own words.
2. Name a good with **elastic** demand at its current price.
3. Why is demand for home heating fuel **inelastic** in cold weather?
4. How do we calculate **total revenue?**

Applying Economic Concepts

5. *Math Practice* Use the formula in Figure 4.7 to calculate the exact elasticity of demand in the following examples. Then tell if, in each case, demand is elastic, inelastic, or unitary elastic. **(a)** When the price of a deluxe car wash rises from $10.00 to $11.00, the number of daily customers falls from 60 to 48. **(b)** A dentist with 80 patients cuts his fee for a cleaning from $60.00 to $54.00 and attracts two new patients.

6. *Try This* Interview a manager at a local restaurant or store. Ask if he or she has changed the price of any good or service in the past year, and if so, how sales were affected. Is demand for each of these goods or services elastic or inelastic? What factors might explain your answer?

7. *Critical Thinking* Think of a good, like gasoline, for which demand can become more elastic over time. What changes can take place in the long term to affect demand?

Take It to the NET Petroleum and petroleum products are important to our everyday lives. Find out how much oil is demanded by North America and how much is demanded by one other continent. Is each demand elastic or inelastic? Use the links provided in the Social Studies area at the following Web site for help in completing this activity. **www.phschool.com**

What Makes a Person an Entrepreneur?

Entrepreneurs come in all shapes and sizes. Some have become very wealthy and well known, such as Andrew Carnegie who built a successful steel company in the 1800s, and Mary Kay Ash who founded Mary Kay Cosmetics. Most entrepreneurs, however, are involved in much smaller ventures, but all entrepreneurs have many things in common.

Traits Entrepreneurs have the ability to see a business opportunity where others do not. In other words, they recognize an existing or potential demand for which there is no supply. Most of all, entrepreneurs possess a willingness to take risks and an ability to learn from the mistakes that they make.

Vision A classic story of entrepreneurial success is that of Charles Darrow. In 1933, Darrow found himself out of work. To support his family, he took whatever odd jobs he could find, but he had a brilliant business idea. He wanted to create a compelling board game in which people could live the fantasy of acquiring land, houses, and hotels which they could rent or sell to fellow players. Recalling a vacation he had once taken in Atlantic City, New Jersey, Darrow named the real estate featured in his game after places in that city. He called the game Monopoly®.

▲ A vacation spent strolling the Boardwalk in Atlantic City gave Charles Darrow the idea for a game.

Perseverance Although many people told him he was wasting his time, Darrow spent months developing Monopoly. He then took his game to Parker Brothers, a leading board game company, which rejected the game because it found 52 flaws in it. Undaunted, Darrow corrected every one of the flaws. Then, with help from a friend who was a printer, he produced several Monopoly sets, which he tried to sell to local stores.

Finally, after weeks of pounding the pavement, a Philadelphia department store agreed to buy 5,000 of the Monopoly sets. The store sold all of the games so quickly that Parker Brothers reconsidered and agreed to produce the game. Within a year, more than 800,000 sets were sold, and soon Charles Darrow became a millionaire. Since that time, some 100 million sets of Monopoly have been sold worldwide.

Applying Economic Ideas

1. What entrepreneurial traits did Darrow use to make Monopoly a success?

2. For Darrow, what were the benefits and drawbacks of being an entrepreneur?

Chapter Summary

A summary of major ideas in Chapter 4 appears below. See also the **Guide to the Essentials of Economics,** which provides additional review and test practice of key concepts in Chapter 4.

Section 1 Understanding Demand (pp. 79–83)

Demand describes the ability and desire to buy a good or service. The **law of demand** says that the quantity demanded of a good will fall as the good's price increases. Two possible responses to a change in price, the **substitution effect** and the **income effect,** work together to create the law of demand. You can list demand for a good at all possible prices in a **demand schedule** and chart these points on a **demand curve.** Every individual has a demand schedule for a good, and you can find the demand schedule for the entire market by adding up all individual demand.

Section 2 Shifts of the Demand Curve (pp. 85–88)

A demand curve shows demand when price varies, but all other factors stay the same. When other factors change, the demand curve shifts to the left or to the right. When a rise in income leads a consumer to increase consumption of a good, that good is a **normal good.** If a higher income leads to lower consumption of a good, it is called an **inferior good.** Other factors that can affect demand are changes in population, tastes, and the prices of other goods.

Section 3 Elasticity of Demand (pp. 90–96)

Elasticity of demand describes how strongly buyers will react to a change in a good's price. When demand is **elastic,** buyers will make relatively big changes to their consumption of a good when its price rises or falls. When demand is **inelastic,** consumers will only change their consumption slightly relative to the change in price. Demand will be more elastic if the good has many substitutes, is considered a luxury, or accounts for a large share of the buyer's income. Entrepreneurs can estimate the elasticity of demand for some goods and use this number to make pricing decisions.

Key Terms

Complete each sentence by choosing the correct answer from the list of terms below. You will not use all of the terms.

normal good	inferior good
complements	law of demand
income effect	unitary elastic
demand curve	elastic
inelastic	elasticity of demand

1. You would refer to a(n) _____ to find the quantity that a person would purchase at each price that could be offered in a market.
2. For a(n) _____, a consumer's demand will increase as his or her income increases.
3. The _____ occurs when an increase in price decreases a consumer's real income.
4. Demand for goods that are necessities is usually _____.
5. If the elasticity of demand of a good is equal to 1, it is described as _____.
6. According to the _____, when prices increase, quantity demanded will decrease.
7. Two goods that are bought and used together are _____.

Using Graphic Organizers

8. On a separate sheet of paper, copy the multi-flow map below. Organize information on shifts in the demand curve for cars by completing the multiflow map with possible causes and effects for shifts in the demand curve.

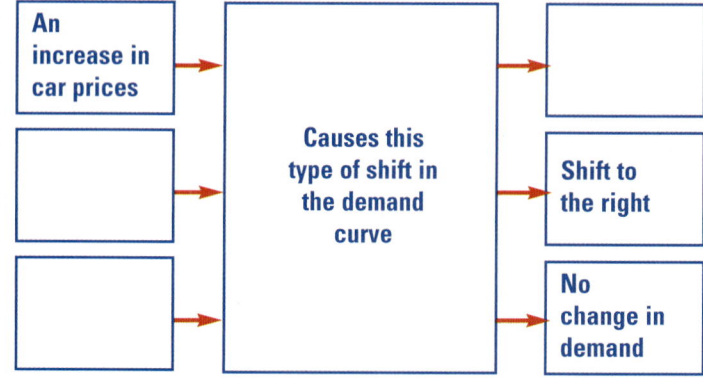

Reviewing Main Ideas

9. Describe the substitution effect in your own words, and give one example.
10. List and describe three causes for shifts in the demand curve.
11. Why do economists use percentage change to calculate elasticity of demand?
12. What are four factors that affect elasticity?

Critical Thinking

13. **Predicting Consequences** Will there always be a demand for inferior goods? How could demand for an inferior good decrease?
14. **Drawing Conclusions** Do you agree or disagree with the following statement? *An increase in income will shift the demand curve for a normal good to the left.* Explain your answer.
15. **Testing Conclusions** Choose three goods. Then predict whether they have elastic or inelastic demand at their current price. Next, determine their elasticity by creating a demand schedule and curve for each one. Gather information for the demand schedules from your classmates.

Problem-Solving Activity

16. As a business owner, you are always concerned about how much of your good or service is demanded. If there is an increase in your production costs, what options do you have to keep your product in demand?

Skills for Life

Analyzing Tables Review the steps shown on page 84; then answer the following questions using the table below.

17. How many urban residents would take a taxi ride that costs $20?
18. List two outside factors that may be used to help interpret this table.
19. Which service has equally low demand in both regions at $30?
20. Compare lawn mowing and taxi rides. What reason could there be for such different demands in different areas?
21. Which service has inelastic demand in both urban and suburban areas?

▼ 100 people in an urban area and 100 people in a suburban or rural area were asked if they were willing to pay $10, $20, or $30 for several services. The number willing to pay each price is listed below.

Demand Schedule for Selected Services

Service	Urban			Suburban and Rural		
	$10	$20	$30	$10	$20	$30
Lawn mowing	15	8	2	82	71	42
Taxi ride	84	78	37	10	8	1
Haircut	92	61	18	88	57	19

Economics Journal

Essay Writing Return to the list of five goods you recently bought. For each item, explain whether you consider your demand for that good to be relatively elastic or inelastic, and why. List two factors for each item that could change your demand for that item.

Take It to the NET

Chapter 4 Self-Test As a final review activity, take the Chapter 4 Self-Test in the Social Studies area at the Web site listed below, and receive immediate feedback on your answers. The test consists of 20 multiple-choice questions designed to test your understanding of the chapter content.
www.phschool.com

Chapter 5 Supply

A family buys a half-gallon of orange juice at the supermarket. An author hires a graduate student to translate a book. A store sells a bicycle to a woman over the Internet.

Each of these exchanges involves a buyer and a seller. In this chapter you'll read about the "supply side" of the marketplace, where sellers decide how much to produce or supply. After reading the chapter, you'll better understand the factors that influence sellers' decisions on how much orange juice to produce, how many hours a week to work as a translator, or how many bicycles to export.

Economics Journal

Write down a list of three goods: one that is usually available and "on sale," another that is popular but difficult to find, and a third that falls somewhere in between. What prices do stores charge for these goods?

Keep It Current

Items marked with this logo are periodically updated on the Internet. Keep up-to-date with what's in the news. To get current information on supply go to www.phschool.com

Preview

Objectives

After studying this section you will be able to:

1. **Explain** the law of supply.
2. **Interpret** a supply graph using a supply schedule.
3. **Explain** the relationship between elasticity of supply and time.

Section Focus

The law of supply predicts that producers will offer more of a good as its price goes up. How strongly producers react to a change in price depends on their ability to raise or lower output.

Key Terms

supply
law of supply
quantity supplied
supply schedule
variable
market supply schedule
supply curve
market supply curve
elasticity of supply

If you were running a business, what would you do if you discovered that customers were suddenly willing to pay twice as much for your product? If you were like most entrepreneurs, you would try to produce more in order to take advantage of the higher prices. Even if you used the higher prices as a way to work fewer hours while earning the same income, you could be sure that someone else would jump into the market and start selling the same good.

The Law of Supply

Supply is the amount of goods available. How do producers decide how much to supply? According to the **law of supply,** the higher the price, the larger the quantity produced. Economists use the term **quantity supplied** to describe how much of a good is offered for sale at a specific price.

The law of supply develops from the choices of both current and new producers of a good. As the price of a good rises, existing firms will produce more in order to earn additional revenue. At the same time, new firms will have an incentive to enter the market to earn a profit for themselves. If the price of a good falls, some firms will produce less, and others might drop out of the market.

These two movements—individual firms changing their level of production and firms entering or exiting the market—combine to create the law of supply.

Higher Production

If a firm is already earning a profit by selling a good, then an increase in the price—*ceteris paribus*—will increase the

supply *the amount of goods available*

law of supply *tendency of suppliers to offer more of a good at a higher price*

quantity supplied *the amount a supplier is willing and able to supply at a certain price*

Figure 5.1 Law of Supply

Price As price increases ... Supply Quantity supplied increases

Price As price falls ... Supply Quantity supplied falls

The law of supply predicts that higher prices lead to more production.
Supply and Demand How is the law of supply different from the law of demand?

firm's profits. The promise of higher revenues for each sale also encourages the firm to produce more. Consider the pizzeria you read about in Chapter 4. The pizzeria is probably making a reasonable profit by selling a certain number of slices a day at the market price. If the pizzeria weren't making a profit, the owner would soon try to raise the price or switch from pizzas to something more profitable.

If the price of pizza rises, but the firm's cost of making pizza stays the same, then the pizzeria will earn a higher profit on each slice of pizza. A sensible entrepreneur would try to produce and sell more pizza to take advantage of the higher prices.

Similarly, if the price of pizza goes down, the pizzeria will earn less profit per slice or even lose money. The owner will choose to sell less pizza and produce something else,

such as calzones or sandwiches, that will yield more profit.

In both cases, the search for profit drives the supplier's decision. When the price goes up, the supplier recognizes the chance to make more money and works harder to produce more pizza. When the price falls, the same entrepreneur is discouraged from producing as much as before.

Market Entry

Profits appeal both to producers already in the market and people who may decide to join the market. As you have seen, when the price of pizza rises, a pizzeria stands out as a good opportunity to make money. If you were considering opening a restaurant of your own, a pizzeria would look like a safe bet. In this way, rising prices draw new firms into a market and add to the quantity supplied of the good.

Consider the market for music. In the late 1970s, disco music became popular among young people. The music industry quickly recognized the popularity of disco, and more and more groups began releasing disco recordings. Even some groups that once performed soul music and rhythm and blues chose to record disco albums. New entrants crowded the market to take advantage of the potential for profit. Disco, however, proved to be a short-lived fad. By the early 1980s, disco music was gone from the radio, and stores couldn't sell the albums on their shelves.

▶ **The music industry illustrates how profit drives suppliers' decisions. As different musical styles become popular, new groups make recordings to profit from the current fad.**

This pattern of sharp increases and decreases in supply occurs again and again in the music industry. In the early 1990s, "grunge" music emerged from Seattle to become widely popular among high school and college students across the country. How did the market react? Record labels soon hired many grunge groups. Music stores devoted more and more space to this style of music. Within a few years, however, grunge lost its appeal, and many groups disbanded or moved on to new styles. Swing music enjoyed a smaller peak of popularity in the late 1990s.

In each of the examples above, many musicians joined the market for a particular style of music to profit from a trend. Their actions reflected the law of supply, which says that the output or quantity supplied of a good increases as the price of the good increases.

The Supply Schedule

Similar to a demand schedule, a **supply schedule** shows the relationship between price and quantity supplied for a specific good. The pizzeria discussed earlier might have a supply schedule that looks like the one in Figure 5.2. This table compares two **variables,** or factors that can change. These variables are the price of a slice and the number of slices supplied by a pizzeria. We could collect this information by asking the pizzeria owner how many slices she is willing and able to make at different prices, or we could look at records to see how the quantity supplied has varied as the price has changed. We will almost certainly find that at higher prices, the pizzeria owner is willing to make more pizza. At a lower price she prefers to make less pizza and to devote her limited resources to other, more profitable, items.

Like a demand schedule, a supply schedule lists supply for a very specific set of conditions. The schedule shows how the price of pizza, and only the price of pizza, affects the pizzeria's output. All of the other factors that could change the restaurant's output decisions, such as the costs of

Figure 5.2 Supply Schedule

Price per slice of pizza	Slices supplied per day
$ .50	100
$1.00	150
$1.50	200
$2.00	250
$2.50	300
$3.00	350

This supply schedule lists how many slices of pizza one pizzeria will offer at different prices. **Incentives What does this chart tell you about the pizzeria owner's decisions?**

tomato sauce, labor, and rent, are assumed to remain constant.

A Change in the Quantity Supplied

Economists use the word *supply* to refer to the relationship between price and quantity supplied, as shown in the supply schedule. The pizzeria's supply of pizza includes all possible combinations of price and output. According to this supply schedule, the pizzeria's supply is 100 slices at $ .50 a slice, 150 slices at $1.00 a slice, 200 slices at $1.50 a slice, and so on. The number of slices that the pizzeria offers at a specific price is called the quantity supplied at that price. At $2.50 per slice, the pizzeria's quantity supplied is 300 slices per day.

A rise or fall in the price of pizza will cause the quantity supplied to change, but not the supply schedule. In other words, a change in a good's price moves the seller from one row to another in the same supply schedule, but does not change the supply schedule itself. When a factor other than the price of pizza affects output, we have to build a whole new supply schedule for the new market conditions.

Market Supply Schedule

All of the supply schedules of individual firms in a market can be added up to create a **market supply schedule**. A market supply schedule shows the relationship between prices and the total quantity supplied by all

supply schedule *a chart that lists how much of a good a supplier will offer at different prices*

variable *a factor that can change*

market supply schedule *a chart that lists how much of a good all suppliers will offer at different prices*

Figure 5.3 Market Supply Schedule

Price per slice of pizza	Slices supplied per day
$ .50	1,000
$1.00	1,500
$1.50	2,000
$2.00	2,500
$2.50	3,000
$3.00	3,500

A market supply schedule represents all suppliers in a market.
Supply and Demand How does this market supply schedule compare to the individual supply schedule?

supply curve *a graph of the quantity supplied of a good at different prices*

market supply curve *a graph of the quantity supplied of a good by all suppliers at different prices*

elasticity of supply *a measure of the way quantity supplied reacts to a change in price*

firms in a particular market. The information in a market supply schedule becomes important when we want to determine the total supply of pizza at a certain price in a large area, like a city.

The market supply schedule for pizza resembles the supply schedule at a single pizzeria, but the quantities are much larger. Figure 5.3 shows the supply of pizza for a hypothetical city.

This market supply schedule lists the same prices as those in the supply schedule for the single pizzeria, since all restaurants will charge prices within the same range. The quantities supplied are much larger because there are many pizzerias in the community. Like the individual supply schedule, this market supply schedule reflects the law of supply. Pizzerias supply more pizza at higher prices.

The Supply Graph

When the data points in the supply schedule are graphed, they create a **supply curve**. A supply curve is very similar to a demand curve, except that the horizontal axis now measures the quantity of the good supplied, not the quantity demanded. Figure 5.4 shows a supply curve for one pizzeria and a **market supply curve** for all the pizzerias in the city. The data used to draw the two curves are from the supply schedules in Figures 5.2 and 5.3. The prices

shown along the vertical axes are the same in both graphs. However, the quantities of pizza supplied at each price are much larger in the market supply curve.

The key feature of the supply curve is that it always rises from left to right. As your finger traces the curve from left to right, it moves toward higher and higher output levels (on the horizontal axis) and higher and higher prices (on the vertical axis). This illustrates the law of supply, which says that a higher price leads to higher output.

Supply and Elasticity

In Chapter 4, you learned that elasticity of demand measures how consumers will react to a change in price. **Elasticity of supply** is based on the same concept. Elasticity of supply is a measure of the way suppliers respond to a change in price.

Elasticity of supply tells how firms will respond to changes in the price of a good. The labels *elastic, inelastic,* and *unitary elastic* represent the same values of elasticity of supply as those of elasticity of demand. When elasticity is greater than one, supply is very sensitive to changes in price and is considered elastic. If supply is not very responsive to changes in price, and elasticity is less than one, supply is considered inelastic. When a percentage change in price is perfectly matched by an equal percentage change in quantity supplied, elasticity is exactly one, and supply is unitary elastic.

Elasticity of Supply and Time

What determines whether the supply of a good will be elastic or inelastic? The key factor is time. In the short run, a firm cannot easily change its output level, so supply is inelastic. In the long run, firms are more flexible, so supply is more elastic.

Elasticity of Supply in the Short Run

An orange grove is one example of a business that has difficulty adjusting to a change in price in the short term. Orange trees take several years to mature and grow

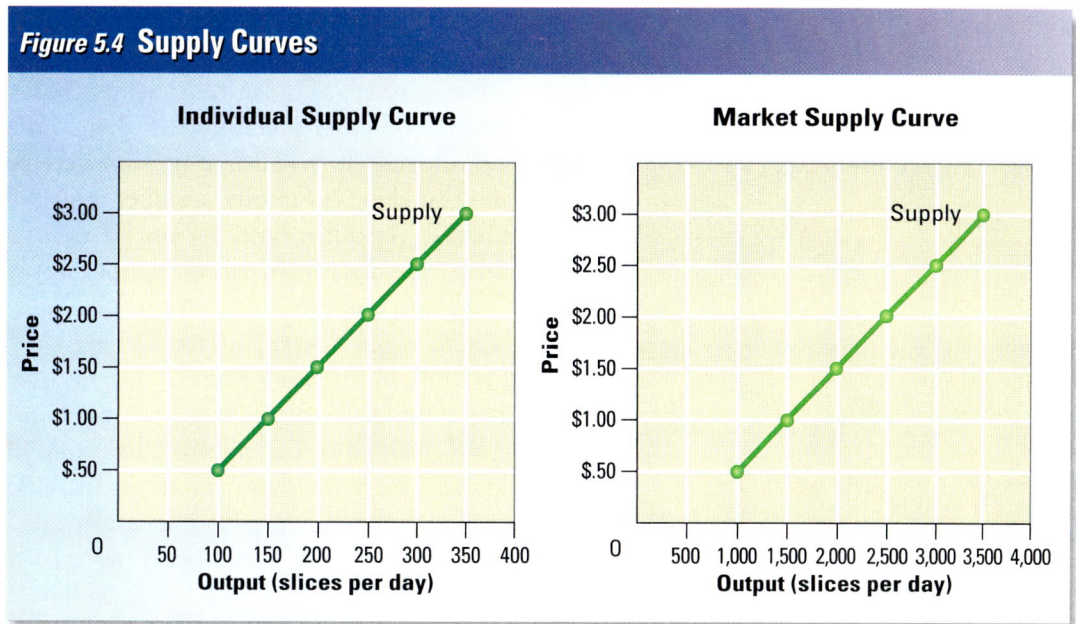

Figure 5.4 Supply Curves

Individual Supply Curve

Market Supply Curve

Supply curves always rise from left to right, as predicted by the law of supply. As price increases, so does the quantity supplied.

Supply and Demand
How many slices will one pizzeria produce at $2.00 a slice?

fruit. If the price of oranges goes up, an orange grower can buy and plant more trees, but he will have to wait several years for his investment to pay off. In the short term, the grower could take smaller steps to increase output. For example, he could use a more effective pesticide. While this step might increase his output somewhat, it would probably not increase the number of oranges by very much. Economists would say that his supply is inelastic, because he cannot easily change his output. The same factors that prevent the owner of the orange grove from expanding his supply will also prevent new growers from entering the market and supplying oranges in the short term.

In the short run, supply is inelastic whether the price increases or decreases. If the price of a crate of oranges falls, the grove owner has few ways to cut his supply. He invested years ago in land and trees, and his grove will provide oranges no matter what the price is. Even if the price drops drastically, the grove owner will probably pick and sell nearly as many oranges as before. The grove owner's competitors have also invested heavily in land and trees and won't drop out of the market if they can survive. In this case, supply is inelastic whether prices rise or fall.

While orange groves illustrate a business in which supply is inelastic, other businesses benefit from more elastic supply. For example, a business that provides a service, such as a haircut, is highly elastic. Unlike oranges, the supply of haircuts is easily expanded or reduced. If the price of a haircut rises, barber shops and salons can hire new workers quickly. In addition,

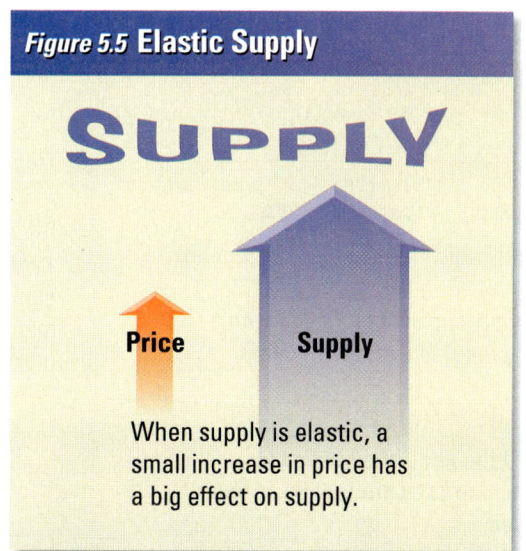

Figure 5.5 Elastic Supply

SUPPLY

Price **Supply**

When supply is elastic, a small increase in price has a big effect on supply.

When supply is elastic, it reacts strongly to changes in price.
Supply and Demand **If supply is inelastic, how will supply react to a small increase in price?**

▶ While the supply of oranges is inelastic, the supply of goods made from oranges is elastic. For example, producers can choose whether to produce more or less orange juice from the oranges.

new barber shops and salons will open, and existing businesses might stay open later in the evening. This means that a small increase in price will cause a large increase in quantity supplied, even in the short term.

If the price of a haircut drops, some barbers will close their shops earlier in the day, and others will leave the market for jobs elsewhere. Quantity supplied will fall quickly. Because haircut suppliers can quickly change their operations, the supply of haircuts is elastic.

Elasticity in the Long Run

Like demand, supply can become more elastic over time. Consider the example of the orange grower who could not increase his output much when the price of oranges rose. Over time, he could plant more trees to increase his supply of oranges. These changes will become more effective over time as trees grow and bear fruit. After several years, he will be able to sell many more oranges at the high market price.

If the price drops and stays low for several years, orange growers who survived the first two or three years of losses might decide to give up and grow something else. Given five years to respond instead of six weeks, the supply of oranges will be far more elastic. Just like demand, supply becomes more elastic if the supplier has a long time to respond to a price change.

Section 1 Assessment

Key Terms and Main Ideas

1. Explain the **law of supply** in your own words.
2. What is the difference between supply and **quantity supplied**?
3. How does the quantity supplied of a good with a large **elasticity of supply** react to a price change?

Applying Economic Concepts

4. *Problem Solving* If the price of oil rises around the world, what will happen to oil production in Texas? Explain your answer.

5. *Decision Making* Explain whether you think the supply of the following goods is elastic or inelastic, and why. **(a)** hotel rooms **(b)** taxi rides **(c)** photographs

6. *Critical Thinking* When the price of a good rises, total supply in the market will rise, but some entrepreneurs might actually choose to work less. Why might they make this choice?

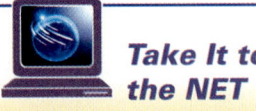

Take It to the NET

Scarcity can influence the elasticity of the supply of a good or service. Investigate two of our sources of energy (petroleum, natural gas, hydropower, nuclear, geothermal), and determine whether supply is elastic or inelastic. Use the links provided in the Social Studies area at the following Web site for help in completing this activity. **www.phschool.com**

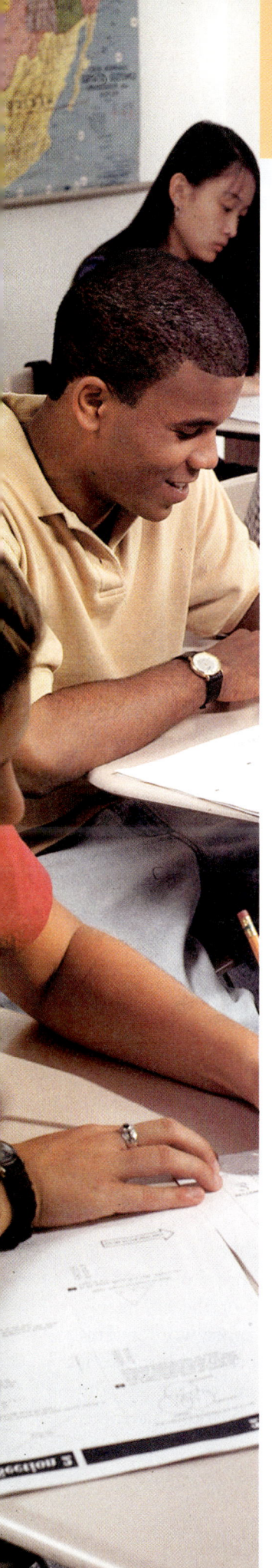

Skills for LIFE

Critical Thinking   Graphs and Charts

Social Studies   Technology

Test-Taking

Successful test-taking involves more than studying at home the night before the test. You can take steps to prepare for a test well before the test day arrives. You can also follow some specific practices while taking the test to ensure your success. Use the following steps to help you complete a checklist like the one below for an upcoming test in one of your classes.

1. **Long-Term Planning** Give yourself plenty of time to prepare for a test. (a) Ask your teacher when the next test will be given. (b) Block off specific times to study before the test date.

TEST PREPARATION CHECKLIST

Long-Term Planning
1. Test date: _____
2. Allocated study time: _____

**Short-Term Planning
(Day Before the Test)**
1. Have you studied enough? _____
2. What will you do to relax? _____
3. What will you eat for breakfast? _____
4. What will you wear so that you will be
   comfortable during the test? _____
5. List the materials you will need for the test:
   pencils, pens, erasers, a watch _____
   _____

During-the-Test Reminders
1. I should answer these questions first
   because I know these subjects the best:
2. I need more time to think about these
   subjects:_____

After the Test
1. Which questions were the most difficult?
   _____
2. What could I have done to prepare better
   for these questions? _____

2. **Short-Term Planning** Now that it is the day before the test, what are you going to do? Plan the next morning's events so you are not stressed. Eat a healthy breakfast. Plan to wear comfortable clothing and to have the necessary equipment for taking the test. (a) Think of three activities to do to stay relaxed. (b) Refer to a checklist of things to do the day before the test.

3. **Taking the Test** During the test, follow some basic strategies to achieve better results. Read all directions and questions carefully before you answer them. Judge your time limit so you have enough time to complete all parts. Complete all the "easy" questions first.

4. **After the Test** Evaluate your test performance to determine how to improve your skills in the future. (a) Looking at your own test-taking experience, what types of questions give you the most difficulty? (b) Make a list of these types of questions, and determine how you can be better prepared for these questions.

Additional Practice

Create your own schedule or checklist for an upcoming essay or research paper. Use a format similar to the one shown here.

Section 2 — Costs of Production

Preview

Objectives

After studying this section you will be able to:

1. **Explain** how firms decide how much labor to hire to produce a certain level of output.
2. **Analyze** the production costs of a firm.
3. **Understand** how a firm chooses to set output.
4. **Explain** how a firm decides to shut down an unprofitable business.

Section Focus

Entrepreneurs consider marginal benefits and costs when deciding how much output to produce. Ordinarily, firms earn their highest profits when the cost of making one more unit is the same as the market price of the good.

Key Terms

marginal product of labor
increasing marginal returns
diminishing marginal returns
fixed cost
variable cost
total cost
marginal cost
marginal revenue
operating cost

---

marginal product of labor *the change in output from hiring one additional unit of labor*

In Section 1, we identified how producers respond to a change in price. The law of supply states that producers will offer more goods as the price goes up and fewer as the price falls. In this section, we will explain how a supplier decides *how much* to produce.

Consider a firm that produces beanbags. The firm's factory has one sewing machine and one pair of scissors. The firm's inputs are workers and materials, including cloth, thread, and beans. Assume that each beanbag requires the same amount of materials. As the number of workers increases, what happens to the quantity of beanbags produced?

The supply of beanbag chairs in the market depends on several factors, including the cost of labor and capital. ▼

Labor and Output

One of the basic questions any business owner has to answer is how many workers to hire. To answer this question, owners have to consider how the number of workers they hire will affect their total production. For example, at the beanbag factory, one worker can produce four beanbags per hour. Two workers can make a total of ten bags per hour, and three can make a total of seventeen beanbags an hour. As new workers join the company, total output increases. After the seventh worker is hired, production peaks at 32 beanbags per hour. When the firm hires the eighth worker, however, total output drops to 31 bags per hour.

Figure 5.6 shows the relationship between labor, measured by the number of workers in the factory, and the number of beanbags produced.

Marginal Product of Labor

The third column of Figure 5.6 shows the **marginal product of labor,** or the change in output from hiring one more worker. This is called the marginal product because it measures the change in output at the margin, where the last worker has been hired or fired.

The first worker to be hired produces four bags an hour, so her marginal product is four bags. The second worker raises total output from four bags an hour to ten, so her marginal product of labor is six. Looking at this column, we see that the marginal product of labor increases for the first three workers, rising from four to seven.

Increasing Marginal Returns

The marginal product of labor increases for the first three workers because there are three tasks involved in making a beanbag. Workers cut and sew cloth into the correct shape, stuff it with beans, and sew the bag closed. In our example, a single worker performing all these tasks would only produce four bags per hour. Adding a second worker would allow each worker to specialize in one or two tasks. If each worker focuses on only one part of the process, she will waste less time switching between tasks and will become more skillful at her assigned tasks. In other words, specialization increases output per worker, so the second worker adds more to output than the first. The firm enjoys **increasing marginal returns**.

In our example, there are benefits from specialization for the first three workers. The firm enjoys a rising marginal product of labor for the first three workers.

Diminishing Marginal Returns

When the fourth through the seventh workers are hired, the marginal product of labor is still positive. Each new worker still adds to total output. However, the marginal product of labor shrinks as each worker joins the company. The fourth worker increases output by six bags, while the seventh increases output by only one bag. Why?

After the beanbag firm hires its first three workers, one for each task, the benefits of specialization end. At that point, adding more workers increases total output, but at a decreasing rate. This situation is known as **diminishing marginal returns**. A firm with diminishing marginal returns of labor will

produce less and less output from each additional unit of labor added to the mix.

The firm suffers from diminishing marginal returns from labor because its workers must work with a limited amount of capital. Remember that capital is any human-made resource that is used to produce other goods. In this example, capital is represented by the factory's single sewing machine and pair of scissors. When there are three workers, but only one needs to use the sewing machine, this worker will never have to wait to get to

Figure 5.6 Marginal Product of Labor

Labor (number of workers)	Output (beanbags per hour)	Marginal product of labor
0	0	—
1	4	4
2	10	6
3	17	7
4	23	6
5	28	5
6	31	3
7	32	1
8	31	-1

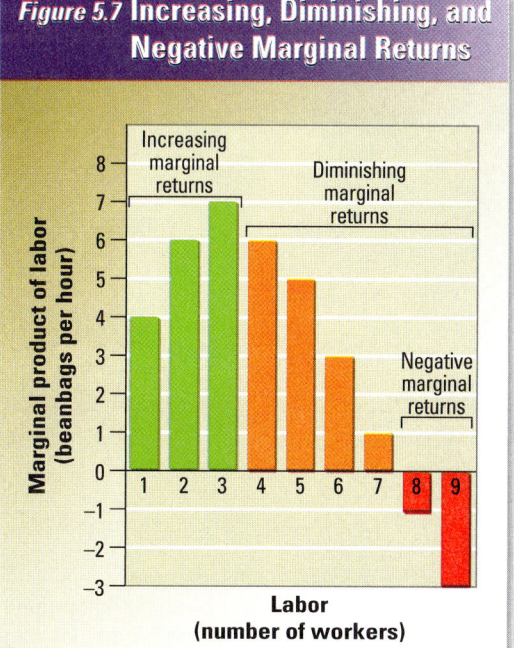

Figure 5.7 Increasing, Diminishing, and Negative Marginal Returns

The marginal product of labor is the increase in output added by the last unit of labor.

Specialization
Why does the marginal product of labor decrease with more than four workers in this example?

increasing marginal returns *a level of production in which the marginal product of labor increases as the number of workers increases*

diminishing marginal returns *a level of production in which the marginal product of labor decreases as the number of workers increases*

Labor has increasing and then diminishing marginal returns.
Opportunity Cost
What is the marginal product of labor when the factory currently employs five workers?

work. When there are more than three workers, the factory will assign more than one to work at the sewing machine. While one is working, the other will have to wait. She may be able to help cut fabric or stuff bags in the meantime, but every bag must be sewn up at some point, so she cannot greatly increase the speed of the production process.

The problem gets worse as more workers are hired and the amount of capital remains constant. Wasted time waiting for the sewing machine or scissors means that additional workers will add less and less to total output at the factory.

Negative Marginal Returns

As the table in Figure 5.6 shows, adding the eighth worker at the beanbag factory can actually decrease output by one bag. At this stage, workers get in each other's way and disrupt the production process, so overall output decreases. Of course, few companies ever hire so many workers that their marginal product of labor becomes negative.

Production Costs

Paying workers and purchasing capital are all costs of producing goods. Economists

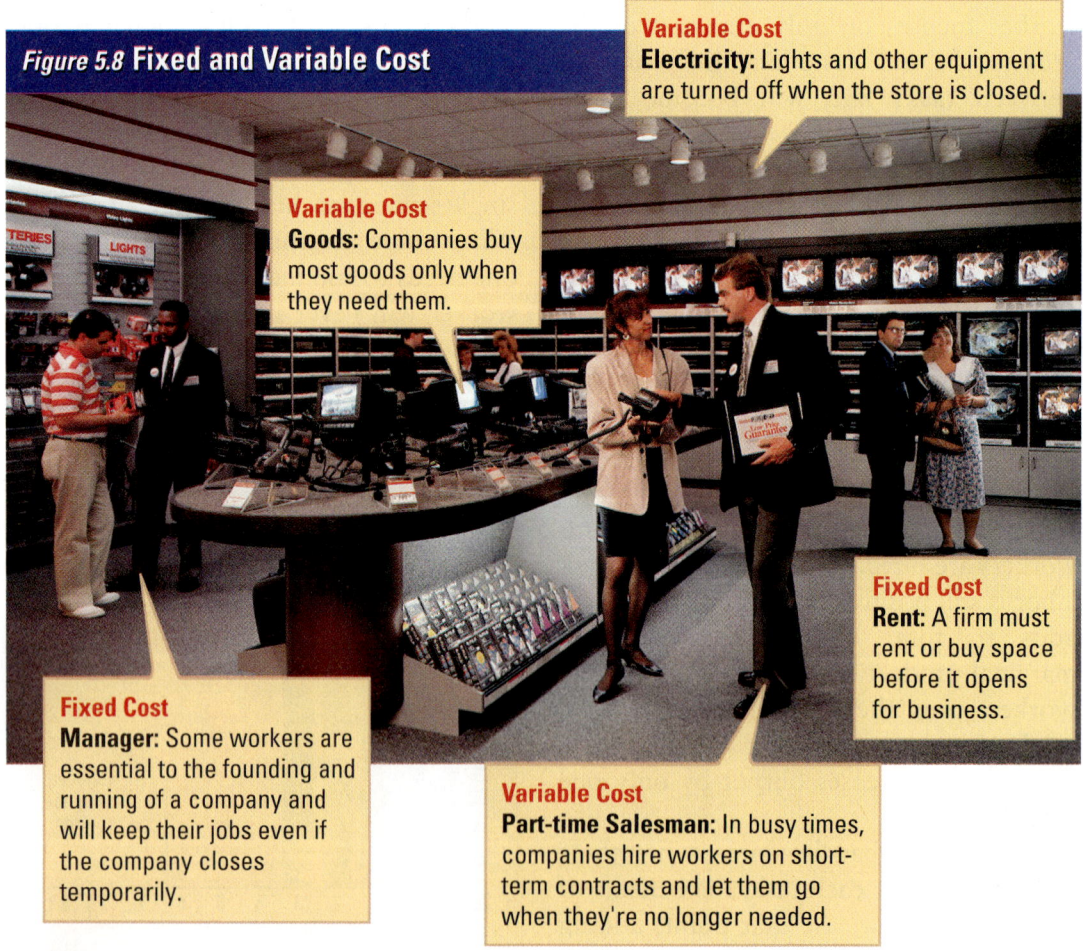

Figure 5.8 Fixed and Variable Cost

Variable Cost
Electricity: Lights and other equipment are turned off when the store is closed.

Variable Cost
Goods: Companies buy most goods only when they need them.

Fixed Cost
Rent: A firm must rent or buy space before it opens for business.

Fixed Cost
Manager: Some workers are essential to the founding and running of a company and will keep their jobs even if the company closes temporarily.

Variable Cost
Part-time Salesman: In busy times, companies hire workers on short-term contracts and let them go when they're no longer needed.

Firms must separate fixed costs from variable costs to determine whether or not to produce at a given market price.
Entrepreneurs Why are some employees considered variable costs?

Figure 5.9 Production Costs

Beanbags (per hour)	Fixed cost	Variable cost	Total cost (fixed cost + variable cost)	Marginal cost	Marginal revenue (market price)	Total revenue	Profit (total revenue – total cost)
0	$36	$0	$36	—	$24	$0	$–36
1	36	8	44	$8	24	24	–20
2	36	12	48	4	24	48	0
3	36	15	51	3	24	72	21
4	36	20	56	5	24	96	40
5	36	27	63	7	24	120	57
6	36	36	72	9	24	144	72
7	36	48	84	12	24	168	84
8	36	63	99	15	24	192	93
9	36	82	118	19	24	216	98
10	36	106	142	24	24	240	98
11	36	136	172	30	24	264	92
12	36	173	209	37	24	288	79

BUILDING KEY CONCEPTS

Firms consider a variety of costs when deciding how much to produce.
Markets and Prices
Why is the marginal revenue always equal to $24?

divide a producer's costs into two categories: fixed costs and variable costs.

Fixed Costs

A **fixed cost** is a cost that does not change, no matter how much of a good is produced. Most fixed costs involve the production facility, the cost of building and equipping a factory, office, store, or restaurant. Examples of fixed costs include rent, machinery repairs, property taxes on a factory, and the salaries of workers who keep the business running even when production temporarily stops.

Variable Costs

Variable costs are costs that rise or fall depending on the quantity produced. They include the costs of raw materials and some labor. For example, to produce more beanbags, the firm must purchase more beans and hire more workers to stuff the beanbags. If the company wants to produce less and cut costs, it can stop buying beans or have some workers work fewer hours a week. The cost of labor is a variable cost because it changes with the number of workers, which changes with the quantity produced. Electricity and heating bills are also variable costs, because the company can cut off heat and

electricity for the factory and its machines when they are not in use.

Total Cost

Figure 5.9 shows some cost data for the firm that produces beanbags. The firm has a factory that is fully equipped to produce beanbags. How does the cost of producing beanbags change as the output increases?

In our example, the fixed costs are the costs of the factory building and all the machinery and equipment inside. As shown in the second column in Figure 5.9, the fixed costs are $36.00 per hour.

Variable costs include the cost of beans, fabric, and most of the workers hired to produce the beanbags. As shown in the third column, variable costs rise with the number of beanbags produced. Fixed costs and variable costs are added together to find **total cost**. Total cost is shown in the fourth column.

Marginal Cost

If we know the total cost at several levels of output, we can determine the **marginal cost** of production at each level. Marginal cost is the additional cost of producing one more unit.

As shown in Figure 5.9, even if the firm is not producing a single beanbag, it still

fixed cost *a cost that does not change, no matter how much of a good is produced*

variable cost *a cost that rises or falls depending on how much is produced*

total cost *fixed costs plus variable costs*

marginal cost *the cost of producing one more unit of a good*

must pay $36.00 an hour for fixed costs. If the firm decides to produce just one beanbag an hour, its total cost rises $8.00 from $36.00 to $44.00 an hour. The marginal cost of the first beanbag is $8.00.

For the first three beanbags, the marginal cost falls as output increases. The marginal cost of the second beanbag is $4.00, and the marginal cost of the third beanbag is $3.00. Each additional beanbag is cheaper to make because of increasing marginal returns resulting from specialization.

With the fourth beanbag, the marginal cost starts to rise. The marginal cost of the fifth per hour is $7.00, the sixth costs $9.00, and the seventh costs $12.00. The rising marginal cost reflects diminishing returns to labor. The benefits of specialization are exhausted when the firm reaches three beanbags, and diminishing returns set in as more and more workers share a fixed production facility.

Setting Output

Behind all of the decisions about how many workers to hire is the firm's basic goal: to maximize profits. Profit is defined as total revenue minus total cost. As you read in Chapter 4, a firm's total revenue is the money the firm gets by selling its product. Total revenue is equal to the price of each good multiplied by the number of goods sold. Figure 5.9 shows total revenue when the price of a beanbag is $24.00. To find the level of output with the highest profit, we look for the biggest gap between total revenue and total cost. The gap is biggest and profit is highest when the firm makes 9 or 10 beanbags per hour. At this rate, the firm can expect to make a profit of $98.00 an hour.

Marginal Revenue and Marginal Cost

Another way to find the best level of output is to find the output level where **marginal revenue** is equal to marginal cost. Marginal revenue is the additional income from selling one more unit of a good. If the firm has no control over the market price, marginal revenue equals the market price. Each beanbag sold at $24.00 increases the firm's total revenue by $24.00, so marginal revenue is $24.00. According to the table, price equals marginal cost with 10 beanbags, so that's the quantity that maximizes profit at $98 an hour.

To understand how an output of 10 beanbags maximizes the firm's profits, suppose that the firm picked a different level of output. If the firm made only 4 beanbags per hour, is it making as much money as it can?

From Figure 5.9, we know that the marginal cost of the fifth beanbag is $7.00. The market price for a beanbag is $24.00, so the marginal revenue from that beanbag is $24.00. The $17.00 difference between the marginal revenue and marginal cost represents pure profit for the company from making and selling the fifth beanbag. The company should increase its production to five beanbags an hour to capture that profit on the fifth beanbag.

If we do the same calculations for a sixth beanbag, we find that the company can capture a profit of $15.00 by producing the sixth beanbag per hour. The price of the seventh beanbag is $12.00 higher than its marginal cost, so that beanbag earns an

Figure 5.10 Marginal Cost Curve

Marginal cost (in dollars) vs. Output (beanbags per hour)

Marginal cost

For most firms, the marginal cost of production falls as output rises from zero, but eventually begins to rise.

Markets and Prices How many beanbags an hour should this firm make to produce at the lowest possible marginal cost?

additional $12.00 in profit for the company. The profit is available any time the company receives more for the last beanbag than it cost to produce. Any rational entrepreneur would take this opportunity to increase profit.

Now suppose that the firm is producing so many beanbags an hour that marginal cost is *higher* than price. If the firm produces eleven beanbags an hour, it receives $24.00 for that eleventh beanbag, but the $30.00 cost of that beanbag wipes out the profit. The firm actually loses $6.00 on the sale of the eleventh beanbag. Because marginal cost is increasing, and price is constant in this example, the losses would get worse at higher levels of output. The company would be better off producing less and keeping costs down.

The ideal level of output is where marginal revenue (price) is equal to marginal cost. Any other quantity of output would generate less profit.

Responding to Price Changes

What would happen if the price of a beanbag suddenly rose from $24.00 to $37.00? Thinking at the margin, we would predict that the firm would increase production to twelve beanbags per hour. That's the quantity at which the marginal cost is equal to the new, higher price. At the original price of $24.00, the firm would not produce more than ten beanbags, according to the graph in Figure 5.11. When the price rises to $37.00, marginal revenue soars above marginal cost at that level of output. Raising production to twelve beanbags an hour would allow the firm to capture profits on the eleventh and twelfth beanbags.

This example shows the law of supply in action. An increase in price from $24.00 to $37.00 causes the firm to increase the quantity supplied from ten to twelve beanbags an hour.

The Shutdown Decision

Consider the problems faced by a factory that is losing money. The factory is

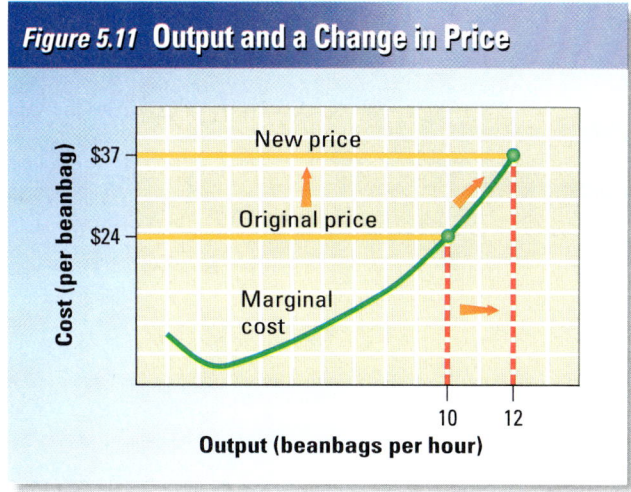

Figure 5.11 **Output and a Change in Price**

The most profitable level of output is where price (or marginal revenue) is equal to marginal cost.
Markets and Prices What would happen to output if the market price fell to $20?

producing at a level of output at which marginal revenue is equal to marginal cost. As you have read, this is the most profitable level of output. However, the market price is so low that the factory's total revenue is still less than its total cost, and the firm is losing money. Should this factory continue to produce goods and lose money, or should its owners shut the factory down?

This may seem like a silly question. In fact, there are times when keeping a money-losing factory open is the best choice. The firm should keep the factory open if the total revenue from the goods and services the factory produces is greater than the cost of keeping it open.

For example, if the price of beanbags drops to $7, and the factory produces at the profit-maximizing level of five beanbags per hour, the total revenue of the business is $35 per hour. Weigh this against the factory's **operating cost,** or the cost of operating the facility. The operating cost includes the variable costs the owners must pay to keep the factory running, but not the fixed costs, which the owners must pay whether the factory is open or closed.

According to Figure 5.9, if the factory produces five beanbags, the variable cost is $27 per hour. Therefore, the benefit of operating the facility (total revenue of $35)

operating cost *the cost of operating a facility, such as a store or factory*

▲ **When a factory begins losing money, the owner must consider its operating cost and revenue when deciding what to do.**

is greater than the variable cost ($27), so it makes sense to keep the facility running.

Consider the effects of the other choice. If the firm were to shut down the factory, it would still have to pay all of its fixed costs. The factory's total revenue would be zero because it would be producing nothing for

sale. Therefore, the firm would lose an amount of money equal to its fixed costs.

For this beanbag factory, the fixed costs equal $36 per hour, so the factory would lose $36 for each hour it is closed. If the factory were to keep producing five beanbags per hour, its total cost would be $63 ($36 in fixed costs plus $27 in variable costs) per hour, but it would lose only $28 ($63 in total cost minus $35 in revenue) for each hour it is open. The factory would lose less money while producing because the total revenue ($35) would exceed the variable costs ($27), leaving $8 to cover some of the fixed costs. Although the factory would lose money in either situation, it would lose less money by continuing to produce and sell beanbags.

How long will a business continue to operate a factory at a loss before it decides to replace the facility? The firm will build a new factory and stay in the market only if the market price of beanbags is high enough to cover all the costs of production, including the cost of building a new factory.

Section 2 Assessment

Key Terms and Main Ideas

1. How does the **marginal product of labor** change as more workers are hired?

2. What is the impact of **diminishing marginal returns** on labor?

3. Give an example of a **fixed cost** and a **variable cost** of a bakery.

4. How does a firm calculate **marginal cost**?

Applying Economic Concepts

5. *Critical Thinking* A firm has two factories, one twice as large as the second. As the number of workers at each factory increases, which factory will experience diminishing returns first?

6. *Decision Making* Explain whether each of these expenses of a textile mill is a fixed cost or a variable cost, and why. **(a)** repairs to a leaking roof **(b)** cotton **(c)** food for the mill's cafeteria **(d)** night security guard **(e)** electricity

7. *Math Practice* Use the table below to answer the following questions. **(a)** What is the total cost when output is 2? **(b)** What is the marginal cost of the third unit? **(c)** How much should this firm produce if the market price is $24?

Output	Fixed Cost	Variable Cost
1	$5	$10
2	$5	$27
3	$5	$55
4	$5	$91
5	$5	$145

Take It to the NET Firms must consider their fixed and variable costs when they set their budgets and supply. Create your own virtual factory and determine three fixed and variable costs. Use the links provided in the Social Studies area at the following Web site for help in completing this activity. **www.phschool.com**

Robert L. Johnson (b. 1946)

In 1979, while working as chief lobbyist for the National Cable Television Association, Robert Johnson was asked by a businessman to support a proposed cable channel for older Americans. Existing channels targeted young white viewers, leaving older Americans underserved. Johnson immediately realized that this statement applied to African Americans as well. In that moment, the idea for Black Entertainment Television—BET—was born.

Launching BET

Searching for investors, Johnson approached Tele-Communications Incorporated (TCI), a large cable operator that was hoping to expand. He pointed out that a cable company supplying quality programming with appeal to the African American community would have an advantage over its competitors in cities with large black populations. TCI bought a 20 percent stake in his venture.

In January 1980, Johnson launched BET—the first black-owned and -operated television network. Its first broadcasts were limited to two hours each Friday night on another cable network's channel. However, he soon added a gospel show, coverage of college sports, and a music program featuring black recording artists. By 1982, using music videos that record companies provided for free, BET had increased its airtime to six hours a day.

In 1984, Johnson sold another share in BET to Home Box Office (HBO), a division of Time Warner. This provided the money he needed to expand his programming. Johnson now had access to the country's two largest cable providers, Time Warner and TCI, as well as to HBO's satellite, so he could broadcast 24 hours a day. By 1989,

BET was reaching 23 million homes. Ten years later, that figure had grown to nearly 58 million households, including more than 90 percent of African American households with cable.

Creating a Brand

"When I see BET, I don't see a cable network," Johnson says. "I see a black media conglomerate." In the 1990s, Johnson used the network's commercial airtime and its strong reputation among African Americans to create a BET "umbrella brand."

Besides adding four more cable channels, Johnson launched BET Arabesque Films to produce movies for theaters and for his cable network. Arabesque Books, a line of African American romance novels that Johnson purchased in 1998, provided the material for the first movies. In 1997, Johnson launched the first of his BET Soundstage restaurants, an African American version of the Hard Rock Cafe restaurant chain. Other ventures include a clothing line, a health and fitness magazine, and a newsmagazine directed at African Americans. "I want to grow my brand to be like Disney," Johnson says of his goals.

CHECK FOR UNDERSTANDING

1. Source Reading Describe how Johnson's BET affected the supply of television entertainment available to cable viewers.

2. Critical Thinking Using clues in the text above, explain the meaning of the term *umbrella brand.*

3. Learn More Use the Internet and other sources to research and report on the variety of products and services that BET currently has or is planning for the future.

Objectives

After studying this section you will be able to:

1. **Identify** how determinants such as input costs create changes in supply.

2. **Identify** three ways that the government can influence the supply of a good.

3. **Understand** supply and demand in the global economy.

4. **Analyze** the effects of other factors that affect supply.

Section Focus

Changes in the costs of inputs can raise or lower the supply of a good at all prices. The number of firms in a market and the price and supply of other goods can also have an effect on the supply of a good.

Key Terms

subsidy
excise tax
regulation

Just as several factors can affect demand at all price levels, a separate set of factors can affect supply. In this section, you will read about these factors that can affect supply, and the factors that shift an entire supply curve to the left or right.

▲ **New technology has lowered the costs of production in many markets.**

Input Costs

Any change in the cost of an input used to produce a good—such as raw materials, machinery, or labor—will affect supply. A rise in the cost of an input will cause a fall in supply at all price levels because the good has become more expensive to produce. On the other hand, a fall in the cost of an input will cause an increase in supply at all price levels.

Effect of Rising Costs

Think of the effects of input costs on the relationship between marginal revenue (price) and marginal cost. A supplier sets output at the most profitable level, where price is equal to marginal cost. Marginal cost includes the cost of the inputs that go into production, so a rise in the cost of labor or raw materials will translate directly into a higher marginal cost. If the cost of inputs increases enough, the marginal cost may become higher than the price, and the firm may not be as profitable as it could be.

If a firm has no control over the price, the only solution is to cut production and lower marginal cost until marginal cost equals the lower price. Supply falls at each price, and the supply curve shifts to the left, as illustrated in Figure 5.12.

Figure 5.12 Shifts in the Supply Curve

Increase in Supply

Supply Curve

New Supply Curve

Price

Output

Decrease in Supply

New Supply Curve

Supply Curve

Price

Output

BUILDING KEY CONCEPTS

Factors that reduce supply shift the supply curve to the left, while factors that increase supply move the supply curve to the right.

Supply and Demand Which graph best represents the effects of higher costs?

Technology

Input costs can drop as well. Advances in technology, for example, can lower production costs in many industries. Sophisticated robots have replaced many workers on assembly lines and allowed manufacturers to spend less on salaries. Computers have simplified tasks and cut costs in fields as diverse as journalism and architecture. E-mail that can be sent and received in an instant can replace slowly delivered letters and expensive long-distance phone calls.

Technology lowers costs and increases supply at all price levels. This effect is seen in a rightward shift in the supply curve in Figure 5.12.

Government's Influence on Supply

The government has the power to affect the supplies of many goods. By raising or lowering the cost of producing goods, the government can encourage or discourage an entrepreneur or an industry within the country or abroad.

Subsidies

One method used by governments to affect supply is to give subsidies to the producers of a good, particularly food. A **subsidy** is a government payment or discounted loan that supports a business or market. The government often pays a producer a set subsidy for each unit of a good produced.

Governments have several reasons for subsidizing producers. European countries faced food shortages during and after World War II. Although imported food is cheaper, European governments protect farms so that some will be available to grow food in case imports are ever cut off. The government of France also subsidizes small farms because French citizens want to protect the lifestyle and character of the French countryside.

Governments in developing countries often subsidize manufacturers to protect young, growing industries from strong foreign competition. In the past, countries such as Indonesia and Malaysia have subsidized a national car company as a source of pride, even though imported cars were less expensive to build. In Western Europe, banks and national airlines were allowed to suffer huge losses with the assurance that the government would cover their debts. In many countries, governments have stopped providing industrial subsidies in the interest of free trade and fair competition.

In the United States, the federal government subsidizes producers in many industries. Farm subsidies are particularly controversial, however, especially when farmers are paid to take land out of cultivation to keep prices high. In these cases, more efficient farmers are penalized, and farmers use more herbicides and pesticides

subsidy *a government payment that supports a business or market*

Common Agricultural Policy The European Union, a group of fifteen countries in Europe, protects its farms through its Common Agricultural Policy (CAP). Under CAP, the European Union **subsidizes** farms to keep them running and to encourage farmers to produce more food. Although this may have made sense in difficult times after World War II, farms have since modernized, and subsidies have led to a tremendous amount of unneeded food. In 1994, the CAP cost Europe $40 billion while producing a "wine lake" and "butter mountain" that no one would buy. Since then, Europe has tried to cut subsidies and introduce voluntary limits on production.

excise tax *a tax on the production or sale of a good*

regulation *government intervention in a market that affects the production of a good*

on lands they do cultivate to compensate for production lost on the acres the government pays them not to plant.

Taxes

A government can reduce the supply of some goods by placing an **excise tax** on them. An excise tax is a tax on the production or sale of a good. An excise tax increases production costs by adding an extra cost for each unit sold.

Excise taxes are sometimes used to discourage the sale of goods that the government thinks are harmful to the public good, like cigarettes, alcohol, and high-pollutant gasoline. Excise taxes are built into the prices of these and other goods, so consumers may not realize that they are paying them. Like any increase in cost, an excise tax causes the supply of a good to decrease at all price levels. The supply curve shifts to the left.

Regulation

Subsidies and excise taxes represent ways that government directly affects supply by changing revenue or production costs. Government can also raise or lower supply through indirect means. Government regulation often has the effect of raising costs. **Regulation** is government intervention in a market that affects the price, quantity, or quality of a good.

For many years, pollution from automobiles harmed the environment. Starting in 1970, the federal government required car manufacturers to install technology to reduce pollution from auto exhaust. For example, new cars had to use lead-free fuel because scientists linked health problems to

▲ Although other countries can grow food more cheaply, the French government keeps its farmers in business by offering subsidies.

lead in gasoline. Regulations such as these increased the cost of manufacturing cars and reduced the supply. The supply curve shifted to the left.

Supply in the Global Economy

As you read in earlier chapters, a large and rising share of goods and services is produced in one country and imported by another to be sold to consumers. The supplies of imported goods are affected by changes in other countries. Here are some examples of possible changes in the supply of products imported by the U.S.

- The U.S. imports carpets from India. An increase in the wages of Indian workers would decrease the supply of carpets to the U.S. market, shifting the supply curve to the left.
- The U.S. imports telephones from Japan. A new technology that decreases the cost of producing telephones would increase the supply of telephones to the U.S. market, shifting the supply curve to the right.
- The U.S. imports oil from Russia. A new oil discovery in Russia would increase the supply of oil to the U.S. market and shift the supply curve to the right.

Import restrictions also affect the supply curves of restricted goods. The total supply of a product equals the sum of imports and domestically produced products. An import ban on sugar would eliminate foreign sugar suppliers from the market, shifting the market supply curve to the left. At any price, a smaller quantity of sugar would be supplied. If the government restricted imports by establishing an import quota, the supply curve would shift to the left, but the shift would be smaller than it would be for an absolute ban on sugar imports.

Other Influences on Supply

While government can have an important influence on the supply of goods, there are also other important factors that influence

▲ As prices for fossil fuels have risen, electric companies have looked to alternative sources of supply, such as wind.

supply. First, producers' expectations of future prices affect their output decisions. Second, the supply of goods increases with the number of firms producing the good.

Future Expectations of Prices

If you were a soybean farmer, and you expected the price of soybeans to double next month, what would you do with the crop that you just harvested? Would you sell it right now, or hold on to it until soybean prices rise? Most farmers would store their soybeans until the price rose, cutting back supply in the short term.

If a seller expects the price of a good to rise in the future, the seller will store the goods now in order to sell more in the future. On the other hand, if the price of the good is expected to drop in the near future, sellers will earn more money by placing goods on the market immediately before the price falls. Expectations of higher prices will reduce supply now and increase supply later, and expectations of lower prices will have the opposite effect.

Inflation is a condition of rising prices. During periods of inflation, the value of cash in a person's pocket decreases from day to day as prices rise. Not too long ago, one dollar could buy a movie ticket or a small meal, but inflation over many years

▲ High levels of inflation, like those Russia faced in the 1990s, can cause suppliers to hoard their goods to sell later.

During the Civil War, the South faced terrible inflation. The prices of most goods rose very quickly. There were shortages of food, and shopkeepers knew that prices on basic food items like flour, butter, and salt would rise each month. A few decided to hoard their food and wait for higher prices. They succeeded too well; the supply of food fell so much that prices rose out of the reach of many families. Riots broke out in Virginia and elsewhere when hungry people decided they weren't going to wait for the food to be released from the warehouses, and the shopkeepers lost their goods and their profits.

has reduced the value of the dollar. However, a good will continue to hold its value, provided that it can be stored for a long period of time. When faced with inflation, suppliers prefer to hold on to goods that will maintain their value rather than sell them for cash that loses its value rapidly. As a result, inflation can affect supply by encouraging suppliers to hold on to goods as long as possible. In the short term, supply can fall dramatically.

Number of Suppliers

One final factor to consider when looking at changes in supply is the number of suppliers in the market. If more suppliers enter a market to produce a certain good, the market supply of the good will rise, and the supply curve will shift to the right. On the other hand, if suppliers stop producing the good and leave the market, the supply will decline. There is a positive relationship between the number of suppliers in a market and the market supply of the good.

Section 3 Assessment

Key Terms and Main Ideas

1. How does a **subsidy** affect supply?
2. Why does the government impose **excise taxes?**
3. How can **regulation** affect a producer's output decisions?

Applying Economic Concepts

4. *Using the Databank* Turn to the graph on page 534 that lists the production of the American agriculture, timber, and mining industries. If the government wanted the mining industry to produce $120 billion next year, what step could it take?

5. *Decision Making* Decide whether each of these events would cause an increase or decrease in the supply of American-made backpacks. **(a)** The government raises the minimum wage of backpack workers to $40 an hour. **(b)** A new regulation requires firms to make backpacks out of expensive clear plastic. **(c)** An engineer invents a machine that can sew ten backpacks a minute, speeding up production.

6. *Critical Thinking* Explain why a change that lowers the marginal revenue (price) changes the quantity produced in the same direction as a change that raises the marginal cost of production.

Take It to the NET

Throughout history, artists have looked to governments and private donors for financial support. Determine what effect government and private donations to the arts have on the supply of cultural activities in the United States. Use the links provided in the Social Studies area at the following Web site for help in completing this activity. **www.phschool.com**

Are Baseball Players Paid Too Much?

Major league baseball provides us with a prime example of the ways in which supply and demand affect wages. Millions of people are willing to buy tickets to watch major leaguers in person. Even more watch the games on television. Most team owners make enormous amounts of money from the sale of tickets and television rights, as well as licensing fees.

Supply and Demand The salaries of top baseball players are determined by supply and demand. The public creates a high demand for watching professional sports, but the supply of truly talented athletes is relatively small. This drives their salaries up. On the other hand, most people could be trained to work as store clerks or fast-food restaurant employees, so wages for those positions tend to be low.

Free Agency Up until the 1970s, players received relatively low salaries. This was because most were required to play only for the team that first signed them to a contract, or to the team that they had been traded to. In the mid-1970s, players went to court seeking the right to become "free agents." Free agency would allow them, after playing for a team for a certain number of years, to sell their services to any other team willing to pay them the salaries they asked for. Although team owners strongly opposed free agency, the players won their case.

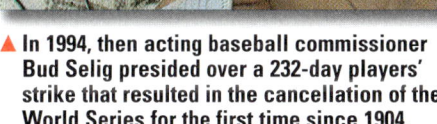

▲ In 1994, then acting baseball commissioner Bud Selig presided over a 232-day players' strike that resulted in the cancellation of the World Series for the first time since 1904.

A Price to Pay This victory has led to bidding wars which have resulted in the astronomical salaries that top stars now receive. Yet, while these players have benefited greatly from free agency, both fans and major league baseball itself have had to pay a price. The intense loyalty that fans once demonstrated toward their favorite teams has diminished as players switch from one team to another in search of higher salaries. Owners have sharply increased ticket prices to afford the huge increases in players' salaries.

Now, only teams that operate in the largest television markets or have the wealthiest owners can afford to pay the best players. Some fans believe that only the richest teams can make it to the World Series, while the less-wealthy teams are left behind. The result of this development has been a growing cynicism on the part of many fans who feel—rightly or wrongly—that baseball championships are now purchased rather than won.

Applying Economic Ideas

1. What arguments might players make for free agency?

2. How do the laws of supply and demand affect baseball players' salaries?

Chapter Summary

A summary of major ideas in Chapter 5 appears below. See also the **Guide to the Essentials of Economics**, which provides additional review and test practice of key concepts in Chapter 5.

Section 1 Understanding Supply (pp. 101–106)

The **law of supply** states that when the price of a good rises, the **quantity supplied** of that good also rises because existing firms produce more and new firms join the market. Economists list the quantity supplied of a good at each price in a **supply schedule** and graph this data on a **supply curve** that rises from left to right. Supply can be elastic or inelastic depending upon how easily a producer can change the level of output.

Section 2 Costs of Production (pp. 108–114)

As an entrepreneur invests more in labor while keeping capital constant, the **marginal product of labor** first increases, then falls. A firm adds its **fixed costs** and **variable costs** to determine its **total cost** at each level of output. The most profitable level of output is where the **marginal cost** of producing the last unit is the same as the **marginal revenue** the firm receives when that unit is sold.

Section 3 Changes in Supply (pp. 116–120)

Several factors can raise or lower the supply of a good at all prices. When inputs such as capital and labor become more expensive, supply falls and the supply curve shifts to the left. New technology can lower the cost of production and increase supply, shifting the supply curve to the right. Government encourages suppliers with **subsidies** and reduces supply with **excise taxes**. Other factors that affect supply are the number of suppliers in the market and competition from suppliers in other countries.

Key Terms

Match the following definitions with the terms listed below. You will not use all of the terms.

marginal costs	supply schedule
marginal revenue	regulation
elasticity of supply	excise tax
law of supply	variable costs
subsidy	fixed cost

1. An expense that costs the same whether or not a firm is producing a good or service
2. The income that the supplier receives from selling one more unit
3. A tax on the sale or manufacture of a good
4. A measure of how suppliers will respond to a change in price
5. A government payment to support a business or market
6. The tendency of suppliers to offer more of a good at a higher price
7. The additional cost of producing one more unit of output

Using Graphic Organizers

8. On a separate sheet of paper, copy the multi-flow map below. Organize information on how firms determine their total costs by completing the multiflow map with examples of fixed and variable costs.

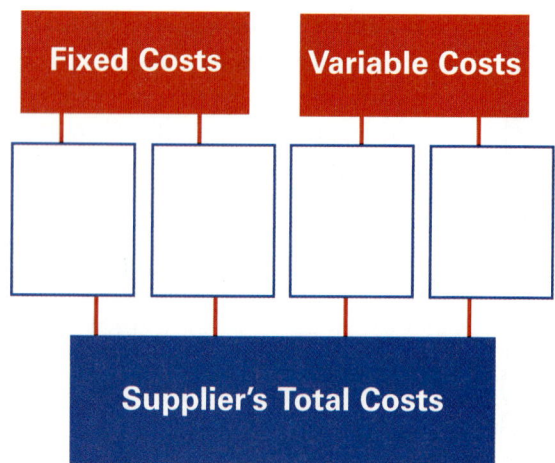

Reviewing Main Ideas

9. How does the marginal product of labor change as more people are hired?
10. What categories of costs combine to create a firm's total cost?
11. Name and describe three factors that can cause a change in supply.
12. What circumstances cause a firm to experience diminishing marginal returns?
13. How can the global economy affect the supply of a good in the United States?

Critical Thinking

14. **Recognizing Cause and Effect** Assume that a $1 per pound tax has been placed on fish. What effect will this have on the supply curve for fish?
15. **Analyzing Information** A local coffee shop has the following expenses: $5,000 a month for rent; $3,000 a month for a full-time manager; $4,000 a month for part-time workers; and $2,000 a month for coffee beans, milk, and cups. In July, the owner can expect to earn $7,000 in revenue. If she chooses to close down the store, she will not have to pay for part-time workers or supplies. Explain whether she should close the shop for the month of July, and why or why not.
16. **Making Comparisons** Compare the two terms *increasing marginal returns* and *diminishing marginal returns*. Describe two scenarios, one to explain and demonstrate each term.

Problem-Solving Activity

17. Suppose that you plan to open a T-shirt factory. Create a list of fixed costs and variable costs that you would encounter. How would each of these costs affect the number of T-shirts you make?

Economics Journal

Recognizing Cause and Effect For each item on your list, explain if you think supply is elastic or inelastic, and why. Brainstorm five specific events that could increase the supply of each item.

Skills for Life

Test-Taking Skills Review the steps shown on page 107, and then complete the following activity based on your own experiences.

18. Having time that is free of distractions is essential. List three possible distractions that you face while studying, and one way you could reduce or eliminate each one.
19. Create a list of three stress-free activities you can do for brief study breaks.
20. Compare the list of distractions and study break activities. Are there any similarities? How can you use both lists to make your studying more efficient and effective?
21. Think of yourself as an individual economic system. Your time is in limited supply. How would you describe the supply of study time? Prepare a supply schedule. Does your study time have an elastic or inelastic supply? Draw a supply curve to illustrate your ideas.

ROTHCO Baloo

"I can't understand it -- I always get the answers right when I watch <u>game shows</u>!"

Take It to the NET

Chapter 5 Self-Test As a final review activity, take the Chapter 5 Self-Test in the Social Studies area at the Web site listed below, and receive immediate feedback on your answers. The test consists of 20 multiple-choice questions designed to test your understanding of the chapter content.
www.phschool.com

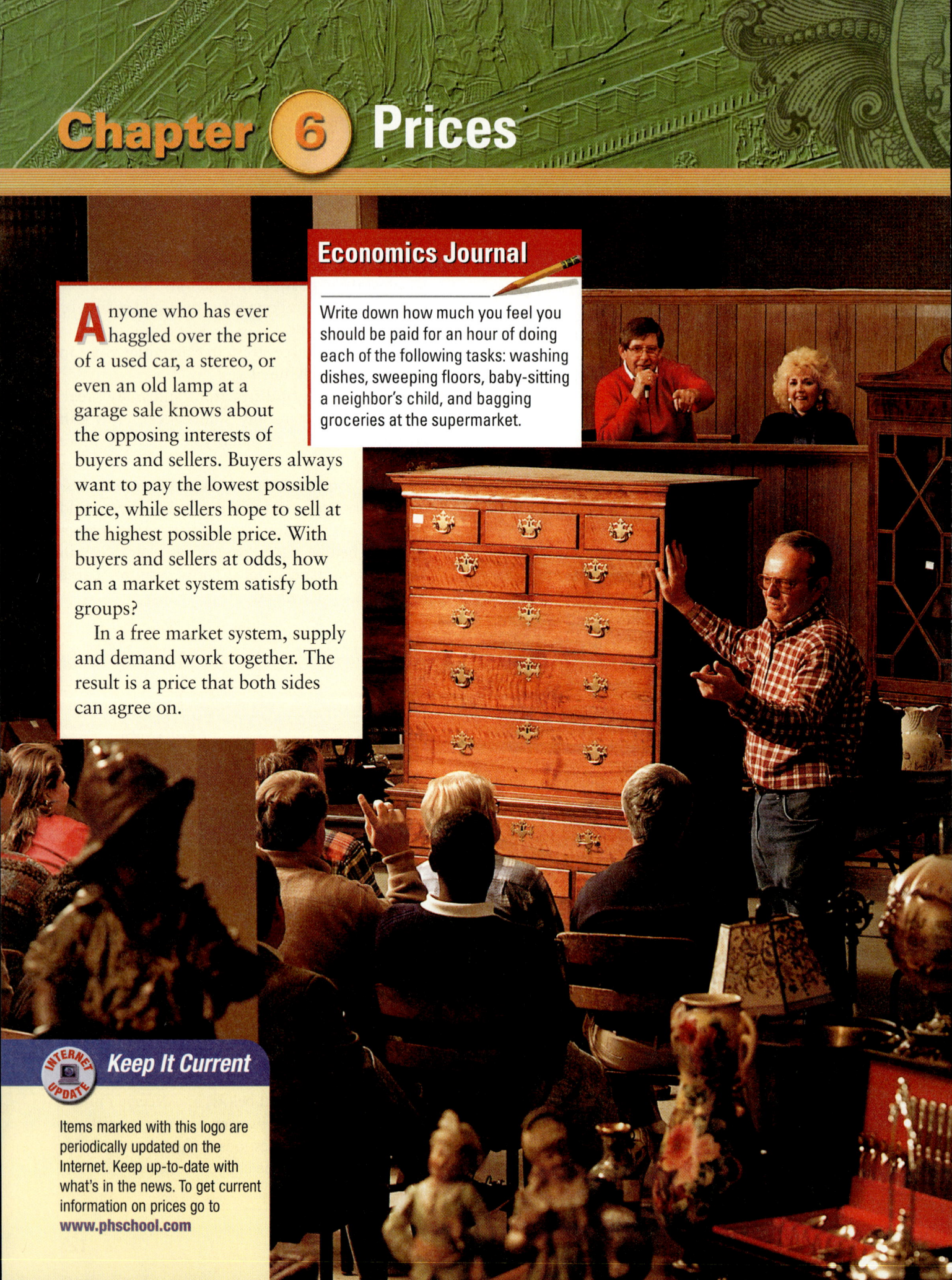

Chapter 6 Prices

Anyone who has ever haggled over the price of a used car, a stereo, or even an old lamp at a garage sale knows about the opposing interests of buyers and sellers. Buyers always want to pay the lowest possible price, while sellers hope to sell at the highest possible price. With buyers and sellers at odds, how can a market system satisfy both groups?

In a free market system, supply and demand work together. The result is a price that both sides can agree on.

Economics Journal

Write down how much you feel you should be paid for an hour of doing each of the following tasks: washing dishes, sweeping floors, baby-sitting a neighbor's child, and bagging groceries at the supermarket.

Combining Supply and Demand

Objectives

After studying this section you will be able to:

1. **Explain** how supply and demand create balance in the marketplace.
2. **Compare** a market in equilibrium with a market in disequilibrium.
3. **Identify** how the government sometimes intervenes in markets to control prices.
4. **Analyze** the effects of price ceilings and price floors.

Section Focus

In an uncontrolled market, the price of a good and quantity sold will settle at a point where the quantity supplied equals the quantity demanded. The government can set a maximum or minimum price, but that can lead to an imbalance between supply and demand.

Key Terms

equilibrium
disequilibrium
excess demand
excess supply
price ceiling
price floor
rent control
minimum wage

The market system makes certain that consumers can buy the products they want, that sellers make enough profit to stay in business, and that sellers respond to changing needs and tastes of consumers. Other economic systems have been tried—most notably, central planning—and have been judged by most observers to be less successful than the market system.

In this section we will combine our tools for studying demand and supply to learn how markets operate and how markets can turn competing interests into a positive outcome for both sides. In the process we will discover that free markets usually produce some of their best outcomes when they are left alone, without government intervention.

Balancing the Market

Just as buyers and sellers come together in a market, the study of demand and supply will come together in this section. We begin by looking at the supply and demand schedules. As you will recall, a demand schedule shows how much consumers are willing to buy at various prices. A supply schedule shows how much sellers are willing to sell at various prices. Comparing these schedules should allow us to find common ground for the two sides of the market.

The combined supply and demand schedule in Figure 6.1 combines the market demand and supply schedules for pizza slices that you saw in Chapters 4 and 5. For each price, this schedule lists both the number of slices that consumers are willing to buy and the number of slices that pizzerias are willing to supply.

Defining Equilibrium

The point where demand and supply come together at the same number of slices is called the **equilibrium**. Equilibrium is the point of balance between price and quantity. At equilibrium, the market for a good is stable.

equilibrium *the point at which quantity demanded and quantity supplied are equal*

▼ In the market equilibrium, prices adjust to make the quantity supplied equal to the quantity demanded.

Figure 6.1 **Finding Equilibrium**

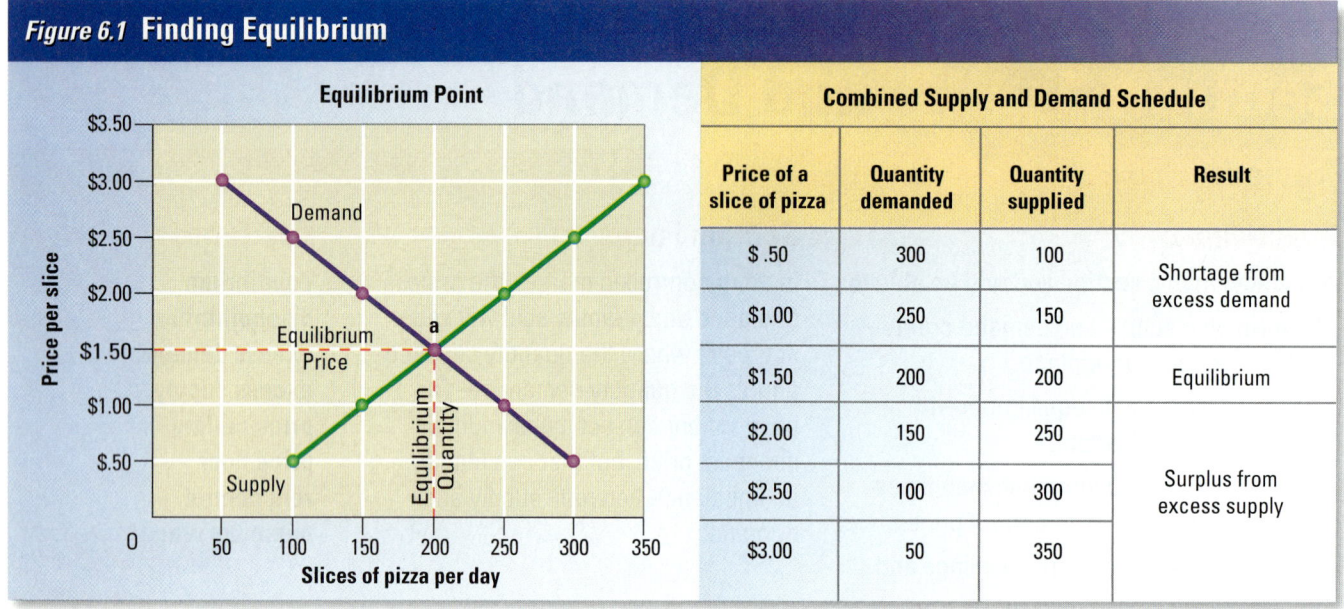

Equilibrium Point

Combined Supply and Demand Schedule

Price of a slice of pizza	Quantity demanded	Quantity supplied	Result
$ .50	300	100	Shortage from excess demand
$1.00	250	150	
$1.50	200	200	Equilibrium
$2.00	150	250	Surplus from excess supply
$2.50	100	300	
$3.00	50	350	

Market equilibrium will be found at the price at which the quantity demanded is equal to the quantity supplied. **Markets and Prices** How many slices are sold at $2.50 a slice? How many slices are sold at equilibrium?

To find the equilibrium price and equilibrium quantity, simply look for the price at which the quantity supplied equals the quantity demanded. Do you see that in Figure 6.1 this occurs at a price of $1.50 per slice? At that price, and only at that price, the quantity demanded and the quantity supplied are equal, at 200 slices per day. This is the market equilibrium.

In the market for pizza, as in any market, quantities supplied and demanded will be equal at only one price and one quantity. At this equilibrium price, buyers will purchase exactly as much of the product as firms are willing to sell. Buyers who are willing to purchase the goods at the equilibrium price will find ample supplies on store shelves. Firms that are willing to sell at the equilibrium price will find enough buyers for their goods.

Graphing Equilibrium
We can also illustrate equilibrium with a supply and demand graph. In Figure 6.1, we have plotted on the same graph the market supply curve and the market demand curve for slices of pizza. The equilibrium price and quantity can be found where quantity supplied equals quantity

demanded, or the point where the supply curve crosses the demand curve. On the graph, this is point a.

Disequilibrium

If the market price or quantity supplied is anywhere but at the equilibrium, the market is in a state that economists call **disequilibrium**. Disequilibrium occurs when quantity supplied is not equal to quantity demanded in a market. In the above example, disequilibrium will occur with any price other than $1.50 per slice or any quantity other than 200 slices. Disequilibrium can produce one of two outcomes, excess demand or excess supply.

Excess Demand
The problem of **excess demand** occurs when quantity demanded is more than quantity supplied. When the actual price in a market is below the equilibrium price, you have excess demand, because a low price encourages buyers and discourages sellers.

For example, in Figure 6.1, a price of $1.00 per slice of pizza will lead to a quantity demanded of 250 slices per day and a quantity supplied of only 150 slices

disequilibrium
describes any price or quantity not at equilibrium; when quantity supplied is not equal to quantity demanded in a market

excess demand *when quantity demanded is more than quantity supplied*

per day. At this price, there is excess demand of 100 slices per day.

When customers want to buy 100 more slices of pizza than restaurants are prepared to sell, these customers will have to wait in long lines for their pizza, and some will have to do without. In Figure 6.2, below, we have illustrated the excess demand at $1.00 per slice by drawing a dotted line across the graph at that price. As you can see, at $1.00 a slice, the quantity demanded is 250 slices, and the quantity supplied is 150 slices.

If you were running the pizzeria, and you noticed long lines of customers waiting to buy your pizza at $1.00 per slice, what would you do? Assuming that you like to earn profits, you would probably raise the price. As you increased the price of pizza, you would be willing to work harder and bake more, because you would know you could earn more money for each slice you sell.

Of course, as the price rises, customers will buy less pizza, since it is becoming relatively more expensive. When the price reaches $1.50 per slice, you will find that you are earning more profits and can keep up with demand, but the lines are much shorter. Some days you may throw out a few leftover slices, and other days you have to throw an extra pizza or two in the oven to keep up with customers, but on the whole, you are meeting the needs of your customers. In other words, the market is now at equilibrium.

As long as there is excess demand, and the quantity demanded exceeds the quantity supplied, suppliers will keep raising the price. When the price has risen enough to close the gap, suppliers will have found the

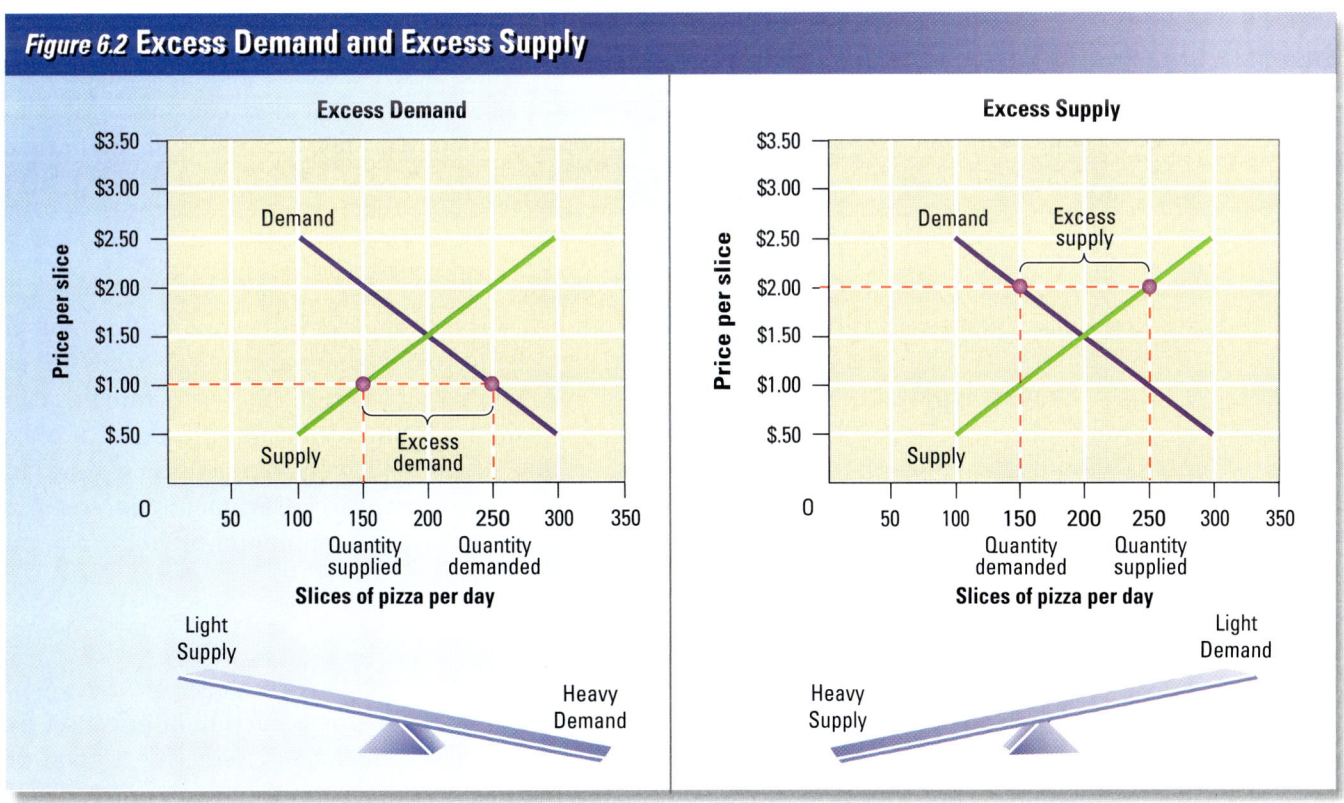

Figure 6.2 Excess Demand and Excess Supply

Excess demand and excess supply both lead to a market with fewer sales than at equilibrium.
Supply and Demand Why are sales lower at $1.00 a slice than at $2.00 a slice?

▼ How much would you be willing to pay to live in one of these apartments?

highest price that the market will bear. They will continue to sell at that price until one of the factors described in Chapter 4 or 5 changes the demand or supply curve and creates new pressures to raise or lower prices, and eventually, a new equilibrium.

Excess Supply

If the price is too high, then the market will face a problem of excess supply. **Excess supply** occurs when quantity supplied exceeds quantity demanded. For example, at a price of $2.00 per slice of pizza, the quantity supplied of 250 slices per day is much greater than the quantity demanded of 150 slices per day. This means that pizzeria owners will be making 100 more slices of pizza each day than they can sell at that price. The relatively high price encourages pizzeria owners to work hard and bake lots of pizza, but it discourages customers from buying pizza, since it is relatively more expensive than

other menu items. Some customers will buy one slice instead of two, while others will eat elsewhere. The problem is shown graphically in Figure 6.2. At the end of the day, it is likely that 100 slices will have to be thrown out.

After a short time, pizzeria owners will get tired of throwing out unsold pizza at closing time and will cut their prices. As the price falls, the quantity demanded will rise, and more customers will buy more pizza. At the same time, pizzeria owners will prepare fewer pizzas. As the price of pizza falls, the quantity demanded rises and the quantity supplied falls. This process will continue until the price reaches $1.50 per slice. At that price, the amount of pizza that pizzeria owners are willing to sell is exactly equal to the amount that their customers are willing to buy.

Whenever the market is in disequilibrium and prices are flexible, market forces will push the market toward the equilibrium. Sellers do not like to waste their resources on excess supply, particularly when the goods cannot be stored for long, like pizza. And when there is excess demand, profit-seeking sellers realize that they can raise prices to earn more profits. In this way, market prices move toward the equilibrium level.

Government Intervention

Markets tend toward equilibrium, but in some cases the government steps in to control prices. The government can impose a **price ceiling**, or a maximum price that can be legally charged for a good. In other cases, the government can create a **price floor**, or a minimum price for a good or service.

Price Ceilings

A price ceiling is a maximum price, set by law, that sellers can charge for a good or service. The government places price ceilings on some goods that are considered "essential" and might become too expensive for some consumers. For example, some local governments, notably New York City, have

excess supply when quantity supplied is more than quantity demanded

price ceiling a maximum price that can be legally charged for a good or service

price floor a minimum price for a good or service

experimented with ceilings on apartment rents, called **rent control**. Rent control was introduced to prevent inflation during a housing crisis in the early 1940s and continued after World War II. More recently, other cities imposed rent control, often motivated by a desire to help poor households by cutting their housing costs and permitting them to live in neighborhoods they could otherwise not afford. As we'll see, rent control reduces the quantity and quality of housing, so it helps some households but harms others, including many poor households. If the ceiling is established below the equilibrium price, the result will look like graph A in Figure 6.3 below.

In this market, the supply and demand curves for two-bedroom apartments meet at the equilibrium shown at point c in graph B. At this point, rents are $900 a month. Consumers will demand 30,000 apartments and suppliers will offer 30,000 apartments for rent.

Suppose that the city government passes a law that limits the rent on two-bedroom apartments to $600 per month. At that price, the quantity of apartments demanded is 40,000 (point b), and the quantity supplied is 20,000 (point a). At such a low price, apartments seem inexpensive, and many people will try to rent apartments instead of living with their families or investing in their own houses.

However, some landlords will have difficulty earning profits or breaking even at these low rents. Fewer new apartment buildings will be built, and older ones might be converted into offices, stores, or condominiums.

As you can see in graph A of Figure 6.3, the result is excess demand of 20,000 apartments. The price ceiling increases the quantity demanded but decreases the quantity supplied. Since rents are not allowed to rise, this excess demand will last as long as the price ceiling holds.

The Cost of Price Ceilings
When the price cannot rise to the equilibrium level, the market must determine which 20,000 of the 40,000 households will get an apartment, and which 20,000 will do without. Although governments usually pass rent control laws to help renters with the greatest need, few of these renters benefit from rent control. Methods besides prices, including long waiting lists, discrimination by landlords, and even bribery, are used to allocate the scarce supply of apartments among the many people who want them. Luck becomes an important factor, and sometimes the only way to get a rent-controlled apartment is to inherit it from a parent or grandparent.

New York City revised its laws in the 1990s to exclude the wealthiest renters

rent control *a price ceiling placed on rent*

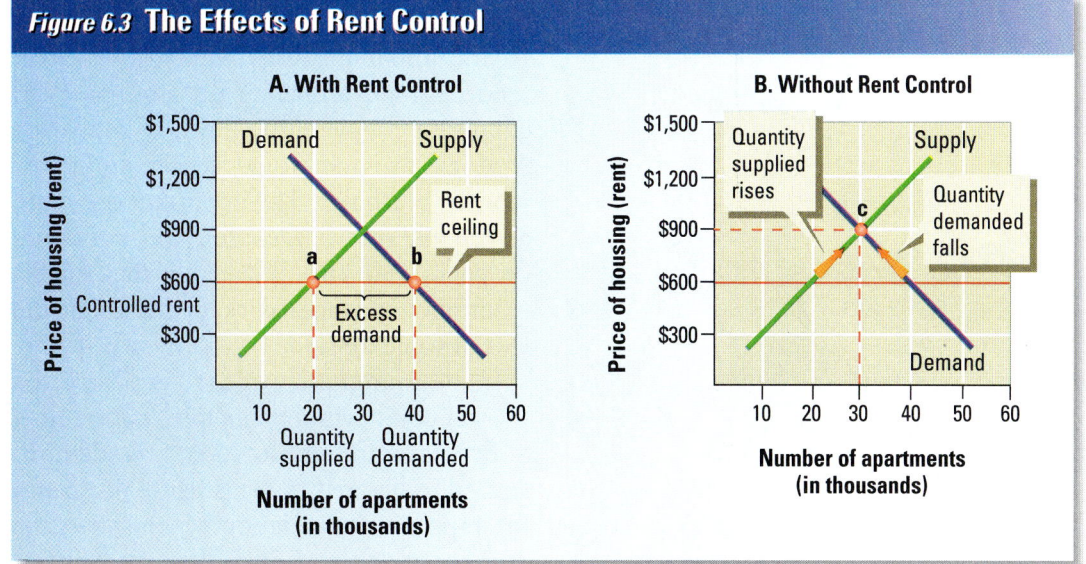

Figure 6.3 The Effects of Rent Control

A. With Rent Control

B. Without Rent Control

Rent control helps some people, but it also creates a housing market with fewer, less-desirable homes.

Supply and Demand
At what price does the market for apartments reach equilibrium without rent control?

from rent control protection after newspapers discovered that some very wealthy people rented spacious apartments at prices much less than market value.

Additionally, since the rent controls limit landlords' profits, landlords may try to increase their income by cutting costs. Why should a landlord give a building a fresh coat of paint and a new garden if he or she can't earn the money back through higher rent? Besides, if there's a waiting list to get an apartment, the landlord has no incentive to work hard and attract renters. As a result, many rent-controlled apartment buildings become run-down, and renters may have to wait months to have routine problems fixed.

Ending Rent Control

If rents were allowed to rise to the market equilibrium level, which is $900 per month, the quantity of apartments in the market would actually rise to 30,000 apartments. The market would be in equilibrium, and people who could afford $900 a month would have an easier time finding vacant apartments. Instead of spending time and money searching for apartments, and then having to accept an apartment in a poorly maintained building, many renters would be able to find a wider selection of apartments. Landlords would also have a

greater incentive to properly maintain their buildings and invest in new construction.

On the other hand, people lucky enough to live in a rent-controlled apartment may no longer be able to afford to stay there once rent control is ended and the landlord can legally raise the rent. As soon as the neighborhood improves, these renters may be priced out of their own apartments, to be replaced by people willing to pay the equilibrium price. Remember that ending rent control increases the number of apartments on the market by 10,000.

Certainly, the end of rent control benefits some people and hurts others. Economists agree that the benefits of ending rent control exceed the costs, and suggest that there are better ways to help poor households find affordable housing.

Price Floors

A price floor is a minimum price, set by the government, that must be paid for a good or service. Price floors are often imposed when government wants sellers to receive some minimum reward for their efforts.

The Minimum Wage

One well-known price floor is the **minimum wage**, which sets a minimum price that an employer can pay a worker for an hour of labor. The federal government sets a base level for the minimum wage, and states can set their own minimum wages even higher. A full-time worker being paid the federal minimum wage will earn less than the federal government says is necessary to support a couple with one child. However, it does provide some lower limit for workers' earnings. The important question, as you will read in *Debating Current Issues* on pages 180–181, is whether the benefits to minimum wage workers outweigh the loss of some jobs.

If the minimum wage is set above the market equilibrium wage rate, the result is a decrease in employment, as demonstrated in Figure 6.4. This figure illustrates the supply curve of labor, which shows the number of worker-hours offered at various

▼ The minimum wage has a strong impact on teens in the work force.

wage rates, and a demand curve for labor, which shows the number of workers employers will hire at various wages.

If the market equilibrium wage for low-skilled labor is $4.50 per hour, and the minimum wage is set at $5.15, the result is an excess supply of labor. There are now 4 million more people looking for work than employers are willing to hire. (Remember that in this example, the worker is the supplier because he or she supplies labor that is bought by an employer.) Firms will employ 2 million fewer workers than they would at the equilibrium wage rate because the price floor on labor keeps the wage rate artificially high. If the minimum wage is below the equilibrium rate, it will have no effect because employers would have to pay at least the equilibrium rate anyway to find workers in a free market.

Price Supports in Agriculture

Price floors are used for many farm products around the world. Until 1996, the United States set minimum prices for several commodities, although these price floors were not legal limits. Instead, whenever the price fell below the price floor, the government created demand by buying excess crops.

Although Congress abolished price supports in 1996, several states in the Northeast have formed the Northeast Dairy Compact to guarantee a minimum price for milk produced on farms in these states.

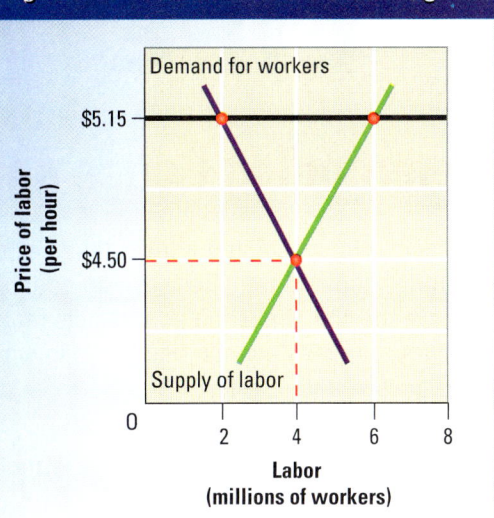

Figure 6.4 Effects of Minimum Wage

A minimum wage law can set the price of labor above the equilibrium price, leading to a labor surplus.

Supply and Demand According to this graph, how big is the surplus of workers when the minimum wage is $5.15 per hour?

Section 1 Assessment

Key Terms and Main Ideas

1. What is unique about an **equilibrium** price?
2. What situation can lead to **excess demand?**
3. How is a **price floor** different from a **price ceiling?**
4. How does **rent control** work?

Applying Economic Concepts

5. *Using the Databank* Turn to the graph of median weekly earnings on page 536 in the Databank. Suppose that the federal government has raised the minimum wage to $500 per week. **(a)** Which category of jobs would be least affected by the change? **(b)** Which two categories would be most affected by the new minimum wage? **(c)** What are the likely consequences for workers in these two fields?

6. *Critical Thinking* What are the benefits and drawbacks of a price ceiling?

7. *Math Practice* The graph below shows supply and demand curves in the notebook market. Use what you have learned in this section to identify the following elements of the graph: price floor, supply curve, equilibrium point, disequilibrium point, demand curve, price ceiling.

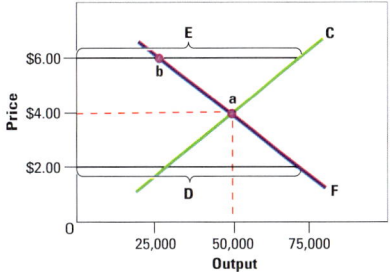

Take It to the NET

Rent control is one example presented in this section of ways in which the government acts to control prices. Investigate some recent rent control issues. Use the links provided at the following Web site for help in completing this activity. **www.phschool.com**

Determining Cause and Effect

Recognizing cause and effect means examining how one event or action brings about others. Because an economy is a complex web of choices and events, one challenge economists face is finding and defining the relationships between events. Use the following steps to learn how to determine causes and effects.

1. **Identify the two parts of a cause-effect relationship.** A cause is an event or an action that brings about an effect. Words such as *because*, *due to*, and

STATEMENTS LIST

A. Because of floods in South America, last year's coffee crop was poor.

B. Coffee is grown in Brazil, Colombia, and several countries in West Africa.

C. Because of the poor harvest, there was not enough good coffee available for American distributors to buy. As a result, prices went up, and many stores chose to stop selling the most expensive blends.

D. Many Americans drink coffee in the morning to wake up, while others drink coffee in the afternoon or after dinner.

E. The poor state of this year's crop led coffee shops to raise prices even as the quality of their coffee declined. When a heat wave hit the Northeast in July and August, sales dropped by 30 percent, many servers lost their jobs, and a major chain decided to delay opening new stores in Philadelphia and Washington, D.C.

F. When high quality coffee became expensive and difficult to find, many consumers switched to tea and soft drinks instead. Importers bought more tea in Southeast Asia to meet the new demand, and tea plantations planted more crops for the following year. While farmers in South America struggled to rebuild, farmers in India and Indonesia made more money and were able to invest in new machinery.

on account of signal causes. Words such as *so*, *thus*, *therefore*, and *as a result* signal effects. Read statements A through F at the left and answer the following: (**a**) Which statements are cause-effect statements? (**b**) Identify the cause and the effect in each cause-effect statement. (**c**) Which word or words signal the cause-effect relationship?

2. **Remember that an event can have more than one cause and more than one effect.** Read statement E at the left and answer the following questions. (**a**) What are the causes presented in the statement? (**b**) What are the effects of those causes?

3. **An event can be both a cause and an effect.** Causes and effects can form a chain of events. Read statement F at the left and use arrows to draw a diagram of the causes and effects that show the chain of related events.

Additional Practice

Based on what you have learned in this chapter, construct a chain of events to show the impact of a new tax on the coffee market.

Objectives

After studying this section you will be able to:

1. **Identify** the determinants that create changes in price.
2. **Explain** how a market reacts to a fall in supply by moving to a new equilibrium.
3. **Explain** how a market reacts to shifts in demand by moving to a new equilibrium.

Section Focus

When a supply or demand curve shifts, a new equilibrium occurs. The market price and quantity sold move toward the new equilibrium.

Key Terms

surplus
shortage
search costs

Economists say that a market will tend toward equilibrium, which means that the price and quantity will gradually move toward their equilibrium levels. Why does this happen? Remember that excess demand will lead firms to raise prices. Higher prices induce the quantity supplied to rise and the quantity demanded to fall until the two values are equal.

On the other hand, excess supply will force firms to cut prices. Falling prices will cause quantity demanded to rise and quantity supplied to fall until, once again, they are equal. Through these relationships, the market price and quantity sold of a good will move toward their equilibrium values.

Remember from Chapters 4 and 5 that all of the changes in demand and supply described above are changes along a demand or supply curve. Assuming that a market starts at equilibrium, there are two factors that can push it into disequilibrium: a shift in the entire demand curve and a shift in the entire supply curve.

Changes in Price

In Chapter 5, you read about the different factors that shift a supply curve to the left or to the right. These factors include advances in technology, new government taxes and subsidies, and changes in the prices of the raw materials and labor used to produce the good.

Since market equilibrium occurs at the intersection of a demand curve and a supply curve, a shift of the entire supply curve will change the equilibrium price and quantity. A shift in the supply curve to the left or the right creates a new equilibrium. Since markets tend toward equilibrium, a change in supply will set market forces into motion that lead the market to this new equilibrium price and quantity sold.

◀ A functioning market will carefully balance supply and demand.

BUILDING KEY CONCEPTS

As CD players become cheaper to produce, the supply increases at all but the lowest prices.

Supply and Demand
Why do the 1982 and 1987 supply curves begin so high up on the graph?

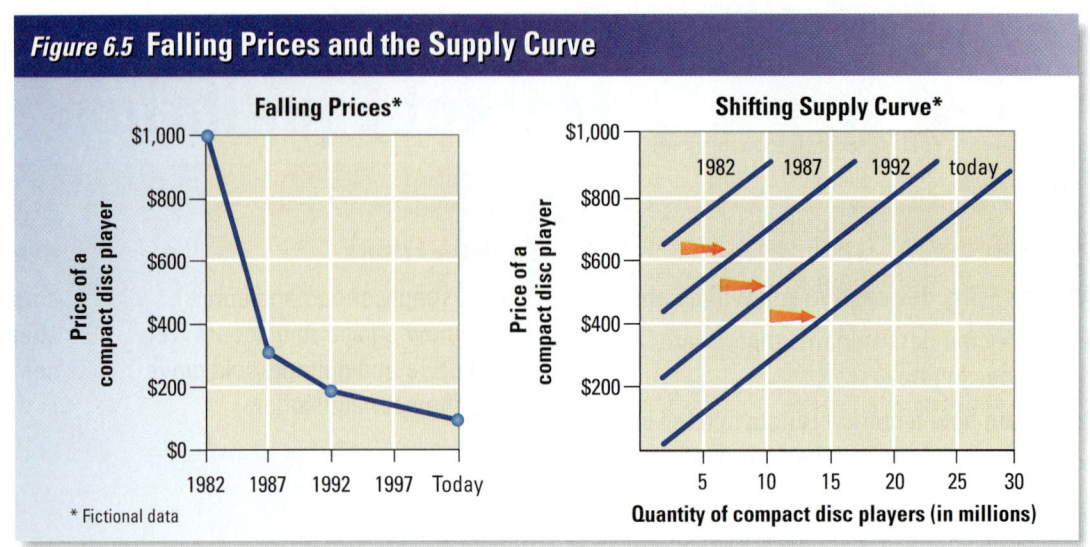

Figure 6.5 Falling Prices and the Supply Curve

Falling Prices*

Price of a compact disc player / 1982 1987 1992 1997 Today

* Fictional data

Shifting Supply Curve*

Price of a compact disc player / Quantity of compact disc players (in millions)

Understanding a Shift in Supply

When compact disc players were first introduced in the early 1980s, a basic, single-disc machine cost around $1,000. The early compact disc players were much more expensive and less sophisticated than the compact disc players people use today. Gradually, as firms developed better technology for producing compact disc players, their prices fell. In 1987, a consumer could purchase a fancy single-disc player for $300; just five years later, in 1992, a similar player could be purchased for about $200. Today, consumers can buy a compact disc player for around $100.

Not only have the prices of compact disc players fallen, but the machines on sale today have many more features and options than the original $1,000 machine. Technology has lowered the cost of manufacturing compact disc players and has also reduced the costs of some of the inputs, like computer chips. These advances in production have allowed manufacturers to produce compact disc players at lower costs. Producers have passed on these lower costs to consumers in the form of lower market prices.

We can use the tools developed in Chapter 5 to graph the effect of these changes on the CD market's supply curve. Figure 6.5 shows how the supply curve shifted outward, or to the right, as manufacturers offered more and more CD players at lower prices. In the early 1980s, no compact disc players were offered for $300. They were simply too expensive to develop and manufacture. Today, manufacturers can offer millions of CD players at this price.

Finding a New Equilibrium

Picture the point in time when compact disc players were evolving from an expensive luxury good to a mid-priced good. A new generation of computer chips has just reduced the cost of production. These lower costs have shifted the supply curve to the right where at each price, producers are willing to supply a larger quantity.

This shift, shown in Figure 6.6 using fictional quantities, has thrown the market into disequilibrium. At the old equilibrium price, suppliers are now willing to offer 4,000,000 compact disc players, up from 2,000,000.

In Figure 6.6, the increase in quantity supplied at the old equilibrium price is shown as the change from point a to point b. However, the quantity demanded at this price has not changed, and consumers will only buy 2,000,000 compact disc players. At this market price, unsold compact disc players will begin to pile up in the warehouse. When quantity supplied exceeds quantity demanded at a given price, economists call this a **surplus**. The surplus compact disc players are

surplus *situation in which quantity supplied is greater than quantity demanded; also known as excess supply*

134 Prices

excess supply, so something will have to change to bring the market to equilibrium.

As you read in Section 1, suppliers will respond to excess supply by reducing prices. As the price falls from $600 to $400, more consumers decide to buy compact disc players, and the quantity demanded rises. The combined movement of falling prices and increasing quantity demanded can be seen in Figure 6.6 as a change from point a to point c. Notice that this change is a movement along the demand curve, not a shift of the entire demand curve.

Eventually, the price falls to a point where quantity supplied and quantity demanded are equal, and excess supply is no longer a problem. This new equilibrium point, shown at point c in Figure 6.6, marks a lower equilibrium price and a higher equilibrium quantity sold than before the supply curve shifted. This is how equilibrium changes when supply increases, and the entire supply curve shifts to the right.

Changing Equilibrium

As the price of compact disc players fell due to better technology, more and more people bought them. The equilibrium in this market, then, started moving gradually downward and to the right. This is where the quantities demanded and supplied are higher, and the prices are lower.

The supply curve for compact disc players has been moving to the right ever since the first $1,000 compact disc players were sold. The curve continues to shift today as new technology continues to drive down the production cost and market price of the most basic machines.

Equilibrium is usually not an unchanging, single point on a graph. The equilibrium in the compact disc player market has always been in motion. The market equilibrium follows the intersection of the demand curve and the supply curve as that point moves downward along the demand curve.

Equilibrium is a "moving target" that changes as market conditions change. Manufacturers and retail sellers of compact

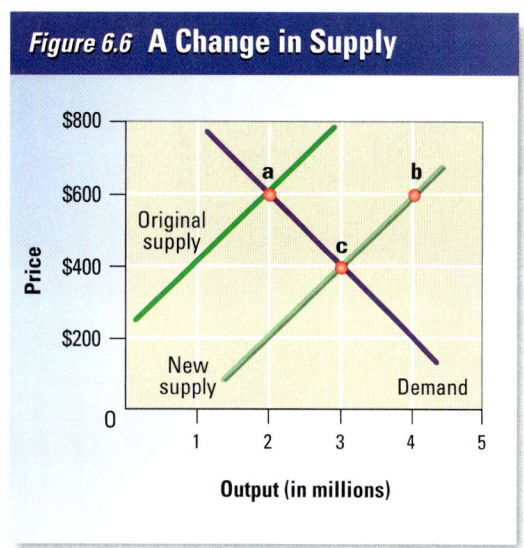

Figure 6.6 A Change in Supply

Output (in millions)

When supply increases, prices fall, and quantity demanded increases to reach a new equilibrium.

Supply and Demand
How would you compare the location of the new equilibrium to that of the old equilibrium?

disc players are constantly searching for a new equilibrium as technology and methods of production change. Consumers recognize this "searching" by the frequent price changes, sales, and rebates on compact disc players. Each of these tactics is designed to keep the machines moving out of stores as fast as new machines come in.

A Fall in Supply

Just as new technology or lower costs can shift the supply curve to the right, so other factors that reduce supply can shift the supply curve to the left. Consider the market for cars. If the price of steel rises, automobile manufacturers will produce fewer cars at all price levels, and the supply curve will shift to the left. If auto workers strike for higher wages, and the company must pay more for labor to build the same number of cars, supply will decrease. If the government imposes a new tax on car manufacturers, supply will decrease. In all of these cases, the supply curve will move to the left, because the quantity supplied is lower at all price levels.

▲ Almost every fall, a trendy toy emerges as one that every child "must have." Demand for these toys increases.

shortage *situation in which quantity demanded is greater than quantity supplied; also known as excess demand*

search costs *the financial and opportunity costs consumers pay when searching for a good or service*

When the supply curve shifts to the left, the equilibrium price and quantity sold will change as well. This process is the exact opposite of the change that results from an increase in supply. As the supply curve shifts to the left, suppliers raise their prices and the quantity demanded falls. The new equilibrium point will be at a spot along the demand curve above and to the left of the original equilibrium point. The

market price is higher than before, and the quantity sold is lower.

Shifts in Demand

Almost every year, around November, a new doll or toy emerges as a nationwide fad. People across the country race to stores at opening time and stand in long lines to buy that year's version of Tickle Me Elmo or Pokémon.

As you read in Chapter 4, these fads reflect the impact of consumer tastes and advertising on consumer behavior. Fads like these, in which demand rises quickly, are real-life examples of a rapid, rightward shift in a market demand curve. Figure 6.7 shows how a rapid, unexpected increase in market demand will affect the equilibrium in a market for a hypothetical, trendy toy.

The Problem of Excess Demand

In Figure 6.7, the fad causes a sudden increase in market demand, and the demand curve shifts to the right. This shift leads to excess demand at the original price of $24 (point b). Before the fad began, quantity demanded and quantity supplied were equal at 300,000 dolls, shown at point a. On the graph, excess demand appears as a gap between the quantity supplied of 300,000 dolls and the new quantity demanded of 500,000 at $24, shown at point b. This is an increase of 200,000 in the quantity demanded. Economists would also describe this as a **shortage** of 200,000 dolls.

In the stores that carry the dolls, excess demand appears as bare shelves and long lines. Excess demand also appears in the form of **search costs**—the financial and opportunity costs consumers pay in searching for a good or service. Driving to different stores and calling different towns to find an available doll are both examples of search costs.

In the meantime, the available dolls must be rationed, or distributed, in some other manner. In this case, long lines, limits on the quantities each customer may buy, and

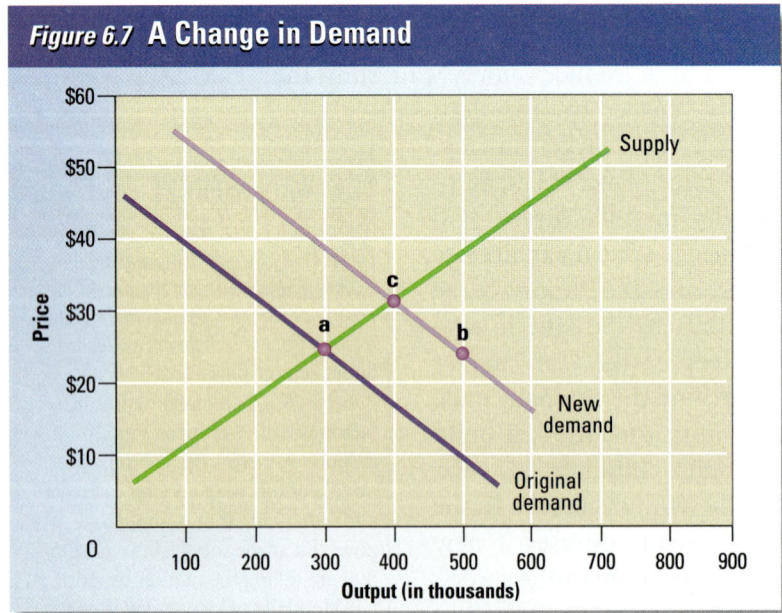

Figure 6.7 A Change in Demand

[Graph showing Price (in dollars from $0 to $60) on vertical axis and Output (in thousands, from 100 to 900) on horizontal axis. Lines shown: Supply, New demand, Original demand, with points a, b, and c marked.]

When demand shifts, price and quantity supplied change to create a new equilibrium.
Prices and Markets What happens to prices when the demand curve shifts to the right?

"first come, first serve" policies are used to distribute the dolls among customers.

Return to Equilibrium

As time passes, firms will react to the signs of excess demand and raise their prices. In fact, customers may actually push prices up on their own if there is "bidding" in the market, as there is for real estate, antiques, fine art, and hard-to-find items.

If a parent cannot find the doll he wants at the store, he might offer the store keeper an extra $5 to guarantee him a doll from the next shipment. Through these methods, the market price will rise until the quantity supplied equals the quantity demanded at 300,000 dolls. All of these dolls are sold at the new equilibrium price of $30, shown at point c in Figure 6.7.

When demand increases, both the equilibrium price and the equilibrium quantity also increase. The demand curve has shifted, and the equilibrium point has moved, setting in motion market forces that push the price and quantity toward their new equilibrium values.

A Fall in Demand

When a fad passes its peak, demand can fall as quickly as it rose. Excess demand turns into excess supply for the once-popular toy as parents look for a new, more trendy gift for their children. Overflowing store shelves and silent cash registers, the symptoms of excess supply, replace long lines and bidding wars.

When demand falls, the demand curve shifts to the left. Suppliers respond by cutting prices on their inventory. Price and quantity sold slide down along the supply curve to a new equilibrium point at point a in Figure 6.7. The end of the fad restores the original price and quantity supplied.

Section 2 Assessment

Key Terms and Main Ideas

1. What conditions lead to a **surplus**?
2. What is an example of a **search cost**?

Applying Economic Concepts

3. *Decision Making* Explain how the equilibrium price and quantity sold of eggs will change in the following cases. Remember that they need not move in the same direction. **(a)** An outbreak of food poisoning is traced to eggs. **(b)** Scientists breed a new chicken that lays twice as many eggs each week. **(c)** A popular talk show host convinces her viewers to eat an egg a day.

4. *Critical Thinking* What will happen to suppliers in a market if there is a surplus of the good they sell, but no supplier can afford to lower prices?

5. *Math Practice* The graph at the right shows the effects of a demand shift on a particular market. **(a)** Has demand increased or decreased? Explain. **(b)** What are the original equilibrium price and quantity sold? **(c)** What are the new equilibrium price and quantity sold? **(d)** A new tax raises the cost of production. How does the supply curve react? **(e)** Give a market price and quantity sold that might be a new equilibrium point after this cost increase.

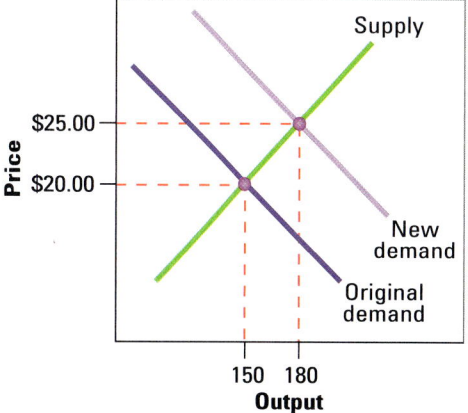

Take It to the NET Search costs are continually dropping as computers and the Internet make searching easier and easier. Choose an item you or a classmate plans to purchase within the next month and find the best price using the Internet. Use the links provided at the following Web site for help in completing this activity. **www.phschool.com**

ECONOMIC

Profile

Economist

Entrepreneur

Michael Dell (b. 1965)

In 1984, Michael Dell took $1,000 and an idea, and began to build a computer business. Defying the odds against the success of a new business, Dell built what is now the largest direct-sale computer manufacturer in the world. In the process, he made millionaires out of investors who had faith in a young person and his ideas.

From Out of a Dorm Room

"I often wonder what new development will come along and totally change the face of our industry," says computer magnate Michael Dell. This visionary Texan has not only adapted well to change, he has revolutionized the way products are marketed and sold. Dell has been called the Henry Ford of the computer industry.

As a teenager in the early 1980s, Dell saw a future in personal computers (PCs). During his freshman year at the University of Texas, he sold PCs from his dorm room. Business was so good that the next year he quit school and, with $1,000 in capital, started a company. Fifteen years later, Dell Computer Corporation was a $19.9 billion business, with more than $18 million a day in sales on its Internet site alone.

Direct From Dell

When Dell started his company in 1984, PC manufacturers were all selling standard models through retail stores. Dell's vision was to sell his computers directly to consumers. This approach allowed him to customize each computer to the customer's needs. It also enabled Dell to sell PCs for less than his competitors did because there were no retailers marking up his prices to make a profit for their stores.

Dell's direct-marketing model had cost advantages as well. By custom-building each computer, he did not have to maintain warehouses full of unsold goods. The company took each order by phone or fax and shipped the finished computer within two weeks. The low inventory costs were also reflected in Dell's pricing. Not only did Dell's customers receive exactly what they needed, they got it at a lower price than that of his competitors' standard PCs.

Dell in Cyberspace

As the Internet grew in the early 1990s, Dell saw new opportunities. Most people at the time viewed the Internet as a source of information. "Commerce . . . was pretty much restricted to ordering T-shirts," Dell says. "But it . . . struck me that if you could order a T-shirt online, you could order anything—including a computer." In 1996, Dell became one of the first manufacturers to offer products via the Internet. The Dell Web site allows visitors to create a computer system, calculate its price, place an order, pay, and even arrange financing online.

The success of this "Dell direct" approach to the sale of computers has shaped how other business sectors, such as banking and the auto industry, market and sell their products.

CHECK FOR UNDERSTANDING

1. Source Reading Summarize the factors that allowed Dell Computer Corporation to sell personal computers at lower prices than its competitors could.

2. Critical Thinking What would be likely to happen to its prices if Dell Computer Corporation opened stores across the country? Explain why.

3. Learn More How has Dell Computer Corporation strived to maintain its success against competitors who have imitated the Dell direct sales approach?

138

The Role of Prices

Objectives

After studying this section you will be able to:

1. **Analyze** the role of prices in a free market.
2. **List** the advantages of a price-based system.
3. **Explain** how a price-based system leads to a wider choice of goods and more efficient allocation of resources.
4. **Describe** the relationship between prices and the profit incentive.

Section Focus

Goods and services can be divided up among buyers and sellers by a central plan or a price-based market system. Prices allow an efficient, flexible exchange of goods.

Key Terms

supply shock
rationing
black market
spillover costs

In Section 1, you read how supply and demand interact to determine the equilibrium price and quantity sold in a market. You also read about how those prices change over time. Prices are a key element of equilibrium. Price changes can move markets toward equilibrium and solve problems of excess supply and excess demand. In this section we will discuss the importance of prices and the role they play.

In a free market, prices are a tool for distributing goods and resources throughout the economy. Prices are nearly always the most efficient way to allocate, or distribute, resources. The alternative method for distributing goods and resources, namely a centrally planned economy, is not nearly as efficient as a market system based on prices.

Kevin decides to buy a sweater for his sister for her birthday next month. He goes to a nearby shopping center and compares the prices of several different sweaters. Kevin finds that a department store offers cotton cable-knit sweaters for $30 to $50 and soft cashmere sweaters for $110. He visits other stores and finds that he can spend as little as $20 for an acrylic sweater or as much as $350 for a designer cashmere sweater. Kevin considers his sister's tastes and his own income and buys his sister one of the less expensive cotton sweaters.

Later, Kevin uses his computer to browse catalogs of mail-order stores. He's surprised to find a sweater very similar to the one he bought, but it's on sale for $5 less, shipping

Prices in the Free Market

Prices serve a vital role in a free market economy. Prices help move land, labor, and capital into the hands of producers, and finished goods into the hands of buyers. The following example shows the benefits of a system based on free market prices.

▼ **Sweaters sell for different prices, depending on quality, style, and type of yarn.**

included. Kevin decides to buy the sweater on-line with his credit card and return the sweater he bought at the mall.

Kevin's story, familiar to anyone who has shopped for a gift, demonstrates the importance of prices to the free market system. The simple process of buying a gift for a friend or relative would be much more complicated and inefficient without the price system.

The Advantages of Prices

Prices provide a language for buyers and sellers. Could you conceive of a market-place without prices? Without prices as a standard measure of value, a seller would have to barter for goods by bidding shoes or apples to purchase a sweater. A sweater might be worth two pairs of shoes to one customer, but another customer might be willing to trade three pairs of shoes for the same sweater. The supplier would have no consistent and accurate way to measure demand for a product.

Price as an Incentive

Buyers and sellers alike look at prices to find information on a good's demand and supply. The law of supply and the law of demand describe how people and firms respond to a change in prices. In these cases, prices are a signal that tell a consumer or producer how to adjust. Prices communicate to both buyers and sellers whether goods are in short supply or readily available.

In the example of the popular doll discussed in Section 2, the increased demand for the doll told suppliers that people wanted more dolls, and soon! However, the signal that producers respond to is not simply the demand, but the high price consumers are willing to pay for the doll, well above the usual retail price. This higher price tells firms that people want more dolls, but also that the firms can earn more profit by producing more dolls, because they are in demand. Therefore, rising prices in a market will cause existing firms to produce more goods and will attract new firms to enter a market.

Prices as Signals

Think of prices as a traffic light. A relatively high price is a green light that tells producers that a specific good is in demand and that they should use their resources to produce more. New suppliers will also join the market. A low price, however, is a red light to producers that a good is being overproduced. In this case, low prices tell a supplier that he or she might earn higher profits by using existing resources to produce a different product.

For consumers, a low price is a green light to buy more of a good. A low price indicates that the good carries a low opportunity cost for the consumer, and offers a good buying opportunity. By the same token, a high price is a red light to stop and think carefully before buying.

Flexibility

Another important aspect of prices is that they are flexible. When a supply shift or a demand shift changes the equilibrium in a market, price and quantity supplied need to change to solve problems of too much or too little demand. In many markets, prices are much more flexible than output levels.

▼ Drought, floods, or frost can kill crops and cause a supply shock.

Prices can be easily increased to solve a problem of excess demand, and they can be just as easily decreased to eliminate a problem of excess supply.

For example, a **supply shock** is a sudden shortage of a good, such as gasoline or wheat. A supply shock creates a problem of excess demand because suppliers can no longer meet the needs of consumers. The immediate problem is how to divide up the available supply among consumers.

What are the options? Increasing supply can be a time-consuming and difficult process. For example, wheat takes time to plant, grow, and harvest. **Rationing,** or dividing up goods and services using criteria other than price, is expensive and can take a long time to organize. Rationing is the basis of central planning, which you read about in Chapter 2.

Raising prices is the quickest way to resolve excess demand. A quick rise in prices will reduce quantity demanded to the same level as quantity supplied and avoid the problem of distribution. The people who have enough money and value the good most highly will pay the most for the good. These consumers will be the only consumers still in the market at the higher price, and the market will settle at a new equilibrium.

Price System Is "Free"

Unlike central planning, a distribution system based on prices costs nothing to administer. Central planning requires central planners who collect information on production and decide how resources are to be distributed. In the former Soviet Union, the government employed thousands of bureaucrats in an enormous agency called GOSPLAN to organize the economy. During World War II, the United States government set up the Office of Price Administration to prevent inflation and coordinate rationing of important goods.

On the other hand, free market pricing distributes goods through millions of decisions made daily by consumers and suppliers. Kevin, from the beginning of the section, looks at the prices of sweaters and decides which one to buy for his sister and

which supplier to buy it from. A farmer reads the reports from the commodity exchanges and decides whether to grow corn instead of soybeans next year. Everyone is familiar with how prices work and knows how to use them. In short, prices help goods flow through the economy without a central plan.

A Wide Choice of Goods

One of the benefits of a market-based economy is the diversity of goods and services consumers can buy. Price gives suppliers a way to allow consumers to choose among similar products. Kevin could buy his sister an acrylic sweater for $20, a cotton sweater for $40, or a cashmere sweater for much more. Based on his income and his sister's tastes, Kevin decided on a cotton sweater at the lower end of the price range. The prices provided an easy way for Kevin to narrow his choices to a certain price range. Prices also allow producers to target the audience they want with the products that will sell best to that audience.

In a command economy, however, one organization decides what goods are produced and how much stores will charge for these goods. To limit their costs,

supply shock *a sudden shortage of a good*

rationing *a system of allocating scarce goods and services using criteria other than price*

▼ During the World War II era, civilians could only buy a certain amount of meat and other goods each month. People needed both cash and ration points to buy.

and the government controlled the distribution of food and consumer goods. Choices were limited, and consumers felt, rightly or wrongly, that some people fared better than others. However, rationing was chosen because a price-based system might have put food and housing out of the reach of some Americans, and the government wanted to guarantee every civilian a minimum standard of living in wartime.

▲ North Korea's Communist government has built identical apartment blocks for its citizens, who do not get to choose where to live.

central planners restrict production to a few varieties of each product. As a result, consumers in the former Communist states of Eastern Europe and the Soviet Union had far fewer choices of goods than consumers in Western Europe and the United States. You may ask why Communist governments used a command economic system. The answer is, in part, that they hoped to distribute wealth evenly throughout their society. As a result, the government of the Soviet Union built whole neighborhoods of identical apartment blocks and supermarkets with names such as "Supermarket No. 3."

Rationing and Shortages

Although goods in the Soviet Union were inexpensive, consumers could not always find them. When they did, they often had to wait hours for eggs or soap, years for apartments or telephones. The United States experienced similar problems, although far less severe, when the government instituted temporary price controls during World War II.

Although rationing in the United States was only a short-term hardship, like rationing in the Soviet Union it was expensive and left many consumers unhappy. The needs of the U.S. armed forces for food, metal, and rubber during World War II created tremendous shortages at home,

black market *a market in which goods are sold illegally*

The Black Market

Despite the ration system, the federal government was unable to control the supply of all goods passing through the economy. A butcher could sell a steak without asking for ration points, or a landlord might be willing to rent an apartment at the rate fixed by the government only if the renter threw in a cash "bonus" or an extra two months' rent as a "deposit."

When people conduct business without regard for government controls on price or quantity, they are said to do business on the **black market**. Black markets allow consumers to pay more so they can buy a good when rationing makes it otherwise unavailable. Although black markets are a nearly inevitable consequence of rationing, such trade is illegal and strongly discouraged by governments.

Efficient Resource Allocation

All of the advantages of a free market allow prices to allocate resources efficiently. Efficient resource allocation means that economic resources—land, labor, and capital—will be used for their most valuable purposes. A market system, with its freely changing prices, ensures that resources go to the uses that consumers value most highly. A price-based system also ensures that resource use will adjust to the changing demands of consumers.

These changes take place without any central control, because the people who own resources—landowners, workers who sell their labor, and people who provide capital to firms—seek the largest possible returns. How do people earn the largest returns? By selling their resources to the highest bidder. The highest bidder will be that firm that produces goods that are in the highest demand. Therefore, the resources will flow to the uses that are most highly valued by consumers. This flow is the most efficient way to use our society's scarce resources.

Prices and the Profit Incentive

Suppose that scientists predicted extremely hot weather for the coming summer. In most parts of the country, consumers would buy up air conditioners and fans, to prepare for the heat. Power companies would buy reserves of oil and natural gas to supply these appliances with enough power. Since demand would exceed supply, consumers would bid up the price of fans, and power plants would bid up the price of fuel. Suppliers would recognize the possibility for profit in the higher prices charged for these goods, and they would produce more fans and air conditioners. Oil and natural gas fields would hire workers to pump more fuel for power plants. Eventually, more fans, air conditioners, and fuel would move into the market. The potential heat wave would have created a need for certain goods, and the rise in prices would have given producers an incentive to meet this need.

As we previously noted, efficient resource allocation occurs naturally in a market system as long as the system works reasonably well. Landowners tend to use their scarce property

Global Connections

Rationing and Prices Cuba has two different systems for distributing goods. Some goods are rationed, while many others are sold in stores at different prices. The difference between the two systems is that the price-based system uses not Cuba's currency, the peso, but the United States dollar. Many Cubans earn dollars by working in tourism or as gifts from family members outside the country. Cubans with dollars can buy a variety of food and clothing at stores and restaurants that only accept dollars. Cubans who are paid in pesos must get their food through the state's rationing system. Prices are very low, but food is rationed, and the government provides each person with a limited amount of grain, coffee, salt, and other basic foods.

in the most profitable manner. Workers usually move toward high-paying jobs, and capital will be invested in the firms that pay the highest returns.

The Wealth of Nations

Adam Smith made this point in his famous book *The Wealth of Nations*, published in 1776. Smith explained that it was not because of charity that the baker and the butcher provided people with their food. Rather, they provide people with bread and meat because prices are such that they

▼ **The People's Republic of China is moving away from a command economy and rationing to a more market-based economy.**

▲ The price of water affects how efficiently it is used. When water is provided to farmers at a higher price, they have an incentive to irrigate more efficiently.

spillover costs *costs of production that affect people who have no control over how much of a good is produced*

will profit from doing so. In other words, businesses prosper by finding out what people want, and then providing it. This has proved to be a more efficient system than any other that has been tried in the modern era.

Market Problems

There are some exceptions to the general idea that markets lead to an efficient allocation of resources. The first problem, imperfect competition, can affect prices, and higher prices can affect consumer decisions.

If only a few firms are selling a product, there might not be enough competition among sellers to lower the market price down to the cost of production. When only one producer sells a good, this producer will usually charge a higher price than we would see in a market with several competitive businesses. In the following chapter, you will read more about how markets behave under conditions of imperfect competition.

A second problem can involve **spillover costs,** also known as externalities, that include costs of production, such as air and water pollution, that "spill over" onto people who have no control over how much of a good is produced. Since producers do not have to pay spillover costs, their total costs seem artificially low, and they will produce more than the equilibrium quantity of the good. The extra costs will be paid by consumers.

Imperfect information is a third problem that can prevent a market from operating smoothly. If buyers and sellers do not have enough information to make informed choices about a product, they may not make the choice that is best for them.

Section 3 Assessment

Key Terms and Main Ideas

1. How does a **supply shock** affect equilibrium price and quantity?

2. How is **rationing** different from a price-based market system?

Applying Economic Concepts

3. *Decision Making* List three reasons why a price-based system works more efficiently than central planning.

4. *Critical Thinking* Give two examples of situations in which prices gave you an incentive to purchase or not purchase a good or service.

5. *Try This* Distribute $50 in play money to each student in your class. Then, ask students to bid for items from the following basket of goods and services: 10 pairs of movie tickets, 20 fine restaurant dinners, 40 bagels, 5 pairs of running shoes, and 30 hours of dog walking. **(a)** What prices were bid for these goods? **(b)** Why do you think some goods received higher bids than others? **(c)** What do you think would happen to the bids if the number of items for sale doubled?

6. *Critical Thinking* What do you think Adam Smith would think of rationing? Explain.

Take It to the NET

The gasoline crisis of the 1970s is one of the most memorable supply shocks in recent history. Why did it happen? How did it affect people's lives? Are we using resources more efficiently now? Prepare an outline to answer these questions. Use the links provided at the following Web site for help in completing this activity. **www.phschool.com**

What Made Beanie Babies So Successful?

Sarah Stephens has a passion—she loves Beanie Babies. Sarah is far from alone. She is one of millions of people—girls, boys, teenagers, and adults—caught up in the mania that made Beanie Babies the best-selling collectible toy animal in history.

Innovation Beanie Babies were the brainchild of Ty Warner, the founder and owner of Ty, Inc. In late 1993, he and his staff developed a line of beanbag animals. They made the toys more appealing than ordinary stuffed animals by giving each one a name and a birth date. The retail price they set for each animal was $4.99.

Pricing Within two years of the introduction of Beanie Babies, sales exceeded $100 million dollars annually. What were the reasons for this extraordinary success? It all began with pricing. From the beginning, Ty, Inc., decided to sell Beanie Babies at a modest price in order to sell a large number of Beanies. Even when sales started jumping through the roof, Ty resisted the natural temptation to raise the price of the product and stuck to the original price of $4.99. The affordability of the toy animals was one important key to their success.

▲ The success of Beanie Babies helped Ty Warner amass a personal fortune of more than a billion dollars.

Supply and Demand Another important factor was supply and demand. On a regular basis, Ty, Inc. withdrew some of the 250 different animals from the marketplace while introducing new ones, thus promoting Beanie Babies as collectibles. This, along with the company's strict policy of limiting the number of Beanie Babies it would sell each month to any one store, continued to fuel the demand for the product.

Ty's success with Beanie Babies led other toy makers to introduce similar toys to challenge Ty's place in the market. Finally in 1999, Ty announced that it was stopping production of Beanie Babies. To many market analysts, it was a bold move designed to rekindle intense demand for a possible comeback for Beanies.

"I know they'll bring them back," says Sarah Stephens. "And who knows, the ones I own may now be worth even more some day." In early 2000, Ty announced it would begin production of Beanie Babies again.

Applying Economic Ideas

1. What role did pricing play in the Beanie Baby success story?

2. How did Ty, Inc., employ the principles of supply and demand?

Chapter 6 Assessment

Chapter Summary

A summary of major ideas in Chapter 6 appears below. See also the **Guide to the Essentials of Economics,** which provides additional review and test practice of key concepts in Chapter 6.

Section 1 Combining Supply and Demand (pp. 125–131)

In an uncontrolled market, the price and quantity sold of a good will move to an **equilibrium** point where the quantity supplied equals the quantity demanded. The government can set a maximum price in a market with a **price ceiling,** or a minimum price with a **price floor.** Although some consumers or producers benefit, these moves distort the market and lead to **excess demand** or **excess supply.**

Section 2 Changes in Market Equilibrium (pp. 133–137)

A market moves to a new equilibrium when there is a shift in either supply or demand. In the short term, a **shortage** will occur if quantity demanded exceeds quantity supplied, or a **surplus** will occur if quantity supplied exceeds quantity demanded. Market price and quantity sold adjust, and buyers and sellers change their behavior over time.

Section 3 The Role of Prices (pp. 139–144)

In a free market, prices provide a common language that enables land, labor, and capital to flow into the hands of those who value them most. Prices tell consumers and suppliers which goods are in short supply and which are plentiful. Individual decisions lead to an efficient market with a wide choice of goods. The alternative to a price-based market, **rationing,** is inefficient and difficult to carry out successfully.

Key Terms

Match the following definitions with the terms listed below. You will not use all the terms.

price ceiling	shortage
excess supply	price floor
supply shock	search costs
equilibrium	rationing

1. The point at which quantity demanded and quantity supplied are equal
2. The financial and opportunity costs consumers pay in searching for a good or service
3. A system of allocating scarce goods and services by criteria other than price
4. A sudden drop in the supply of a good
5. Any situation in which quantity supplied exceeds quantity demanded
6. Any situation in which quantity demanded exceeds quantity supplied
7. A government-mandated minimum price that must be paid for a good or service

Using Graphic Organizers

8. On a separate sheet of paper, copy the tree map below. Then complete it with examples of how government actions can affect prices. Include whether prices are in equilibrium or disequilibrium before and after the government's actions.

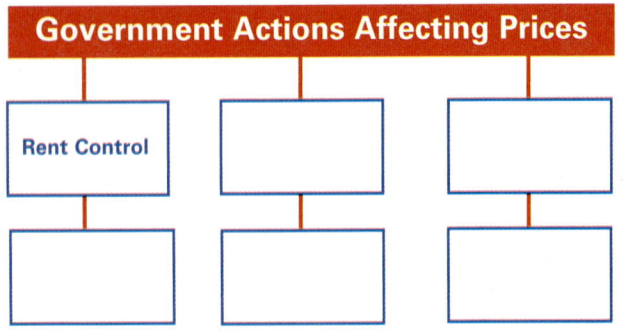

Government Actions Affecting Prices

Rent Control

Reviewing Main Ideas

9. What factors can lead to disequilibrium? Describe these factors in your own words.
10. What role does the government play in determining some prices?
11. What problem can a price floor cause?
12. How do prices act as a "language" in the free market?
13. Turn to Figure 6.1 on page 126. Explain how to interpret the supply and demand graph (left), using the supply and demand schedule (right).

Critical Thinking

14. **Recognizing Cause and Effect** Why have some cities and towns passed rent control laws? How do these laws affect price equilibrium? What happens when these laws are repealed?
15. **Drawing Inferences** How do computers lower search costs for producers and consumers? What effect does this have on price equilibrium?
16. **Synthesizing Information** How do prices in the free market lead to efficient resource allocation? Describe an example from your experience.

Problem-Solving Activity

17. Suppose that a recent snowstorm has caused a supply shock in the market for sugar in the United States. How would you attempt to solve the problems that follow the storm? What actions are available to both consumers and producers?

Economics Journal

Essay Writing Compare your list of minimum wages for chores with the lists of other students. How do they compare? Use your classroom data to create four supply curves, one for each task. How might the minimum wage affect the supply of labor for these chores? Draw a line representing the current minimum wage in your city or state as a price floor.

Skills for Life

Determining Cause and Effect Review the steps shown on page 132; then answer the following questions using the statements below.

18. Which of the statements describe cause-effect relationships?
19. Identify three phrases used to identify the cause of a cause-effect relationship in these statements.
20. Identify three terms used to identify the effect of a cause-effect relationship in these statements.
21. Which statement includes more than one cause-effect relationship?
22. Read statement (f). Create a flowchart describing the cause-effect relationships shown.

STATEMENTS
a) Oranges are grown mainly in the South and West, especially Florida and California.
b) The price of oranges in the United States rose this year because of a small harvest.
c) Some people enjoy orange juice with breakfast, while others like to drink it after exercise.
d) Due to the early frost in much of the South, this year's orange crop was poor.
e) Overall orange juice production was down this year, and several national brands lost money. However, the American dairy industry saw an increase in milk sales. Americans did not drink as much orange juice as they had in recent years.
f) This year's disastrous orange crop caused many brands to raise their prices. Because of the high prices, many consumers switched to other juices. Several national brands reduced orange juice production and researched new products that would meet this alternative demand.

Take It to the NET

Chapter 6 Self-Test As a final review activity, take the Chapter 6 Self-Test in the Social Studies area at the Web site listed below, and receive immediate feedback on your answers. The test consists of 20 multiple-choice questions designed to test your understanding of the chapter content.
www.phschool.com

Market Equilibrium

The supply of a good (or service) and the demand for it interact in the market. If the quantity supplied or demanded goes up or down, the price of that good or service will also be affected. Similarly, changes in supply or demand influence the quantity produced. At a certain point, the quantity that people want is equal to the quantity available, and the price stabilizes. This situation is called *market equilibrium*.

Preparing the Simulation

How does the market reach a state of equilibrium? In this simulation, you and your peers will act as apple producers and consumers. You will meet in the market to agree on an exchange of apples at a certain price. You'll see how both producers and consumers change their requirements in order to reach an agreement.

Step 1: Your class will be divided into two equal groups, Producers and Consumers.

Step 2: The Consumers group will prepare 20 slips of colored paper that represent the prices a Consumer is willing to pay for a bushel of apples. Consumers will number the first 10 slips from $4 to $40 by fours ($4, $8, and so on), and repeat for the second 10 slips. Meanwhile, the Producers group will prepare 20 slips of paper in a contrasting color that represent the cost of producing a bushel of apples. Producers will number the first 10 slips from $5 to $50 by fives ($5, $10, and so on), and repeat for the second 10 slips.

Step 3: Put the Consumer slips into a box. Each person in the Consumer group should draw a slip. If you are a Consumer, the amount on the slip is the maximum price you are willing to pay for a bushel of apples.

Step 4: Put the Producer slips into a box. Each person in the Producer group should

▲ The profit from the sale of these apples is the difference between the sale price and the cost to produce the apples.

draw a slip from the box. If you are a Producer, the amount on the slip is your cost of producing a bushel of apples.

Conducting the Simulation

There will be three trading periods. Your goal is to make the best deal you can—to buy below your maximum price if you are a Consumer, and to sell for more than your cost if you are a Producer.

If you are a Consumer, your score will be the difference between the price you are willing to pay for apples and the price you actually pay. For example, if the price on your slip is $50, and you buy apples for $30, your score is $20. If you are an apple Producer, your score is your profit—the difference

Materials

20 slips of paper (one color)

20 slips of paper (contrasting color)

2 small boxes

notebook paper

Trading Period 1

Producers and Consumers will meet in a trading area and try to make deals. Each person can buy or sell one bushel of apples in each period. When you reach an agreement, report the price and your own score to the teacher. The trading period will end when no more pairs of Producers and Consumers can make a deal.

Trading Period 2

Negotiate as in Trading Period 1. You have another chance to save money (Consumers) or increase your profits (Producers). Again, report your deals to your teacher.

Trading Period 3

Before this trading period begins, one third of the Producers will move into the Consumer group. (The costs on their slips of paper now become the maximum prices they are willing to pay.) Then make trades as in the first two periods. This trading period will end when no more pairs of Producers and Consumers can make a deal. Take note of any price differences produced by an increase in the number of Consumers and a decrease in the number of Producers. Record your transaction with your teacher.

between your cost of producing the apples and the price at which you can sell them.

You do not have to buy or sell apples in any trading period. If you do not, however, your score for that round will be $0. Your teacher will keep a record of all the transactions made. You should also keep a record of your own scores. The final score is the sum of all your savings (Consumers) or profits (Producers).

Transaction Chart

	Trading Period 1	Trading Period 2	Trading Period 3
Number of deals made			
Number of Consumers unable to buy			
Number of Producers unable to sell			
Average price for a bushel of apples			
Lowest price			
Highest price			

Simulation Analysis

On a sheet of notebook paper, create a transaction chart like the one on this page. As a class, complete the transaction chart using information that you reported to your teacher. Then discuss the following questions as a group.

1. In Trading Periods 1 and 2, when was it a good idea for a Consumer not to buy apples?
2. When might a Producer choose not to sell his or her apples?
3. What was the effect of increasing the total number of Consumers in Trading Period 3? What would happen to the apple market if the number of Producers increased instead?
4. **Predicting Consequences** What would happen in this market if all the Producers got together and agreed on one price for apples?

149

If a single firm produced all computer software, life might be easier because all software would be compatible. So why has the government tried to prevent one company from dominating the software market? When there are only one or two firms in a market, consumers have fewer choices, and prices are likely to be higher.

In this chapter you will read about four different types of markets, or market structures. The four structures differ mainly in the number of firms that compete within them.

Economics Journal

Write down the names of three major companies: one with very little competition, one with one or two important competitors, and one with many competitors. Which situation do you think describes most markets?

Keep It Current

Items marked with this logo are periodically updated on the Internet. Keep up-to-date with what's in the news. To get current information on market structures go to www.phschool.com

Section 1   Perfect Competition

Preview

Objectives

After studying this section you will be able to:

1. **Describe** the four conditions that are in place in a perfectly competitive market.
2. **List** two common barriers that prevent firms from entering a market.
3. **Describe** prices and output in a perfectly competitive market.

Section Focus

Perfect competition exists when a market has many buyers and sellers of the same good. Few markets are perfectly competitive because barriers keep companies from entering or leaving the market easily.

Key Terms

perfect competition
commodity
barrier to entry
imperfect competition
start-up costs

The simplest market structure is known as **perfect competition**. It is also called pure competition. A perfectly competitive market is one with a large number of firms all producing essentially the same product. Pure competition assumes that the market is in equilibrium and that all firms sell the same product for the same price. However, each firm produces so little of the product compared to the total supply that no single firm can hope to influence prices. The only decision such producers can make is how much to produce, given their production costs and the market price.

Four Conditions for Perfect Competition

While very few industries meet all of the conditions for perfect competition, some come close. Examples include the markets for many farm products and the stocks traded on the New York Stock Exchange. Both of these examples fulfill four strict requirements for a perfectly competitive market:

1. Many buyers and sellers participate in the market.
2. Sellers offer identical products.
3. Buyers and sellers are well informed about products.
4. Sellers are able to enter and exit the market freely.

Many Buyers and Sellers

Perfectly competitive markets require many participants on both the buying and the selling sides. No individual can be powerful enough to buy or sell enough goods to influence the total market quantity or the market price. Everyone in the market must accept the market price as given.

As we saw in Chapter 6, supply and demand interact to determine both price and output. If a market has many independent buyers and sellers, it is not very likely that large enough groups of either buyers or sellers will work together to bargain for better prices. Instead, the market determines price without any influence from individual suppliers or consumers.

perfect competition
a market structure in which a large number of firms all produce the same product

▼ **The market for tomatoes comes close to perfect competition because a large number of firms sell tomatoes, and one tomato is very much like another.**

► A pushcart business is easy and inexpensive to begin, while a steel mill requires a large building and costly machinery.

commodity *a product that is the same no matter who produces it, such as petroleum, notebook paper, or milk*

Identical Products

In a perfectly competitive market, there are no differences between the products sold by different suppliers. This is the second condition for perfect competition. If a rancher needs to buy corn to feed his cattle, he will not care which farmer grew the corn, as long as every farm is willing to deliver the corn he needs for the same price. If an investor buys a share of a company's stock, she will not care which particular share she is buying.

A product that is considered the same regardless of who makes or sells it is called a **commodity**. Examples of commodities include low-grade gasoline, notebook paper, and milk. Identical products are key to perfect competition for one reason: the buyer will not pay extra for one particular

company's goods. The buyer will always choose the supplier with the lowest price.

Informed Buyers and Sellers

The third condition for a perfectly competitive market is that buyers and sellers know enough about the market to find the best deal they can get. Under conditions of perfect competition, the market provides the buyer with full information about the features of the product and its price. For the market to work effectively, both buyers and sellers have clear incentives to gather as much information as possible.

In most markets, a buyer's willingness to find information about prices and availability represents a trade-off. The time spent gathering information must be worth the amount of money that will be saved. For example, most buyers would not search the Internet or visit a dozen convenience stores to save five cents on a pack of chewing gum.

Free Market Entry and Exit

The final condition of perfectly competitive markets is that firms must be able to enter them when they can make money and leave them when they can't earn enough to stay in business. For example, when the first pioneering companies began earning a lot of money selling frozen dinners, several competitors jumped into the market with

Global Connection

Informed Buyers The French government ensures that travelers will have complete information about the market for hotel rooms and restaurant meals. While hotels in the United States usually advertise only special discounts, every hotel in France must post in its lobby a list of rates for single and double rooms, with and without a sink, shower, or full bathroom. Restaurants must go further and post a long list of prices for dozens of items, leaving spaces blank if some common items are not on the menu.

their own products. Later, the firms withdrew from the market those dinners that consumers didn't buy.

Studies show that markets with more firms, and thus more competition, have lower prices. When one firm can keep others out of the market, it can sell its product at a higher price.

Barriers to Entry

Factors that make it difficult for new firms to enter a market are called **barriers to entry**. Barriers to entry can lead to **imperfect competition**. Common barriers to entry include start-up costs and technology.

Start-Up Costs

Entrepreneurs need to invest money in a new firm long before they can start earning income. Before a new sandwich shop can open, the owner needs to rent a store, buy a refrigerator, freezer, and oven, and print menus. The expenses that a new business must pay before the first product reaches the customer are called **start-up costs**.

When the start-up costs in a market are high, entrepreneurs are less likely to enter that market. As a result, markets that involve high start-up costs are less likely to be perfectly competitive markets. For example, the costs of starting up a sandwich shop are much lower than those involved in starting up a lumber mill or a giant supermarket. So, an entrepreneur with a small income is much more likely to try her luck with a sandwich shop.

The growth of the Internet has reduced the start-up costs in many markets, including the markets for books and music. The entrepreneur no longer needs to rent or buy a store in a good location. The shop window has moved to the Web. As a result, many markets have become more competitive.

Technology

When a school group needs to raise money, its members could sell goods like flowers, cookies, or candy. Some technically skilled students could offer to fix cars or bicycles. Very few student groups would be able to create and sell a new word-processing program.

Some markets require a high degree of technological know-how. A carpenter, pharmacist, or electrician can spend years in training before he or she has learned all the important skills. As a result, new entrepreneurs cannot easily enter these markets without a lot of preparation and study. Barriers of technology and know-how can keep a market from becoming perfectly competitive.

Price and Output

One of the primary characteristics of perfectly competitive markets is that they are efficient. Competition within these markets keeps both prices and production costs low. Firms must use all inputs—land, labor, organizational skills, machinery and equipment—to their best advantage. As a

barrier to entry *any factor that makes it difficult for a new firm to enter a market*

imperfect competition *a market structure that does not meet the conditions of perfect competition*

start-up costs *the expenses a firm must pay before it can begin to produce and sell goods*

Figure 7.1 Perfect Competition

Number of firms: Many

Variety of goods: None

Brand A Brand B Brand C Brand D Brand E Brand F

Barriers to entry: None

ENTRY

Control over prices: None

No Control

BUILDING KEY CONCEPTS

A perfectly competitive market must include a large number of suppliers selling the same good.
Competition What prevents any one firm from raising its prices?

In a perfectly competitive market, price and output reach their equilibrium levels.

Competition What factors allow a perfectly competitive market to reach equilibrium?

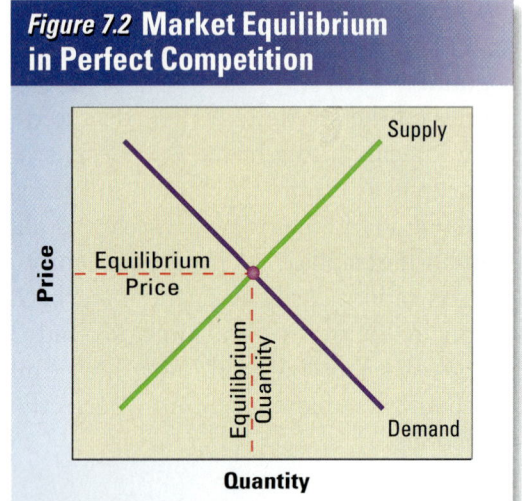

Figure 7.2 Market Equilibrium in Perfect Competition

result, the prices that consumers pay and the revenue that suppliers receive accurately reflect how much the market values the resources that have gone into the product. In a perfectly competitive market, prices correctly represent the opportunity costs of each product.

Prices in a perfectly competitive market are the lowest sustainable prices possible. Because many sellers compete to offer their commodities to buyers, intense competition forces prices down to the point where the prices just cover the most-efficient sellers' costs of doing business. As you read in Chapter 6, this equilibrium is usually the most efficient state a market can achieve.

We saw in Chapter 5 that producers earn their highest profits when they produce enough that their cost to produce one more unit exactly equals the market price of the unit. Since no supplier can influence prices in perfectly competitive markets, producers will make their output decisions based on their most efficient use of available land, labor, capital, and management skills.

In the long run, output will reach the point where each supplying firm just covers all of its costs, including paying the firm's owners enough to make the business worthwhile.

Section 1 Assessment

Key Terms and Main Ideas

1. Describe characteristics and give examples of **perfect competition** (pure competition).

2. How do **start-up costs** discourage entrepreneurs from entering a market?

3. What are two examples of **barriers to entry** in the magazine market?

4. Why must perfectly competitive markets always deal in **commodities**?

Applying Economic Concepts

5. *Decision Making* Which of these markets come close to perfect competition? **(a)** televisions **(b)** bottled water **(c)** pizza **(d)** school buses **(e)** white socks **(f)** baseballs **(g)** paper clips

6. *Try This* Suppose that you and your friends plan to open a new convenience store. Brainstorm a list of ten expenses that would be your start-up costs. Next, use the Sunday newspapers and the Internet to estimate how much each item on your list will cost. How much do you estimate you will spend before the store can open?

7. *Critical Thinking* Other than technology and start-up costs, what are two specific examples of barriers that could prevent a company or individual from entering a market?

Take It to the NET

Perfect competition requires that buyers be well informed about products. Assume that you are about to buy a new car or truck. Gather and analyze information from the Internet on three different models. Then make an informed decision about which model to buy. Use the links provided in the Social Studies area at the following Web site for help in completing this activity. **www.phschool.com**

Analyzing Political Cartoons

Political cartoons express the cartoonist's opinion on a recent issue or current event. The artist's purpose is to sway the opinions of the reader. To achieve this goal, cartoonists often use humor and exaggeration. When analyzing a political cartoon, be sure to examine all the images and words to help you fully understand the artist's intent. Use the following steps to analyze the cartoon below.

1. **Identify the symbols in the cartoon.** Symbolism plays a major role in helping political cartoons convey their messages. For example, Uncle Sam is often used as a symbol for the federal government of the United States. (**a**) What company's symbol is depicted in this cartoon? (**b**) Who is the old man?

2. **Analyze the meaning of the cartoon.** (**a**) What industry is being represented in this cartoon? (**b**) Why would the artist use Alexander Graham Bell? (**c**) What is Mr. Bell reading? Why is that relevant to this cartoon?

3. **Draw conclusions about the cartoonist's intent.** (**a**) What point is the artist trying to make about AT&T's telephone rates? (**b**) Does the artist believe the telephone industry has perfect competition? (**c**) Are you swayed by the cartoonist's opinion?

Additional Practice

Create your own political cartoon based on a current economic event or issue. Include symbolism, humor, and exaggeration in your cartoon.

Monopoly

Objectives

After studying this section you will be able to:

1. **Describe** characteristics and give examples of monopoly.
2. **Describe** how monopolies are formed, including government monopolies.
3. **Explain** how a firm with a monopoly sets output and price, and why companies practice price discrimination.

Section Focus

A firm has a monopoly when it controls an entire market. Because a monopolist controls the price of its product, a monopoly produces less and charges higher prices than would a perfectly competitive firm.

Key Terms

monopoly
economies of scale
natural monopoly
government monopoly
patent
franchise
license
price discrimination
market power

---

monopoly *a market dominated by a single seller*

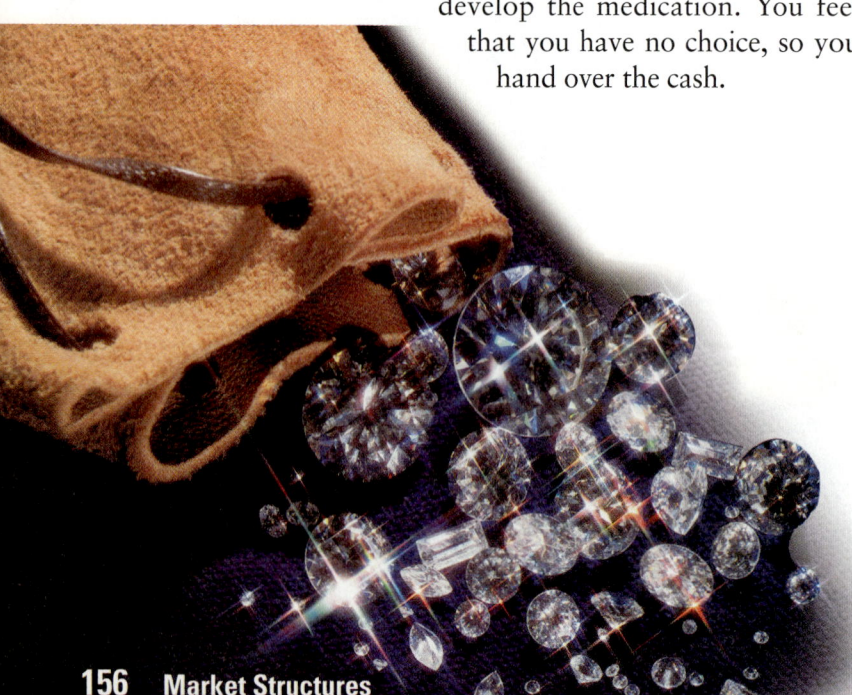

▼ One company, DeBeers of South Africa, has almost total control over the world's diamond supply.

You've gone to the emergency room with a high fever and a sharp pain in your leg. The doctor diagnoses a rare infection and writes a prescription for ten pills of a new medication that the government approved just last year. The doctor tells you that without this medication, your recovery will be slow.

At the pharmacy, you find that the medicine costs $97.35, or nearly ten dollars a pill! The pharmacist tells you that only one company has the right to produce the medicine, and it charges a high price because its scientists worked for years to develop the medication. You feel that you have no choice, so you hand over the cash.

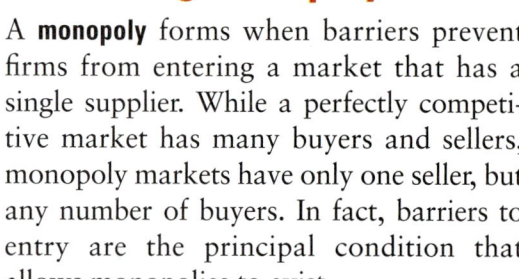

The market for prescription medicines is one of many markets in which monopolies can develop. In this section you will read about different types of monopolies and how they form.

Describing Monopoly

A **monopoly** forms when barriers prevent firms from entering a market that has a single supplier. While a perfectly competitive market has many buyers and sellers, monopoly markets have only one seller, but any number of buyers. In fact, barriers to entry are the principal condition that allows monopolies to exist.

While you can probably think of several companies that look and act like monopolies, economists use a strict set of requirements to define a monopoly. If we define the good or service provided by a company broadly enough, we can usually find substitute goods from a different source. For example, you might think that a convenience store on a highway in the middle of the desert has a monopoly. However, you could have carried more water in the car, or, if you had enough money, you might have flown across the desert instead of paying high prices for food and water during the car trip.

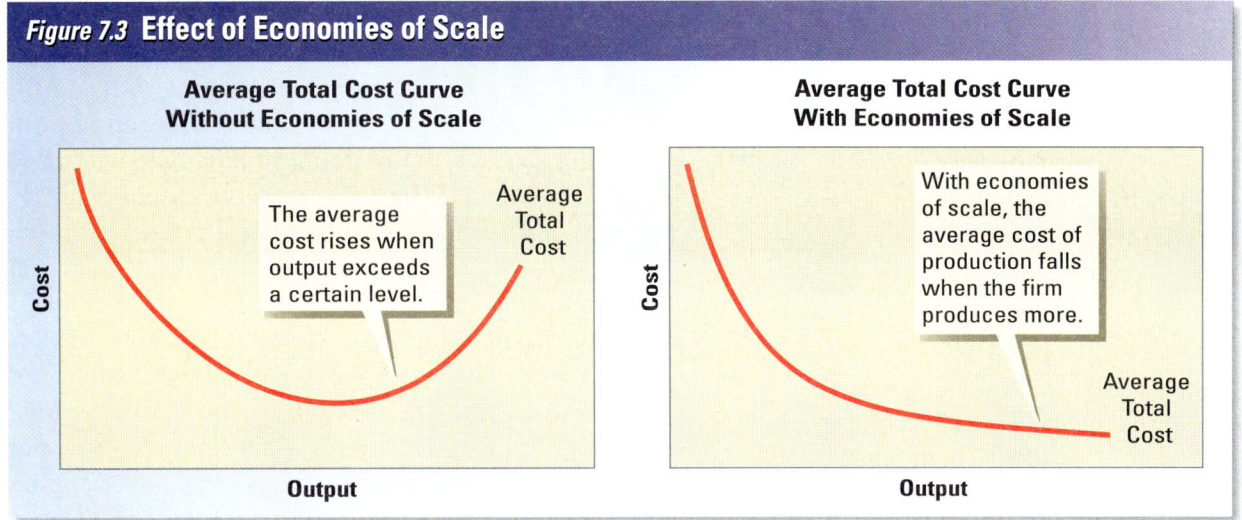

Figure 7.3 Effect of Economies of Scale

Average Total Cost Curve Without Economies of Scale

Cost

The average cost rises when output exceeds a certain level.

Average Total Cost

Output

Average Total Cost Curve With Economies of Scale

Cost

With economies of scale, the average cost of production falls when the firm produces more.

Average Total Cost

Output

With economies of scale, production costs continue to fall as output increases.
Markets and Prices Describe the cost curve for a firm without economies of scale.

The problem with monopolies is that they can take advantage of their market power and charge high prices. Given the law of demand, this means that the quantity of goods sold is lower than in a market with more than one seller. For this reason, the United States has outlawed some monopolistic practices, as you will read in Section 4.

Forming a Monopoly

All monopolies have one trait in common: a single seller in a market. However, different market conditions can create different types of monopolies.

Economies of Scale

If a firm's start-up costs are high, and its average costs fall for each additional unit it produces, then it enjoys what economists call **economies of scale**. Economies of scale are characteristics that cause a producer's average cost to drop as production rises.

The graph on the left in Figure 7.3 above shows an average total cost curve for a firm without economies of scale. Follow the curve from left to right. As output increases from zero, the average cost of each good drops, and the curve initially slopes

downward. This is because large, initial, fixed costs, like the cost of the factory and machinery, can be spread out among more and more goods as production rises. If the factory cost $1,000 to build and each unit of output costs $10 to make, producing one unit will cost $1,010, but producing two units will cost $1,020, or only $510 each. However, if the industry has limited economies of scale, output will eventually rise to a level at which the limited scale economies are exhausted, and the cost of making each unit will rise. The average cost of producing each good increases as output increases, and the curve slopes upward to match the rising cost per unit.

A factory in an industry with economies of scale never reaches this second stage of rising costs per unit. As production increases, the firm becomes more efficient, even at a level of output high enough to supply the entire market. The graph on the right in Figure 7.3 above shows how cost and output are related in economies of scale. Follow the curve from left to right. As output increases, the cost per unit falls, and continues to fall.

A good example is a hydroelectric plant, which generates electricity from a dam on a river. A large dam is expensive to build.

economies of scale *factors that cause a producer's average cost per unit to fall as output rises*

Figure 7.4 Monopoly

Number of firms:
One

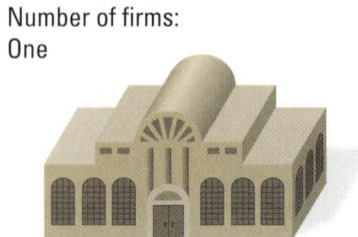

Variety of goods:
None

Barriers to entry:
Complete

Control over prices:
Complete

BUILDING KEY CONCEPTS

In a monopoly, one company controls the market.
Markets and Prices Why is public water a monopoly?

However, once the dam is built, the plant can produce energy at a very low additional cost simply by letting water flow through the dam. The average cost of the first unit of electricity produced is very high because the cost of the dam is so high. As output increases, the fixed costs of the dam can be spread over more units of electricity, so the average cost drops. In a market with economies of scale, bigger is better. An industry that enjoys economies of scale can easily become a natural monopoly.

Natural Monopolies

A **natural monopoly** is a market that runs most efficiently when one large firm provides all of the output. If a second firm enters the market, competition will drive down the market price charged to customers and decrease the quantity each firm can sell. One or both of the firms will not be able to cover their costs and will go out of business.

Public water provides a good example of a natural monopoly. In a competitive market, different water companies would dig reservoirs and set up overlapping networks of pipes and pumping stations to deliver water to the same town. Companies would use more land and water than necessary. Each company would have to pay for all of the unneeded pipes and would serve customers no better than a single network.

In cases like this, the government often steps in to allow just one firm in each geographic area to provide these necessary services. The government action ensures that we don't waste resources building additional plants when only one is needed. In return for monopoly status, a firm with a natural monopoly agrees to let government control the prices it can charge and what services it must provide.

Technology and Change

Sometimes the development of a new technology can destroy a natural monopoly. A new innovation can cut fixed costs and make small companies as efficient as one large firm.

▶ Before cellular phones became popular, telephone service was a natural monopoly because no one wanted to build more than one network of wires.

When telephone calls were carried by thick copper wires, local telephone service was considered a natural monopoly. No one wanted to build more than one network of wires to connect thousands of homes and businesses. In the 1980s and 1990s, consumers began using cellular phones, which were portable and could carry phone calls via radio waves rather than through wires. Cellular technology reduced the barriers to entry in the local telephone market. Now that cellular phone companies can link to thousands or millions of customers with a few, well-placed towers, they don't need to invest in an expensive infrastructure of cables and telephone poles. Cellular phone companies are becoming as efficient as traditional wire-based phone services.

Government Monopolies

In the case of a natural monopoly, the government allows the monopoly to form and then regulates it. In other cases, however, government actions themselves can create barriers to entry in markets and thereby create monopolies. A **government monopoly** is a monopoly created by the government.

Technological Monopolies

One way that the government can give a company monopoly power is by issuing a **patent**. A patent gives a company exclusive rights to sell a new good or service for a specific period of time. Suppose that Leland Pharmaceuticals developed a new asthma medication called BreatheDeep that helped people with asthma develop stronger lungs. If Leland's researchers could prove to the government that they had invented BreatheDeep, the Food and Drug Administration would grant Leland a patent. This patent would give Leland the exclusive right to sell BreatheDeep for twenty years.

Why would the government want to give a company monopoly power? Patents guarantee that companies can profit from their own research without competition. For this reason, patents encourage firms to research and develop new products that benefit society as a whole, even though the research and development costs may be very high. The market power that comes with the patent allows firms to set prices that maximize their opportunity to make a profit.

Franchises and Licenses

A **franchise** is a contract issued by a local authority that gives a single firm the right to sell its goods within an exclusive market. For example, the National Park Service picks a single firm to sell food and other goods at national parks, such as Yellowstone, Yosemite, and the Everglades. Your school may have contracted with one soft-drink company to install and stock vending machines. The franchise may include a condition that no other soft drinks will be sold in the building. Governments, parks, and schools use franchises to keep small markets under control.

On a larger scale, governments can issue a **license** granting firms the right to operate a business. Examples of scarce resources that require licensing include radio and television broadcast frequencies

▲ **A national park can give one company a franchise for, or monopoly over, food service within the park.**

government monopoly *a monopoly created by the government*

patent *a license that gives the inventor of a new product the exclusive right to sell it for a certain period of time*

franchise *the right to sell a good or service within an exclusive market*

license *a government-issued right to operate a business*

FAST FACT

*Many villages in India and Bangladesh have never had phone service, even though most of the population lives in the countryside. Stretching a cable to every village was too expensive and inefficient, even for a **natural monopoly**. Using a cellular network, Grameen Telecom now plans to bring pay phones to 68,000 villages in Bangladesh and serve 100 million new customers.*

and land. The Federal Communications Commission issues licenses for individual radio and television stations. Some cities select a single firm to own and manage all of their public parking lots.

Industrial Organizations

In rare cases, the government allows the companies in an industry to restrict the number of firms in a market. For example, the United States government lets Major League Baseball and other sports leagues restrict the number and location of their teams. The government allows team owners of the major professional sports leagues to choose new cities for their teams and does not charge them with violating the laws that prevent competitors from working together.

Major League Baseball has an exemption from these laws, which are known as antitrust laws, because they were originally passed to break up an illegal form of monopoly known as a trust. Other sports leagues do not have an official exemption, but the government treats them as it treats baseball. The restrictions that the leagues impose help keep team play orderly and stable by preventing other cities from starting their own major league teams and crowding the schedule.

The problem with this type of monopoly is that team owners may charge high prices for tickets. In addition, if you're a sports fan in a city without a major league team, you're out of luck.

Output Decisions

If you had severe asthma, which can be fatal, what would BreatheDeep be worth to you? You would probably want the medicine no matter how much it cost. So Leland, the company that invented and patented the drug, could charge a very high price for its new medication. In fact, they

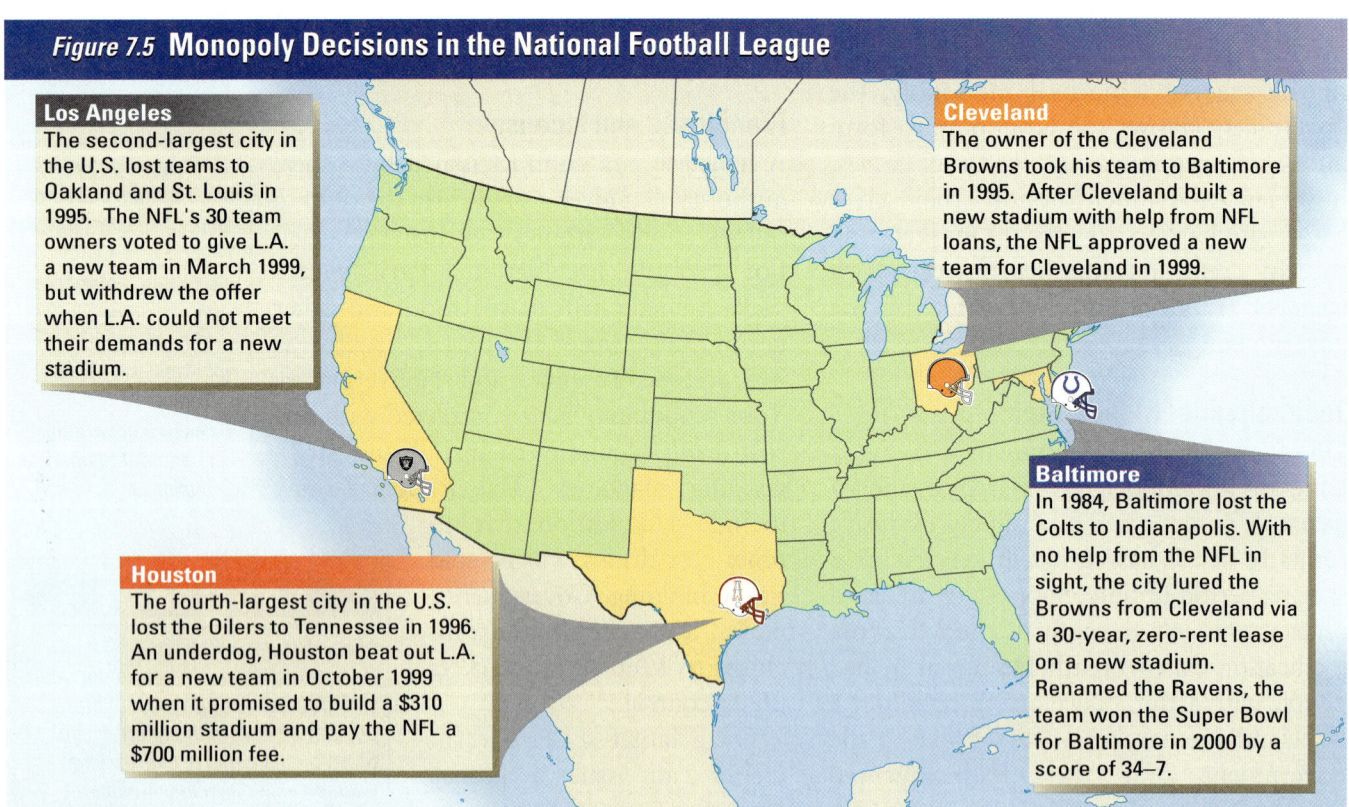

Figure 7.5 Monopoly Decisions in the National Football League

Los Angeles
The second-largest city in the U.S. lost teams to Oakland and St. Louis in 1995. The NFL's 30 team owners voted to give L.A. a new team in March 1999, but withdrew the offer when L.A. could not meet their demands for a new stadium.

Cleveland
The owner of the Cleveland Browns took his team to Baltimore in 1995. After Cleveland built a new stadium with help from NFL loans, the NFL approved a new team for Cleveland in 1999.

Houston
The fourth-largest city in the U.S. lost the Oilers to Tennessee in 1996. An underdog, Houston beat out L.A. for a new team in October 1999 when it promised to build a $310 million stadium and pay the NFL a $700 million fee.

Baltimore
In 1984, Baltimore lost the Colts to Indianapolis. With no help from the NFL in sight, the city lured the Browns from Cleveland via a 30-year, zero-rent lease on a new stadium. Renamed the Ravens, the team won the Super Bowl for Baltimore in 2000 by a score of 34–7.

The owners of professional football teams have a monopoly over membership in the National Football League. Cities have to apply to the NFL for a new team or pay top dollar for an existing team.
Supply and Demand Why do team owners limit the number of teams?

Figure 7.6 Demand Schedule for BreatheDeep

Price	Weekly Demand	Total Revenue	Change in Revenue	Marginal Revenue (per dose)
$12	8,000	$96,000	—	—
$11	9,000	$99,000	$3,000	$3
$10	10,000	$100,000	$1,000	$1
$9	11,000	$99,000	–$1,000	–$1
$8	12,000	$96,000	–$3,000	–$3

When 8,000 doses are made, the market price is $12.

As production rises to 11,000 doses, the price falls to $9.

Demand

Price (in dollars)

Output (in thousands of doses)

By increasing output, a monopolist lowers the price of the good. Above a certain level of output, revenue also begins to decrease.
Markets and Prices Why does revenue fall when production increases from 10,000 doses to 11,000 doses?

could charge enough to earn well above what it cost to research and manufacture the drug. The resulting profits would give the company a reason, or incentive, for inventing the new medication in the first place. But could Leland sell as much medication as it wanted to at whatever price it chose?

Even a monopolist faces a limited choice—it can choose either output or price, but not both. The monopolist looks at the big picture and tries to maximize profits. This usually means that, compared to a perfectly competitive market for the same good, the monopolist produces fewer goods at a higher price.

The Monopolist's Dilemma
The law of demand states that buyers will demand more of a good at lower prices and less at higher prices. Figure 7.6 shows a possible demand curve for BreatheDeep, with prices in dollars on the vertical axis and doses on the horizontal axis. Many people with life-threatening asthma will pay whatever the medicine costs. But some people with milder asthma will choose a cheaper, weaker medicine if the price rises too high.

Trace the demand curve from left to right. At $12 per dose, consumers might demand 8,000 doses of BreatheDeep each

week. But at $9 per dose, as many as 11,000 doses will sell. The law of demand means that when the monopolist increases the price, it will sell less, and when it lowers the price, it will sell more. Another way to interpret this graph is that if a monopolist produces more, the price of the good will fall, and if it produces less, the price will rise.

Falling Marginal Revenue
Remember from Chapter 5 that to maximize profits, a seller should set its marginal revenue, or the amount it earns from the last unit sold, equal to its marginal cost, or the extra cost from producing that unit. This same rule applies to a firm with a monopoly. The key difference is that in a perfectly competitive market, marginal revenue is always the same as price, and each firm receives the same price no matter how much it produces. Neither assumption is true in a monopoly.

To understand how this happens, consider the demand schedule for BreatheDeep in Figure 7.6. When BreatheDeep is sold at $12 a dose, consumers buy 8,000 doses, providing $96,000 in revenue. If Leland lowers the price to $11 a dose, 9,000 doses will be bought for a total revenue of $99,000. The sale of 1,000 more doses brought Leland $3,000 in new revenue.

In Chapter 5, you read that marginal revenue in most markets is equal to price. In this monopoly, the marginal revenue at a market price of $11 is roughly $3 a dose, far below the price. This is because the lower market price affects both the 1,000 new doses sold and the 8,000 doses people buy for $11 each instead of $12.

Now suppose that Leland lowers the price of BreatheDeep from $11 to $10 a dose. 10,000 doses will be bought, giving a total revenue of $100,000. This time, the sale of 1,000 more doses brought only $1,000 in additional revenue. $10,000 in revenue from 1,000 new sales barely exceeds the $9,000 fall in revenue from the 9,000 doses which are sold for $10, not $11. The market price is $10 a dose, but the marginal revenue has fallen to a mere $1 for each dose of BreatheDeep sold.

As you've seen, when a firm has some control over price—and can cut the price to sell more—marginal revenue is *less* than price. In contrast, in a perfectly competitive market, the price would not drop at all as output increased, so marginal revenue would remain the same as price. The firm's total revenue would increase at a steady rate with production.

The table in Figure 7.6 lists marginal revenues for several different prices. Note that marginal revenue actually becomes negative when the quantity demanded is greater than 10,000 doses a week.

Setting a Price

Leland will choose a level of output that yields the highest profits. As you read in Chapter 6, this is the point at which marginal revenue is equal to marginal cost.

In Figure 7.6 we have plotted the demand for BreatheDeep at market prices of $8, $9, $10, $11, and $12 a dose. According to Figure 7.6, output at these prices will be 12,000, 11,000, 10,000, 9,000, and 8,000 doses, respectively. These points form the market demand curve for BreatheDeep shown in purple.

Then, based on this data, we plotted Leland's marginal revenue at these levels of output. These points form the marginal revenue curve shown in blue in Figure 7.7. The marginal revenue curve is at the bottom of the graph because a monopolist's marginal revenue is lower than the market price.

Marginal cost equals marginal revenue at point a in Figure 7.7. This is the most profitable level of output. The monopolist produces 9,000 units, the quantity at which marginal revenue and marginal cost are both $3. According to the market demand curve, the market price is $11 when 9,000 units are sold (point b). Therefore, the monopolist will set the price of each dose at $11 or set production at 9,000 units.

Figure 7.7 also shows how price and output would be different if dozens of firms sold BreatheDeep and the market were perfectly competitive. In a perfectly competitive market, marginal revenue is always equal to market price, so the marginal revenue curve would be the same as the purple demand curve. Firms will set output where marginal revenue is equal to marginal cost, shown at point c. As you can see, a perfectly competitive market for BreatheDeep would have more units sold *and* a lower market price than a monopoly.

How much profit does a monopolist earn? The profit per dose is the difference between the market price and the average total cost at that level of production.

A monopolist sets output at a point (a) where marginal revenue is equal to marginal cost.

Markets and Prices
How does this affect output and price compared to a perfectly competitive market?

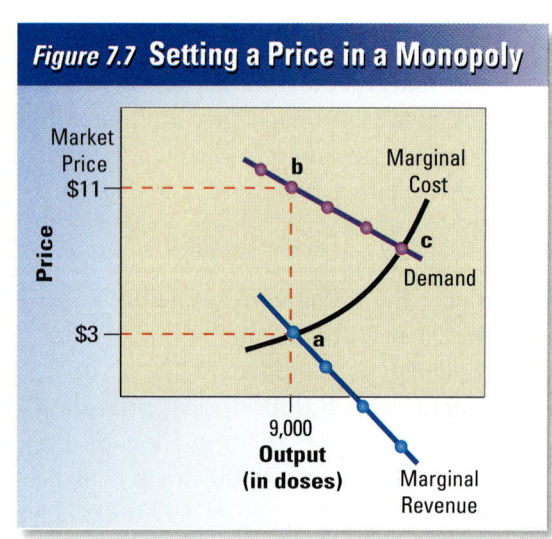

Figure 7.7 **Setting a Price in a Monopoly**

Suppose the average total cost of 9,000 doses is $5 per dose. Each dose is sold for $11, so the monopolist will earn $6 of profit per dose. Total profit is $54,000, or $6 per dose for 9,000 doses.

Price Discrimination

The previous example assumed that the monopolist must charge the same price to all consumers. But in some cases, the monopolist may be able to divide consumers into two or more groups and charge a different price to each group. This practice is known as **price discrimination**.

Price discrimination is based on the idea that each customer has his or her own maximum price he or she will pay for a good. If a monopolist sets the good's price at the highest maximum price of all the buyers in the market, the monopolist will only sell to the one customer willing to pay that much. If the monopolist sets a low price, the monopolist will gain a lot of customers, but the monopolist will lose the profits it could have made from the customers who bought at the low price but were willing to pay more.

Although price discrimination is a feature of monopoly, it can be practiced by any company with **market power**. Market power is the ability to control prices and total market output. As you will read in the next section, many companies have some market power without having a true monopoly.

Market power and price discrimination may be found in any market structure except for perfect competition.

Targeted Discounts

In the monopolist's ideal world, the firm could charge each customer the maximum that he or she is willing to pay, and no less. However, this is impractical, so companies divide consumers into large groups and design pricing policies for each group. One common form of price discrimination identifies some customers who are not willing to pay the regular price and offers those customers a discount. Price discrimination can also mean that a company finds the customers who need the good the most, and charges them more for that good. Here are some examples of price discrimination.

1. *Discounted airline fares* Airlines offer discounts to travelers who buy tickets several weeks in advance or are willing to spend a Saturday night at their destinations. Business travelers would prefer not to stay over on a Saturday night, but these tickets are appealing to vacationers who wouldn't otherwise pay to fly and don't mind the restrictions.

2. *Manufacturers' rebate offers* At times, manufacturers of refrigerators, cars, televisions, and other items will refund a small part of the purchase price to buyers who fill out a form and mail it back. People who take the time to fulfill the rebate requirements are likely more

▲ **Price discrimination can take the form of discounts for senior citizens, children, and students.**

price discrimination *division of customers into groups based on how much they will pay for a good*

market power *the ability of a company to change prices and output like a monopolist*

price-conscious than those who don't, and may be unwilling to pay full price.

3. *Senior citizen or student discounts* Many senior citizens or students have lower incomes than people who work full time. Zoos, theaters, and restaurants often offer discounts to senior citizens and students because they are unlikely to be able to pay full price for what some consider luxuries.

4. *Children fly or stay free promotions* Families with young children spend more of their income on food, clothing, and school expenses. As a result, they have less to spend on vacations. Once again, firms would rather have their business and earn lower profits than earn no profits at all, so they offer discounts for families with children.

Limits of Price Discrimination

For price discrimination to work, a market must meet three conditions. Firms that use price discrimination must have some market power, customers must be divided into distinct groups, and buyers must not be in a position in which they can easily resell the good or service.

1. *Some market power* Price-discriminating firms must have some control over prices. For this reason, price discrimination is rare in highly competitive markets.

2. *Distinct customer groups* The price-discriminating firm must be able to divide customers into distinct groups based on their sensitivity to price. In other words, monopolists must be able to guess the demand curves of different groups, one of which is more elastic, or price-sensitive, than the others.

3. *Difficult resale* If one set of customers could buy the product at the lower price and then resell the product for a profit, the firm could not enforce its price discrimination. Because consumer goods like shoes, groceries, and clothes are easily resold, price discrimination works best in marketing services that are consumed on the spot. Examples include theme park admissions and restaurant meals. Airlines can offer senior discounts because the company can ask for identification and proof of age before letting the customer board.

Although most forms of price discrimination are perfectly legal, sometimes firms use price discrimination to drive other firms out of business. This illegal form of the practice is called predatory pricing, and you will read more about it in Section 4.

Section 2 Assessment

Key Terms and Main Ideas

1. What can a firm with **market power** do?
2. Why does government usually approve of **natural monopolies?**
3. What are three different forms of **price discrimination?**
4. Define the term *economies of scale* in your own words.

Applying Economic Concepts

5. *Try This* Look through a recent newspaper for advertisements and coupons. List five examples of price discrimination.
6. *Decision Making* Suppose that you are the mayor of your town, and a local butcher asks you to **franchise** his shop as the only approved butcher shop in town. List a reason for and a reason against granting his request.
7. *Critical Thinking* Do you believe that public education is a natural monopoly? Why or why not?

 **Take It to the NET** Find two cases in which the federal government has challenged possible monopolies. How did the government define these companies as monopolies? Use the links provided in the Social Studies area at the following Web site for help in completing this activity. **www.phschool.com**

Profile

Economist

Entrepreneur

Bill Gates (b. 1955)

When Bill Gates was 12 years old, the school he attended in Seattle, Washington, bought a computer terminal that was connected to a large computer at a local company. He immediately became hooked on computers and their potential uses. Today, as the Chief Executive Officer and Chairman of Microsoft, the world's largest software company, Gates says his goal is "to have a computer on every desk and in every home, all running Microsoft software."

A Young Entrepreneur

While still a teenager, Gates and some friends developed a computer program to analyze and graph traffic data. In marketing the completed system to city governments, Gates and his friends rang up $20,000 in sales before customers realized they were dealing with students. The company soon folded, but Gates never lost his entrepreneurial spirit.

Growing a Company

In 1975, longtime friend Paul Allen learned that a company in New Mexico was manufacturing a kit to build a small computer. Allen convinced 19-year-old Gates to leave Harvard University and form a company to produce an operating system for this first personal computer, or PC. They named their venture Microsoft.

Five years later, Microsoft landed the contract to develop the operating system for computer giant IBM's new line of PCs. By 1983, 40 percent of all personal computers were running on Microsoft's operating system.

In the late 1980s, Gates launched Windows, a new, PC-compatible operating system that used graphics and a mouse to

perform computer functions. Microsoft's market share for operating systems jumped to 70 percent. Windows also allowed Gates to capture the market for software such as word processing programs, because competitors' products still depended on Microsoft's old, less user-friendly operating system. Those competitors began to complain that Microsoft had a monopoly.

Defending Microsoft

In 1997, the U.S. government claimed that by linking Microsoft's Internet browser to its operating system, Microsoft was unfairly using Windows' huge market share against rival browser companies. Gates angrily denied the charge. "Any operating system without a browser is going to be . . . out of business," he said. "Shall we improve our product or go out of business?"

Some former associates have another view. "He doesn't look for win-win situations with others," one says of Gates, "but for ways to make others lose. Success is defined as flattening the competition." Gates rejects such assessments. However, even today, surrounded by the success that being the world's richest person represents, he maintains his hard competitive edge.

CHECK FOR UNDERSTANDING

1. Source Reading Identify and explain the steps by which Microsoft used its operating systems to gain what critics called a monopoly of the entire computer software industry.

2. Critical Thinking Gates claims that his competitive practices improve the industry. His critics claim that they damage it. With which side do you agree, and why?

3. Decision Making How important do you think competitiveness is in building a successful company? Why?

Monopolistic Competition and Oligopoly

Objectives

After studying this section you will be able to:

1. **Describe** characteristics and give examples of monopolistic competition.

2. **Explain** how firms compete without lowering prices.

3. **Understand** how firms in a monopolistically competitive market set output.

4. **Describe** characteristics and give examples of oligopoly.

Section Focus

Monopolistic competition is similar to perfect competition, except that companies sell slightly different goods. Oligopoly, which is closer to monopoly, describes a market with only a few large producers.

Key Terms

monopolistic competition
differentiation
nonprice competition
oligopoly
price war
collusion
price fixing
cartel

---

monopolistic competition *a market structure in which many companies sell products that are similar but not identical*

So far, you have studied the two extremes of the range of market structures: perfect competition and monopoly. Very few markets fall into either of these categories. Instead, most fall into two additional categories that economists call monopolistic competition and oligopoly.

Monopolistic Competition

In **monopolistic competition,** many companies compete in an open market to sell products that are similar but not identical. Each firm holds a monopoly over its own particular product. You can think of monopolistic competition as a modified version of perfect competition with minor differences in products.

The differences between perfect competition and monopolistic competition arise because monopolistically competitive firms sell goods that are similar enough to be substituted for one another but are not identical. Monopolistic competition does not involve identical commodities. An example of a monopolistically competitive market is the market for jeans. All jeans can be described as denim pants, but in the shops, buyers can choose from a variety of colors, brand names, styles, and sizes.

Unlike perfect competition, monopolistic competition is a fact of everyday life. You

▼ The market for jeans is monopolistically competitive because jeans can vary by size, color, style, and designer.

and your friends probably buy from monopolistically competitive firms several times a week. Common examples include bagel shops, ice cream stands, gas stations, and retail stores.

Four Conditions of Monopolistic Competition

Monopolistic competition develops from four conditions. As you read about the types of markets that favor monopolistic competition, note how similar they are to the rules that define perfect competition.

1. *Many firms* As a rule, monopolistically competitive markets are not marked by economies of scale or high start-up costs. Because firms can start selling goods and earning money after a small initial investment, new firms spring up quickly to join the market.

2. *Few artificial barriers to entry* Firms in a monopolistically competitive market do not face the high barriers to entry discussed in Section 1. Patents do not protect anyone from competition, either because they have expired or because each firm sells a product that is distinct enough to fall outside the zone of patent protection. Just like a perfectly competitive market, a monopolistically competitive market includes so many competing firms that producers cannot work together to keep out new competitors.

3. *Slight control over price* Firms in a monopolistically competitive market structure have some freedom to raise or lower their prices because each firm's goods are a little different from everyone else's, and some people are willing to pay more for the difference. However, unlike a monopoly, a monopolistically competitive firm has only limited control over price. This is because consumers will substitute a rival's product if the price rises too high. For example, many customers will choose a can of brand-name cola over a generic cola even if it costs a quarter more per can. If the

Figure 7.8 Monopolistic Competition

Number of firms: Many

Variety of goods: Some

Barriers to entry: Low

Control over prices: Little

Many firms provide a variety of goods in a monopolistically competitive market.
Competition Why do firms in monopolistic competition have some control over prices?

brand-name cola cost $5 more per can, however, most people would buy the cheaper cola or drink something else.

4. *Differentiated products* Firms have some control over their selling price because they can differentiate, or distinguish, their goods from the other products in the market. The main difference between perfect competition and monopolistic competition is that **differentiation** enables a monopolistically competitive seller to profit from the differences between his or her products and competitors' products.

Nonprice Competition

Firms try not to compete on price alone. The alternative is **nonprice competition,** or competition through ways other than lower prices. Nonprice competition takes several different forms.

1. *Physical characteristics* The simplest way for a firm to distinguish its products is to offer a new size, color, shape,

differentiation *making a product different from other similar products*

nonprice competition *a way to attract customers through style, service, or location, but not a lower price*

texture, or taste. Running shoes, pens, cars, and toothpaste are good examples of products that can be easily differentiated by their physical characteristics. A pen is always a writing tool that uses ink, but many people will pay extra for a pen that looks or writes differently. Similarly, you can probably describe a "car" in only a few words, but factories around the world manufacture thousands of car models to fit a range of personalities, jobs, families, and incomes.

2. *Location*   Real estate agents say that the three most important factors when buying property are "location, location, location." Some goods can be differentiated by *where* they are sold. Gas stations, movie theaters, and grocery stores succeed or fail based on their locations. A convenience store in the middle of a desert differentiates its product simply by selling it hundreds of miles away from the nearest competitor. Such a location allows the seller to charge a lot more for a quart of water.

3. *Service level*   Some sellers can charge higher prices because they offer their customers a high level of service. Conventional restaurants and fast-food restaurants both offer meals to customers. However, conventional restaurants provide servers who bring the food to your table, whereas fast-food restaurants offer a more barebones, do-it-yourself atmosphere. Conventional restaurants and fast-food chains sell many of the same food items, but fast-food chains sell their meals for less. Customers at conventional restaurants pay more for the service and the relaxing atmosphere.

4. *Advertising, image, or status*   Some firms use advertising to create apparent differences between their own offerings and other products in the marketplace. These product differences are often more a matter of perception than reality. For example, a designer can apply his or her name to a plain white T-shirt and charge a higher price, even if the quality of fabric and stitching is no different than what generic T-shirts offer. Customers who pay extra for a designer T-shirt do so because the image and status that go with the designer's name are worth the extra money to them.

Price, Output, and Profits

When economists look at price, output, and profits under monopolistic competition, they find the market looks very much as it would under perfect competition.

Prices

Prices under monopolistic competition will be higher than they would be in perfect competition, because firms have some power to raise prices. However, the number of firms and ease of entry prevent companies

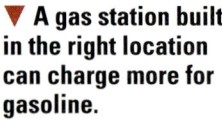

▼ A gas station built in the right location can charge more for gasoline.

NEXT GAS 112 MILES

from raising prices as high as they would if they were a true monopoly. As you have read, if a monopolistically competitive firm raised prices too high, most customers would ignore any differences and buy the cheaper product. Because customers can choose among many substitute products, monopolistically competitive firms face more elastic demand curves than true monopolists do.

Output

The law of demand says that output and price are negatively related. As one rises, the other falls. Because monopolistically competitive firms sell their products at higher prices than do perfectly competitive firms, but at lower prices than a monopoly, total output under monopolistic competition falls somewhere between that of monopoly and that of perfect competition.

Profit

Like perfectly competitive firms, monopolistically competitive firms earn just enough to cover all of their costs, including salaries for the workers. If a monopolistically competitive firm started to earn profits well above its costs, two market trends would work to take those profits away.

First, fierce competition would encourage rivals to think of new ways to differentiate their products and lure customers back. If one company hires a basketball star to promote its soft drink, a rival might hire a popular singer, while another rival could invest in an advertising blitz on television. The rivalries among firms prevent any one firm from earning excessive profits for long.

Secondly, new firms will enter the market with slightly different products that cost a lot less than the market leaders. If the original good costs too much, consumers will switch to these substitutes. You've seen this happen when a brand-name line of clothing, video games, or stuffed animals becomes popular. Competitors quickly flood the market with cheap imitations for people who can't afford the original or don't know or care about the difference.

Figure 7.9 Oligopoly

Number of firms:
A few

Variety of goods:
Some

Barriers to entry:
High

Control over prices:
Some

In an oligopoly, a few large firms dominate a market.
Competition Why are high barriers to entry an important part of oligopoly?

While monopolistically competitive firms can earn profits in the short run, they have to work hard to keep their product distinct to stay ahead of their rivals. Often, they don't succeed.

Production Costs and Variety

Some economists note that firms in monopolistic competition may not be able to produce their goods at the lowest possible average cost. Monopolistically competitive markets have many firms, each producing too little output to minimize costs and use resources efficiently. On the other hand, consumers in these markets enjoy a wide variety of goods to choose from.

Oligopoly

Oligopoly describes a market dominated by a few large, profitable firms. Oligopoly looks like an imperfect form of monopoly. Economists usually call an industry an oligopoly if the four largest firms produce at least 70 to 80 percent of the output.

oligopoly *a market structure in which a few large firms dominate a market*

BUILDING KEY CONCEPTS

Markets can be grouped into four basic structures: perfect competition, monopolistic competition, oligopoly, and monopoly.

Competition
How does a monopolistic competition differ from monopoly?

Figure 7.10 Comparison of Market Structures

	Perfect Competition	Monopolistic Competition	Oligopoly	Monopoly
Number of firms	Many	Many	A few dominate	One
Variety of goods	None	Some	Some	None
Control over prices	None	Little	Some	Complete
Barriers to entry	None	Low	High	Complete
Examples	Wheat, shares of stock	Jeans, books	Cars, movie studios	Public water

Acting on their own or as a team, the biggest firms in an oligopoly may well set prices higher and output lower than in a perfectly competitive market. Examples of oligopolies in the United States include the markets for air travel, breakfast cereals, and household appliances.

Barriers to Entry

An oligopoly can form when significant barriers to entry keep new companies from entering the market to compete with existing firms. Sometimes these barriers are created by a system of government licenses or patents.

In other cases, the economic realities of the market lead to an oligopoly. High start-up costs, such as expensive machinery or a large advertising campaign, can scare firms away from the market. Many small airlines have had trouble competing with larger, better-financed rivals because airplanes are very expensive to buy and maintain. The biggest airlines compound the problem because they often own the most desirable gates at the airport, and already enjoy name recognition and the trust of the consumer. As another example, the two big cola manufacturers have invested so much money in their brand names and sales

networks over the last century that few companies think they can successfully challenge their grip on the market.

Some oligopolies occur because of economies of scale. As you have read, when a firm experiences economies of scale, the average cost of production decreases as output increases. In a monopoly market, only one company can produce enough goods to earn a profit. In an oligopoly, perhaps three or four companies can reach a profitable level of output before the market becomes too crowded and revenue falls below costs.

Cooperation and Collusion

Oligopoly presents a big challenge to government, because oligopolistic firms often *seem* to work together to form a monopoly, even when they are not actually doing so. Many government regulations try to make oligopolistic firms act more like competitive firms. When determined oligopolists work together illegally to set prices and bar competing firms from the market, they can become as damaging to the consumer as a monopoly.

The three practices that concern government the most are price leadership, collusion, and cartels. While these three practices represent ways that firms in an oligopoly can try to control a market, they don't always work. Each tactic includes an incentive for firms to cheat and undo any benefits.

Sometimes the market leader in an oligopoly can start a round of price increases and cuts by making its plans clear to other firms. Price leaders can set prices and output for entire industries as long as other member firms go along with the leader's policy. But disagreements among member firms can spark a **price war,** when competitors cut their prices very low to win business. A price war is harmful to producers but good for consumers.

Collusion refers to an agreement among members of an oligopoly to set prices and production levels. One outcome of collusion is called **price fixing,** an agreement among firms to sell at the same or very similar prices. Collusive agreements set prices and output at the levels that would be chosen by a monopolist. Collusion is illegal in the United States, but the lure of monopolistic profits can tempt businesses to make such agreements despite the illegality and risks.

Collusion is not, however, the only reason for identical pricing in oligopolistic industries. Such pricing may actually result from intense competition, especially if advertising is vigorous and new lines of products are being introduced.

◄ **A computer manufacturer can distinguish its computers with bright colors or a sleek design.**

Cartels

Stronger than a collusive agreement, a **cartel** is an agreement by a formal organization of producers to coordinate prices and production. Although other countries and international organizations permit them, cartels are illegal in the United States. Cartels can only survive if every member keeps to its agreed output levels and no more. Otherwise, prices will fall, and firms will lose profits. However, each member has a strong incentive to cheat and produce more than its quota. If every cartel member cheats, too much product reaches the market, and prices fall. Cartels can also collapse if some producers are left out of the group and decide to lower their prices below the cartel's levels. Therefore, cartels usually do not last very long.

price war *a series of competitive price cuts that lowers the market price below the cost of production*

collusion *an agreement among firms to divide the market, set prices, or limit production*

price fixing *an agreement among firms to charge one price for the same good*

cartel *a formal organization of producers that agree to coordinate prices and production*

Section 3 Assessment

Key Terms and Main Ideas

1. What are the four conditions of **monopolistic competition?**
2. How do economists determine whether a market is an **oligopoly?**
3. Give three examples of **nonprice competition.**
4. How would **price fixing** and **collusion** help producers?

Applying Economic Concepts

5. *Using the Databank* The map on page 545 indicates which countries are members of OPEC, a cartel made up of oil-exporting countries. In the 1970s, OPEC successfully raised oil prices by cutting production. Based on what you have read in this section, explain how this situation illustrates **(a)** how cartels operate **(b)** why cartels can be dangerous.

6. *Decision Making* Would you describe the following markets as monopolistic competition or oligopoly? **(a)** refrigerators **(b)** video game systems **(c)** gourmet ice cream **(d)** sunscreen **(e)** cable sports channels

7. *Critical Thinking* Which of the four forms of nonprice competition described on pp. 167–168 would you emphasize for the following products? Explain your reasoning. **(a)** a new brand of bottled water **(b)** in-home computer repair **(c)** protein bars

Take It to the NET

Cartels, aside from OPEC, are not seen often in today's world. This has not always been the case. Choose one historical cartel, and report on how it functioned. Use the links provided in the Social Studies area at the following Web site for help in completing this activity.
www.phschool.com

Preview

Objectives

After studying this section you will be able to:

1. **Understand** how firms use market power.
2. **List** three market practices that the government regulates or bans to protect competition.
3. **Define** deregulation, and list its effects on several industries.

Section Focus

The federal government sometimes steps into markets to promote competition and the lower prices it brings. In recent years, the government has also deregulated several markets to promote competition.

Key Terms

predatory pricing
antitrust laws
trust
merger
deregulation

It's 1946. The soldiers have come home from World War II, the cities are booming, and you're a city planner who needs to get people to work each morning. You can build wide roads and parking lots and encourage people to buy cars, you can invest in a fleet of buses, or you can expand the streetcar lines and train tracks that already criss-cross the town center. Ideally, you will choose the most efficient system.

However, you never get to decide. A company called National City Lines (NCL) buys your city's streetcar network and decides to raise fares and shut down several lines. Service gets so bad that commuters stay away, and NCL soon shuts down the system. It's now 1966, and your streetcars are gone. Since the roads are too crowded for more cars, you must buy buses.

▼ **After World War II, National City Lines used its mass transit monopoly to shut down streetcar lines.**

In the newspaper, you read that National City Lines was secretly funded by companies that make tires, automobiles, and gasoline—the same companies that now offer to sell you 200 new buses.

This really happened in cities like Los Angeles and Baltimore, where National City Lines turned a mass transit oligopoly into a monopoly by buying up its rivals. National City Lines then used its monopoly to close down the streetcar lines. Although some experts argue that the streetcars might have died out anyway, many critics blame National City Lines for the end result. No one can know what might have happened in a competitive market.

If you think what National City Lines did was unfair, the federal government agrees. In this section, you will read about anticompetitive practices and the tools the government uses to stop them.

Market Power

As you have read, monopoly and oligopoly can sometimes be bad for the consumer and the economy as a whole. Markets dominated by a few large firms tend to have higher prices and lower output than markets with many sellers. Before we look at antitrust policies, let's think about how a firm might try to increase its market power.

To control prices and output like a monopoly, the leading firms in the market can form a cartel, merge with one another, or set the market price below their costs for the short term to drive competitors out of business. The last practice is known as **predatory pricing**. Economists are skeptical about most claims of predatory pricing because the predator loses money each time it drives an endless series of rivals out of business.

Government and Competition

The federal government has a number of policies that keep firms from controlling the price and supply of important goods. If a firm controls a large share of a market, the Federal Trade Commission and the Department of Justice's Antitrust Division will watch that firm closely to ensure that it does not unfairly force out its competitors. These government policies are known as **antitrust laws** because a **trust** is a business combination similar to a cartel.

In 1890, Congress passed the Sherman Antitrust Act, which outlawed mergers and monopolies that limit trade between states. This and other laws gave the government the power to regulate industry, to stop firms from forming cartels or monopolies, and to break up existing monopolies. Over the years, Congress passed new laws to outlaw other anticompetitive practices.

Despite the antitrust laws, companies have used many strategies to gain control over their markets. Some firms require a customer who buys one product to buy other products from the same company, whether or not the customer wants them. For example, a tennis shoe manufacturer can demand that a chain buy and resell its brand-name shirts, windbreakers, and watches if it wants to sell its shoes. Another tactic, the one employed by National City Lines, is to buy out competitors.

Regulating Business Practices

The government has the power to regulate all of these practices if these practices give too much power to a company that already

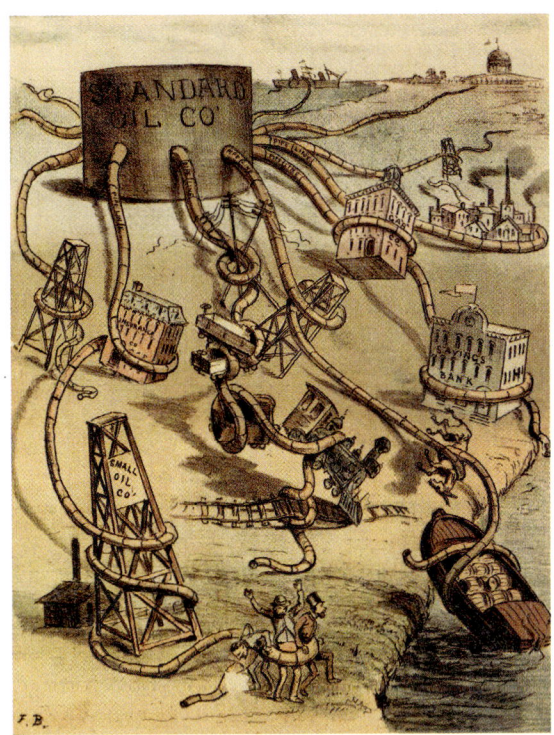

◄ **Public outrage with powerful trusts in the late 1800s led Congress to pass antitrust legislation.**

has few competitors. Microsoft sells operating systems, software that tells a computer how to run. In 1997, the Department of Justice accused Microsoft of using a monopoly in operating systems to illegally extend its control over the market for a program known as a browser that allows people to use the World Wide Web.

Microsoft insisted that computer manufacturers that sold its operating system also include its browser. The government accused Microsoft of predatory pricing because the company gave away its browser for free, which would ruin the other browser company, Netscape. Microsoft's power in one market gave it a big—and possibly unfair—advantage in related markets.

The government sued Microsoft so other companies would have more opportunities to bring new software to the market. Microsoft argued that the browser was part of its operating system and could not be sold separately. Microsoft's defenders pointed out that other companies *do* compete with Microsoft, and people buy Microsoft software because they like it. In November 1999, a federal judge ruled that Microsoft was a monopoly and began taking steps to weaken the company.

predatory pricing *selling a product below cost to drive competitors out of the market*

antitrust laws *laws that encourage competition in the marketplace*

trust *like a cartel, an illegal grouping of companies that discourages competition*

Figure 7.11 Key Events in Federal Antitrust Policy

1911
Supreme Court breaks up John D. Rockefeller's Standard Oil Trust

1900   **1915**   **1925**   **1940**

1901 Theodore Roosevelt becomes President and begins enforcing the 1890 Sherman Antitrust Act, which outlaws mergers and monopolies that restrain trade between states

1914 Clayton Antitrust Act outlaws practices that limit competition or lead to monopoly

1936 Robinson-Patman Act defines and outlaws several forms of price discrimination

▲ Over the past century, the federal government has acted often to promote competition in American industry.

Breaking Up Monopolies

The government used antitrust legislation to break up existing monopolies such as the American Tobacco Company and John D. Rockefeller's Standard Oil Trust in 1911. In 1982, the government broke American Telephone and Telegraph (AT&T) into seven regional phone companies, including BellSouth, USWest, and PacificBell. Because the government treated local telephone service as a natural monopoly, AT&T legally controlled all the cables and networks that linked telephones in homes and businesses. The government stepped in only when AT&T used its legal monopoly in local phone service to take control of other markets for long-distance phone calls and communications equipment. Today, there are many firms in the market for long-distance service and the market is more competitive. Although thousands of workers lost their jobs, consumers benefit from lower prices and better technology.

Blocking Mergers

In addition to breaking up monopolistic companies, the government has the power to prevent the rise of monopolies. The government does this by blocking company **mergers** that might reduce competition

and lead to higher prices. A merger occurs when a company joins with another company or companies to form a single firm. Government regulators also follow the effects of past mergers to check that they did not lead to unfair market control. You read in Section 1 that prices often fall when the number of firms in a market increases. The reverse is also true. Prices often rise when the number of firms in an industry falls.

The government tries to predict the effects of a merger on prices and service when it decides whether or not to approve a merger. Recently, the Department of Justice has looked at data collected by scanners at supermarket check-out lines to see how prices vary when two competitors join forces. In 1997, the Justice Department examined the proposed merger of two companies that sell office supplies. Their studies showed that one company charged less in cities where the other company also had stores. Using this data, the Federal Trade Commission (FTC) convinced the courts that the merger would hurt competition and force customers to pay higher prices. In the end, the Department of Justice did not allow the two companies to merge.

merger *combination of two or more companies into a single firm*

1974 Department of Justice sues to end AT&T's monopoly over local phone service

1999 A Federal judge finds that Microsoft is a monopoly

1955   **1970**   **1985**   **2000**

1950 Celler-Kefauver Act allows government to stop mergers that could hurt competition

1982 AT&T agrees to break up its local phone service into several companies

Preserving Incentives

While some mergers hurt the consumer by reducing competition, others can actually leave the consumer better off. In these cases, corporate mergers will lower overall average costs and lead to lower prices, more reliable products or service, and a more efficient industry. The government must act carefully to make the right decision. In 1997, the Justice Department and the FTC released new guidelines for proposed mergers. Now, companies that want to merge have the chance to prove that the merger would lower costs and consumer prices or lead to a better product.

Deregulation

In the late 1970s and 1980s, Congress passed laws to deregulate several industries. **Deregulation** means that the government no longer decides what role each company can play in a market and how much it can charge its customers. Over several years, the government deregulated the airline, trucking, banking, railroad, natural gas, and television broadcasting industries. Depending on the degree of deregulation, the government's action allowed—or forced—firms in these industries to

compete more in markets by eliminating many entry barriers and price controls.

While deregulation weakens government control, antitrust laws strengthen it. Yet the government uses both of these tools, deregulation and antitrust laws, for the same purpose: to promote competition.

Many critics say that government efforts to regulate industries have created inefficiencies. In some cases, the economic facts or technological limits that created the need for regulation in the first place have changed. For example, in Section 1 you read how the invention of cellular phones challenged the natural monopoly of local phone service and opened the market to new companies. The trucking industry was also regulated as a natural monopoly from the early 1900s until 1978. By then, many had decided that the government was regulating industries that were not natural monopolies at all.

Judging Deregulation

Deregulation has met with mixed success. In most cases, many new firms entered the

deregulation the removal of some government controls over a market

THE WALL STREET JOURNAL.

CLASSROOM EDITION

In the News As this excerpt from a Wall Street Journal Classroom Edition *article notes, although the trucking industry has been* **deregulated,** *the government still regulates safety for truckers.*

"...a survey by the Insurance Institute for Highway Safety concluded that as many as three fourths of drivers violate federal driving-hours restrictions, which include limiting a driving stretch to 10 hours."

▲ After the September 11, 2001, hijackings and attacks, the National Guard began patrolling airports. The impact of fewer people flying was felt throughout the airline industry.

Airlines: A Complicated Deregulation

Many new airlines started operating after President Carter deregulated the industry in 1978, but some eventually failed or were acquired. Freed from regulatory restriction, many of the large airlines competed aggressively for the busiest routes. For most travelers, the increased competition created lower prices. The result is that many busy airports now have one dominant airline, and in some cases fares are actually higher than before deregulation.

By the early 2000s, however, airlines were feeling less secure. Over-expansion drove up their operating costs, and sharply rising labor costs squeezed profits even more. Finally, the terrorist hijackings on September 11, 2001, caused many people to stop flying. Revenues plunged while costs of security and insurance rose.

With President Bush's support, Congress gave the airlines a $5 billion bailout and created a three-person board to administer another $10 billion in federal loan guarantees. The Departments of Transportation, Treasury, and the Fed each have a seat on the board. Because some airlines were already weak, the board's decisions about loan support may ultimately determine which companies stay in business and which fail.

deregulated industries right away. Competition certainly increased in the airline, trucking, and banking industries. Typically, this period of wild growth was followed by the widespread disappearance of some firms in each industry. This weeding out of weaker players is considered healthy for the economy, but it can be hard on workers in the short term.

Section 4 Assessment

Key Terms and Main Ideas

1. What is the purpose of **antitrust laws?**
2. Under what conditions will the government approve a **merger?**
3. How does **predatory pricing** hurt competition?
4. How did **deregulation** change the banking and air travel industries?

Applying Economic Concepts

5. *Decision Making* Why did government once regulate the banking, trucking, and airline industries?
6. *Try This* Use the library to find an editorial from 1911 in support of the breakup of Standard Oil, and compare it to a recent editorial that criticizes Microsoft. Which arguments are the same? Which are different?
7. *Critical Thinking* Why does the government believe it has the right to intervene in markets to promote competition? Is this consistent with the idea of laissez faire and free markets?

Take It to the NET

Deregulation in the public utility market (gas, electric, telephone) is intended to help you as a consumer by providing broader selection and lower rates. Research utility deregulation, and find out how it will affect you as a consumer in the future. Use the links provided in the Social Studies area at the following Web site for help in completing this activity. **www.phschool.com**

Regulating Cable Television

Cable television systems offer more than 100 channels featuring continuous news, sports, weather, business reports, and coverage of local activities. This growth in popularity, however, has led to a need for regulation.

The FCC The Federal Communication Commission (FCC) oversees the cable industry. During the 1950s, the FCC maintained a "hands-off" policy. In the 1960s, however, the FCC began to impose regulations. Responding to complaints from over-the-air broadcasters that cable stations were refusing to carry local stations, the FCC ruled that every cable system had to carry the programs of all local stations as well as those of their own.

By the 1970s, the FCC began to impose more regulations. The agency mandated that cable systems provide at least 20 channels in major markets, provide public access channels, and obtain public approval of changes in their rates.

▲ Many cable channels run specialized programming, such as all home improvement shows or all sports.

Deregulation In the 1980s, the FCC ruled that rates for cable services would be deregulated. This led to skyrocketing cable rates and poor service in certain parts of the country. This resulted in a move in the 1990s to regulate the industry once more.

The Cable Television Consumer Protection Act of 1992 allowed competition in the cable industry for the first time. It was hoped that competition would cause cable rates to stabilize or even decrease, while service would improve.

Today, cable television has grown so popular that cable networks now challenge and often surpass the popularity of the original broadcast giants ABC, CBS, and NBC. How much further will cable television grow? No one is sure. What seems certain, however, is that with growth will come further regulation.

Applying Economic Ideas

1. Should government regulate the cable television industry? Why or why not?

2. The table at the right shows the number of cable subscribers from 1970 to 2000. What do you think accounts for the increase in subscribers in the 1980s and 1990s?

Cable TV Subscribers, 1970–2000

Year	Number of Subscribers
1970	4,500,000
1975	9,800,000
1980	16,000,000
1985	32,000,000
1990	50,000,000
1995	58,000,000
2000	70,000,000 (est.)

Source: *Statistical Abstract of the United States*

Chapter Summary

A summary of major ideas in Chapter 7 appears below. See also the **Guide to the Essentials of Economics,** which provides additional review and test practice of key concepts in Chapter 7.

Section 1 Perfect Competition (pp. 151–154)

Perfect competition describes a market with many well-informed buyers and sellers, identical goods, and no **barriers to entry** to stop companies from joining the market. Perfect competition is only found in markets that deal in **commodities,** or goods that are identical no matter who produces or sells them. These markets are efficient at setting output and prices at a level that is beneficial to all.

Section 2 Monopoly (pp. 156–164)

A firm is a monopolist when it is the only seller in a market. A **natural monopoly** is an industry that works best when only one firm serves the entire market. Government can create a monopoly by issuing a **patent, franchise,** or a **license.** A monopolist can set prices or output. Firms use **price discrimination** to divide consumers into groups based on their ability to pay, and then offer a different price to each group.

Section 3 Monopolistic Competition and Oligopoly (pp. 166–171)

Most markets fall somewhere between perfect competition and monopoly. **Monopolistic competition** is similar to perfect competition, except that companies sell slightly different goods and have a little power to set prices. Closer to monopoly, **oligopoly** describes a market dominated by a few large producers. Firms in an oligopoly can practice **collusion** or form a **cartel** to set prices like a monopoly.

Section 4 Regulation and Deregulation (pp. 172–176)

Firms in an oligopoly can merge to try to gain monopoly power. Because monopoly power can lead to inefficient markets, the federal government has passed laws to promote competition and break up monopolies. In the late 1970s and 1980s, government gave up power to regulate several markets. **Deregulation** has led to lower prices in most deregulated markets.

Key Terms

Complete each sentence by choosing the correct answer from the list of terms below. You will not use all of the terms.

perfect competition	natural monopoly
oligopoly	economies of scale
patent	price fixing
commodities	deregulation
price discrimination	collusion

1. _____ is when a monopolist divides consumers into groups and charges different prices for the same good.
2. A market with many firms producing the same good is in _____.
3. Economists define _____ as a market structure with a few large firms, each of which has some market power.
4. _____ are products that are identical no matter who produces them.
5. A(n) _____ grants the right to sell an invention without competition.
6. A(n) _____ may exist in markets where it is most efficient for only one large firm to provide a product.
7. Economists use the term _____ to describe agreements among firms to set prices and production levels.

8. Using Graphic Organizers

On a separate sheet of paper, copy the multi-flow map below. Organize information on government deregulation by completing the map with causes for deregulation on the left and possible effects on the right. You may add more causes or effects.

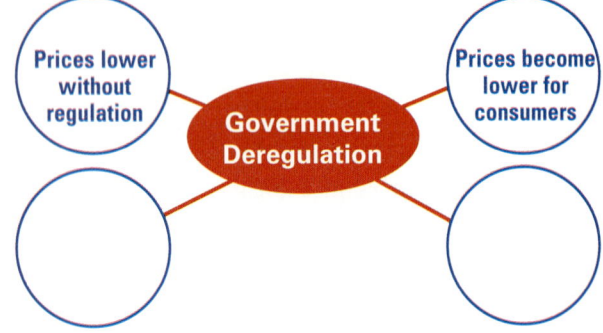

Reviewing Main Ideas

9. How does the buying and selling of stock fit the model for perfect competition?
10. Compare and contrast the characteristics of natural monopolies and monopolies created by government.
11. What four conditions are necessary for a market to be considered monopolistically competitive?
12. How does the United States government intervene in the economy in regard to monopolies and competition?

Critical Thinking

13. **Making Comparisons** How do prices, output, and profits differ between monopolies and monopolistically competitive firms? Are there similarities?
14. **Synthesizing Information** What are the trade-offs between free enterprise and government intervention associated with the United States' antitrust policies?
15. **Analyzing Information** Using the reference to the hydroelectric plant found in Section 2 as an example of economies of scale, think of three examples of industries that benefit from economies of scale.

Problem-Solving Activity

16. Assume that you are the owner of the only music store in town because your town limits the number of shops. The town now wants to repeal that law and allow more music stores to open. Describe what actions you could take as a business owner once the law is repealed.

Economics Journal

Brainstorming Reread your Economics Journal entry for Chapter 7. Write a paragraph for each of the three companies you listed, explaining what market structure each company competes in and how you came to this decision.

Skills for Life

Analyzing Political Cartoons Review the steps shown on page 155; then answer the following questions using the cartoon below.

17. Identify the symbols in the cartoon. What is symbolized by the icons pictured on the man's head?
18. Analyze the intent of the cartoon. **(a)** Who is being represented in the cartoon? **(b)** What is the cartoonist implying about that person?
19. Draw conclusions about the cartoonist's intent. **(a)** Does the artist believe the computer industry has perfect competition? **(b)** Were you swayed or convinced of the cartoonist's opinion in this case?

Take It to the NET

Chapter 7 Self-Test As a final review activity, take the Chapter 7 Self-Test in the Social Studies area at the Web site listed below, and receive immediate feedback on your answers. The test consists of 20 multiple-choice questions designed to test your understanding of the chapter content.
www.phschool.com

DEBATING CURRENT ISSUES: *The Minimum Wage*

In 1938, President Franklin D. Roosevelt signed into law a bill that established a federal minimum wage of 25 cents an hour. This wage initially applied to employees involved in interstate commerce or production of goods for interstate commerce. Later it was extended to include employees of companies doing at least $500,000 in business a year and also to employees of government agencies, hospitals, and schools.

Congress and the President have raised the minimum wage over time to reflect changes in the cost of living. Here are two excerpts from *The Wall Street Journal Classroom Edition*. One, written by Clinton administration officials, supports an increase; the other, written by a restaurant manager, argues against it.

YES *Should the Minimum Wage Be Increased?*

BY ROBERT E. RUBIN, RONALD BROWN, ROBERT B. REICH, JOSEPH E. STIGLITZ, AND LAURA D'ANDREA TYSON

STAGNANT WAGES ARE a 20-year problem that won't be solved overnight. Addressing this long-term challenge will require a persistent and comprehensive economic-growth agenda.

One action we can take right now is to insist that the minimum wage be a living wage. Every member of the president's economic team believes this step will increase wages without costing jobs.

The president has proposed a 90-cent increase in the minimum wage, to $5.15 from $4.25, spread over two years. This is the same plan that won overwhelming bipartisan support when Congress voted to raise the minimum wage in 1989.

Indeed, the first 45 cents of the new increase wouldn't even restore the buying power the minimum wage has lost since the last increase five years ago. And if we don't act this year, it will fall to a 40-year low in terms of purchasing power.

Of the 10 million workers who would benefit from Mr. Clinton's minimum-wage increase, 69 percent are age 20 and older. The average minimum-wage worker brings home half of the family's earnings. And, according to the Bureau of Labor Statistics, 59 percent are women—many of whom shoulder most of the burden at home.

A minimum-wage increase can make a real difference. For a full-time minimum-wage worker, it means an additional $1,800 in earnings—enough to buy seven months of groceries or several months of child care.

According to proponents of a minimum wage hike, people with few job skills—such as this worker—would benefit most from an increase.

Should the Minimum Wage Be Increased?

By Dee Dee Stanback

I HAVE ONE WORD OF advice for those who would raise the minimum wage: Don't.

In 1979, I was a single mother with two children, just barely surviving on welfare. The monthly AFDC check was enough to pay the rent with just a little left over for food, clothes, and other necessities.

Today, I'm a manager at a popular restaurant. I help supervise nearly 200 employees. My family has a good roof over its head, insurance, everything we need. One of my children plans to go to college; the other is an honor-roll student. I'm very proud of my family, my career, and the turn my life has taken.

What made the difference for me? A minimum-wage job. I was scared to death when I went to interview for a dishwasher's position at this restaurant. I had no education, no experience, no training, and few skills. But I had the determination and drive to persuade the general manager to give me a chance.

Just getting the job in the first place was more important to me than the salary level. That dishwashing job was the first rung on the ladder of opportunity for me. And once I got my hands on that ladder, I never let go.

With every new position, I acquired new skills to become a more valuable worker: personal responsibility, a commitment to excellence, self-esteem, pride. That's a lot more than you learn on welfare.

But raising the minimum wage will destroy the kind of entry-level jobs that gave me, and millions like

me, a chance. The people who will get hurt the most are the people with the fewest skills, least experience, and most-limited education—those who enter the job market with the least to offer, but the most to gain.

Value of the Federal Minimum Wage, 1980–1997

Year	Nominal Dollars*	1998 Dollars**
1980	3.10	6.13
1981	3.35	6.01
1982	3.35	5.66
1983	3.35	5.48
1984	3.35	5.26
1985	3.35	5.07
1986	3.35	4.98
1987	3.35	4.81
1988	3.35	4.62
1989	3.35	4.40
1990	3.80	4.74
1991	4.25	5.09
1992	4.25	4.94
1993	4.25	4.79
1994	4.25	4.67
1995	4.25	4.55
1996	4.75	4.93
1997	5.15	5.23

* Face-value dollars

** Dollars adjusted for inflation using the Consumer Price Index (CPI-U)

Note: Years in which the Fair Labor Standards Act was amended to raise the minimum wage are indicated by the gold shading.

Source: Bureau of Labor Statistics, 2001

Even though the minimum wage has increased since 1980, its value has not increased because of inflation.

DEBATING THE ISSUE

1. According to the authors of the "Yes" excerpt, how would employees benefit from a higher minimum wage?

2. Why is Dee Dee Stanback afraid employers won't hire people like her for entry-level jobs if the minimum wage is raised?

3. **Critical Thinking** In what ways might a higher minimum wage help the economy grow?

4. **Reading Graphs** Based on the table above, has the buying power of minimum-wage workers, as reflected by the minimum wage in 1998 dollars, increased or decreased since 1980?

 Take It to the Net Visit **www.phschool.com** for additional resources relating to this debate.

UNIT

3
Business and Labor

Chapters in This Unit

You've graduated; *you're off to work . . .*

Most Americans spend a large proportion of their lives working. Picture yourself going off to work when you finish your education.

- What type of business do you work for?
- Who are your co-workers?
- Who's your boss? Are you in business for yourself?
- How much do you earn?

Economists categorize businesses according to the way they are organized. Economists also study the composition of the country's labor force and the impact of supply and demand on labor and wages. In this unit you'll read about possible answers you might be giving years from now to the questions above.

Focus Activity

Write down five occupations that you're considering for your future. Categorize each of your choices based on who your employer might be for each job.

Chapter 8 Business Organizations

Taking care of business can mean working by yourself out of your home or managing a company with thousands of employees and offices across the globe. It can mean being the sole owner of a company or one of thousands. It can also mean working for something other than a for-profit business.

Economics Journal

List the four businesses you and your family visit the most often. Are they local businesses or national chains? Describe each one in a few sentences.

THE VERMONT COUNTRY STORE

THE ORTON FAMILY BUSINESS

Keep It Current

Items marked with this logo are periodically updated on the Internet. Keep up-to-date with what's in the news. To get current information on business organizations go to
www.phschool.com

Preview

Objectives

After studying this section you will be able to:

1. **Explain** the characteristics of sole proprietorships.
2. **Analyze** the advantages of a sole proprietorship.
3. **Analyze** the disadvantages of a sole proprietorship.

Section Focus

A business is an economic institution that seeks a profit by allocating resources to satisfy customers. Sole proprietorships are the most common form of business in the United States. They are easy to establish and offer owners both the benefits and drawbacks that come with full control of a business.

Key Terms

business organization
sole proprietorship
business license
zoning law
liability
fringe benefit

Entrepreneurs must make many decisions as they start up new businesses. One of the first decisions they face is what form of business organization best serves their interests. A **business organization** is an establishment formed to carry on commercial enterprise. In other words, a business organization is a company, or firm. Sole proprietorships are the most common forms of business organization.

The Role of Sole Proprietorships

A **sole proprietorship** is a business owned and managed by a single individual. That person earns all of the firm's profits and is responsible for all of the firm's debts. This type of firm is by far the most popular in the United States. According to the Internal Revenue Service, about 75 percent of all businesses are sole proprietorships. Most sole proprietorships are small, however. All together they generate only about 6 percent of all United States sales.

Many types of businesses can flourish as sole proprietorships. Look around your town. Chances are good that your local bakery, your barber shop or hair salon, your bike-repair shop, and the corner store are all sole proprietorships.

Advantages of Sole Proprietorships

While you need to do more than just hang out a sign to start your own business, a sole proprietorship is simple to establish. It also offers the owner numerous advantages.

business organization *an establishment formed to carry on commercial enterprise*

sole proprietorship *a business owned and managed by a single individual*

◀ Personal pride motivates many sole proprietors.

It takes a certain type of personality to start up a business.

Entrepreneurs
Describe some times when you exhibited entrepreneurial spirit.

business license
authorization to start a business issued by the local government

Ease of Start-Up

Easy start-up is one of the main advantages of the sole proprietorship. With just a small amount of paperwork and legal expense, just about anyone can start a sole proprietorship.

To start a new business, a sole proprietor must meet a small number of government requirements, which can vary from city to city and state to state. Typically, sole proprietors must meet the following minimum requirements:

1. *Authorization* Sole proprietors must obtain a **business license**, which is an authorization from the local government. Certain professionals, such as doctors and day-care providers, may also be required to obtain a special license from the state.
2. *Site permit* If not operating out of the home, a sole proprietor must obtain a certificate of occupancy to use another building for business.
3. *Name* If not using his or her own name as the name of the business, a sole proprietor must register a business name.

This paperwork often takes only a day or two to complete. The most difficult part of starting a new business is coming up with a good idea!

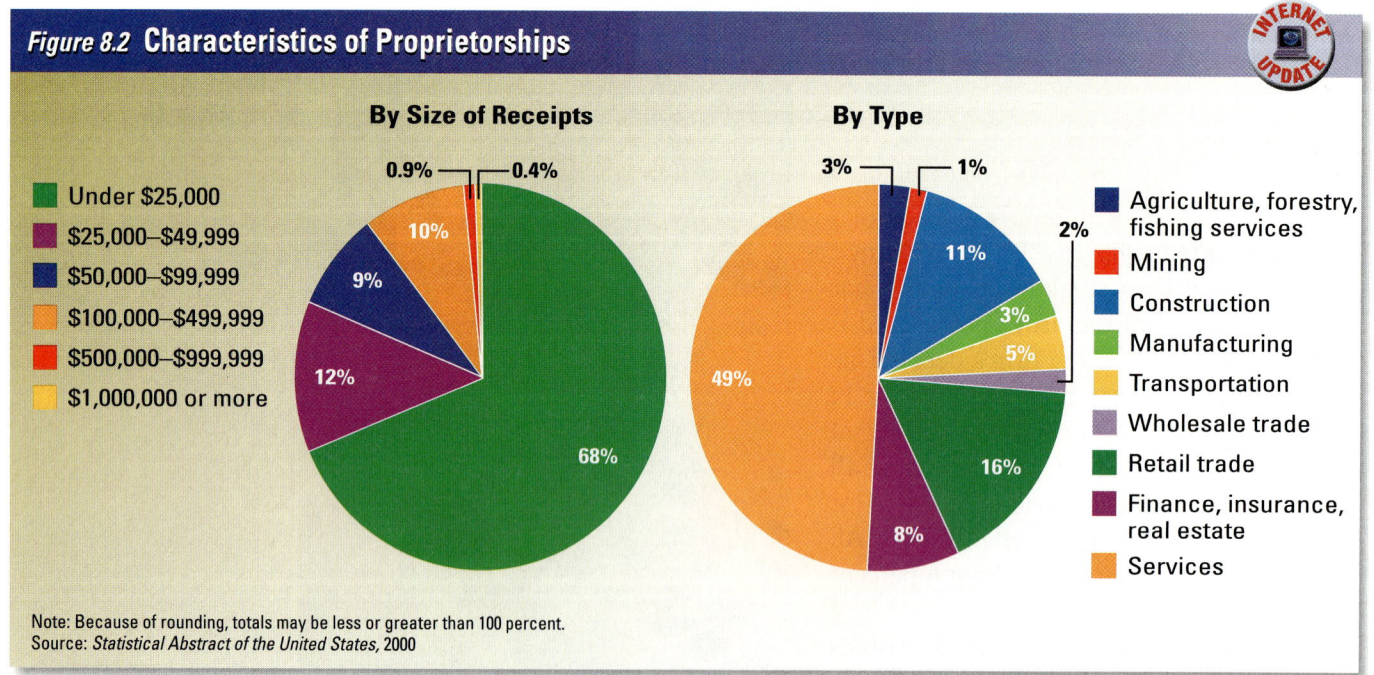

Figure 8.2 Characteristics of Proprietorships

By Size of Receipts

- Under $25,000
- $25,000–$49,999
- $50,000–$99,999
- $100,000–$499,999
- $500,000–$999,999
- $1,000,000 or more

0.9% 0.4%
10%
9%
12%
68%

By Type

3% 1%
11%
2%
3%
5%
49%
16%
8%

- Agriculture, forestry, fishing services
- Mining
- Construction
- Manufacturing
- Transportation
- Wholesale trade
- Retail trade
- Finance, insurance, real estate
- Services

Note: Because of rounding, totals may be less or greater than 100 percent.
Source: *Statistical Abstract of the United States*, 2000

Most sole proprietorships take in relatively small amounts of money, or receipts. Many proprietors run their businesses part-time.
Specialization What percentage of sole proprietorships is engaged in retail trade? Why might more sole proprietors be engaged in services rather than manufacturing?

Relatively Few Regulations

A proprietorship is the least-regulated form of business organization. Even the smallest business, however, is subject to some regulation, especially industry-specific regulations. For example, a gourmet soft pretzel stand would be subject to health codes, and a furniture refinishing business would be subject to codes regarding dangerous chemicals.

Sole proprietorships may also be subject to local **zoning laws**. Cities and towns often designate separate areas, or zones, for residential use and for business. Zoning laws may prohibit sole proprietors from operating businesses out of their homes.

Otherwise, these small businesses face few legal requirements. Because they require little legal paperwork, sole proprietorships are usually the least expensive form of ownership to establish.

Sole Receiver of Profit

A major advantage of the sole proprietorship is that the owner gets to keep all profits after paying income taxes. Potential profits motivate many people to start their own businesses. If the business succeeds, the owner does not have to share the success with anyone else.

Full Control

Another advantage of sole proprietorship is that sole proprietors can run their businesses as they wish. This means that they can respond quickly to changes in the marketplace. Such a degree of freedom appeals to entrepreneurs. Fast, flexible decision making allows sole proprietorships to take full advantage of sudden opportunities.

Easy to Discontinue

Finally, if sole proprietors decide to stop operations and do something else for a living, they can do so easily. They must, of course, pay all debts and other obligations like taxes, but they do not have to meet any other legal obligations to stop doing business.

▲ **What are the benefits of running a business from home?**

Disadvantages of Sole Proprietorships

As with everything else, there are trade-offs with sole proprietorships. The independence of a sole proprietorship comes with a high degree of responsibility.

Unlimited Personal Liability

The biggest disadvantage of sole proprietorship is unlimited personal liability. **Liability** is the legally bound obligation to pay debts. Sole proprietors are fully and personally responsible for all their business debts. If the business fails, the owner may have to sell personal property to cover any outstanding obligations.

For example, let's say you took out a loan to buy a ride-on lawn mower as part of your landscaping business. Even if you don't make enough money to stay in business, you must still repay the loan for the lawn mower. Business debts can ruin a sole proprietor's personal finances.

Limited Access to Resources

If your landscaping business takes off and grows quickly, you might need to expand

zoning law *law in a city or town that designates separate areas for residency and for business*

liability *the legally bound obligation to pay debts*

fringe benefit *payment
other than wages or
salaries*

your business by buying more equipment. But as a sole proprietor, you may have to expand by paying for the equipment out of your own pocket. This is because banks are sometimes unwilling to offer financing in the early days of a business. Many small business owners use all of their available savings and other personal resources to start up their businesses. This makes it difficult or impossible for them to expand quickly.

Physical capital may not be the only factor resource in short supply. Human capital may be lacking, too. A sole proprietor, no matter how ambitious, may lack some of the skills necessary to run a business successfully. All individuals have strengths and weaknesses. Some aspects of your business may suffer. For example, you may be great at sales, but not at bookkeeping and accounting. You may love working outdoors landscaping, but hate to call on people to drum up business.

Finally, as a sole proprietor, you may have to turn down work because you simply don't have enough hours in the day or enough workers to keep up with demand. A small business often presents its owner with too many demands, and that can be exhausting both personally and financially.

Lack of Permanence

A sole proprietorship has a limited life. If a sole proprietor dies or closes shop due to retirement, illness, loss of interest in the business, or for any other reason, the business simply ceases to exist.

Sole proprietorships often have trouble finding and keeping good employees. Small businesses generally cannot offer the security and advancement opportunities that many employees look for in a job. In addition, many sole proprietorships are able to offer employees little in the way of fringe benefits. **Fringe benefits** are payments to employees other than wages or salaries, such as paid vacation, retirement pay, and health insurance. Lack of experienced employees can hurt a business. Once again, the flip side of total control is total responsibility: a sole proprietor cannot count on anyone else to maintain the business.

Section 1 Assessment

Key Terms and Main Ideas

1. What is a **business organization**?
2. What is a **sole proprietorship**?
3. What role do **business licenses** and **zoning laws** play in sole proprietorships?
4. What kinds of **liabilities** are sole proprietors subject to?
5. Why do you think many sole proprietorships are able to offer few **fringe benefits** to workers?

Applying Economic Concepts

6. *Using the Databank* Examine the graph "Fastest-Growing Occupations" on page 537. Which of these occupations do you think could operate successfully as sole proprietorships? Explain your reasoning.
7. *Try This* Refer to Figure 8.1, "The Entrepreneurial Spirit," on page 186. How many of these traits do you have? Would you like to start your own business someday? Why or why not?

 *Take It to
the NET* Suppose that you will be opening a business of your own soon. First, decide what the business will be. Next, write down three questions you have about starting your own business, such as "Where will I get the money to start up my business?" Answer your questions using Internet resources. Use the links provided in the Social Studies area at the following Web site for help in completing this activity. **www.phschool.com**

ECONOMIC
Profile

Economist

Entrepreneur

Jerry Yang (b. 1968)

When 10-year-old Jerry Yang arrived in California from Taiwan with his brother, mother, and grandmother, the only English word he knew was shoe. *Some 15 years later he had mastered the language well enough to come up with "Yet Another Hierarchical Officious Oracle!" as the name for an on-line directory of Internet addresses that he and his friend David Filo had developed. The initials gave the directory the name Yang really wanted: Yahoo!*

The Birth of Yahoo!

Yang and Filo were graduate students in engineering and shared an office at Stanford University in 1993. At the time, the World Wide Web was in its infancy, and the two office mates began to spend time exploring the new Web. When they could not remember the addresses of interesting Web sites they had visited, they decided to make a reference list. In early 1994, they put their list on-line for friends to use. As the list got longer, Filo and Yang divided it into categories, and the Internet directory Yahoo! was born.

A Hobby Becomes a Business

By the end of 1994, word of a great, free catalog of Web pages had spread well beyond the university. Yang and Filo's site was getting a million visits a day, and Stanford began to rethink letting the university's equipment be tied up in this way. Yahoo! produced no revenue to cover expenses, so Yang and Filo began to consider how they might turn their hobby into a self-sustaining company. With the help of a business student friend, they developed a business plan and began to look for financing.

In April 1995, a California investment firm put up $1 million to get Yahoo! Corporation started. At the same time, the company's success was assured. America Online (AOL), already the world's largest Internet service provider, asked Yahoo! to be its search engine for the Web. The prospect of visits from millions of AOL subscribers convinced Filo and Yang to sell advertising space on the Yahoo! site. The idea quickly spread across the Web.

The Yahoo! Explosion

In 1996, Yang and Filo offered Yahoo! stock to the public for the first time. The money raised allowed the company to greatly expand its services. Although going public eventually reduced their ownership in Yahoo! to about 25 percent, the founders remained active in the company. Yang remained involved in business operations and Filo in technical development. By 1999, the company had become a $30 billion business. Except for the fact that both were now multimillionaires, little had changed since 1994 for the laid-back pair. Yahoo!'s success "hasn't changed my life at all," reports Yang, "except that I think more about taxes."

CHECK FOR UNDERSTANDING

1. **Source Reading** Explain why Yahoo!'s agreement with AOL assured that Yahoo! would be a success.

2. **Critical Thinking** Why are Yang and Filo much wealthier today than they were when they owned 100 percent of the company?

3. **Learn More** Use the Internet and other sources to learn more about Yahoo!'s legal status as a business organization. Has the company's business organization changed over time?

189

Preview

Objectives

After studying this section you will be able to:

1. **Compare and contrast** the different types of partnerships.
2. **Analyze** the advantages of partnerships.
3. **Analyze** the disadvantages of partnerships.

Section Focus

Partnerships let individuals pool their resources and share responsibility for the forming and running of a business.

Key Terms

partnership
general partnership
limited partnership
limited liability
  partnership (LLP)
articles of partnership
Uniform Partnership Act
  (UPA)
assets

---

partnership *a business organization owned by two or more persons who agree on a specific division of responsibilities and profits*

general partnership *partnership in which partners share equally in both responsibility and liability*

limited partnership *partnership in which only one partner is required to be a general partner*

limited liability partnership (LLP) *partnership in which all partners are limited partners*

A **partnership** is a business organization owned by two or more persons who agree on a specific division of responsibilities and profits. In the United States, partnerships account for about 7 percent of all businesses. They generate about 5 percent of all sales and about 10 percent of all income.

Types of Partnerships

Partnerships fall into three categories: general partnerships, limited partnerships, and limited liability partnerships. Each divides responsibility and liability differently.

◀ Sometimes three heads are better than one.

General Partnership

The most common type of partnership is the **general partnership**. Partners in a general partnership share equally in both responsibility and liability. Many of the same kinds of businesses that operate as sole proprietorships could operate as general partnerships. Doctors, lawyers, accountants, and other professionals often form partnerships with colleagues. Small retail stores, farms, construction companies, and family businesses often form partnerships as well.

Limited Partnership

In a **limited partnership,** only one partner is required to be a general partner. That is, only one partner has unlimited personal liability for the firm's actions. The remaining partner or partners contribute only money. They do not actively manage the business. Limited partners can lose only the amount of their initial investment. A limited partnership must have at least one general partner, but may have any number of limited partners. The main advantage of being a general partner is in having control of the business. The main drawback, of course, is the extent of liability.

Limited Liability Partnerships

The **limited liability partnership (LLP)** is a newer type of partnership recognized by

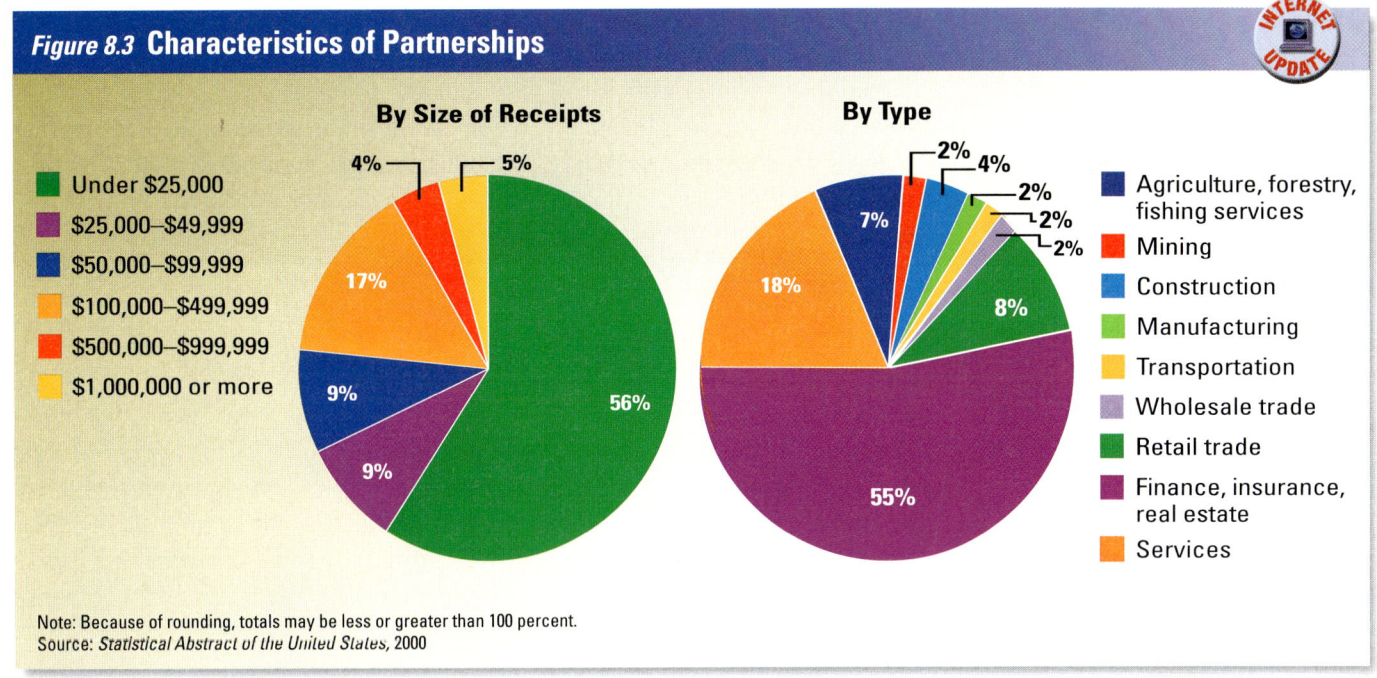

Figure 8.3 Characteristics of Partnerships

By Size of Receipts

- Under $25,000
- $25,000–$49,999
- $50,000–$99,999
- $100,000–$499,999
- $500,000–$999,999
- $1,000,000 or more

4%
5%
17%
9%
9%
56%

By Type

- Agriculture, forestry, fishing services
- Mining
- Construction
- Manufacturing
- Transportation
- Wholesale trade
- Retail trade
- Finance, insurance, real estate
- Services

2%
4%
2%
2%
2%
7%
18%
8%
55%

Note: Because of rounding, totals may be less or greater than 100 percent.
Source: *Statistical Abstract of the United States*, 2000

Partnerships can range in size from a pair of house painters to an accounting firm with thousands of partners.

Specialization Using the information in these graphs, describe partnerships in terms of industry and income.

many states. In this type of partnership, all partners are limited partners. An LLP functions like a general partnership, except that all partners are limited from personal liability in certain situations, such as another partner's mistakes. Not all types of businesses are allowed to register as limited liability partnerships. Most states allow professionals such as attorneys, physicians, dentists, and accountants to register as LLPs.

Advantages of Partnerships

Partnerships are easy to establish and are subject to few government regulations. They provide entrepreneurs with a number of advantages.

Ease of Start-Up

Like proprietorships, partnerships are easy and inexpensive to establish. The law does not require a written partnership agreement. Most small business experts, however, advise partners to work with an attorney to develop **articles of partnership,** or a partnership agreement. This legal document spells out each partner's rights and responsibilities. It outlines how partners will share profits or losses. Partnership agreements may also address other details, such as the ways new partners can join the firm, duration of the partnership, and tax responsibilities.

If partners do not establish their own articles of partnership, they will fall under the rules of the **Uniform Partnership Act (UPA)**. The Uniform Partnership Act is a uniform state law adopted by most states to establish rules for partnerships. The UPA requires common ownership interests, profit and loss sharing, and shared management responsibilities.

Like sole proprietorships, partnerships are subject to little government regulation. The government does not dictate how partnerships conduct business. Partners can distribute profits as they wish, as long as they abide by the partnership agreement or by the UPA.

articles of partnership *a partnership agreement*

Uniform Partnership Act (UPA) *act ordering common ownership interests, profit and loss sharing, and shared management responsibilities in a partnership*

assets *money and other valuables belonging to an individual or business*

Shared Decision Making and Specialization

In a sole proprietorship, the individual owner has the sole burden of making all the business decisions. In a partnership, the responsibility for the business may be shared. A sole proprietorship requires the owner to wear many hats, some of which might not fit very well. In a successful partnership, however, each partner brings different strengths and skills to the business.

Larger Pool of Capital

Each partner's **assets**, or money and other valuables, improve the firm's ability to borrow funds for operations or expansion. Partnership agreements can also allow firms to add limited partners to raise funds.

Partnerships offer more advantages to employees, enabling them to attract and keep talented employees more easily than proprietorships can. Graduates from top accounting schools, for example, often seek jobs with large and prestigious accounting LLPs, hoping to become partners themselves someday.

Taxation

Partnerships, like sole proprietorships, are not subject to any special taxes. Partners pay taxes on their share of the income that the partnership generates. The business itself, however, does not have to pay taxes.

Disadvantages of Partnerships

Partnerships also present some disadvantages. Many of the disadvantages of sole proprietorships are present in partnerships. Limited liability partnerships have fewer disadvantages than partnerships with general partners. All partnerships, however, have the potential for conflict.

Unlimited Liability

Unless the partnership is an LLP, at least one partner has unlimited liability. As in a sole proprietorship, any general partner could lose everything, including personal property, in paying the firm's debts. Limited partners do not face the same threat. They can lose only their investment.

In a partnership, each general partner is bound by the acts of all other general partners. If one partner's actions cause the firm losses, then all of the general partners suffer. If one doctor in a partnership is

Like sole proprietors, ▶ partners must maintain their entrepreneurial spirit to stay in business.

▲ These partners must find positive ways to deal with conflict if they want to keep their business running smoothly.

sued for malpractice, all of the doctors in the partnership stand to lose. General partners do not enjoy absolute control over the firm's actions like sole proprietors do. The risk from other people's actions means that people must choose their business partners carefully.

Potential for Conflict

As in any close relationship, partnerships have the potential for conflict. Partnership agreements address technical aspects of the business, such as profit and loss. Many important considerations exist outside these legal guidelines, however. Partners need to ensure that they agree about work habits, goals, management styles, ethics, and general business philosophies. Still, friction between partners often arises and can be difficult to resolve. Many partnerships dissolve because of interpersonal conflicts. Partners must learn to communicate openly and find ways to resolve conflicts.

Section 2 Assessment

Key Terms and Main Ideas

1. Explain the characteristics of **partnerships.**
2. How do **general partnerships, limited partnerships,** and **limited liability partnerships** differ?
3. What issues are addressed in **articles of partnership?**
4. What is the purpose of the **Uniform Partnership Act?**

Applying Economic Concepts

5. *Critical Thinking* Why might accountants and physicians find limited liability partnerships attractive?

6. *Critical Thinking* Do you think the advantages of partnerships outweigh the disadvantages? Why or why not?

7. *Problem Solving* You and your general partners are operating under the Uniform Partnership Act, not your own articles of partnership. Now you cannot agree who should be responsible for which duties. How will you resolve your conflict?

8. *Try This* With a partner or two, draw up articles of partnership for a fictional business. Decide which type of partnership best suits your business and your personal preferences and skills.

Take It to the NET Choose a classmate and suppose that the two of you have just decided to form a new partnership for a business venture. Find out what's required in your state to start your new business. Use the links provided in the Social Studies area at the following Web site for help in completing this activity. **www.phschool.com**

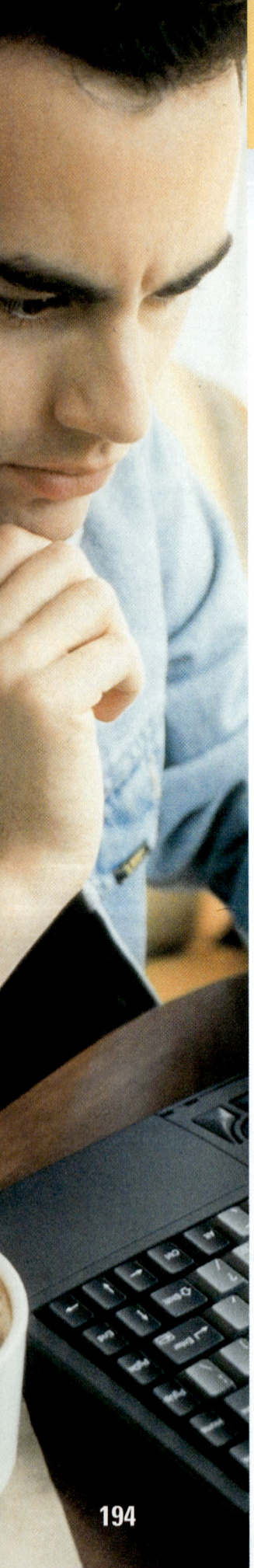

Using the Internet for Research

The Internet is a comprehensive network of computers that links businesses, universities, and individuals around the world. The World Wide Web is one part of the Internet. Because the Internet has no central organization, finding a Web page with the information you need can be difficult. Search engines, databases that track thousands of Web pages by subject, can help you focus your search.

In addition to advertising and product information, many corporations use their Internet sites to post corporate ethics statements like the one below. An ethics statement typically describes how the company approaches the law, the community in which it works, and its employees. Use the steps below to locate a corporate ethics statement on the Web.

1. Prepare your search. American companies can face ethical dilemmas over issues like pollution, safety, and working conditions. (a) Identify two companies that you think might face ethical issues. (b) How could you use the Internet to find these companies?

2. Refine your search. Many search engines offer an advanced search option that allows you to refine your search. (a) Which words other than "ethics," "statement," and the company name might help you find the documents you are looking for? (b) Based on your first set of results, what word could you *exclude* from your search to eliminate inappropriate listings?

3. Analyze the document. Answer the following questions using the ethics statement at left. (a) List three significant phrases that the company uses in its ethics statement. (b) Do you find the company's statement convincing? Why or why not? (c) Which words or phrases are not convincing?

ETHICS STATEMENT OF ALPINE INVESTMENTS, INC.

Alpine Investments, Inc., and each of its employees will:

- Individually and collectively maintain a high level of ethical conduct with clients, coworkers, members of allied professions, and the public.
- Practice a method of financial planning founded on a legal and practical basis, not voluntarily associating with anyone who violates this principle.
- Seek advice in doubtful or difficult cases, and whenever it appears that the services of members of other professions would provide more complete and better quality or degree of advice.
- Not reveal the private information we may observe in any client's affairs, unless required to do so by law.
- Obey all laws and uphold the dignity and honor of the profession and accept the profession's self-imposed rules.
- Oppose, without hesitation, illegal or unethical conduct of fellow members of our profession.

Additional Practice

Use the Internet to find an ethics statement for a company that has recently been in the news for a controversial decision or action.

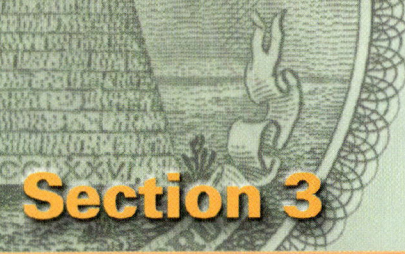

Corporations, Mergers, and Multinationals

Preview

Objectives

After studying this section you will be able to:

1. **Explain** the characteristics of corporations.
2. **Analyze** the advantages of incorporation.
3. **Analyze** the disadvantages of incorporation.
4. **Compare and contrast** corporate combinations.
5. **Describe** the role of multinational corporations.

Section Focus

Corporations are complex business organizations that can be combined to form even larger businesses. Some corporate enterprises span the globe.

Key Terms

corporation
stock
closely held corporation
publicly held corporation
bond
certificate of incorporation
dividend
horizontal merger
vertical merger
conglomerate
multinational corporation (MNC)

Businesses often rely on investment to expand operations. One way for a business to increase investment is to form a corporation. A corporation can grow even larger by combining with other corporations. Some corporations are so large that they do business all over the world.

Corporations

The most complex form of business organization is the corporation. A **corporation** is a legal entity, or being, owned by individual stockholders, each of whom faces limited liability for the firm's debts. Stockholders own **stock,** a certificate of ownership in a corporation. In other words, if you own

stock in a corporation, you are a part-owner of that corporation. If a corporation issues 1,000 shares of stock, and you purchase 1 share, you own 1/1000th of the company.

Corporations differ from sole proprietorships, which have no identity beyond that of the owners. A corporation is defined as an "entity" because it has a legal identity separate from those of its owners. Legally, it is regarded much like an individual. A

corporation *a legal entity owned by individual stockholders*

stock *a certificate of ownership in a corporation*

Many corporations make their headquarters in large cities.
▼

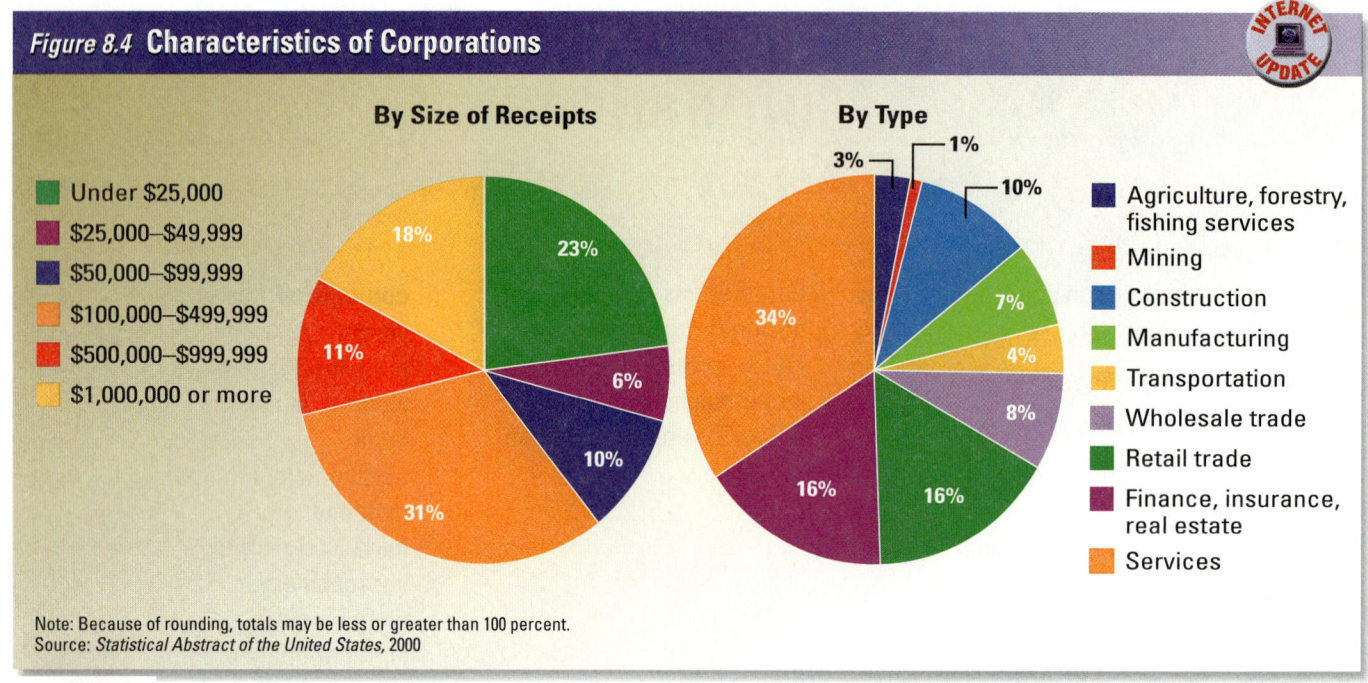

Figure 8.4 Characteristics of Corporations

By Size of Receipts

- Under $25,000
- $25,000–$49,999
- $50,000–$99,999
- $100,000–$499,999
- $500,000–$999,999
- $1,000,000 or more

23%, 6%, 10%, 31%, 11%, 18%

By Type

3%, 1%, 10%, 7%, 4%, 8%, 16%, 16%, 34%

- Agriculture, forestry, fishing services
- Mining
- Construction
- Manufacturing
- Transportation
- Wholesale trade
- Retail trade
- Finance, insurance, real estate
- Services

Note: Because of rounding, totals may be less or greater than 100 percent.
Source: *Statistical Abstract of the United States,* 2000

Notice that over 60 percent of corporations are engaged in services, manufacturing, wholesale trade, and retail trade.
Incentives What incentives do businesses in these particular industries have to form corporations?

closely held corporation
corporation that issues stock to only a few people, often family members

publicly held corporation
corporation that sells stock on the open market

corporation pays taxes, may engage in business, make contracts, sue other parties, and get sued by others.

In the United States, corporations account for about 20 percent of all businesses, yet sell about 90 percent of all products sold in the nation. They generate about 70 percent of the net income earned in the nation. Because of the advantages of corporations, most large business firms do incorporate. Supermarkets, high-tech companies, and machinery manufacturers are just some of the types of firms that usually form corporations. Corporations' profits are about ten percent of their income.

Types of Corporations

Some corporations issue stock to only a few people, often family members. These stockholders rarely trade their stock, but pass it on within families. Such corporations are called **closely held corporations**. They are also known as privately held corporations.

A **publicly held corporation**, on the other hand, has many shareholders who can buy or sell stock on the open market. Stocks are bought and sold at financial markets called stock exchanges, such as the New York Stock Exchange. You will read about these financial markets in Chapter 11.

Corporate Structure

While the exact organization varies from firm to firm, all corporations have the same basic structure. Corporation owners—the stockholders—elect a board of directors. The board of directors makes all the major decisions of the corporation. It appoints corporate officers, who run the corporation and oversee production. Corporate officers, in turn, hire managers and employees, who work in various departments like finance, sales, research, marketing, and production.

Advantages of Incorporation

Incorporation, or forming a corporation, offers advantages to both the individual owners, or stockholders, and to the corporation itself. These include

- limited liability for owners
- transferable ownership
- ability to attract capital
- long life

Advantages for Stockholders

The primary reason that entrepreneurs choose to incorporate, or form a corporation, is to gain the benefit of limited liability. Individual investors do not carry responsibility for the corporation's actions. They can lose only the amount of money they have invested in the business.

Corporations usually also provide stockholders with more flexibility than other ownership forms. Shares of stock are transferable, which means that stockholders can sell their stocks to others and get money in return.

Advantages for the Corporation

The corporate structure also presents advantages for the firm itself. Corporations have more potential for growth than other business forms. By selling shares on the stock market, corporations can raise money to purchase capital. A corporation can offer as many shares of stock as its corporate charter allows. As long as investors have confidence in the firm's success, companies should be able to sell stock fairly easily.

Corporations can also raise money by borrowing it. They do this by selling bonds. A **bond** is a formal contract to repay borrowed money with interest at fixed intervals.

Because ownership is separate from the running of the firm, corporation owners— that is, stockholders—do not need any special managerial skills. Instead, the corporation can hire various experts—the best financial analysts, the best engineers, and so forth—to create and market the best services or goods possible.

Corporations also have the advantage of long life. Unlike a sole proprietorship, the company does not end with the death of an owner. Because stock is transferable, that is, it can be bought and sold, corporations are able to exist longer than simple proprietorships. Unless it has stated in advance a specific termination date, the corporation can continue doing business indefinitely.

Disadvantages of Incorporation

Corporations are not without their disadvantages. These include

- expense and difficulty of start-up
- double taxation
- potential loss of control by the founders
- more legal requirements and regulations

Difficulty and Expense of Start-Up

Corporate charters can be difficult, expensive, and time consuming to establish. Though most states allow people to form corporations without legal help, few experts would recommend this cheaper shortcut. Applications are complex and confusing.

Firms that wish to incorporate must first file for a state license known as a **certificate of incorporation**, or corporate charter. The application includes crucial information such as

- the corporate name
- statement of purpose
- length of time that the business will run (usually "for perpetuity," or without limit)
- founders' names and addresses
- headquarters' business address
- method of fund-raising
- the rules for the corporation's management

Once state officials review and approve the application, they grant a corporate charter. Then the corporation may organize itself to produce and sell a good or service.

Double Taxation

The law considers corporations legal entities separate from their owners. Corporations, therefore, must pay taxes on their income.

bond *a formal contract to repay borrowed money with interest at fixed intervals*

certificate of incorporation *license to form a corporation issued by state government*

dividend *the portion of corporate profits paid out to stockholders*

Profit is a form of income. When stockholders receive income from the corporation in the form of **dividends**—the portion of corporate profits paid out to stockholders—the stockholders must pay personal income tax on those dividends. This double taxation keeps many firms from incorporating.

Stockholders may face an additional tax if they sell their shares. When stockholders sell their shares, they must pay a special tax, called a capital gains tax, if they have made a profit.

Loss of Control

Unlike the owner of a sole proprietorship, the original owners of a corporation often lose control of the company. Managers and boards of directors, not owners, manage corporations. These professional managers do not always act in the owners'

best interests. They might be more interested in protecting their own jobs or salaries today than in making difficult decisions that would benefit the firm tomorrow.

More Regulation

Corporations also face more regulations than other kinds of business organizations. Corporations must hold annual meetings for shareholders and keep careful records of all business transactions. Publicly held corporations are required to file quarterly and annual reports to the Securities and Exchange Commission (SEC). The SEC is a federal agency that regulates the stock market.

Corporate Combinations

As a corporation continues to grow, managers and owners may decide it makes

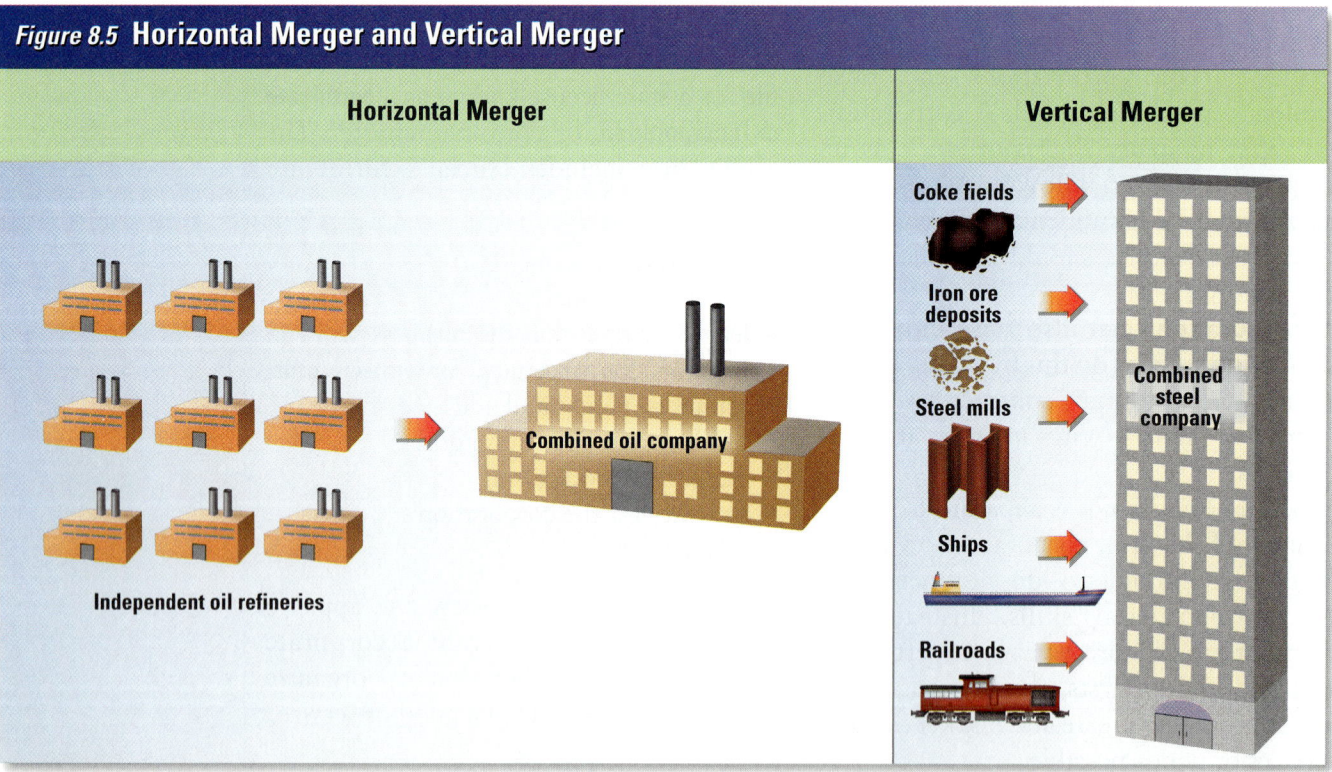

Figure 8.5 Horizontal Merger and Vertical Merger

Horizontal Merger

Independent oil refineries

Combined oil company

Vertical Merger

Coke fields

Iron ore deposits

Steel mills

Ships

Railroads

Combined steel company

Beginning in the 1880s, John D. Rockefeller's Standard Oil Company combined horizontally (left) with 40 other oil refineries. The power gained by Standard Oil and similar monopolies prompted passage of the Sherman Antitrust Act in 1890. In 1899, Andrew Carnegie established the Carnegie Steel Company. He used the vertical merger (right) to purchase ore mines, furnaces and mills, and even the shipping and railroad lines needed to transport his products to market. Within a short time, Carnegie controlled the steel industry. Most vertical mergers, however, do not result in monopolies. **Competition** **Explain the difference between horizontal and vertical mergers.**

sense to merge, or combine, the firm with another company or companies. The three kinds of mergers are horizontal mergers, vertical mergers, and conglomerates.

Each of these corporate combinations can lead to larger, more efficient firms. Often, larger firms can produce and sell their products at lower prices. However, their size can also give some of these combinations more monopoly power, as discussed in Chapter 7.

Horizontal mergers

Horizontal mergers join two or more firms competing in the same market with the same good or service. For example, in late 1998, two giant automakers, Chrysler Corporation and Daimler-Benz, merged to form DaimlerChrysler.

Two firms might choose to merge if the newly resulting firm would result in economies of scale or would otherwise improve efficiency. At the time of the merger, Chrysler Corporation and Daimler-Benz predicted that their merger would reduce costs and boost revenues as much as $3 billion dollars annually.

As you read in Chapter 7, the federal government watches horizontal mergers carefully. The resulting single firm might gain monopoly power in its market.

Vertical Mergers

Vertical mergers join two or more firms involved in different stages of producing the same good or service. A vertical merger can allow a firm to operate more efficiently. A vertically combined firm can control all phases of production, rather than rely on the goods or services of outside suppliers. Sometimes firms combine vertically out of fear that they may otherwise lose crucial supplies. To ensure production, these firms simply buy their suppliers.

Antitrust regulators become concerned when many firms in the same industry merge vertically if that merger drives supplying firms out of business. Most vertical mergers do not substantially lessen competition, however, so they are usually allowed.

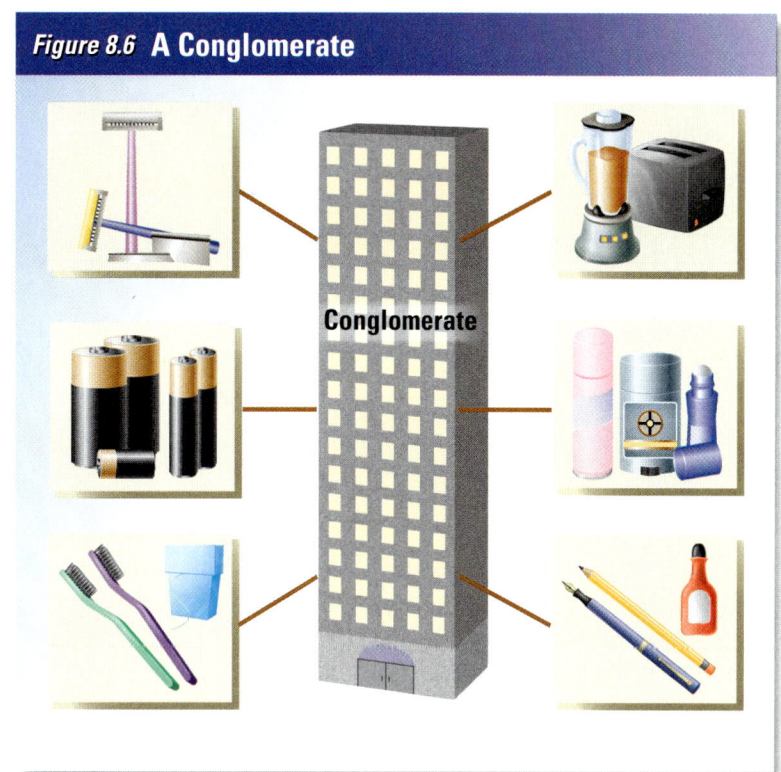

Figure 8.6 A Conglomerate

Conglomerate

Conglomerates combine diverse businesses.
Competition Why don't conglomerates generally decrease competition?

Conglomerates

Sometimes firms buy other companies that produce totally unrelated goods or services. These combinations, called **conglomerates**, have more than three businesses that make unrelated products. In a conglomerate, no one business earns the majority of the firm's profits. The government usually allows this kind of merger, because it does not result in decreased competition.

Multinational Corporations

The world's largest corporations produce and sell their goods and services throughout the world. They are called **multinational corporations (MNCs)**. MNCs are corporations that operate in more than one country at a time. They usually have headquarters in one country and branches in other countries. Multinationals, which are sometimes called transnational corporations, must obey laws and pay taxes in each country in which they operate. In the

horizontal merger *the combination of two or more firms competing in the same market with the same good or service*

vertical merger *the combination of two or more firms involved in different stages of producing the same good or service*

conglomerate *business combination merging more than three businesses that make unrelated products*

multinational corporation (MNC) *large corporation that produces and sells its goods and services throughout the world*

▲ **Multinational corporations make their presence felt throughout the world.**

1980s. The picture today shows many different home countries for these giants, including Japan, South Korea, the Netherlands, and Italy.

Advantages of Multinationals

Multinationals benefit consumers and workers worldwide by providing jobs and products around the world. They also spread new technologies and production methods across the globe. Often the jobs they provide help poorer nations gain better living standards for their people.

Disadvantages of Multinationals

On the downside, many people feel that multinational firms unduly influence the culture and politics in the countries in which they operate. While some people feel that MNCs provide much needed jobs, critics are concerned about the low wages and poor working conditions provided by MNCs in some poorer countries. Whatever the advantages and disadvantages, trends suggest that MNCs will become increasingly visible and important in the world economy in the years ahead.

late 1990s, an estimated 63,000 multinational firms operated about 690,000 foreign branches. They accounted for more than $3 trillion of worldwide assets. Many multinational corporations have operating budgets much bigger than most governments' budgets.

Corporations in the United States and Great Britain operated the world's largest multinationals in the 1970s and early

---

Section 3 Assessment

Key Terms and Main Ideas

1. How does a **corporation** differ from a sole proprietorship or partnership?
2. What is the difference between a **closely held corporation** and a **publicly held corporation**?
3. What information is required in a **certificate of incorporation**?
4. What is **stock**?
5. Why must stockholders pay taxes on **dividends**?
6. What is a merger? How do **horizontal mergers, vertical mergers,** and **conglomerates** differ?
7. Why are some corporations called **multinational corporations**?

Applying Economic Concepts

8. *Critical Thinking* Suppose you are deciding whether to incorporate your house-cleaning business. Analyze the consequences of this economic decision.
9. *Try This* Identify several sole proprietorships and partnerships in your neighborhood or town. Which of these businesses might benefit from incorporation? Explain your reasoning.
10. *Critical Thinking* How might a corporation benefit by being multinational?
11. *Problem Solving* You want to incorporate your family business. Will you form a closely held corporation or a publicly held corporation? Explain your reasoning.

Take It to the NET Use the Internet to identify a company that has been accused of exploiting foreign labor. What specific criticisms have been made? What is the company's response? Who do you think is right? Use the links provided in the Social Studies area at the following Web site for help in completing this activity. **www.phschool.com**

Other Organizations

Preview

Objectives

After studying this section you will be able to:

1. **Understand** how a business franchise works.
2. **Identify** the different types of cooperative organizations.
3. **Understand** the purpose of nonprofit organizations, including professional and business organizations.

Section Focus

Some organizations exist to aid business owners, consumers, producers, industries, workers, or society at large. Many operate without the aim of earning a profit.

Key Terms

business franchise
royalty
cooperative
consumer cooperative
service cooperative
producer cooperative
nonprofit organization
professional organization
business association
trade association

Why would a person with dreams of running her own business turn to a multinational company for help? Why would a customer pay a fee for the privilege of shopping at a certain store? Why would an organization have no intention of earning a profit at all?

There are sound answers for all of these questions. As you read this section, you will discover many kinds of organizations that serve many kinds of interests. You are probably already familiar with a number of them.

Business Franchises

In Chapter 7, you learned about franchises issued by government authorities. These franchises give only one firm the right to sell its goods within a limited market, such as within a national park. In business, too, a franchise signals exclusive rights. A **business franchise** is a semi-independent business that pays fees to a parent company. In return, the business is granted the exclusive right to sell a certain product or service in a given area.

Parent companies are called *franchisers*. The franchiser develops the products and business systems. They then work with the

local franchise owners to help them produce and sell their products.

The image that leaps to mind when discussing franchises is the fast-food restaurant. However, franchises offer a wide array of goods and services, from diamonds to day-care centers.

> **business franchise** *a semi-independent business that pays fees to a parent company in return for the exclusive right to sell a certain product or service in a given area*

◄ Competing restaurant franchises often cluster together along highways.

royalty share of earnings given as payment

cooperative a business organization owned and operated by a group of individuals for their mutual benefit

Franchising has become popular in recent years. This is because small franchise businesses allow owners a degree of control. At the same time, the owners benefit from the support of the parent company. As with any other form of business organization, franchises offer both advantages and disadvantages.

Advantages of Franchises

For a small business owner, a franchise can provide advantages a completely independent business cannot. A franchise comes with a built-in reputation. Consumers may already be familiar with the product and brand of the franchise. Other benefits include

1. *Management training and support* Franchisers help inexperienced owners gain the experience they need to succeed.
2. *Standardized quality* Most parent companies require franchise owners to follow certain rules and processes to guarantee product quality.

▲ What advantages do co-ops offer consumers?

3. *National advertising programs* Parent companies pay for far-reaching advertising campaigns to establish their brand names.
4. *Financial assistance* Some franchisers provide financing to help franchise owners start their businesses.
5. *Centralized buying power* Franchisers buy materials in bulk for all of their franchise locations. They pass on the savings to their franchise owners.

Disadvantages of Franchises

The biggest disadvantage of a franchise is that the franchise owner must sacrifice some freedom in return for the parent company's guidance. Other disadvantages include

1. *High franchising fees and royalties* Franchisers often charge high fees for the right to use the company name. They also charge franchise owners a share of the earnings, or **royalties**.
2. *Strict operating standards* Franchise owners must follow all of the rules laid out in the franchising agreement for such matters as hours of operation, employee dress codes, and operating procedures. Otherwise, an owner may lose the franchise.
3. *Purchasing restrictions* Franchise owners must often buy their supplies from the parent company or from approved suppliers.
4. *Limited product line* Franchise agreements allow stores to offer only approved products.

Cooperative Organizations

A **cooperative** is a business organization owned and operated by a group of individuals for their shared benefit. In other words, working together, the individuals can provide themselves with certain advantages. Cooperatives, or co-ops, fall into three main categories: consumer, or purchasing cooperatives; service cooperatives; and producer cooperatives.

Consumer Cooperatives

Retail outlets owned and operated by consumers are called **consumer cooperatives,** or purchasing cooperatives. Consumer cooperatives sell merchandise to their members at reduced prices. By making large purchases, consumer cooperatives can obtain goods at a lower cost. They then pass the savings on to members. Examples of consumer cooperatives include discount price clubs, compact disc or book clubs, some health food stores, and housing cooperatives. Some co-ops require members to work a small number of hours per year to maintain their memberships. Others require membership fees instead. For example, your local health food store may require you to work 20 hours per month in order to maintain your membership. Giant discount price clubs, on the other hand, require annual membership fees.

Service Cooperatives

Cooperatives that provide a service, rather than goods, are called **service cooperatives.** Some service co-ops offer discounted insurance, banking services, health care, legal help, or baby-sitting services. Credit unions, or financial cooperatives, lend money to their members at reduced rates.

Producer Cooperatives

Producer cooperatives are agricultural marketing cooperatives that help members sell their products. These co-ops allow members to focus their attention on growing their crops or raising their livestock. The co-ops, meanwhile, market these goods for the highest prices possible.

Nonprofit Organizations

Some institutions function much like business organizations, but do not operate for the purpose of generating profit. These **nonprofit organizations** are usually in the business of benefiting society. Nonprofit organizations include museums, public schools, the American Red Cross, hospitals, adoption agencies, churches, synagogues, YMCAs, and many other groups.

Global Connection

Nonprofits on a Global Scale Some nonprofit organizations focus on both local and global concerns. Recently, a global nonprofit organization, the Conservation International Foundation, joined efforts with one of the nation's largest coffee retailers to promote and sell "shade-grown coffee," which is currently grown in the Americas and other parts of the globe. In conjunction with the coffee retailer, this nonprofit organization is supporting a style of growing coffee that reduces the environmental impact of coffee growing in biologically sensitive regions. The foundation is also helping coffee growers sell directly to retailers, rather than through a third party. This arrangement brings greater profits to the coffee growers. **What are the local benefits of this program? What are the global benefits?**

The government exempts nonprofit organizations from income taxes. Many nonprofit organizations operate with partial government support. Almost all of them provide services rather than goods.

Other nonprofit organizations provide support to particular occupations or geographical areas. These include professional organizations, business associations, trade associations, and labor unions.

Professional Organizations

Professional organizations work to improve the image, working conditions, and skill levels of people in particular occupations. Examples include the National Education Association for public school and college

consumer cooperative *retail outlet owned and operated by consumers*

service cooperative *cooperative that provides a service, rather than a good*

producer cooperative *agricultural marketing cooperative that helps members sell their products*

nonprofit organization *institution that functions much like a business, but does not operate for the purpose of generating profits*

professional organization *nonprofit organization that works to improve the image, working conditions, and skill levels of people in particular occupations*

▲ **What might motivate these Red Cross volunteers?**

◄ **Many nonprofit organizations serve business interests.**

business association
nonprofit organization that promotes collective business interests for a city, state, or other geographical area, or for a group of similar businesses

trade association
nonprofit organization that promotes the interests of a particular industry

and university workers, American Veterinary Medical Association for veterinary professionals, the American Bar Association for lawyers, and the American Management Association for business professionals.

Professional organizations keep their members up-to-date on industry trends. They help them identify and follow codes of conduct. For example, the American Medical Association opposes advertising. It believes that doctors present a less professional, authoritative, and caring image if they advertise for patients. Likewise, the American Bar Association frowns upon law firms that advertise their services for personal injury complaints.

Business Associations

Business associations promote the collective business interests of a city, state, or other geographical area, or of a group of similar businesses. They may also address codes of conduct, just as professional associations do.

Your local Better Business Bureau, sponsored by local businesses, is a nonprofit group. It aims to protect consumers by promoting an ethical and fair marketplace. Your state's or city's chamber of commerce works to attract new businesses to your area.

Trade Associations

Nonprofit organizations that promote the interests of particular industries are called **trade associations**. The American Marketing Association, for example, aims to improve marketers' and marketing firms' images. All kinds of industries, from publishing to food processing, enjoy the support of trade associations.

Labor Unions

A labor union is an organized group of workers whose aim is to improve working conditions, hours, wages, and fringe benefits. In the next chapter, you will read about the history and role of labor unions.

Section 4 Assessment

Key Terms and Main Ideas

1. How does a **business franchise** work?
2. What are **royalties**?
3. What is a **cooperative**?
4. How do **consumer cooperatives, service cooperatives,** and **producer cooperatives** differ?
5. What is a **nonprofit organization**?
6. What is the purpose of **professional organizations, business associations,** and **trade associations**?

Applying Economic Concepts

7. *Critical Thinking* Do you think the advantages of owning a franchise outweigh the disadvantages? Explain your reasoning.
8. *Critical Thinking* Do you think professional and business associations benefit consumers? Explain your reasoning.
9. *Try This* Make a list of the types of organizations described in this section. Next to each type, write down an example with which you are familiar.

Take It to the NET

Many nonprofit organizations are charitable organizations. Find two charities from your state and list their mission statements and organizational goals. Use the links provided in the Social Studies area at the following Web site for help in completing this activity.
www.phschool.com

Business and Ethics

Statement of Principles and Code of Conduct

WE EMBRACE RESPONSIBILITY.

WE ACT IN GOOD FAITH, HONESTLY AND FAIRLY.

WE HONOR THE LAW.

WE NURTURE ACHIEVEMENT.

WE DELIVER QUALITY AND VALUE.

WE RESPECT THE EARTH.

WE ADVANCE TECHNOLOGY.

WE ARE GOOD CITIZENS.

WE GUARD OUR INTEGRITY.

When George Abbot Morison retired to the family farm in Peterborough, New Hampshire, in the 1940s, the state had high unemployment and very little industry. Morison decided to do something that would create new jobs and help revitalize the state's industrial base. He had read about Hitchiner Manufacturing Company, Inc., a small company that specialized in producing metal parts. Morison saw a growing need for precision metal parts and realized that Hitchiner's metal casting process had great commercial potential. In 1949, he and his son John H. Morison bought the company, and John became president.

Rights and Responsibilities For the Morisons' investment to pay off, they had to develop the company so that it would make money. To do so, they benefited from their rights to enter into contracts, to use the courts to enforce their contractual rights, and to receive equal protection of law.

Hitchiner also had responsibilities. It had to comply with health and safety laws to reduce the chances of on-the-job injuries. The company had to pay employees at least minimum wage and had to make contributions to the state workers compensation fund. It also had to pay taxes on its profits.

Most importantly, the company strove to maintain "the highest standards of ethical and good-spirited conduct." Key points of its ethics policy appear in the Statement of Principles and Code of Conduct on this page.

Helping Employees Morison realized that the company's success depended on having an educated and trained work force. Hitchiner began sending employees for courses in many disciplines, from basic literacy and mathematics to statistical process control, for apprenticeships in specialized technical fields, and for business-management seminars. In 1953, Hitchiner became one of the first American companies to give its employees an ownership interest in the company.

▼ **Hitchiner uses the latest technologies in metal casting.**

Continued Success Today, Hitchiner markets its metal castings and licenses its technology and processes worldwide. Its current sales total about $200 million a year.

Applying Economic Ideas

1. **(a)** How were the Morisons able to help themselves and help their community at the same time? **(b)** What were their rights and responsibilities?

2. Analyze Hitchiner's ethics policy. Why was this policy an important part of its business success?

Chapter Summary

A summary of major ideas in Chapter 8 appears below. See also the **Guide to the Essentials of Economics**, which provides additional review and test practice of key concepts in Chapter 8.

Section 1 Sole Proprietorships (pp. 185–188)

Sole proprietorships are the most common form of business in the United States. They are easy to establish and offer owners both the benefits and drawbacks that come with full control of the business.

Section 2 Partnerships (pp. 190–193)

Partnerships let individuals pool their resources and share responsibility in the forming and running of a business. Three types of partnerships are the **general partnership**, the **limited partnership**, and the **limited liability partnership**.

Section 3 Corporations, Mergers, and Multinationals (pp. 195–200)

Corporations are complex business organizations that can be owned by a few or a great many individuals. **Mergers** combine corporations in various ways to form even larger businesses. Some corporate enterprises, the **multinationals**, span the globe.

Section 4 Other Organizations (pp. 201–204)

Business franchises are business organizations that give business owners support from a parent company. Other types of organizations serve to aid business owners, consumers, producers, industries, workers, or society at large. Many operate as **nonprofit organizations**.

Key Terms

Match the following definitions with the terms listed below. You will not use all of the terms.

liability	limited partnership
corporation	royalties
conglomerate	nonprofit
general partnership	organization
sole proprietorship	consumer
vertical merger	cooperative

1. the combination of two or more firms involved in different stages of producing the same good or service
2. the legally bound obligation to pay debts
3. a legal entity owned by individual stockholders
4. a business owned and managed by a single individual
5. a retail outlet owned and operated by consumers
6. a business combination merging more than three businesses that make unrelated products
7. share of earnings given as payment
8. a form of partnership in which only one partner is required to be a general partner

Using Graphic Organizers

9. On a separate sheet of paper, copy the flowchart below. Use the flowchart to organize information about how a business might grow. Complete the flowchart by writing descriptions and examples for each cell in the chart. You may add cells to the chart.

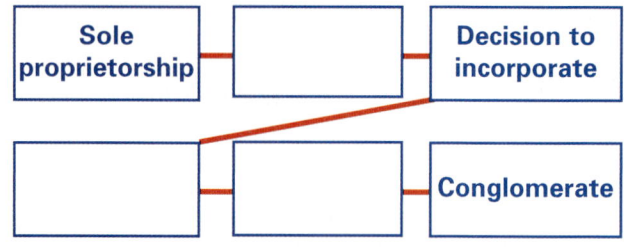

Reviewing Main Ideas

10. List three trade-offs of running a sole proprietorship.
11. What are the advantages of forming a partnership when creating a new business?
12. What benefits do corporations bring to their stockholders?
13. Compare the advantages and disadvantages of opening a business franchise.
14. Describe the difference between vertical mergers, horizontal mergers, and conglomerates.
15. What are multinational corporations?
16. What are the advantages of cooperatives?
17. Identify and evaluate the ordinances and regulations that apply to the various types of businesses described in the chapter.

Critical Thinking

18. **Drawing Conclusions** Suppose you are opening a new business. List three choices that you would need to make to decide what style of business organization to form.
19. **Analyzing Information** How are the three types of corporate combinations usually affected by antitrust policy?
20. **Making Comparisons** Compare the different levels of individual liability among the three main types of business organizations: sole proprietorships, partnerships, and corporations.
21. **Drawing Inferences** How can stockholders influence the actions of the corporation they own?

Problem-Solving Activity

22. Recommend a cooperative for your community. Describe the type of cooperative it would be (consumer, service, or producer) and how your community could benefit from it.

Economics Journal

Identifying Alternatives Revisit your list of local businesses. Pick one and recommend a particular business form for it. Draft a proposal outlining why you think the business or the owner(s) would benefit from your plan.

Skills for Life

Using the Internet for Research Review the steps shown on page 194. Then complete the following activity.

Mergers lead to the formation of new business organizations. Corporate mergers sometimes have far-reaching effects on the companies and employees involved. Use the steps below to prepare a summary of one recent corporate merger and its effects on the employees of the companies involved.

23. **Prepare your search.** Identify one recent merger that has taken place. The Federal Trade Commission (FTC) oversees all mergers to make sure that they do not interfere with competition. Begin by visiting the FTC Web site. **(a)** How can you use the Internet to obtain information about these mergers? **(b)** List three key terms you might use in your search.
24. **Refine your search.** Once you have identified one merger to research, you need to refine your search. **(a)** How can you refine your search? **(b)** Identify two Internet sources that contain specific information about the merger.
25. **Analyze your results.** After you have located specific documents referring to the merger you have selected, you can begin to analyze the information. Print the documents if possible. **(a)** Look at the source of your documents. Could the source be biased? **(b)** What effect has the merger had on employees?

Take It to the NET

Chapter 8 Self-Test As a final review activity, take the Chapter 8 Self-Test at the Web site listed below and receive immediate feedback on your answers. The test consists of 20 multiple-choice questions designed to test your understanding of the chapter content. **www.phschool.com**

Be an Entrepreneur!

Many people dream of starting their own businesses. Here's your chance to practice doing just that. In this simulation, you and your classmates will form a partnership to run a small business. You plan to sell a line of souvenir baseball caps out of a rented vendor's cart in a nearby shopping mall.

Each partnership group will work independently. First, you will calculate your monthly costs. Then, you will price your product. Next, you will try to project how you would do in the first month of business. At the end of the simulation, all the partnerships will compare results.

▲ Careful planning will improve your business's chances of success.

Preparing the Simulation

Step 1: Form groups of four to six people. Each group will be a separate business partnership.

Step 2: Choose a name for your company.

Materials
Paper
Calculator

Conducting the Simulation

Step 1: Now, get started with your business plan! You and your partners already have $3,000 in start-up capital. Before you spend any of it, you need to figure out what your expenses will be. On a piece of paper, make a monthly expenses chart like the one on the next page. As you figure out each monthly expense, record it on the chart.

Business Loan Should you work within your $3,000 budget, or should you borrow money? You have learned that the best small-business loan that you qualify for charges an interest rate of 10% and requires monthly payments over 5 years:
   $5,000 loan: $106 per month
   $10,000 loan: $212 per month

Vendor License Your community requires you to get a vendor license. This will cost you $60 per year.

Banking Costs You need a business checking account. This will cost $12 per month.

Business Space The monthly rental costs for the vendor's cart depend on size and location:
   Cart in well-traveled, central location: $2,000 per month
   Cart in low-traffic area: $600 per month

Advertising Should you advertise? If you think you'll get enough "walk-in" traffic in the mall, you may not need to. Or, you may want to be more aggressive and use advertising to bring people directly to you:
   Medium-sized ad in the major city newspaper: $400 per week
   Small ad in neighborhood newspaper: $40 per week

Labor Should you and your partners work the cart, or should you hire a salesperson? Your vendor's cart will need to be staffed from 9:30 A.M. to 9:30 P.M. If you hire a salesperson, you will need to pay wages plus another 25 percent for benefits and taxes. Use the following formula:

Number of hours per month × hourly wage × 1.25 = total monthly labor cost

Step 2: Now you need to make decisions about your inventory. How many caps will you order from the manufacturer? Refer to the catalog page at right to determine which kind you'll order. Make an order/pricing form like the one on this page, and record the quantities and costs of the caps you want to buy.

Step 3: Next, you need to set a price for your caps. Keep in mind what the caps cost you and what you think people will pay for them. Add the prices to the order/pricing form and calculate your profit per cap.

Step 4: Finally, you need to determine how many caps you need to sell in order to make a profit after having paid your monthly expenses. Assume, for the moment, that you sell equal numbers of each cap. How many caps do you need to sell each month to break even?

How many do you need to sell to make a profit large enough to pay salaries to you and your partners?

Step 5: Present your business plan to the rest of your class.

Good Quality! Cotton caps with plastic snap tabs
Colors: khaki, green, blue, charcoal, red

Item Number	Quantity	Price per cap
Style 101 Silk Screened	100	$2.53
	500	$2.37
	1,000	$2.09
Style 102 Embroidered	100	$5.20
	500	$4.82
	1,000	$4.60

Best Quality! Cotton twill caps with adjustable leather strap and brass buckle
Colors: black, white, navy blue, pine green

Item Number	Quantity	Price per cap
Style 202 Embroidered	100	$6.05
	500	$5.60
	1,000	$5.40

Monthly Expenses for Cap Business

Expense	Monthly Expense
Banking Costs	$
Loan Repayment	$
Vendor's License	$
Business Space	$
Advertising	$
Labor	$
Total Monthly Expenses	$

Simulation Analysis

After all the partnerships in your class have presented their business plans, answer the following questions.

1. Which business plan was the most cautious? Which group took the most chances?
2. Where do you get the greatest savings for additional quantities—the least-expensive or most-expensive caps?
3. Suppose that you began the first month with equal numbers of silk-screened and embroidered caps. At the end of the month, you sold out of caps with silk-screened designs but had 20 embroidered caps left. What would this tell you about your market?
4. **Formulating Questions** What other information would you need if you were actually going to set up a small business?

Why do some people earn a lot of money while others work hard and earn little?

This question relates to labor markets, the subject of this chapter. With a little information, and a little theory, you can begin answering this and other puzzling questions. In the process, you will learn how the government measures the unemployment rate, how workers' wages are determined, and how labor unions influence workers' earnings, job security, and benefits in today's economy.

Economics Journal

Interview a parent, grandparent, or other older adult, and ask that person to describe his or her first job. Ask about hours, pay, working conditions, and co-workers. Take detailed notes of the responses to your questions.

Keep It Current

Items marked with this logo are periodically updated on the Internet. Keep up-to-date with what's in the news. To get current information on labor, go to **www.phschool.com**

Objectives

After studying this section you will be able to:

1. **Describe** how trends in the labor force are tracked.
2. **Analyze** past and present occupational trends.
3. **Summarize** how the U.S. labor force is changing.
4. **Identify and explain** trends in the wages and benefits paid to U.S. workers.

Section Focus

The Bureau of Labor Statistics (BLS) tracks trends in the labor market. These trends include the movement toward a service economy, the hiring of more college graduates, women, and temporary employees, an overall decline in real wages, and rising costs for employee benefits.

Key Terms

labor force
learning effect
screening effect
contingent employment

What are the hottest jobs for the new millennium? If you guessed computer-related occupations, you are right. The number of computer engineers and computer support specialists are expected to grow by over 100 percent between 1998 and 2008. (See "Fastest-Growing Occupations" in the Economic Atlas and Databank on page 537 for more information on the ten fastest-growing occupations.)

The labor force is being transformed right before our eyes. Soaring growth in computer-related jobs is just one of the ways in which the job market in the United States is changing.

Tracking the Labor Force

How do we know the direction of changes in the job market? Each month, the Bureau of Labor Statistics (BLS) of the United States Department of Labor surveys households to assemble information on the labor force. Economists define the **labor force** as all nonmilitary people who are employed or unemployed.

Employment

Economists consider people to be employed if they are 16 years or older and meet at least one of the following requirements:

- they worked at least one hour for pay within the past week;
- they worked 15 or more hours without pay in a family business, such as a farm;
- they held jobs but did not work due to illnesses, vacations, labor disputes, or bad weather.

Unemployment

People who do not meet these criteria are counted as unemployed if they are either temporarily without work or are not working but have looked for jobs within the last 4 weeks. So to be counted as unemployed, a person either must have work lined up for the future, or must be actively searching for a new job.

The labor force is made up of people with jobs and those who are looking for jobs or are waiting to report to work. Some examples of people outside the labor force are full-time students, parents who stay at home to raise children, and retirees. These people are not considered unemployed, and thus are not counted in employment statistics.

labor force *all nonmilitary people who are employed or unemployed*

▼ **The labor force includes many small business owners.**

"Discouraged workers," people who once sought work but have given up looking for a job, are not counted in employment statistics either.

The Bureau of Labor Statistics

The Bureau of Labor Statistics (BLS) provides answers to two important economic questions: How many people are in the labor force? How many are employed and unemployed at any given time? You can find BLS data in the Census Bureau's *Statistical Abstract of the United States,* available in print or on the Internet.

The BLS provides information about historical trends. For example, the percentage of the U.S. population in the labor force has increased steadily from 59.2 percent in 1950 to 67.1 percent in 1999. In 2000, the national unemployment rate of 4.0 percent was as low as that of any year since the 1960s. The number of employed civilians in the U.S. in 2000 was about 141,489,000.

The BLS also reports the unemployment rate each month. Economists studying the health of the macroeconomy monitor these monthly unemployment figures, which indicate the health of the labor market.

Occupational Trends

Shifts in the job market reflect major shifts in what our economy produces. To understand these changes, let's look at them in a historical context.

A Changing Economy

At its founding, the United States was a nation of farmers. Most people had few job opportunities beyond the corn, wheat, cotton, and tobacco fields. In the 1800s in the North, however, this agricultural tradition gradually yielded to the Industrial Revolution. The coming of the machine age energized the economy and created new jobs in textile mills, shoe factories, and other new manufacturing enterprises.

By the early decades of the 1900s, heavy manufacturing had become the powerhouse of the U.S. economy. New corporate empires were born, employing thousands of workers: John D. Rockefeller's Standard Oil in 1863; Andrew Carnegie's steelworks in the 1870s; Henry Ford's automobile company in 1903.

The mid-twentieth-century boom in electronics—led by radio and television—produced a new surge of factory jobs. Employment growth centered in the Northeast and Midwest, in companies such as General Electric, Westinghouse, Carrier, and Goodyear.

In the 1970s, the revolution in personal computers opened another new horizon for employment. As computer use continues to rise in businesses, government, and households, computer-related occupations are booming. Many of the new jobs involve the storage, use, and transfer of information. In this "Information Age," even some

Figure 9.1 Composition of the U.S. Labor Force

Total U.S. population

Total civilian, noninstitutionalized U.S. population

Military, institutionalized

Nonlabor force

Total U.S. labor force

Employed

Unemployed

This flowchart shows how the Bureau of Labor Statistics defines who is in the U.S. labor force and who in the labor force is employed and unemployed.
Economic Systems How does being unemployed differ from not being part of the labor force?

traditional jobs, from trucking to farming to car sales, now require some computer skills. By the late 1900s, over half of American workers reported some use of computers on the job.

Fewer Goods, More Services

The increase in information management jobs is part of an overall shift in the United States from a manufacturing economy to a service economy. Our production of services is increasing faster than our production of goods. Jobs in the service sector include financial services (banking, insurance, investment), online services (Web design, online marketing, advertising, research), consulting services, health care, and desktop publishing.

Effects of International Competition

As service jobs increase, the United States is losing manufacturing jobs. Between January 1997 and December 1999, about 3,275,000 employees were laid off from jobs they had held for at least 3 years because of plant closings or moves, too little work, or the elimination of their positions. Much factory work formerly done in the United States by American firms is now being done overseas, where labor costs are often lower.

As less-skilled manufacturing jobs move overseas, there is less and less demand for the services of unskilled American workers. These employees may receive lower pay or may lose their jobs entirely. This decrease in demand for less-skilled workers pushes these workers to go back to school or to enter job-training programs to gain new skills.

Notice that these shifts in demand for workers are another example of supply and demand in operation. Demand for skilled labor is rising, so wages for skilled workers go up, and the supply of skilled workers increases to meet the demand. Meanwhile, as demand for low-skilled labor drops off, there is a surplus of less-skilled workers who find that they must become more skilled in order to compete in the job market.

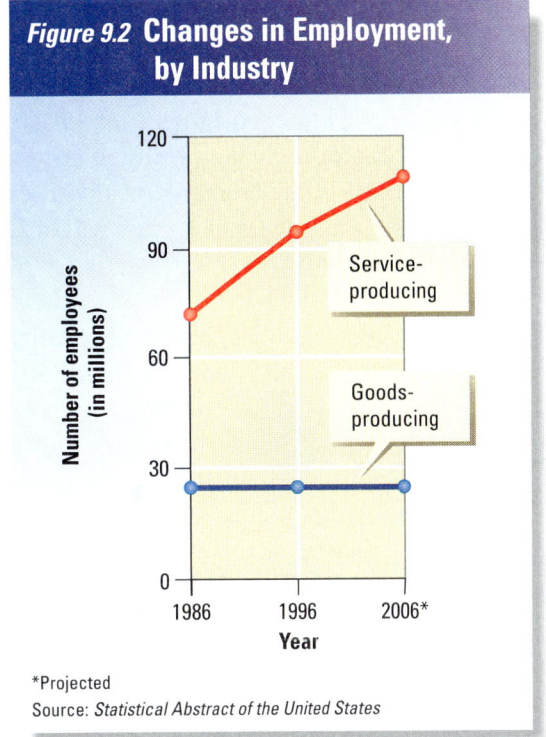

Figure 9.2 Changes in Employment, by Industry

*Projected
Source: *Statistical Abstract of the United States*

This chart shows the shift from a goods-producing, or manufacturing, economy to a service economy in the United States. **Supply and Demand** Describe the changes in the U.S. economy during the period shown on the graph.

The Changing Labor Force

In the 1950s, a typical American worker was a white man who had graduated from high school and had found a secure 40-hour-a-week job where he would hope to stay until retiring at age 65. Not anymore. Today, someone entering the work force can expect to have four or five different jobs during his or her working life and retire at around age 62, or even earlier. The face of the U.S. labor force has changed.

College Graduates

To get jobs, people must have human capital—the education, training, and experience that make them useful in the workplace. More and more, a high-school diploma alone won't prepare a person for financial success. Getting a good education, however, is costly. It requires money, time, and effort. (See "Paying for Education" in the Personal Finance Handbook on page 516.) Relatively few people become highly educated; thus, there is a smaller supply of such workers. Higher earnings compensate these workers for their high training costs.

The theory that education increases productivity and results in higher wages is called the **learning effect**. The statistics in Figure 9.3 support this theory. They show that college-educated workers typically earn more than high-school dropouts. People with professional degrees, such as doctors and lawyers, tend to earn more than people with bachelor's degrees.

Another theory about the relationship of education to wages is called the **screening effect**. This theory suggests that the completion of college indicates to employers that a job applicant is intelligent and hard-working. The skills and determination necessary to complete college may also be useful qualities for employees. According to the screening theory, a college degree does not increase productivity, but

simply identifies people who may be good employees because of their innate skills.

Women at Work

The changing face of the labor force can be seen right at your local bank. A few decades ago, men greeted customers at the tellers' windows and served as loan officers. Today, most bank tellers and many loan officers are women.

Figure 9.4 shows that in 1960, almost 38 percent of women belonged to the labor force. By 1995, that rate had jumped to over 58 percent.

The increase may be due to several factors. One is that women were encouraged to get a higher education and add to their human capital. By increasing their human capital, they increased their productivity and thus increased their earnings. In addition, as more and more jobs become available in the service sector of the economy, fewer jobs call for physical strength. Instead, jobs require brainpower

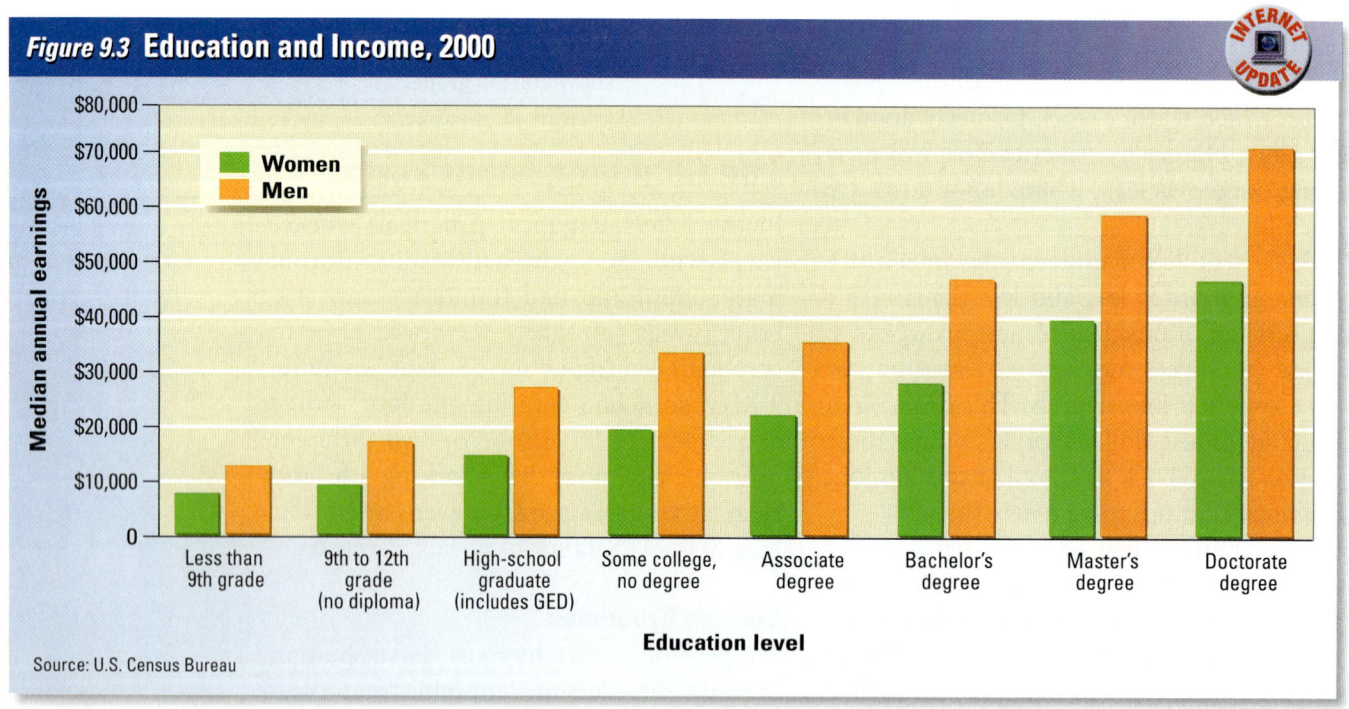

Figure 9.3 Education and Income, 2000

Source: U.S. Census Bureau

As you make your career plans, one factor to consider is the statistic shown here: Education has a big effect on earnings.

Incentives (a) As a man moves up one educational level at a time, when is he likely to see the greatest potential increase in earnings? (b) When is a woman likely to see the greatest potential increase in earnings? (c) What can you conclude about the opportunity costs for men and women of moving up to that higher-paying level?

and personal skills, placing men and women on equal footing.

The presence of women in the labor market is expected to continue rising. The BLS projects that the rate of participation of women in the labor force will inch even higher, to more than 61 percent by 2006.

Temporary Workers

In another important trend both in the United States and abroad, more and more businesses are replacing permanent, full-time workers with part-time and temporary workers. Some temporary workers come from "temp" agencies. Others are hired directly by firms as contract workers, people hired for a specified time period or to complete a certain task. These temporary and part-time jobs are known as **contingent employment**.

Contingent employment is becoming more common even in white-collar, professional occupations that have traditionally offered some of the most secure jobs in the economy. For example, some software engineers and attorneys are now hired as contract workers, paid a certain amount of money to complete a certain project, and then released. Such highly skilled workers, when hired directly by employers, are well paid. Some earn as much as permanent workers. On the other hand, workers who get their jobs through temp agencies tend to earn less compared to both permanent employees and directly hired temporary workers.

Why are some companies relying more on temporary employees? Several reasons have been suggested.

1. Flexible work arrangements allow a firm to easily adjust its work force to changing demands for its output. During off-peak seasons or times of reduced demand for their products, companies can easily lay off temporary workers or reduce workers' hours instead of keeping idle employees on the payroll. When business picks up, companies can rehire whatever workers they need.

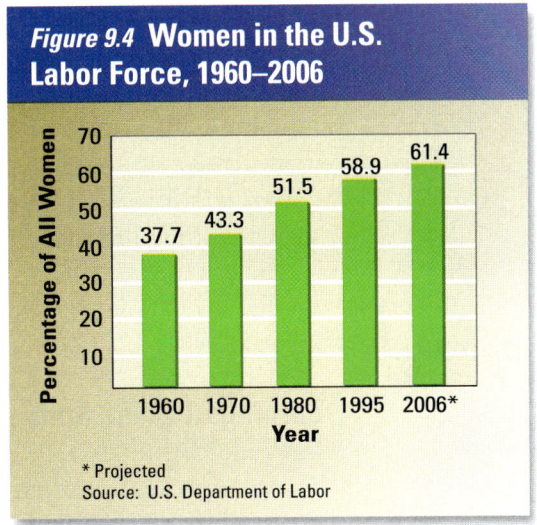

Figure 9.4 Women in the U.S. Labor Force, 1960–2006

Percentage of All Women:
- 1960: 37.7
- 1970: 43.3
- 1980: 51.5
- 1995: 58.9
- 2006*: 61.4

* Projected
Source: U.S. Department of Labor

Participation by women in the labor force has climbed steadily in recent decades.
Income By what percent will the number of women in the work force have changed between 1960 and 2006?

2. Discharging temporary workers is much easier than discharging regular, permanent employees, since temporary workers do not receive severance pay (money that companies give to employees who are laid off), and temporary workers have fewer legal rights in the workplace.

3. Temporary workers in many industries are paid less and given fewer benefits (if any) than their permanent, full-time counterparts. This advantage has become more important as the cost of medical insurance has risen.

4. Some workers actually prefer these flexible arrangements to traditional, permanent jobs; thus, the market reflects their preferences.

Some people enter and exit the labor force regularly, or prefer the freedom to move from one job to another. However, BLS studies show that a majority of temporary workers would prefer permanent jobs.

contingent employment
a temporary or part-time job

THE WALL STREET JOURNAL.
CLASSROOM EDITION

In the News As this excerpt from a Wall Street Journal Classroom Edition article shows, temping has some advantages for the employee, not just the firm.

"Temporary workers once were at the low end of the workplace food chain. But in today's fast-changing high-technology world, a growing number of techies . . . are discovering that today's job market rewards rather than punishes workers who move frequently between jobs, mastering new skills in the process. . . .

"By changing jobs, tech specialists can build networks of contacts who can help them land more lucrative postings."

Trends in Wages and Benefits

Labor economists study not only who is in and out of the work force, but how they are doing in terms of earnings and benefits. Today, the picture is mixed.

Earnings Up for Some, Down for Others

While American workers are well paid compared to their counterparts in some other countries, the trend over the last 20 years has been toward slightly lower earnings. The Bureau of Labor Statistics reports that average weekly earnings in the United States decreased from $275 in 1980 to $271 in 1999, as measured in inflation-adjusted dollars.

The slightly lower *average* earnings don't tell the whole story, however. In the past, most employees were paid in wages. Today, added benefits such as health insurance, retirement funds, employee stock options, and year-end bonuses mean that average weekly earnings are higher than BLS statistics suggest. Many employees today also enjoy the intangible benefits of telecommunicating from their homes and "flex-time," or flexible working hours. Overall, the earnings of college graduates actually increased, while the earnings of workers without college degrees decreased.

Why have average wages decreased in the last couple of decades? One reason, as you have read, is that greater competition from foreign companies has decreased the demand for low-skilled workers. For example, the last 30 years have brought foreign competition in such industries as steel, textiles, and auto production. Deregulation of many domestic industries, such as trucking, air travel, and telecommunications, may have forced firms to cut employees' wages as competition has intensified.

Cost of Benefits

For many workers, benefits such as pensions and health insurance are a significant share of total compensation. This share rose fairly steadily during the 1900s and early 2000s. Benefits now make up about 28 percent of total compensation in the United States economy today. This adds up to a large cost for employers—especially

▲ Employers may offer a wide range of benefits, including medical insurance, life insurance, and retirement savings plans.

▲ The downsizing trend in the 1990s was caused in part by employers wanting to hire cheaper temporary workers instead of permanent full-time employees.

since many benefits are becoming more expensive.

Company payments into the Social Security system may also be regarded as benefits, since they will be used to pay benefits to retired and disabled workers. Most employees know that Social Security taxes are deducted from their paychecks each month, but may not realize that their employers are also paying a matching amount. Thus, workers and employers share this cost. In addition, Social Security tax rates have risen substantially since the program was created during the 1930s, causing further increases in employers' benefits costs.

Employers are finding that these rising benefits costs increase the cost of doing business and thus cut into their profits. The use of contingent employment is one way some firms are cutting their benefits expenses. Other responses include moving production facilities overseas, where wages are lower and benefits often are nonexistent.

If benefits costs continue to rise, companies will be pressured to respond even further. These responses are likely to be unpopular with workers.

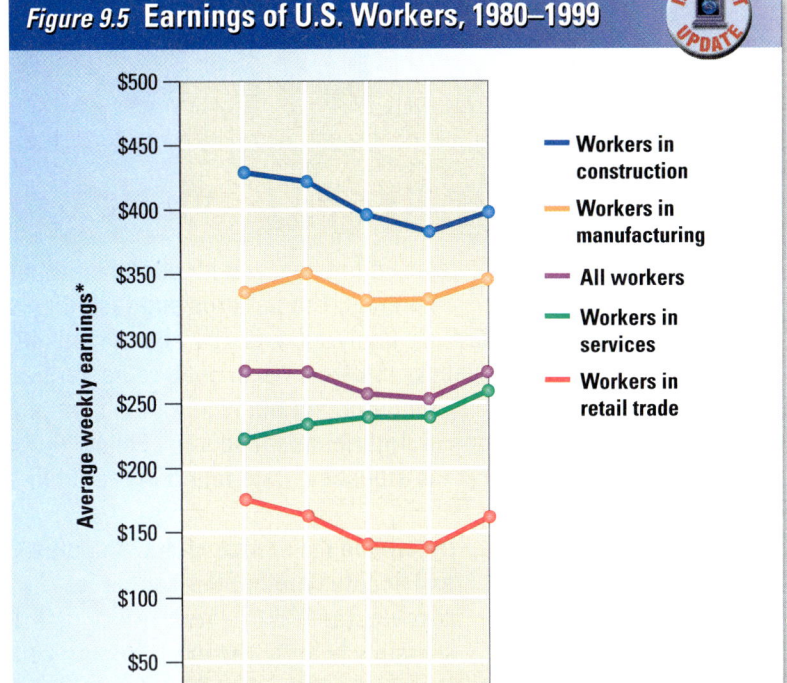

Figure 9.5 Earnings of U.S. Workers, 1980–1999

Legend:
- Workers in construction
- Workers in manufacturing
- All workers
- Workers in services
- Workers in retail trade

Y-axis: Average weekly earnings*
X-axis: Year

*Constant (1982) dollars
Source: *Statistical Abstract of the United States*, 2000

This graph shows the differences in average weekly earnings among workers who are paid hourly or weekly wages. **Markets and Prices** Why might wages for workers in retail be much lower than those for workers in construction?

Section 1 Assessment

Key Terms and Main Ideas

1. What groups of people does the government consider to be **(a)** in the **labor force**; **(b)** employed; **(c)** unemployed?

2. What were the major steps in the United States' progression from an agricultural economy to a service economy?

3. How does the **screening effect** differ from the **learning effect**?

Applying Economic Concepts

4. *Critical Thinking* Are you part of the labor force? If so, would the government consider you employed during the past week, or unemployed? If not, explain why.

5. *Problem Solving* Would you hire permanent workers or contingent workers if you owned **(a)** a pool and garden shop in Minnesota; **(b)** an architectural firm **(c)** a laundromat **(d)** a tax preparation service? Explain your reasoning.

6. *Decision Making* You are the manager of a medium-sized publishing company with 90 permanent employees, all of whom receive competitive wages, health insurance, and retirement benefits. The health insurance provider announces a 20 percent increase. Describe at least two possible ways you could respond.

Take It to the NET

The Bureau of Labor Statistics releases monthly reports on employment. Find the most current data on the Web. What time period does it cover? How many Americans were unemployed at this time? What percentage of the work force was unemployed? Did unemployment go up or down from the previous month? Use the links provided in the Social Studies area at the following Web site for help in completing this activity. **www.phschool.com**

Analyzing Statistics

Statistics provide us with useful information about economic and historical trends. The patterns suggested by statistics, however, must be carefully analyzed, and sources of statistics must be carefully evaluated for reliability. Statistics also need to be verified by other forms of evidence.

During a recent economic boom, unemployment rates dropped as millions of Americans found jobs. Follow the steps below to read and interpret the statistical data found in the table.

1. **Determine the source of the statistics and decide whether the source is reliable.** (a) What is the source of the statistics below? (b) In your opinion, is the source reliable?

2. **Study the statistics to determine what information they provide.** Read the row and column titles carefully, and answer the following questions. (a) What do the data describe? (b) What groups of people are described by the data?

3. **Analyze the data to determine social trends or patterns.** You may be able to use statistical data to draw conclusions about trends or patterns. Answer the following questions: (a) How did the unemployment rate for all workers change between 1992 and 2000? (b) Was the change even

across all groups in the work force? (c) Which group suffered from the highest unemployment in 2000? (d) Why do you think this group had the most difficulty finding work? (e) Women who maintain families have a higher rate of unemployment than married women who live with their husbands. Why might this be? (Note: Remember that the unemployment rate only includes people looking for work, not all Americans.)

Additional Practice

Use the Internet to find the most recent government statistics on unemployment, and compare them to the data shown here. What changes do you find? What do these changes indicate about the economy?

Unemployment Rates for U.S. Workers		
	Spring 1992	Spring 2000
All workers	7.4%	4.0%
Men, age 20 and up	7.1%	3.3%
Women, age 20 and up	6.3%	3.6%
Both sexes, 16 to 19 years	18.5%	12.8%
Married women, spouse present	5.1%	2.7%
Women who maintain families	10.0%	6.2%

Sources: Bureau of Labor Statistics

Section 2   Labor and Wages

Objectives

After studying this section you will be able to:

1. **Analyze** the relationship between supply and demand in the labor market.
2. **Understand** the connection between wages and skill levels.
3. **Explain** how laws against wage discrimination affect wage levels.
4. **Describe** other factors affecting wages, such as minimum wage and workplace safety laws.

Section Focus

In a competitive labor market, laws of supply and demand are the main factors responsible for determining wages. Wages are also affected by skill levels and legislation prohibiting wage discrimination. Other factors, such as minimum wage laws, workplace safety laws, and labor unions also affect wages.

productivity
equilibrium wage
unskilled labor
semi-skilled labor
skilled labor
professional labor
glass ceiling
labor union
featherbedding

If you are considering what career to pursue, you've probably thought about how much money you can earn in various professions. Most surgeons, for example, earn a lot of money. Social workers generally do not. Why? What determines the size of our paychecks?

It's a matter of supply and demand. Like eggs or airplanes or pet iguanas, labor is a commodity that is bought and sold. Wages are high in professions where supply is low and demand is high. Doctors, for example, are in relatively short supply but in high demand. Relatively large numbers of people become social workers compared to the number of social work jobs available. Hardly anyone needs a widget maker, so widget makers earn very little if anything at all. Thus workers' earnings—the price of labor—depend on conditions in the labor market.

Supply and Demand for Labor

Employment or unemployment in a labor market depends on how closely the demand for workers—the number of available jobs—meets the supply of workers seeking jobs. Let's examine how supply and demand operate in labor markets.

Labor Demand

The demand for labor comes from private firms and government agencies that hire workers to produce goods and services. In most labor markets dozens, or sometimes hundreds, of firms compete with one another to hire workers.

In a competitive labor market, workers are usually paid according to the value of what they produce. For example, competition among restaurants results in a wage for cooks that reflects the cook's productivity. **Productivity** is the value of output, which in this example is the cost of a meal. Suppose that most of the restaurants in your city pay $12 an hour for cooks who generate $20 an hour in revenue for the restaurants. An entrepreneur who set up a new restaurant and offered $15 an hour could attract cooks from other restaurants and still make a profit of $5 an hour per cook.

This possibility of profit will attract other restaurant entrepreneurs. The competition among the growing number of restaurants will push up the wage for cooks to nearly $20. As a result, cooks will be paid close to the value of their productivity. The flowchart in

productivity *value of output*

FAST FACT

The top three employers in the United States are Wal-Mart, General Motors, and McDonald's, respectively. Wal-Mart employs more than three times as many workers (1,244,000) as General Motors (386,000), its closest competitor in the labor market.

Figure 9.6 Effects of Competition

Cooks are paid less than their productivity (the value of output).

↓

A new restaurant opens in town, offering higher wages for cooks.

↓

Other restaurants raise wages for cooks to compete for scarce labor.

↓

Cooks are paid closer to their productivity (the value of output).

BUILDING KEY CONCEPTS

This flowchart shows how competition causes workers to be paid a wage close to their productivity.

Markets and Prices Explain how the outcome of this scenario affects (a) the cooks, (b) the restaurants.

equilibrium wage *the wage rate that produces neither an excess supply of workers nor an excess demand for workers in the labor market*

Figure 9.6 (above) shows the ripple effect that occurs when the new restaurant hires cooks at a higher wage.

Now look at the demand curve for labor, shown in the right-hand graph of Figure 9.7 on page 221. Notice that it is negatively sloped, reflecting the law of demand. The higher the price of labor, the smaller the quantity of labor demanded by firms and government.

Labor Supply

The supply of labor comes from people who provide labor in exchange for wages. As the left-hand graph in Figure 9.7 shows, the supply curve is positively sloped, reflecting the law of supply. In other words, the higher the wage, the larger the quantity of labor supplied.

This is sensible because the higher the wage for a job, the greater the number of people attracted to the job. A higher wage for cooks encourages people who would choose other occupations to acquire the training—that is, the human capital—required to become a cook. For example, if the wage for chefs were high enough, some servers and other staff would be willing to invest the time and money required to complete cooking school.

Equilibrium Wage

We know that at the market equilibrium, the quantity of a good supplied will equal the quantity demanded. Because the equilibrium price makes the quantity that suppliers want to sell equal to the quantity that demanders want to buy, there is no tendency for the price or quantity to change. Economic factors—the supply of labor and the demand for it—combine to determine an equilibrium price. These factors may be different in different parts of the country, or at different times.

The **equilibrium wage** is the wage rate that produces neither an excess supply of workers nor an excess demand for workers in the labor market. On a graph, the equilibrium wage is shown by the intersection of the supply and demand curves. (See Figure 9.8.) At equilibrium, there is no pressure to raise or lower the price.

How do these theories affect how much you should expect to earn working in a pet store or a grocery store next summer? It depends on the supply and demand conditions in your area. If your local pet stores and grocery stores won't hire many additional workers during the summer and a lot of teenagers will be looking for work, the wage will be relatively low. On the other hand, if stores want to hire a lot of teenagers and not many teens want to work, the wage will be higher.

Wages and Skill Levels

Why do lawyers earn more money than carpenters, and carpenters more than cashiers? Wages vary according to workers'

Figure 9.7 Labor Supply and Demand

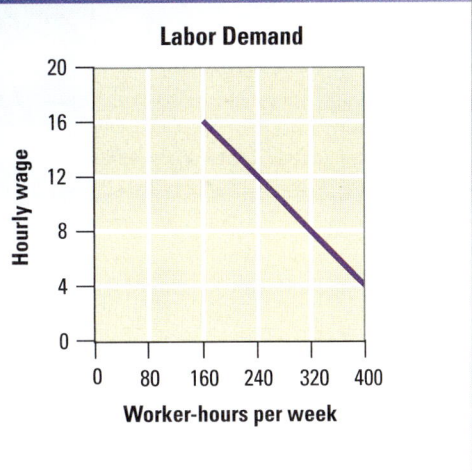

The graph on the right shows how the quantity of labor demanded varies depending on the price of labor. The graph on the left shows how the labor supply varies depending on the wage rate. **Supply and Demand (a) According to the demand curve, if each cook works a 40-hour week, how many cooks will be hired at $12 an hour and at $20 an hour? (b) Why is the supply curve positively sloped?**

skill levels and education, as well as according to supply and demand. Jobs are often categorized into four skill levels:

1. **Unskilled labor** requires no specialized skills, education, or training. Workers in these jobs usually earn an hourly wage. They include dishwashers, messengers, janitors, and many factory and farm workers.

2. **Semi-skilled labor** requires minimal specialized skills and education, such as operation of certain types of equipment. Semi-skilled workers usually earn an hourly wage. They include lifeguards, word processors, short-order cooks, and some construction workers.

3. **Skilled labor** requires specialized abilities and training to do tasks such as operating complicated equipment. Skilled workers need little supervision, yet usually earn an hourly wage rather than a salary. They include auto mechanics, bank tellers, plumbers, firefighters, chefs, and carpenters.

4. **Professional labor** demands advanced skills and education. Professionals are usually white-collar workers who receive a salary. Professionals include managers, teachers, bankers, doctors,

actors, professional athletes, and computer programmers.

We can graph the difference in pay scales for workers with various skills. The left-hand graph in Figure 9.9 shows the labor

Figure 9.8 Equilibrium Wage

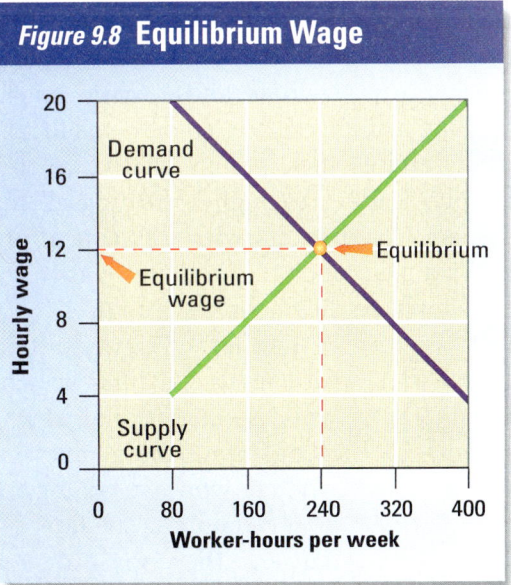

This graph shows the wage at which the quantity demanded equals the quantity supplied. **Supply and Demand Explain why a stable wage means stable restaurant prices.**

unskilled labor *labor that requires no specialized skills, education, or training*

semi-skilled labor *labor that requires minimal specialized skills and education*

skilled labor *labor that requires specialized skills and training*

professional labor *labor that requires advanced skills and education*

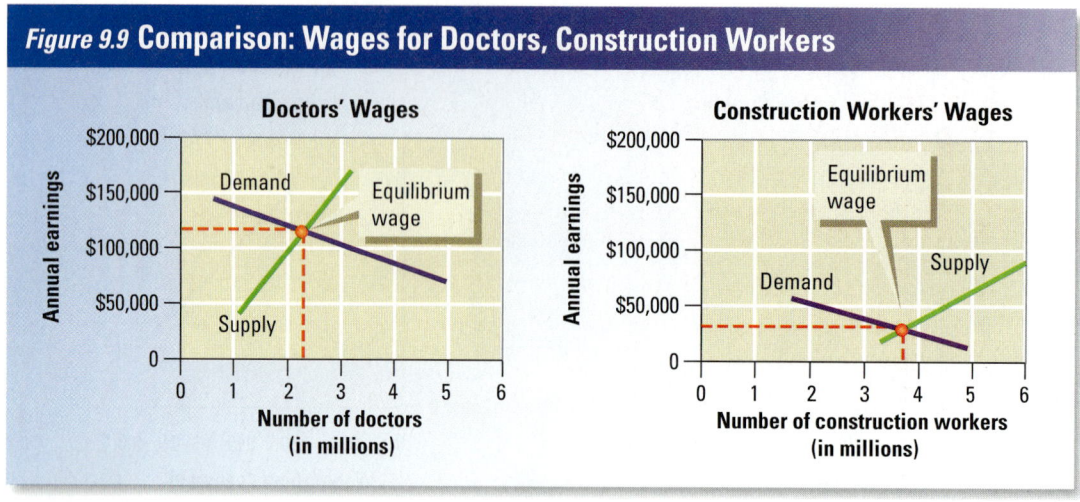

Figure 9.9 Comparison: Wages for Doctors, Construction Workers

Doctors' Wages

Annual earnings: $200,000 / $150,000 / $100,000 / $50,000 / 0

Demand, Supply, Equilibrium wage

Number of doctors (in millions): 0 1 2 3 4 5 6

Construction Workers' Wages

Annual earnings: $200,000 / $150,000 / $100,000 / $50,000 / 0

Equilibrium wage, Demand, Supply

Number of construction workers (in millions): 0 1 2 3 4 5 6

BUILDING KEY CONCEPTS

Anyone who pays doctors' bills already knows what the graph on the left shows: Wages for doctors are high. By comparison, construction workers' wages are lower, as shown in the graph on the right. **Supply and Demand** **Give reasons to explain why the supply of doctors is low and the supply of construction workers is high.**

market for medical doctors. Note that the supply of doctors is relatively low and the demand is relatively high. This produces a high equilibrium wage.

By comparison, the right-hand graph in Figure 9.9 shows that the supply of construction workers is high relative to the demand for them. Hence, the equilibrium wage for construction workers is lower than that for doctors.

Doctors and other highly educated workers, as well as those with much training and experience, enjoy demand for their services that is high relative to the supply, leading to higher earnings. The demand for workers with less education and training tends to be lower relative to the supply, so their earnings are lower.

Another reason that earnings vary is differences in working conditions. Many factors affect the number of workers who are willing to do a certain job: the level of danger, the physical or emotional stress involved, the location, and weather conditions in the area.

Economic studies have shown that jobs with high accident and fatality rates

pay relatively high wages. Workers who do dangerous jobs require compensation for the risks they take. Thus, there is a higher equilibrium wage rate for dangerous jobs, as shown in Figure 9.10.

Wage Discrimination

By seeing labor as something that is bought and sold, we have seen that wages for a particular job should end up at the equilibrium price of labor for that job, depending on the supply and demand for workers in that field. In some situations, however, national or state legislators have decided that there are policy reasons for interfering with the "invisible hand" that sets the wage level. One example is legislation prohibiting wage discrimination.

Wage discrimination occurs when people with the same job, same skills and education, same job performance, and same seniority receive unequal pay. Some companies, for example, have paid lower wages to women and minority employees.

Some employers defended wage discrimination against women by claiming that men needed the money to support families, while women were simply working to earn some extra cash. Job discrimination was also based on the assumption that women would leave their jobs at some point to have children. Discrimination against African Americans and other minority workers reflected racial and ethnic prejudice in society.

Laws Against Wage Discrimination

In the 1960s, the United States Congress passed several anti-discrimination laws that prevent companies from paying lower wages to some employees based on factors like gender or race that are not related to skill or productivity. The Equal Pay Act of 1963 required that male and female employees in the same workplace performing the same job receive the same pay. Title VII of the Civil Rights Act of 1964 prohibited job discrimination on the basis of race, sex, color, religion, or nationality. (Religious institutions and small businesses are exempt from the law.) The Civil Rights Act also created the Equal Employment Opportunity Commission (EEOC) to enforce the law's provisions. The EEOC handles complaints of job discrimination. If necessary, it takes companies to court to force them to comply with the law.

Pay Levels for Women

Despite these protections, the earnings gap that many people see between the wages of men and women is only gradu-ally being closed. Historically, this gap has been the result of social conditions for women.

1. *"Women's work."* Women have historically been denied entrance to certain high-paying occupations, such as doctors, lawyers, and corporate managers. Instead, they have been encouraged to pursue careers in lower-paying fields such as teaching, nursing, and clerical work. With so many women seeking work in these occupations, the labor supply has been generally high. A large supply of labor tends to produce a relatively low equilibrium wage.

2. *Human capital.* Overall, women have had less education, training, and experience in certain occupations than men. This lack of human capital makes women's labor, in economic terms, less productive. As a result, fewer women are eligible for the higher-paying, traditionally male-dominated jobs in fields such as engineering.

3. *Women's career paths.* Even today, some employers assume that female employees are not interested in career advancement. This perception can be a roadblock for women in the workplace. The difficulty many women face in trying to balance child rearing and a career adds to this perception.

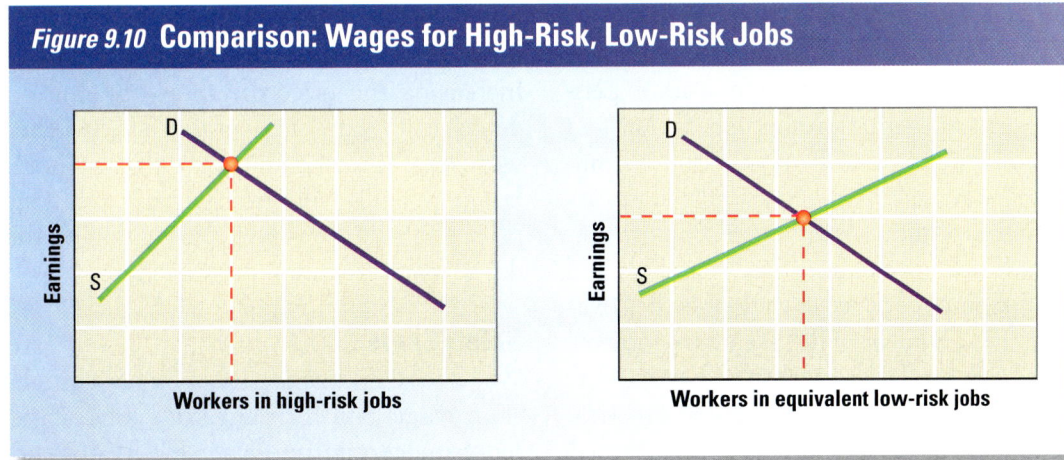

Figure 9.10 Comparison: Wages for High-Risk, Low-Risk Jobs

These graphs show how wages compare for similar jobs with different degrees of risk.
Supply and Demand Write one sentence that compares the demand curves on the two graphs and one sentence that compares the two supply curves.

Despite much progress made toward eliminating wage discrimination, significant wage differences exist between men and women and among workers of various ethnic groups. **Markets and Prices** According to the graph, which group has the lowest earnings?

Figure 9.11 **Median Earnings for U.S. Workers, by Gender and Ethnicity, 2000**

Group	Median annual earnings
Hispanic women	$21,026
African American women	$25,745
White women	$29,659
Hispanic men	$25,041
African American men	$30,893
White men	$40,350

Source: U.S. Census Bureau

glass ceiling *an unofficial, invisible barrier that prevents women and minorities from advancing in businesses dominated by white men*

Much progress has been made in creating job opportunities for women. Yet some qualified women still find that they cannot advance beyond a certain level in the companies they work for. In some companies, men dominate the high managerial positions, and women find it difficult to receive top-level promotions. This unofficial, invisible barrier that sometimes prevents some women and minorities from advancing to the top ranks of business is called a **glass ceiling**.

Pay Levels for Minorities
Minorities tend to earn lower pay than whites do. Income differences between minority workers and white workers are caused partly by productivity differences. On average, whites historically have had access to more education and work experience, giving them more human capital and hence higher wages. In part, non-discrimination laws are designed to help minority workers get more access to job opportunities where they can improve their skills and build their experience. The goal is that over time these workers will be able to compete equally in the labor market and contribute more to the productive capacity of America.

Other Factors Affecting Wages
In addition to laws forbidding discrimination, several other factors can affect wages.

These include minimum wage laws, workplace safety laws, employer decisions, and labor unions.

Minimum Wage Laws
In 1938, Congress passed the Fair Labor Standards Act. This law created a minimum wage—the lowest amount employers could lawfully pay for most types of work—and required employers to pay overtime for work beyond 40 hours a week. Many states also have their own minimum wage laws. Because of these laws, employers may be forced to pay more than the equilibrium wage for unskilled labor.

Supporters of the minimum wage argue that it helps the poorest American workers earn enough to support themselves. Opponents point out that artificially increasing the price of labor will cause a decrease in quantity demanded. In other words, individual employees will earn more, but companies will hire fewer of them. (See pages 180–181 for more information on the debate over the minimum wage.)

Safety Laws
We have seen that there is a higher equilibrium wage rate for dangerous jobs. Laws requiring certain minimum levels of workplace safety may also have an effect on wages. If a law or policy increases safety at work, it may also decrease wages because workers are willing to work for lower

wages when jobs are safer. It thus would lower the employer's costs. Of course, the employer will usually have to spend money to comply with safety regulations, which may more than offset the employer's savings from any wage reduction.

Employers Respond to Wage Levels

Employers may also take actions to try to affect wage levels. For example, a company might try to cut labor costs by substituting machines for people. In other words, employers can replace human capital with physical capital.

Take furniture, for example. In countries where labor is relatively cheap, furniture may be hand-made by workers. In the United States, where labor is relatively expensive, manufacturers have substituted sophisticated machinery for more expensive human labor. Other examples of substituting physical for human capital include automated teller machines (ATMs) and mechanized assembly lines (such as in automobile manufacturing plants). These technological advances have greatly reduced the number of employees that banks and manufacturing companies hire.

Even if firms cannot use technology to replace labor, they may be able to reduce their labor costs in other ways. Companies may build production plants in other parts of the world where labor is more plentiful, and therefore cheaper. Check the labels on your jeans and shirts to see where they come from!

Similarly, employees who are unhappy with their wages have several choices. In a competitive labor market, they might get higher-paying jobs elsewhere. Other people may change careers entirely, either by choice or out of necessity. Although labor unions are becoming less of a force in the American economy, workers might decide to join a union and press for higher pay.

Unions

An organization of workers that tries to improve working conditions, wages, and benefits for its members is called a **labor union**. Although labor unions today have fewer members than in the past, they are another force that may affect the level of wages for certain jobs. One of the key goals of unions is to get wage increases for their members. As you will see in Section 3, unions allow workers to negotiate wage levels as a group rather than having to deal individually with employers.

Nationally, union members do tend to earn higher wages than nonunion workers in similar jobs. In 1999, the average weekly union wage was $672, compared with $516 a week for nonunion wage earners.

Some evidence suggests that unions depress the wages of nonunion workers. Consider this reasoning:

1. Unions press employers to raise their members' wages.
2. When wages go up, the quantity of labor demanded goes down. Thus, the number of union jobs decreases.
3. As union jobs are cut, more workers are forced to seek nonunion jobs.
4. An increase in the supply of available nonunion workers causes the wage rate for nonunion jobs to fall.

In addition, some unions have engaged in **featherbedding,** negotiating labor contracts that keep unnecessary workers on the company payroll. A notable example of featherbedding occurred in the railroad industry.

In the early days of railroads, a "cabooseman" had to ride at the back of the train to operate a rear brake that stopped the train. Yet even after design

labor union *an organization of workers that tries to improve working conditions, wages, and benefits for its members*

featherbedding *the practice of negotiating labor contracts that keep unnecessary workers on a company's payroll*

Global Connections

Wages Worldwide An average production worker in the United States makes $31,300 a year, according to the U.S. Census Bureau. If you were a worker in a country other than the United States, what would you earn? An average production worker in Germany makes the equivalent of $35,863 a year, while the average worker in Hungary makes $9,916 a year. Wages in Western Europe range from $40,995 in Belgium to $28,198 in France. A worker in Japan makes $27,664, in Turkey $15,825, and in Mexico, just $8,662. These figures are adjusted according to the relative purchasing power in the various countries.

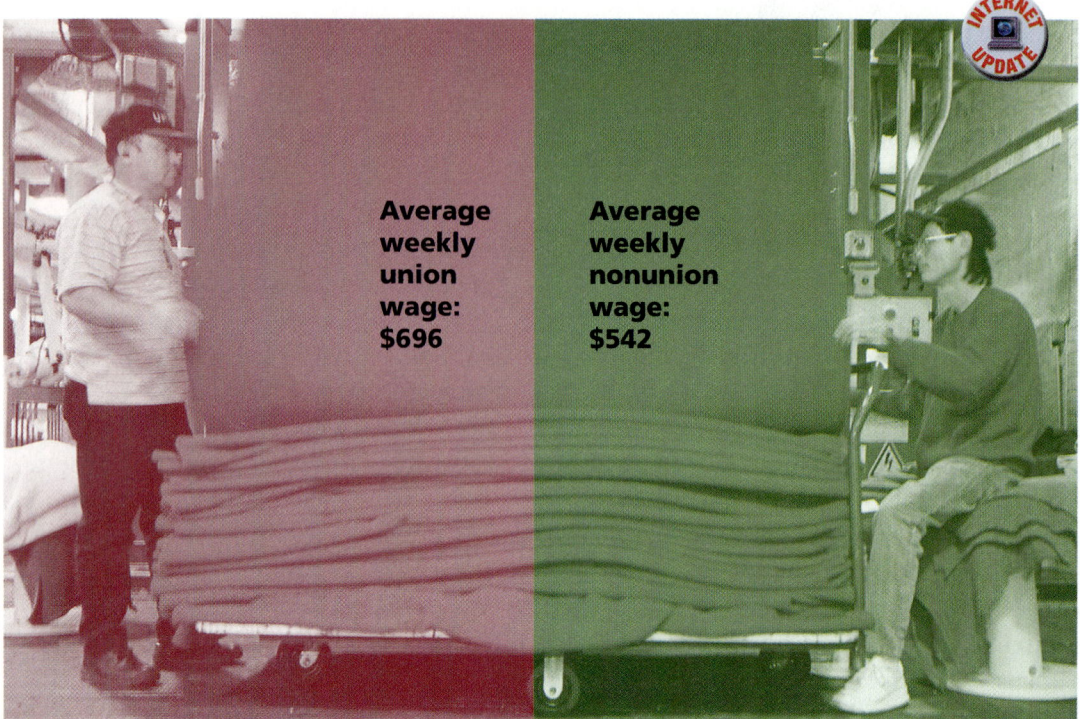

Average
weekly
union
wage:
$696

Average
weekly
nonunion
wage:
$542

▲ In 2000, union workers earned higher wages than nonunion workers.

changes allowed the engineer at the front of the train to operate rear brakes, unions managed to keep caboosemen on the payroll, receiving full wages and benefits for doing nothing.

Unions have been criticized not only for featherbedding, but also because the above-market union wages they negotiate can curtail capital formation. In addition, higher prices for union-made goods can cut sales and consumer purchasing power. The next section will trace the history of unions in the United States and further describe their advantages and disadvantages.

Section 2 Assessment

Key Terms and Main Ideas

1. How do the laws of supply and demand affect the labor market?

2. What generally happens to the **equilibrium wage** when **(a)** demand for workers is low and supply is high; **(b)** demand for workers is high and supply is low?

3. How does **skilled labor** differ from **professional labor**? Give an example of each.

4. How do minimum wage and safety laws affect wages?

Applying Economic Concepts

5. *Critical Thinking* Choose two occupations, one that pays high wages and one that pays low wages. Explain the reasons for the difference in wages in terms of supply and demand. Are there any additional factors that could also help explain the difference?

6. *Using the Databank* Turn to the chart of "Fastest-Growing Occupations" on page 537. **(a)** What types of jobs are being created at the fastest pace? **(b)** Are the fastest-growing occupations in traditionally unionized industries?

Take It to the NET Choose three careers you might consider pursuing and find out their average salaries. Use the links provided in the Social Studies area at the following Web site for help in completing this activity. **www.phschool.com**

Profile

Karl Marx (1818–1883)

While Adam Smith described the orderliness and benefits of a free market economy, Karl Marx focused on its disorders. Marx looked at the factories and slums of nineteenth-century Europe and created a controversial new way to look at economics. Marx's radical ideas eventually led to his exile from his homeland and the eruption of violent revolutions in Russia and China.

Marx the Revolutionary

Karl Marx studied philosophy in his native Germany and earned a doctorate at the age of 23. However, because his radical writings criticized the government, he could find no work as a teacher and was soon forced to flee to Paris. There, in 1848, he and Friedrich Engels published the pamphlet for which Marx is best known: the *Communist Manifesto*.

In the *Communist Manifesto*, Marx argued that history is a struggle between the owners of capital, or "capitalists," and the workers, or "proletariat." He believed that as wealth became concentrated in the hands of the capitalists, the proletariat would become more and more dissatisfied. The result, he predicted, would be revolution and a classless society.

Marx returned to Germany after the publication of his pamphlet, but was soon expelled. In 1849, he settled permanently in London.

Das Kapital

Although Marx is known more for his social and political theories than for his economic ideas, much of his work concerned economics. In 1867, Marx completed the first volume of *Das Kapital*, a three-volume study of the economics of capitalism. Drawing heavily on the writings of Adam Smith and David Ricardo, Marx explored the relationship between labor, profit, and the distribution of wealth. By the time the final volume appeared in 1894, *Das Kapital* had established Marx as one of the most prominent economists of the nineteenth century.

The Theory of Surplus Value

In *Das Kapital*, Marx claimed that human labor is the source of all added value. Marx used the textile industry as an example. The capitalist buys cotton thread and pays workers in his factory to weave it into fabric. The capitalist then sells the fabric for more than the combined value of the thread and the workers' wages. The workers' labor has therefore added value to the capitalist's goods. However, the capitalist does not return this "surplus value" to the workers, but keeps it as profit, thereby "exploiting" the workers. This conclusion was the basis for Marx's radical social and political views.

CHECK FOR UNDERSTANDING

1. Source Reading Explain the following passage from *Das Kapital* in your own words: "Capital buys the labour power and pays the wages for it. By means of his work the labourer creates new value which does not belong to him, but to the capitalist."

2. Critical Thinking If, as Marx advocated, "surplus value" were returned to the workers, how might this retard economic growth and development?

3. Problem Solving Research "profit sharing" and explain how you think Marx would have viewed this method of compensation.

Preview

Objectives

After studying this section you will be able to:

1. **Describe** why historically some American workers have joined labor unions.

2. **Trace** the history of the labor movement in the United States.

3. **Analyze** reasons for the decline of the labor movement.

4. **Explain** how labor and management negotiate contracts.

Section Focus

Historically, American workers have tried to gain some control over their working conditions by joining together in labor unions. Labor unions rose to great power and economic influence in the mid-1900s, but have declined since then.

Key Terms

strike
right-to-work law
blue-collar worker
white-collar worker
collective bargaining
mediation
arbitration

Today we think of Labor Day as the traditional end of the summer, a time for picnicking and perhaps shopping for school supplies. You might not know that the holiday has its roots in 1882, when labor leader Peter J. McGuire suggested a day celebrating the American worker. On September 5, 1882, some 10,000 workers took to the streets of New York City in a parade sponsored by a labor group called the Knights of Labor. The Knights later proposed making the first Monday in September a Labor Day holiday. The idea caught on quickly. In 1894, Congress made Labor Day a federal holiday.

Labor and Labor Unions

As you read in Section 2, wages are determined by the forces of supply and demand.

Competition among firms keeps a worker's wages close to his or her level of productivity. In general, workers who command the highest wages are workers with specialized skills and who are in short supply—brain surgeons, for example.

What if, however, an individual employee feels that he or she is being paid too little, working too many hours, or working under unsafe conditions? One option is for the worker to quit his or her current job and find an employer who offers better wages and working conditions. Many economists, in fact, argue that it is a competitive labor market that helps prevent low pay and dangerous working conditions because workers will leave such firms to work elsewhere.

Historically, American workers have also tried to gain some control over their working conditions by joining together to bring their concerns to the attention of company management. Today, only about one out of seven workers in the United States belongs to a labor union. However, this number does not accurately reflect the strong influence that unions have had on the nation's economy in the past. In order to understand the role of labor unions today, we will look at how labor unions rose to power in the United States.

▼ In 1998, United Auto Workers in Flint, Michigan, went on strike against General Motors to force the company to address "unresolved health and safety, subcontracting and production standards issues."

The Labor Movement

The union movement took shape over the course of more than a century. It faced many obstacles along the way, including violence and legal opposition from companies. Figure 9.12 highlights some of the major events in the history of organized labor.

Workers in the 1800s

Labor unions arose largely in response to changes brought by the Industrial Revolution in the early and mid-1800s. Manufacturing brought a new type of occupation to America: the factory job.

By today's standards, it was not an enviable job. In garment factories, iron plants, and gunpowder mills, laborers worked 12 to 16-hour days, 7 days a week, for meager wages. The long workday was not new to those who had worked on farms, but the working conditions were. Men, women, and children as young as age 5 operated clattering machines so dangerous that many people lost their sight, their hearing, even fingers and limbs. Injured workers often lost their jobs.

Today, many firms emphasize that one of their major goals is to attract, hire, and retain the most highly skilled workers. This means treating workers well. In 1855, however, a factory boss bluntly summarized his attitude toward workers:

> " I regard people just as I regard my machinery. So long as they can do my work for what I choose to pay them, I keep them, getting out of them all I can. "
>
> —Manager of a textile mill in Fall River, Massachusetts, 1855

Unions Take Hold

As early as the 1790s, whispers of worker discontent grew into organized protests. Skilled workers such as shoemakers and carpenters began to form unions in order to protect their interests. The tool of unions was the **strike**, an organized work stoppage intended to force an employer to address union demands. Initially, the courts regarded unions as illegal. Employers simply fired and replaced workers who caused trouble by trying to organize.

The man who truly started the United States labor movement was Samuel Gompers. The young cigarmaker in New York City rose within union ranks, focusing on three workplace reforms: higher wages, shorter hours, and safer work environments. In 1886, he founded the American Federation of Labor (AFL).

strike *an organized work stoppage intended to force an employer to address union demands*

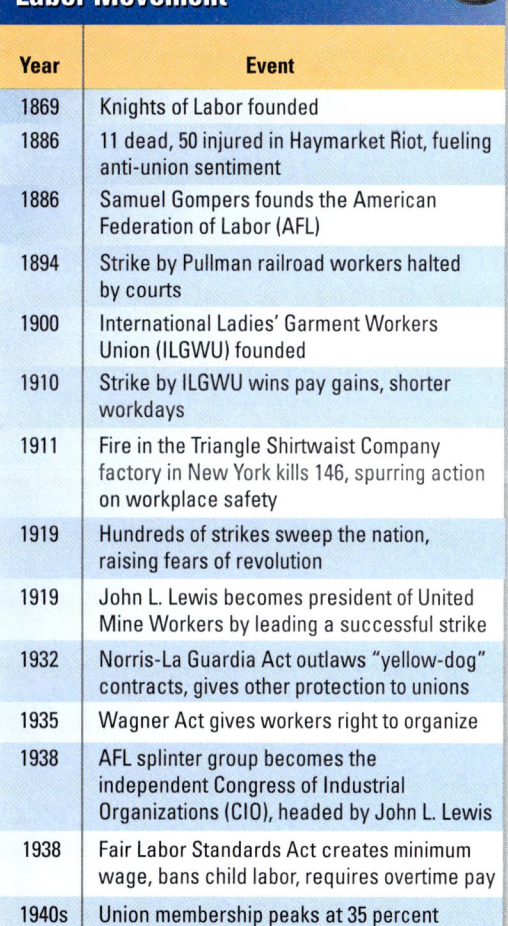

Figure 9.12 Key Events in the U.S. Labor Movement

Year	Event
1869	Knights of Labor founded
1886	11 dead, 50 injured in Haymarket Riot, fueling anti-union sentiment
1886	Samuel Gompers founds the American Federation of Labor (AFL)
1894	Strike by Pullman railroad workers halted by courts
1900	International Ladies' Garment Workers Union (ILGWU) founded
1910	Strike by ILGWU wins pay gains, shorter workdays
1911	Fire in the Triangle Shirtwaist Company factory in New York kills 146, spurring action on workplace safety
1919	Hundreds of strikes sweep the nation, raising fears of revolution
1919	John L. Lewis becomes president of United Mine Workers by leading a successful strike
1932	Norris-La Guardia Act outlaws "yellow-dog" contracts, gives other protection to unions
1935	Wagner Act gives workers right to organize
1938	AFL splinter group becomes the independent Congress of Industrial Organizations (CIO), headed by John L. Lewis
1938	Fair Labor Standards Act creates minimum wage, bans child labor, requires overtime pay
1940s	Union membership peaks at 35 percent
1947	Taft-Hartley Act allows states to pass right-to-work laws
1955	AFL and CIO merge to create AFL-CIO
1960s	Government employees begin to organize
1962	Cesar Chavez begins organizing the first farmworkers' union, which eventually establishes the first labor agreement with growers
1970s	Rise in anti-union measures by employers
1990s	Increase in public-sector unions, including teaching assistants at some universities

The American labor movement had its roots in the 1800s, when the rise of factories led to difficult and dangerous working conditions. **Economic Institutions** **Describe the relationship shown here between labor laws and union membership in the 1900s.**

▲ At left, this poster of the United Mine Workers union, founded in 1890, celebrates its efforts to secure fair pay, safe working conditions, and other benefits for mine workers. The photograph at right shows the aftermath of the Triangle Shirtwaist Factory fire of 1911 in which 146 workers died. The tragedy brought national attention to the issues of workplace safety and workers' rights.

Employer Resistance

Attempts to unionize brought swift responses from employers. Viewing strikers as threats to free enterprise and social order, companies identified and fired union organizers. They forced workers to sign so-called yellow-dog contracts, agreements in which workers promised not to join a union. (*Yellow* was slang for "coward.") Companies also used court orders called *injunctions* to order striking employees back to work. Some companies hired their own private militias to harass union organizers.

Congressional Protections

As the nation struggled through the effects of the Great Depression in the 1930s, Congress took up the labor cause, passing a number of pro-union measures. The expansion of workers' rights in the 1930s contributed to a new rise in union strength. Membership peaked in the 1940s at about 35 percent of the nation's non-farm work force.

Unions became a dominant force in many industries. They controlled the day-to-day operations of businesses from shipyards to garbage collection to steel production. Unions amassed billions of dollars in union dues to cover the costs of union activities including organizing, making political donations, and providing aid to striking workers.

Decline of the Labor Movement

As they grew, some unions began to abuse their new power. Some sought to preserve outdated and inefficient production methods in order to protect jobs and benefits. As you read in Section 2, sometimes unions even negotiated to preserve job positions that were really unnecessary—called "featherbedding"—in order to keep more union members employed.

As a result, companies that badly needed to improve efficiency to stay competitive found that unions could be an obstacle.

The reputation of unions suffered further because of their links to organized crime. Corrupt crime bosses gained a foothold in many local unions and used union funds to finance illegal operations. In time, corruption reached the very top of major unions, including the Teamsters, the nation's largest union by 1940.

"Right to Work" Laws

In an effort to curb union power, Congress passed the Taft-Hartley Act in 1947. This act allowed states to pass **right-to-work laws,** measures that ban mandatory union membership. Today, most right-to-work states are in the South, which has a lower level of unionism than other regions.

Right-to-work laws may be one of several reasons for a decline in union membership in recent decades. By 2000, union membership had dropped to just 13.5 percent of the labor force.

Today, unionism in the United States is far more limited than in many other countries. For example, organized labor does not have its own political party, such as Great Britain's Labour Party, which holds top positions in government.

Loss of Traditional Strongholds

One theory for the decline of unions suggests that structural changes in the U.S. economy have reduced union membership. The charts in Figure 9.13 illustrate these influential economic trends. For example:

1. Unions have traditionally been strongest in the manufacturing sector. This sector has a high proportion of **blue-collar workers,** those who work in industrial jobs, often in manufacturing, and who

right-to-work law *a measure that bans mandatory union membership*

blue-collar worker *someone who works in an industrial job, often in manufacturing, and who receives wages*

▲ In loud, dirty factories, young children were once forced to work long hours in hazardous conditions. The boys in this photo of a Georgia cotton mill, taken between 1908 and 1912, were so small they had to climb onto the machinery. Pressure from unions helped win passage of the 1938 Fair Labor Standards Act, which made most forms of child labor illegal.

Figure 9.13 U.S. Economic Changes That Have Affected Unions

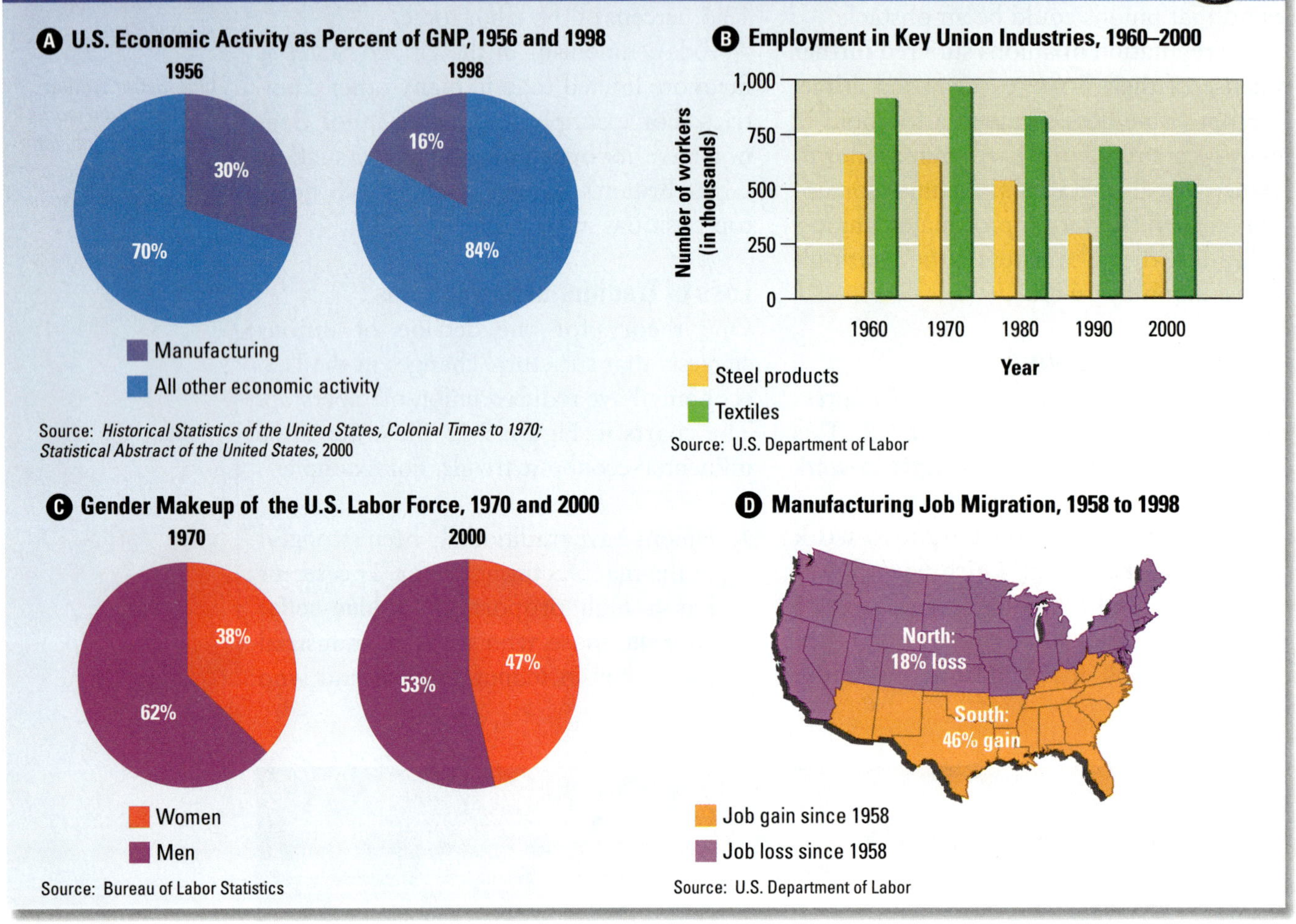

Ⓐ U.S. Economic Activity as Percent of GNP, 1956 and 1998

1956
- 30% Manufacturing
- 70% All other economic activity

1998
- 16% Manufacturing
- 84% All other economic activity

■ Manufacturing
■ All other economic activity

Source: *Historical Statistics of the United States, Colonial Times to 1970;*
Statistical Abstract of the United States, 2000

Ⓑ Employment in Key Union Industries, 1960–2000

Number of workers (in thousands) vs. Year (1960, 1970, 1980, 1990, 2000)

■ Steel products
■ Textiles

Source: U.S. Department of Labor

Ⓒ Gender Makeup of the U.S. Labor Force, 1970 and 2000

1970
- 38% Women
- 62% Men

2000
- 47% Women
- 53% Men

■ Women
■ Men

Source: Bureau of Labor Statistics

Ⓓ Manufacturing Job Migration, 1958 to 1998

North: 18% loss
South: 46% gain

■ Job gain since 1958
■ Job loss since 1958

Source: U.S. Department of Labor

BUILDING KEY CONCEPTS

These charts show changes in industry and in the labor force that have lessened the strength of unions. **Incentives** **Identify the change indicated in each chart and explain how it affected union membership.**

---

white-collar worker
someone in a professional or clerical job who usually earns a salary

receive wages. Blue-collar manufacturing jobs have been declining, as shown in Chart A in Figure 9.13, causing union jobs to disappear.

Unions are weakest in white-collar professions. A **white-collar worker** is someone in a professional or clerical job who usually earns a salary. White-collar employment—traditionally nonunion—is on the rise partly because of jobs in high technology companies.

2. Certain manufacturing industries, such as automobiles, steel, and textiles, have traditionally employed large numbers of union workers. (See Chart B in Figure

9.13.) These industries have been hurt by foreign competition in recent years. As a result, many industries have laid off union workers. Some have shifted operations to countries where labor is cheaper.

3. The rising proportion of women in the labor force (see Chart C in Figure 9.13) has affected union membership, since women are less likely to join unions. Fewer women work in blue-collar, unionized industries than in white-collar jobs.

4. Seeking to reduce their production costs, some industries have relocated from the

Northeast and Midwest to the South, which has historically been less friendly to unions. (See Chart D in Figure 9.13.) In fact, some firms may have moved to the South in part because of the decreased union activity there.

Another theory for union decline is that other organizations now provide many of the services that had been won in the past through union activity. Thus, the need for unions has decreased. For example, the government has passed laws setting workplace safety standards and a shorter workweek. It provides unemployment insurance and Social Security. More corporations now offer benefits such as medical insurance and pension plans.

While overall union membership is on the decline, public sector unionization has increased, due to new laws and changing attitudes in the 1960s and 1970s. Thus, over the last few decades, growth of unions among governmental employees has partially made up for losses in the private sector.

Labor and Management

A union gains the right to represent workers at a company when a majority of workers in a particular work unit vote to accept the union. After that, the company is required by law to bargain with the union in good faith to negotiate an employment contract.

Collective Bargaining

Picture a room, a table, and, on each side, a team of lawyers and trained negotiators determined to get what they want—or at least part of it. This is **collective bargaining,** the process in which union and company representatives meet periodically to negotiate a new labor contract.

Union contracts generally last two to five years and can cover hundreds of issues. The resulting contract spells out each side's rights and responsibilities for the length of the agreement.

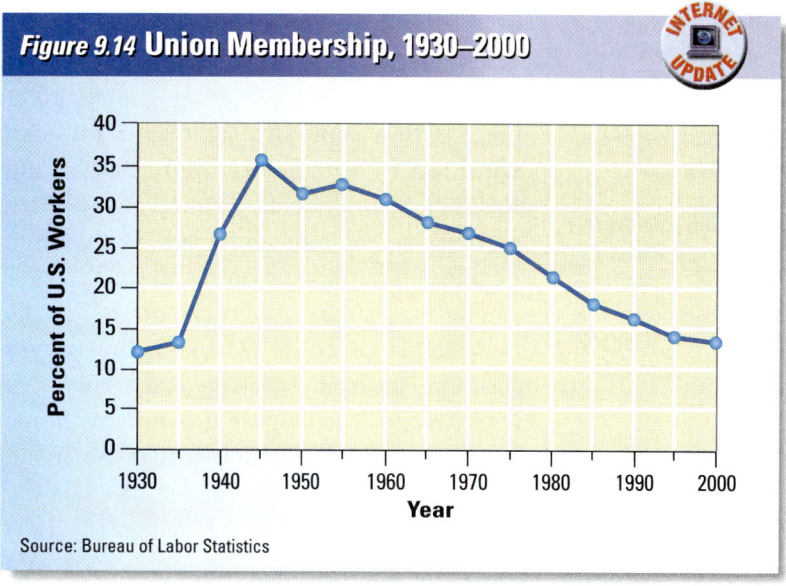

Figure 9.14 Union Membership, 1930–2000

Source: Bureau of Labor Statistics

Union membership reached its peak in the 1940s.
Competition What is the trend in union membership today?

Generally the union comes to the bargaining table with certain goals that set the agenda for collective bargaining talks. Let's examine those goals.

- *Wages and Benefits.* The union negotiates on behalf of all members for wage rates, overtime rates, planned raises, and benefits. In seeking higher wages, the union is aware that if wages go too high, the company may lay off workers to reduce costs.
- *Working Conditions.* Safety, comfort, worker responsibilities, and many other workplace issues are negotiated and written into the final contract.
- *Job Security.* One of the union's primary goals is to secure its members' jobs, so the contract spells out the conditions under which a worker may be fired.

If a union member is discharged for reasons that the union believes to be in violation of the contract, the union might file a grievance, or formal complaint. The union contract specifies how grievances will be handled. The procedure usually involves hearings by a committee of union and company representatives.

collective bargaining
the process in which union and company representatives meet to negotiate a new labor contract

mediation *a settlement technique in which a neutral mediator meets with each side to try to find a solution that both sides will accept*

arbitration *a settlement technique in which a third party reviews the case and imposes a decision that is legally binding for both sides*

Strikes and Settlements

When a contract is about to expire, or when the union is negotiating its first agreement with a company, the negotiators can wind up in tough late-night bargaining sessions. Most of the time, the parties manage to reach an agreement. But when a deadlock occurs, tensions escalate.

The union may ask its members to vote on whether to strike. A strike is the union's ultimate weapon. A strike, particularly a lengthy one, can cripple a company. Some firms can continue to function by using managers to perform key tasks, or by hiring nonunion "strikebreakers." If a company can withstand a strike, it is in a good bargaining position. Most firms, however, cannot produce goods and services without their union workers.

A long strike can also be devastating to workers, since they do not get paid while they are not working. Many unions provide some financial aid to their members during lengthy strikes, but the payments are generally much smaller than what the members would have earned while working.

To avoid the economic losses of a strike both to workers and management, a third party is sometimes called in to settle a dispute. The two sides might agree to **mediation,** a settlement technique in which a neutral mediator meets with each side to try to find a solution that both sides will accept. A mediator often can help each side understand the other's concerns, leading to an agreement. However, the decision reached by the mediator is nonbinding—that is, neither side is required to accept it. If mediation fails, the talks may go into **arbitration,** a settlement technique in which a neutral third party reviews the case and imposes a decision that is legally binding for both sides.

The collective bargaining process usually goes smoothly, with few strikes. It may seem as though workers strike frequently since strikes are often front-page news when they do occur.

In 1999, there were 17 major strikes, involving about 73,000 workers. Keep in mind that this number involved only a small fraction of the nation's work force, however.

Section 3 Assessment

Key Terms and Main Ideas

1. What are some of the key goals of labor unions?
2. How are **strikes** damaging to workers and companies?
3. What is a **right-to-work law?**
4. How do **mediation** and **arbitration** differ?
5. How do **blue-collar workers** and **white-collar workers** differ in the types of work they perform? Give examples of each.

Applying Economic Concepts

6. *Critical Thinking* Create a time line in which you trace the history of labor unions in the United States from the 1800s to the present.

7. *Decision Making* In recent years, some manufacturing firms have moved their factories to countries where nonunion labor is cheap. The companies say they need to make such moves to reduce costs and compete with foreign companies. American unions have fiercely opposed the cuts in American jobs, saying companies must care for their workers. Which side would you support if you were **(a)** a U.S. worker; **(b)** a consumer; **(c)** an investor in the company? Explain your reasoning for each response.

8. *Critical Thinking* Turn to the graph on page 233 showing Union Membership, 1930–2000. Give reasons to explain the rise and fall of union membership shown on the graph.

 **Take It to the NET**

Find an example of a major labor conflict in U.S. history. Write a summary of the conflict, identifying **(a)** the major participants; **(b)** the position of each side; **(c)** techniques used to resolve the conflict; **(d)** the outcome of the situation. Use the links provided in the Social Studies area at the following Web site for help in completing this activity. **www.phschool.com**

Americans Improve Their Working Conditions

In the early days of our country, farming was the most common job. Then during the Industrial Revolution of the 1800s, large numbers of people began moving from farms to cities. They took jobs in the new factories, where they worked 10 hours a day during the week and a half day on Saturday. Work was hard, repetitive, and often dangerous. People went home exhausted, and sometimes injured.

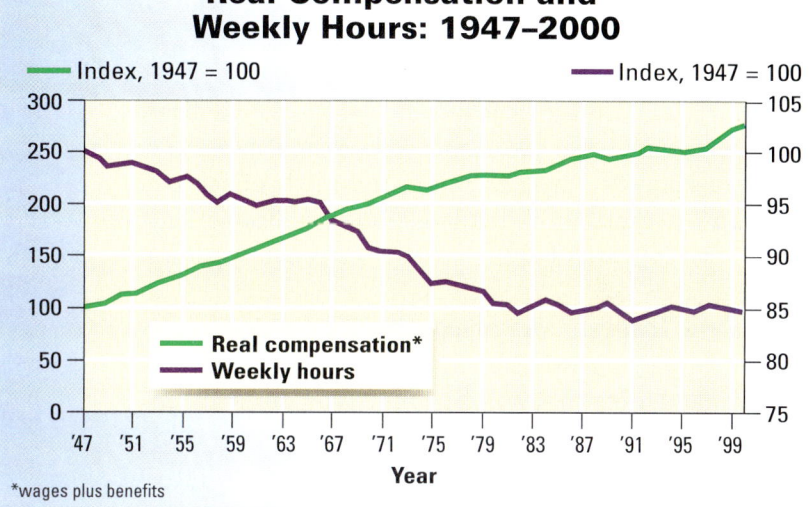

Real Compensation and Weekly Hours: 1947–2000

Index, 1947 = 100   Index, 1947 = 100

- Real compensation*
- Weekly hours

*wages plus benefits
Source: Federal Reserve Bank of Dallas

Better Jobs Through Technology

In the early part of the Industrial Revolution, workers performed boring and repetitive jobs in order to make the most efficient use of newly developed machinery. Gradually, however, machines were created to do the dullest tasks with less and less human involvement. People worried that the increase in automation would mean that machines would take away their jobs. In the long run, however, automation freed American workers to pursue more interesting and rewarding technical and professional careers.

In addition, in the last 25 years, rates of injury in dangerous industries such as construction and manufacturing have been cut nearly in half due to safety rules and safer equipment. Workers have also moved to lower-risk jobs in areas such as finance, insurance, and real estate.

New Working Environments During the 1990s, computers gave rise to a whole new field of work for millions of Americans. Younger workers led the way, creating new companies to develop hardware and software and to harness the power of the Internet. Many of these new companies also developed new rules for working: flexible hours, casual clothes, informal supervision, and the chance of becoming rich if the company was successful.

▼ **Many of today's workers enjoy a relaxed work environment.**

Applying Economic Ideas

1. Examine the graph on Real Compensation and Weekly Hours. Explain the relationship between compensation and hours during the time period shown.

2. How has technology helped Americans improve their working conditions?

Chapter Summary

A summary of major ideas in Chapter 9 appears below. See also the **Guide to the Essentials of Economics,** which provides additional review and test practice of key concepts in Chapter 9.

Section 1 Labor Market Trends (pp. 211–217)

The **labor force** is all nonmilitary people who are employed or unemployed. As America becomes more of a service economy, employers are hiring more college graduates and women. **Contingent employment** is on the rise. The **learning effect** and the **screening effect** help to raise wages for college graduates. Other labor trends include decreasing wages in some jobs and rising costs of employee benefits.

Section 2 Labor and Wages (pp. 219–226)

In a competitive labor market, laws of supply and demand determine wages based on how much a worker produces. At **equilibrium wage** there is neither an excess demand for labor nor an excess supply of labor. Historically, wage rates have been affected by workplace conditions, discrimination, and union **featherbedding.**

Section 3 Organized Labor (pp. 228–234)

Labor unions began in the mid-1800s. Using **strikes** to gain better wages and working conditions, unions made great gains in the mid-1900s. **Right-to-work laws** and other anti-union measures have curbed union influence. Unions and management engage in **collective bargaining.** Some disputes are resolved through **mediation** or **arbitration.**

Key Terms

Complete each sentence by choosing the correct answer from the list of terms below. You will not use all of the terms.

strike	collective
arbitration	bargaining
labor force	learning effect
equilibrium wage	screening effect
labor union	glass ceiling
contingent	
employment	

1. In the _____ process, a third party reviews a case and renders a legally binding decision.
2. The _____ is the theory that the completion of college tells employers that a job applicant is reasonably intelligent and hard-working.
3. An organized work stoppage intended to force an employer to address union demands is called a(n) _____.
4. The _____ consists of all nonmilitary people that are employed or unemployed.
5. The _____ is an unofficial, invisible barrier that prevents some women and minorities from advancing to top-level corporate positions in businesses dominated by white men.
6. The wage rate that produces neither a surplus nor a shortage of workers in the labor market is called the _____.
7. The use of temporary and/or part-time workers instead of permanent, full-time employees is known as _____.

Using Graphic Organizers

8. On a separate sheet of paper, copy the web map below. Then fill in the ovals with examples of factors that affect wage rates.

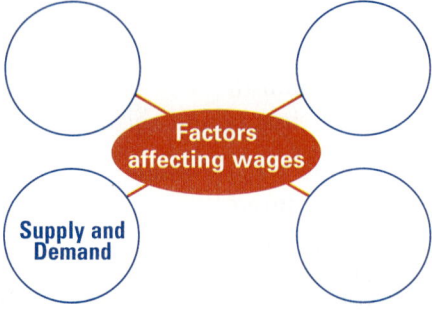

Reviewing Main Ideas

9. Who does the government include in its definition of the labor force?
10. What is a labor union?
11. Describe how collective bargaining works.
12. Why is the equilibrium wage high for some workers and low for others?
13. Why is the United States producing fewer goods and more services?
14. How do wage increases affect the demand for and supply of labor?
15. How does discrimination affect wages?
16. How does education affect wages?

Critical Thinking

17. **Predicting Consequences** How might technological changes affect labor demand in the future? Give specific examples.
18. **Drawing Conclusions** Reread the Fast Fact on page 212 describing how the invention of a punch card tabulator sped up data analysis after the 1880 Census. **(a)** What types of information related to labor might the new tabulator have helped to analyze? **(b)** Give other examples of types of economic information available as a result of technological innovations.
19. **Analyzing Information** Describe the reasons why companies are turning to contingent labor. How might this trend affect the work force in the future?

Problem-Solving Activity

20. Suppose you are a business owner competing for employees in a tight labor market. How might you attract employees without raising wages?

Economics Journal

Essay Writing Review your interview of an older adult. Interview a young adult about his or her job, or compare your own job experience to that of your interview subject. Write an essay describing your impressions of how the workplace has changed over the years.

Skills for Life

Analyzing Statistics Review the steps shown on page 218; then answer the following questions using the statistics in the table below.

21. What is the source of these statistics?
22. What is being shown by these data?
23. According to the table, who has the lower earnings, a man without a college education or a woman without a college education?
24. Which category of worker shown has the lowest percentage of low-wage employment?
25. Which category of worker shown has the highest percentage of low-wage employment?

Education and Employment

Adult men, ages 25 – 54		
	No low-wage employment	Low-wage* employment
College or more	90.6%	9.4%
High school or less	70%	30%

Adult women, ages 25 – 54		
	No low-wage employment	Low-wage* employment
College or more	83.1%	16.9%
High school or less	57.9%	42.1%

*average hourly earnings below $5.70
Source: U.S. Census Bureau

Take It to the NET

Chapter 9 Self-Test As a final review activity, take the Chapter 9 Self-Test in the Social Studies area at the Web site listed below, and receive immediate feedback on your answers. The test consists of 20 multiple-choice questions designed to test your understanding of the chapter content.
www.phschool.com

DEBATING CURRENT ISSUES: *Child Labor*

In 1997, the U.S. Congress amended a 1930 trade law banning imports made with child labor. According to *The Wall Street Journal Classroom Edition* article "Trading Places: Brazilian Program Tries to Put Child Laborers Back in School" by Matt Moffett, Staff Reporter of *The Wall Street Journal*, this law turned a spotlight on the labor practices of citrus-producing companies in Brazil. Brazil is the world's largest exporter of orange juice and a supplier for major U.S. orange juice brands.

Children continue to work in Brazilian groves picking oranges. Does this mean juice imports from Brazil should be banned? These excerpts from "Trading Places" examine both sides of the question.

YES Should the U.S. Ban Juice Imports From Brazil?

IN 1990, ODED GRAJEW walked away from the presidency of a toy company to form an advocacy group, the Abrinq Foundation for the Rights of the Child. Says Mr. Grajew: "Brazil's chronically unequal wealth distribution has one root cause: Millions of children are working instead of studying."

He cites the citrus business as an industry with an especially severe child-labor problem. Orange picking is harsh work. Pickers stand on ladders leaning perilously in the treetops. They earn about 20 cents for each 60-pound box they fill, about $5 a day.

Yielding to pressure from Mr. Grajew, the Brazilian Association of Citrus Exporters in 1996 publicly pledged that the industry would refrain from employing children as pickers. Three juice companies that made special contributions to children's causes got the right to stamp their products with Abrinq's "Child Friendly" seal.

But some children's activists say Abrinq's efforts fall short in a critical area: enforcement. They note that after dispensing its seals of approval, Abrinq doesn't do any follow-up monitoring of corporate compliance. The foundation concedes this but contends enforcement is the job of the government, the unions, and the press.

And there are signs the industry would just as soon not know who is picking its oranges. Where pickers had traditionally been hired directly by juice makers or landowners, the industry recently began exploiting a legal loophole that allows workers to be grouped into supposedly autonomous cooperatives.

Many children in developing countries work in order to help their families survive, but their long working hours often deprive them of a good education.

Under the co-op system, workers generally get paid more money up front but give up union representation and, in many cases, health and pension benefits. Several Brazilian courts have declared the co-ops illegal.

NO *Should the U.S. Ban Juice Imports From Brazil?*

IRONICALLY, THE ORANGE-JUICE flap has all but overshadowed the progress being made by Brazil's own programs to curb rural child labor.

In central Brazilian farm communities far from the international spotlight, a diverse group of activists and educators is making major strides toward eradicating child labor in the orange groves.

In one crackdown in Catanduva, a score of police and labor inspectors stopped buses, vans, and trucks headed for the fields. They uncovered numerous irregularities, ranging from dangerous transport of workers to improperly stored pesticides. But among the 2,200 workers who passed through the checkpoint, only four children were found.

"I didn't think I would ever say this, but after lots of work, we are making significant progress," says Walter Hipolito, a rural union leader who himself began picking oranges at age nine.

Prodded by Brazil's major child-advocacy group, the town's largest juice producer, Citrovita Agro Industrial Ltd., has funded an educational center for underprivileged youth. In addition, local educational authorities are offering financial aid to poor families that might otherwise have to send their children into the fields.

The local government gives needy parents whose children maintain good school-attendance records stipends of $45 a month per child—a significant sum here, where adult orange pickers earn about $100 a month.

The scholarship saved 13-year-old Marcella Carla Goncalves from following in the footsteps of her father, who quit school after the fourth grade to work in the fields. "My job is going to class," she says.

In the year since the program started, truancy in Catanduva schools has been reduced to less than 1 percent from 18 percent.

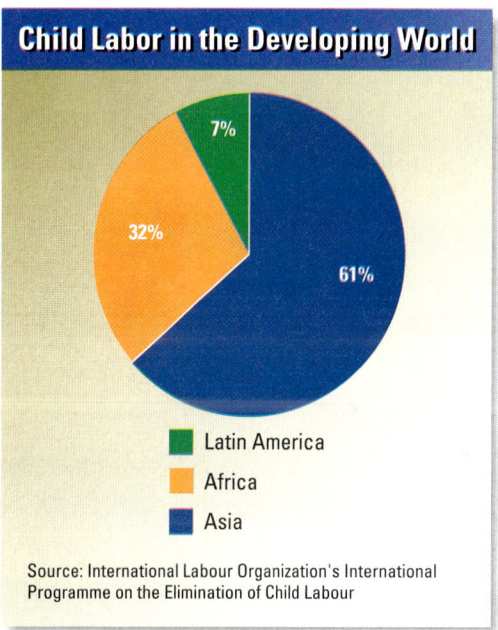

Child Labor in the Developing World

- 7%
- 32%
- 61%

■ Latin America
■ Africa
■ Asia

Source: International Labour Organization's International Programme on the Elimination of Child Labour

In developing countries in Latin America, Africa, and Asia, some 250 million children between the ages of 5 and 14 work.

DEBATING THE ISSUE

1. Why does Brazil's citrus industry have especially severe child-labor problems?

2. What evidence indicates Brazil is trying to reduce the number of children who work?

3. **Drawing Conclusions** Why is it ironic that Brazil is the focus of this trade debate?

4. **Reading Graphs** Use the pie chart and the caption below it to calculate the number of Latin American children between the ages of 5 and 14 who work.

 Take It to the Net Visit **www.phschool.com** for additional resources relating to this debate.

UNIT 4
Money, Banking, and Finance

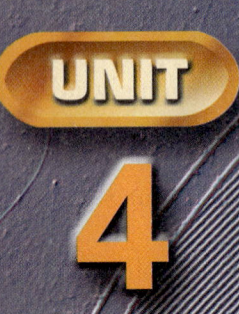

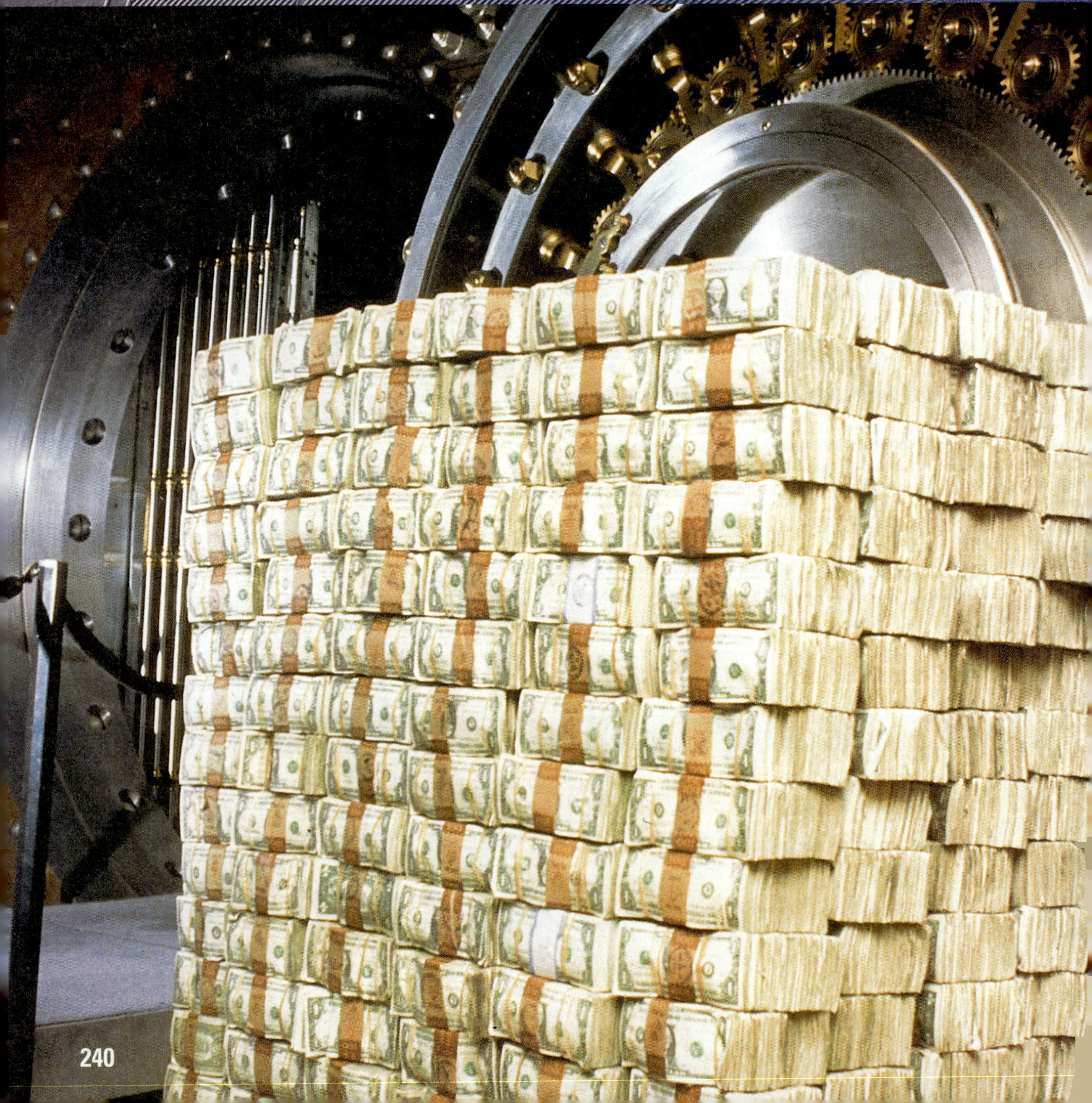

You've just won a million dollars . . .

While most people work to earn wages, you've just been handed a check for a million dollars. Now it's time to go to the bank and collect your winnings.

- ■ Where does the bank get the money to cash your check?
- ■ Should you be investing your money in stock or bonds instead of keeping it in a savings account?
- ■ What happens to the money you've deposited in your savings account? Is it safe?

Money plays a central role not just in economic theory, but also in our lives. For economists, "money" has a special meaning, though. In this unit you'll read about how economists define money, as well as how banks and other institutions help channel money from savers to investors.

Focus Activity

Create a flowchart showing some of the possible paths that a one-dollar bill might take over the course of two days. Include different paths showing how the money may be spent or saved.

Chapter 10 Money and Banking

Picture shopping at an Egyptian market and paying with a packet of salt, or walking into the bank with paper money and walking out with a pouch of gold. Seem unlikely? Actually, these scenarios might well have happened at various times in the past. They illustrate how much money and banking have changed over the centuries to meet society's changing needs.

Economics Journal

Record each time you use cash, checks, credit cards, and ATM cards during an average week. Include any trips you make to a bank or ATM.

Keep It Current

Items marked with this logo are periodically updated on the Internet. Keep up-to-date with what's in the news. To get current information on money and banking go to **www.phschool.com**

Section 1   Money

Preview

Objectives

After studying this section you will be able to:

1. **Describe** the three uses of money.
2. **Explain** the six characteristics of money.
3. **Understand** the sources of money's value.

Section Focus

Money serves as a medium of exchange, a unit of account, and a store of value. Although many objects have served as money in the past, the coins and bills we use today meet the needs of modern society.

Key Terms

money
medium of
 exchange
barter
unit of
 account
store of
 value

currency
commodity
 money
representative
 money
fiat money

Suppose you have just arrived at your neighborhood store after playing basketball on a hot day. You grab a soda and fish around in your jeans pockets for some money. You find a pen, keys, and a chewing gum wrapper, but, unfortunately, no money. Then you reach into your jacket pocket. Finally!—a crumpled dollar bill. You hand the money to the clerk and take a long, cold drink.

Money is a part of our daily lives. Without it, we can't get the things we need and want. That's not the whole story of money, however. In fact, money has functions and characteristics that you might never have thought about.

The Three Uses of Money

If you were asked to define money, you would probably think of the coins and bills in your wallet or the paychecks you receive for your part-time job. Economists define money in terms of its three uses. For an economist, **money** is anything that serves as a medium of exchange, a unit of account, and a store of value.

Money as a Medium of Exchange

A **medium of exchange** is anything that is used to determine value during the exchange of goods and services. Without money, people acquire goods and services

through **barter**, or the direct exchange of one set of goods or services for another. Barter is still used in many parts of the world, especially in traditional economies in Asia, Africa, and Latin America. It is also sometimes used informally in the United States. For example, a person might agree to help paint a neighbor's house in exchange for vegetables from the neighbor's garden. In general, however, as an economy becomes more specialized, bartering becomes too difficult and time-consuming to be practical.

To appreciate how much easier money makes exchanges, suppose that money did not exist, and that you wanted to trade your video cassette recorder (VCR) for an audio CD player. You probably would have a great deal of trouble making the exchange. First, you would need to find someone who wanted to both sell the model of CD player you want and buy your particular VCR. Second, this person would need to agree that your VCR is worth the same as his or her CD player. As you might guess, people in barter economies spend a great deal of time and effort exchanging the goods they have for the goods they need and want. That's why barter generally works well only in small, traditional economies.

Now consider how much easier your transaction would be if you used money as

money *anything that serves as a medium of exchange, a unit of account, and a store of value*

medium of exchange *anything that is used to determine value during the exchange of goods and services*

barter *the direct exchange of one set of goods or services for another*

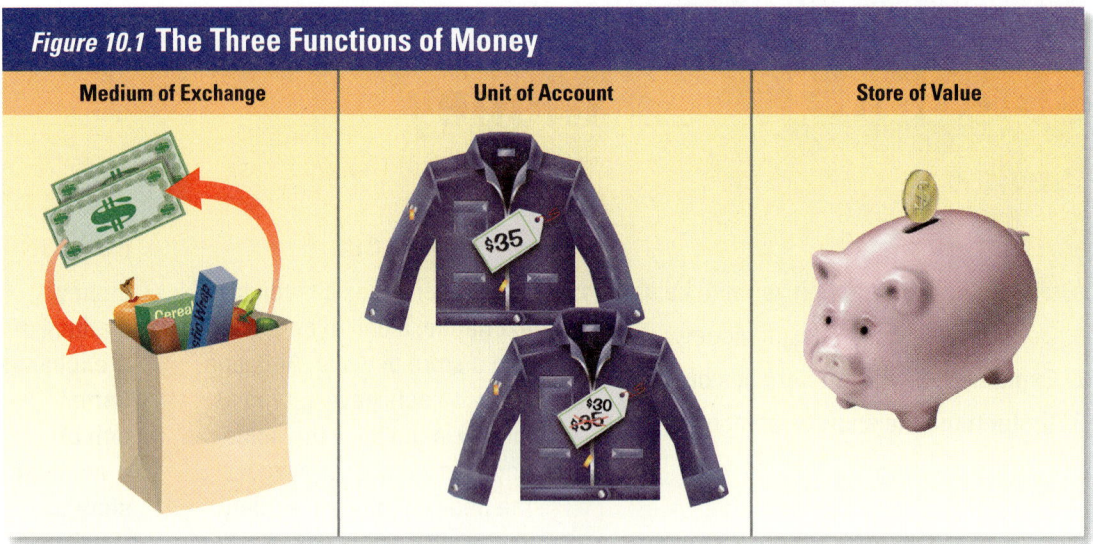

Figure 10.1 The Three Functions of Money

| Medium of Exchange | Unit of Account | Store of Value |

Money serves as a medium of exchange, a unit of account, and a store of value.
Money How does each illustration represent a characteristic of money?

unit of account *a means for comparing the values of goods and services*

store of value *something that keeps its value if it is stored rather than used*

a medium of exchange. All you would have to do is find someone who is willing to pay you $100 for your VCR. Then you could use that money to buy a CD player from someone else. The person selling you the CD player can use the $100 however he or she wishes. By the same token, the person who buys your VCR can raise that money however he or she wishes. Because money makes exchanges so much easier, people have been using it for thousands of years.

Money as a Unit of Account

In addition to serving as a medium of exchange, money serves as a **unit of account**. In other words, money provides a means for comparing the values of goods and services. For example, suppose you see a jacket on sale for $30. You know this is a good price because you have checked the price of the same or similar jackets in other stores. You can compare the cost of the jacket in this store with the cost in other stores because the price is expressed in the same way in every store in the United States—in terms of dollars and cents. Similarly, you would expect a movie in the theater to cost about $7.00, a video rental about $3.50, and so forth.

Other countries have their own forms of money that serve as units of account. The Japanese quote prices in terms of yen, the Russians in terms of rubles, Mexicans in terms of nuevo pesos, and so forth.

Money as a Store of Value

Money also serves as a **store of value**. This means that money keeps its value if you decide to hold on to—or store—it instead of spending it. For example, when you sell your VCR to purchase a CD player, you might not have a chance to purchase a CD player right away. In the meantime, you can keep the money in your wallet or in a bank. The money will still be valuable and will be recognized as a medium of exchange weeks or months from now when you go to buy the CD player.

Money serves as a good store of value with one important exception. Sometimes economies experience a period of rapid inflation, or a general increase in prices. For example, suppose the United States experiences 10 percent inflation during a particular year. If you sold your VCR at the beginning of that year for $100, the money you received would have 10 percent less value, or buying power, at the end of the year. This is because the price of the CD player would have increased by 10 percent during the year, to $110. The $100 you received at the beginning of the year would no longer be enough to buy the CD player.

In short, when an economy experiences inflation, money does not function as well as a store of value. You will read more about the causes and effects of inflation in Chapter 13.

The Six Characteristics of Money

The coins and paper bills used as money are called **currency**. In the past, societies have also used an astoundingly wide range of other objects as currency. Cattle, salt, dried fish, furs, precious stones, gold, and silver have all served as currency at various times in various places. So have porpoise teeth, rice, wheat, shells, tulip bulbs, and olive oil. These items all worked well in the societies in which they were used. None of them, however, would function very well in our economy today. Each lacks at least one of the six characteristics that economists use to judge how well an item serves as currency. These six characteristics are durability, portability, divisibility, uniformity, limited supply, and acceptability.

Durability

Objects used as money must withstand the physical wear and tear that comes with being used over and over again. If money wears out or is easily destroyed, it cannot be trusted to serve as a store of value.

Unlike wheat or olive oil, coins last for many years. In fact, some collectors have ancient Roman coins that are more than 2,000 years old. While our paper money may not seem very durable, its rag (cloth) content helps $1 bills typically last at least a year in circulation. When paper bills wear out, the United States government can easily replace them.

Portability

People need to be able to take money with them as they go about their daily business. They also must be able to easily transfer money from one person to another when they use money for purchases. Paper money and coins are very portable, or easily carried, because they are small and light.

Divisibility

To be useful, money must be easily divided into smaller denominations, or units of value. When money is divisible, people only have to use as much of it as necessary for any exchange. In the 16th and 17th centuries, people actually used pieces of coins to pay exact amounts for their purchases. Spanish coins called doubloons had lines scored or etched on

currency *coins and paper bills used as money*

▼ **Roman coins**

Figure 10.2 Roman Empire, About Second Century A.D.

Coins used throughout the Roman Empire provide a good example of the six characteristics of money. They were durable, portable, divisible into denominations, uniform, in limited supply, and accepted throughout the Empire.
Money What does the fact that Roman coins have been found in places as far from Rome as Britain and Egypt suggest about how well the coins served as currency?

them so that they could be easily divided into eight parts. Spanish coins, in fact, came to be called "pieces of eight."

Today, of course, if you use a $20 bill to pay for a $5 lunch, the cashier will not rip your bill into four pieces in order to make change. That's because American currency, like currencies around the world, consists of various denominations—$5 bills, $10 bills, and so on.

Uniformity

Any two units of money must be uniform—that is, the same—in terms of what they will buy. In other words, people must be able to count and measure money accurately.

Suppose everything were priced in terms of dried fish. One small dried fish might buy an apple. One large dried fish might buy a sandwich. This method of pricing is not a very accurate way of establishing the standard value of products because the size of a dried fish can vary. Picture the arguments people would have when trying to agree whether a fish was small or large. A dollar bill, however, always buys $1 worth of goods.

Limited Supply

Suppose a society uses certain pebbles as money. These pebbles have only been found on one beach. One day, however, someone finds an enormous supply of similar pebbles on a different beach. Now anyone can scoop up these pebbles by the handful. Since these pebbles are no longer in limited supply, they are no longer useful as currency.

In the United States, the Federal Reserve System controls the supply of money in circulation. By its actions, the Federal Reserve is able to keep just the right amount of money available. You'll read more about how the Federal Reserve monitors and adjusts the money supply in Chapter 16.

Acceptability

Finally, everyone in an economy must be able to exchange the objects that serve as money for goods and services. When you go to the store, why does the person behind the counter accept your money in exchange for a carton of milk or a box of pencils? After all, money is just pieces of metal or paper. Your money is accepted because the owner of the store can spend it elsewhere to buy something he or she needs or wants.

In the United States, we expect that other people in the country will continue to accept paper money and coins in exchange for our purchases. If people suddenly lost confidence in our currency's value, they would no longer be willing to sell goods and services in return for dollars. (See *Global Connections* below to learn more about what happens when people lose confidence in their country's currency.)

Sources of Money's Value

Think about the bills and coins in your pocket. They are durable and portable. They are also easily divisible, uniform, in limited supply, and accepted throughout the country. As convenient and practical as they may be, however, bills and coins have very little value in and of themselves. What, then, makes money valuable? The answer is that there are actually several possible sources of money's value, depending on whether the money is commodity, representative, or fiat money.

Commodity Money

A commodity is an object. **Commodity money** consists of objects that have value in and of

commodity money
objects that have value in themselves and that are also used as money

Global Connections

The Ruble Russia's currency is facing trouble as a store of value. In 1998, it was devalued by the official Russian state bank from 6.3 rubles to the dollar to 9.5 rubles to the dollar. This slippage hurt average Russians, as their savings were now worth only two thirds of their previous value. Many Russians turned to buying American dollars with the rubles they had left, fearing another devaluation and having more faith in the stability of the dollar. By 2001, the ruble was valued at 29 to the dollar, or about 3.4 cents.

Figure 10.3 Sources of Money's Value

Commodity money	Representative money	Fiat money

Objects like this shock of wheat once served as commodity money.

Representative money like this silver certificate could be exchanged for silver.

Today, Federal Reserve notes are fiat money, decreed by the federal government to be an acceptable way to pay debts.

BUILDING KEY CONCEPTS

Americans used both commodity and representative money during the colonial period. Representative money was used until 1913, when the first Federal Reserve notes were issued. **Money** **What are the advantages of fiat money over commodity and representative money?**

themselves and that are also used as money. For example, salt, cattle, and precious stones have been used in various societies as commodity money. These objects have other uses as well. If not used as money, salt can preserve food and make it tastier. Cattle can be slaughtered for their meat, and gems can be made into jewelry. Tobacco, corn, and cotton all served as commodity money in the American colonies.

As you can guess, commodity money tends to lack several of the characteristics that make objects good sources of money. For example, it is often not portable, durable, or divisible. That's why commodity money only works in simple economies. As the American colonies developed more complex economic systems, tobacco and other objects were no longer universally accepted as money. The colonies needed a more convenient payment system. They turned to representative money to meet their needs.

Representative Money

Representative money makes use of objects that have value because the holder can exchange them for something else of value.

For example, if your brother gives you an IOU, the piece of paper itself is worth nothing. The promise that he will do all of your chores for a month may be worth quite a lot, however. The piece of paper simply represents his promise to you.

Early representative money took the form of paper receipts for gold and silver. Gold or silver money was heavy and thus inconvenient for customers and merchants to carry around. Each time someone made a transaction, the coins would have to be weighed and tested for purity. People therefore started to leave their gold in goldsmiths' safes. Customers would carry paper ownership receipts from the goldsmith to show how much gold they owned. After a while merchants began to accept goldsmiths' receipts instead of the gold itself. In this way, the paper receipts became an early form of paper money.

Colonists in the Massachusetts Bay Colony first used representative money in the late 1600s when the Colony's treasurer issued bills of credit to lenders to help finance King William's War. The bills of credit showed the exact amount that colonists had loaned to the Massachusetts government. Billholders could redeem the

representative money *objects that have value because the holder can exchange them for something else of value*

fiat money *money that has value because the government has ordered that it is an acceptable means to pay debts*

paper for specie, that is, gold and silver coins.

Representative money was not without its problems. During the American Revolution, the Second Continental Congress issued representative money called Continentals to finance the war against England. Unfortunately, few people were able to redeem these early paper currencies for specie because the federal government had no power to collect taxes. Until the Constitution replaced the Articles of Confederation in 1789, the federal government depended on the states' voluntary contributions to fill the treasury. As a result, the federal treasury held very little gold or silver. Continentals became worthless because people came to believe that they would not be able to redeem their bills for gold and silver coins. People even began to use the phrase "not worth a Continental" to refer to something useless.

Later, the United States government issued representative money in the form of silver and gold certificates. These certificates were "backed" by gold or silver. In other words, holders of such certificates could redeem them for gold or silver at a local bank. The United States government thus had to keep vast supplies of gold and silver on hand to be able to convert all paper dollars to gold if the demand arose. Some silver certificates circulated until 1971, but for the most part, the government stopped converting paper money into silver or gold in the 1930s.

Fiat Money

If you examine a dollar bill, you will see George Washington's picture on one side, and on the other side the words, "This note is legal tender for all debts, public and private." In essence, these words mean that our money is valuable because our government says it is.

United States money today is fiat money. A fiat is an order or decree. **Fiat money**, also called "legal tender," has value because the government has decreed that it is an acceptable means to pay debts. It remains in limited supply, and therefore valuable, because the Federal Reserve controls its supply. This control of the money supply is essential for a fiat system to work.

Section 1 Assessment

Key Terms and Main Ideas

1. How does **money** serve as a **store of value**?
2. Give examples of **(a)** commodity money, **(b)** representative money, and **(c)** fiat money.
3. Why does United States **currency** have value?
4. What are the disadvantages of **commodity money**?
5. Why did Continentals become worthless?

Applying Economic Concepts

6. *Critical Thinking* Suppose you are shopping for a new backpack and want to get the best value for your money. Explain how the fact that money functions as a unit of account helps you to make your choice.

7. *Try This* Would movie tickets or popcorn make good money? Describe how well these items meet each of the six characteristics of an ideal currency.

8. *Decision Making* Suppose you need a graphing calculator. Should you plan to trade your hockey stick for one or should you try to sell your hockey stick and use the money to buy one from a classmate? Explain your reasoning.

9. *Problem Solving* What material(s) would you use if you were creating a new United States coin? Why?

10. *Critical Thinking* Suppose you live in a society that has a barter economy. What difficulties might you encounter in paying for such services as medical care and education?

Take It to the NET Think of an item you have bought recently and find out how much it cost the year you were born. Use the links provided in the Social Studies area at the following Web site for help in completing this activity. **www.phschool.com**

Understanding Public Opinion Polls

Public opinion polls measure what people think about a particular subject. Although pollsters take several steps to ensure that their results mirror the population as a whole, there are many pitfalls. For example, the same question phrased in different ways can result in widely different answers, even if all the questions are essentially the same. Because a poll can only measure a small sample of the population, pollsters include a statistical margin of error that indicates the degree to which the poll is accurate for the entire population. Public opinion polls should be read critically to understand exactly what they say. Use the following steps to analyze the hypothetical poll below.

1. Establish the purpose of the poll. Read the statements in the poll. (**a**) What is the subject of the poll. (**b**) What, specifically, were people asked?

2. Analyze the response. Look at the change in the rate of people who agreed with the statements as the statements changed. A politician reading only the responses to the first question might assume that the American people would support an expensive system of free clinics.

(**a**) Which details seemed to provoke a negative reaction? (**b**) Can we say that a majority of Americans would agree with statement B? Why or why not?

3. Expand upon the original question. The lessons learned from one poll can help make the next poll more accurate. If you were a politician trying to obtain accurate and precise information about the public's opinions on health care, how might you rephrase the questions in the poll?

Health Care Poll

"The government today does not spend enough to provide all Americans, including the 40 million Americans without health insurance, with good health care. Keeping this in mind, do you agree or disagree with the following statements?"

	I Agree	I Disagree
A. "Every American should have access to good health care."	64%	36%
B. "The government should guarantee that every American has good health care."	53%	47%
C. "The government should spend more to guarantee that every American has good health care."	42%	58%

Note: Random sample of 1,400 people surveyed by phone; margin of error ± 4 percent

Additional Practice

Use the Internet to find the results of a recent poll. Look at the question or questions asked. How does the pollster try to keep the question as neutral as possible?

The History of American Banking

Objectives

After studying this section you will be able to:

1. **Describe** the shifts between centralized and decentralized banking before the Civil War.
2. **Explain** how the banking system was stabilized in the later 1800s.
3. **Describe** developments in banking during the twentieth century.

Section Focus

The history of banking in the United States is the story of shifts between a centralized, national banking system and independent state and local banks. Out of these shifts has developed the stable banking system in which we place our confidence today.

Key Terms

bank
national bank
bank run
greenback
gold standard
Federal Reserve System
central bank
member bank
Federal Reserve note
Great Depression
Federal Deposit Insurance Corporation (FDIC)

---

bank *an institution for receiving, keeping, and lending money*

▲ What were the views of Alexander Hamilton (top) and Thomas Jefferson (bottom) on the creation of a national bank?

Chances are there is at least one **bank**—an institution for receiving, keeping, and lending money—near your home. That's because banks have become a fact of everyday life in the United States. This was not always the case, however. American banking as we know it today has developed over the course of the nation's history to meet the needs of a growing and changing population.

American Banking Before the Civil War

During the first part of our nation's history, banks were very informal businesses that merchants managed in addition to their regular trade. For example, a merchant who sold cloth, grain, or other goods might allow customers to deposit money. He would then charge a small fee to keep the money safe. He would also charge a fee if a customer wanted to take out a loan. These informal banks were not completely safe, however. If a merchant went out of business or was untrustworthy, customers could lose all of their savings.

Two Views of Banking

After the American Revolution, the leaders of the new nation agreed that one of their main goals must be to establish a safe, stable banking system. Such a system was important for increasing trade with other countries and ensuring the economic growth of the new United States. The nation's leaders did not, however, agree on how that goal should be accomplished. Their debate on banking during the 1780s and 1790s was part of a larger political debate about the role of government in the young country.

As you may remember from your study of American history, the Federalists believed that the country needed a strong central government to establish economic and social order. The Antifederalists favored leaving most powers in the hands of the states. These two groups viewed the country's banking needs quite differently.

The Federalists, led by Alexander Hamilton, believed that a centralized banking system was necessary for the United States to develop healthy industries and trade. When President Washington appointed Hamilton as Secretary of the Treasury in 1789, Hamilton proposed a

national bank (a bank chartered, or licensed, by the national government) that could issue a single currency for the entire nation, manage the federal government's funds, and monitor other banks throughout the country.

The Antifederalists, however, led by Thomas Jefferson, supported a decentralized banking system. In this system, the states would establish and regulate all banks within their borders.

The First Bank of the United States
At first, the Federalists were successful in creating a strong central bank. In 1791, Congress set up the Bank of the United States, granting it a twenty-year charter, or license to operate. The United States Treasury used the Bank for the following purposes:

- to hold the money that the government collected in taxes
- to help the government carry out its powers to tax, borrow money in the public interest, and regulate interstate and foreign commerce
- to issue representative money in the form of bank notes, which were backed by gold and silver
- to ensure that state-chartered banks held sufficient gold and silver to exchange for bank notes should the demand arise

The Bank succeeded in bringing order and stability to American banking. Many people worried, however, that the Bank would lend only to wealthy people and large businesses. They feared that ordinary people who needed to borrow money to maintain or expand their farms and small businesses would be refused loans. In addition, Jefferson and other Antifederalists pointed out that the Constitution does not explicitly give Congress the power to create a national bank. Therefore, they argued, the creation of a national bank was unconstitutional. When Alexander Hamilton died in a famous duel with Vice President Aaron Burr in 1804, the Bank lost its main backer. The Bank functioned only until 1811, when its charter ran out.

Chaos in American Banking
Once the Bank's charter expired, state banks (banks chartered by state governments) began issuing bank notes that they could not back with specie, or gold and silver coins. The states also chartered many banks without considering whether these banks would be stable and creditworthy.

Without any kind of supervision or regulation, financial confusion resulted. Prices rose rapidly. Neither merchants nor customers had confidence in the value of the paper money in circulation. Different banks issued different currencies, and bankers always faced the temptation to print more money than they had gold and silver to back. Merchants had to keep lists of which notes were redeemable by gold and silver and which were not.

The Second Bank of the United States
To eliminate this financial chaos, Congress chartered the Second Bank of the United States in 1816. Like the first Bank, the Second Bank was limited to a twenty-year charter. The Second Bank slowly managed to rebuild the public's confidence in a national banking system, although many people, including President Andrew Jackson, continued to oppose the idea.

national bank *a bank chartered, or licensed, by the national government*

▲ In this cartoon, Andrew Jackson drags bank supporter Henry Clay behind him as he attacks the monster national bank. How does the artist suggest that the danger is not real?

▲ During the Free Banking Era (1837–1863), state-chartered banks and even individual companies issued their own currency. What were some of the difficulties that arose from this practice?

bank run *widespread panic in which great numbers of people try to redeem their paper money*

Nicholas Biddle, the Second Bank's president starting in 1823, was responsible for restoring stability. If Biddle thought that a particular state bank was issuing bank notes without enough reserves (that is, gold and silver to back them), he would surprise the bank with a great number of its notes all at once, asking for gold or silver in return. Some state banks, caught without the necessary reserves, went out of business. Others quickly learned to limit how many notes they issued.

Despite the difficulties arising from decentralized banking, many people continued to distrust the federal government's banking power. In addition, although the Supreme Court had ruled a national bank constitutional in 1819, the same groups who had opposed the first Bank also opposed the Second Bank. Finally, President Jackson's extreme distrust of the Second Bank led him to veto the renewal of the Bank in 1832.

The Free Banking Era

The fall of the Second Bank once again triggered a period dominated by state-chartered banks. For this reason, the period between 1837 and 1863 is known as the Free Banking, or "Wildcat," Era. Between 1830 and 1837 alone, the number of state-chartered banks nearly tripled. As you might expect, the sheer number of banks and currencies gave rise to a variety of problems.

1. *Bank runs and panics* State-chartered banks often did not keep enough gold and silver to back the paper money that they issued. Customers found it increasingly difficult to exchange their paper money for gold and silver, setting off **bank runs**. These were widespread panics in which great numbers of people tried to redeem their paper money at once. Many banks failed as a result, and public confidence plummeted. An especially severe panic occurred in 1837.
2. *Wildcat banks* Some banks were located on the edges of settled areas. They were called "wildcat banks" because people joked that only wildcats lived in such remote areas. Wildcat banks had a high rate of failure.
3. *Fraud* A few banks engaged in out-and-out fraud, or cheating. They issued bank notes, collected gold and silver money from customers who bought the notes, and then disappeared. Anyone who had bought the notes lost their money.
4. *Many different currencies* State-chartered banks—as well as cities, private banks, railroads, stores, churches, and individuals—were allowed to issue currency. Notes of the same denominations often had different values, so that a dollar issued by the "City of Atlanta" was not necessarily worth the same as a dollar issued by the "City of New York." Many notes were counterfeits, or worthless imitations of real notes.

The Later 1800s

By 1860, an estimated 8,000 different banks were circulating currency. To add to the confusion, the federal government played no role in providing paper currency or regulating reserves of gold or silver. The

Civil War, which erupted in 1861, made existing problems worse.

Currency in the North and South

During the Civil War, both the Union and Confederacy needed to raise money to finance their military efforts. In 1861, the United States Treasury issued its first paper currency since the Continental. The official name of the currency was "demand notes," but they were called **"greenbacks"** because they were printed with green ink.

In the South, the Confederacy issued currency backed by cotton, hoping that a Confederate victory would ensure the currency's value. As the Confederate economy suffered under the strain of the war, however, Confederate notes became worthless.

Unifying American Banks

With war raging, the federal government enacted reforms aimed at restoring confidence in paper currency. These reforms resulted in the National Banking Acts of 1863 and 1864. Together, these Acts gave the federal government three important powers:

1. the power to charter banks
2. the power to require banks to hold adequate gold and silver reserves to cover their bank notes
3. the power to issue a single national currency

The new national currency led to the elimination of the many different state currencies in use and helped stabilize the country's money supply.

The Gold Standard

Despite the reforms made during the Civil War, the country was still plagued by money and banking problems. In the 1870s, the nation adopted a **gold standard**— a monetary system in which paper money and coins are equal to the value of a certain amount of gold. The gold standard had two advantages:

1. It set a definite value for the dollar, so

that one ounce of gold equaled about $20. Since the value was set, people knew that they could redeem the value of their paper money at any time. Confident in that knowledge, people felt comfortable carrying around the lighter and more convenient paper money.
2. The government could issue currency only if it had gold in the treasury to back the notes. Because of the limited supply of gold, the government was prevented from printing an unlimited number of notes.

The gold standard thus fulfilled an essential requirement of a banking system: a stable currency that inspires the confidence of the public.

Banking in the Early Twentieth Century

Reforms such as the creation of a single national currency and the gold standard helped stabilize American banking. They did not, however, provide for a central decision-making authority. Such an authority could help banks provide funds

greenback *paper currency issued during the Civil War*

gold standard *a monetary system in which paper money and coins are equal to the value of a certain amount of gold*

▲ **The National Banking Acts of 1863 and 1864 required banks to hold enough gold and silver reserves to cover their bank notes.**

Figure 10.4 Developments in American Banking

Date	Development	Example
1780s	The nation has no reliable medium of exchange. Federalists and Antifederalists disagree about a banking system.	▶ 1780s Continental
1791	First Bank of the United States is established.	
1811–1816	Period of instability follows expiration of first Bank's charter.	
1816	Second Bank of the United States reestablishes stability.	
1830s–1860s	President Jackson vetoes recharter of Second Bank in 1832, giving rise to Free Banking Era.	
1861–1863	Civil War makes clear the need for a better monetary and banking system.	◀ 1861–1863 Greenback
1863–1864	National Banking Acts of 1863 and 1864 establish national banking system and uniform national currency.	
1907	Panic of 1907 leads to creation of the Federal Reserve System.	
1913	President Wilson signs the Federal Reserve Act.	▶ 1933 FDIC
1929	The Great Depression begins.	
1933	President Roosevelt helps restore confidence in the nation's banks by establishing the FDIC.	
1940s–1960s	Period of government regulation and long-term stability	
Late 1960s–1970s	New laws make clear the rights and responsibilities of banks and consumers.	
1980s	Period of deregulation; S&Ls face bankruptcies	
1990s	Banks enter a period of financial health and mergers.	

BUILDING KEY CONCEPTS

The history of American banking shows a series of shifts between stability and instability.
Government What does the chart suggest about the role of government in banking during the twentieth century?

---

for growth and manage the money supply based on what the economy needed.

Continuing problems in the nation's banking system resulted in the Panic of 1907. Because they lacked adequate reserves, many banks had to stop exchanging gold for paper money. Several long-standing New York banks failed, and many people lost their jobs because businesses did not have access to money for investing in future projects. Clearly, the economy needed a central banking system so that the country could avoid such panics in the future. As a result of the 1907 crisis, the government made plans to reinstate a central bank.

The Federal Reserve System

Passed in late 1913, the Federal Reserve Act established the **Federal Reserve System.** The Federal Reserve System, or Fed, served as the nation's first true **central bank,** or bank that can lend to other banks in time of need. It reorganized the federal banking system as follows:

- *Member banks* The system created up to twelve regional Federal Reserve Banks throughout the country. All banks chartered by the national government were required to become members of the Fed. The Federal Reserve Banks were the central banks for their districts. **Member banks**—banks that belong to the Fed— stored some of their cash reserves at the Federal Reserve Bank in their district.
- *Federal Reserve Board* All of the Federal Reserve Banks were supervised by a Federal Reserve Board appointed by the President of the United States.
- *Short-term loans* Each of the regional Federal Reserve Banks allowed member

Federal Reserve System *the nation's central banking system*

central bank *bank that can lend to other banks in times of need*

member bank *bank that belongs to the Federal Reserve System*

banks to borrow money to meet short-term demands. This helped to prevent bank failures that occurred when large numbers of depositors withdrew funds during a panic.

- *Federal Reserve notes* The system also created the national currency we use today in the United States—**Federal Reserve notes**. This allowed the Federal Reserve to increase and decrease the amount of money in circulation according to business needs.

You will read more about the role of the Federal Reserve and how the system works today in Chapter 16.

Banking and the Great Depression

The Fed helped to restore confidence in the nation's banking system. It was unable, however, to prevent the terrifying **Great Depression**—the severe economic decline that began in 1929 and lasted more than a decade.

During the 1920s, banks loaned large sums of money to many high-risk businesses. Many of these businesses proved unable to pay back their loans. Farmers were also unable to pay back loans due to crop failures and hard times on the nation's farms. In addition, the 1929 stock market crash resulted in widespread bank runs as nervous depositors rushed to withdraw their money. The combination of unpaid loans and bank runs resulted in the failure of thousands of banks across the country.

Banking Reforms

After becoming President in 1933, Franklin D. Roosevelt acted to restore public confidence in the nation's banking system. On March 5, 1933, Roosevelt declared a national "bank holiday" and closed the nation's banks. Within a matter of days, sound banks began to reopen. The "bank holiday" was not a time of festivities, as the name implies, but a desperate last resort to restore trust in the nation's financial system.

Later in 1933, Congress passed the act that established the **Federal Deposit Insurance**

Corporation (FDIC). The FDIC insures customer deposits if a bank fails. At first, FDIC insurance covered losses up to $2,500. Today the amount insured has risen to $100,000 per account.

In addition, federal legislation passed during the Great Depression severely restricted individuals' ability to redeem dollars for gold. Eventually, currency became fiat money backed only by the government's decree that establishes its value. In this way, the Federal Reserve could maintain a money supply at adequate levels to support a growing economy.

Banking in the Later Twentieth Century

As a result of the many bank failures of the Great Depression, banks were closely regulated from 1933 through the 1960s. Restrictions included the interest rates banks could pay depositors and the rates that banks could charge consumers for loans. Banks could also lend money only to customers who had a history of paying back loans on time.

By the 1970s, banks were eager for relief from federal regulation. In the late 1970s and 1980s, Congress passed laws to deregulate several industries. Deregulation

Federal Reserve note *the national currency we use today in the United States*

Great Depression *the severe economic decline that began in 1929 and lasted for more than a decade*

Federal Deposit Insurance Corporation (FDIC) *the government agency that insures customer deposits if a bank fails*

▼ **Widespread bank runs at the start of the Great Depression led to the failure of thousands of banks nationwide.**

▲ What does the cartoonist suggest about the large number of bank mergers during the 1990s?

is the removal, or relaxation, of government restrictions on business. Unfortunately, this deregulation contributed to a crisis in a class of banks known as Savings and Loans (S&Ls).

The Savings and Loan Crisis

Deregulation was one cause of the S&L crisis. High interest rates, inadequate capital, and fraud were others.

1. *Deregulation* Deregulation contributed to the crisis because S&Ls had previously been protected by government regulation. S&Ls were unprepared for competition.
2. *High interest rates* During the 1970s, S&Ls had made long-term loans at low rates. By the 1980s, interest rates had skyrocketed. This meant that S&Ls had to pay out high interest rates to their depositors. At the same time, however, they were receiving low rates on the money they had loaned out in the 1970s.

3. *Bad loans* Risky loans made in the early 1980s hit the S&L industry especially hard, forcing many out of business, as the graph on page 176 of Chapter 7 shows.
4. *Fraud* A few financially important institutions fraudulently made large loans to businesses that had little chance of succeeding. When these businesses failed, a tremendous drain was put on the reserves of the FSLIC, the federal agency that insured S&Ls.

In 1989, Congress passed the Financial Institutions Reform, Recovery, and Enforcement Act (FIRREA). This Act essentially abolished the independence of the savings and loan industry and transferred insurance responsibilities to the FDIC.

Banking in the 1990s

In 1999, in some of the most sweeping legislation since the Great Depression, Congress repealed the 1933 Glass-Steagall Act. This action paved the way for banks to sell financial assets such as stocks and bonds. In addition, the 1990s saw a growing trend toward bank mergers. You can read more about these mergers in the Case Study on page 265.

Section 2 Assessment

Key Terms and Main Ideas

1. What was the purpose of the first Bank of the United States?
2. What were three results of the National Banking Acts of 1863 and 1864?
3. Explain the purpose of the **Federal Deposit Insurance Corporation (FDIC)**.

Applying Economic Concepts

4. *Critical Thinking* Use evidence from your reading to explain how the role of financial institutions has changed over time.

5. *Decision Making* Picture yourself living in the period following the Civil War. Would you support a central banking system? Why or why not?
6. *Try This* Suppose you are a Federalist or Antifederalist. Write notes for one side of a debate on the creation of a national bank. Then organize a classroom debate.
7. *Critical Thinking* Suppose you were living during the Great Depression. How might the events of that era have affected your future banking decisions?

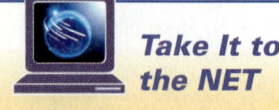

Take It to the NET

Find out more about the history of our nation's currency. Identify and describe one form of currency from each of three different centuries. Use the links provided in the Social Studies area at the following Web site for help in completing this activity. **www.phschool.com**

ECONOMIC
Profile

Amadeo P. Giannini (1870–1949)

When other banks refused to make loans to working-class people, this son of immigrants established one that would. On the strength of his low-income customer base, Amadeo Peter Giannini built the largest commercial bank in the world and contributed to the United States' economic development.

From Dockworker to Banker

Giannini was born in San Jose, California, to Italian immigrant parents. After his father died, his mother remarried, and the family moved to San Francisco. At age 12, Giannini went to work on the docks, loading and unloading fruits and vegetables for his stepfather's produce market. As a young man, he traveled throughout the state, signing farmers to contracts to supply him with produce. Over time, Giannini gained a reputation as a shrewd but honest businessman. He also developed a respect for people who worked with their hands.

In 1902, Giannini's business success led him to be invited to join the board of directors of a local bank. As a director he learned that the bank would loan only to wealthy San Franciscans. When the other bank directors refused to make loans to low-income workers, he quit the board to start his own bank.

Founding a Community Bank

In 1904, Giannini opened the Bank of Italy in San Francisco's heavily Italian North Beach section. He went door-to-door in the neighborhood, explaining to immigrant workers what the bank could do for them if they were to become customers.

About 18 months later, a devastating earthquake destroyed much of the city, including Giannini's bank. While other banks stayed closed, Giannini put a plank across two barrels in front of his ruined bank and made loans from this "desk." As a result, working-class North Beach was the first section of the city to be rebuilt.

The Bank of America

The earthquake bolstered Giannini's belief that banks should serve the public at large, and he decided to offer his banking services in other communities. In 1909, he opened his first branch in nearby San Jose. By 1918, the Bank of Italy had expanded across California, becoming the first bank in America with a statewide system of branches. In the 1920s, Giannini started a new bank network, which he named the Bank of America. In 1930, he merged the Bank of Italy into this new bank.

Giannini had retired in 1930, but his successor's conservative policies soon brought him out of retirement to retake control. In the 1930s, he made the Bank of America the world's largest commercial bank. At the time of Giannini's death, the Bank of America had roughly 500 branches and $6 billion in deposits.

CHECK FOR UNDERSTANDING

1. Source Reading In your own words, summarize Amadeo Giannini's ideas about a bank's function and role in society.

2. Critical Thinking How does the establishment of new branches benefit both a bank and the public?

3. Learn More Use the Internet and other sources to learn about the Community Reinvestment Act. Write a brief report on what it requires banks to do.

Objectives

After studying this section you will be able to:

1. **Explain** how the money supply in the United States is measured.
2. **Explain** the functions of financial institutions.
3. **Identify** different types of financial institutions.
4. **Understand** the changes brought about by electronic banking.

Section Focus

Banking has changed greatly in recent decades. Today, many people are likely to use credit or debit cards instead of cash or checks. Banks provide a large array of services, and electronic banking is revolutionizing the way people conduct banking transactions.

Key Terms

money supply
liquidity
demand
 deposit
money market
 mutual fund
fractional
 reserve
 banking

default
mortgage
credit card
interest
principal
debit card
creditor

---

money supply *all the money available in the United States economy*

liquidity *the ability to be used as, or directly converted to, cash*

demand deposit *the money in checking accounts*

Do you have a checking account, credit card, or ATM card? If you don't, you most likely will in the near future. As this question suggests, people in the United States today use more than just paper currency and coins to pay for purchases.

Measuring the Money Supply

You are familiar with paying for the items you need with currency—the bills and coins in your pocket. Money consists of currency. It also consists of traveler's checks, checking account deposits, and a variety of other components. All of these components make up the United States **money supply**—all the money available in the United States economy. To more easily keep track of these different kinds of money, economists divide the money supply into several categories. The main categories are called M1 and M2.

M1

M1 represents money that people can gain access to easily and immediately to pay for goods and services. In other words, M1 consists of assets that have **liquidity,** or the ability to be used as, or directly converted into, cash.

As you can see from Figure 10.5, about 48 percent of M1 is made up of currency

held by the public, that is, all currency held outside of bank vaults. Another large part of M1 is deposits in checking accounts. Funds in checking accounts are also called **demand deposits** because checks can be paid "on demand," that is, at any time. Until the 1980s, checking accounts did not pay interest, and a new category, called *other checkable deposits,* was introduced to describe checking accounts that did pay interest. Today this distinction is not as meaningful as it once was since many checking accounts pay interest if your balance is sufficiently high.

Traveler's checks make up a very small component of M1. Unlike personal checks, traveler's checks can be easily turned into cash.

M2

M2 consists of all the assets in M1 plus several additional assets. These additional M2 funds cannot be used as cash directly, but can be converted to cash fairly easily. M2 assets are also called *near money.*

For example, deposits in savings accounts are included in M2. They are not included in M1 because they cannot be used directly in financial exchanges. You cannot hand a sales clerk your savings account passbook to pay for a new backpack. You can, however, withdraw

▲ Assets that have liquidity include currency, funds in checking accounts, and traveler's checks.

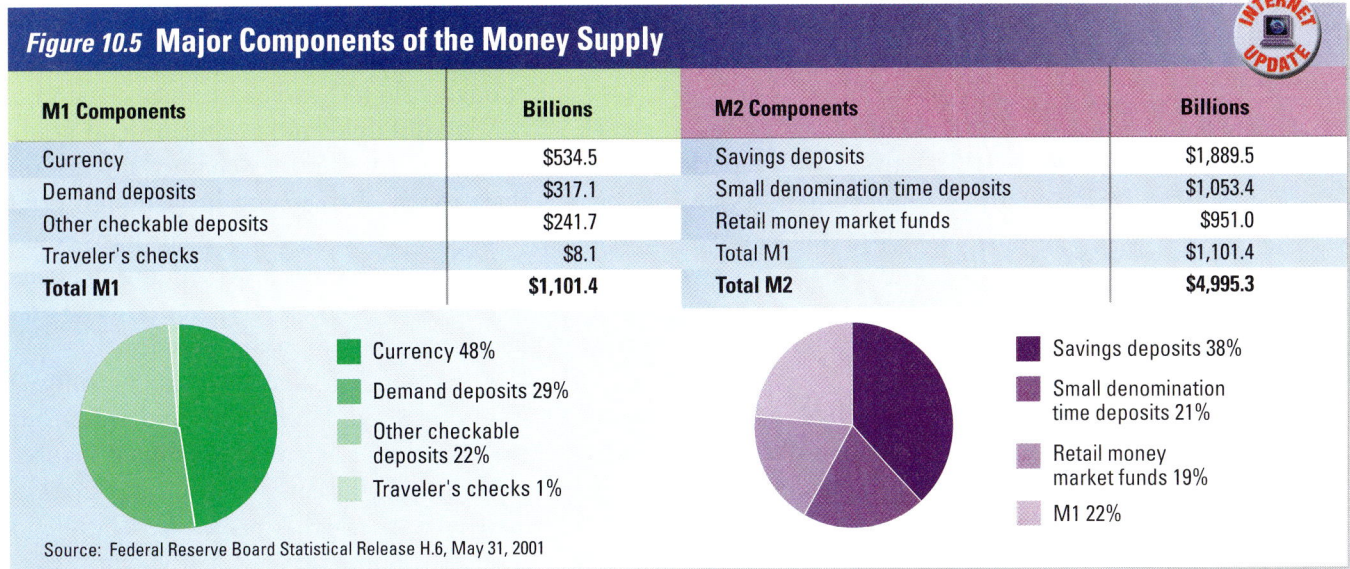

Figure 10.5 Major Components of the Money Supply

M1 Components	Billions	M2 Components	Billions
Currency	$534.5	Savings deposits	$1,889.5
Demand deposits	$317.1	Small denomination time deposits	$1,053.4
Other checkable deposits	$241.7	Retail money market funds	$951.0
Traveler's checks	$8.1	Total M1	$1,101.4
Total M1	**$1,101.4**	**Total M2**	**$4,995.3**

Currency 48%
Demand deposits 29%
Other checkable deposits 22%
Traveler's checks 1%

Savings deposits 38%
Small denomination time deposits 21%
Retail money market funds 19%
M1 22%

Source: Federal Reserve Board Statistical Release H.6, May 31, 2001

The components of M1 can be used as cash or can be easily converted into cash. M2 consists of the assets in M1 plus assets that can be converted to cash fairly easily.
Money What is the largest component of M1? Of M2?

money from your savings account and then use that money to buy a backpack.

Deposits in **money market mutual funds** are also included as part of M2. These are funds that pool money from small savers to purchase short-term government and corporate securities. They earn interest and can be used to cover checks written over a certain minimum amount, such as $250. You will read more about money market mutual funds in Chapter 11.

Functions of Financial Institutions

Banks and other financial institutions are essential to managing the money supply. They also perform many functions and offer a wide range of services to consumers.

Storing Money

Banks provide a safe, convenient place for people to store money. Banks keep cash in fireproof vaults and are insured against the loss of money in the event of a robbery. As you read in Section 2, FDIC insurance protects people from losing their money if the bank is unable to repay funds.

Saving Money

Banks offer a variety of ways for people to save money. Four of the most common ways are the following:

- *Savings accounts*
- *Checking accounts*
- *Money market accounts*
- *Certificates of deposit (CDs)*

Savings accounts and checking accounts are the most common types of bank accounts. They are especially useful for people who need to make frequent withdrawals. Savings accounts and most checking accounts pay a small amount of interest at an annual rate.

Money market accounts and certificates of deposits (CDs) are special kinds of savings accounts that pay a higher rate of interest than do savings and checking accounts. Money market accounts allow you to save and to write a limited number of checks. Interest rates are not fixed, but can move up or down. CDs, on the other hand, offer a guaranteed rate of interest over a certain period of time. Funds placed in a CD, however, cannot be removed until the end of a certain time period, such as one or two years. Customers who remove their

money market mutual fund *a fund that pools money from small savers to purchase short-term government and corporate securities*

fractional reserve banking *a banking system that keeps only a fraction of funds on hand and lends out the remainder*

money before that time pay a penalty for early withdrawal.

Loans

Banks also perform the important service of providing loans. As you have read, the first banks started doing business when goldsmiths issued paper receipts. These receipts represented gold coins that the goldsmith held in safe storage for his customers. He would charge a small fee for this service.

In early banks, those receipts were fully backed by gold—every customer who held a receipt could be sure that the goldsmith kept the equivalent amount of gold in his safe. Gradually, however, goldsmiths realized that their customers seldom, if ever, asked for all of their gold on one day. Goldsmiths could

thus lend out half or even three quarters of their gold at any one time and still have enough gold to handle customer demand.

Why did goldsmiths want to lend gold? The answer is that they charged interest on their loans. By keeping just enough gold reserves to cover demand, goldsmiths could run a profitable business lending deposits to borrowers and earning interest. The first banks were based on this practice.

A banking system that keeps only a fraction of funds on hand and lends out the remainder is called **fractional reserve banking**. Like the early banks, today's banks also operate on this principle. They lend money to homeowners for home improvements, to families to pay for college tuition, and to businesses. The more money a bank lends out, and the higher the interest rate it charges borrowers, the more profit a bank is able to make.

By making loans, banks help new businesses get started, and they help established businesses grow. When a business gets a

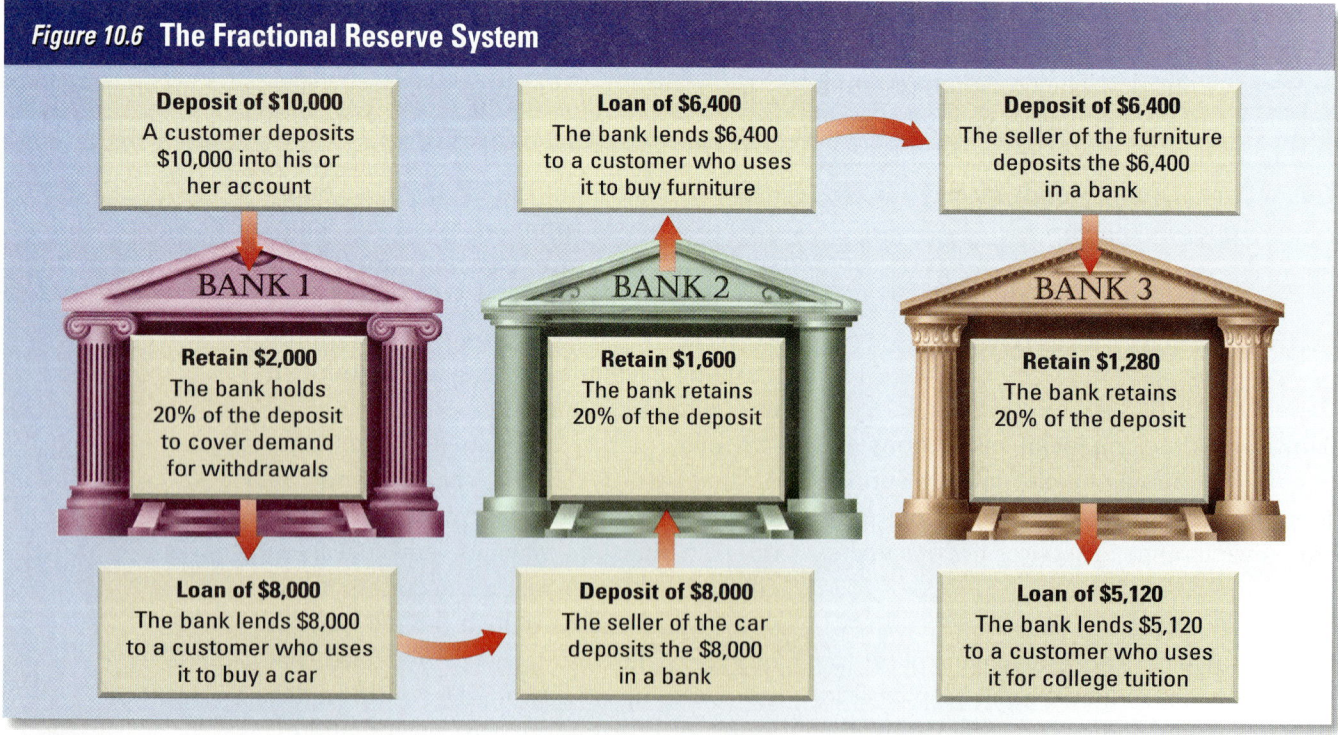

Figure 10.6 The Fractional Reserve System

Deposit of $10,000
A customer deposits $10,000 into his or her account

Loan of $6,400
The bank lends $6,400 to a customer who uses it to buy furniture

Deposit of $6,400
The seller of the furniture deposits the $6,400 in a bank

BANK 1

BANK 2

BANK 3

Retain $2,000
The bank holds 20% of the deposit to cover demand for withdrawals

Retain $1,600
The bank retains 20% of the deposit

Retain $1,280
The bank retains 20% of the deposit

Loan of $8,000
The bank lends $8,000 to a customer who uses it to buy a car

Deposit of $8,000
The seller of the car deposits the $8,000 in a bank

Loan of $5,120
The bank lends $5,120 to a customer who uses it for college tuition

BUILDING KEY CONCEPTS

In a fractional reserve system, banks keep only a fraction of funds on hand and lend out the rest. The funds lent out fuel the economy and ensure continued growth. **Money** Why does the bank retain a percentage of the money it receives from depositors?

loan, that business can create new jobs by hiring new workers or investing in physical capital in order to increase production.

A business that gets a loan may also help other businesses grow. For example, suppose you and a friend want to start a window-washing business. Your business will need supplies like window cleaner and ladders, so the companies that make your supplies will also benefit. They may even hire workers to expand their businesses.

Bankers must, however, consider the security of the loans they make. Suppose borrowers **default**, or fail to pay back their loans? Then the bank loses money. Bankers therefore always face a trade-off between profits and safety. If they make too many bad loans—loans that are not repaid—they may go out of business altogether. (See pages 510–511 of the Personal Finance Handbook to learn more about banks and the services they offer.)

Mortgages

A **mortgage** is a specific type of loan that is used to buy real estate. Suppose the Lee family wants to buy a house for $200,000. They are unlikely to have the cash on hand to be able to pay for the house. Like almost all home-buyers, they will need to take out a mortgage.

The Lees can afford to make a down payment of 20 percent of the price of the house, or $40,000. After investigating the Lees's creditworthiness, their bank agrees to lend them the remaining $160,000 so that they can purchase their new house. Mortgages usually last for 15, 25, or 30 years. According to the terms of their loan, the Lees are responsible for paying back the loan plus whatever interest the bank charges over a period of 25 years.

Credit Cards

If you look at a credit card, somewhere you will see the name of a bank printed on it. Another service that banks provide is issuing **credit cards**—cards entitling their holders to buy goods and services based on the cardholder's promise to pay for these goods and services.

Figure 10.7 Compound Interest

Start of year	Principal amount	Interest earned at 5%	Principal at end of year
–	$100.00	$5.00	$105.00
1	$105.00	$5.25	$110.25
2	$110.25	$5.51	$115.76
3	$115.76	$5.79	$121.55
4	$121.55	$6.08	$127.63
5	$127.63	$6.38	$134.01
6	$134.01	$6.70	$140.71
7	$140.71	$7.04	$147.75
8	$147.75	$7.39	$155.14
9	$155.14	$7.76	$162.90
10	$162.90	$8.14	$171.04
11	$171.04	$8.55	$179.59
12	$179.59	$8.98	$188.57
13	$188.57	$9.43	$198.00
14	$198.00	$9.90	$207.90
15	$207.90	$10.39	$218.29

This chart shows the money earned on a $100 deposit when interest is compounded yearly at 5 percent.

Income How many years does it take for the original deposit to double?

How do credit cards work? Suppose you buy a sleeping bag and tent for $100 on May 3. You do not actually pay for the gear until you receive your credit-card bill and pay it in June. In the meantime, however, the credit-card issuer (the bank) will have paid the sporting goods store. Your payment repays the bank for the "loan" of $100.

Simple and Compound Interest

As you have read, **interest** is the price paid for the use of borrowed money. The amount borrowed is called the **principal**. Simple interest is interest paid only on principal. For example, if you deposit $100 in a savings account at 5 percent simple interest, you will make $5 in a year (assuming that interest is paid annually).

Suppose that you leave the $5 in interest in the bank, so that at the end of the year you have $105 in your account—$100 in principal and $5 in interest. Compound interest is interest paid on both principal and accumulated interest. That means that in the second year, as long as you leave both the principal and the interest in your account, interest will be paid on $105. Figure 10.7 shows how an account paying compound interest grows over time.

default *failure to pay back a loan*

mortgage *a specific type of loan that is used to buy real estate*

credit card *a card entitling its holder to buy goods and services based on the holder's promise to pay for these goods and services*

interest *the price paid for the use of borrowed money*

principal *the amount of money borrowed*

After customers deposit money, a bank lends it to businesses and other borrowers and collects interest. The bank uses this income from interest to cover its costs and make a profit.

Income What are the sources of a bank's income?

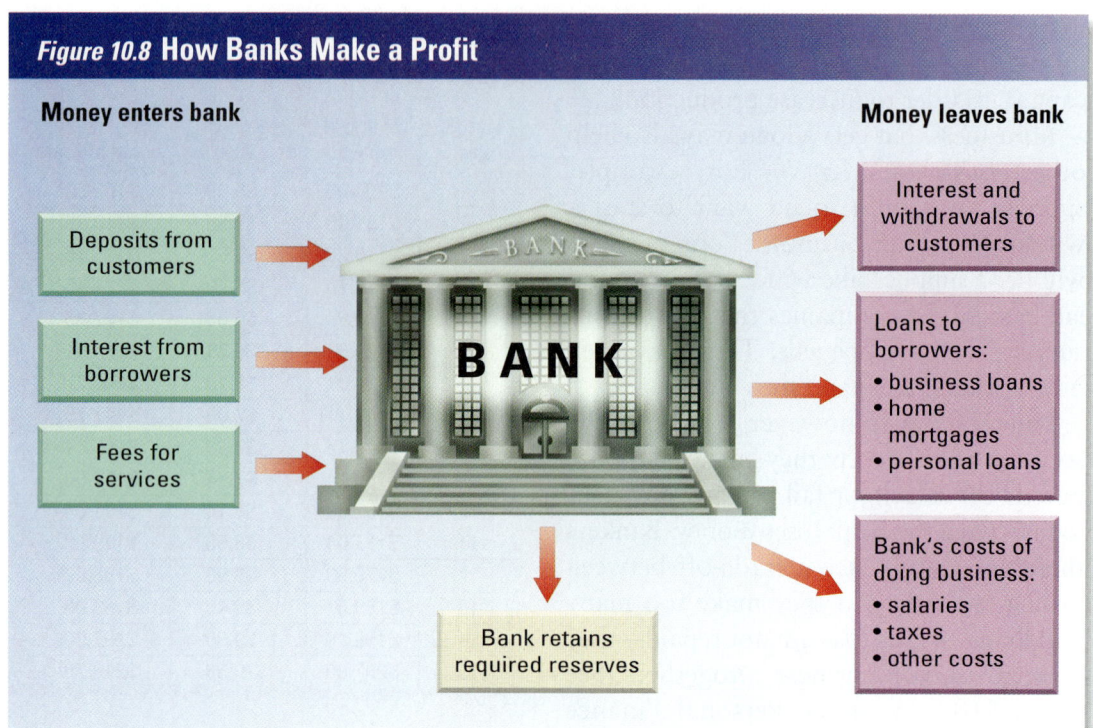

Figure 10.8 **How Banks Make a Profit**

Money enters bank   **Money leaves bank**

Deposits from customers → **BANK** → Interest and withdrawals to customers

Interest from borrowers → Loans to borrowers:
• business loans
• home mortgages
• personal loans

Fees for services → Bank's costs of doing business:
• salaries
• taxes
• other costs

Bank retains required reserves

Banks and Profit

The largest source of income for banks is the interest they receive from customers who have taken loans. Banks, of course, also pay out interest on customers' savings and most checking accounts. The amount of interest they pay out, however, is less than the amount of interest they charge on loans. The difference in the amounts is how banks cover their costs and make a profit.

Types of Financial Institutions

Several kinds of financial institutions operate in the United States. These include commercial banks, savings and loan associations, mutual savings banks, and credit unions. During the 1990s, these financial institutions became more similar than dissimilar, although differences still remain.

Commercial Banks

Commercial banks, which traditionally provided services to businesses, offer a wide range of services today. Commercial banks offer checking services, accept deposits, and make loans. Some commercial banks are chartered by states and are regulated by state authorities and by the Federal Deposit Insurance Corporation (FDIC). About one third of all commercial banks are national banks and are part of the Federal Reserve System. Commercial banks provide the most services and play the largest role in the economy of any type of bank.

Savings and Loan Associations

Savings and Loan Associations (S&Ls), which you read about in Section 2, were originally chartered to lend money for building homes during the mid-1800s. Members of Savings and Loan Associations deposited funds into a large general fund and then borrowed enough money to buy their own houses. Savings and Loans are also called *thrifts* because they originally enabled "thrifty" working-class people—that is, people who were careful with their money—to save up and borrow enough to buy their own homes. Over time, Savings and Loan Associations have taken on many of the same functions as commercial banks.

Savings Banks

Mutual savings banks (MSBs) originated in the early 1800s to serve people who made smaller deposits and transactions than commercial banks wished to handle. Mutual savings banks were owned by the depositors themselves, who shared in any profits. Later, many MSBs began to sell stock to raise additional capital. These institutions became simply savings banks because depositors no longer owned them.

Although savings banks were traditionally concentrated in the Northeast, they had an important influence on the national economy. In 1972, the Consumer's Savings Bank of Worcester, Massachusetts, introduced a Negotiable Order of Withdrawal (NOW) account, a type of checking account that pays interest. NOW accounts became available nationwide in 1980.

Credit Unions

Credit unions are cooperative lending associations for particular groups, usually employees of a specific firm or government agency. Credit unions are commonly fairly small and specialize in home mortgages and car loans, usually at interest rates favorable to members. Some credit unions also provide checking account services.

Finance Companies

Finance companies make installment loans to consumers. These loans spread the cost of major purchases like computers, cars, refrigerators, and recreational vehicles over a number of months. Because people who borrow from finance companies more frequently fail to repay the loans, finance companies generally charge higher interest rates than banks do.

Electronic Banking

Banks began to use computers in the early 1970s to keep track of transactions. As computers have become more common in the United States, their role in banking has also increased dramatically. In fact, computerized banking may revolutionize banking in much the same way that paper currency changed banking long ago.

Automated Teller Machines

If you use an Automated Teller Machine (ATM), you are already familiar with one of the most common types of electronic banking. ATMs are computers that customers can use to deposit money, withdraw cash, and obtain account information at their convenience. Instead of having to go to the bank during the bank's hours of operation to conduct banking business face–to–face with a teller, you can take care of your finances at an ATM.

ATMs are convenient for both banks and for customers, since they are available 24 hours a day and reduce banks' labor costs. The overwhelming popularity of ATMs suggests that they are likely to be a permanent feature of modern banking.

Debit Cards

Debit cards are used to withdraw money. You may use a debit card to withdraw

debit card *a card used to withdraw money*

◀ **Electronic banking has greatly changed the way customers interact with their banks.**

money at an ATM. You may also use a debit card in stores equipped with special machines. When you "swipe" your card through one of these machines, your debit card sends a message to your bank to transfer money from your checking account directly into the store's bank account. For security, debit cards require customers to use personal identification numbers, or PINs, to authorize financial transactions.

Home Banking

More and more people are using the Internet to conduct their financial business. Many banks, credit unions, and other financial institutions allow people to check account balances, transfer money to different accounts, pay their bills, and automatically deposit their paychecks via computer.

Automatic Clearing Houses

Automatic Clearing Houses (ACHs), located at Federal Reserve Banks and their

creditor *person or institution to whom money is owed*

branches, allow customers to pay bills without writing checks. An ACH transfers funds automatically from customers' accounts to creditors' accounts. (A **creditor** is a person or institution to whom money is owed.) People usually use ACHs to pay regular monthly bills like mortgage payments, rent, utility bills, and insurance premiums. They save time, postage costs, and any worries about forgetting to make a payment.

Stored Value Cards

Stored value cards, or smart cards, are similar to debit cards. These cards are embedded with either magnetic strips or computer chips with account balance information. Smart cards include cards issued to college students living in dormitories to pay for cafeteria food, computer time, or photocopying. Phone cards, with which customers prepay for a specified amount of long-distance calling, are also smart cards.

Will stored value smart cards someday replace cash altogether? No one can know for sure, but you can read more about this question in the Debating Current Issues on pages 268–269.

Section 3 Assessment

Key Terms and Main Ideas

1. What is the difference between M1 and M2? Give an example of each.
2. How does a **debit card** differ from a **credit card?**
3. Describe three services that banks provide.
4. Explain why banks must balance profit and security when making loans.

Applying Economic Concepts

5. *Try This* Suppose you are setting up a classroom bank. What incentives will you offer so your classmates will use your bank? How will your bank make a profit?

6. *You Decide* Suppose that you are planning to open a checking account so you can deposit checks from your summer job. How will you decide on a bank?

7. *Using the Databank* Turn to the graph entitled "Personal Savings as a Percentage of Disposable Income" on page 540. **(a)** Describe the pattern of personal savings shown on the graph. **(b)** What factors could have caused the steady drop in savings since the 1970s?

8. *Critical Thinking* Write a paragraph in which you analyze how financial institutions affect households and businesses.

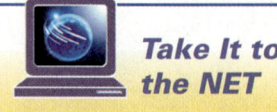

Take It to the NET

Research the current state of electronic money and banking. Then, describe one concern that has arisen about the use of electronic money. Use the links provided in the Social Studies area at the following Web site for help in completing this activity. **www.phschool.com**

Big Banks and Small

Since the 1980s, bank mergers have been taking place at a rapid rate. By 1999, there were only half as many banks in existence as there had been 20 years earlier. Larger banks mean larger profits, as banks acquire more customers through each successive merger. This certainly benefits the banks' shareholders, but what about consumers?

Large Banks These giant banks offer many benefits to their customers, such as computerized banking, conveniently located branch banks, and far-reaching ATM networks. However, after mergers, many banks have increased fees for services or tightened credit restrictions. Many customers are unhappy about the impersonal nature of some larger banks.

Small-Bank Networks A positive outcome of the merger mania has been growth among small banks. The federal government has forced many large banks to divest some of their branch banks in order to avoid having a monopoly in any given location. In some areas, banking companies have formed small regional networks by buying some of these banks.

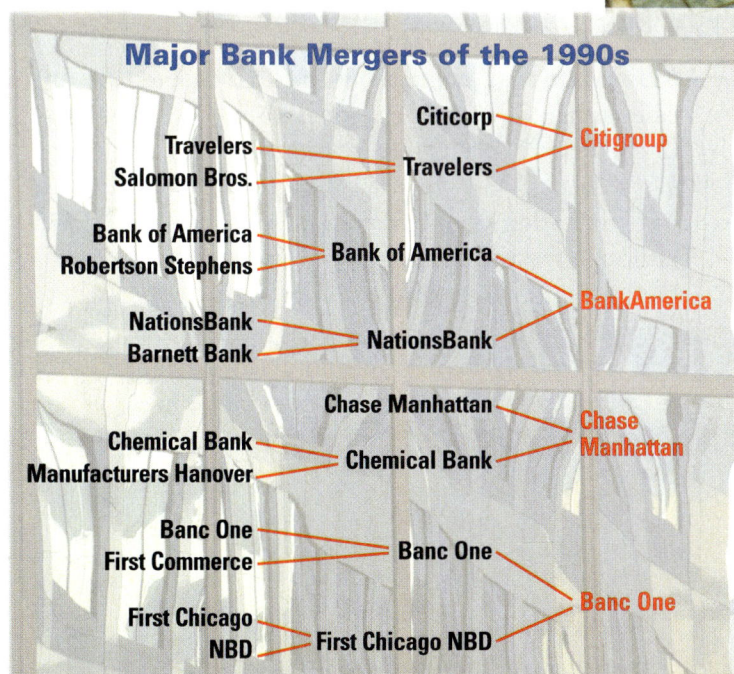

▲ Some small depositors like the personalized service of a small bank.

Community Banks In addition, new community banks have started up. In the 1990s, an average of 200 new bank charters were issued every year. Small banks have capitalized on their small size, emphasizing personalized service and their ties to the local community.

Over the last two decades, the merger mania has made some people fear the end of all competition in the banking industry. But as large banks grow ever larger, new community banks have stepped in to ensure that many people still have a choice of where to bank.

Applying Economic Ideas

1. What are the benefits and drawbacks of using one of the big banks?

2. The chart shows some of the major banking mergers of the 1990s. What do you think are the advantages and disadvantages to a bank entering into a major merger?

Major Bank Mergers of the 1990s

	Citicorp	**Citigroup**
Travelers	Travelers	
Salomon Bros.		
Bank of America	Bank of America	
Robertson Stephens		**BankAmerica**
NationsBank	NationsBank	
Barnett Bank		
	Chase Manhattan	**Chase Manhattan**
Chemical Bank	Chemical Bank	
Manufacturers Hanover		
Banc One	Banc One	
First Commerce		**Banc One**
First Chicago	First Chicago NBD	
NBD		

Chapter Summary

A summary of major ideas in Chapter 10 appears below. See also the **Guide to the Essentials of Economics**, which provides additional review and test practice of key concepts in Chapter 10.

Section 1 *Money (pp. 243–248)*

Money has three main functions in our economy. It serves as a **medium of exchange,** a **unit of account,** and a **store of value.** Economists use six characteristics to judge how well an item serves as **currency:** durability, portability, divisibility, uniformity, limited supply, and acceptability. U.S. currency has value because the United States government has given it value by fiat, or decree.

Section 2 *The History of American Banking (pp. 250–256)*

American banking has gone through several shifts between centralized and decentralized systems throughout our nation's history. Before the Civil War, banking was largely fragmented. A more stable, centralized system emerged after the conflict. The twentieth century has seen American banking become more stable, with the development of the **Federal Reserve System** in 1913 and the **Federal Deposit Insurance Corporation (FDIC)** in 1933.

Section 3 *Banking Today (pp. 258–264)*

Many different components are considered when calculating the country's money supply. M1 consists of currency, deposits in checking accounts, and traveler's checks. M2 consists of all the components of M1 plus additional assets. Banks vary in function, although the various banks and financial institutions have become increasingly similar in the services they provide. These services include storing money safely and providing loans. Technological advances are furthering a shift toward electronic banking.

Key Terms

Choose the italicized term in parentheses that best completes each sentence.

1. Using corn, cattle, or cotton as a medium of exchange is an example of *(representative money/commodity money).*
2. *(Currency/Greenback)* is a term that refers to bills and coins.
3. A *(debit card/credit card)* allows you to withdraw money directly from your checking account.
4. When buying a house, you obtain a *(unit of account/mortgage)* to help pay for it.
5. The *(Federal Reserve System/FDIC)* guarantees a bank deposit up to $100,000.
6. The money held in a checking account can be referred to as a *(demand deposit/gold standard).*
7. *(Barter/Fiat money)* holds its value because a government has deemed it acceptable as a form of payment.
8. *(Liquidity/Money supply)* refers to how easily assets can be converted into cash.

Using Graphic Organizers

9. On a separate sheet of paper, copy the web map below to summarize the services that banks provide. Complete the web map by writing an example of a banking service and a brief description of it in each oval. You may add more ovals as necessary.

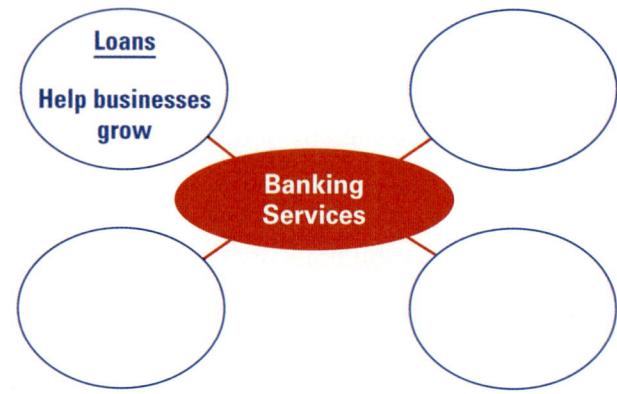

Reviewing Main Ideas

10. In your own words, describe the three functions of money.

11. Explain how a $1 bill has all six characteristics of money.

12. Name two measures that have been taken to stabilize American banking since the Great Depression.

13. What is fractional reserve banking?

14. What is electronic banking?

Critical Thinking

15. Predicting Consequences What would happen if the dollar lost its store of value? What could you substitute as a medium of exchange?

16. Recognizing Cause and Effect What were the effects of the following events on the history of banking? **(a)** expiration of the charter of the Second Bank of the United States **(b)** Panic of 1907 **(c)** Great Depression

17. Drawing Conclusions Some economists have predicted a "cashless society" in which all banking will be done electronically. Do you think this will be true of the United States economy? Support your conclusion with specific examples.

18. Synthesizing Information List three of your personal financial goals (for example, paying for education beyond high school). What role might banks have in helping you achieve those goals?

Problem-Solving Activity

19. Make a list of the problems associated with debit cards, such as forgotten PINs, lost cards, and so forth. What steps could be taken to eliminate some of these problems?

Economics Journal

Writing Essays Review your list of the times that you used money and its substitutes during an average week. Then write an essay describing how your week would have been different if you had bartered for your purchases instead of using money.

Skills for Life

Understanding Public Opinion Polls Review the steps shown on page 249; then answer the following questions using the hypothetical opinion poll results below.

20. What is probably the purpose of this public opinion poll? For whom might the results of this public opinion poll be useful?

21. Do the questions asked provide a valid indicator of overall public opinion? Why or why not?

22. Describe the public's general feelings about ATM user fees charged by banks based on the results of this poll.

23. Think of two more questions that this poll could ask to make it more useful in evaluating public opinion toward ATM user fees.

ATM User Fees Poll

"Many banks charge fees of $1.00 or more for ATM use. Keeping this in mind, do you agree or disagree with the following statements?"

	I Agree	I Disagree
A. Banks have no right to charge ATM user fees.	48%	52%
B. Banks should charge ATM user fees, but they should be lower.	63%	37%
C. Banks are charging an appropriate amount for ATM user fees.	19%	81%

Note: Random sample of 2,000 people surveyed by phone; margin of error is ± 5%.

Take It to the NET

Chapter 10 Self-Test As a final review activity, take the Chapter 10 Self-Test in the Social Studies area at the Web site listed below, and receive immediate feedback on your answers. The test consists of 20 multiple-choice questions designed to test your understanding of the chapter content.
www.phschool.com

THE WALL STREET JOURNAL.

DEBATING CURRENT ISSUES: *The Future of Money*

> As commerce becomes increasingly electronic, what will happen to the paper and coins we now trade for goods and services? One alternative is a "stored value" smart card: a bank card equipped with a microchip.
>
> The consumer could load money directly onto the microchip from his or her account using an ATM, a special telephone line, or a computer. Because of the versatility of the microchip, the same card could handle both credit and cash transactions, as well as serving as a digital identity card that could even contain medical information about the owner.
>
> Will such cards someday replace cash? These excerpts from *The Wall Street Journal Classroom Edition* article "Future Shop" by Nicholas Bray, Staff Reporter of *The Wall Street Journal*, look at both sides of this question.

YES *Will Smart Cards Replace Cash?*

JOHN CASTLE, A BAKER in the English town of Swindon, has just sold an almond-and-jam cookie. To his delight, the transaction involved no coins, bank notes, or credit cards. Instead, the customer used Mondex, a cash card equipped with a microchip, and Mr. Castle booked the sale on a terminal resembling a calculator.

"It's going to save me a lot of time counting change," Mr. Castle says. "It will also be a lot more hygienic than using coins and bank notes."

Launched by two of Britain's leading banks—National Westminster Bank and the HSBC Holdings unit of Midland Bank—Mondex looks and works something like a debit card. The thinking behind the project is simple: In a world of electronic cash, banks and other organizations will be able to charge individual and corporate users for providing and processing the electronic signals that replace coins and paper money. Among other things, predict NatWest executives, electronic cash will play a major role in payments for goods and services bought over interactive-television channels or the Internet.

Mondex's promoters maintain that adequate safeguards can be built into the system to prevent fraud and criminal misuse.

Tim Jones, a NatWest executive who is one of Mondex's two co-inventors, explains that because each card is really a minicomputer in its own right, it can send signals to other cards telling them how it is being used. Such signals would

Smart cards will likely become a common convenience for many consumers, but will they replace cash entirely?

ultimately reach the issuing bank, which could then respond by sending out signals of its own—for example, to warn users that a specific card is being used fraudulently.

With other electronic-cash products under development, it is hard to predict which will emerge as the winner. Indeed, analysts say, there may be room for several competing products, providing they all respect common standards.

Ultimately, this battle may well be decided by shopkeepers, rather than by banks or consumers. Take Mr. Castle, the baker. He currently pays several thousand pounds a year in bank charges for his small business in the center of Swindon's shopping district, and he figures he could cut these charges if he didn't have to handle so much cash.

NO Will Smart Cards Replace Cash?

SEAN LANGLANDS, a construction consultant, says cards such as Mondex are "pointless." He is standing outside a McDonald's restaurant in Swindon where cashiers are already busy selling hamburgers for electronic cash. Pulling a wallet full of credit and debit cards from his pocket, he says he definitely doesn't want yet another one. "It's a waste of time."

What is more, critics argue that Mondex opens the door to all sorts of abuses, from money laundering to fraud. In one of its key features, money loaded onto one card can be transmitted electronically to another card over phone wires using specially adapted telephones, without the intervention of a bank.

This makes Mondex "totally unaccounted and not auditable," says Richard Phillimore, head of chip-card development at Europay, the European franchising arm of MasterCard International. If large sums of money are involved, he warns, the result could be a major headache for banks and regulators worldwide.

The fruit of more than five years of research and development, Mondex basically consists of a card and a card reader. The reader, which resembles a thick dog tag, has a liquid-crystal display window that shows how much money is loaded into the card. Card holders also can buy special "wallets," resembling minicalculators, in which they can store electronic cash before loading it onto their cards.

Using these wallets, holders can make money transfers and receive payments directly from other cardholders—precisely the characteristic that lies at the root of Mr. Phillimore's concerns. Because of this feature, Mondex "is just like cash," says Mr. Jones, the co-inventor.

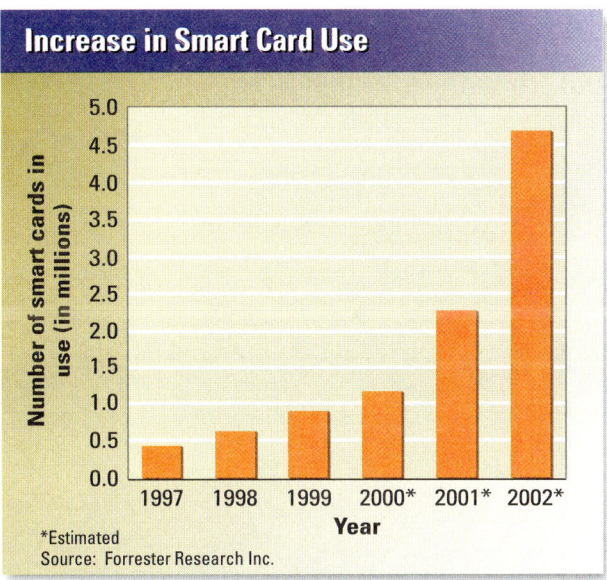

Increase in Smart Card Use

*Estimated
Source: Forrester Research Inc.

As retailers and consumers grow more familiar with smart cards, it is expected that smart card use will increase rapidly.

DEBATING THE ISSUE

1. Why does baker John Castle like using a microchip-equipped cash card for transactions?

2. What kinds of abuses do critics say Mondex will encourage?

3. **Critical Thinking** How are advances in technology affecting the potential use of electronic cash?

4. **Reading Graphs** According to the chart, how many smart cards were expected to be in use in 2002?

Take It to the Net Visit **www.phschool.com** for additional resources relating to this debate.

Chapter 11 Financial Markets

What is the Dow? Where is Wall Street? What does a daytrader do? You may have heard these terms but be unsure of exactly what they mean. In this chapter you will learn the meaning of these and other terms from the world of investment. You will also learn how the stock market works and how investors choose from among stocks, bonds, and other investments.

Economics Journal

Look through the financial pages of a major newspaper for stock and bond reports. Jot down the kinds of information you find. Then make a list of questions about the information that you don't understand.

Keep It Current

INTERNET UPDATE

Items marked with this logo are periodically updated on the Internet. Keep up-to-date with what's in the news. To get current information on financial markets go to **www.phschool.com**

Saving and Investing

Objectives

After studying this section you will be able to:

1. **Understand** how investing contributes to the free enterprise system.
2. **Explain** how the financial system brings together savers and borrowers.
3. **Describe** how financial intermediaries link savers and borrowers.
4. **Identify** the trade-offs among risk, liquidity, and return.

Section Focus

Investment promotes economic growth and contributes to a nation's wealth. The financial system includes savers and borrowers, as well as the institutions that transfer savers' dollars to borrowers. When borrowers invest these funds, they fuel economic growth.

Key Terms

investment
financial system
financial asset
financial intermediary
mutual fund
diversification
portfolio
prospectus
return

If you go to school today, you give up your time now so that you will be prepared for a career in the future. If a firm builds a new plant, it spends money today for the sake of earning more money in the future. A government may spend money today to build a dam to ensure that people will have a source of hydroelectric power in the future. All of these actions represent investments.

In its most general sense, **investment** is the act of redirecting resources from being consumed today so that they may create benefits in the future. In more narrow, economic terms, investment is the use of assets to earn income or profit.

Investing and Free Enterprise

As you have read, one of the chief advantages of the free enterprise system is that it allows people to make a profit. This profit motive leads individuals and businesses to make investments. Investing, in fact, is an essential part of the free enterprise system.

Investment promotes economic growth and contributes to a nation's wealth. When people deposit money in a savings account in a bank, for example, the bank may then lend the funds to businesses. The busi-

nesses, in turn, may invest that money in new plants and equipment to increase their production. As these businesses use their investments to expand and grow, they create new and better products and provide new jobs.

investment *the act of redirecting resources from being consumed today so that they may create benefits in the future; the use of assets to earn income or profit*

◄ How does this illustration suggest that investment promotes economic growth?

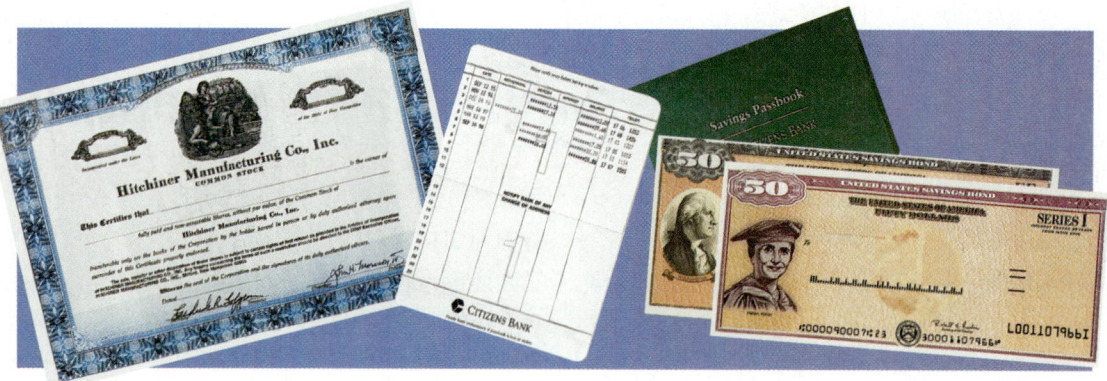

► Documents such as (from left to right) a stock certificate, a savings passbook, and savings bonds are financial assets.

financial system *the system that allows the transfer of money between savers and borrowers*

financial asset *claim on the property or income of a borrower*

financial intermediary *institution that helps channel funds from savers to borrowers*

mutual fund *fund that pools the savings of many individuals and invests this money in a variety of stocks, bonds, and other financial assets*

The Financial System

In order for investment to take place, an economy must have a financial system. A **financial system** includes savers and borrowers and allows the transfer of money between them to take place.

Financial Assets

When people save, they are, in essence, lending funds to others. As you read in Chapter 10, people can save money in a variety of ways. They may put money in a savings account, purchase a certificate of deposit, or buy a government or corporate bond. In each case, savers obtain a document that confirms their purchase or deposit. These documents may be passbooks, computer printouts, bond certificates, or other records.

Such documents represent claims on the property or income of the borrower. These claims are called **financial assets,** or securities. If the borrower fails to pay back the loan, these documents can serve as proof in court that money was borrowed and that repayment is expected.

For example, suppose you have $100 in a savings account at your local bank. Your passbook (or computer printout) is proof of the money in your account.

The Flow of Savings and Investments

Figure 11.1 shows how the financial system brings together savers and borrowers, fueling investment and economic growth. On one side are savers—households, individuals, and businesses that lend out their savings in return for financial assets. On the other side are borrowers—governments and businesses—who invest the money they borrow to build roads, factories, and homes. Borrowers may also use these funds to develop new products, create new markets, or provide new services.

Financial Intermediaries

Savers and borrowers may be linked directly. As you examine Figure 11.1, you will notice that borrowers and savers may also be linked through a variety of institutions pictured as "in between" the two. These **financial intermediaries** are institutions that help channel funds from savers to borrowers. They include the following:

- *Banks, Savings and Loan Associations, and Credit Unions* As you read in Chapter 10, banks, S&Ls, and credit unions take in deposits from savers, then lend out some of these funds to businesses and individuals.
- *Finance companies* Finance companies make loans to consumers and small businesses. Because finance companies sometimes lend money to people who do not repay their loans, they take on a high degree of risk. Finance companies, therefore, charge borrowers higher fees and interest rates to cover their losses from the loans that are not repaid.
- *Mutual funds* **Mutual funds** pool the savings of many individuals and invest this money in a variety of stocks, bonds, and other financial assets. Mutual funds allow people to invest in a broad range of companies in the stock market. This way,

investors do not risk their savings by purchasing the stock of only one or two companies that might do poorly.

- *Life insurance companies* The main function of life insurance is to provide financial protection for the family or other beneficiaries of the insured. Working members of a family, for example, may buy life insurance policies so that if they die, money will be paid to survivors to make up for lost income. Insurance companies collect payments called premiums from the people who buy insurance. They lend out part of the premiums they collect to investors.
- *Pension funds* A pension is income that a retiree receives after working a certain number of years or reaching a certain age. In some cases, injuries may qualify a working person for pension benefits. Employers may contribute to the pension fund on behalf of their employees, they may withhold a percentage of workers' salaries to deposit in a pension fund, or they may do both. Employers set up pension funds to collect deposits and distribute payments. Pension fund managers invest these deposits in stocks, bonds, and other financial assets.

Now that you know something about the types of financial intermediaries, you may wonder why savers don't deal directly with investors. The answer is that, in general, dealing with financial intermediaries offers three advantages. Intermediaries share risks, provide information, and provide liquidity to investors.

Sharing Risk

As a saver, you may not want to invest your entire life savings in a single company or enterprise. For example, if you had $500 to invest and your neighbor was opening a new restaurant, would you give her the entire $500? Since it is estimated that more than half of all new businesses fail, you probably would not want to risk all of your money. Instead, you would want to spread the money around to various businesses to reduce the chances of losing your entire investment.

This strategy of spreading out investments to reduce risk is called **diversification**. If you deposited $500 in the bank or bought shares of a mutual fund, those institutions could pool your money with other people's savings and put your money to work by making a variety of investments.

diversification
spreading out investments to reduce risk

Figure 11.1 Financial Intermediaries

Savers make deposits to . . .

Financial Institutions that make loans to . . .

Commercial banks
Savings & loan associations
Savings banks
Mutual savings banks
Credit unions

Life insurance companies
Mutual funds
Pension funds
Finance companies

Investors

Financial intermediaries, including banks and other financial institutions, accept funds from savers and make loans to investors. Investors include entrepreneurs, businesses, and other borrowers.

Economic Institutions **What advantages do financial intermediaries provide for savers?**

Investors must weigh the risks explained in this chart against the potential rate of return on their investment. **Income** What additional examples can you think of to illustrate each of the types of risk explained in the chart?

Figure 11.2 Types of Risk

Name	Description	Example
Credit risk	Borrowers may not pay back the money they have borrowed, or they may be late in making payments.	You lend $20 to your cousin, who promises to pay you back in two weeks. When your cousin fails to pay you on time, you don't have money for the basketball tickets you had planned to buy.
Liquidity risk	You may not be able to convert the investment back into cash quickly enough for your needs.	Your CD player is worth $100. You need cash to buy concert tickets, so you decide to sell your CD player. To convert your CD player into cash on short notice, you have to discount the price to $75.
Inflation rate risk	Inflation rates erode the value of your assets.	Ricardo lends Jeff $1,000 for one year at 10 percent interest. If the inflation rate is 12 percent, Ricardo loses money.
Time risk	You may have to pass up better opportunities for investment.	Lili invests $100 in May's cleaning business, to be repaid at 5 percent interest one year later. Six months later, Lili is unable to invest in Sonia's pet-sitting business, which pays 10 percent interest, because she has already invested her savings.

portfolio *a collection of financial assets*

prospectus *an investment report to potential investors*

return *the money an investor receives above and beyond the sum of money initially invested*

In other words, financial intermediaries diversify your investments and thus reduce the risk that you will lose all of your funds if a single investment fails.

Providing Information

Financial intermediaries are also good sources of information. Your local bank collects information about borrowers by monitoring their income and spending. So do finance companies when borrowers fill out credit applications. Mutual fund managers know how the stocks in their **portfolios,** or collections of financial assets, are performing. As required by law, all intermediaries provide this information to potential investors in an investment report called a **prospectus.** Financial intermediaries reduce the costs in time and money that lenders and borrowers would pay if they had to search out such information about investment opportunities on their own.

Providing Liquidity

Financial intermediaries also provide investors with liquidity. (Recall that liquidity is the ease with which people can convert an asset into cash.) It is intermediaries that provide this liquidity in the financial system.

Suppose, for example, that you decide to invest in a mutual fund. You keep the investment for two years, but then must sell it to pay your college tuition. If you had purchased an investment-quality painting instead, you would need to find another investor who would buy the art from you. As you can see, financial intermediaries and the liquidity they provide are crucial to meeting borrowers' and lenders' needs in our increasingly complex financial system.

Risk, Liquidity, and Return

As you have read, most decisions involve trade-offs. For example, the trade-off for going to a movie may be two additional hours of sleep. Saving and investing involves trade-offs as well.

Return and Liquidity

Suppose you save money in a savings account. Savings accounts are good ways to save when you need to be able to get to your cash for immediate use. On the other hand, savings accounts pay relatively low interest rates, about 2 to 3 percentage points below a certificate of deposit (CD). In other words, savings accounts are liquid, but they have a low return. **Return** is the money an investor receives above and beyond the sum of money initially invested.

What if, however, you suddenly inherit $5,000? You do not need ready access to those funds, since your part-time job pays your day-to-day expenses. If you are willing to give up some degree of ready access to your money, you can earn higher interest rates than offered by a savings account. For example, you can invest your money in a certificate of deposit that pays 6 percent interest. You would not be allowed to withdraw your money for, say, two years without paying a penalty. Therefore, before buying the CD, you would want to weigh the greater return on your investment against the loss of liquidity.

Return and Risk

Certificates of deposit (up to $100,000) are considered very safe investments because they are insured by the federal government. When you buy a CD, you are giving up liquidity for a certain period of time, but you are not risking losing any money. What if, however, you decided to invest the money in a new Web page development company that your friends are starting? If the company succeeds, you could double your investment. If it fails, however, you could lose all or part of your money.

To take another example, suppose your savings account is earning 4 percent interest. Would you be willing to lend money to your friend Emily for that same 4 percent interest rate, knowing that she rarely pays back loans on time? Probably not. For you to lend Emily the money, she would have to offer you a higher return than the bank could offer. This higher return would help offset the greater risk that Emily will not repay the loan on time. Likewise, investors and lenders must consider the degree of risk involved in an investment and decide what return they would require to make up for that risk.

The higher the potential return, the riskier the investment. Whenever individuals evaluate an investment, they must balance the risks involved with the rewards they expect to gain from the investment.

Section 1 Assessment

Key Terms and Main Ideas

1. How does investing promote financial growth?
2. Explain how savers, borrowers, and **financial intermediaries** contribute to the **financial system**.
3. Describe three roles of financial intermediaries.
4. Explain the following statement in your own words. "The higher the potential **return** on an **investment**, the higher the risk."

Applying Economic Concepts

5. *Critical Thinking* Explain why a student with $500 in a savings account is participating in the American financial system.

6. *You Decide* Suppose your cousin Bill asks to borrow $50 from you for concert tickets. Bill has offered to pay you interest on the loan. What factors should you consider before you decide how much interest to charge?
7. *Try This* What are three questions concerning risk, return, and liquidity that you would ask a financial advisor before investing your savings?
8. *You Decide* Explain the potential risks and returns of the following savings plans and investments. **(a)** a savings account **(b)** a certificate of deposit **(c)** your neighbor's successful pet care service

Take It to the NET Choose one form of investing described in this section and find out more about it. Do you think you might choose this form of investing in the future? Summarize your research in a well-organized paragraph. Use the links provided at the following Web site for help in completing this activity. **www.phschool.com**

Profile

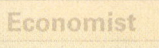

Warren Buffett (b. 1930)

When Warren Buffett was 5 years old, he set up a stand to sell lemonade—not in front of his own house, but at a friend's house on another street, where the traffic was heavier. The son of an Omaha, Nebraska, stockbroker, Buffett announced while still in grade school that he intended to be rich before he was 35. Today, Buffett is widely considered to be a financial genius and is one of the most successful investors in the world.

The Oracle of Omaha

At age 14, Warren Buffett bought 40 acres of land and rented it to a farmer. By the age of 21, Buffett had accumulated nearly $10,000. Nearly every dollar of the $20 billion he is worth today can be traced back to that original bankroll. Because of this phenomenal success, he is known as the financial "Oracle of Omaha."

Investing the Buffett Way

Buffett learned how to invest at Columbia University, where he earned a master's degree in business in 1951. A professor taught him to pick his investments by doing his own research. "You're not right or wrong because 1,000 people agree with you or disagree with you," the professor told him. "You're right because your facts and reasoning are right."

Buffett has continued to follow that advice to this day. He will not invest in a business he does not understand. For this reason, he has shied away from high-tech companies and focuses on communications, retail, and insurance companies.

Buffett also looks for companies whose stock is selling for less than it is worth. If such a company is well managed, has few competitors, and is concentrating on what it does best, he will buy that stock and wait for it to go up.

For example, many analysts predicted in 1963 that American Express charge card company would go out of business after it suffered a major financial setback. In Omaha, Buffett saw that people were still using their American Express cards. Ignoring the experts, he bought 5 percent of American Express. Five years later, the stock was worth nearly six times what he paid for it.

The Berkshire Hathaway Company

Buffett objects to those who label his Berkshire Hathaway investment company a mutual fund. Because it owns Dairy Queen, GEICO Insurance, and Executive Jet outright—and holds controlling interests in other corporations—Buffett prefers to think of it as a holding company.

The cost of Berkshire Hathaway stock, as much as $70,900 a share in 2001, puts it beyond the reach of most investors. That's fine with Buffett. Not only does the high price make Berkshire Hathaway the "Rolls Royce" of investing, it also limits trading in the company's shares on the stock market.

CHECK FOR UNDERSTANDING

1. Source Reading Summarize Warren Buffett's approach to investing by creating a list of his "dos" and "don'ts" when deciding whether to buy stock in a company.

2. Critical Thinking Why might it be a plus for a company to have such a high share price that trading in its stock is discouraged? What drawbacks might there be for a company in this situation?

3. Problem Solving Is Buffett's firm a mutual fund or a holding company? Use the Internet and other resources to learn more about Berkshire Hathaway in order to support your response.

Bonds and Other Financial Assets

Objectives

After studying this section you will be able to:

1. **Describe** the characteristics of bonds as financial assets.
2. **Identify** different types of bonds.
3. **Describe** the characteristics of other types of financial assets.
4. **Explain** four different types of financial asset markets.

Section Focus

Corporations and governments borrow money by selling bonds and other financial assets. The corporation or government pays the purchaser interest on the bonds and repays the principal, or money borrowed, at a specified time.

Key Terms

coupon rate
maturity
par value
yield
savings bond
municipal bond
corporate bond

Securities and Exchange Commission
junk bond
capital market
money market
primary market
secondary market

How do borrowers raise money for investment? One of the most important ways is by selling bonds. As you read in Chapter 8, bonds are certificates sold by a company or government to finance projects or expansion.

For example, starting in 1942, the United States Department of Treasury launched bond drives to encourage Americans to buy "war bonds"—government savings bonds that helped finance World War II. Movie stars and war heroes urged the public to buy bonds. Even school children brought their dimes and quarters to school each week, buying defense stamps that would eventually add up to the price of a war bond.

Bonds as Financial Assets

Bonds are basically loans, or IOUs, that represent debt that the government or a corporation must repay to an investor. Bonds typically pay the investor a fixed amount of interest at regular intervals for a fixed amount of time. Bonds are generally lower-risk investments. As you might expect from your reading about the relationship between risk and return, the rate of return on bonds is usually also lower than for other investments.

The Three Components of Bonds

Bonds have three basic components:

- *Coupon rate* The **coupon rate** is the interest rate that the bond issuer will pay to the bondholder.
- *Maturity* **Maturity** is the time at which payment to the bondholder is due.

coupon rate *the interest rate that a bond issuer will pay to a bondholder*

maturity *the time at which payment to a bondholder is due*

Don't Let That Shadow Touch Them
Buy **WAR BONDS**

◄ This poster used powerful images to convince people to buy war bonds during World War II.

par value *the amount that an investor pays to purchase a bond and that will be repaid to the investor at maturity*

yield *the annual rate of return on a bond if the bond were held to maturity*

Different bonds have different lengths of maturity. Bonds typically mature in 10, 20, or 30 years.

- *Par value* A bond's **par value** is the amount that an investor pays to purchase the bond and that will be repaid to the investor at maturity. Par value is also called *face value* or *principal*.

Suppose that you buy a $1,000 bond from the corporation Jeans, Etc. The investor who buys the bond is called the "holder." The seller of a bond is called the "issuer." You are therefore the holder of the bond, and Jeans, Etc. is the issuer. The basic components of this bond are as follows:

- *Coupon rate:* 5 percent, paid to the bondholder annually
- *Maturity:* 10 years
- *Par Value:* $1,000

Figure 11.3 Discounts from Par

1. Sharon buys a bond with a par value of $1,000 at 5 percent interest.

$1,000 = $1,000 Bond

Bond purchase without discount from par

2. Interest rates go up to 6 percent.

3. Sharon needs to sell her bond. Nate wants to buy it, but is unwilling to buy a bond at 5 percent interest when the current rate is 6 percent.

4. Sharon offers to discount the bond, taking $40 off the price and selling it for $960.

5. Nate accepts the offer. He now owns a $1,000 bond paying 5 percent interest, which he purchased at a discount from par.

$960 = $1,000 Bond

Bond purchase with discount from par

Investors can earn money by buying bonds at a discount, called a discount from par.
Interest Rates How do interest rates affect bond prices?

How much money will you earn from this bond, and over what period of time? The coupon rate is 5 percent of $1,000 per year. This means that you will receive a payment of $50 (.05 times $1,000) each year for ten years, or a total of $500 in interest. In ten years, the bond will have reached maturity, and Jeans, Etc. will retire the debt. This means that the company's debt to you will have ended, and that Jeans, Etc. will pay you the par value of the bond, or $1,000. Thus, for your $1,000 investment, you will have received $1,500 over a period of ten years.

Not all bonds are held to maturity. Over their lifetime they might be bought or sold, and their price may change. Because of these shifts in price, buyers and sellers are interested in a bond's yield, or yield to maturity. **Yield** is the annual rate of return on the bond if the bond were held to maturity (5 percent in the example above involving Jeans, Etc.).

Buying Bonds at a Discount

Investors earn money from interest on the bonds they buy. They can also earn money by buying bonds at a discount, called a discount from par. In other words, if Nate were buying a bond with a par value of $1,000, he may be able to pay only $960 for it. When the bond matures, Nate will redeem the bond at par, or $1,000. He will thus have earned $40 on his investment, in addition to interest payments from the bond issuer.

Why would someone sell a bond for less than its par value? The answer lies in the fact that interest rates are always changing. For example, suppose that Sharon buys a $1,000 bond at 5 percent interest, which is the current market rate. A year later, she needs to sell the bond to help pay for a new car. By that time, however, interest rates have risen to 6 percent. No one will pay $1,000 for Sharon's bond at 5 percent interest when they could go elsewhere and buy a $1,000 bond at 6 percent interest. For Sharon to sell her bond at 5 percent, she will have to sell it at a discount. (See Figure 11.3.)

Figure 11.4 Bond Ratings

Standard & Poor's		Moody's	
Highest investment grade	AAA	Best quality	Aaa
High grade	AA	High quality	Aa
Upper medium grade	A	Upper medium grade	A
Medium grade	BBB	Medium grade	Baa
Lower medium grade	BB	Possesses speculative elements	Ba
Speculative	B	Generally not desirable	B
Vulnerable to default	CCC	Poor, possibly in default	Caa
Subordinated to other debt rated CCC	CC	Highly speculative, often in default	Ca
Subordinated to CC debt	C	Income bonds not paying income	C
Bond in default	D	Interest and principal payments in default	D

BUILDING KEY CONCEPTS Standard & Poor's and Moody's rate bonds according to their assessments of the issuer's ability to make interest payments and to repay the principal when the bond matures.
Income **What bond rating carries the least risk?**

Bond Ratings

How does an investor decide which bonds to buy? Investors can check bond quality through two firms that publish bond ratings. Standard & Poor's and Moody's rate bonds on a number of factors, including the issuer's ability to make future interest payments and to repay the principal when the bond matures. These companies' rating systems rank bonds from the highest investment grade (AAA in the Standard & Poor's system or Aaa in the Moody's rating system) to the lowest (D in both systems). A bond rating of D generally means that the bond is in default—that is, the issuer has not kept up with interest payments or has defaulted on paying principal.

The higher the bond rating, the lower the interest rate the company usually has to pay to get people to buy its bonds. For example, a AAA bond may be issued at a 5 percent interest rate. A BBB bond, however, may be issued at a 7.5 percent interest rate. The buyer of the AAA bond trades off a lower interest rate for lower risk. The buyer of the BBB bond trades greater risk for a higher interest rate.

Similarly, the higher the bond rating, the higher the price at which the bond will sell. For example, a $1,000 bond with an AAA (or "triple A") rating may sell at $1,100. A $1,000 bond with a BBB rating may sell for only $950 because of the increased risk that the seller could default.

In essence, holders of bonds with high ratings who keep their bonds until maturity face relatively little risk of losing their investment. Holders of bonds with lower ratings, however, take on more risk in return for potentially higher interest payments.

Advantages and Disadvantages to the Issuer

From the point of view of the investor, bonds are good investments because they are relatively safe. Bonds are desirable from the issuer's point of view as well, for two main reasons:

1. Once the bond is sold, the coupon rate for that bond will not go up or down. For example, when Jeans, Etc. sells bonds, it knows in advance that it will be making fixed payments for a specific length of time.
2. Unlike stockholders, bondholders do not own a part of the company. Therefore, the company does not have to share profits with its bondholders if the company does particularly well.

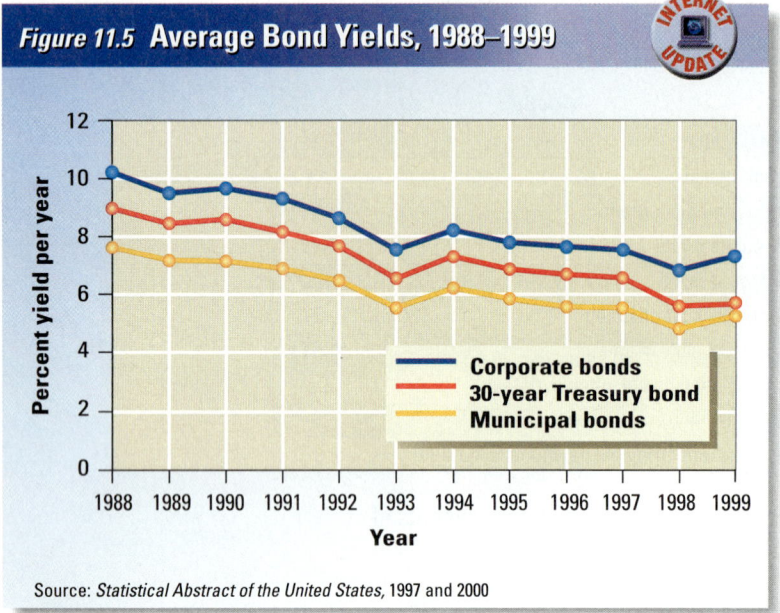

Figure 11.5 Average Bond Yields, 1988–1999

Percent yield per year (vertical axis): 0, 2, 4, 6, 8, 10, 12
Year (horizontal axis): 1988 1989 1990 1991 1992 1993 1994 1995 1996 1997 1998 1999

- Corporate bonds
- 30-year Treasury bond
- Municipal bonds

Source: *Statistical Abstract of the United States,* 1997 and 2000

BUILDING KEY CONCEPTS

From the end of the 1980s to the end of the 1990s, bond yields dipped slightly for all three types of bonds shown. Corporate bonds, however, continued to have the highest yield. **Income Which of the three types of bonds would you expect to carry the least risk? Explain your answer.**

savings bond
low-denomination bond issued by the United States government

On the other hand, bonds also pose two main disadvantages to the issuer:

1. The company must make fixed interest payments, even in bad years when it does not make money. In addition, it cannot change its interest payments even when interest rates have gone down.

Figure 11.6 Treasury Bonds, Notes, and Bills

	Treasury Bond	Treasury Note	Treasury Bill
Term	long-term	intermediate-term	short-term
Maturity	from 10 to 30 years	from 2 to 10 years	3, 6, or 12 months
Liquidity and safety	safe	safe	liquid and safe
Minimum purchase	$1,000	$1,000	$1,000
Denomination	$1,000	$1,000	$1,000

BUILDING KEY CONCEPTS

Treasury bonds, notes, and bills represent debt that the government must repay the investor.
Government How do these three types of government securities differ?

2. If the firm does not maintain financial health, its bonds may be downgraded to a lower bond rating and thus may be harder to sell unless they are offered at a discount.

Types of Bonds

Despite these risks to the issuer, when corporations or governments need to borrow funds for long periods, they often issue bonds. There are several different types of bonds.

Savings Bonds

You may already be familiar with savings bonds, which are sometimes given to young people as gifts. **Savings bonds** are low-denomination ($50 to $10,000) bonds issued by the United States government. The government uses funds from the sale of savings bonds to help pay for public works projects like buildings, roads, and dams. Like other government bonds, savings bonds have virtually no risk of default, or failure to repay the loan.

The federal government pays interest on savings bonds. However, unlike most other bond issuers, it does not send interest payments to bondholders on a regular schedule. Instead, the purchaser buys a savings bond for less than par value. For example, you can purchase a $50 savings bond for only $25. When the bond matures, you receive the $25 you paid for the bond plus $25 in interest.

Treasury Bonds, Bills, and Notes

The United States Treasury Department issues Treasury bonds, as well as Treasury bills and notes (T-bills and T-notes). These investments offer different lengths of maturity, as shown in Figure 11.6. Backed by the "full faith and credit" of the United States government, these securities are among the safest investments in terms of default risk. For this reason, many Americans invested in government bonds (driving bond prices up) after the September 2001 terrorist attacks.

▲ Municipal bonds, or munis, help finance local projects such as libraries and schools.

Municipal Bonds

State and local governments and municipalities (government units with corporate status) issue bonds to finance such improvements as highways, state buildings, libraries, parks, and schools. These bonds are called **municipal bonds,** or "munis."

Because state and local governments have the power to tax, investors can assume that these governments will be able to keep up with interest payments and repay the principal at maturity. Standard & Poor's and Moody's therefore consider most municipal bonds to be safe investments, depending upon the financial health of a particular state or town. In addition, the interest paid on municipal bonds is not subject to income taxes at the federal level or in the issuing state. Because they are relatively safe and are tax-exempt, "munis" are very attractive to investors.

Corporate Bonds

As you read in Chapter 8, corporations issue bonds to help raise money to expand their businesses. These **corporate bonds** are issued in fairly large denominations, such as $1,000, $5,000, and $10,000. The interest on corporate bonds is taxed as ordinary income.

Unlike city and other governments, corporations have no tax base to help guarantee their ability to repay their loans, so these bonds have moderate levels of risk. Investors in corporate bonds must depend on the success of the corporation's sales of goods and services to generate enough income to pay interest and principal.

Corporations that issue bonds are watched closely not only by Standard & Poor's and Moody's, but also by the **Securities and Exchange Commission** (SEC). The SEC is an independent government agency that regulates financial markets and investment companies. It enforces laws prohibiting fraud and other dishonest investment practices.

Junk Bonds

Junk bonds, or high-yield securities, are lower-rated, and potentially higher-paying, bonds. They became especially popular investments during the 1980s and 1990s,

municipal bond *a bond issued by a state or local government or municipality to finance such improvements as highways, state buildings, libraries, parks, and schools*

corporate bond *a bond that a corporation issues to raise money to expand its business*

Securities and Exchange Commission *an independent agency of the government that regulates financial markets and investment companies*

junk bond *a lower-rated, potentially higher-paying bond*

International Bonds The United States government isn't the only government that issues bonds. Many other countries, including Saudi Arabia, Germany, and Japan, also issue bonds. International bonds are usually issued in large denominations, starting at $1 million. In addition, principal and coupon payments are often made in foreign currencies. The investors, therefore, cannot know what the value of payments will turn out to be. **What are two drawbacks to buying international bonds?**

when large numbers of aggressive investors made—but also sometimes lost—large sums of money buying and selling these securities.

Junk bonds have been known to pay over 12 percent interest at a time when government bonds are yielding only about 8 percent interest. On the other hand, junk bonds also carry bond ratings of "lower medium grade" or "speculative" (BB, Ba, or lower). Investors in junk bonds therefore face a strong possibility that some of the issuing firms will default on their debt.

Nevertheless, in many cases junk bonds have enabled companies to undertake activities that would otherwise have been impossible to complete. (For more information on how to follow the progress of a stock by reading stock market reports, see page 284.)

Other Types of Financial Assets

In addition to bonds, investors may choose other financial assets. These include certificates of deposit and money market mutual funds, as well as stock. You will read more about stock in Section 3.

Certificates of Deposit

Certificates of deposit (CDs) are one of the most common forms of investment. As you read in Chapter 10, CDs are available through banks, which lend out the funds deposited in CDs for a fixed amount of time, such as 6 months or a year.

CDs are attractive to small investors because they cost as little as $100. Investors can also choose among many terms of maturity. This means that if an investor foresees a future expenditure, such as college tuition or a major home improvement, he or she can buy a CD that matures just before the expenditure is due.

Money Market Mutual Funds

Money market mutual funds are special types of mutual funds. As you read in Section 1, businesses collect money from individual investors and then buy stocks, bonds, or other financial assets to form a mutual fund.

In the case of money market mutual funds, intermediaries buy short-term financial assets. Investors receive higher interest on a money market mutual fund than they would receive from a savings account. On the other hand, money market mutual funds are not covered by FDIC insurance. (As you read in Chapter 10, FDIC insurance protects bank deposits up to $100,000 per account). This makes them slightly riskier than savings accounts.

"Gee, fellas - junk bonds."

▲ **From what you have read, how accurate is the cartoonist's view of junk bonds?**

Financial Asset Markets

Financial assets, including bonds, certificates of deposit, and money market mutual funds, are traded on financial asset markets. The various types of financial asset markets are classified in different ways.

Capital and Money Markets

One way to classify financial asset markets is according to the length of time for which funds are lent. This type of classification includes capital markets and money markets.

- *Capital markets* Markets in which money is lent for periods longer than a year are called **capital markets.** Financial assets that are traded in capital markets include long-term CDs and corporate and government bonds that require more than a year to mature.
- *Money markets* Markets in which money is lent for periods of less than a year are called **money markets.** Financial assets that are traded in money markets include short-term CDs, Treasury bills, and money market mutual funds.

Primary and Secondary Markets

Markets may also be classified according to whether assets can be resold to other buyers. This type of classification includes primary and secondary markets.

- *Primary markets* Financial assets that can be redeemed only by the original holder are sold on **primary markets.** Examples include savings bonds, which are non-transferable (that is, the original buyer cannot sell them to another buyer). Small certificates of deposit are also in the primary market because investors would most likely cash them in early rather than try to sell them to someone else.
- *Secondary markets* Financial assets that can be resold are sold on **secondary markets.** This option for resale provides liquidity to investors. If there is a strong secondary market for an asset, the investor knows that the asset can be resold fairly quickly without a penalty, thus providing the investor with ready cash. The secondary market also makes possible the lively trade in stock that is the subject of the next section.

capital market *market in which money is lent for periods longer than a year*

money market *market in which money is lent for periods of less than a year*

primary market *market for selling financial assets that can only be redeemed by the original holder*

secondary market *market for reselling financial assets*

Section 2 Assessment

Key Terms and Main Ideas

1. Describe two ways in which investors can earn money from bonds.
2. Why are bond ratings useful to investors?
3. Describe five different types of bonds.
4. How do **capital markets** and **money markets** differ?

Applying Economic Concepts

5. *Math Practice* Suppose that you buy a bond for $100 that pays 4 percent interest per year. How much money will you have earned when the bond reaches maturity in five years?

6. *Decision Making* Suppose that you have saved $1,000. In which of the financial assets described in this section would you invest? Explain your choice.

7. *Critical Thinking* Which bond would you expect to be more expensive, a bond with a AAA rating or a bond with a BBB rating? (Assume that both bonds pay the same rate of interest.)

8. *Try This* Assume that you are an investment advisor with a client who is interested in buying bonds. Create a fact sheet that shows your client the different types of bonds and their characteristics.

Take It to the NET Use the Internet to learn more about bonds. Then answer the following question: If you were given a $100 savings bond when you were born, what would it be worth now? (Remember that you need to find the interest rate being offered on your birthday.) Use the links provided at the following Web site for help in completing this activity. **www.phschool.com**

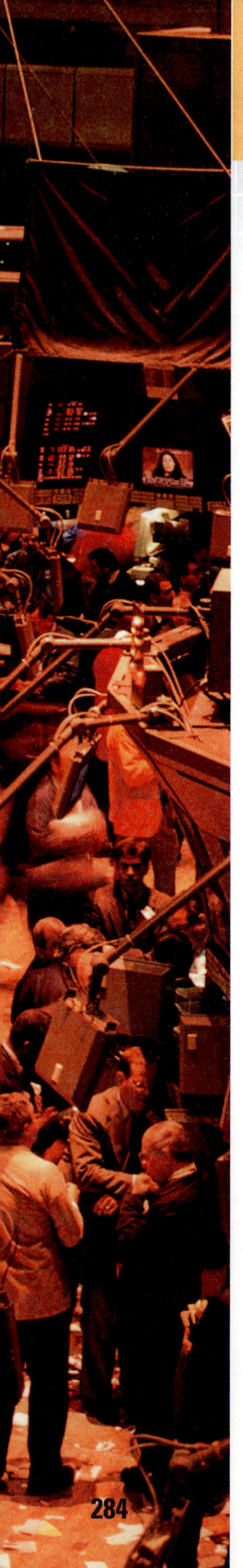

Skills for LIFE

Critical Thinking | Graphs and Charts

Social Studies | **Technology Skills**

Reading an Online Stock Market Report

Many Web sites provide stock prices from today's trading. To save space, stock reports use symbols and abbreviations to convey important facts about each stock. Follow the steps below to read the sample online stock market report.

1. **Identify the stocks and the information presented.** The stock listing below includes a shortened version of each company's name. Use Figure 11.7 on page 287 to learn what the other abbreviations stand for and what all of the data mean. (a) How many shares of Toro (TTC) were traded on this day? (b) What was the highest price paid for a share of Timberland (TBL) on this day? In the past 52 weeks?

2. **Compute the value of your stock.** Some online stock reports provide prices in real time, while others have a delay of 15 or 20 minutes. If you check stock prices after the market has closed, the prices listed will be those from the end of the day.
(a) How much did one share of Toro cost? (b) If you bought 50 shares of Titan International (TWI) at its highest price that day, how much would you have paid? (c) Suppose that you own 20 shares of Timberland and 40 shares of Tupperware (TUP). How much was your portfolio worth? (d) Based on the change in stock prices, how much did the value of your portfolio go up from the previous day?

3. **Determine general trends in the stock market.** Past success does not guarantee that a stock will continue to do well, but an investor can track a stock's performance to see if its price has generally been going up or down. (a) Which stock is trading for close to its highest price for the year? (b) Which stock is closest to its low price for the past year? (c) How much were 100 shares of Thor Industries worth at its peak? (d) How much were those shares worth at the lowest price for Thor?

Additional Practice

Using online stock quotes track the price and trading volume of a specific stock for one week. Based on your notes, list five facts about the stock.

Back	Next	Reload	Home					

| 52 week | | | | | Sales | | | | |
High	Low	Stock	Div	PE	100s	High	Low	Last	Chg
42.38	14.00	TBL		13	461	35.88	35.00	32.25	-0.88
32.00	20.19	THO	.08	10	244	25.94	24.50	25.94	+1.25
39.50	16.50	TTC	.48	22	477	37.38	36.88	37.06	-0.38
25.50	11.88	TUP	.88	18	1,914	20.81	19.13	19.19	-1.69
14.50	6.63	TWI	.06		953	11.00	10.75	11.00	+0.06

Preview

Objectives

After studying this section you will be able to:

1. **Understand** the benefits and risks of buying stock.
2. **Describe** how stocks are traded.
3. **Identify** how stock performance is measured.
4. **Explain** the causes and effects of the Great Crash of 1929.

Section Focus

Corporations sell stock to raise money for starting, running, or expanding their businesses. Investors buy stocks to profit through regular payments, called dividends, or by selling the stock at a price higher than the purchase price. Stocks are traded on secondary markets called stock exchanges.

Key Terms

share	futures
equities	options
capital gain	call option
capital loss	put option
stock split	bull market
stockbroker	bear market
brokerage firm	The Dow
stock exchange	S & P 500
Nasdaq	Great Crash
OTC market	speculation

The New York Stock Exchange is a tangle of telephones, video monitors, computer screens, and frantic activity. The wrong decision may mean the difference between gaining or losing thousands of dollars. This is one of the places where stock is bought and sold—and fortunes are made and lost. Just what is stock, exactly how is it traded, and when is it a good investment?

Buying Stock

Besides bonds, corporations can raise funds by issuing stock, which represents ownership in the corporation. Stock is issued in portions known as **shares.** By selling shares of stock, corporations raise money to start, run, and expand their businesses. Stocks are also called **equities,** or claims of ownership in the corporation.

Benefits of Buying Stock

There are two ways for stockholders to make a profit:

• *Dividends* As you read in Chapter 8, many corporations pay out part of their profits as dividends to their stockholders. Dividends are usually paid four times a

year (quarterly). The size of the dividend depends on the corporation's profit. The higher the profit, the larger the dividend per share of stock.

share *portion of stock*

equities *claims of ownership in a corporation*

▲ **Daytime at the Chicago Board of Trade (top photo) shows the frantic pace of trade. The frenzied pace of a day of trading is perhaps even better suggested by a view of the Chicago Stock Exchange at night (bottom photo).**

capital gain *the difference between a higher selling price and a lower purchase price, resulting in a financial gain for the seller*

capital loss *the difference between a lower selling price and a higher purchase price resulting in a financial loss to the seller*

stock split *the division of a single share of stock into more than one share*

stockbroker *a person who links buyers and sellers of stock*

• *Capital gains* A second way an investor can earn a profit is to sell the stock for more than he or she paid for it. The difference between the higher selling price and the lower purchase price is called a **capital gain**. An investor who sells a stock at a price lower than the purchase price, however, suffers a **capital loss**.

Types of Stock

Stock may be classified in several ways, such as whether or not it pays dividends.

• *Income stock* This stock pays dividends at regular times during the year.
• *Growth stock* This stock pays few or no dividends. Instead, the issuing company reinvests its earnings in its business. The business (and its stock) thus increases in value over time.

Stock may also be classified as to whether stockholders have a vote in company policy.

• *Common stock* Investors who buy common stock are voting owners of the company. They usually receive one vote for each share of stock owned. They may use this vote, for example, to elect the company's board of directors. In some cases, a relatively small group of people may own enough shares to give them control over the company.
• *Preferred stock* Investors who buy preferred stock are nonvoting owners of the company. Owners of preferred stock, however, receive dividends before the owners of common stock. If the company goes out of business, preferred stockholders get their investments back before common stockholders.

Stock Splits

Owners of common stock may sometimes vote on whether to initiate a stock split. A **stock split** means that each single share of stock splits into more than one share. A company may seek to split a stock when the price of stock becomes so high that it discourages potential investors from buying it.

For example, suppose you own 200 shares in a sporting goods company called Ultimate Sports. Each share is worth $100. After the split, you own two shares of Ultimate Sports stock for every single share you owned, so that you now own 400 shares. Because the price is divided along with the stock, however, each share is now worth only $50. Although the split has not immediately resulted in any financial gain, shareholders like stock splits because prices tend to rise afterward.

Risks of Buying Stock

Purchasing stock is risky because the firm selling the stock may earn lower profits than expected, or it may lose money. If so, the dividends will be smaller than expected or nothing at all, and the market price of the stock will probably decrease. If the price of the stock decreases, investors who choose to sell their stock will get less than they paid for it, experiencing a capital loss.

How do the risk and rate of return on stocks compare to the risk and rate of return on bonds? As you have read, investors expect higher rates of return when they take on greater risk. Because of the laws governing bankruptcy, stocks are more risky than bonds. When a firm goes bankrupt, it sells its assets (such as land and equipment) and then pays its creditors, including bondholders, first. Stockholders receive dividends only if there is money left over after bondholders are paid. As you might expect, because stocks are riskier than bonds, the returns on stocks are generally higher.

How Stocks Are Traded

Suppose you decide that you want to buy stock. Do you call up the company and place an order? Probably not, because very few companies sell stock directly. Instead, you would contact a **stockbroker,** a person who links buyers and sellers of stock.

Stockbrokers usually work with individual investors, advising them to buy or sell particular stocks.

Stockbrokers work for **brokerage firms,** or businesses that specialize in trading stocks. Stockbrokers and brokerage firms cover their costs and earn a profit by charging a commission, or fee, on each stock transaction. Sometimes they also act as dealers of stock, meaning that they buy shares at a lower price and sell them to investors at a slightly higher price, profiting from the difference, or "spread."

Stock Exchanges

Stock is bought and sold on **stock exchanges,** or markets for buying and selling stock. These markets act as secondary markets for stocks and bonds. Most newspapers publish data on transactions in major stock exchanges. (See Figure 11.7 to learn how to read a newspaper stock market report.)

Major United States stock exchanges include the New York Stock Exchange (NYSE) and Nasdaq. In addition, a growing number of people trade stocks on the Internet. (See Skills for Life on page 284 to learn more about reading a stock market report on the Internet.)

The New York Stock Exchange

The New York Stock Exchange (NYSE) is the country's largest and most powerful exchange. The NYSE began in 1792 as an informal, outdoor exchange under a now-famous buttonwood tree in New York's financial district. Over time, as the financial market developed and the demand to buy and sell financial assets grew, the exchange moved indoors and became restricted to a limited number of members, who buy "scats" allowing thcm to tradc on the exchange. Today, new technologies make trading so fast that a transaction takes only an instant.

The NYSE handles stock and bond transactions for only the largest and most established companies in the country. The largest and best-known companies listed

brokerage firm *a business that specializes in trading stocks*

stock exchange *a market for buying and selling stock*

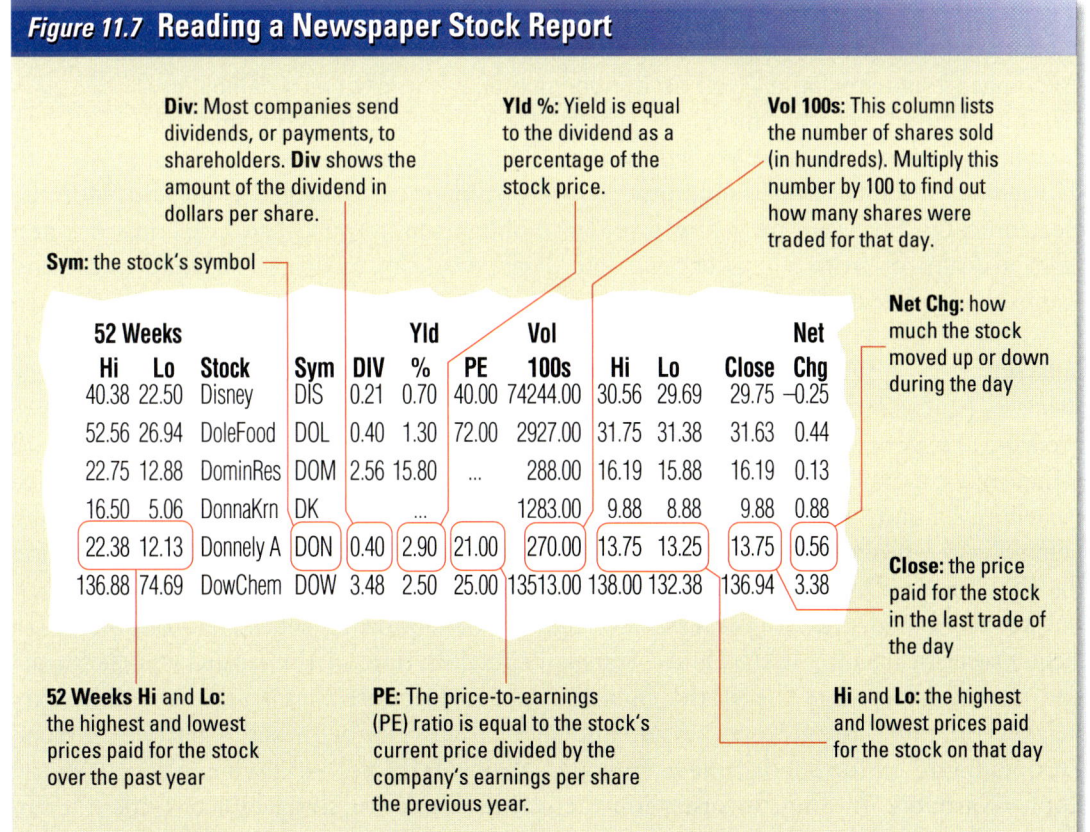

Figure 11.7 Reading a Newspaper Stock Report

Div: Most companies send dividends, or payments, to shareholders. **Div** shows the amount of the dividend in dollars per share.

Yld %: Yield is equal to the dividend as a percentage of the stock price.

Vol 100s: This column lists the number of shares sold (in hundreds). Multiply this number by 100 to find out how many shares were traded for that day.

Sym: the stock's symbol

Net Chg: how much the stock moved up or down during the day

52 Weeks											
Hi	Lo	Stock	Sym	DIV	Yld %	PE	Vol 100s	Hi	Lo	Close	Net Chg
40.38	22.50	Disney	DIS	0.21	0.70	40.00	74244.00	30.56	29.69	29.75	−0.25
52.56	26.94	DoleFood	DOL	0.40	1.30	72.00	2927.00	31.75	31.38	31.63	0.44
22.75	12.88	DominRes	DOM	2.56	15.80	...	288.00	16.19	15.88	16.19	0.13
16.50	5.06	DonnaKrn	DK		...		1283.00	9.88	8.88	9.88	0.88
22.38	12.13	Donnely A	DON	0.40	2.90	21.00	270.00	13.75	13.25	13.75	0.56
136.88	74.69	DowChem	DOW	3.48	2.50	25.00	13513.00	138.00	132.38	136.94	3.38

52 Weeks Hi and **Lo:** the highest and lowest prices paid for the stock over the past year

PE: The price-to-earnings (PE) ratio is equal to the stock's current price divided by the company's earnings per share the previous year.

Hi and **Lo:** the highest and lowest prices paid for the stock on that day

Close: the price paid for the stock in the last trade of the day

Many newspapers publish daily reports of stock market transactions. The explanations of the abbreviations in this sample report will help you read stock market reports in your own daily paper.

Income Which of the companies listed pays the highest dividend?

▲ **Stockbrokers link buyers and sellers of stock.**

OTC market *an electronic marketplace for stocks and bonds*

Nasdaq *American market for OTC securities*

futures *contracts to buy or sell at a specific date in the future at a price specified today*

options *contracts that give investors the choice to buy or sell stock and other financial assets*

call option *the option to buy shares of stock at a specified time in the future*

put option *the option to sell shares of stock at a specified time in the future*

on the NYSE are referred to as blue chip companies. Blue chip stocks are often in high demand because investors expect the companies to continue to do business profitably for a long time.

The OTC Market

Despite the importance of organized stock exchanges like the New York Stock Exchange, many stocks, as well as bonds, are not traded on the floor of stock exchanges. Instead, they are traded on the **OTC market**, that is, over-the-counter, or electronically. Investors may buy directly from a dealer or from a broker who will search the market for the best price.

Nasdaq

Nasdaq (the National Association of Securities Dealers Automated Quotations) is the American market for over-the-counter securities. Nasdaq was created in 1971 to help solve the problem of fragmentation in the OTC market by using automation. By the 1990s, it had grown into the second largest securities market in the United States and the third largest in the world, linking markets in the United States, Asia, and Europe. Because it does not have a trading floor, Nasdaq's trading information is simultaneously broadcast to some 360,000 computer terminals throughout the world.

Futures and Options

Futures are contracts to buy or sell commodities at a specific date in the future at a price specified today. For example, a buyer and seller might agree today on a price of $4.50 for a bushel of soybeans six or nine months in the future. The buyer would pay some portion of the money today, and the seller would deliver the goods in the future. Many of the markets in which futures are bought and sold are associated with grain and livestock exchanges. These markets include the New York Mercantile Exchange and the Chicago Board of Trade.

Similarly, **options** are contracts that give investors the choice to buy or sell stock and other financial assets. Investors may buy or sell a particular stock at a particular price up until a certain time in the future—usually three to six months. The option to buy shares of stock at a specified time in the future is known as a **call option**.

For example, you may pay $10 per share today for a call option. The call option gives you the right, but not the obligation, to purchase a certain stock at a price of, say, $100 per share. If at the end of six months, the price has gone up to $115 per share, your option still allows you to purchase the stock for the agreed-upon $100. You thus earn $5 per share ($15 minus the $10 you paid for the call option). If, on the other hand, the price has dropped to $80, you can throw away the option and buy the stock at the going rate.

The option to sell shares of stock at a specified time in the future is called a **put option**. Suppose that you, as the seller, pay $5 for the right to sell a particular stock that you do not yet own at $50 per share. If the price per share falls to $40, you can buy the share at that price and require the contracted buyer to pay the agreed-upon $50. You would then make $5 on the sale ($10 minus the $5 you paid for the put option). If the price rises to $60, however, you can throw away the option and sell the stock for $60.

Daytrading

Most people who buy stock hold their investment for a period of time—sometimes many years—with the expectation that it will grow in value. Recently, however, a different type of stock trading, called daytrading, has become popular. Daytraders try to predict minute-by-minute price changes based on computer programs that tell the trader when to buy and sell. These traders might make dozens of trades a day in hopes of making a profit. Unfortunately, daytrading is a risky business in which traders can lose a great deal of money.

Measuring Stock Performance

You may have heard newscasters speak of a "bull" or "bear" market or of the market rising or falling. What do these terms mean and how are increases and decreases in the sale of stocks measured?

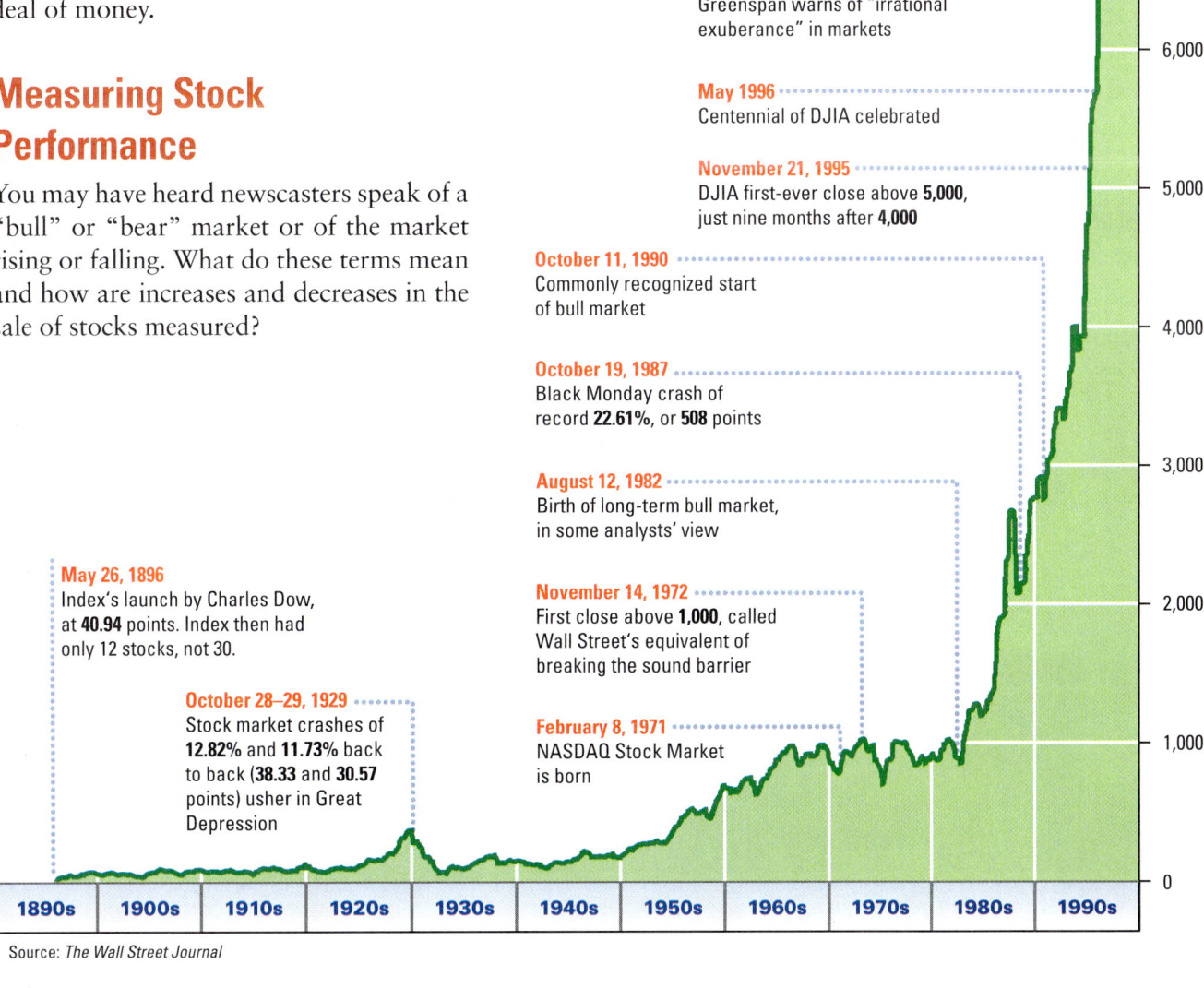

Figure 11.8 The Dow, 1896–1999

May 3, 1999
DJIA reaches **11,014.69**, breaking the **11,000** points mark. It will attain an all-time high of **11,722.98** on January 14, 2000

March 29, 1999
DJIA jumps **184.54**, or **1.88%**, to **10,006.78** amid tech-stock rally

September 8, 1998
Biggest-ever point gain, **380.53**, or **4.98%**, after seven weeks of decline

October 27–28, 1997
Biggest-ever point loss, **554.26** (but only **7.18%**), followed by then-biggest point gain, **337.17** (**4.71%**)

December 5, 1996
Greenspan warns of "irrational exuberance" in markets

May 1996
Centennial of DJIA celebrated

November 21, 1995
DJIA first-ever close above **5,000**, just nine months after **4,000**

October 11, 1990
Commonly recognized start of bull market

October 19, 1987
Black Monday crash of record **22.61%**, or **508** points

August 12, 1982
Birth of long-term bull market, in some analysts' view

November 14, 1972
First close above **1,000**, called Wall Street's equivalent of breaking the sound barrier

February 8, 1971
NASDAQ Stock Market is born

May 26, 1896
Index's launch by Charles Dow, at **40.94** points. Index then had only 12 stocks, not 30.

October 28–29, 1929
Stock market crashes of **12.82%** and **11.73%** back to back (**38.33** and **30.57** points) usher in Great Depression

1890s 1900s 1910s 1920s 1930s 1940s 1950s 1960s 1970s 1980s 1990s

Source: *The Wall Street Journal*

Bull and Bear Markets

When the stock market rises steadily over a period of time, a **bull market** exists. On the other hand, when the stock market falls for a period of time, people call it a **bear market**. In a bull market, investors expect an increase in profits and thus buy stock. During a bear market, investors sell stock in expectation of lower profits. The 1980s and 1990s brought the longest sustained bull market in the nation's history.

The Dow Jones Industrial Average

The Dow (The Dow Jones Industrial Average) has shown how certain stocks have traded on every business day since 1896. To make sure that the stocks remain representative of the stock market as a whole, over the years the companies on the Dow have changed. Today, the stocks on the Dow represent 30 large companies in various industries, such as food, entertainment, and technology.

S & P 500

The **S & P 500** (Standard & Poor's 500) gives a broader picture of stock performance. It tracks the price changes of 500 different stocks as a measure of overall stock market performance. The S&P 500 reports mainly on stocks listed on the NYSE, but some of its stocks are traded on the Nasdaq and OTC markets.

The Great Crash of 1929

Like the 1980s and 1990s, the 1920s saw a long-term bull market. Unfortunately, this period ended in a horrifying collapse of the stock market known as the **Great Crash**. The causes of this collapse contain important lessons for investors today.

Investing During the 1920s

When President Herbert Hoover took office in 1929, the United States economy seemed to be in excellent shape. The stock market is widely viewed as the nation's main economic indicator, and the stock market was soaring. In 1925, the market value of all stocks had been $27 billion. By early October 1929, combined stock values had hit $87 billion, rising by almost $11.4 billion in 1928 alone.

Signs of Trouble

Despite widespread optimism about continuing prosperity, there were signs of trouble. A relatively small number of companies and families held much of the nation's wealth. Many farmers and workers, on the other hand, were suffering financially. In addition, many ordinary people went into debt buying consumer goods such as refrigerators and radios—new and exciting inventions at the time—on credit. Finally, industries were producing more goods than consumers could buy. As a result, some industries, including the important automobile industry, developed large surpluses of goods, and prices began to slump.

Another economic danger sign was the debt that investors were piling up by playing the stock market. The dizzying climb of stock prices encouraged widespread **speculation**, the practice of making high-risk investments with borrowed money in hopes of getting a big return. To make matters worse, before World War I, only the wealthy had bought and sold

▲ As stock market prices fell in 1929, nervous investors crowded onto Wall Street hoping to hear the latest news.

shares in the stock market. Now, however, the press was reporting stories of ordinary people making fortunes in the stock market. Small investors thus began speculating in stocks, often with their life savings.

To attract less-wealthy investors, stockbrokers encouraged a practice called buying on margin. Buying on margin allowed investors to purchase a stock for only a fraction of its price and borrow the rest from the brokerage firm. Brokers' loans to these investors went from about $5 million in mid-1928 to $850 million in September 1929. The Hoover administration did little to discourage such borrowing.

The Crash

By September 3, 1929, the Dow had reached an all-time high of 381. The rising stock prices dominated the news. Eager investors filled brokerage firms to catch the latest news coming in on ticker tape. Prices for many stocks soared far above their real values in terms of the company's earnings and assets.

After their peak in September, stock prices began to fall. Some brokers demanded repayment of loans. When the stock market closed on Wednesday, October 23, 1929, the Dow had dropped 21 points in an hour. The next day, worried investors began to sell, and stock prices fell further. Business and political leaders told the public not to worry about their losses, but widespread panic began.

By Monday, October 28, 1929, the value of shares of stock were dropping to a fraction of what people had paid for them. Investors all over the country were therefore racing to get what was left of their money out of the stock market. On October 29, 1929, known as Black Tuesday, a record 16.4 million shares were sold, compared with the average 4 to 8 million shares per day earlier in the year. The Great Crash had begun.

The Aftermath of the Crash

During the bull market that led up to the Crash, about 4 million people had invested in the stock market. Although they were

10/26/98

▲ What does the cartoonist suggest about investors who assume that the stock market will only keep climbing?

the first to feel the effects of the Crash, eventually the whole country was affected. The Crash contributed to the Great Depression, in which millions of Americans lost their jobs, homes, and farms.

Mistakes in monetary policy slowed the nation's recovery. In 1929, the Fed had begun limiting the money supply in order to discourage excessive lending. With too little money in circulation, individuals and businesses could not spend enough to help the economy improve.

After the Depression, many people saw stocks as risky investments to be avoided. In 1980, only about 2.5 percent of American households held stock. Gradually, however, attitudes began to change. The development of mutual funds also made it easy to own a wide range of stocks. Americans became more comfortable with stock ownership.

After a period of very strong growth, stocks crashed again on "Black Monday," October 18, 1987. The Dow Jones

FAST FACT

The story of the rise, fall, and recovery of General Motors offers a lesson for investors who saw technology stocks soar, then rapidly lose value in the late 1990s and early 2000s. When William C. Durant founded General Motors in the early 1900s, investment capital poured in. GM stock rose more than 5,500% from 1914 to 1920. When the overcrowded auto industry began to disappoint investors in the early 1920s, however, auto stocks plummeted, and GM stock lost two-thirds of its value in six months. Eventually, of course, GM recovered and prospered.

▶ Following the September 11, 2001, terrorist attacks, the American flag draped over the New York Stock Exchange symbolized American unity and patriotism.

lost 22.6% of its value that day—nearly twice the one-day loss that began the Crash of 1929. This time the market rebounded on each of the next two days, and impact on the economy was much less severe. The Fed moved quickly to add liquidity and reduce interest rates to stimulate economic growth. Within two years, the Dow returned to pre-crash levels.

The Market Today

During the second half of the 1990s, stock prices rose dramatically. Technology companies (especially Internet companies) were particularly successful. Many people bought stock for the first time or changed their investments to new technology companies. By the end of the twentieth century, almost half of American households owned mutual funds.

In 2000, however, investors became worried that most companies could not make enough money to justify their high stock prices. Stocks fell, and many investors lost most or all of their prior gains. Economic growth slowed, and in early 2001 the country entered a recession.

Stock prices dropped even more sharply after the September 11, 2001, terrorist attacks on the World Trade Center and the Pentagon. Investors worried that the American economy would be seriously disrupted by the rise of terrorism. However, the market returned to pre-crash levels within a month. Stock prices continued to rise gradually as investors gained confidence that the current recession would be a mild one.

Section 3 Assessment

Key Terms and Main Ideas

1. What are two benefits and two risks of buying stock?
2. Identify two **stock exchanges** and describe the differences between them.
3. Describe two popular indexes of stock performance.
4. What were three causes of the **Great Crash**?

Applying Economic Concepts

5. *Critical Thinking* Many people believe that electronic trading services will replace stockbrokers in the future. What might be the advantages and disadvantages of this development?

6. *Critical Thinking* What might be the advantages and disadvantages of trading in futures and options? Choose a specific example to support your conclusions.

7. *Try This* What three questions would you ask a stockbroker before buying a company's stock?

8. *You Decide* Would you advise a friend to become a daytrader? Explain your answer.

9. *You Decide* Suppose you were given $1,000 to invest in the stock market. How would your choice of stock be influenced by the fact that you will soon need to pay college tuition?

Take It to the NET

Even with the current trend of daytrading, most people use a stockbroker to purchase their stocks. How could you know that a certain stockbroker is reliable? Would a certain broker provide sound advice? Describe the process you would use to find a reliable stockbroker. Use the links provided at the following Web site for help in completing this activity.
www.phschool.com

Real-life Case Study

The Fate of the Dot-Coms

The "dot-coms" are companies that sprang up to take advantage of the potential business opportunities offered by the Internet. The first of these companies to take off provided services directly relating to the Internet—companies like America Online and Netscape. Right behind them came a big group of "B2C" companies, businesses marketing products to consumers. Amazon.com is the best known of these, but there were hundreds—even thousands—more looking for a share of consumers' spending.

Unlimited Potential? Many dot-coms were started by young entrepreneurs with more vision than experience. Companies like Amazon declared that making a profit in the short term was less important than developing a large market share for the long run. Even though the companies were losing money, and often did not expect to be profitable for years, excited investors flocked to the stocks. Stock prices soared, which in turn generated more excitement, attracted more investors, and pushed stock prices even higher. Venture capitalists funded fledgling companies and pushed them quickly to market in order to take advantage of the hot stock market.

The Fall of the Dot-Coms In the middle of 2000, Internet stocks fell sharply as investors became concerned about the lack of profits. The companies could stay in business if investors were willing to put up more money or if they had profits to reinvest. Otherwise, they could quickly run out of money. Many dot-coms filed for bankruptcy protection or closed their doors entirely. Investors saw the value of their holdings plummet.

The Future of the Dot-Coms After the fall of technology stocks, many formerly enthusiastic entrepreneurs and investors began to think that dot-coms would never be a good investment. In reality, they were probably never as good as people thought at the height of the market, or as bad as people thought after the fall. Certainly the Internet will continue to expand, and its use in business will grow. Companies that are able to develop useful Web-based services may find that they grow more steadily, but more reliably, than during the boom years.

Dry Bones

IF I HAD SAVED UP ANY MONEY AT ALL...

I'D HAVE INVESTED IT IN HIGH TECH STOCKS...

AND I'D HAVE BEEN RUINED IN THE STOCK MARKET CRASH!

YOU MEAN?

YUP...POVERTY HAS KEPT ME FROM FINANCIAL RUIN!

YOU LUCKY DOG!

CARTOONISTS & WRITERS SYNDICATE http://CartoonWeb.com

KIRSCHEN
JERUSALEM POST
Jerusalem
ISRAEL

http://drybones.org

▲ What does the cartoon suggest about investing in dot-coms?

Applying Economic Ideas

1. Why did the initial success of dot-coms make it easier for other dot-com companies to get started?

2. What might a dot-com entrepreneur have done to avoid the "boom and bust" cycle that many technology stocks experienced?

▼ One technology stock, Cisco Systems, reflected the decline of the value of dot-coms in early 2001.

Cisco Systems, 2000–2001

Price per sale: $75, $60, $45, $30, $15, 0

Month: Jul, Sep, Nov, Jan, Mar, May, Jul

Source: Nasdaq

Chapter Summary

A summary of major ideas in Chapter 11 appears below. See also the **Guide to the Essentials of Economics,** which provides additional review and test practice of key concepts in Chapter 11.

Section 1 *Saving and Investing (pp. 271–275)*

Saving and **investment** are essential parts of the American free enterprise system. In our financial system, institutions called **financial intermediaries** bring together savers and borrowers to channel funds for investment. Investors must weigh potential risks and **returns** when choosing among the many types of investments available.

Section 2 *Bonds and Other Financial Assets (pp. 277–283)*

Businesses and governments issue bonds and other financial assets in order to finance expansion. Bonds are relatively low-risk investments for purchasers, who generally receive the purchase price of the bond plus interest when the bond matures. Other financial assets, such as money market mutual funds and certificates of deposit, offer additional investment opportunities.

Section 3 *The Stock Market (pp. 285–292)*

The stock market is another way for people to invest their earnings. Stocks offer possibilities for high return, but also present certain risks. Major **stock exchanges** in the United States include the New York Stock Exchange and the **Nasdaq,** an electronic stock exchange. Stock performance is measured by **The Dow** and the **S & P 500.** The **Great Crash** of 1929 dealt the stock market one of its worst economic blows in our history. Following a period of distrust of the stock market in the decades after the Crash, however, investors returned to the stock market in great numbers.

Key Terms

Match the following terms with the definitions listed below. You will not use all of the terms.

brokerage firm	portfolio
junk bonds	financial
bull market	intermediary
coupon rate	maturity
investment	diversification
speculation	capital gain

1. Spreading out your investments to reduce risk
2. Difference between a higher selling price and a lower purchase price
3. The interest rate to be paid to the bondholder
4. A period of time during which the stock market steadily rises
5. An action taken today that will create benefits in the future
6. Institution that helps channel funds from savers to investors
7. Lower-rated, higher-paying bonds
8. The practice of making high-risk investments in hopes of getting a big return
9. Collection of financial assets

Using Graphic Organizers

10. On a separate sheet of paper, copy the web map below. Complete the web map by writing and describing examples of investment options in the circles. More circles may be added.

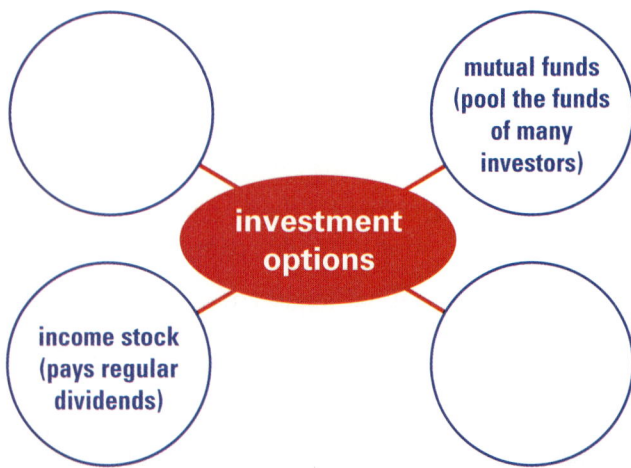

investment options

mutual funds (pool the funds of many investors)

income stock (pays regular dividends)

Reviewing Main Ideas

11. What do financial intermediaries do?
12. How do bond ratings influence which bonds investors buy? How are bond ratings established?
13. Describe three ways that stocks are traded.
14. How does diversification strengthen an investor's portfolio?

Critical Thinking

15. **Drawing Conclusions** Using evidence from the chapter, support the following statement: Savings and investments play an essential role in the free enterprise system.
16. **Making Comparisons** Compare different means by which savings can be invested and the risks each strategy poses to the consumer.
17. **Drawing Conclusions** Review the causes of the Great Crash of 1929. What lessons can investors learn from the Crash?
18. **Demonstrating Reasoned Judgment** Analyze the economic impact of investing in the stock and bond market.

Problem-Solving Activity

19. Suppose that you have been handed $10,000. Now, create your own hypothetical investment portfolio that best suits your needs and goals. What types of financial intermediaries will you use? Will you invest more money in stocks, bonds, or other financial assets?

Skills for Life

Reading an Online Stock Market Report Review the steps shown on page 284; then answer the following questions using the stock listing below.

20. Which company uses the symbol GT?
21. Of these companies, which one had the most shares traded?
22. What is the actual dollar value of one share of Guess at the closing value?
23. If you could own 10 shares of GucciCp or 50 shares of Griffon, which would you choose (based on closing value)?
24. Which stock(s) appear(s) to be on an upward trend? A downward trend?

◁Back	Next ▷		⟳Reload	🏠Home							
52 week				YTD			Vol				Net
Hi	Lo	Stock	Sym	Div	%	PE	100s	Hi	Lo	Close	Chg
64.38	35.31	Gillette	G	0.59	1.20	53.00	12159.00	51.37	50.75	51.12	-0.31
52.63	26.50	Goodrich	GR	1.10	2.70	14.00	3436.00	41.93	41.43	41.44	-0.13
72.88	45.43	Goodyear	GT	1.20	2.00	18.00	5345.00	61.25	60.31	61.12	0.25
14.19	6.25	Griffon	GFF			11.00	403.00	8.06	7.43	7.68	-0.50
85.50	31.50	GucciCp	GUC	0.40	0.60	20.00	2330.00	65.75	65.81	65.00	-0.69
11.50	3.62	Guess	GES			17.00	1175.00	11.75	10.87	11.56	0.81

Economics Journal

Synthesizing Information Review the list of questions you created at the beginning of the chapter. Use what you have learned in the chapter to answer your questions. Research any remaining questions in the library or on the Internet.

Take It to the NET

Chapter 11 Self-Test As a final review activity, take the Chapter 11 Self-Test in the Social Studies area at the Web site listed below, and receive immediate feedback on your answers. The test consists of 20 multiple-choice questions designed to test your understanding of the chapter content.
www.phschool.com

Economics
Simulation
Making Investment Decisions

Long ago, many people saved their money by tucking it away in a sugar bowl or underneath a mattress. These are relatively safe, but not very profitable, options for savings. Today, there are a wide number of investment options available to help your savings multiply. Banks offer various types of savings accounts and certificates of deposit (CDs). These are safe and accrue small amounts of interest. More agressive investments, such as mutual funds, government bonds, and stocks and bonds, potentially offer greater returns, but are relatively risky.

In this simulation, you and your group are trying to raise enough money to pay for all 100 students in your senior class to visit a nearby amusement park. You plan to take the trip in one year, and you have already saved some money. You want to earn as much interest or dividends as you can, but you only have one year. How will you make your money grow?

Materials
Paper
Calculator

▲ How will you raise enough money to pay for a senior class trip to an amusement park?

Preparing the Simulation

The best way to make sound investments is to understand your choices thoroughly. Your task in this simulation is to determine the best way to raise enough money for your senior trip in only one year.

Step 1: First, form fundraising groups of five to eight students. Each fundraising group will begin with $5,000 to invest for one year.

Step 2: Your goal is to raise enough money for everyone in your senior class to spend a Senior Weekend at a nearby amusement park. There are 100 students in your senior class, and you have figured out that it will cost $8,000 to buy two-day passes for everyone.

Conducting the Simulation

The simulation will consist of two parts. First, you will discuss your investment options and make your choices. Then you will calculate the results and discover how much you would have made—or lost.

Step 1: First, examine your investment options. Of all the options available, you have narrowed down your choices to the five shown in the investment choices chart. Some of your choices have guaranteed returns on your investment, but others do not. Be sure you understand the risks as well as the potential returns of each kind of investment.

Step 2: As a group, discuss your philosophy of investing. Do you want to take risks in hopes of a higher return? Would you rather avoid risk in your investments, but earn a smaller return?

As you discuss each fundraising choice, keep these questions in mind:
- Does this alternative guarantee a certain rate of return, or might the rate of return vary?
- Is this choice aggressive enough to earn the necessary amount of money in one year?
- What is the risk associated with this investment choice?

Step 3: Decide how to invest your group's $5,000. Make an investments and returns chart like the one on this page, and record your investment choices.

Step 4: Now, suppose it is one year later, and it is time to analyze the results of your investment decisions. Your teacher will provide you with the performance figures for each investment option. Using that information, calculate your profits and losses on stock and mutual funds. Figure out the interest you would have accumulated from bank deposits or CDs.

Fundraising Options

Options	Potential Return
Deposit the money in a bank	
Gibraltar Bank Savings Acount A traditional savings account at your local bank is fully guaranteed by the FDIC, and deposits can be withdrawn at any time.	2% guaranteed
One-Year Certificate of Deposit This CD is fully guaranteed by the FDIC, but deposits may only be withdrawn after the end of one full year.	4% guaranteed
Invest in the stock market	
Rock Solid Mutual Fund This mutual fund invests in blue chip stocks, which are stocks for large, well-established companies that expect slow and steady growth.	8% return last year; return not guaranteed
Hurrah! (individual company stock) This brand-new technology company has been all over the news in the last few weeks. The new technology it developed has revolutionized how companies conduct business across the Internet.	brand new; no data to determine how this stock will perform
Wycombe and Marlow Health Care This company is in financial trouble but could turn itself around. The bonds it has issued are considered junk bonds; if the company is able to pay interest on the bonds, investors will make a healthy profit.	15%, if the company can pay the interest when it is due

Investments and Returns Chart

Choices	Amount Invested	Amount of Return
Gibraltar Bank Savings Account	$	$
One-Year Certificate of Deposit (CD)	$	$
Rock Solid Mutual Fund	$	$
Hurrah! Stock	$	$
Wycombe and Marlow Health Care	$	$
Totals	$	$

Simulation Analysis

As a final step, meet with the other fundraising groups and compare your investment choices and their results.

1. How many of the groups met their goal of turning their $5,000 into $8,000 in one year?
2. Which group's investments earned the most? Did this group take risks or make "safe" choices?
3. Did any groups lose money? Was it because they took risks? Or were there changes in the economy over the year?
4. **Identifying Alternatives** If you could do this simulation again, would you have made different investment choices? Why or why not?

UNIT 5

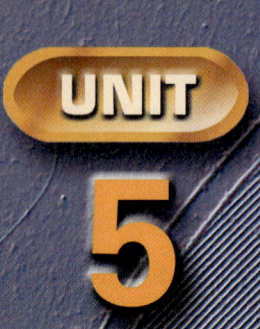

Measuring Economic Performance

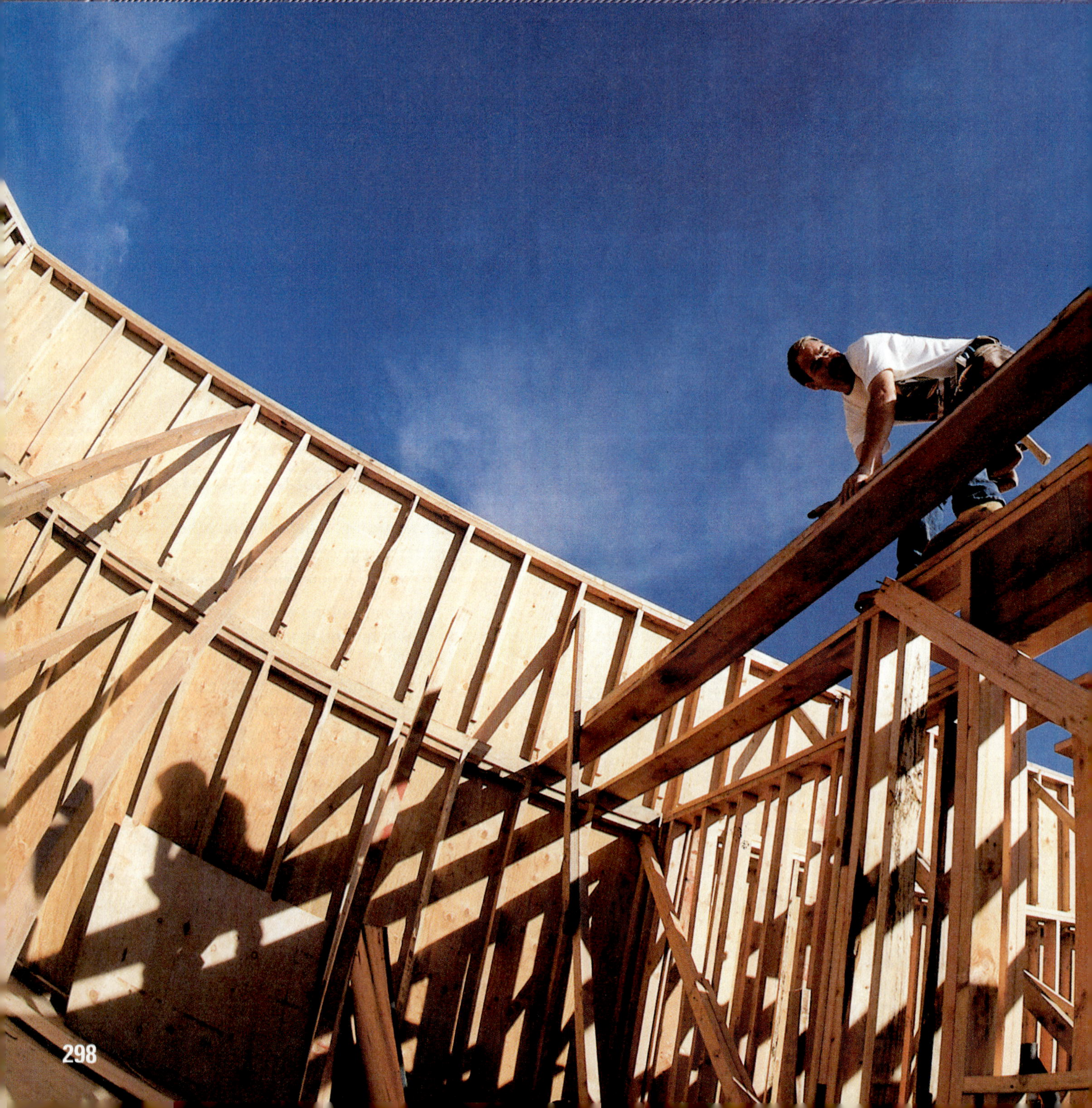

New housing *starts are up . . .*

Every day, news reporters tell us how well or poorly the economy is performing. Analyzing an entire economy is a challenging task. However, there are key indicators such as the number of new housing starts, unemployment rates, and inflation rates that provide clues. After listening to the financial news, you may wonder:

- How do economists measure the health of the economy?
- What impact would a recession have on workers and businesses?
- What is inflation?
- What makes the economy grow?

In this unit, you'll read about the answers to these questions as you are introduced to macroeconomics—the branch of economics that looks at an economy as a whole.

Focus Activity

Summarize one recent news article that refers in some way to the health of the economy of the United States. Then share your article with a classmate.

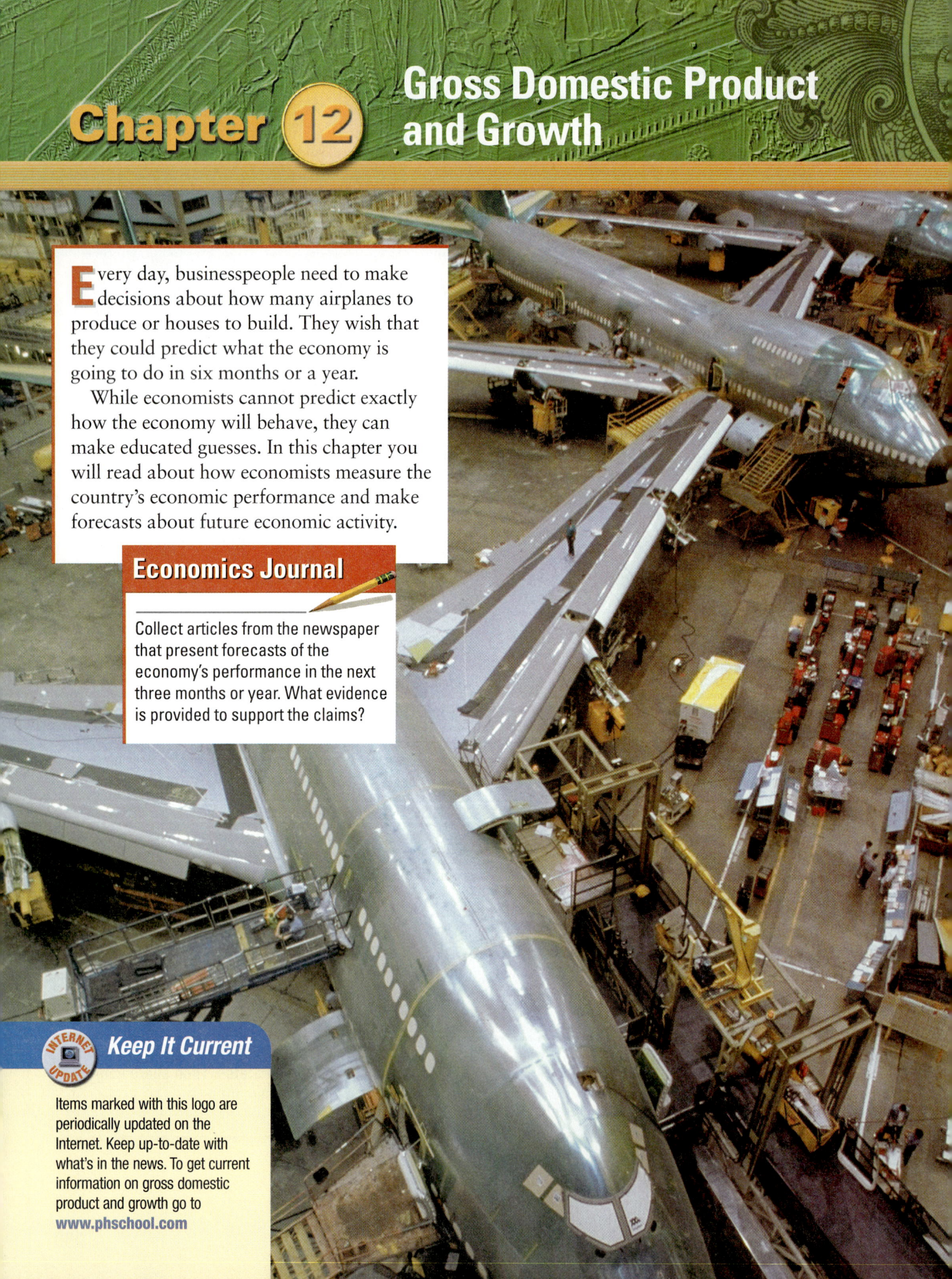

Chapter 12

Gross Domestic Product and Growth

Every day, businesspeople need to make decisions about how many airplanes to produce or houses to build. They wish that they could predict what the economy is going to do in six months or a year.

While economists cannot predict exactly how the economy will behave, they can make educated guesses. In this chapter you will read about how economists measure the country's economic performance and make forecasts about future economic activity.

Economics Journal

Collect articles from the newspaper that present forecasts of the economy's performance in the next three months or year. What evidence is provided to support the claims?

Keep It Current

Items marked with this logo are periodically updated on the Internet. Keep up-to-date with what's in the news. To get current information on gross domestic product and growth go to
www.phschool.com

Gross Domestic Product

Objectives

After studying this section you will be able to:

1. **Identify** National Income and Product Accounts (NIPA).
2. **Explain** how gross domestic product (GDP) is calculated.
3. **Explain** the difference between nominal and real GDP.
4. **List** the main limitations of GDP.
5. **Describe** other income and output measures.
6. **Identify** factors that influence GDP.

Section Focus

There are several ways to evaluate a nation's economic performance. Gross domestic product (GDP) is the most important, despite its limitations. GDP changes in response to shifts in aggregate supply or aggregate demand.

Key Terms

national income accounting
gross domestic product
intermediate goods
durable goods
nondurable goods
nominal GDP
real GDP
gross national product
depreciation
price level
aggregate supply
aggregate demand

Early economists believed that a national economy would regulate itself. Periods of high unemployment and low income and output would be temporary and short-lived and would be corrected automatically.

These ideas about the economy lasted until the Great Depression, a severe economic decline that started in 1929 and lasted for over a decade. This economic avalanche, touched off by the Great Crash of the stock market in October 1929, devastated the U.S. economy. The length and depth of the Great Depression convinced many economists that they must find a way to monitor the macroeconomy's performance so that they could predict economic downturns and try to prevent them.

National Income and Product Accounts

Keeping track of the U.S. economy is an enormous task. Today, economists monitor important macroeconomic data using **national income accounting,** a system that collects statistics on production, income, investment, and savings. The data are compiled and presented in the form of National Income and Product Accounts (NIPA), which are maintained by the U.S. Department of Commerce. NIPA data are used to determine economic policies that you will read about in Chapters 15 and 16.

Gross Domestic Product

The most important of the measures in NIPA is **gross domestic product (GDP),** the dollar value of all final goods and services produced within a country's borders in a given year. This carefully worded definition conveys a lot of information that we should consider piece by piece.

Dollar value is the total of the selling prices of all goods and services produced in a country in one calendar year, which are added up to calculate GDP. *Final goods and services* are products in the form sold to consumers, as opposed to **intermediate goods,** which are used in the production of final goods. *Produced within a country's borders* is especially important to remember. For example, U.S. GDP includes cars made in Ohio by a Japanese car company.

national income accounting *a system that collects macroeconomic statistics on production, income, investment, and savings*

gross domestic product (GDP) *the dollar value of all final goods and services produced within a country's borders in a given year*

intermediate goods *goods used in the production of final goods*

durable goods *goods that last for a relatively long time, such as refrigerators, cars, and DVD players*

nondurable goods *goods that last a short period of time, such as food, light bulbs, and sneakers*

U.S. GDP does not include cars made in Brazil by an American automaker. You'll be able to see shortly why this distinction is important.

Let's look at the housing market for more examples of how GDP is compiled. Suppose that your neighbor sold his house this year. When the house was built, say in 1982, it was counted in that year's GDP. Thus, it would be inaccurate to count it again this year just because it changed hands. However, the fee paid to the real estate agent who handled the resale of the house would come from services performed this year, so that fee would be included in GDP.

Meanwhile, your neighbor has bought a newly built house. Would the lumber, nails, shingles, windows, and other items used to produce that house be included in GDP? No. Those are intermediate goods, and their value would be included in the price of the completed house. Thus, only the price of the completed house would be added to GDP.

Expenditure Approach

One way government economists calculate GDP is by using the expenditure approach, sometimes called the output-expenditure approach. It works this way: First, economists estimate the annual expenditures, or amounts spent, on four categories of final goods and services:

1. consumer goods and services
2. business goods and services
3. government goods and services
4. net exports or imports of goods and services

Consumer goods include **durable goods**, those goods that last for a relatively long time, such as refrigerators, cars, and DVD players. Consumer goods also include **nondurable goods**, those goods that last a short period of time, such as food, light bulbs, and sneakers.

Then, economists add together the amounts spent on all four categories to arrive at the total expenditures on goods

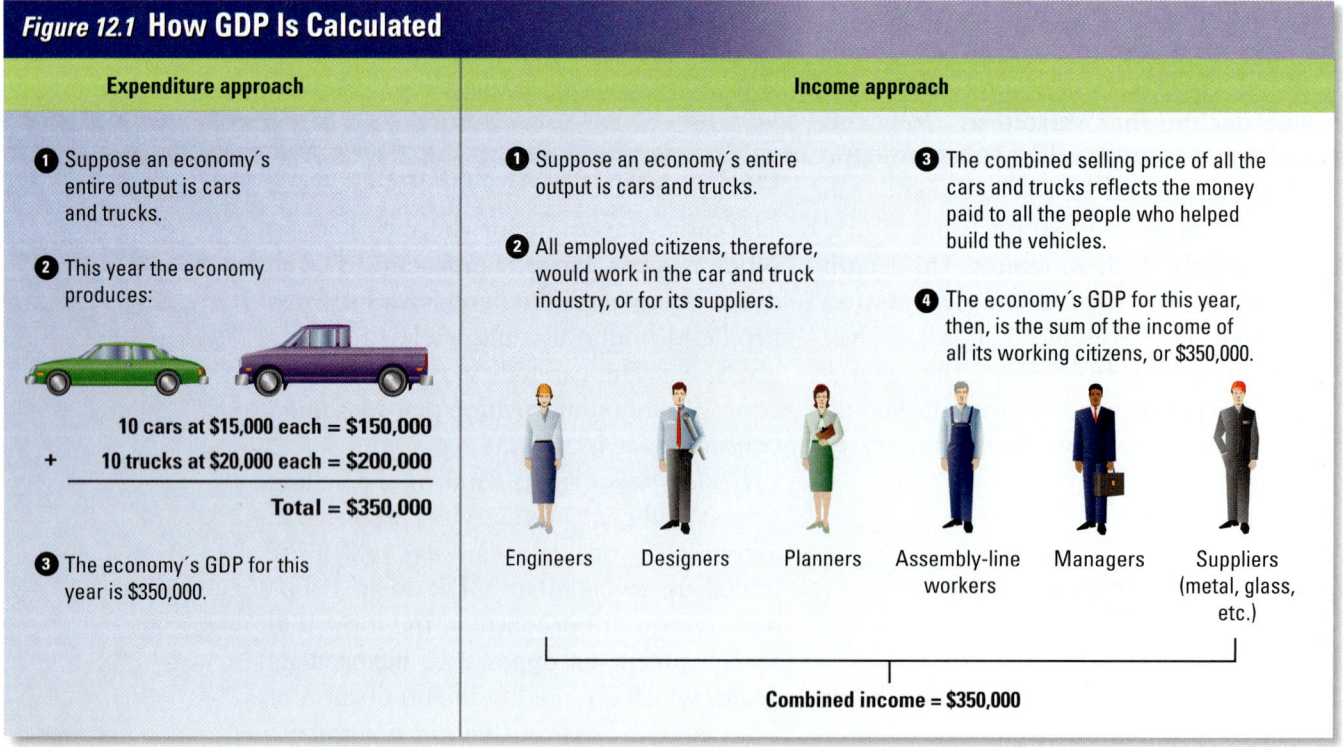

Figure 12.1 How GDP Is Calculated

Expenditure approach

① Suppose an economy's entire output is cars and trucks.

② This year the economy produces:

10 cars at $15,000 each = $150,000
+ 10 trucks at $20,000 each = $200,000
Total = $350,000

③ The economy's GDP for this year is $350,000.

Income approach

① Suppose an economy's entire output is cars and trucks.

② All employed citizens, therefore, would work in the car and truck industry, or for its suppliers.

③ The combined selling price of all the cars and trucks reflects the money paid to all the people who helped build the vehicles.

④ The economy's GDP for this year, then, is the sum of the income of all its working citizens, or $350,000.

Engineers   Designers   Planners   Assembly-line workers   Managers   Suppliers (metal, glass, etc.)

Combined income = $350,000

BUILDING KEY CONCEPTS

The two ways of measuring gross domestic product are shown here. The expenditure approach is a practical way of calculating GDP. The income approach is generally more accurate.
Gross Domestic Product Apply the example shown in the diagram by using the expenditure approach and the income approach to explain how a brand-new housing complex would add to GDP.

and services produced during the year. This total equals GDP. Figure 12.1 provides a simplified example of calculating GDP with the expenditure approach.

Income Approach

The expenditure approach gives economists a practical way to measure GDP. If they want better accuracy, however, they use the income approach. The income approach calculates GDP by adding up all the incomes in the economy.

Here's how it works: When a firm sells its product, the selling price represents income for the firm's owners and employees. For instance, suppose that your neighbor's newly built house sold for $115,000. This amount is added to GDP under the expenditure approach.

However, that $115,000 is also income that was shared by all of the people who helped build the house. The contractor, the bricklayer, the roofers, the window installers, and everyone else who worked on the house received some income directly from the house's selling price. Also, let's not forget the people who supplied the lumber, the nails, and all of the other materials that went into the house. The money that they received for these goods all comes from the selling price of the house, even though they may have been paid before the house was sold.

Each of these people may get only a small share of the house's selling price. However, if we added up all the shares, we would see that $115,000 of income was generated by the sale. In other words, the house's selling price is equal to the amount of income earned by all of the people who helped, however indirectly, to build the house. This same logic holds for all goods and services produced in the economy. Thus, we may calculate GDP by adding up all income earned in the economy. This process is the income approach, shown in Figure 12.1.

In theory, we can calculate GDP with either the income approach or the expenditure approach. Both calculations should give us the same total. In fact, federal economists often determine GDP using both approaches. Then they compare the two totals and make adjustments to offset any mistakes. This gives them a better result.

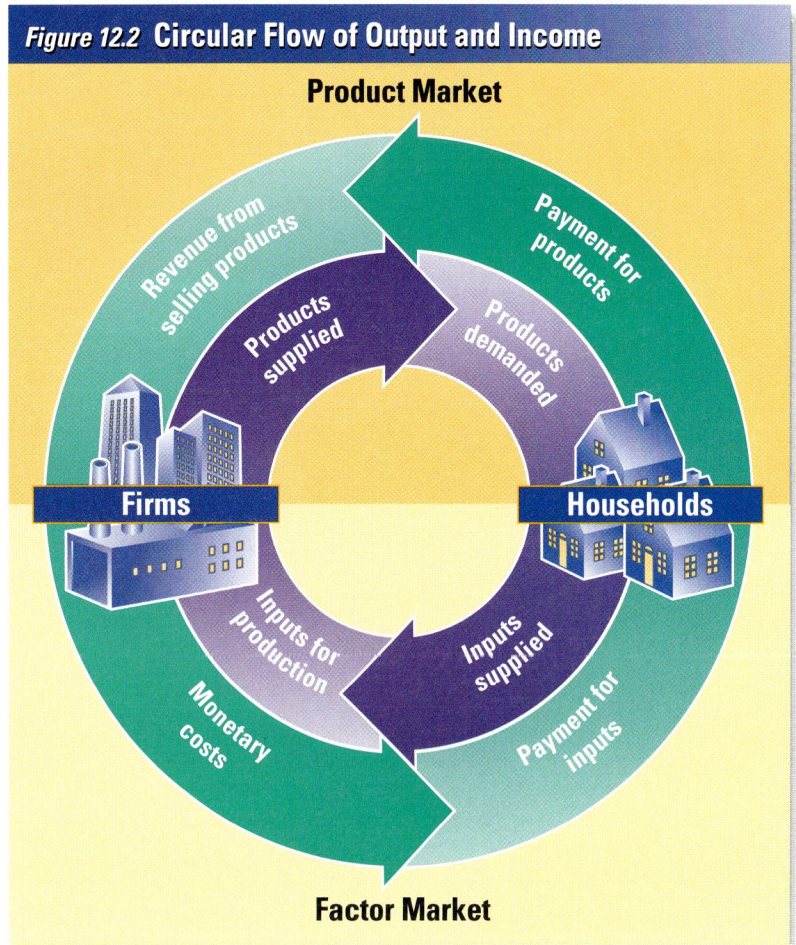

Figure 12.2 Circular Flow of Output and Income

Product Market

Revenue from selling products

Payment for products

Products supplied

Products demanded

Firms

Households

Inputs for production

Inputs supplied

Monetary costs

Payment for inputs

Factor Market

BUILDING KEY CONCEPTS

This circular flow diagram shows how the production of goods and services generates income for households and how households purchase goods and services produced by firms. **Gross Domestic Product (a) Which part of this diagram would you use to calculate GDP using the expenditure approach? (b) Which part would you use for the income approach?**

Nominal Versus Real GDP

Government policymakers measure gross domestic product to find out how well the economy is performing. The measurement must be as accurate as possible. Comparing the results of the expenditure and income approaches is one way to judge accuracy. To develop additional information about the economy, economists distinguish between two measures of GDP, nominal and real.

Figure 12.3 Nominal and Real GDP

Year 1 Nominal GDP	Year 2 Nominal GDP	Year 2 Real GDP
1 Suppose an economy's entire output is cars and trucks. **2** This year the economy produces: 10 cars at $15,000 each = $150,000 + 10 trucks at $20,000 each = $200,000 _____ Total = $350,000 **3** Since we have used the current year's prices to express the current year's output, the result is a nominal GDP of $350,000.	**1** In the second year, the economy's output does not increase, but the prices of the cars and trucks do: 10 cars at $16,000 each = $160,000 + 10 trucks at $21,000 each = $210,000 _____ Total = $370,000 **2** This new GDP figure of $370,000 is misleading. GDP rises because of an increase in prices. Economists prefer to have a measure of GDP that is not affected by changes in prices. So they calculate real GDP.	**1** To correct for an increase in prices, economists establish a set of constant prices by choosing one year as a base year. When they calculate real GDP for other years, they use the prices from the base year. So we calculate the real GDP for Year 2 using the prices from Year 1: 10 cars at $15,000 each = $150,000 + 10 trucks at $20,000 each = $200,000 _____ Total = $350,000 **2** Real GDP for Year 2, therefore, is $350,000.

This example shows the different results that come from calculating nominal GDP and real GDP. Real GDP reflects actual increases in output without the misleading effects of price increases.

Gross Domestic Product Using Year 1 as the base year, calculate real GDP for Year 3, in which 15 cars and 14 trucks were sold.

nominal GDP *GDP measured in current prices*

real GDP *GDP expressed in constant, or unchanging, prices*

Nominal GDP

In Figure 12.1, we calculated **nominal GDP**—that is, GDP measured in current prices. (Sometimes it is called "current GDP.") To calculate nominal GDP, we simply use the current year's prices to calculate the value of the current year's output. Figure 12.3 shows how the definition of nominal GDP applies to the small economy that produces only cars and trucks.

Real GDP

Study how nominal GDP is calculated in Year 1 and Year 2. The diagram points out a problem with nominal GDP: A general increase in prices *appears* to make GDP rise, when in fact output has not risen. To correct for this distortion, economists determine **real GDP**. This is defined as GDP expressed in constant, or unchanging, prices.

Look again at Figure 12.3 and see how real GDP is calculated in Year 2. When real GDP rises, we can be certain whether an economy is producing more goods and services, regardless of changes in the prices of those items. In this example, we learn from calculating real GDP that output did not increase in Year 2.

Limitations of GDP

Even though economists can calculate it accurately, GDP is still not a perfect yardstick. For instance, GDP does not take into account certain economic activities, such as:

- *Nonmarket activities* GDP does not measure goods and services that people make or do themselves, such as caring for children, mowing the lawn, cooking dinner, washing the car. GDP *does* rise, however, when people pay someone else to do these things for them. When nonmarket activities are shifted to the market, GDP is pushed up somewhat, even though production has not really increased.

- *The underground economy* A large amount of production and income is never recorded or reported to the government: for instance, transactions on the *black market,* the market for illegal goods, such as drugs, weapons, stolen cars, and exotic animals. Income from illegal gambling goes unreported. So do "under the table" wages paid by some companies to avoid paying business and income taxes.

Many legal, informal transactions are not reported, as well, such as selling your car to a friend or trading your stereo for a bike, or hiring someone to baby-sit, mow lawns, or shovel snow. Underground transactions add nothing to the GDP figure, even though goods and services were produced and income was earned.

- *Negative externalities* Unintended economic side effects, or externalities, have a monetary value that often is not reflected in GDP. (See Chapter 3, Section 3, for a discussion of externalities.) For example, if a power plant spends money to reduce damage caused by pollution, those expenditures will be added to GDP. However, the value of a clean environment is not counted in GDP, even though a cleaned-up lake or restored wetlands have considerable social value.

- *Quality of life* Although some economists and politicians interpret rising GDP as a sign of rising well-being, we should remember that additional goods and services do not necessarily make people any happier. In fact, some things that are not counted in GDP contribute greatly to most people's quality of life, such as pleasant surroundings, ample leisure time, and personal safety. GDP measures output and income within an economy, not individuals' quality of life.

All of these limitations suggest that GDP is a poor measure of people's well-being and a somewhat flawed measure of output and income. Nevertheless, while the measure itself may be imperfect, when calculated consistently over time, it helps reveal economic growth rates. For this reason, GDP is closely watched by economists and policymakers.

Other Income and Output Measures

As you have read, our system of National Income and Product Accounts provides numerous measurements of the macroeconomy's performance. While gross domestic product is the primary measure of income and output, sometimes other measures are more useful. Many of these other yardsticks are derived *from* GDP. Figure 12.4 (on the next page) shows how GDP is used to determine five other economic measures.

The first is **gross national product** (GNP), the annual income earned by U.S.-owned firms and U.S. citizens. GNP is a measure of the market value of all goods and services produced by Americans in one year. Study the diagram on the next page to see how GNP is derived from GDP.

GNP does not account for **depreciation**, the loss of the value of capital equipment that results from normal wear and tear. The cost of replacing this physical capital slightly reduces the value of what we

gross national product (GNP) the annual income earned by U.S.-owned firms and U.S. citizens

depreciation the loss of the value of capital equipment that results from normal wear and tear

▲ When people go to grocery stores to buy food, their efforts are not counted in GDP; however, when they pay someone else, like this on-line grocery service, to do their shopping, the expense does get counted in GDP.

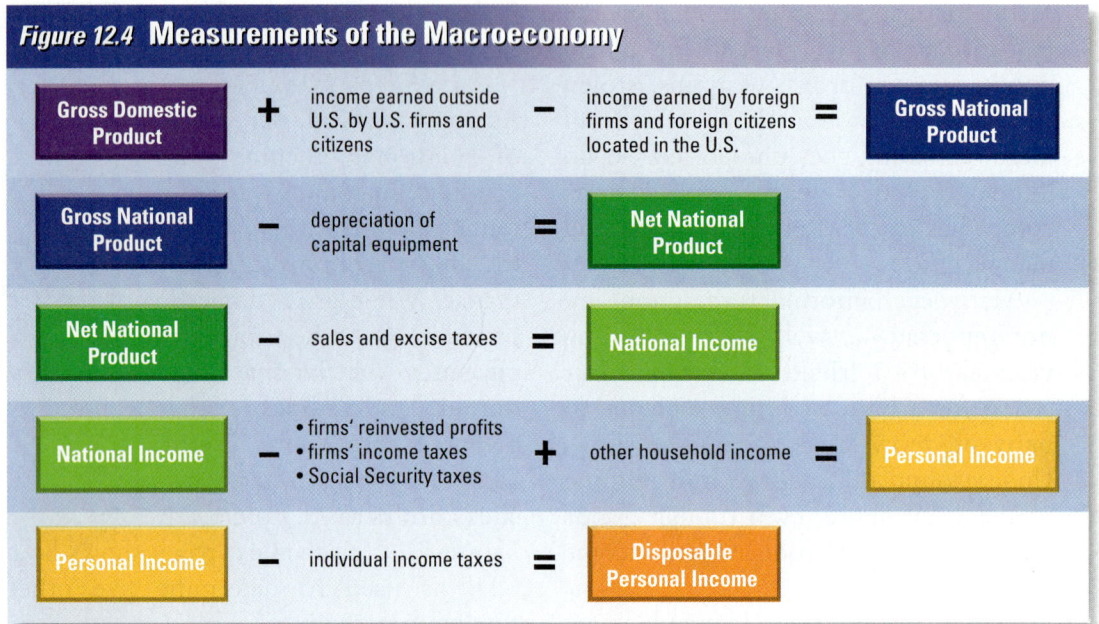

Figure 12.4 Measurements of the Macroeconomy

Gross Domestic Product	+	income earned outside U.S. by U.S. firms and citizens	−	income earned by foreign firms and foreign citizens located in the U.S.	=	Gross National Product
Gross National Product	−	depreciation of capital equipment	=	Net National Product		
Net National Product	−	sales and excise taxes	=	National Income		
National Income	−	• firms' reinvested profits • firms' income taxes • Social Security taxes	+	other household income	=	Personal Income
Personal Income	−	individual income taxes	=	Disposable Personal Income		

These equations summarize the formulas for calculating some of the key macroeconomic measurements.
Economic Systems Why might economists track so many different indicators of the nation's economic health?

produce. GNP minus the cost of depreciation of capital equipment is called *net national product (NNP)*. NNP is a measure of the net output for one year, or the output made after the adjustment for depreciation.

NNP does not reflect another cost of doing business: taxes. After subtracting sales and excise taxes and making some other minor adjustments to NNP, we get another important statistic, called *national income (NI)*.

From NI, we can find out how much pretax income businesses actually pay to U.S. households after reinvesting some of their income and paying additional taxes. That amount, as calculated in Figure 12.4, is called *personal income (PI)*.

Finally, we want to know how much money people actually have to spend after they pay their taxes, a figure called *disposable personal income (DPI)*. To find DPI, we take personal income and subtract individual income taxes.

See how far we have come. Beginning with GDP, the value of all goods and services produced in a year—a very large number—we wind up knowing how much

cash Americans have to spend or put in the bank. As you might suppose, this data is extremely valuable to economic planners, legislators, investors, and businesses.

Influences on GDP

So far, we have defined GDP, calculated it, and learned about its limitations. One important issue, however, remains: What influences GDP? That is, in a real economy, what factors can change the level of GDP? These questions go to the heart of macroeconomics.

In Chapters 4 and 5 we learned about demand and supply as they relate to individual markets. Now we will look at supply and demand on a nationwide scale to see how large-scale changes in supply and demand can affect GDP.

Aggregate Supply

As you read earlier, market supply is the amount of a particular good or service available for purchase at all possible prices in an individual market. But how do we look at supply and prices on a macroeconomic level? Think of aggregate supply as a supply curve for the whole economy.

First, economists add up the total supply of goods and services produced for sale in the economy—in other words, GDP. Then they calculate the **price level**, the average of all prices in the economy. Now they can determine **aggregate supply**, the total amount of goods and services in the economy available at all possible price levels.

In a macroeconomy, as the prices of most goods and services change, the price level changes. Firms respond by changing their output—that is, their production, or real GDP, which is aggregate supply. For example, if the price level rises, it means that the prices of most goods and services are rising. Rising prices give firms an incentive to increase their output. After all, at higher prices, more goods and services sold means greater profits, at least until producers are forced to pay higher prices for intermediate goods. Similarly, as prices throughout the economy fall, companies' profits shrink. In response, they reduce their output.

The aggregate supply (AS) curve on a graph illustrates the relationship between prices and output supplied. Look at the aggregate supply curve in Figure 12.5. As the price level rises, real GDP, or aggregate supply, rises. As the price level falls, real GDP falls.

Aggregate Demand

Aggregate demand is the amount of goods and services in the economy that will be purchased at all possible price levels. As price levels in the macroeconomy move up and down, individuals and businesses change how much they buy.

For example, a lower price level translates into greater purchasing power for households, because the real value of money rises as price levels drop. The dollars that we hold are worth more at lower price levels than they are at higher price levels. Therefore, falling prices increase wealth and demand. This scenario is known as the wealth effect.

On the other hand, as the price level rises, purchasing power declines, causing a reduction in the quantity of goods and services demanded. The aggregate demand (AD) curve shows this relationship between price and real GDP demanded. As you can see from Figure 12.5, this curve (right-hand

price level *the average of all prices in the economy*

aggregate supply *the total amount of goods and services in the economy available at all possible price levels*

aggregate demand *the amount of goods and services in the economy that will be purchased at all possible price levels*

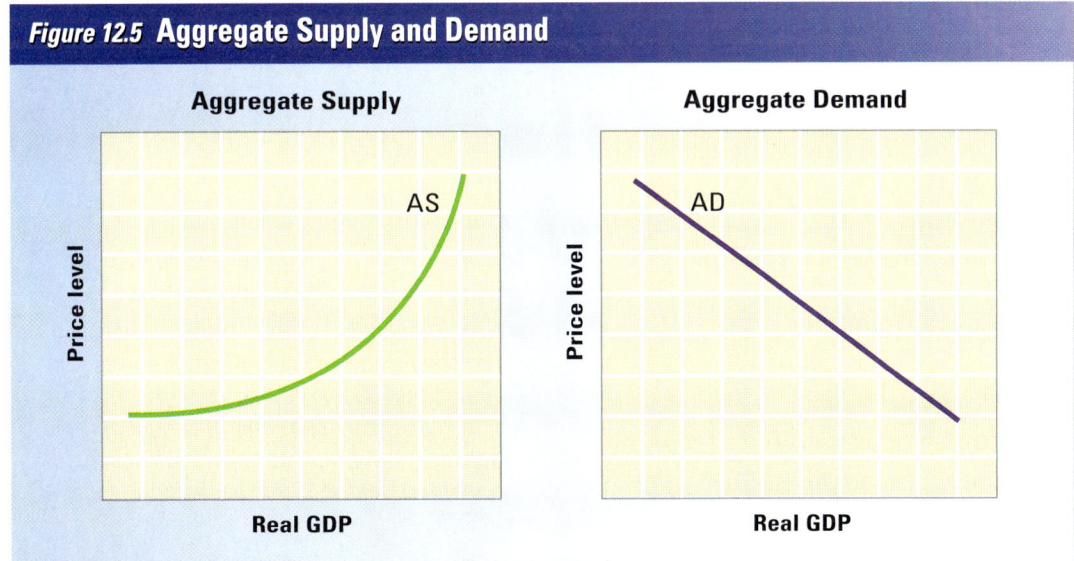

Figure 12.5 Aggregate Supply and Demand

Aggregate Supply

Aggregate Demand

These graphs show an aggregate supply curve and an aggregate demand curve.
Supply and Demand Explain what the positive (upward to the right) and negative (downward to the right) slopes of these curves mean.

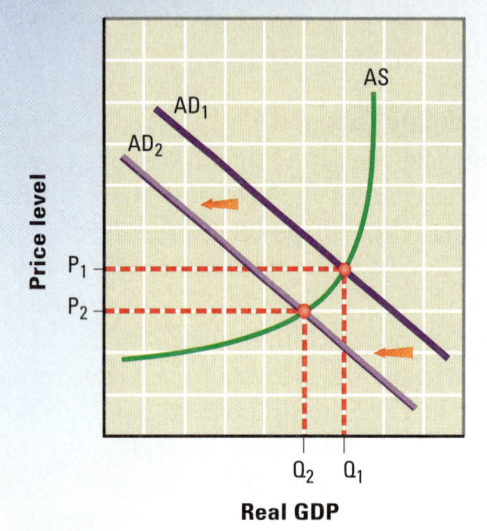

Figure 12.6 Equilibrium Aggregate Supply and Demand

Price level

AS

AD₁

AD₂

P₁

P₂

Q₂ Q₁

Real GDP

BUILDING KEY CONCEPTS

This graph shows AS/AD equilibrium. It also shows what happens to GDP and to the price level when aggregate demand shifts from AD₁ to AD₂.

Supply and Demand If a country goes to war, causing an increase in government demand for durable and nondurable goods, how might real GDP and price levels be affected?

graph) plots the total amount of goods and services demanded in the economy at various price levels. Like all demand

curves, it is negatively sloped (downward to the right).

Aggregate demand is made up of the same types of spending discussed earlier under the expenditure approach to calculating GDP. Consumers account for most of aggregate demand, but business spending on capital investment, government spending, and foreigners' demand for export goods all play roles, too.

Aggregate Supply/Aggregate Demand Equilibrium

When we put together the aggregate supply (AS) and aggregate demand (AD) curves, we can find the AS/AD equilibrium in the macroeconomy. Look at Figure 12.6. The intersection of the AS and AD₁ curves indicates an equilibrium price level of P₁ and an equilibrium real GDP of Q₁.

Now consider how GDP might change. Any shift in either the AS or AD curve will cause real GDP to change. For example, the graph shows aggregate demand falling from line AD₁ to line AD₂. As a result, the equilibrium GDP (Q₂) falls, and so does the equilibrium price level (P₂).

Any shift in aggregate supply or aggregate demand will have an impact on real GDP and on the price level. In the next section we will discuss some factors that may cause such shifts.

Section 1 Assessment

Key Terms and Main Ideas

1. What is the difference between **intermediate goods** and **final goods**?

2. How does **gross domestic product (GDP)** differ from **gross national product**?

3. How does **nominal GDP** differ from **real GDP**?

4. What economic activities are not included in GDP?

5. If **aggregate demand** rises, what happens to real GDP? What happens to the **price level**?

Applying Economic Concepts

6. *Critical Thinking* Why is GDP calculated by both the expenditure approach and the income approach?

7. *Math Practice* Suppose that a very small economy produces only televisions and computers. Determine nominal GDP and real GDP in Year 4, using the following information: *In Year 1, the base year, 10 computers sold at $2,000 each, and 15 televisions sold at $500 each. In Year 4, 17 computers sold at $2,200 each and 20 televisions sold at $550 each.*

Take It to the NET Collect real GDP data for the last six months. Analyze the data to determine what part of the business cycle the country is in right now. Use the links provided in the Social Studies area at the following Web site for help in completing this activity. **www.phschool.com**

Skills for
LIFE

Critical Thinking

Graphs and Charts

Social Studies

Technology

Predicting Consequences

Economists, politicians, and entrepreneurs use economic data as a window into the future. On the basis of past events and the current situation, they sometimes try to predict how an economy or an individual market will behave. Thousands of variables and events have an impact on an economy, so predictions will not always come true. However, one can observe broad trends in an economy and try to imagine what will happen if these trends continue into the future. Follow the steps below to analyze the table and use the data to make predictions about the American economy.

1. Identify the kinds of information in the table. The table below lists the number of new businesses started each year during a recent American economic boom. Also listed is the discount lending rate, one of the key factors that determines how expensive it is to borrow money to start a new business. The higher the discount rate, the more expensive it is to borrow money. Because the discount rate can rise or fall during the year, rates are given for January and December. Read the column headings and introductory notes for the table. (a) What information does this table give you for each year? (b) How much did the number of business starts change between 1997 and 1998?

2. Look for relationships within the data. Lower interest rates encourage people to invest in new businesses because the cost of borrowing money is lower. Because too much borrowing can lead to inflation, the Federal Reserve Bank will raise the discount rate if there is a lot of new investment in the economy. (a) How did the interest rates in 1993 and early 1994 compare with rates in other years? (b) How did the number of new businesses change between 1993 and 1994? (c) What is the relationship between interest rates and business starts from 1993 to 1995?

Additional Practice

Using the Internet or your local library, locate recent articles about the state of the economy and interest rates. What indicators do economists use to judge the health of the economy? Based on these indicators, do you think interest rates will go up, stay the same, or go down in the near future? Explain.

New Businesses, 1993–1999

Year	New Businesses Started	Discount Rate on January 1	Discount Rate on December 31	Rate Change
1993	166,154	3%	3%	0%
1994	188,387	3%	4.75%	+1.75%
1995	168,158	4.75%	5.25%	+0.5%
1996	170,475	5.25%	5%	-0.25%
1997	166,740	5%	5%	0%
1998	155,141	5%	4.5%	-0.5%
1999	151,016	4.5%	5%	+0.5%

Sources: Federal Reserve Bank of Minneapolis; *Statistical Abstract of the United States*, 2000

Business Cycles

Objectives

After studying this section you will be able to:

1. **Identify** the phases of the business cycle.

2. **Describe** four key factors that keep the business cycle going.

3. **Explain** how economists forecast fluctuations in the business cycle.

4. **Analyze** the impact of business cycles in U.S. history.

5. **Analyze** why U.S. business cycles may change in the future.

Section Focus

A business cycle consists of successive periods of improvement and decline in a macroeconomy. Policymakers study business cycles to try to predict declines, lessen their effects, and speed economic recovery.

Key Terms

business cycle
expansion
economic growth
peak
contraction
trough
recession
depression
stagflation
leading indicators

---

business cycle *a period of macro-economic expansion followed by a period of contraction*

expansion *a period of economic growth as measured by a rise in real GDP*

economic growth *a steady, long-term increase in real GDP*

peak *the height of an economic expansion, when real GDP stops rising*

contraction *a period of economic decline marked by falling real GDP*

Many economic analysts and historians of the nineteenth century recognized economic panics and collapses. But most did not see a pattern in the occurrence of these changes.

One early economist did see a pattern, however. He attributed it to, of all things, sunspots. In a way, his theory wasn't so crazy. William Stanley Jevons, a British economist of the mid-1800s, believed that periodic sunspot activity affected crop harvests. In the 1800s, when most people worked on farms, crop surpluses and shortages would have had widespread economic effects.

Economists long ago dismissed Jevons's sunspot theory, but they embraced his notion that the economy undergoes periodic changes. A modern industrial economy repeatedly experiences cycles of good times, then bad times, and then good times again. Business cycles are of major interest to macroeconomists, who study their causes and effects. In this section we will learn about these periodic swings in economic performance: how we describe them, what might cause them, and how they have shaped the country's economy.

Phases of a Business Cycle

As you read in Chapter 3, a **business cycle** is a period of macroeconomic expansion followed by a period of macroeconomic contraction. Figure 12.7 illustrates the phases of a business cycle.

Business cycles are not minor ups and downs. They are major changes in real GDP above or below normal levels. The typical business cycle consists of four phases: expansion, peak, contraction, and trough.

1. *Expansion*   An **expansion** is a period of economic growth as measured by a rise in real GDP. In economists' terms, **economic growth** is a steady, long-term increase in real GDP. In the expansion phase, the economy as a whole enjoys plentiful jobs, a falling unemployment rate, and business prosperity.

2. *Peak*   When real GDP stops rising, the economy has reached its **peak**, the height of an economic expansion.

3. *Contraction*   After reaching its peak, the economy enters a period of **contraction**, an economic decline marked by falling real GDP. Falling output generally causes unemployment to rise.

Figure 12.7 Tracking a Business Cycle

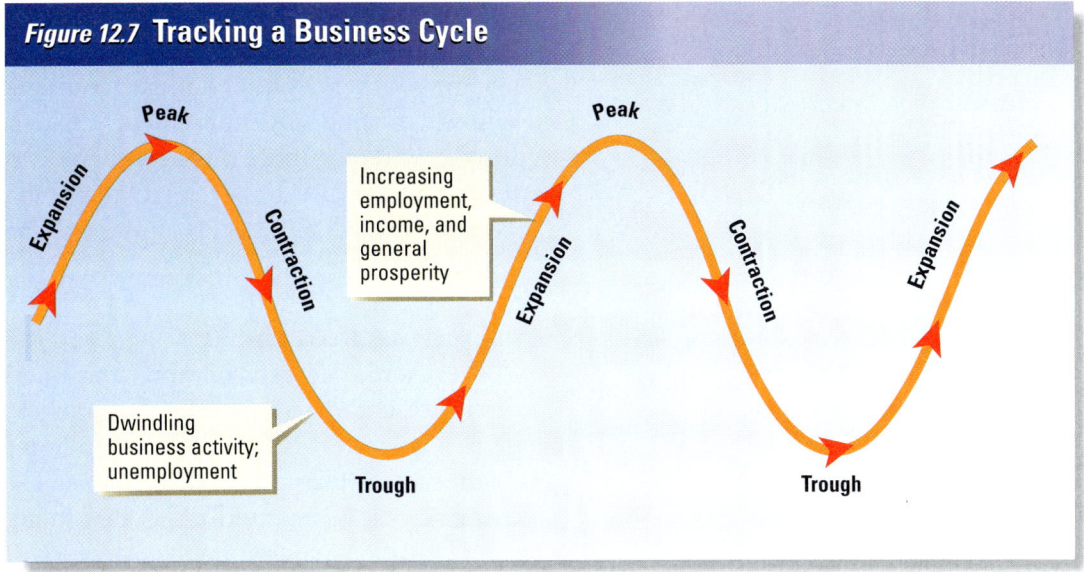

BUILDING KEY CONCEPTS

In a business cycle, a period of rising real GDP reaches a peak, then falls into a contraction. When the contraction reaches the low point, or trough, a new expansion begins. From 1854 to 1991, the United States had 31 business cycles. Excluding wartimes, the cycles averaged 48 months. **Gross Domestic Product** **In which part of a business cycle do you think the United States is right now—expansion or contraction? Give evidence to support your conclusion.**

4. *Trough* When the economy has "bottomed out," it has reached the **trough** (TRAWF), the lowest point in an economic contraction, when real GDP stops falling.

During the contraction phase, GDP is always falling. But other conditions, such as price levels and unemployment, may vary. Economists created terms to describe contractions with different characteristics and levels of severity. They include:

- *Recession* If real GDP falls for two consecutive quarters (at least six straight months), the economy is said to be in a recession. A **recession** is a prolonged economic contraction. Generally lasting from 6 to 18 months, recessions are typically marked by unemployment rising into the range of 6 percent to 10 percent.
- *Depression* If a recession is especially long and severe, it may be called a **depression**. The term has no precise definition but usually refers to a deep recession with features such as high unemployment and low factory output.

- *Stagflation* This term combines *stagnant*—a word meaning unmoving or decayed—and *inflation*. **Stagflation** is a decline in real GDP (output) combined with a rise in the price level (inflation).

Although economists know much about business cycles, they cannot predict any one cycle's behavior, nor can they tell exactly how long its phases will last. The only certainty is that a growing economy will eventually experience a downturn and will later bounce back.

What Keeps a Business Cycle Going?

The shifts that occur during a business cycle have many causes, some more predictable than others. Often, two or more factors will combine to push the economy into the next phase of a business cycle. Typically, a sharp rise or drop in some important economic variable will set off a series of events that bring about the

trough *the lowest point in an economic contraction, when real GDP stops falling*

recession *a prolonged economic contraction*

depression *a recession that is especially long and severe*

stagflation *a decline in real GDP combined with a rise in the price level*

next phase. Business cycles are affected by four main economic variables:

1. *business investment*
2. *interest rates and credit*
3. *consumer expectations*
4. *external shocks*

Business Investment

When the economy is expanding, firms expect sales and profits to keep rising. Therefore, they may invest heavily in new plants and equipment. Or they may invest in the expansion of old plants in order to increase the plants' productive capacity. All of this investment spending creates additional output and jobs, helping to increase GDP and maintain the expansion.

At some point, however, firms may decide that they have expanded enough or that demand for their products is dropping. They cut back on investment spending; as a result, aggregate demand falls. As Figure 12.8 shows, the result is a decline in the price level and in GDP. The drop in business spending reduces output and income in other sectors of the economy.

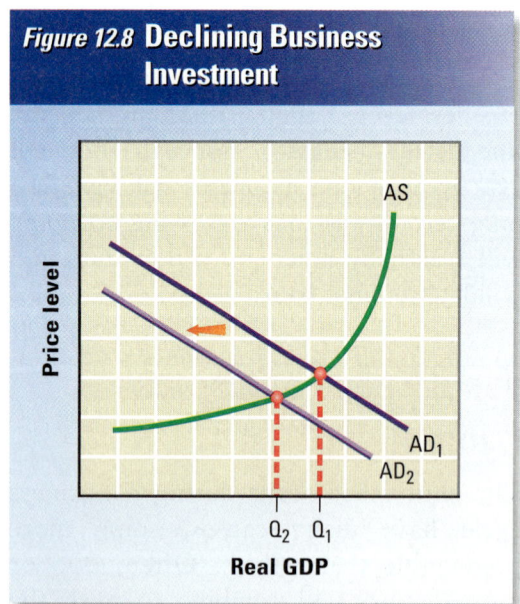

Figure 12.8 Declining Business Investment

Real GDP

This graph shows how a drop in business investment can affect the business cycle.

Supply and Demand On this graph, when business investment declines, what happens to (a) aggregate demand? (b) real GDP? (c) the price level?

Then industries that produce capital goods slow production down and begin to lay off workers. Other industries might follow, causing unemployment to rise. Jobless workers cannot buy new cars, eat at restaurants, or perhaps even pay their rent. The downward spiral picks up speed, and we find ourselves in a recession.

Interest Rates and Credit

In the United States economy, consumers often use credit to purchase "big ticket" items—from new cars and houses to home electronics, appliances, and vacations. The cost of credit is the interest rate that financial institutions charge their customers. If the interest rate rises, consumers are less likely to buy those new cars and homes and appliances.

Businesses, too, look to interest rates in deciding whether or not to purchase new equipment, expand their facilities, or make any other large investments that must be financed. For businesses, interest rates are a part of the opportunity cost of making investments.

When interest rates are low, companies borrow money to make new investments, often adding jobs to the economy. When interest rates climb, investment dries up, as does job growth. One result of rising interest rates, then, is less output and employment in the industries producing consumer and business goods. Such actions may lead to a contraction of the entire economy.

Consider a recent example of the impact of interest rates on the business cycle. In the early 1980s, high consumer interest rates helped bring on the worst economic slump in the United States since the Great Depression of the 1930s. Some credit-card interest rates reached 21 percent, and interest rates on home loans climbed as high as 17 percent. As a result, the cost of expensive items usually bought on credit was too high for many Americans.

As consumers reduced their spending, the economy entered a recession. The recession eventually drove up unemployment rates to over 9 percent—the highest since the Depression.

You can see, therefore, why economists watch interest rates closely. The rise and fall of borrowing rates has a great impact on the level of spending and real GDP in the economy.

Consumer Expectations

Consumer spending is determined partly by consumers' expectations. Fears of a weakening economy can cause consumer confidence to fall, meaning that a majority of people expect the economy to begin contracting. If that happens, consumers may start "saving for a rainy day," reducing their spending because they expect layoffs and lower incomes.

This reduced spending can actually help bring on a contraction, as firms respond to reduced demand for their products. Thus consumer expectations often become self-fulfilling prophecies, creating the very outcome that consumers fear.

Of course, the opposite can occur, too. If people expect a robust and rapidly growing economy, they will also expect abundant job opportunities and rising incomes. Thus, they will buy more goods and services. The rise in spending will create high aggregate demand, pushing up GDP. In other words, consumers can help create the very prosperity they anticipate!

External Shocks

Of all of the factors that affect the business cycle, perhaps most difficult to predict are external shocks, which you read about in Chapter 6. External shocks can dramatically affect an economy's aggregate supply.

Examples of negative external shocks include disruptions of the oil supply, wars that interrupt normal trade relations, and droughts that severely reduce crop harvests.

Let's consider what might happen if one of these shocks occurred. Suppose that the nation's oil supply were suddenly cut off. Immediately, the price of any remaining oil skyrockets.

This shock has a powerful effect on the economy. Oil is used to produce many

Figure 12.9 Negative External Shock

 Difficulties such as hurricanes, drought, war, and trade disputes can cause negative external shocks to the economy. **Supply and Demand** Compare the results of the negative shock shown on this graph with the results of declining business investment shown in Figure 12.8.

goods, and petroleum products fuel the trucks, trains, and airplanes that transport goods from factories to stores. The oil shortage forces firms to reduce production and raise prices for their goods. In other words, GDP declines and the price level rises.

Figure 12.9 illustrates this scenario. The negative shock raises costs of production and prices of final goods throughout the economy. The aggregate supply (AS) curve shifts to the left, reflecting higher prices and lower real GDP. This is the stagflation that you read about on page 311. It is particularly harmful to businesses and households and difficult for policymakers to fix.

Of course, an economy may also enjoy *positive* external shocks to its aggregate supply. The discovery of a large deposit of oil or minerals will contribute to a nation's wealth. A growing season with a perfect mix of sun and rain may create bountiful harvests that drive food prices down. Positive shocks tend to shift the AS curve to

THE WALL STREET JOURNAL.

CLASSROOM EDITION

In the News *As this excerpt from a Wall Street Journal Classroom Edition article shows, business cycles influence people's spending and borrowing habits, incomes, and employment.*

"Consumers [pay] off their credit-card bills faster than ever, as a strong economy and low borrowing costs [leave] many families flush with cash. . . .

"'Late in an economic expansion, the vast majority of consumers are in the best shape they are ever going to be in. In this expansion, consumers are in great shape, home values are high, incomes are up and jobs are plentiful,' says Robert Barbera, chief economist at Hoenig & Co., an investment and economic consulting firm."

leading indicators *key economic variables that economists use to predict a new phase of a business cycle*

the right, lowering the price level and increasing real GDP.

External shocks usually come without much warning. The other key factors capable of pushing an economy from one phase of the business cycle to another are more predictable. So economists track business investment, interest rates, and consumer expectations in order to more accurately forecast changes in the business cycle.

Business Cycle Forecasting

Predicting changes in a business cycle is difficult for a number of reasons. To predict the next phase of a business cycle, forecasters must anticipate movements in real GDP before they occur. This is no easy task, given the large number of factors that influence the level of output in a modern economy.

Government and business decision makers need accurate economic predictions to respond to changes in a business cycle. For instance, if businesses expect a contraction, they may reduce inventories and postpone building new factories. If government policymakers expect a contraction,

they may launch spending and taxation measures to try to prevent a recession.

Economists have many tools available for making these predictions. The **leading indicators** are a set of key economic variables that economists use to predict a new phase of a business cycle.

The stock market is one leading indicator. Typically, the stock market turns sharply downward a short time before a recession begins. Recessions do not *always* follow downturns in the stock market, but the pattern is fairly regular. Combined with other leading indicators, stock market movements can help economists predict a contraction.

The Conference Board, a private business research organization, maintains an index of ten leading economic indicators, including stock prices, interest rates, and manufacturers' new orders of capital goods. Economists and policymakers closely watch this index, which is updated monthly. However, like the other important tools used to forecast changes in the business cycle, it is not altogether reliable, since it sometimes predicts events that don't occur. (See "Economic Indicators" in the Economic Atlas and Databank, pages 538–539, for data relating to the Index of Leading Economic Indicators and other economic measures.)

Business Cycles in American History

Economic activity in the United States has indeed followed a cyclical pattern. Periods of GDP growth alternate with periods of GDP decline.

The Great Depression

As you read earlier, before the 1930s many economists believed that when an economy declined, it would quickly recover on its own. This explains why, when the U.S. stock market crashed in 1929, and the economy took a nosedive, President Herbert Hoover felt little need to

Global Connections

Global Economic Decline Like a deadly virus, the Great Depression quickly spread throughout much of the world. Latin America took a hard hit when U.S. markets for its goods dried up. Europeans depended on the United States for investments and loans, which became scarce. Industrial production fell by 40 percent in Germany, 14 percent in Britain, and 29 percent in France. "Hoovervilles," the makeshift shelters of the homeless named after President Hoover, sprang up in cities around the world. A photo from the era shows a British man wearing a sign that described the plight of many: "I know 3 trades / I speak 3 languages / Fought for 3 years / Have 3 children / And no work for 3 months / But I only want one job."

change his economic policies. The crisis, however, did not just go away.

One look at Figure 12.10 shows that the Great Depression did not rapidly cure itself. Rather, it was the most severe economic downturn in the history of industrial capitalism. Between 1929 and 1933, GDP fell by almost one third, and unemployment rose to about 25 percent. One out of every four workers was jobless, and those who could find work often earned very low wages.

As the effects of the Great Depression spread throughout the world, it affected economists' beliefs about the macroeconomy. The Depression, along with the publication of John Maynard Keynes's *The General Theory of Employment, Interest, and Money*, pushed economists to consider the idea that modern market economies could fall into long-lasting contractions.

In addition, many economists accepted Keynes's idea that government intervention might be needed to pull an economy out of a depression. You'll read more about Keynes and his ideas in Chapter 15.

The depression also affected American politics. Rejecting Hoover, voters in 1932 elected the Democratic governor of New York, Franklin Delano Roosevelt, to the presidency. Roosevelt soon began a series of government programs designed to get people back to work.

Programs such as the Works Progress Administration and the Civilian Conservation Corps got able-bodied workers back on the job and earning income, which they would then spend supporting their families. In this way, spending increased throughout the economy.

Not until the United States entered into World War II did the country completely recover from the Great Depression. The sudden surge in government defense spending boosted real GDP well above pre-depression levels.

Some Later Recessions

Thankfully, no economic downturns since the 1930s have been nearly as severe as the

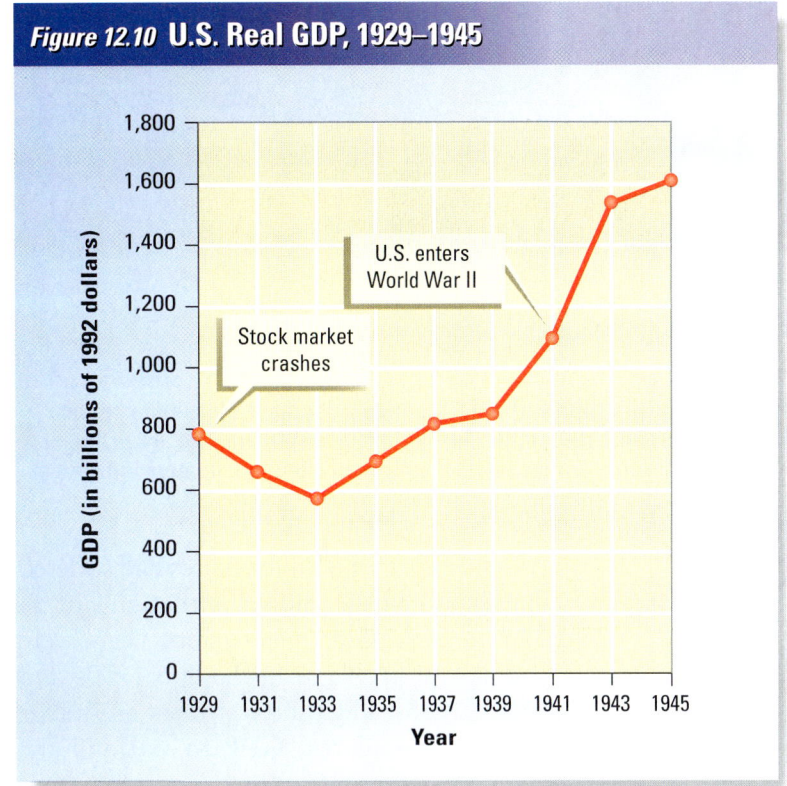

Figure 12.10 U.S. Real GDP, 1929–1945

As this graph shows, output (real GDP) dropped dramatically during the Great Depression. With factories idle, thousands of Americans lost their jobs and their homes. **Unemployment What accounts for the rise in real GDP in the early 1940s?**

Great Depression. We have had recessions, though.

In the 1970s, an international cartel, the Organization of Petroleum Exporting Countries (OPEC), launched an embargo on oil shipped to the United States and quadrupled the price of its oil. These actions caused external shocks in the American oil market. As oil prices skyrocketed, raw material costs rose, and the economy quickly contracted into a period of stagflation.

Reeling from higher-than-ever prices for gasoline and heating fuel prices, Americans began looking for ways to conserve energy. They turned down their heat, bought smaller, more fuel-efficient cars, and began researching energy alternatives to petroleum. When the United States and other nations developed more of their own energy resources, OPEC finally lowered its oil prices.

▲ When the supply of OPEC petroleum decreased, gasoline prices shot up. Limited supplies closed some gas stations. The green flag at this California gas station meant that only those customers with even-numbered license plates could buy rationed gas that day.

mists began to suggest that the nature of the business cycle had changed. Perhaps we had learned how to control recessions and promote long-term growth.

In early 2001, however, the U.S. growth slowed. Companies began predicting reduced profits. Economists hoped the decline would be short lived, but then the terrorist attacks of September 11 on the World Trade Center and the Pentagon resulted in a sharp drop in consumer spending. The economy fell into a recession. The hotel, airline, and tourism industries were especially affected. Unemployment rose as many hard hit companies laid off employees. Although spending gradually increased following the attacks, many companies blamed their performance problems on September 11.

Many economists expect steady improvement and predict that the recession will be relatively mild. The economic slowdown in 2001, however, suggests that the economy will continue to experience the normal patterns of peaks and troughs during the 21st century. The terrorist attacks remind us that there will always be unexpected events that affect economic performance. Still, the active role of the Fed in cutting interest rates and the government's commitment to stabilize the economy through fiscal policy may help to reduce the severity of recessions in the future.

Once again the United States had suffered an economic downturn, although not as severe as the Great Depression. There were additional problems in the late 1970s and early 1980s. High interest rates and other factors caused real GDP to fall and the unemployment rate to rise to over 9 percent in the early 1980s.

The Future of U.S. Business Cycles

Following a brief recession in 1991, the U.S. economy grew steadily, with real GDP rising each year during the 1990s. The country enjoyed record growth, low unemployment, and low inflation. Some econo-

Section 2 Assessment

Key Terms and Main Ideas

1. Which phase of a **business cycle** can lead an economy into recession?

2. How can interest rates push a business cycle into a **contraction?**

3. Why is the stock market considered to be a **leading indicator** of economic change?

4. How did the Great Depression affect economists' beliefs about the macroeconomy?

Applying Economic Concepts

5. *Critical Thinking* At which point in a business cycle would you prefer to be, the peak or the trough? Why?

6. *Try This* Draw a line graph of a business cycle in which the peak occurs when the real GDP reaches $4.9 trillion ($4,900 billion) and the trough occurs at $4.3 trillion. Label the expansion, peak, contraction, and trough. Use Figure 12.10 as a model.

Take It to the NET Find a first-person description of life during the Great Depression. Briefly describe the conditions the person faced, and explain how he or she was affected by the business cycle. Use the links provided in the Social Studies area at the following Web site for help in completing this activity. **www.phschool.com**

Profile

ANDREW CARNEGIE (1835–1919)

Andrew Carnegie's hard work and determination helped him rise from poverty to wealth and power. He inherited a strong commitment to workers from his father, but he also was ruthless when dealing with his own employees. He was deeply committed to charity, and is remembered today for the his huge charitable endowments.

Escape from Poverty

If you had known the Carnegie family when Andrew was born, you would never have predicted his financial success. The Carnegies lived in Dunfermline, Scotland. The town formerly produced the finest damask linens in England, but the industry had declined and Andrew's father, a weaver, did not have enough work to support his family. Hearing that conditions were better in America, the family left Scotland and arrived in Pittsburgh, Pennslyvania, in 1848.

Pittsburgh was a booming industrial city, growing rapidly but suffering the effects of pollution. Carnegie later wrote that "if you washed your face and hands they were as dirty as ever in an hour. The soot gathered in the hair and irritated the skin . . . ." Carnegie was determined to improve his life.

At first, Carnegie worked as a telegraph messenger, then as the personal telegrapher to the superintendent of the western division of the Pennsylvania Railroad. Eventually, he became superintendent himself. By 1856, he had saved enough money to begin investing in other companies, and by 1863 he was earning $40,000 a year from his investments. In 1899, he founded the company that grew into Carnegie Steel Co., Ltd.

Mixed Treatment of Workers

Carnegie often spoke out in support of working people, no doubt remembering his own humble beginnings. But he ran his own business ruthlessly. In a brutal confrontation between striking workers and management guards, three workers and seven guards were killed. Carnegie expressed horror at the bloodshed. Once the union was crushed, however, Carnegie cut wages and imposed longer workdays. He gave his steel workers only one day off during the entire year: the Fourth of July.

Charitable Commitments

In 1901, Carnegie sold Carnegie Steel to J.P. Morgan. Carnegie personally earned $250 million from the sale—or about $4.5 billion in today's dollars. He then retired from business as one of the wealthiest people in the world.

In retirement, Carnegie gave more than $350 million to a wide range of philanthropic causes—over $3 billion in current dollars. He supported education, world peace, libraries, and research. Today, he is also remembered for creating music halls (the most famous one, in New York City, bears his name) and over 3,000 public libraries.

CHECK FOR UNDERSTANDING

1. Source Reading How did Andrew Carnegie use the technological developments of the Industrial Revolution to become one of the richest people in the world?

2. Critical Thinking Are today's entrepreneurs able to make the same degree of charitable contributions as Carnegie? Why or why not?

3. Learn More Use the Internet to learn more about major Carnegie endowments such as the Carnegie Endowment for International Peace.

Preview

Objectives

After studying this section you will be able to:

1. **Analyze** how economic growth is measured.
2. **Understand** capital deepening and how it contributes to economic growth.
3. **Analyze** how saving and investment are related to economic growth.
4. **Summarize** the impact of population growth, government, and foreign trade on economic growth.
5. **Identify** the causes and impact of technological progress.

Section Focus

Economic growth is a steady, long-term increase in a nation's real GDP that tends to raise living standards. Primary contributors to long-term growth include capital deepening, saving and investing, and advances in technology. The other factors that affect economic growth are population, government, and foreign trade.

Key Terms

real GDP per capita
capital deepening
saving
savings rate
technological progress

Most of us would agree that as far as material possessions go, Americans are much better off today than they were 100 years ago. Why is this so?

Economic growth has allowed successive generations to have more and better goods and services than their parents. Long-term increases in real GDP allow an entire society to improve its quality of life, especially its standard of living. (See Chapter 3.)

A hundred years ago, most American families would have been able to own an icebox, a wood-burning stove, and a horse or bicycle. For most of us today, those necessities of life have turned into a refrigerator-freezer, a microwave oven, and a car or two. Think about the differences between these two sets of products!

Americans have been enjoying a fairly steady rise in their standard of living.
Standard of Living By about how much did real GDP per capita increase between 1970 and 2000?

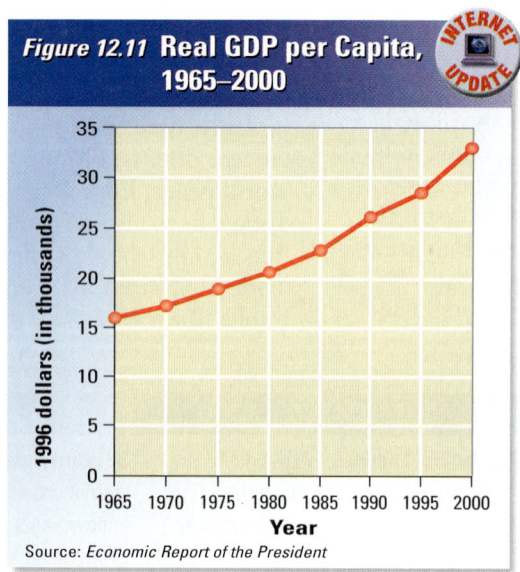

Figure 12.11 Real GDP per Capita, 1965–2000

1996 dollars (in thousands)

Year

Source: *Economic Report of the President*

Measuring Economic Growth

The basic measure of a nation's economic growth rate is the percentage change of real GDP over a given period of time. For example, the real GDP in 1990 was $6.7 billion, and in 2000, it was $9.3 billion. The economic growth rate for this time period was about 38 percent (($9.3 billion – $6.7 billion) ÷ $6.7 billion × 100).

GDP and Population Growth

Over time, a nation's population tends to grow. Real gross domestic product, if it is to satisfy the needs of a nation's growing population, must keep up with the growth

Figure 12.12 Economic Health of Selected Countries

Country	GDP per capita (2000 dollars, in thousands)	GDP growth (average annual % change in growth, 1990–2000)	Secondary-school expenditure per student, 1998 (in dollars)	Life expectancy at birth, 1998 (men/women)	Unemployment rate (% of labor force, 1998, men/women)	% change in consumer prices, 2000
U.S.	36.0	+3.3	7,764	73.9/79.4	4.1/4.3	2.1
Czech Rep.	14.0	+0.2	3,182	71.1/78.1	7.4/10.5	4.5
France	23.2	+1.8	6,605	74.6/82.2	9.9/13.1	1.8
Germany	24.9	+1.7	6,209	74.5/80.5	8.3/9.3	2.0
Japan	25.6	+1.3	5,890	77.2/84.0	4.8/4.5	-0.8
Korea	17.7	+6.1	3,544	70.6/78.1	7.1/5.1	3.4
Mexico	9.0	+3.5	1,586	72.4/77.0	1.8/2.6	5.9
Turkey	6.8	+3.5	not available	66.4/71.0	7.6/6.6	67.3
U.K.	23.9	+2.2	5,230	74.6/79.7	6.8/5.1	1.6

Source: Organization for Economic Cooperation and Development, 2001

The statistics shown here are typically used as indicators of a country's living standards. **Standard of Living (a) How does the economic health of the United States compare to that of the other countries shown here? (b) What countries seem to have the most-healthy and the least-healthy economies?**

rate of the population. This is one reason that economists prefer a measure that takes population growth into account. For this, they rely on **real GDP per capita**, which is real GDP divided by the total population (*per capita* means "for each person").

This measure is considered the best measure of a nation's standard of living. As long as real GDP is rising faster than the population, real GDP per capita will rise, and so will the standard of living. Economists can see how the standard of living has changed over time by comparing real GDP per capita from two different time periods. They can also use per capita growth rates to compare the economies of two different nations.

GDP and Quality of Life

We can use GDP to measure standard of living, which relates to material goods. We cannot use it, however, as a complete measure of people's quality of life. As you read in Section 1, GDP excludes many factors that affect the quality of life, such as the state of the environment or the level of stress that individuals feel in their daily lives. In addition, while real GDP per capita represents the average output per person in an economy, it tells us nothing about how the output is distributed. A nation may have relatively high real GDP per capita, but if most of the income goes to relatively few people while the majority earn next to nothing, the typical person will not enjoy a very high standard of living.

Despite these facts, real GDP per capita is a good starting point for measuring a nation's quality of life. Nations with greater availability of goods and services usually enjoy better nutrition, safer and more comfortable housing, longer life spans, better education, and other indicators of a favorable quality of life.

Since economic growth has an enormous impact on quality of life, economists devote significant resources to figuring out what causes the nation's real GDP to rise. They

real GDP per capita
real GDP divided by the total population

capital deepening
process of increasing the amount of capital per worker

saving *income not used for consumption*

savings rate *the proportion of disposable income that is saved*

focus on the roles of capital goods, technology, and a few related factors.

Capital Deepening

Physical capital, the equipment used to produce goods and services, makes an important contribution to the output of an economy. With more physical capital, each worker can be more efficient and productive, producing more output per hour of work. Economists use the term *labor productivity* to describe the amount of output produced per worker.

With a labor force of a given size, more physical capital will lead to more output—in other words, to economic growth. This process of increasing the amount of capital per worker, called **capital deepening,** is one of the most important sources of growth in modern economies. (See Figure 12.13.)

Figure 12.13 Effects of Capital Deepening

Labor force

+

Human capital → Physical capital

↓

Increased labor productivity

↓

Increased output

↓ ↓

Increased wages | Increased labor demand

This diagram shows the beneficial effects of capital deepening.
Money Suppose you own a small clothing shop. Why should buying a new line of clothes for an upcoming season and providing special training for sales staff result in capital deepening?

Human capital, the productive knowledge and skills acquired by a worker through education and experience, also contributes to output. Firms, and employees themselves, can deepen human capital through training programs and on-the-job experience. Better-trained and more-experienced workers can produce more output per hour of work. As the United States moves toward a service-oriented economy, human capital becomes another vital source of growth.

Capital deepening—whether it be physical capital or human capital—increases output per worker. It also tends to increase workers' earnings. To understand why this happens, consider the effect of greater worker productivity on the demand for workers. As you read in Chapter 9, if workers can produce more output per hour, they become more valuable to their employers. As a result, employers will demand more workers. This increase in demand will increase the equilibrium wage rate in the labor market.

So, with a labor force of a given size, capital deepening will increase output and workers' wages. But how does an economy increase its stock of capital per worker? It does so through saving and investment.

Saving and Investment

To help us understand how saving and investment are related, let's consider an economy with no government sector and no foreign trade. In this simplified economy, consumers and business firms purchase all output. In other words, output can be used for consumption (by consumers) or investment (by firms). Income that is not used for consumption is called **saving.**

Since output can only be consumed or invested, whatever is not consumed must be invested. Therefore, in this simplified economy, saving is equal to investment. The proportion of disposable income that is saved is called the **savings rate.**

To see this another way, look at an individual's decision, as shown in Figure 12.14.

Shawna had an after-tax income of $30,000 last year, but she spent only $25,000. That left her with $5,000 available for saving. She used some of her leftover income to purchase shares in a mutual fund (stocks and bonds). She put the rest of the money into her bank account.

Through her mutual-fund firm, her bank, and other intermediaries, Shawna's $5,000 was made available to businesses. The firms used the money to invest in new plants and equipment. So, when Shawna chose not to spend her entire income and decided instead to save some of it, the amount that she saved became available for business investment.

If we consider the economy as a whole, the process works the same way. If total saving rises, more investment funds become available to business firms, and they will spend more on capital. Those firms will use most of these funds for capital investment—for expanding the stock of capital in the business sector.

Higher saving, then, leads to higher investment, and thus to higher amounts of capital per worker. In other words, higher saving leads to capital deepening. Now we can understand why most nations promote saving. In the long run, more saving will lead to higher output and income for the population, raising GDP and the standard of living.

Population, Government, and Trade

Now we will consider a slightly more realistic economy that has population growth, a government sector, and foreign trade. First, think about the effect of the population growth on capital accumulation.

Population Growth

Population growth does not necessarily preclude economic growth. However, if the population grows while the supply of capital remains constant, the amount of capital per worker will shrink. This process, the opposite of capital deepening,

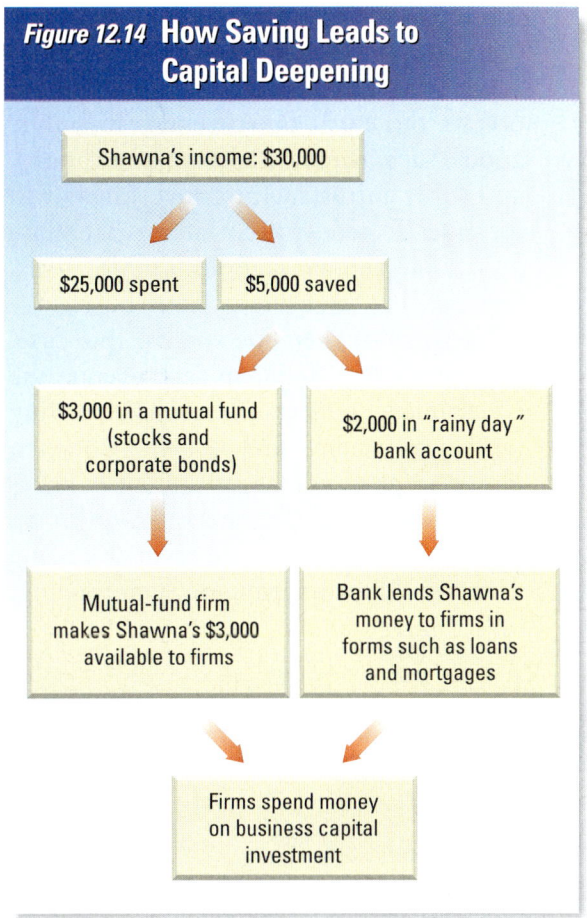

Figure 12.14 How Saving Leads to Capital Deepening

Shawna's income: $30,000

$25,000 spent $5,000 saved

$3,000 in a mutual fund (stocks and corporate bonds) $2,000 in "rainy day" bank account

Mutual-fund firm makes Shawna's $3,000 available to firms   Bank lends Shawna's money to firms in forms such as loans and mortgages

Firms spend money on business capital investment

This diagram shows how saving adds to GDP by creating capital.
Money If people saved a high proportion of their incomes, how might the economy be affected?

will lead to lower living standards. In fact, some relatively poor countries, such as India, have large labor forces but small capital stocks.

The result is that output per worker—and earnings per worker—are relatively low. Conversely, a nation with low population growth and expanding capital stock will enjoy significant capital deepening.

Government

Government can affect the process of capital deepening in several ways. If government raises tax rates to pay for additional services or to finance a war, households will have less money. People will reduce their saving, thus reducing investment. In these cases, the government is taxing households in order to pay for

technological progress *an increase in efficiency gained by producing more output without using more inputs*

consumption spending, and the net effect is reduced investment.

On the other hand, if government invests the extra tax revenues in public goods, such as roads, telecommunications, and other infrastructure, investment will increase. To see why, consider what share of income the average household saves. Suppose that, on average, households save 10 percent of their income. In this case, for every extra dollar in tax revenue the government collects, household saving (and investment) drops by 10 cents. However, government investment in infrastructure rises by $1. The net result is an increase in total investment of 90 cents. This would promote capital deepening,

since the government is taxing its citizens to provide investment goods.

Foreign Trade

Foreign trade can result in a trade deficit, a situation in which the value of goods a country *imports* is higher than the value of goods it *exports*. (You will read more about trade deficits in Chapter 17.) Running a trade deficit may not seem like a wise practice, but if the imports consist of investment goods, the practice can foster capital deepening. *Investment goods* are the structures and equipment purchased by businesses.

Capital deepening can help a country pay back its creditors because it is a source of economic growth. In the mid-1800s, for example, the United States financed the building of the transcontinental railroad in part by borrowing funds from investors in other countries. (See Figure 12.15.) The borrowing created a trade deficit, but it also helped create a much higher rate of economic growth than would have occurred without the borrowing. The railroad opened up vast areas to farming, which over time helped increase the nation's agricultural output by a huge amount.

Of course, not all trade deficits promote capital deepening. In this regard, trade deficits are similar to government taxation. Whether they encourage capital deepening and economic growth depends on how the funds are used. If they are used for short-term consumption, the economy will not grow any faster, and it will not have any additional GDP to pay back the debts. If the funds are used for long-term investment, however, they will foster capital deepening. The resulting economic growth will bring the country prosperity in the future.

Technological Progress

Another key source of economic growth is technological progress. This term usually brings to mind new inventions or new ways of performing a task, but in economics, it has a more precise definition. **Technological progress** is an increase in efficiency gained

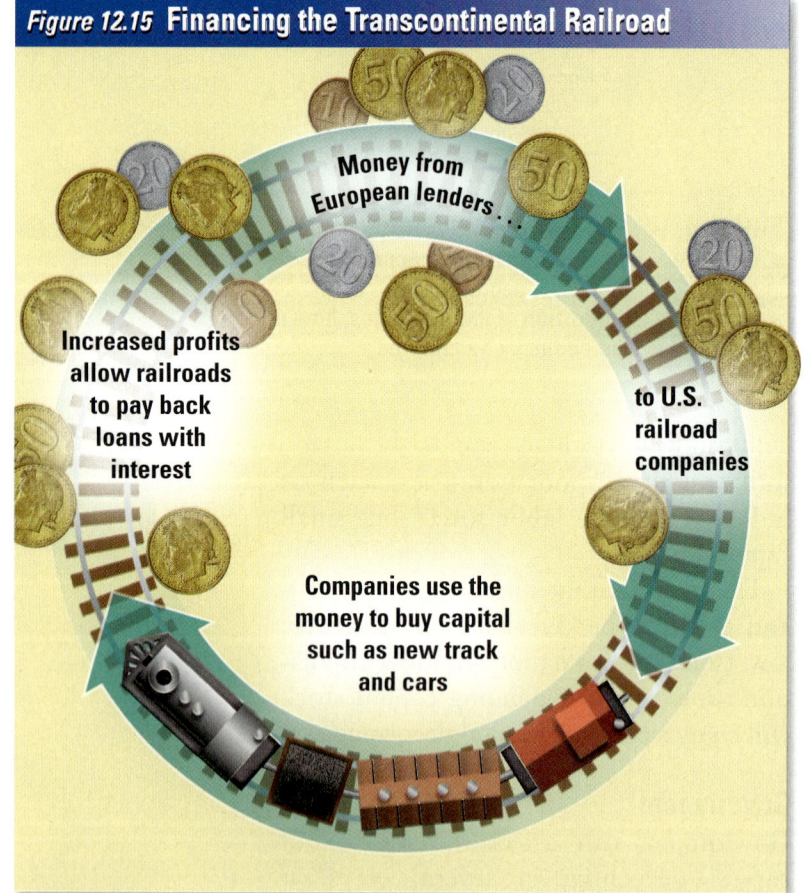

Figure 12.15 Financing the Transcontinental Railroad

Money from European lenders . . .

to U.S. railroad companies

Companies use the money to buy capital such as new track and cars

Increased profits allow railroads to pay back loans with interest

In the mid-1800s, railroad companies, eager to build a transcontinental line, borrowed money from foreign investors. The railroad, which was completed in 1869, made enough money to pay off the loans and return a profit.

Money How is the scenario shown here an example of capital deepening?

▲ Inventions such as desktop computers (right) contribute to America's technological progress. Just as important are new manufacturing processes, such as the use of robots in assembly lines (left), and new knowledge, such as medical breakthroughs.

by producing more output without using more inputs.

Technological progress occurs in many ways, as illustrated in the photographs above. It can come as new scientific knowledge that has practical uses. It can be a new machine that allows goods to be produced more efficiently. It may be a new method for organizing production. All of these advances raise a nation's productivity. Increased productivity means that we can produce more output with the same amounts of land, labor, and capital. With technological progress, a society can enjoy higher real GDP per capita, which leads to a higher standard of living.

Measuring Technological Progress

In most modern economies, the amount of physical and human capital changes all the time. So does the quantity and quality of labor and the technology used to produce goods and services. These interconnected variables work together to produce economic growth. How then can we isolate and measure the effects of technological progress?

Robert Solow, a 1987 Nobel Prize-winning economist from the Massachusetts Institute of Technology, developed a method for measuring the impact of technological progress on economic growth. Solow's method was to determine how much growth in output comes from increases in capital and how much comes from increases in labor. He concluded that any remaining growth in output must then come from technological progress.

Between 1929 and 1982, the average annual growth rate of real GDP was 2.92 percent. Using Solow's method, economist Edward Denison has estimated that technological progress boosted the real GDP 1.02 percent per year, on average. Increases in capital and labor were responsible for 0.56 percent and 1.34 percent of the average annual growth, respectively (2.92 − 0.56 − 1.34 = 1.02).

Causes of Technological Progress

Since technological progress is such an important source of economic growth, economists have looked for its causes. They have found a variety of factors that influence technological progress.

FAST FACT

Innovations in communication and transportation have revolutionized business efficiency in recent decades. Suppose a Michigan manufacturer needs a part from Japan to repair an essential tool on his automobile assembly line. He can contact the parts factory in Japan instantly through phone, fax, or email. Then, instead of waiting a week or more for the new part to arrive, he can receive the part in the morning through an overnight airline express service and have his assembly line up and running by afternoon.

1. Scientific research Scientific research can generate new or improved production techniques, improve physical capital, and result in better goods and services.

2. Innovation When new products and ideas are successfully brought to the market, output goes up, boosting GDP and business profits. Yet innovation often requires costly research. For companies to carry out research, they need some assurance that they will make a profit on the sale of a product.

That's why the government issues patents. A patent is an exclusive right to produce and sell a product for a given period, currently 20 years. A patent helps companies recover the cost of research by earning profits before its competitors are allowed to copy new products.

Government can aid innovation in other ways as well. Through organizations such as the National Science Foundation and the National Institutes of Health, the United States government sponsors so-called basic

research, the theoretical research that is often costly and might not bring a new product to market in a timely way.

3. Scale of the market Larger markets provide more incentives for innovation, since the potential profits are greater. For this reason, larger economies will come up with more technological advances.

4. Education and experience As you read earlier, firms can develop their human capital by providing education and on-the-job experience for workers. Human capital makes workers more productive and thus accelerates economic growth. It can also stimulate growth in another way. A more educated and experienced work force can more easily handle technological advances and may well create some new advances, too.

5. Natural resource use Increased natural resource use can create a need for new technology. For example, new technology can turn previously useless raw materials into usable resources. It can also allow us to obtain and use resources more efficiently, develop substitute new resources, and discover new resource reserves. Because price is based on the cost of obtaining a resource (and not necessarily on its scarcity), new technology can also lead to lower prices.

Section 3 Assessment

Key Terms and Main Ideas

1. **(a)** Why do economists measure **real GDP per capita? (b)** Why does real GDP per capita provide a better way to compare the economies of two different nations than does real GDP alone?

2. What is **capital deepening,** and how does it contribute to economic growth?

3. What role does **saving** play in the process of economic growth?

4. How do patents encourage **technological progress?**

Applying Economic Concepts

5. *Critical Thinking* You have read about the economic effects of the transcontinental railroad. What other communication and transportation systems might have similar effects? Write a paragraph analyzing these effects.

6. *Using the Databank* Turn to the graph "Personal Savings as a Percentage of Disposable Income" on page 540. What was the trend in savings between 1990 and 2000? How might this trend have affected capital deepening? Explain.

Take It to the NET

Create a brief oral presentation analyzing how a technological innovation has changed the way goods are manufactured, marketed, and distributed in the United States. Use the links provided in the Social Studies area at the following Web site for help in completing this activity. www.phschool.com

How Has Technology Affected Productivity?

Technology, according to Peter Zentz, "is the cornerstone of all the products we make." Zentz is an executive with Benthos, Inc., a manufacturer of underwater equipment such as cameras that operate on the ocean floor. Benthos cameras took the first underwater pictures of the RMS *Titanic* after its discovery.

"The technology that continues to be developed in our industry," says Zentz, "is truly remarkable. But what strikes me every day is the way in which other types of technology have enabled us . . . to efficiently serve our customers, communicate effectively with them and our workers . . . and keep precise records."

Teleconferencing Rick Gifford, a Benthos sales executive, believes that one of the greatest advancements for business is the technology that makes teleconferencing possible. "We used to spend hours, even days, bringing our sales representatives, customers, and field workers into our office for important meetings," he explains. "Through teleconferencing we get it done just as effectively, eliminate enormous expense, and no one has to be uprooted."

Photocopiers Zentz and Gifford, however, both agree that the computer is not their most indispensable technological device. "Believe it or not," says Zentz, "we've found that the copy machine is our most important piece of equipment. The thought of hand-copying the thousands of designs, research reports, written correspondence, and other documents that we generate every year boggles my mind."

Zentz is not alone in his opinion. In a recent survey, most office workers indicated that the photocopier is important to their productivity. But whatever the ranking, one thing is certain. Technology has changed the business world forever.

Applying Economic Ideas

1. How has technology affected office productivity?

2. The graph on the right shows annual total spending in the United States economy with and without technology. What can you conclude about the relationship of technology and GDP?

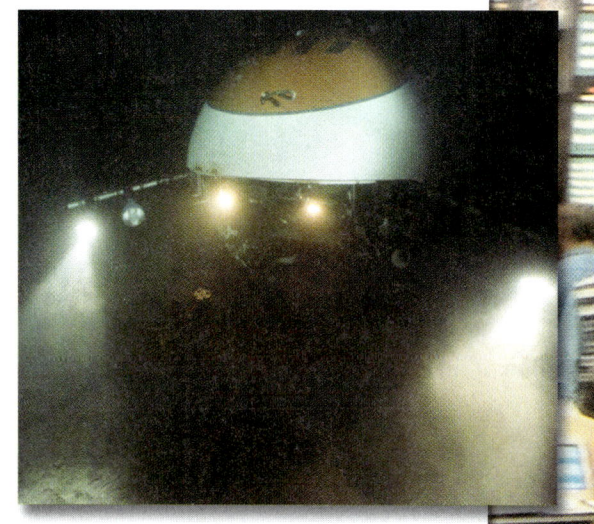

▲ High-tech underwater cameras help researchers study the ocean floor.

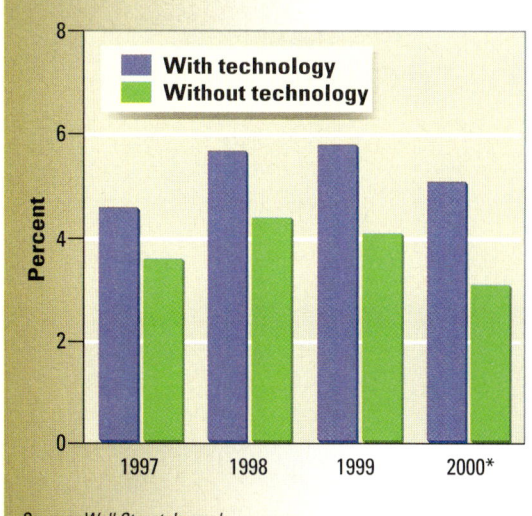

Annual Growth of Total Spending

- With technology
- Without technology

Source: *Wall Street Journal Classroom Edition*, March 2001

* Through third quarter

Chapter 12 Assessment

Chapter Summary

A summary of major ideas in Chapter 12 appears below. See also the **Guide to the Essentials of Economics**, which provides additional review and test practice of key concepts in Chapter 12.

Section 1 *Gross Domestic Product* (pp. 301–308)

Gross domestic product (GDP) is the most important measure of a nation's economic performance. GDP changes in response to shifts in **aggregate supply** and **aggregate demand**. GDP does have its limitations, however. Other measures are often used in addition to GDP when evaluating a nation's economy. **National income accounting** is a system that collects macroeconomic statistics.

Section 2 *Business Cycles* (pp. 310–316)

A business cycle includes four phases: **expansion, peak, contraction,** and **trough.** Policymakers study business cycles to try to predict downturns in the economy and take steps to lessen their effects and speed economic recovery. **Leading indicators** help economists take the pulse of the macroeconomy.

Section 3 *Economic Growth* (pp. 318–324)

Economic growth is a steady, long-term increase in real GDP and often results in higher living standards. **Capital deepening, saving** and investment, population growth, government, foreign trade, and **technological progress** affect economic growth. **Real GDP per capita** is considered the best measure of a nation's standard of living.

Key Terms

Complete each sentence by choosing the correct answer from the list of terms below. You will not use all of the terms.

gross domestic product	recession
	leading indicators
price level	business cycle
capital deepening	gross national
aggregate supply	product
intermediate goods	

1. _____ are goods used in the production of final goods.
2. A _____ can be described as a period of macroeconomic expansion followed by a period of contraction.
3. Economists use the term _____ to describe the dollar value of all final goods and services produced within a country's borders in a given year.
4. _____ occurs when the amount of capital per worker increases.
5. The _____ is the average of all prices in the economy.
6. A prolonged economic contraction is known as a _____.

Using Graphic Organizers

7. On a separate sheet of paper, copy the web map below. Complete the web map by filling in the circles with components of GDP. You may add more circles.

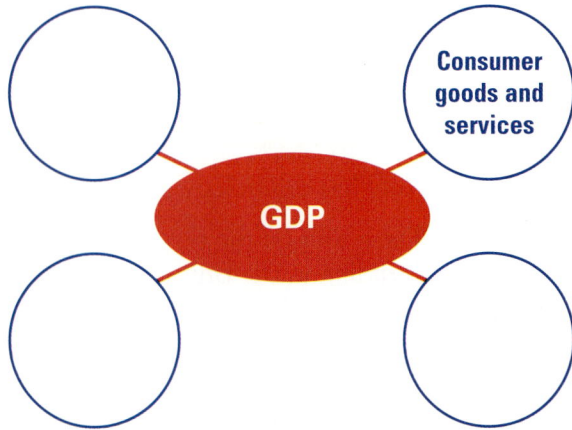

Consumer goods and services

GDP

Reviewing Main Ideas

8. List three limitations of using GDP as a measure of the nation's economy.

9. Identify four factors that keep the business cycle going.

10. Summarize the ways in which economists measure economic growth.

11. What is the difference between nominal GDP and real GDP?

Critical Thinking

12. Making Comparisons Compare the factors that propel the business cycle in peak periods. Which factor affects you most? Which is the most uncontrollable factor?

13. Drawing Inferences Why is real per capita GDP used to measure economic growth? In which ways is this measure more effective than other measures?

14. Synthesizing Information Explain why GDP is an accepted way of measuring the economy, despite its known drawbacks.

Problem-Solving Activity

15. A group of consumers claims that drug companies earn excessive profits because of the patents they have on drugs. They recommend cutting the length of time that a drug company can hold a patent to five years. They argue that this will lead to lower prices for drugs because competitors will enter the market after the five-year period. Are there any drawbacks to this proposal?

Skills for Life

Predicting Consequences Review the steps shown on page 309; then answer the following questions using the table below.

16. What is the topic of the table?

17. What economic indicators does the table show?

18. What time period do the data cover?

19. What trend can you find in these data?

20. How might you explain the trend in these data?

21. What prediction could you make on the state of the economy based on these data?

Economic Indicators

	Manufacturers' orders, consumer goods (1996 dollars, in millions)	Building permits (in thousands)	Money supply, M2 (1996 dollars, in billions)
Nov. 2000	177,156	1,614	4,535.80
Dec. 2000	174,852	1,553	4,565.80
Jan. 2001	167,820	1,724	4,591.20
Feb. 2001	170,582	1,663	4,620.30
March 2001	170,493	1,627	4,674.20

Source: The Conference Board

Economics Journal

Making Comparisons Compare the forecasts you collected. How are they similar? How do they differ? On what indicator does each article base its forecast? Which forecast is considered most reliable?

Take It to the NET

Chapter 12 Self-Test As a final review activity, take the Chapter 12 Self-Test in the Social Studies area at the Web site listed below, and receive immediate feedback on your answers. The test consists of 20 multiple-choice questions designed to test your understanding of the chapter content.
www.phschool.com

Increasing Productivity

Resources are limited, and people's wants and needs often exceed what is available. As a result of scarcity, people "economize" by trying to get the greatest benefits from their limited resources. In other words, they try to get as much as possible from those resources by increasing productivity. Productivity is usually measured by the amount of output per worker. In this lab you will explore how businesses try to obtain the greatest possible benefits from the fewest possible resources.

Materials

50 sheets of plain
8½" x 11" paper
6 student desks
3 scissors
10 pencils

▲ Specialization at this assembly line can lead to increased productivity.

Preparing the Simulation

One way that producers attempt to increase productivity is by dividing production into steps and assigning a step to each worker. Your task in this lab is to determine the impact this specialization, or division of labor, has on productivity.

Step 1: With a group of six of your classmates, form a "company" that builds paper airplanes. As a group, experiment and agree on a simple design for your company's airplane using only one half of an 8½" x 11" piece of paper (8½" x 5½"). Next, choose a company name, and print the name on both sides of the plane's fuselage. Each member of the company should practice making an airplane before beginning the lab activity.

Step 2: Gather your company's production resources as shown in the Materials box above. You already have one factor of production—your group's labor. Select one member to be quality control manager. The other members will be production workers. The quality control manager should inspect each worker's "practice" airplane using the following criteria: The plane must be made

from the correct size paper, it must be properly folded, and the company name should be printed correctly on both sides.

Step 3: As the "workers" assemble the factors of production, the quality control manager should prepare a chart by copying, on a separate sheet of paper, the Productivity Chart shown at right.

Conducting the Simulation

This simulation will consist of three four-minute "shifts," each of which is described on the next page. During each shift the group's six workers will "manufacture" airplanes. All workers must cease work immediately at the end of each shift.

Shift 1

Materials:
1 pair of scissors
1 pencil
2 desks

Procedure: Each worker must work alone to make his or her airplanes. The materials must be shared. After the four minutes is up, the quality control manager should inspect the airplanes and record the number of acceptable airplanes completed in the Shift 1 column on the Productivity Chart.

Shift 2

Materials:
1 pair of scissors
1 pencil
2 desks

Procedure: Before this shift begins, work as a group to break the production process into a series of steps. Include cutting the paper, folding, and writing the company name. Before the shift begins, assign group members to one of the steps and organize the new assembly line. When the shift ends, the quality control manager should record the number of acceptable airplanes completed in the Shift 2 column on the Productivity Chart.

Shift 3

Materials:
Using the costs listed on the Productivity Chart, decide as a group whether to purchase additional desks, scissors, or pencils for the purposes of increasing productivity or of adding a second assembly line. You may acquire a maximum of 6 desks, 3 scissors, and 10 pencils.

Procedure: Before the shift begins, record the costs of any new capital in the Shift 3 column on the chart and reorganize the new assembly line or lines. At the end of the shift, record the number of airplanes completed in the Shift 3 column on the chart.

Productivity Chart

	Shift 1	Shift 2	Shift 3
a number of acceptable airplanes completed			
b number of workers			
c cost of materials (25¢ per plane)			
d wages ($1.00 per worker)			
e factory rent ($1.00 per desk)	2.00	2.00	
f investment in equipment (50¢ per scissors) (25¢ per pencil)	.75	.75	
g total cost (c + d + e + f)			
h cost per airplane (g + a)			
i total time worked (b x 4 minutes)			
j output per minute (a + i)			
k productivity per worker (a + b)			

Simulation Analysis

Complete the productivity chart as a group; then discuss the following questions.

1. What effect did the division of labor in Shift 2 have on productivity?
2. What effect did investing in additional capital goods for Shift 3 have on productivity?
3. For which shift was the cost per airplane the lowest? The highest?
4. **Identifying Alternatives** If instead of making an additional capital investment in Shift 3, the company had laid off one or two workers, how might total production, costs, and productivity per worker (rows a, g, h, j, and k on the productivity chart) have been affected?

329

Chapter 13 Economic Challenges

Even in times of prosperity, unemployment, inflation, and poverty can affect large numbers of Americans. This chapter addresses the causes and effects of these economic challenges.

Economics Journal

The United States Census Bureau indicates that about 13 percent of Americans live in poverty. What images come to mind when you think of poverty? Think about these images. Then answer the following question in your journal: What is poverty?

Keep It Current

Items marked with this logo are periodically updated on the Internet. Keep up-to-date with what's in the news. To get current information on economic challenges go to **www.phschool.com**

Unemployment

Preview

Objectives

After studying this section you will be able to:

1. **Describe** frictional, seasonal, structural, and cyclical unemployment.
2. **Describe** how full employment is measured.
3. **Explain** why full employment does not mean that every worker is employed.

Section Focus

Even in good economic times, unemployment affects millions of Americans. The unemployment rate provides an important clue to the health of the entire economy.

Key Terms

frictional unemployment
seasonal unemployment
structural unemployment
cyclical unemployment
census
unemployment rate
full employment
underemployed
discouraged worker

In the late 1990s and early 2000s, unemployment in the United States hit record lows. Nevertheless, millions of Americans were looking for work, trying their best to get by on limited funds while they searched for a new job.

Unemployment, however, is not just a personal issue. It is an issue for the national economy. Economists can measure how healthy the economy is at any given time by counting the number of people who are unemployed. Congress, the President, and other policymakers pay close attention to these statistics so they can take the necessary action to get people back to work.

Economists look at four basic kinds of unemployment: frictional, seasonal, structural, and cyclical. The various kinds of unemployment have different effects on the economy as well as on the people who are unemployed.

Frictional Unemployment

Unemployment always exists, even in a booming economy. **Frictional unemployment** occurs when people take time to find a job. For example, people might change jobs, be laid off from their current jobs, need some time to find the right job after they finish their schooling, or take time off from working for a variety of other reasons. In the following examples Hannah, Jorge, and Liz are all considered frictionally unemployed.

- Hannah was not satisfied working as a nurse in a large hospital. Last month she left her job to begin looking for a position at a small health clinic.
- Since Jorge graduated from law school three months ago, he has been interviewing with various law firms to find the one that best suits his needs and interests.
- Liz left her sales job two years ago to care for an aging parent. Now she is trying to return to the work force.

None of these three people found work immediately after beginning his or her search. While they are looking for work, they are considered frictionally unemployed. In an economy as large and diverse as that of the United States, economists expect to find many people in this category.

Seasonal Unemployment

Gregory is a brick mason for a small construction company in the northeastern United States. Every winter Gregory's

frictional unemployment *unemployment that occurs when people take time to find a job*

▲ Seasonal unemployment affects migrant farm workers, who can be without work once the harvest season is over.

workers can also have periods of unemployment even during harvest season, depending on weather patterns that year. Heat, cold, rain, and drought can all ruin harvest schedules by causing fruits and vegetables to ripen sooner or later than expected. Instead of moving smoothly from crop to crop, migrant workers might lose work time waiting for a crop to be ready for picking.

Structural Unemployment

As you read in Chapter 9, the structure of the American economy has changed over time. Two centuries ago, people needed basic farming skills to survive. As the country developed an industrial economy, farm workers moved to urban areas to work in factories. Today, service industries are rapidly replacing manufacturing industries, and information services are expanding at breakneck speed.

All these shifts lead to upheavals in the labor market. When the structure of the economy changes, the skills that workers must have in order to succeed in the economy also change. Workers who lack the necessary skills lose their jobs. **Structural unemployment** occurs when workers' skills do not match the jobs that are available.

seasonal unemployment *unemployment that occurs as a result of harvest schedules or vacations, or when industries slow or shut down for a season*

structural unemployment *unemployment that occurs when workers' skills do not match the jobs that are available*

employer lays off all seven of his employees when cold weather forces an end to outdoor work. In the spring, he hires the workers back again to begin a new construction season. Gregory's yearly pattern of steady work followed by a predictable period of unemployment marks him as a seasonal worker.

In general, **seasonal unemployment** occurs when industries slow or shut down for a season or make seasonal shifts in their production schedules. It can also occur as a result of harvest schedules or vacations. When this school year ends, you or your friends may need some time to find the perfect summer job. If so, economists will count you as seasonally unemployed.

As with frictional unemployment, economists expect to see seasonal unemployment throughout the year. Government policymakers do not take steps to prevent this kind of unemployment, because it is a normal part of a healthy economy.

Still, the lives of seasonally unemployed workers can be extremely difficult. Migrant agricultural workers, for example, travel throughout the country to pick fruits and vegetables as various crops come into season. They know that their work will likely end when winter arrives. Migrant

► **With the invention of electric refrigerators, workers no longer made home deliveries of ice. The displacement of these workers is an example of structural unemployment.**

There are five major causes of structural unemployment.

- *The development of new technology* New inventions and ideas often push out older ways of doing things. For example, after the compact disc was introduced in 1982, fewer people bought phonograph records. Many workers who produced records and record players had to look for work in another field.
- *The discovery of new resources* New resources replace old resources and the industries that provide them. The discovery of petroleum in Pennsylvania in 1859 severely hurt the whale-oil industry and put many whaling ship crews out of work.
- *Changes in consumer demand* Consumers often stop buying one product in favor of another. Many people today favor sneakers and other sports shoes over more traditional kinds of shoes. As a result, traditional shoemaking jobs have declined.
- *Globalization* Recent trends in the world economy include a shift from local to global markets. As a result, companies often relocate jobs or entire facilities to another country. Celia, for example, had spent many years working on an automobile assembly line in Michigan. Then, in the late 1990s, the removal of trade barriers between the countries of North America led her company to move much of its auto assembly work to Mexico, where labor is less expensive. Celia lost her job.
- *Lack of education* People who drop out of school or fail to acquire the minimum skills needed for today's job market may find themselves unemployed, employed part-time, or stuck in a low-wage job. For example, Martin only barely managed to graduate from high school. When he was hired as a clerk by a local clothing store, he had trouble using the computerized checkout register. The store manager fired Martin after just two months because Martin lacked the skills needed for the job.

Policymakers in the 1990s recognized that computer technology, globalization, and other structural changes threatened the futures of many workers. As a result, they developed job-training programs to help workers gain new skills, especially computer skills.

Retraining takes a long time, however, and the new skills do not assure the trainees a high-wage job. Some companies have begun offering their own training programs. In this way, they can tailor the training to fit their exact labor needs. This approach gives more trainees the specific skills that can make them valued employees.

Cyclical Unemployment

Unemployment that rises during economic downturns and falls when the economy improves is called **cyclical unemployment**. During recessions, or downturns in the business cycle, the demand for goods and services drops. The resulting slowdown in production causes the demand for labor to drop as well, and companies begin to lay off employees. Many of these laid-off employees will be rehired when the recession ends and the business cycle resumes an upward trend. Although economists expect cyclical unemployment, it can severely

cyclical unemployment
unemployment that rises during economic downturns and falls when the economy improves

◄ Cyclical unemployment can affect workers in industries sensitive to changes in the business cycle, such as workers in the steel industry.

"Our days of living from pay check to pay check are over . . . I was laid-off."

▲ What might be the effects of the mother's job loss on her family?

census *an official count of the population*

unemployment rate *the percentage of the nation's labor force that is unemployed*

strain the economy and greatly distress the unemployed.

The most damaging example of cyclical unemployment in the twentieth century was the Great Depression. During the Great Depression, one out of every four workers was unemployed. Many remained jobless for years. To help these unemployed workers, President Franklin D. Roosevelt proposed, and Congress passed, the Social Security Act of 1935. In addition to providing payments for people who cannot support themselves, this act established a program of unemployment insurance. Today, this insurance provides weekly payments to workers who have lost their jobs. The payments usually provide about half of a worker's lost wages each week for a limited amount of time.

Measuring Employment

The amount of unemployment in the nation is an important clue to the health of the economy. For this reason, the government keeps careful track of how many people are unemployed, and why.

The United States Bureau of the Census conducts a monthly census relating to the size and other characteristics of the population. (A **census** is an official count of the population.) Each month, the Bureau of Labor Statistics (BLS), a branch of the U.S.

Department of Labor, polls a sample of the population. This sample, consisting of about 50,000 families, is designed to represent the entire population of the United States. The interviewers poll families about employment during that month. From this poll, called the Current Population Survey, the BLS identifies how many people are employed and how many are unemployed. Using these numbers, the BLS computes the **unemployment rate**, or the percentage of the nation's labor force that is unemployed.

Determining the Unemployment Rate

As you read in Chapter 9, the labor force is composed of civilians age 16 and older who have a job or are actively looking for a job. To determine the unemployment rate, BLS officials add up the number of employed and unemployed people. That figure equals the total labor force. Then they divide the number of unemployed people by the total labor force and multiply by 100. As Figure 13.1 shows, the result is the percentage of people who are unemployed.

For example, in April 2001, the Current Population Survey showed that 135.3 million people were employed, and 6.4

Figure 13.1 Calculating the Unemployment Rate

To calculate the unemployment rate, use the following formula:

Number of people unemployed **divided by** number of people in the civilian labor force **multiplied by** 100

For example,
if the number of people unemployed = 6.4 million and the number of people in the civilian labor force = 141.7 million

then,
$$6.4 \div 141.7 = .045$$
$$.045 \times 100 = 4.5$$

Therefore,
the unemployment rate is 4.5%.

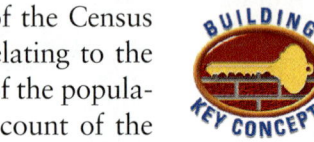

To calculate the unemployment rate, follow the steps above. **Unemployment** In 1982, the civilian labor force was 110.2 million, and 10.68 million people were unemployed. What was the unemployment rate?

million were unemployed. The total labor force, therefore, was 141.7 million. Dividing 6.4 million by 141.7 million, and then multiplying the result by 100, yields an unemployment rate of 4.5 percent for that month.

When you see the unemployment rate for a particular month, it has usually been "seasonally adjusted." This means that the rate has been increased or decreased to take into account the level of seasonal unemployment. Seasonally adjusting unemployment levels allows economists to compare unemployment rates from month to month in order to detect changing economic conditions.

The unemployment rate is only an average for the nation. It does not reflect differences from region to region, state to state, or even city to city. Some areas, such as the coal-mining region of Appalachia in the southeastern United States, have long had a higher-than-average unemployment rate. The BLS and individual state agencies therefore establish unemployment rates for states and other geographic areas. These rates help pinpoint trouble areas on which policymakers can focus attention.

Full Employment

Look at Figure 13.2. Notice the low levels of unemployment in the late 1960s and late 1990s. Do you think it is possible for the economy to reach an unemployment rate of 0 percent? As you read earlier, zero unemployment is not an achievable goal in a market economy, even under the best of circumstances. Economists generally agree that in an economy that is working properly, an unemployment rate of around 4 to 6 percent is normal. Such an economy would still experience frictional, seasonal, and structural unemployment. In other words, **full employment** is the level of employment reached when no cyclical unemployment exists.

Underemployment

Full employment means that nearly everyone who wants a job has a job, but are

Figure 13.2 **Unemployment Rate, 1964–2000**

Source: U.S. Department of Labor

Between 1964 and 2000, the unemployment rate peaked at an alarming 9.7 percent in 1982. **Unemployment** **In what years was the unemployment rate between 4 and 6 percent, the rate considered normal for a healthy economy?**

all those people satisfied with their jobs? Not necessarily. Some people working at low-skill, low-wage jobs may be highly skilled or educated in a field with few opportunities. They are **underemployed,** that is, working at a job for which they are over-qualified, or working part-time when they desire full-time work.

For example, Jim was a philosophy major in college. He went on to earn a graduate degree in philosophy. When he left school, Jim found that although the economy was booming, he could not find

full employment *the level of employment reached when there is no cyclical unemployment*

underemployed *working at a job for which one is over-qualified, or working part-time when full-time work is desired*

Global Connections

A Shorter Workweek During the early months of 1998, protests erupted throughout France. The reason—the nation's high unemployment rate. In response, the French government signed into law a shorter, 35-hour workweek that went into effect in January 2000. This new workweek, down from the standard 39 hours a week, is intended to create more than 200,000 new jobs and ease the country's 12.5 percent unemployment rate. Many economists, however, are skeptical of this solution. **How would a mandatory shorter workweek affect employment?**

discouraged worker *a person who wants a job but has given up looking*

jobs in which he could apply his knowledge of philosophy. Jim had many job choices, but none of them paid very well, and none of them challenged his mind. He was underemployed.

So was Celia, the auto worker described earlier. After her company sent her auto-assembly job to Mexico, she could not find a similar job in the local area, so she was forced to take a low-skill, low-wage job.

Underemployment also describes the situation of people who want a permanent, full-time job but have not been able to find one. Many part-time workers and seasonal workers fit this category.

Discouraged Workers

Some people, especially during a long recession, give up hope of finding work. These **discouraged workers** have stopped searching for employment and may need to rely on other family members or savings to support them. Discouraged workers, although they are without jobs, do not appear in the unemployment rate determined by the Bureau of Labor Statistics because they are not actively looking for work.

Effects of Terrorism

By late 2001, the employment picture had changed from the low levels of unemployment of the late 1990s and 2000. Even before the September 11 attacks on the World Trade Center and the Pentagon, the economic slowdown had brought U.S. unemployment to a four-year high. Studies estimate that the terrorist attacks cost the country an additional 1.5 to 2 million jobs.

Many of the lost jobs were in travel and tourism. The largest drop-off was in air transportation, accounting for about 20 percent of jobs lost.

The area of New York City around the World Trade Center site was especially hard-hit, with New York City losing some 150,000 jobs. Employment in New York City and in the nation as a whole is expected to improve as the economy returns to normal, and New York begins rebuilding.

Section 1 Assessment

Key Terms and Main Ideas

1. How do **frictional** and **structural unemployment** differ? Give an example of each.
2. When does **cyclical unemployment** take place?
3. How is the **unemployment rate** calculated?
4. Why isn't **full employment** the same as zero unemployment?

Applying Economic Concepts

5. *Math Practice* Determine the unemployment rate for a month in which 125.4 million people were employed and 7.3 million people were unemployed.

6. *Critical Thinking* After a car accident, Santo needed six months to recover. Since his recovery, he has spent the last year trying to find work in his former occupation, medical technology. So far, he has failed, even though the economy is booming. Which of the four kinds of unemployment best describes Santo's situation? Explain.

7. *Try This* Create two fictional workers, one a discouraged worker and one an underemployed worker. Write a paragraph explaining each person's employment situation. Include why these workers are discouraged or underemployed, their current financial situation, and their view of the future.

Take It to the NET

The Bureau of the Census and the Bureau of Labor Statistics provide information about unemployment rates. Find the most recent data on national unemployment. Is there a trend upward or downward in the unemployment rate, or has the rate been steady? Use the links provided in the Social Studies area at the following Web site for help in completing this activity.
www.phschool.com

Skills for LIFE

Critical Thinking

Graphs and Charts

Social Studies

Technology

Analyzing Bar Graphs

A bar graph is a useful way to present information visually and to condense large amounts of data. Bar graphs allow us to see the relationships between two or more sets of data, and to discern trends. Use the following steps to study and analyze the bar graph below.

1. Identify the subject. Bar graphs show one or more sets of data for a small group of items, such as cities, countries, or people. The title, axis labels, and key tell the reader what the graph depicts. (**a**) What is the title of the graph below? (**b**) What do the bars represent?

2. Read the data. While some graphs measure all data on the same scale, this bar graph uses two different scales for the *y-*, or vertical, axis. Two different scales are needed to show home prices and average income. Per capita income is shown on the left scale, while home prices are shown on the

right scale. (**a**) What is the per capita income in Houston? (**b**) Which city has the lowest housing costs? (**c**) How much does the average house cost in this city?

3. Interpret the graph. Look at the data and consider what you can learn from the bar graph. (**a**) Judging from the three cities with the least expensive houses, what conclusion can you draw about the relationship between geographic location and housing costs? (**b**) What does it mean if the housing bar is much taller than the income bar? (**c**) Compare the average income and housing cost in Phoenix with those in Houston. Which city is relatively cheaper to live in (housing costs divided by average per capita income)?

Additional Practice

Construct a bar graph using two sets of recent data on the economies of the United States, Canada, Germany, and Japan, such as inflation rate, income per capita, or unemployment rate. What can you infer from your bar graph about these economies? What other statistics might you have used instead?

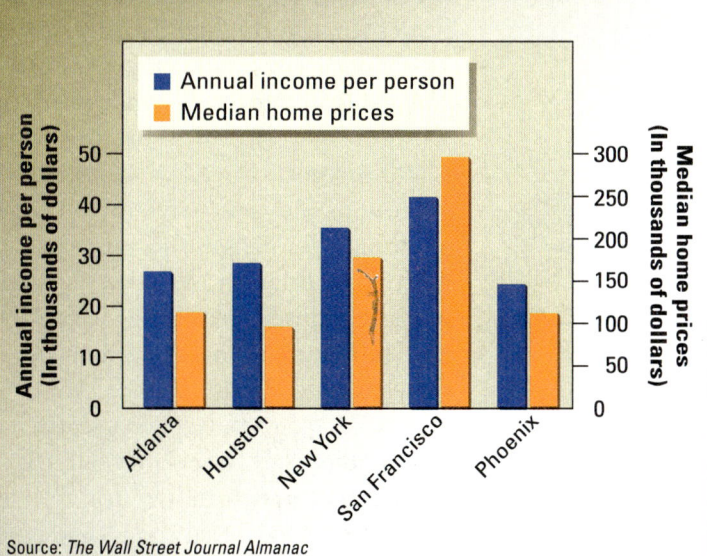

Source: *The Wall Street Journal Almanac*

337

Preview

Objectives

After studying this section you will be able to:

1. **Explain** the effects of rising prices.
2. **Understand** the use of price indexes to compare changes in prices over time.
3. **Identify** the causes and effects of inflation.
4. **Describe** recent trends in the inflation rate.

Section Focus

Economists use indexes to keep track of rising prices and to calculate the inflation rate. The level of inflation in the economy can affect wages, purchasing power, and other aspects of everyday life.

Key Terms

inflation
purchasing
  power
price index
Consumer Price
  Index (CPI)
market basket
inflation rate
core inflation
  rate

hyperinflation
quantity theory
demand-pull
  theory
cost-push
  theory
wage-price
  spiral
fixed income
deflation

---

inflation a general increase in prices

You may have heard your grandparents or other relatives talk about the "good old days," when you could get an ice cream for a nickel or a movie ticket for a quarter. They aren't kidding. Prices really were much lower years ago. On the other hand, although prices have generally risen, wages have risen, too. If you asked your older relatives how much they earned when they were young, you might find that it was difficult to scrape up that quarter for the movie ticket. In this section, you will learn why prices have risen, how economists measure their rise, and the effects of rising prices across the economy.

The Effects of Rising Prices

Josephine and Jack Barrow have owned the same house for 50 years. Recently, they had a real estate agent estimate the house's present market value. The Barrows were astounded. They had bought the house for $12,000, and now it was worth nearly $150,000—a rise in value of more than 1,100 percent.

How could the value of a house, or anything else, increase so much? The main reason is inflation. **Inflation** is a general increase in prices. Over the years prices rise and fall, but in the American economy, they have mostly risen. Since World War II, real estate prices have risen greatly.

The Barrows were pleased that they could get so much money for their house. They also realized that they could not buy a similar house in their area for $12,000 or even $120,000. Inflation had raised the

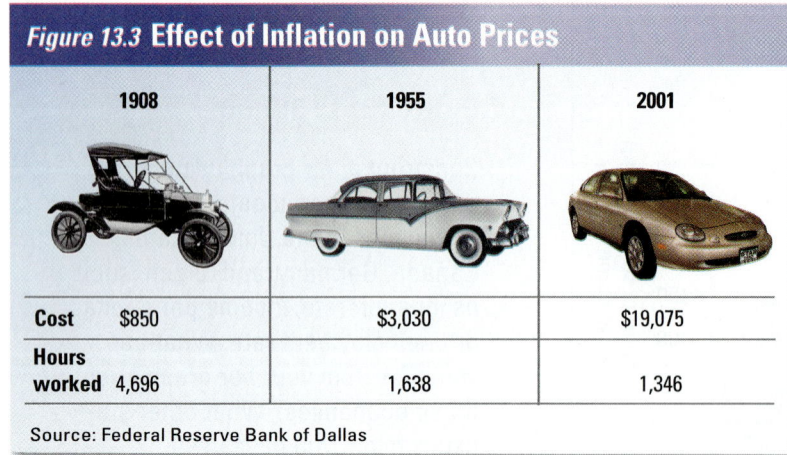

Figure 13.3 Effect of Inflation on Auto Prices

	1908	1955	2001
Cost	$850	$3,030	$19,075
Hours worked	4,696	1,638	1,346

Source: Federal Reserve Bank of Dallas

Inflation has driven up the price of an automobile even though the number of hours a worker must work to earn the money to pay for an automobile has decreased.
Income Why can more people afford automobiles today than they could in 1908, despite much higher auto prices?

prices of all houses, just as it had also raised wages and the price of most other goods and services.

Another way to look at the Barrows' situation is that inflation had shrunk the value, or purchasing power, of the Barrows' money. **Purchasing power** is the ability to purchase goods and services. As prices rise, the purchasing power of money declines. That is why $12,000 can buy much less now than it could 50 years ago.

Price Indexes

Housing costs are just one element that economists consider when they study inflation. The economy has thousands of goods and services, with millions of individual prices. How do economists compare the changes in all these prices in order to measure inflation? The answer is that they do not compare individual prices; instead, they compare price levels. As you read in Chapter 12, price level is the cost of goods and services in the entire economy at a given point in time.

To help them calculate price level, economists usually turn to a price index. A **price index** is a measurement that shows how the average price of a standard group of goods changes over time. A price index produces an average that economists can compare to earlier averages to see how much prices have changed over time.

Using Price Indexes

Price indexes help consumers and businesspeople make economic decisions. For example, after Marina read in the newspaper that consumer prices had been rising, she decided to increase the amount of money she had been saving to buy a new car. She wanted to be sure that when the time came to buy the car, she would have saved enough money for her purchase.

The government also uses indexes in making policy decisions. A member of Congress, for example, might push for an increase in the minimum wage if she thinks inflation has shrunk purchasing power.

Figure 13.4 CPI Market Basket Items

Category	Examples
Food and drinks	cereals, coffee, chicken, milk, restaurant meals
Housing	rent, homeowners' costs, fuel oil
Apparel and upkeep	men's shirts, women's dresses, jewelry
Transportation	airfares, new and used cars, gasoline, auto insurance
Medical care	prescription medicines, eye care, physicians' services
Entertainment	newspapers, toys, musical instruments
Education and communication	tuition, postage, telephone services, computers
Other goods and services	haircuts, cosmetics, bank fees

Source: Bureau of Labor Statistics

The CPI market basket helps economists calculate the average inflation rate for the country. **Inflation** Why might an individual family experience an inflation rate that is higher or lower than the national average?

The Consumer Price Index

Although there are several price indexes, the best-known index focuses on consumers. **The Consumer Price Index (CPI)** is computed each month by the Bureau of Labor Statistics (BLS). The CPI is determined by measuring the price of a standard group of goods meant to represent the "market basket" of a typical urban consumer. This **market basket** is a representative collection of goods and services. By looking at the CPI, consumers, businesses, and the government can compare the cost of a group of goods this month with what the same or a similar group cost months or even years ago.

As you can see from Figure 13.4, the CPI market basket is divided into eight categories of goods and services. Figure 13.4 shows these categories and a few examples of the many items in each group.

About every 10 years, the items in the market basket are updated to account for shifting consumer buying habits. The BLS determines how the market basket should change by conducting a Consumer Expenditure Survey. The BLS conducted one such survey from 1993 to 1995. For

purchasing power *the ability to purchase goods and services*

price index *a measurement that shows how the average price of a standard group of goods changes over time*

Consumer Price Index (CPI) *a price index determined by measuring the price of a standard group of goods meant to represent the "market basket" of a typical urban consumer*

market basket *a representative collection of goods and services*

inflation rate *the percentage rate of change in price level over time*

core inflation rate *the rate of inflation excluding the effects of food and energy prices*

each of these years, 4,800 families provided information on their spending habits. Another 4,800 families kept diaries in which they noted everything they purchased during a two-week period for each of the years. This process resulted in the list of market basket items used today.

Price Indexes and the Inflation Rate

Economists also find it useful to calculate the **inflation rate**, or the percentage rate of change in price level over time. Although there are other price indexes, the CPI is the index you will most often hear about, so we will focus on it. How does the BLS determine the CPI and use it to calculate the inflation rate?

Determining the CPI

To determine the CPI, the BLS establishes a base period to which it can compare current prices. Currently, the base period is 1982–1984. The cost of the market basket for that period is assigned the index number 100. Every month, BLS representatives update the cost of the same market basket of goods and services by rechecking all the prices. Each updated cost is compared with the base-period cost to determine the index for that month. As costs rise, the index rises.

The BLS determines the CPI for a given year using the following formula.

$$CPI = \frac{\text{updated cost}}{\text{base period cost}} \times 100$$

For example, suppose the market basket cost $200 during the base period and costs $330 today. The CPI for today would be:

$$\frac{\$330}{\$200} \times 100 = 165$$

In this example, the CPI rose from 100 in the base period to 165 today.

Calculating the Inflation Rate

To figure the inflation rate from one year to the next, you would use the steps shown in Figure 13.5. You can also determine the rate of inflation from month to month using the same basic formula that you see in this chart. Just substitute "Month A" and "Month B" for "Year A" and "Year B."

Types of Inflation

Inflation rates in the United States have changed greatly over time. From Figure 13.6, you can see that the inflation rate stayed fairly low in the 1960s. When the inflation rate stays low and averages between 1 and 3 percent, it does not typically cause problems for the economy. Businesses and governments can plan in this environment. However, economists have noted that when the inflation rate exceeds 5 percent, the inflation rate itself becomes unstable and unpredictable. This makes planning very difficult.

As you can also see in figure 13.6, the inflation rate sometimes spikes up sharply, as in 1974 and 1980. These sharp increases in the inflation rate were due in part to increases in prices in world food and oil markets. In order to study long-term trends in the inflation rate, analysts need to set aside temporary spikes in food and fuel prices. To do this, economists have developed the concept of core inflation rate. The **core inflation rate** is the rate of inflation excluding the effects of food and energy prices.

To calculate the inflation rate, follow the steps shown in the chart.
Inflation CPI for 1979 was 72.6. For 1980, CPI was 82.4. Calculate the inflation rate for 1980.

Figure 13.5 Calculating the Inflation Rate

To calculate the inflation rate, use the following formula:

CPI for Year A **minus** CPI for Year B **divided by** CPI for Year B **multiplied by** 100

For example,
if the CPI for 1999 (Year A) = 166.6 and the CPI for 1998 (Year B) = 163

then,

166.6 − 163 = 3.6

3.6 ÷ 163 = .022

.022 × 100 = 2.2

Therefore,
the inflation rate for 1999 was 2.2%.

By far the worst kind of inflation is **hyperinflation,** or inflation that is out of control. During periods of hyperinflation, inflation rates can go as high as 100 or even 500 percent per month, and money loses much of its value. This level of inflation is rare, but when it occurs it often leads to a total economic collapse.

Causes of Inflation

Where does inflation come from? Price levels can rise steeply when demand for goods and services exceeds the supply available at current prices, such as during wartime. They can also rise steeply when productivity is restricted, such as when a long drought leads to poor harvests.

Nobody can explain every instance of rising price levels. Economists, however, offer several theories about the causes of inflation. These include the quantity theory, the demand-pull theory, and the cost-push theory.

A full explanation of the reasons for inflation incorporates all three theories. Economists therefore look at all elements of this picture when they try to understand the inflation process.

The Quantity Theory

The **quantity theory** of inflation states that too much money in the economy causes inflation. Therefore, the money supply should be carefully monitored to keep it in line with the nation's productivity as measured by real GDP.

Economists at the University of Chicago developed a popular version of this theory in the 1950s and 1960s. They maintained that the money supply could be used to control price levels in the long term. The key to stable prices, they said, was to increase the supply of money at the same rate as the economy was growing.

Demand-Pull Theory

The **demand-pull theory** states that inflation occurs when demand for goods and services exceeds existing supplies. During wartime, for example, the needs of the

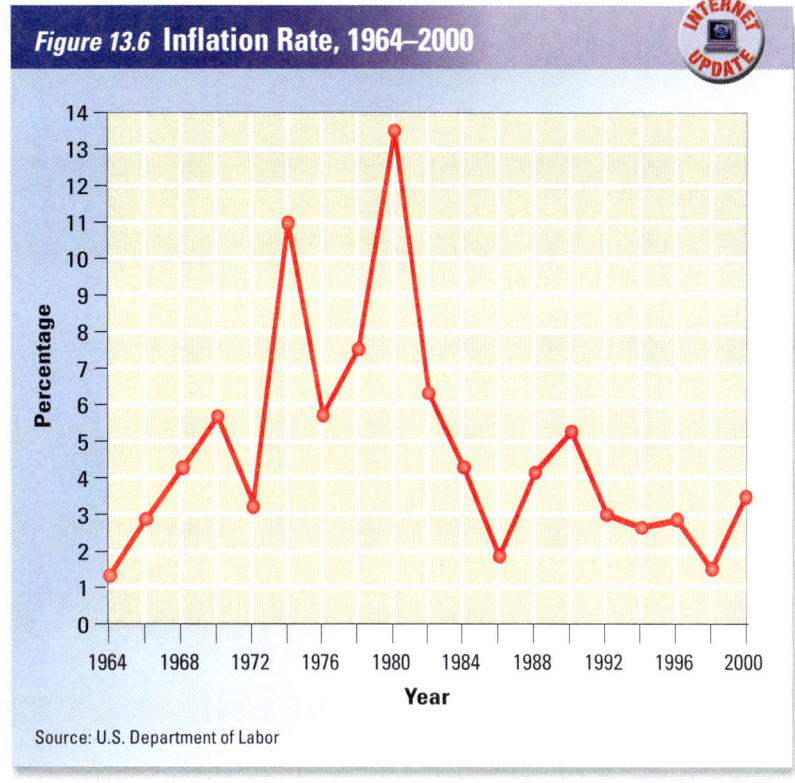

Figure 13.6 Inflation Rate, 1964–2000

Source: U.S. Department of Labor

Sharp inflation rate increases in 1974 and 1980 were due in part to increases in food and oil prices. An inflation rate of 1 to 3 percent does not typically cause economic problems. **Inflation** In what years was the inflation rate at a level where it would not cause problems for the economy?

government put pressure on producers. The heavy demand for new equipment, supplies, and services makes those items more valuable, forcing their prices up. Wages also rise as the demand for labor increases along with the demand for goods.

Cost-Push Theory

According to the **cost-push theory,** inflation occurs when producers raise prices in order to meet increased costs. Higher prices for raw materials can cause costs to increase. Wage increases, however, are most often the biggest reason, since wages are the largest single production cost for most companies.

Wage increases can come when low unemployment leads employers to offer higher wages in an effort to attract workers. Wage increases can also occur as a result of collective bargaining.

Assume, for example, that Jen is a union laborer at Am-Gro Fertilizer. Her

hyperinflation *inflation that is out of control*

quantity theory *theory that too much money in the economy causes inflation*

demand-pull theory *theory that inflation occurs when demand for goods and services exceeds existing supplies*

cost-push theory *theory that inflation occurs when producers raise prices in order to meet increased costs*

Figure 13.7 The Wage-Price Spiral

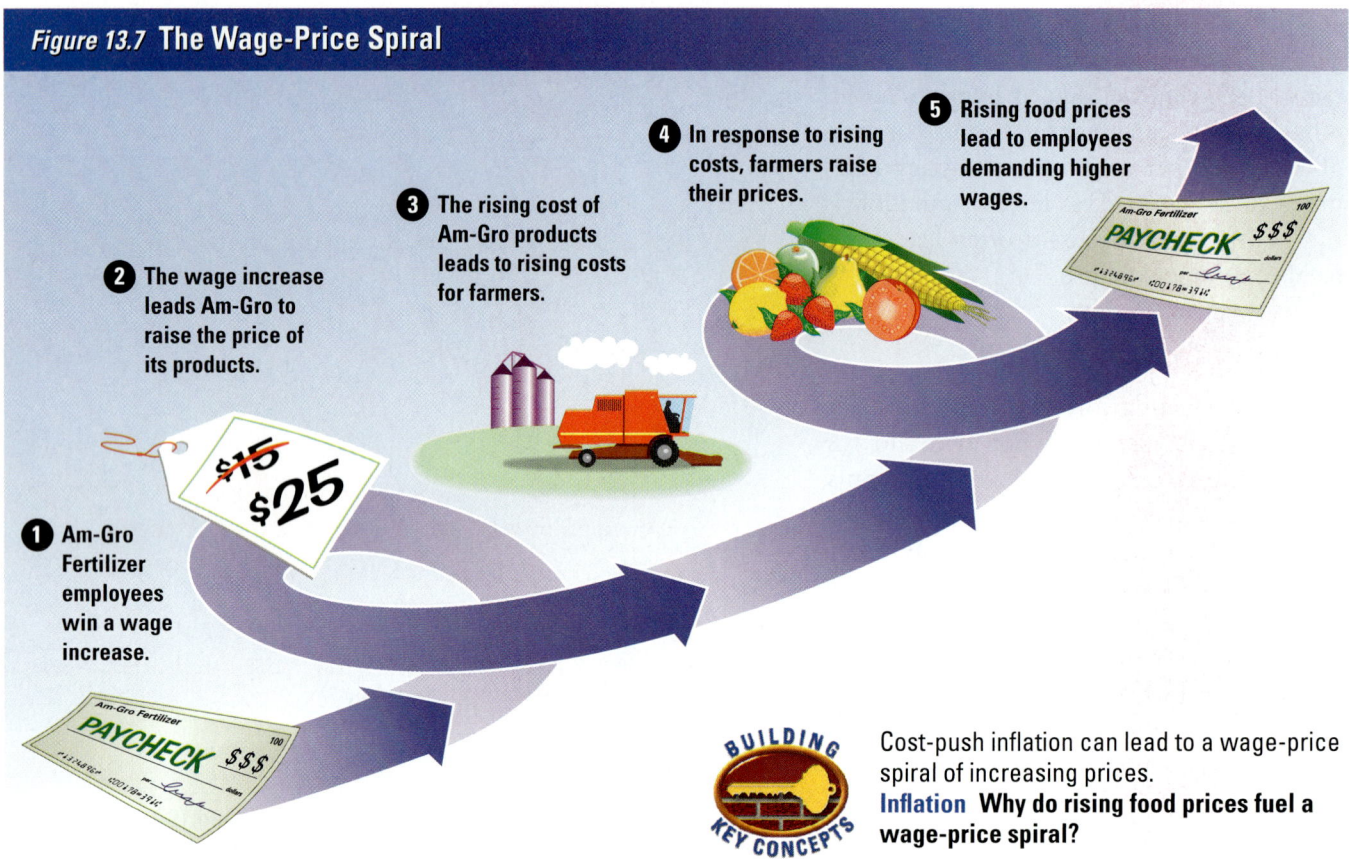

2 The wage increase leads Am-Gro to raise the price of its products.

3 The rising cost of Am-Gro products leads to rising costs for farmers.

4 In response to rising costs, farmers raise their prices.

5 Rising food prices lead to employees demanding higher wages.

1 Am-Gro Fertilizer employees win a wage increase.

BUILDING KEY CONCEPTS

Cost-push inflation can lead to a wage-price spiral of increasing prices.
Inflation Why do rising food prices fuel a wage-price spiral?

wage-price spiral *the process by which rising wages cause higher prices, and higher prices cause higher wages*

union recently won a large wage increase. This new cost has led Am-Gro to raise its prices to meet the higher payroll and maintain its profits.

Cost-push inflation can lead to a spiral of ever-higher prices. That is, one increase in costs leads to an increase in prices, which leads to another increase in costs, and on and on. The process by which rising wages cause higher prices, and higher prices cause higher wages, is known as the **wage-price spiral**. Figure 13.7 above shows how a wage-price spiral would affect Am-Gro Fertilizer.

Effects of Inflation

High inflation is a major economic problem, especially when inflation rates change greatly from year to year. Buyers and sellers find planning for the future difficult, if not impossible. The effects of inflation can be seen mainly in purchasing power, income, and interest rates.

Purchasing Power

You have seen, in the example of Jack and Josephine Barrow's house, how inflation can erode purchasing power. In an inflationary economy, a dollar will not buy the same number of goods that it did in years past. To take a simple example, suppose $1.00 would buy $1.00 worth of goods last year. If the inflation rate is 10 percent this year, however, $1.00 will buy the equivalent of only $.90 worth of goods today.

Income

Inflation sometimes, but not always, erodes income. If wage increases match the inflation rate, a worker's real income stays the same. People who don't receive their income as wages, such as doctors, lawyers, and businesspeople, can often increase their incomes to keep up with inflation by raising the prices they charge.

Not all people are so fortunate. The Barrows, for example, could be hit hard by inflation because they are retired and living on a **fixed income,** or income that does not increase even when prices go up. The portion of their income from Social Security rises with the price level, because the government raises Social Security benefits to keep up with inflation. Much of their income, however, comes from a pension fund that pays them a fixed amount of money each month. Inflation steadily eats away at the real value of that pension check.

Interest Rates

People receive a given amount of interest on money in their savings accounts, but their true return depends on the rate of inflation. For example, Sonia had her savings in an account that paid 7 percent interest. At the same time, the annual inflation rate was 5 percent. The purchasing power of Sonia's savings increased that year by 2 percent, not by 7 percent, because 5 percent of her savings was needed to keep up with inflation.

When a bank's interest rate matches the inflation rate, savers break even. The amount they gain in interest is taken away by inflation. Savers may even lose money if the inflation rate is higher than their bank's interest rate.

Recent Trends

Americans over age 30 have experienced positive inflation rates for most of their lifetimes. In the late 1990s, however, prices at times seemed to be falling. Some experts even predicted a period of **deflation,** or a sustained drop in the price level.

In addition, unemployment levels during the late 1990s and early 2000s remained low. Typically, when unemployment falls to very low levels, inflation increases. This makes sense because high unemployment means that companies have lots of workers to choose from. They do not have to lure skilled workers with high wages. When the pool of available workers shrinks, wages rise. Rising wages can push the inflation rate up, as you know from the discussion of the wage-price spiral.

In the late 1990s, however, unemployment fell to its lowest level in decades, and inflation crept along at less than 3 percent. Economists had different reactions to this phenomenon. Some suggested that the economy was just going through a lucky streak. Others maintained that the economy was returning to the normal levels of unemployment that had existed in the 1950s and 1960s.

fixed income *income that does not increase even when prices go up*

deflation *a sustained drop in the price level*

Section 2 Assessment

Key Terms and Main Ideas

1. How does **inflation** affect **purchasing power**? Give an example.
2. What is the purpose of the **Consumer Price Index (CPI)**?
3. What causes a **wage-price spiral**, and what can it lead to?
4. Why did the existence of low inflation and low unemployment in the 1990s puzzle some economists?

Applying Economic Concepts

5. *Math Practice* Suppose that the CPI for last year was 164 and that for this year it is 168. Calculate the inflation rate from last year to this year.
6. *Critical Thinking* If you had never experienced inflation, how might that affect your expectations about annual wage increases?
7. *Using the Databank* Turn to the chart on page 538 that shows the CPI Market Basket. **(a)** Which category of the CPI receives the highest percentage weighting? **(b)** Does this answer surprise you? Why or why not?

Take It to the NET Using CPI data for the past decade, write a short oral presentation regarding the impact of inflation on the economy. Use the links provided in the Social Studies area at the following Web site for help in completing this activity. **www.phschool.com**

Profile

Oprah Winfrey (b. 1954)

Determination and an uncanny ability to connect with her audience enabled Oprah Winfrey to become one of the richest and most powerful women in America. Remembering her roots, Oprah has used her substantial power in the media to raise awareness of important social and economic issues.

Raised in Poverty

Born in rural Mississippi, Oprah Winfrey spent her early childhood in extreme poverty on a farm, where she was raised by her grandmother after her mother moved north in search of work. At age 6, Winfrey was sent to Milwaukee, Wisconsin, to live with her mother and half brothers. The family struggled to survive on her mother's monthly $50 income as a servant.

Winfrey spent her early teens in and out of trouble until she went to live with her father in Nashville, Tennessee. Winfrey credits his strict discipline with saving her life. He required her to learn five new vocabulary words each day and read one book per week. "Getting my library card was like citizenship," Winfrey recalls. She soon excelled in school, and in her senior year, she got a part-time job reading the news for a local radio station.

The Oprah Winfrey Show

While studying speech and drama at Tennessee State University, Winfrey was offered a job anchoring the evening news at a local TV station. "Sure I was a token," she says, "But, honey, I was one happy token." After graduating in 1976, Winfrey took a job with a station in Baltimore,

Maryland. When the station demoted her from news anchor to talk show host, she discovered what she "was born to do."

In 1984, Winfrey moved to Chicago to take over a similar show. In 1985, it became *The Oprah Winfrey Show,* and the next year it began to air nationwide. By 1987, in a business dominated by white men, this African American woman had the most-watched talk show in America.

Oprah Gives Back

In exploring topics related to family abuse, poverty, and opportunity, Winfrey has confronted her own past in front of a national television audience. By offering a forum for such subjects, she has increased public awareness of important social and economic issues. Winfrey has also shared her success by contributing millions of dollars to schools and to her own Family for Better Lives foundation.

In 1997, Winfrey launched Oprah's Angel Network to encourage people to help those in need. Oprah's Angel Network has raised more than $3.5 million for scholarships for needy students. Working with Habitat for Humanity, Oprah's Angel Network has also built over 200 houses for low-income people across the nation.

CHECK FOR UNDERSTANDING

1. Source Reading Describe three ways in which Oprah Winfrey has used her position to address the issue of poverty in America.

2. Critical Thinking How are poverty and opportunity related? What effects does widespread poverty have on the nation's economy?

3. Learn More Use the Internet and other resources to learn more about efforts to improve the lives of poor people in the United States. Prepare a brief report on one specific public or private program.

Poverty

Objectives

After studying this section you will be able to:

1. **Define** who is poor, according to government standards.
2. **Describe** the causes of poverty.
3. **Analyze** the distribution of income in the United States.
4. **Summarize** government policies intended to combat poverty.

Section Focus

Despite the tremendous success of our nation's economy, millions of Americans remain poor. The government develops public policies and programs to try to combat poverty.

Key Terms

poverty threshold
poverty rate
income distribution
food stamps
Lorenz Curve
enterprise zone
block grant
workfare

What image comes to mind when you think of poverty? You might associate poverty with a homeless person on a city street or a poorly clothed child in a small rural house. Despite the success of the American economy, many Americans lack sufficient food, clothing, and shelter. In this section you'll read about the nature and causes of poverty, the distribution of income in the United States, and government programs designed to combat poverty.

The Poor

As you have read, the United States Bureau of the Census conducts extensive surveys to gather data about the American people. Then its economists analyze the data and organize it to reveal important characteristics, such as how many families and households live in poverty. The Census Bureau defines a family as a group of two or more people related by birth, marriage, or adoption who live in the same housing unit. A household is all people who live in the same housing unit, regardless of how they are related.

The Poverty Threshold

According to the government, a poor family is one whose total income is less than the amount required to satisfy the family's minimum needs. The Census Bureau determines the income level, known as the poverty threshold, needed to meet those minimum needs. The **poverty threshold** is the income level below which income is insufficient to support a family or household.

The poverty threshold, or poverty line, varies with the size of the family. For example, in 2000, the poverty threshold for a single parent under age 65 with one child

poverty threshold *the income level below which income is insufficient to support a family or household*

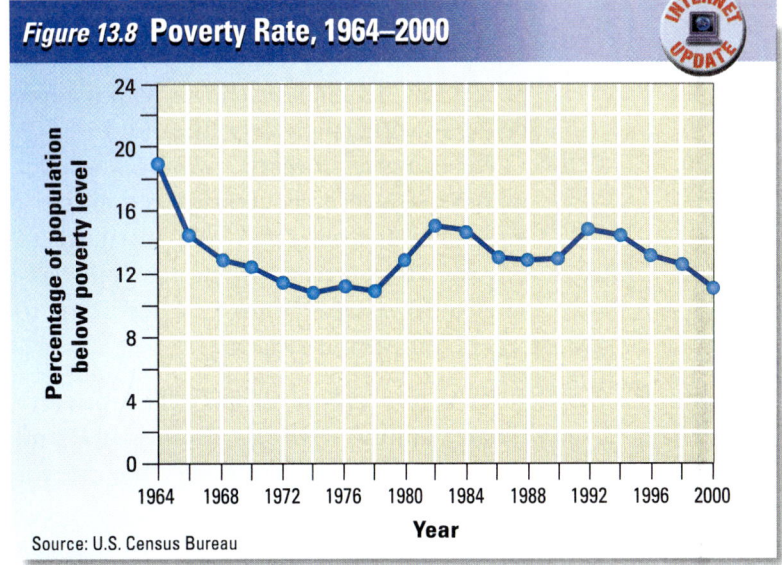

Figure 13.8 Poverty Rate, 1964–2000

Percentage of population below poverty level (y-axis: 0, 4, 8, 12, 16, 20, 24)

Year (x-axis: 1964, 1968, 1972, 1976, 1980, 1984, 1988, 1992, 1996, 2000)

Source: U.S. Census Bureau

The poverty rate began to decline during the 1960s, partly as a result of anti-poverty programs.
Income How did poverty rates during the 1990s compare with poverty rates during the 1960s?

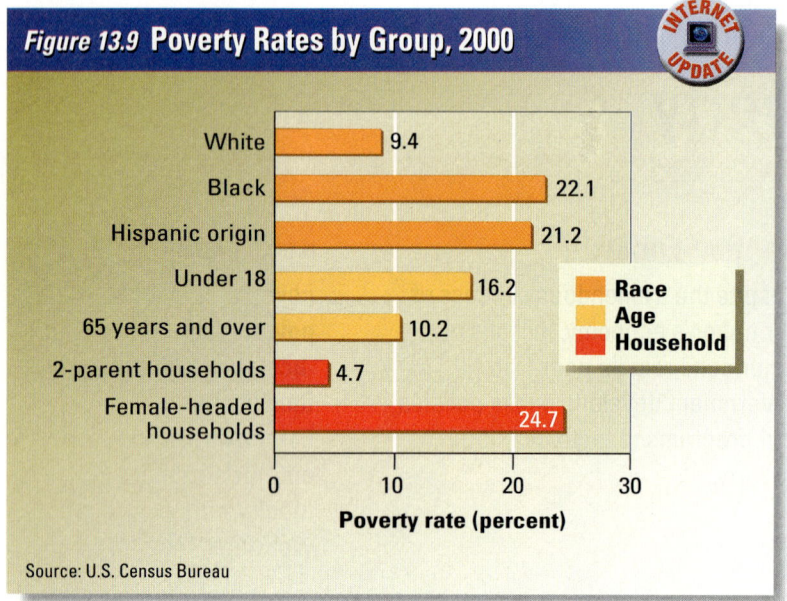

Figure 13.9 Poverty Rates by Group, 2000

INTERNET UPDATE

Group	Poverty rate (percent)
White	9.4
Black	22.1
Hispanic origin	21.2
Under 18	16.2
65 years and over	10.2
2-parent households	4.7
Female-headed households	24.7

Race
Age
Household

Poverty rate (percent)

Source: U.S. Census Bureau

BUILDING KEY CONCEPTS

Households headed by women, African Americans, and Hispanics are more likely than other groups to have incomes below the poverty threshold, as this recent data shows.

Income What percentage of African American families have incomes below the poverty threshold?

poverty rate *the percentage of people who live in households with income below the official poverty line*

was $11,869. For a family of four with two children, it was $17,463. If a family's total income is below the poverty threshold, everyone in the family is counted as poor.

The Poverty Rate

Figure 13.9 shows poverty rates for various groups. The **poverty rate** is the percentage of people who live in households with income below the official poverty threshold.

We can use poverty rates to discover whom the government considers to be poor and what factors seem to contribute to poverty. As you read in Chapter 3, poverty rates differ sharply by groups, according to several different indicators:

- *Race and ethnic origin* The poverty rate among African Americans and Hispanics is more than twice the rate for white Americans.
- *Type of family* Families with a single mother have a poverty rate almost six times greater than that of two-parent families.
- *Age* The percentage of children living in poverty is significantly larger than

that for any other age group. Young adults make up the next largest group in this category.

- *Residence* People who live in the inner city have double the poverty rate of those who live outside the inner city. People who live in rural areas also have a higher poverty rate, especially in regions where job prospects are limited.

Causes of Poverty

Put simply, a family is poor when the adults in the family fail to earn enough income to provide for its members' basic needs. This failure to earn adequate income is often the result of unemployment.

As you read in Section 1, millions of Americans are unemployed, for a variety of reasons. While they are out of a job, their families might well fall below the poverty threshold. Many other poor adults are not even considered a part of the labor force. Some suffer from chronic health problems or disabilities that prevent them from working.

Many poor adults do have jobs, however. In fact, more than half of poor households have someone who works at least part-time, and one in five have a full-time, year-round worker. For these "working poor," the problem is usually low wages or a limited work schedule, rather than the lack of a job. For example, Ray makes $7.90 an hour as a full-time clerk in a clothing store. While he is at work, his wife stays at home with their two young children. Although Ray works 40 hours per week, and his salary is well above minimum wage, his annual earnings amount to just over $16,400, which is below the poverty threshold for a family of four.

Economists agree that poverty and lack of income go hand in hand, but have different ideas about the causes of poverty. Here are some of the most important explanations for why some people are poor.

Lack of Education

The median income of high school dropouts in 1998 was $20,724, which was just above the poverty threshold for a family of five in that year. High-school graduates earned about one third more than dropouts, and college graduates earned about three times as much.

Location

In most cities of the United States, racial minorities are concentrated in the inner cities, far from the higher-wage jobs in suburban areas. Many inner-city residents do not own cars, and mass-transit systems are often not an efficient means of commuting from the inner city to the suburbs. As a result, people who live in the inner city earn less than people living outside the inner city. Similar obstacles exist for many people living in rural areas.

Racial and Gender Discrimination

White workers generally earn more than minority workers, and men generally earn more than women. Much of this income inequality can be explained by differences in hours worked, education, and work experience. Part of the inequality, however, results from racial and gender discrimination. Even when all the workers in a group are equally productive, whites are often paid more than African Americans, and men are often paid more than women. Economists agree, however, that this kind of discrimination has been diminishing.

Economic Shifts

People who lack education and skills are not very productive workers. For this reason they are often the "last hired and first fired." They are hired when the economy is expanding, and workers are hard to find, but they are the first to lose their jobs when the economy slows down. Also, workers without college-level skills have suffered in recent decades from the ongoing decline of manufacturing and the rise of service and high-technology jobs.

Shifts in Family Structure

The divorce rate has risen significantly since the 1960s, as has the number of children born to unmarried parents. These demographic shifts tend to result in more single-parent families and more children living in poverty.

Income Distribution

In 1999, the median household income in the United States was $40,816, which means that half the households earned more than this amount and half earned

▼ **People with college and advanced degrees generally earn much higher incomes than people with only high-school diplomas.**

Education Level: High School Diploma

Education Level: College Degree

Education Level: Advanced Degree

less. This figure, however, tells only part of the income story. In order to fully understand poverty in the United States, you also need to understand **income distribution,** or how the nation's total income is distributed among its population.

Income Inequality

The United States has millions of poor people, but it also has the one of the highest per capita GDPs in the world. How can that be? The answer lies in how the market distributes income. Figure 13.10 shows how income is distributed in the United States. These figures do not take into account the effects of taxes or noncash government aid such as housing subsidies, health care, or food stamps. **Food stamps** are government-issued coupons that recipients exchange for food.

Look at the table on the left side of Figure 13.10. To compute the numbers in the table, economists take four steps.

1. First, they rank the nation's households according to income.
2. Second, they divide the list into fifths, or quintiles, with equal numbers of households in each fifth. The lowest fifth, which appears at the top of the list, includes the poorest 20 percent of households. The highest fifth, which appears at the bottom of the list, includes the richest 20 percent of households. The first column in Figure 13.10 shows this division into quintiles.
3. Next, they compute each group's average income by adding up the incomes of all the households in the group, and then dividing by the number of households.
4. Finally, they compute each group's share, or percentage, of total income by dividing the group's total income by the total income of all the groups. The second column shows each group's share. The third column shows the cumulative total. (For example, the lowest two fifths of households earned 12.5 percent of total income.)

Compare the share of the poorest fifth with that of the richest fifth. If you divide richest by poorest, you will see that the typical household in the richest fifth receives more than 13 times the income of the typical household in the poorest fifth.

Now look at the graph on the right side of Figure 13.10. It shows that the numbers for shares of total income, when they are plotted on a graph, form a curve. This

The table (left side) shows family income ranked by category. When plotted on a Lorenz Curve (right side), these data show the distribution of income in the United States.
Income What percent of total income did the lowest three fifths of households make in 2000?

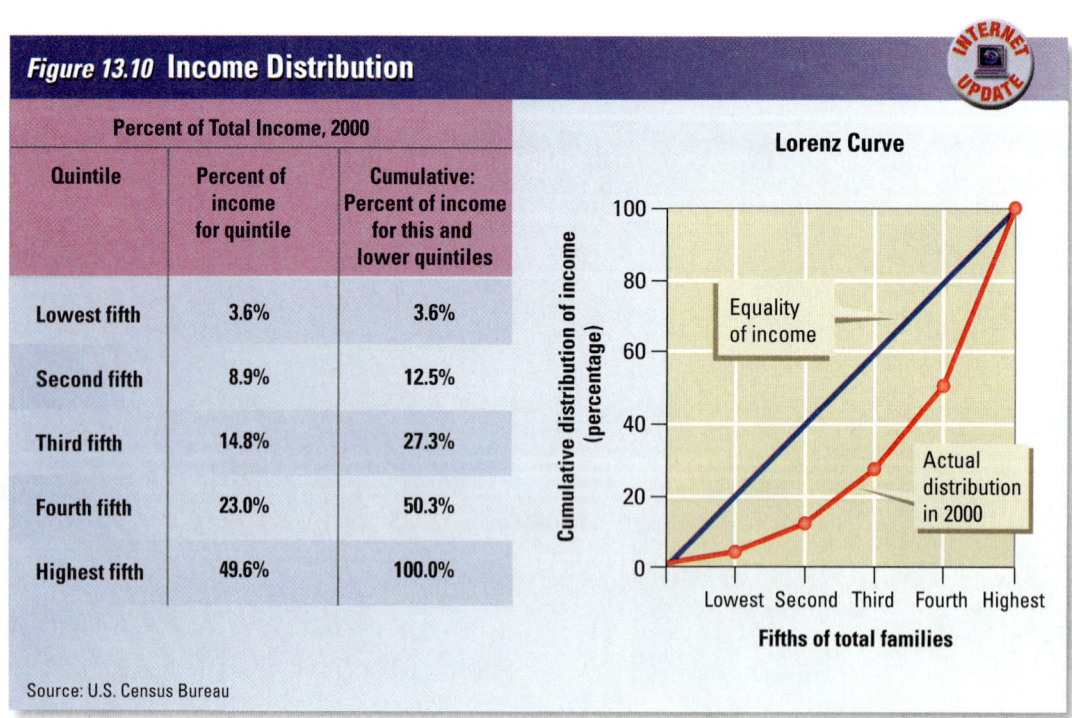

Figure 13.10 Income Distribution

Quintile	Percent of Total Income, 2000	
	Percent of income for quintile	**Cumulative: Percent of income for this and lower quintiles**
Lowest fifth	3.6%	3.6%
Second fifth	8.9%	12.5%
Third fifth	14.8%	27.3%
Fourth fifth	23.0%	50.3%
Highest fifth	49.6%	100.0%

Source: U.S. Census Bureau

Lorenz Curve

Equality of income

Actual distribution in 2000

graph, called the **Lorenz Curve,** illustrates the distribution of income in the economy.

Let's see what this Lorenz Curve tells you. First, read the label on each axis. Then look at the straight line running diagonally across the graph. This reference line represents complete equality. Under conditions of complete equality, each quintile would receive one fifth of total income. That means the lowest 20 percent of households would receive 20 percent of total income, as shown by the point (lowest, 20). Similarly, the lowest 40 percent (the first two quintiles) would receive 40 percent of total income, as shown by the point (second, 40). The lowest 60 percent would receive 60 percent of total income, and so on.

In 1999, the distribution of income was not equal, as the Lorenz Curve indicates. For example, the point (lowest, 3.6) shows that the lowest 20 percent, or one fifth, of households received just 3.6 percent of the nation's total income. The point (second, 12.5) shows that the lowest 40 percent, or two fifths, of households received only 12.5 percent of the income. The area on the graph between the line of equality and the Lorenz Curve represents the amount of inequality in income distribution. The larger the area between the curves, the greater the income inequality.

Income Gap

As you can see from Figure 13.10, the wealthiest fifth of American households earned almost as much income (49.4 percent) as the bottom four-fifths combined (50.6 percent). A study published in 1999 showed that the richest 2.7 million Americans receive as much income after taxes as the poorest 100 million Americans. Why are there such differences in income among Americans? Here are two key factors.

- *Differences in skills and education* Some people are more highly skilled than others, so they earn higher wages. Labor skills are determined in part by education and training and in part by a

worker's natural ability. In addition, some people work in jobs that are in high demand, so they generally earn more income.

- *Inheritances* Some people inherit large sums of money and earn income by investing it. Others inherit businesses that produce income from profits.

In the last two decades, the distribution of income has become less equal. Since 1977, the share of income earned by the lowest three fifths has decreased by 12 percent, while the share earned by the top 1 percent has more than doubled.

Antipoverty Policies

As you read in Chapter 3, the government spends billions of dollars on programs designed to reduce poverty. This money is spent mainly on cash assistance, education, medical benefits, and noncash benefits such as food stamps and subsidized housing.

Many antipoverty programs have drawn criticism from those who say that much of the money is wasted or that the programs themselves harm the very people they are intended to help. In recent years, these criticisms have led to various new policies and proposals for reform. These include the establishment of enterprise zones, job training and other forms of employment assistance, and welfare reform.

▲ **Young adults who volunteer for the government-sponsored AmeriCorps program help combat poverty.**

Lorenz Curve *the curve that illustrates income distribution*

enterprise zone *area where companies can locate free of certain local, state, and federal taxes and restrictions*

block grant *federal funds given to the states in lump sums*

workfare *a program requiring work in exchange for temporary assistance*

Enterprise Zones

Enterprise zones, which became popular in the 1980s, are areas where companies can locate free of certain state, local, and federal taxes and restrictions. These zones benefit businesses and residents because people can find work near their homes. Rundown areas, such as inner cities, can begin to be revitalized.

Employment Assistance

The lack of an adequate income may result from inadequate skills or simply a lack of opportunity. In recent decades, federal and state governments have designed job-training programs to deal with the problem of workers who lack skills. In addition, the federal government has made a minimum wage mandatory since 1938. The minimum wage ensures that workers' hourly pay will not fall below a certain point.

Welfare Reform

Poor people often cannot afford basic needs, such as food and medical care. The United States has long had a welfare system that provides for those basic needs, especially for children and the elderly. That system underwent major reform when President Clinton signed the Personal Responsibility and Work Opportunity Reconciliation Act of 1996. (See Debating Current Issues, pages 354–355.)

This welfare-reform plan responded to criticisms that welfare encouraged poor people to remain unemployed in order to keep receiving aid. It replaced the traditional antipoverty program for poor families (Aid to Families with Dependent Children, or AFDC) with a new program called Temporary Assistance for Needy Families (TANF). TANF eliminated cash assistance for poor families. Instead, the federal government provides **block grants,** or lump sums of money, to the states. As a result of this welfare-reform act, the states are now responsible for designing and implementing programs to move most poor adults from welfare dependence to employment. TANF also set a 5-year limit on receipt of benefits.

How will TANF affect poverty rates? The plan calls for a shift from welfare to **workfare**—a program requiring work in exchange for temporary assistance. The resulting surge of new employees will increase the number of low-skilled people in the labor market. In theory, this could lower the wages of the least-skilled workers. On the other hand, welfare reform has the potential to reduce poverty by providing poor Americans with labor skills and access to a steady, adequate income.

Section 3 Assessment

Key Terms and Main Ideas

1. How is the **poverty threshold** related to the **poverty rate?**
2. Identify five reasons that help account for poverty.
3. What is the **Lorenz Curve,** and what does it suggest about the distribution of income in the United States?
4. How do existing government policies deal with poverty?
5. Explain how a family can include working adults but still have an income below the poverty threshold.

Applying Economic Concepts

6. *Try This* Suppose that you are in charge of creating an antipoverty program for your state. Create a list of at least five proposals for your program.
7. *Math Practice* Do you think the minimum wage in 1997 ($5.15 per hour) was adequate to lift most families out of poverty? Explain your answer.
8. *Critical Thinking* How might the distribution of block grants help the federal government control its budget?

Take It to the NET Poverty rates vary in different regions of the country. Find the most recent national poverty rate and the poverty rate for your region. Use the links provided in the Social Studies area at the following Web site for help in completing this activity. **www.phschool.com**

Unemployment in a Booming Economy

In the late 1990s, the United States found itself in the midst of an economic boom that would have been unimaginable only a decade earlier. Demand for workers continued to grow to such an extent that by 2000, there were more than 122 million jobs in the nation. Meanwhile, the nation's unemployment rate remained well below 5 percent.

Looking for Work During such a period of frenzied demand for workers, some people thought that anyone who wanted a job could get one. They were wrong. Even in periods of so-called full employment, there are always qualified people without jobs. Some companies move, while others fail. Some workers live in areas where there are few jobs available that match their skills.

▲ Job seekers can use the Internet to help them find the right job.

Take Rick Taber, for example, a highly educated, skilled accountant who lives about 100 miles from Boston. When the company he worked for was purchased by another firm, he lost his job. There were jobs available in Boston, but Rick didn't want to move there. He spent almost a year searching for a job near his home that would match his skills and experience, but eventually had to take a job for which he was overqualified.

Older Workers Sometimes older workers have trouble finding jobs because of the emphasis on youth in the job marketplace. Many energetic men and women in their 50s and 60s, with years of experience in their fields, have difficulty finding work because some companies prefer to hire younger employees, who tend to work for smaller salaries.

Effects of Technology In addition, the technology that helped create millions of new jobs in high tech industries has also eliminated jobs in other areas. Many bank tellers, for example, have lost their jobs because computers and machines do many of their tasks more cheaply and efficiently. Telephone operators are being replaced by automated phone systems. As technology continues to perform routine tasks more efficiently, more and more Americans will find themselves switching jobs, and perhaps occupations.

Applying Economic Ideas

1. Why are some people jobless during periods of high employment?

2. How might technological changes in the workplace affect the unemployment rate?

Chapter Summary

A summary of major ideas in Chapter 13 appears below. See also the **Guide to the Essentials of Economics**, which provides additional review and test practice of key concepts in Chapter 13.

Section 1 Unemployment (pp. 331–336)

Unemployment affects millions of Americans each year. Causes of unemployment vary, so unemployment is categorized into **seasonal, frictional, structural,** and **cyclical unemployment.** The Bureau of Labor Statistics tracks unemployment and determines the **unemployment rate.** Economists use the unemployment rate as an indicator of the health of the overall economy.

Section 2 Inflation (pp. 338–343)

A general increase in prices is known as **inflation.** Economists use indexes to measure inflation and its effects on consumers and producers. The best-known index is the **Consumer Price Index (CPI),** which uses prices of a group of consumer goods called the **market basket.** Inflation affects many aspects of our everyday lives, from how much we earn to how much our earnings can purchase.

Section 3 Poverty (pp. 345–350)

Despite the tremendous success of our nation's economy, millions of Americans remain poor. Causes of poverty range from lack of education to racial and gender discrimination. Federal, state, and local governments administer programs to help people whose incomes place them below the **poverty threshold,** the income level needed to meet a family's minimum needs.

Key Terms

Match the following definitions with the terms listed below. You may not use all of the terms.

inflation	discouraged
full employment	workers
poverty rate	deflation
wage-price spiral	price level
structural	Lorenz Curve
unemployment	poverty threshold

1. occurs when the skills that workers have do not match the jobs that are available
2. the percentage of people in a particular group who live in households below the official poverty threshold
3. an increase in the general level of prices
4. process by which rising wages cause higher prices and higher prices cause higher wages
5. an average of the prices of goods and services in the economy
6. the level of employment reached when there is no cyclical unemployment
7. illustrates the distribution of income in the economy

Using Graphic Organizers

8. On a separate sheet of paper, copy the tree map below. Chart the four types of unemployment, and list the causes of each.

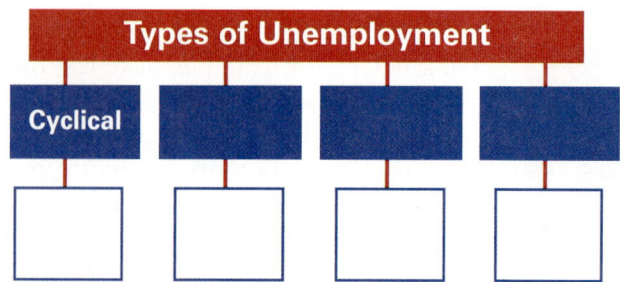

Types of Unemployment

Cyclical

Reviewing Main Ideas

9. What are three effects of inflation? Give an example of each.
10. What role does the Consumer Price Index play in calculating inflation?
11. List and describe at least three ways in which the government combats poverty.
12. What are three causes of inflation, and how do they differ?
13. How is the unemployment rate determined?
14. Which groups are most affected by poverty? Use data from the chapter to support your answer.

Critical Thinking

15. **Analyzing Information** Review the characteristics of the Personal Responsibility and Work Opportunity Reconciliation Act of 1996 decribed on page 350. Do you agree with the basic aim of the program? Explain your answer.
16. **Expressing Problems Clearly** How can full employment be a problem? What issues arise when the economy reaches full employment?
17. **Recognizing Cause and Effect** What cause-and-effect relationship exists in the cost-push theory of inflation?

Problem-Solving Activity

18. Assume you are about to run for local political office. Your area is currently affected by high poverty rates and unemployment. Write a proposal for alleviating poverty and unemployment in your area.

Skills for Life

Analyzing Bar Graphs Review the steps shown on page 337; then answer the following questions using the bar graphs below.

19. What is the subject of these bar graphs?
20. Did the total number of people in poverty in the United States increase or decrease between 1998 and 1999?
21. Which regions of the country had poverty rates lower than the national rate?
22. Did any regions have a poverty rate greater than the national rate? If so, which ones?
23. What additional data might you want to consult to help you interpret these graphs?

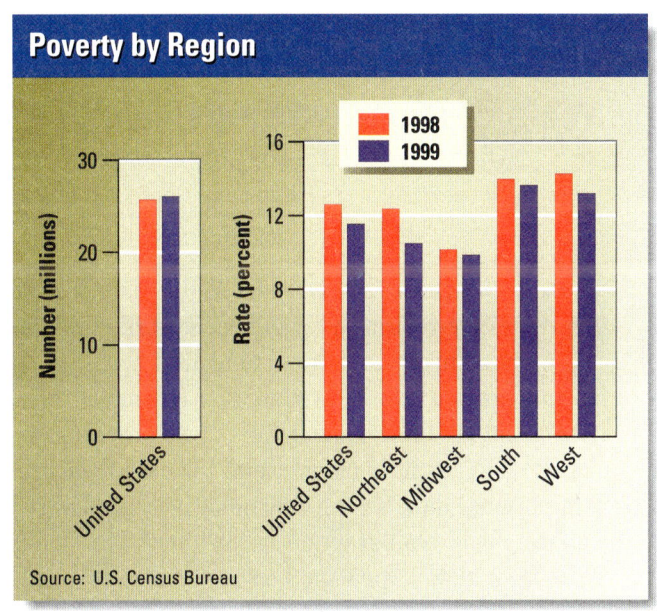

Poverty by Region

Source: U.S. Census Bureau

Economics Journal

Making Comparisons How do your perceptions of poverty in the United States compare with the data presented in this chapter? How does your definition of poverty compare with that of the Bureau of the Census? What do you think are the primary causes of poverty?

Take It to the NET

Chapter 13 Self-Test As a final review activity, take the Chapter 13 Self-Test in the Social Studies area at the Web site listed below, and receive immediate feedback on your answers. The test consists of 20 multiple-choice questions designed to test your understanding of the chapter content.
www.phschool.com

DEBATING CURRENT ISSUES: *Welfare and Work*

In August 1996, President Bill Clinton signed into law a bill that radically restructured the U.S. antipoverty program. The legislation turned welfare programs over to the states and imposed a five-year time limit on benefits. It also required beneficiaries to find work in two years.

Has the welfare-to-work provision succeeded in moving welfare recipients out of poverty? Nancy L. Johnson (R.-Conn.), chair of the Human Resources Subcommittee of the House Ways and Means Committee, says *yes* in this excerpt from "The Results Are In: Welfare Reform Works," an opinion piece from *The Wall Street Journal.* Former welfare recipient Sara Day would say *no* based on the excerpt from *The Wall Street Journal Classroom Edition* article "Why a Welfare Success Story May Go Back on Welfare," by Christina Duff, Staff Reporter of *The Wall Street Journal.*

YES *Has Welfare Reform Cut Poverty Levels?*

BY NANCY L. JOHNSON

ON THE THIRD ANNIVERSARY of the historic 1996 welfare-reform law, the law is working better than anyone ever dared to hope. A host of studies now provide good information on two major questions about the effects on mothers of welfare reform:

1) Do families have more income? There are no reliable national data on the income of mothers leaving welfare. But we can examine changes in the income of all poor and low-income mothers.

According to the Census Bureau, those whose incomes were in the bottom 20 percent of mothers—averaging about $6,500 in 1997—had income increases of nearly $500 between 1993 and 1997. Thus this bottom group, which includes most mothers on welfare and some who left welfare, is somewhat better off than in 1993.

The big story concerns the income of mothers in the next bracket, who had average incomes of $13,500 in 1997. These mothers lost about $1,500 in cash welfare and food stamps but gained nearly $3,000 in earnings and the earned-income tax credit over the period. Combine this with modest increases in child-support payments and nonwelfare government benefits, and these mothers were about $1,500 better off in 1997 than in 1993. Here is the group of mothers that represents the greatest success of welfare reform.

2) Have they escaped poverty? If mothers leaving welfare were falling into the abyss [bottomless hole], poverty rates would increase, or, at best, stagnate.

One important concern for mothers leaving welfare is how to afford child care, which can consume a large portion of a low-income worker's wages.

Opponents of welfare reform predicted it would cast a million children into poverty. In fact, both overall poverty and child poverty declined in 1995 [through 1999], the latest years for which we have data. Poverty among black children declined more in 1997 than in any previous year.

NO — Has Welfare Reform Cut Poverty Levels?

BY CHRISTINA DUFF, STAFF REPORTER OF
THE WALL STREET JOURNAL

SARA DAY COULD BE considered a welfare-reform success story. After 10 years on welfare, she has a two-year-college degree and earns $11 an hour as a secretary at a prep school. Her welfare cash and food stamps stopped a year ago, and her government-paid health care ended in March. Her only major tether is medical care for her children.

So why is the 28-year-old single mom contemplating a return to welfare?

Because her take-home pay and child support total $1,435.50 a month, and food, rent, and other basic expenses total $1,418.37, not counting clothing, diapers or pills for her migraines. To make ends meet, she lets bills go unpaid and sends her children to day care even when she isn't working so they can get the free lunch.

She has no health insurance, and her partially subsidized rent is climbing faster than her paychecks.

Ms. Day is a face behind the statistics cited both by welfare-reform supporters and critics. Her family is one of about 1.6 million families that have left the welfare rolls in the past three years, and she is one of those cited in state surveys that find up to 70 percent of former recipients have found work. Low-wage workers are enjoying solid raises at last, and the federal earned-income tax credit is supplementing their income, as it is Ms. Day's.

But a new study by the Institute for Wisconsin's Future suggests welfare reform may be more successful at moving low-income families off welfare rolls than lifting them out of poverty. The liberal nonprofit group found that the number of welfare recipients in Wisconsin decreased by 67 percent between 1986 and 1997, but that the number of people in poverty fell by only 11.8 percent. Wisconsin launched its welfare reform effort in 1986.

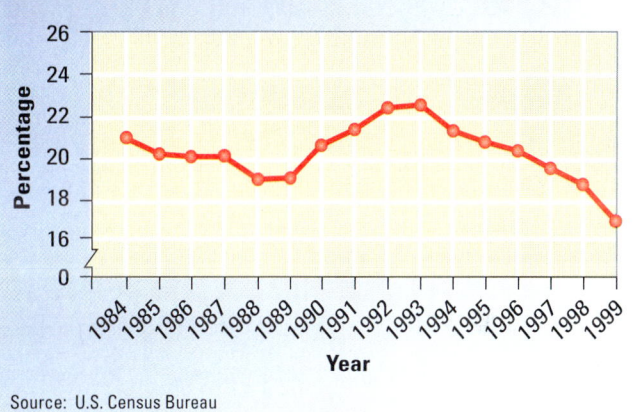

Percentage of U.S. Children in Poverty

Source: U.S. Census Bureau

In most of the 1980s and 1990s, one out of every five or six children lived in poverty in the United States.

DEBATING THE ISSUE

1. What statistics on poverty does Nancy Johnson cite to prove the welfare-to-work provision of welfare reform is successful?

2. What data in the second excerpt indicate that welfare reform may not be successful in moving former welfare recipients out of poverty?

3. **Analyzing Information** How much money does Sara Day have each month for clothing, diapers, and medicine after she pays for food, rent, and other basic expenses? Does your answer support or refute the Wisconsin study that says reform may lift people off welfare rolls but not out of poverty?

4. **Reading Graphs** Was the rate of child poverty rising or falling in the two years before welfare reform began? Can you use this graph to support the opinion that welfare-to-work is lifting people out of poverty?

 Take It to the Net Visit **www.phschool.com** for additional resources relating to this debate.

UNIT 6

Government and the Economy

It's April 15. Where's your tax return?

Every year Americans rush to file their Federal Income Tax return by midnight on or around April 15. Whether you'll be receiving a refund or have to pay, you're probably asking yourself a few questions as you slip the envelope addressed to the IRS into the mail slot:

- What does the government do with all the money it collects?
- Why does the government sometimes spend more than it takes in?
- Is the national debt too large?

Governments, whether federal, state, or local, all need money to operate. This unit focuses on how governments gather financial resources, how they spend these resources, and the actions that the government sometimes takes to help ensure the health of the nation's economy.

Focus Activity

Keep track of all the transactions you make in one day—whether you're buying a bottle of juice or putting money in a parking meter. Calculate what portion of all of your spending goes to the local, state, or federal government.

Chapter 14 Taxes and Government Spending

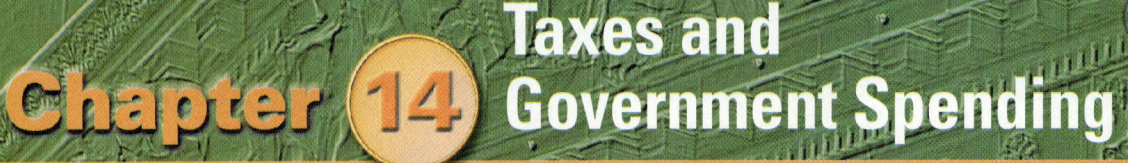

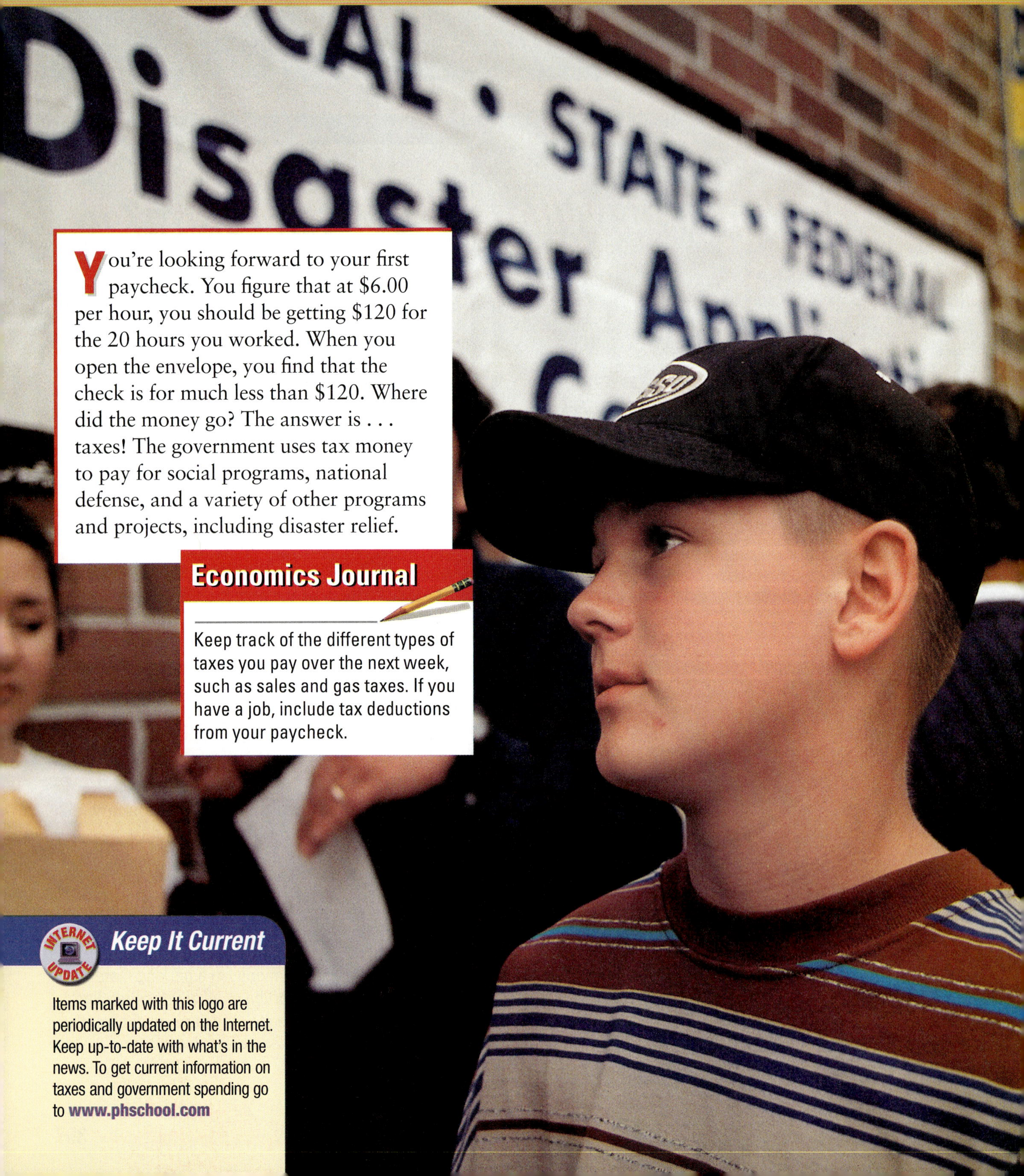

You're looking forward to your first paycheck. You figure that at $6.00 per hour, you should be getting $120 for the 20 hours you worked. When you open the envelope, you find that the check is for much less than $120. Where did the money go? The answer is . . . taxes! The government uses tax money to pay for social programs, national defense, and a variety of other programs and projects, including disaster relief.

Economics Journal

Keep track of the different types of taxes you pay over the next week, such as sales and gas taxes. If you have a job, include tax deductions from your paycheck.

Keep It Current

Items marked with this logo are periodically updated on the Internet. Keep up-to-date with what's in the news. To get current information on taxes and government spending go to **www.phschool.com**

What Are Taxes?

Preview

Objectives

After studying this section you will be able to:

1. **Understand** how the government uses taxes to fund programs.
2. **Identify** the roots of the concept of taxation in the United States Constitution.
3. **Describe** types of tax bases and tax structures.
4. **List** the characteristics of a good tax.
5. **Identify** who bears the burden of a tax.

Section Focus

Local, state, and national governments generate revenue by charging taxes. The Constitution spells out specific limits on governments' powers to tax. Taxation can take several different forms, and people disagree over which method of taxation is most fair.

Key Terms

tax
revenue
tax base
individual income tax
sales tax
property tax
corporate income tax
proportional tax
progressive tax
regressive tax
incidence of a tax

Looking at all of the taxes taken from your paycheck can be discouraging. It can feel like all of that money is being taken from you for someone else's use. Frustration over taxes is, after all, what led American colonists to go to war against Britain and declare independence. How, then, is anything different today?

Although money is taken from your paycheck, it is not done without your consent. As citizens of the United States, we authorize the government, through the Constitution and our elected representatives in Congress, to raise money in the form of taxes. Why?

Funding Government Programs

A **tax** is a required payment to a local, state, or national government. Taxation is the primary way that the government collects money. Taxes give the government the money it needs to operate.

The income received by a government from taxes and other nontax sources is called **revenue**. Without revenue from taxes, the government would not be able to provide the goods and services that we not only benefit from, but that we expect the government to provide. For example, we authorize the government to provide national defense, highways, education, and law enforcement. We also ask the government to provide help to people in need.

All of these goods and services cost money—in workers' salaries, in materials, in land and labor. All members of our society share these costs through the payment of taxes.

Taxes and the Constitution

Taxation is a powerful tool. The founders of the United States did not, without careful consideration, give their new government the power to tax. The Constitution they created spells out specific limits on the government's power to tax.

The Power to Tax

The Framers of the Constitution gave each branch of government certain powers and duties. The first power granted to Congress is the power to tax. This is Article 1, Section 8, Clause 1:

To lay and collect taxes, duties, imposts and excises, to pay the debts, and provide

tax *a required payment to a local, state, or national government*

revenue *income received by a government from taxes and nontax sources*

for the common defense and general welfare of the United States; but all duties, imposts, and excises shall be uniform throughout the United States.

This clause is the basis for federal tax laws.

Limits on the Power to Tax

The Constitution specifically limits certain kinds of taxes. Two of those limits are in the taxation clause. First, the purpose of a tax must be for the "common defense and general welfare." A tax cannot bring in money that goes to individual interests. Second, federal taxes must be the same in every state. The federal gas tax, for example, cannot be $.04 a gallon in Maryland and $.10 a gallon in South Dakota.

Other provisions of the Constitution also limit the kinds of taxes Congress can impose. For example, Congress cannot tax church services because that would violate the freedom of religion promised by the First Amendment. Another clause of the Constitution prohibits taxing exports. The government can collect taxes only on imports—goods brought into the United States. (Congress can limit or prohibit the export of certain goods, however, such as technology or weaponry.)

Yet another clause of the Constitution (Article 1, Section 9, Clause 4) prohibits Congress from levying, or imposing, taxes unless they are divided among the states according to population. Because of this provision, it took the Sixteenth Amendment to legalize the income tax. This amendment was ratified in 1913.

Tax Bases and Tax Structures

Despite these limits, the government actually collects a wide variety of taxes. Economists describe these taxes in different ways. First, they describe a tax according to the value of the object taxed. Second, they describe how the tax is structured.

Tax Bases

A **tax base** is the income, property, good, or service that is subject to a tax. The tax base might be a person's earnings (**individual income tax**), the dollar value of a good or service being sold (**sales tax**), the value of a property (**property tax**), or the value of a company's profits (**corporate income tax**). When government policymakers create a

Figure 14.1 Three Types of Tax Structures

Type of Tax	Description	Example	Ron's taxes on $50,000 income	Mary's taxes on $150,000 income
Proportional	A constant percentage of income is taken in taxes as income increases	"Flat" tax	$7,500, or 15 percent of income	$22,500, or 15 percent of income
Progressive	A larger percentage of income is taken in taxes as income increases	Income tax	$5,000, or 10 percent of income	$45,000, or 30 percent of income
Regressive	A smaller percentage of income is taken in taxes as income increases	Sales tax	$2,000, or 5 percent of total purchases of $40,000; tax bill is 4 percent of income	$3,000, or 5 percent of total purchases of $60,000; tax bill is 2 percent of income

This chart shows how three different tax structures would affect a taxpayer named Ron with an income of $50,000 and a taxpayer named Mary with an income of $150,000. **Income** How does Mary's higher income affect the taxes she pays in each type of tax structure?

new tax, they first decide what the base will be for the tax: income, sales, property, profits, or some other category.

Next, the government decides how to structure the tax on that particular base. As shown in Figure 14.1, economists describe three different tax structures: proportional, progressive, and regressive.

Proportional Taxes

A **proportional tax** is a tax for which the percentage of income paid in taxes remains the same for all income levels. Leslie Wilson, a corporate executive, earns $350,000 a year. Tony Owens, a nurse, earns $50,000 a year. If a 6 percent proportional tax were levied on their incomes, Leslie would pay 6 percent of $350,000, or $21,000, in taxes. Tony would pay 6 percent of $50,000, or $3,000. With a proportional income tax, whether income goes up or down, the percentage of income paid in taxes stays the same.

Progressive Taxes

A **progressive tax** is a tax for which the percentage of income paid in taxes increases as income increases. As income rises, the percentage of income paid in taxes also rises. People with very small incomes might pay no tax at all.

The federal income tax is the clearest example of a progressive tax in the United States. A sample progressive income tax system is shown in Figure 14.2. Notice that the tax rate in this example rises from 15, to 25, and then to 30 percent as income rises. This is a progressive tax rate structure because as income rises, the percentage of income paid in taxes also rises.

Regressive Taxes

A **regressive tax** is a tax for which the percentage of income paid in taxes decreases as income increases. For example, although the sales tax rate remains constant, a sales tax is regressive. This is because higher-income households spend a lower proportion of their incomes on taxable goods and services. As a result, although they may pay more actual dollars in sales taxes, the proportion of their

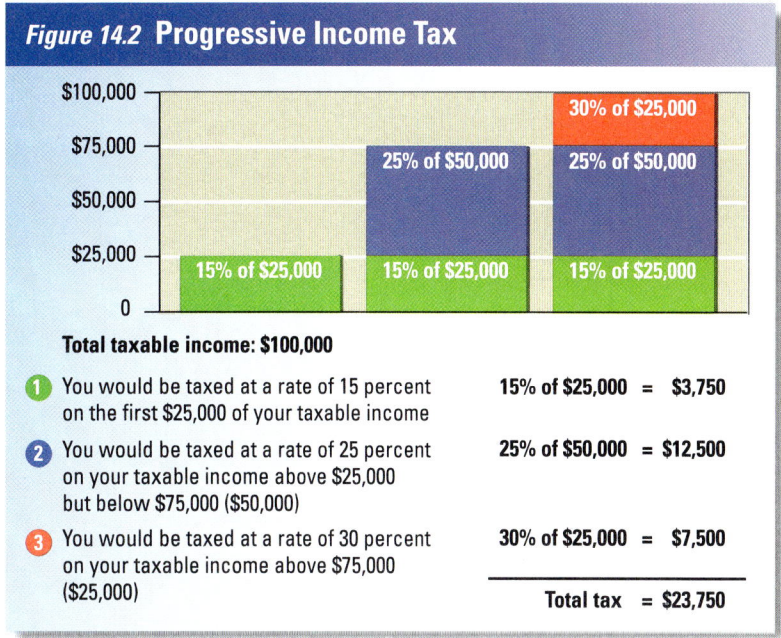

Figure 14.2 Progressive Income Tax

Total taxable income: $100,000

1. You would be taxed at a rate of 15 percent on the first $25,000 of your taxable income — 15% of $25,000 = $3,750

2. You would be taxed at a rate of 25 percent on your taxable income above $25,000 but below $75,000 ($50,000) — 25% of $50,000 = $12,500

3. You would be taxed at a rate of 30 percent on your taxable income above $75,000 ($25,000) — 30% of $25,000 = $7,500

Total tax = $23,750

In a progressive tax structure, the higher a taxpayer's income, the greater percentage he or she must pay in taxes. This chart shows a sample progressive income tax for a taxpayer with total taxable income of $100,000.
Income According to the chart, what would be the total tax on taxable income of $65,000?

income spent on sales taxes is lower than that of lower-income households.

Characteristics of a Good Tax

Though it is sometimes difficult to decide whether a specific tax is proportional, progressive, or regressive, economists do generally agree on what makes a good tax. A good tax should have four characteristics: simplicity, efficiency, certainty, and equity, or fairness.

- *Simplicity* Tax laws should be simple and easily understood. Taxpayers and businesses should be able to keep the necessary records, prepare their own tax forms, and pay the taxes on a predictable schedule.
- *Efficiency* Government administrators should be able to collect taxes without spending too much time or money. Similarly, taxpayers should be able to pay taxes without giving up too much time. They should also not have to pay too much money in fees.

proportional tax *a tax for which the percentage of income paid in taxes remains the same for all income levels*

progressive tax *a tax for which the percentage of income paid in taxes increases as income increases*

regressive tax *a tax for which the percentage of income paid in taxes decreases as income increases*

A STUDY HAS FOUND THAT DEATH AND TAXES ARE THE LEADING CAUSE OF STATISTICS.

SCHWADRON
ROTHCO

▲ This political cartoon makes fun of the saying, "The only sure things in life are death and taxes." Why are taxes necessary?

- *Certainty* Certainty is also a characteristic of a good tax. It should be clear to the taxpayer when a tax is due, how much money is due, and how the tax should be paid.
- *Equity* The tax system should be fair, so that no one bears too much or too little of the tax burden.

Determining Fairness

Although everyone agrees that a tax system should be fair, people often disagree on what "fair" means. Over time, economists have proposed two different ideas about how to measure the fairness of a tax.

The first idea is called the benefits-received principle. According to this principle, a person should pay taxes based on the level of benefits he or she expects to receive. People who drive, for example, pay gasoline taxes that are used to build and maintain highways. In this way, the people who receive the most benefit from the roads also contribute the most to their upkeep.

The second idea about fairness is called the ability-to-pay principle. According to this principle, people should pay taxes according to their ability to pay. The ability-to-pay principle is the idea behind a progressive income tax: people who earn more income pay more taxes.

Balancing Tax Revenues and Tax Rates

How much revenue does a good tax generate? The answer is "enough, but not too much." That is, enough so that citizens' needs are met, but not so much that the tax discourages production. For example, if a company has to pay $100,000 in taxes, it will not be able to use that $100,000 to expand production. If tax rates are lower, however, the company can use more of its income to stimulate production rather than to pay taxes. Ultimately, many people argue, the economy benefits from lower, rather than higher, tax rates.

Who Bears the Burden of a Tax?

To fully evaluate the fairness of a tax, it is important to think about who actually bears the burden of the tax. Taxes affect more than just the people who send in the checks to pay them. Why? The answer lies in supply and demand analysis.

Suppose that the government imposes a gasoline tax of $.50 per gallon and collects the tax from service stations. You may think that the burden of the tax falls only on the service stations, because they mail the checks to the government. Graphs A and B in Figure 14.3, however, provide a different set of answers.

Both Graphs A and B show two supply curves: an original supply line and a line showing the supply after the $.50 tax is imposed. When a tax is imposed on a good, the cost of supplying the good increases. The supply of the good then decreases at each and every price level. This shifts the supply curve to the left.

Before the tax, the market was in equilibrium, and consumers bought gas at $1.00

Figure 14.3 Elasticities of Demand and Tax Effects

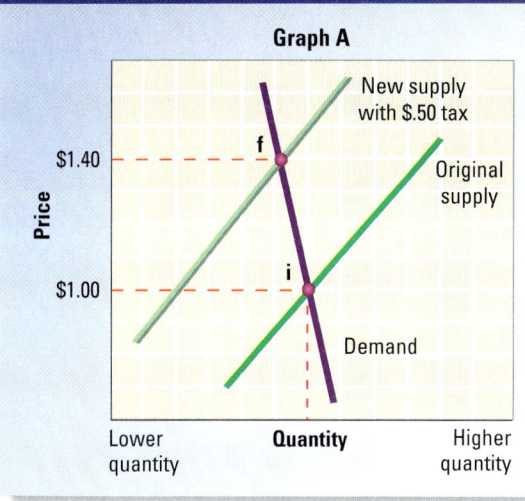

Graph A

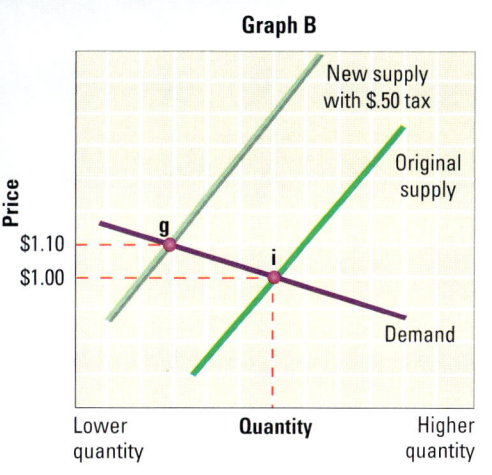

Graph B

If demand for a good is relatively inelastic (Graph A), a new tax will increase the price by a relatively large amount, and consumers will pay a large share of the tax.

Supply and Demand Who bears the burden of a tax if demand is relatively elastic?

per gallon. This is shown as point i on Graph A above. If demand for gas is relatively inelastic (that is, if consumers buy about the same amount no matter what the price), the tax will increase the price of each gallon by a relatively large amount. Consumers will bear a large share of the tax. This is shown in Graph A. Demand is inelastic, so the demand curve is relatively steep, and a $.50 tax increases the equilibrium price by $.40 (from $1.00 to $1.40 from point i to point f). In other words, consumers pay about four fifths of the tax.

In contrast, if demand is relatively elastic, the demand curve will be relatively flat, as in Graph B. Consumers will pay a relatively

small part of the tax. As Graph B shows, a $.50 tax increases the equilibrium price by only $.10 (from $1.00 to $1.10 from point i to point g). In this case, consumers pay only one fifth of the tax. The service stations pay the other four fifths.

This example shows the **incidence of a tax**—that is, the final burden of a tax. When policymakers consider a new tax, they examine who will actually bear the burden. As in the example above, producers can "pass on" the burden to consumers. Generally, the more inelastic the demand, the more easily the seller can shift the tax to consumers. The more elastic the demand, the more the seller bears the burden.

incidence of a tax *the final burden of a tax*

Section 1 Assessment

Key Terms and Main Ideas

1. Why do governments impose taxes?
2. What is the difference between a **progressive tax** and a **regressive tax**?
3. What are the four characteristics of a good tax?
4. Describe the benefits-received principle. How does it differ from the ability-to-pay principle?

Applying Economic Concepts

5. *Try This* Suppose that your town decides to levy a tax to raise funds for construction, maintenance, and other expenses for local schools. Should the tax be proportional, progressive, or regressive? Explain your answer.
6. *Critical Thinking* Analyze the impact of the power to tax as expressed in the Constitution on tax policies today.

Take It to the NET Find out more about the tax-creation process. Then discuss your findings with a classmate. Use the links provided in the Social Studies area at the following Web site for help in completing this activity. **www.phschool.com**

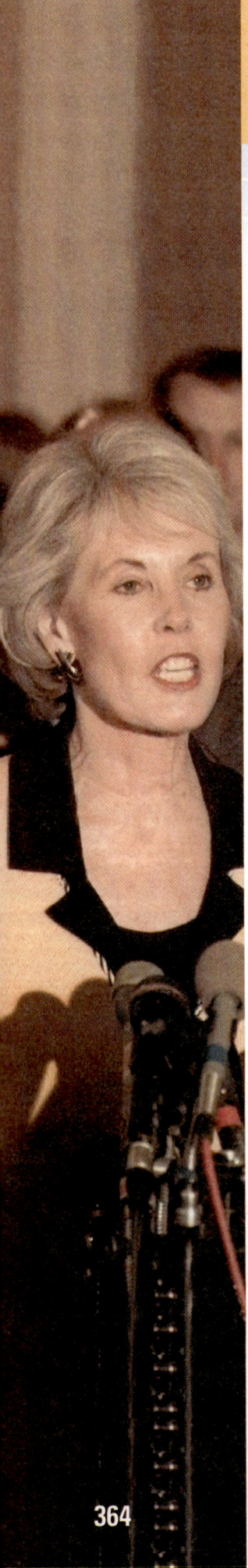

Distinguishing Fact from Opinion

A fact is a statement that can be proved by reliable sources. An opinion is a judgment that reflects a person's beliefs or feelings. It may or may not be provable. Distinguishing fact from opinion is important when studying a political issue like taxation. Read the speech below by a member of Congress about a proposed tax cut; then answer the following questions.

1. **Determine which statements are facts.** Remember that facts can be verified by other sources. (**a**) List three statements about the tax relief bill that appear to be facts. (**b**) How could you prove that each of these statements is a fact?

2. **Determine which statements are opinions.** Sometimes authors signify opinions with phrases such as "I believe" or "I think," but often they do not. Other clues that indicate opinions are sweeping generalizations and emotion-packed words. (**a**) List two statements from the passage that are opinions. (**b**) How do you know that they are opinions?

3. **Determine how the writer uses facts to support her opinions.** Generally, an opinion is more persuasive when an author gives facts to support it. (**a**) How does Representative Dunn support her opinion that this tax relief bill helps women "throughout their lives"? (**b**) Does she present any evidence to support her statement that some people think the tax relief bill is "not good for women"? (**c**) In your opinion, has Representative Dunn supported her opinions well? Explain your answer.

REPRESENTATIVE JENNIFER DUNN, ON A PROPOSED TAX CUT

"…the Republican tax relief bill helps women throughout their lives both at home and in the job market.

The only people who think this tax relief bill is not good for women are those who don't believe we women can manage our own money.

So let's talk first about tax relief at home:

With this bill, the mothers of 41 million American children will be able to keep more of their own money. The $500 per child tax credit…is money mothers surely can use to make ends meet… money that can be used to pay for school clothes, or groceries, or the often unexpected expenses that come with raising children.

Women and their families will also receive help in sending their children to college. The cost of higher education is overwhelming these days.

Women are provided additional options to save for their retirement through expanded IRAs. The fact is that we live longer than men, yet we generally have less savings set aside. Our society shouldn't force women into choosing between shoes for their 8-year-old daughter or saving for their retirement."

Additional Practice

Suppose that you are a member of Congress who opposes the tax relief bill and who will give a speech in response to Representative Dunn. Which of her opinions would you challenge, and how? What sort of facts might you research to support your case?

Section 2 Federal Taxes

Objectives

After studying this section you will be able to:

1. **Describe** the process of paying individual income taxes.
2. **Explain** the basic characteristics of corporate income taxes.
3. **Understand** the purpose of Social Security, Medicare, and unemployment taxes.
4. **Identify** other types of taxes.

Section Focus

The federal income taxes that households and families pay help to fund government programs. Other types of taxes are levied on specific items for specific purposes.

Key Terms

withholding
tax return
taxable
  income
personal
  exemption
deductions
FICA

Social
  Security
Medicare
estate tax
gift tax
tariff
tax incentive

During fiscal year 2001, the federal government took in more than $2 trillion in taxes. If you divide up this federal tax revenue among all the people in the United States, it comes to about $7,100 per person. How does the government get all this money?

The federal government has six major sources of tax revenue. They are individual and corporate income taxes, social insurance taxes, excise taxes, estate and gift taxes, and taxes on imports.

Individual Income Taxes

The federal government levies a tax on individuals' taxable income. As Figure 14.4 shows, individual income taxes make up the federal government's main source of revenue. About 49 percent of the federal government's revenues come from the payment of individual income taxes.

"Pay-As-You-Earn" Taxation

The amount of federal income tax a person owes is determined on an annual basis. In theory, the federal government could wait until the end of the tax year to collect individual income taxes. In reality, that would be a problem for both taxpayers and the government. Like other employers, the government has to pay regularly for rent, supplies, services, and employees' salaries.

A single annual payment from all the nation's taxpayers at once would make meeting these expenses difficult.

Similarly, many people might have trouble paying their taxes in one large sum. For these reasons, federal income tax is collected in a "pay-as-you-earn" system. This means that individuals usually pay

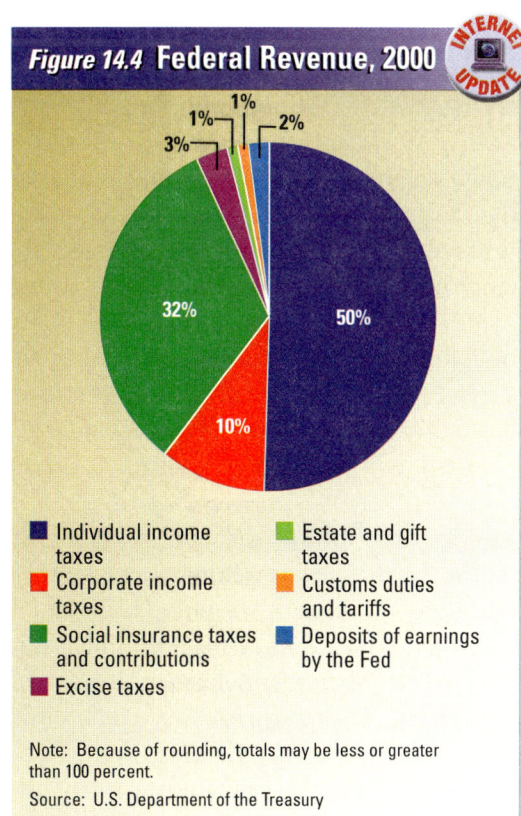

Figure 14.4 Federal Revenue, 2000

- Individual income taxes — 50%
- Corporate income taxes — 10%
- Social insurance taxes and contributions — 32%
- Excise taxes — 3%
- Estate and gift taxes — 1%
- Customs duties and tariffs — 1%
- Deposits of earnings by the Fed — 2%

Note: Because of rounding, totals may be less or greater than 100 percent.

Source: U.S. Department of the Treasury

Sources of government revenue include the taxes shown on this graph. **Government** Analyze the categories of revenue in the federal budget. What are the largest sources of federal revenue?

HOURS AND EARNINGS		TAXES AND DEDUCTIONS	
Hours	Earnings	Description	Amount
20	200.00	FICA	15.20
		Federal	10.25
		State	5.10
		City	1.00
		Total Taxes	**31.55**
TOTAL			
Taxable Wages		**Less Taxes**	**Net Pay**
200.00		31.55	168.45

▲ **This young worker's pay stub shows that her employer, as required by law, has withheld part of her earnings for taxes. What percentage of this worker's pay was withheld for federal taxes? For total taxes?**

most of their income tax throughout the year as they earn income. In mid-April, they pay any additional income taxes they owe.

Tax Withholding

Employers are responsible in part for carrying out the system for collecting federal income taxes. They do so by **withholding,** or taking payments out of your pay before you receive it. The amount they withhold is based on an estimate of how much you will owe in federal income taxes for the entire year. After withholding the money, the employer forwards it to the federal government as an "installment payment" on your upcoming annual income tax bill. On the sample pay stub shown above, the employer has withheld $10.25 in federal income taxes from this employee's paycheck.

Filing a Tax Return

At the end of the year, employers give their employees a report showing how much income tax has already been withheld and sent to the government. The employee then completes a tax return. A **tax return** is a form used to file income taxes. On it you declare your income to the government and figure out your taxable income.

Taxable income is a person's gross (or total) income minus exemptions and deductions. Gross income includes earned income—salaries, wages, tips, and commissions. It also includes income from investments such as interest on savings accounts and dividends from stock.

Personal exemptions are set amounts that you subtract from your gross income for yourself, your spouse, and any dependents. **Deductions** are variable amounts that you can subtract, or deduct, from your gross income. Deductions include such items as interest on a mortgage, donations to charity, some medical expenses, and state and local tax payments.

Completing a tax return allows you to determine whether the amount of income taxes you have already paid was higher or lower than the actual amount of tax you owe. If you have paid more than you owe, the government sends you a refund. If you have paid less than you owe, you must pay the balance to the government. All federal income tax returns must be sent to the Internal Revenue Service, or IRS, by midnight on April 15 (or the next business day if April 15 falls on a weekend).

Tax Brackets

The federal income tax is a progressive tax. In other words, the tax rate rises with the amount of taxable income. The tax rate schedule in Figure 14.5 shows that in 2001, there were five rates. Each applied to a different range of income, or tax bracket. For example, married couples who filed a return together (a joint return) and had a taxable income of $45,200 or less paid 15 percent income tax. The highest rate—39.6 percent—was paid by high-income single people or married couples on the portion of their taxable incomes that exceeded $297,350. Each year, the IRS publishes new tax rate schedules that reflect any changes in the federal tax code.

Corporate Income Taxes

Like individuals, corporations must pay federal income tax on their taxable income. Corporate taxes made up about 10 percent of federal revenues in recent years.

Determining a corporation's taxable income can be a challenge because businesses can take many deductions. That is, they can subtract many expenses from their income before they reach the amount of income that is actually subject to taxation. For example, companies can deduct the cost of their employees' health insurance. Many other costs of doing business can also be used as deductions.

Like individual income tax rates, corporate income tax rates are progressive—that is, tax rates increase as income increases. In 2001, rates began at 15 percent on the first $50,000 of taxable income. The highest rate was 39 percent on taxable corporate incomes between $335,000 and $10 million.

Social Security, Medicare, and Unemployment Taxes

In addition to withholding money for income taxes, employers withhold money for another category of taxes authorized under the Federal Insurance Contributions Act, or FICA. **FICA** taxes fund two large government programs, Social Security and Medicare. Employees and employers share FICA payments.

Social Security Taxes

Most of the FICA taxes you pay go to the Social Security Administration to fund Old-Age, Survivors, and Disability Insurance (OASDI), or **Social Security**. Social Security was established in 1935 to ease the hardships of the Great Depression.

FICA *taxes that fund Social Security and Medicare*

Social Security *Old-Age, Survivors, and Disability Insurance (OASDI)*

Figure 14.5 Federal Income Tax Rates, 2001

Schedule	If your taxable income is over–	but not over–	the tax is	of the amount over–
Schedule X– use if your filing status is **single**	$0	$27,050	.... 15%	$0
	$27,050	$65,550	$4,057.50 plus 28%	$27,050
	$65,550	$136,750	$14,837.50 plus 31%	$65,550
	$136,750	$297,350	$36,909.50 plus 36%	$136,750
	$297,350	....	$94,725.50 plus 39.6%	$297,350
Schedule Y– use if your filing status is **married filing jointly**	$0	$45,200	.... 15%	$0
	$45,200	$109,250	$6,780.00 plus 28%	$45,200
	$109,250	$166,550	$24,714.00 plus 31%	$109,250
	$166,550	$297,350	$42,461.50 plus 36%	$166,550
	$297,350	....	$89,567.50 plus 39.6%	$297,350

According to these sample individual income tax tables, a single individual with $20,000 of taxable income would pay $20,000 X .15, or $3,000, in taxes.

Income What would be the tax for a married couple filing jointly with $75,000 in taxable income?

Value-Added Tax Individual income taxes and sales taxes play a smaller role in generating government revenue in many European nations than they do in the United States. Instead, in much of Europe, a value-added tax, or VAT, has been implemented. A VAT taxes the increase in value that a good gains in each step of its production. For example, in the United States, consumers usually pay taxes when they buy a car. Under a VAT system, the price of a car already includes the tax paid by the mine that extracts the iron ore used to make the car. It also includes the tax the steel mill paid based on the value added to the iron ore when it was turned into steel. Similarly, the car's price includes the tax the car manufacturer paid on the value the steel gained when it was made into a car. In this way, the consumer doesn't directly pay the tax. Rather, the total price of the car already includes the tax. **Would you recommend a VAT for the United States? Why or why not?**

Medicare *a national health insurance program that helps pay for health care for people over age 65 or with certain disabilities*

estate tax *a tax on the estate, or total value of the money and property, of a person who has died*

gift tax *a tax on money or property that one living person gives to another*

Originally, Social Security was simply a retirement fund to provide old-age pensions to workers. Today, it also provides benefits to surviving family members of wage earners and to people whose disabilities keep them from working.

Each year the government establishes an income cap for Social Security taxes. In 2000, the cap was $76,200. No Social Security taxes could be withheld from a taxpayer's wages and salaries above that amount.

Medicare Taxes

FICA taxes also fund Medicare. The **Medicare** program is a national health insurance program that helps pay for health care for people over age 65. It also covers people with certain disabilities.

Both employees and self-employed people pay the Medicare tax on all their earnings. There is no ceiling as for Social Security payments.

Unemployment Taxes

The federal government also collects an unemployment tax, which is paid by employers. In effect, the tax pays for an insurance policy for workers. If workers are laid off from their jobs through no fault of their own, they can file an "unemployment compensation" claim and collect benefits for a fixed number of weeks. In order to collect unemployment benefits, an unemployed person usually must show that he or she is actively looking for another job. The unemployment program is financed by both state and federal unemployment taxes.

Other Types of Taxes

What are the taxes on gasoline and cable television service called? If you inherit money from your great aunt, will you have to pay a tax? Why are some imported products so expensive? To answer these questions, you need to look at excise, estate, gift, and import taxes.

Excise Taxes

As you read in Chapter 5, an excise tax is a general revenue tax on the sale or manufacture of a good. Federal excise taxes apply to gasoline, cigarettes, alcoholic beverages, telephone services, cable television, and other items.

Estate Taxes

An **estate tax** is a tax on the estate, or total value of the money and property, of a person who has died. It is paid out of the person's estate before the heirs receive their share. A person's estate includes not only money, but also real estate, cars, furniture, investments, jewelry, paintings, and insurance.

In 2002, if the total value of the estate is $700,000 or less, there is no federal estate tax. Because an estate tax is a progressive tax, the rate rises with increasing value. That is, a $5 million estate is taxed at a higher rate than a $750,000 estate.

Gift Taxes

The **gift tax** is a tax on money or property that one living person gives to another. The goal of the gift tax, established in 1924, was to keep people from avoiding estate taxes by giving away their money before they died. The tax law sets limits on gifts, but still allows the tax-free transfer of fairly large amounts each year. Under current law, a person can give up to $10,000 a year tax-free to each of several different people.

Import Taxes

Taxes on imported goods (foreign goods brought into the country) are called **tariffs**. Today, most tariffs are intended to protect American farmers and industries from foreign competitors rather than to raise revenue. Tariffs raise the price of foreign items and help keep the price of American products competitive. You will read more about tariffs in Chapter 17.

Taxes That Affect Behavior

The basic goal of taxation is to create revenue. However, governments sometimes use tax policies to discourage the public from buying harmful products. Taxes are also used to encourage certain types of behavior. The use of taxation to encourage or discourage behavior is called a **tax incentive**.

Federal taxes on tobacco products and alcoholic beverages are examples of so-called sin taxes. While they do bring in revenue, their main purpose is to discourage people from buying and using tobacco and alcohol.

▲ The owner of this house is installing solar panels. He or she may be able to take advantage of tax incentives designed to encourage energy conservation.

Taxes have also been imposed on the purchase of vehicles that get low gas mileage. The goal of these taxes is to encourage people to purchase more fuel-efficient cars. Similarly, certain tax deductions encourage energy conservation. Homeowners and businesses may deduct some of the cost of certain improvements, such as adding solar heating, from their taxable income.

tariff *a tax on imported goods*

tax incentive *the use of taxation to encourage or discourage certain behavior*

Section 2 Assessment

Key Terms and Main Ideas

1. Explain "pay-as-you-earn" taxation.
2. Describe **withholding** and explain how it would affect a student with a part-time job.
3. What is the purpose of **FICA**?

Applying Economic Concepts

4. *Critical Thinking* The founders of the United States wanted to avoid establishing a permanent aristocracy, or group of wealthy families who could control a great deal of the nation's wealth. How is this idea related to estate and gift taxes?

5. *Try This* Contributions to organizations such as the American Cancer Society are tax deductible (that is, they can be deducted from taxable income). Explain the reason for this tax policy.

6. *Using the Databank* Study the bar graph showing Government Receipts by Source on page 543 of the Databank. Approximately how much money (in billions of dollars) do the top three sources of government income generate?

7. *You Decide* Reread the Fast Fact on page 368. What factors might account for the differences in tax rates among the countries mentioned? What benefits might you expect as a trade-off with higher tax rates?

Take It to the NET

Explore the services the Internal Revenue Service provides, and learn what the IRS expects from United States citizens. Use the links provided in the Social Studies area at the following Web site for help in completing this activity. **www.phschool.com**

Profile

Henry J. Aaron (b. 1936)

During the 1990s, a movement to "save Social Security" became a major crusade among Washington politicians. The debate worried many Americans, who wondered if the nation's retirement system was about to collapse. A prominent economist says, however, that the Social Security system works, so don't try to fix it.

The Sky Is Not Falling

Many studies predict that the Social Security system will go bankrupt once the Baby Boom generation begins to retire, despite hikes in the Social Security tax and huge surpluses in the program today. Not everyone agrees. Among the harshest critics of this alarming prediction is economist Henry Aaron.

An Expert on Entitlements Issues

Henry Aaron is senior fellow in economic studies at the Brookings Institution, a Washington "think tank" that analyzes economic and social issues. Before joining Brookings, he served on the staff of the Council of Economic Advisors, and in the 1970s, served as Assistant Secretary for Planning in the Department of Health, Education, and Welfare.

In 1978, Aaron was selected to chair the Social Security Advisory Council, which reviews the status of the Social Security system every four years. He has become recognized as an expert on government entitlements and tax policy.

The Dangers of Unwise Reforms

Much of the concern over Social Security has arisen because increasing numbers of retirees are being supported by the taxes of working Americans. Aaron agrees that the ratio of retirees to workers will continue to rise. However, he argues that this increase is offset by a lower ratio of children to workers and by growing numbers of women entering the work force. Both trends reduce the ratio of nonworking dependents per worker, Aaron argues, so the overall tax burden on workers' wages will remain about the same.

One popular proposal is to replace Social Security with a private retirement savings program. Aaron warns that this would require a 50-year transition, during which people would have to make their private contributions while also supporting current retirees through a 10 percent sales tax.

For those who would reform the existing system by raising the retirement age or reducing benefits, Aaron has dire warnings. He notes that no one really knows how expectations about old age affect the saving, working, and spending decisions that people make. Aaron cautions that major changes in the current system could have unforeseen consequences for the entire economy.

CHECK FOR UNDERSTANDING

1. Source Reading   Summarize in your own words the argument that Aaron makes to oppose any major changes in the Social Security system.

2. Critical Thinking   What trends and conditions are responsible for the increase in the ratio of retirees to workers? Why might this development be a potential threat to the future of Social Security?

3. Learn More   Research and report on changes that Congress has made in Social Security in recent years.

Preview

Objectives

After studying this section you will be able to:

1. **Distinguish** between mandatory and discretionary spending.
2. **Describe** major entitlement programs.
3. **Identify** categories of discretionary spending.
4. **Explain** the impact of federal aid to state and local governments.

Section Focus

Although the federal budget is extremely large, about three quarters of the government's spending is required by current laws. Major categories of government spending include Social Security, defense, interest on the national debt, Medicare, and health care.

Key Terms

mandatory spending
discretionary spending
entitlement
Medicaid

Suppose that each year you were given over $2 trillion to spend. So much money! So many choices! In reality, when the federal government receives this amount of revenue in the form of taxes, most of it is already accounted for. That is, after the government fulfills all its legal obligations, only about 40 percent of the money remains. In this section you will look at the many items on which the federal government spends its tax revenues. In Chapter 15, you will read about how the federal government, as part of the budget process, plans for that spending.

Mandatory and Discretionary Spending

The graph in Figure 14.6 shows the major categories of federal spending. Some of these categories, such as Social Security and Medicare, are "mandatory." **Mandatory spending** refers to money that lawmakers are required by existing laws to spend on certain programs or to use for interest payments on the national debt. Others, such as defense and education, are "discretionary." **Discretionary spending** is spending about which government planners can make choices.

In general, the percentage of federal spending that is mandatory has grown in recent years. The percentage of discretionary spending has decreased. These trends worry many budget planners and politicians.

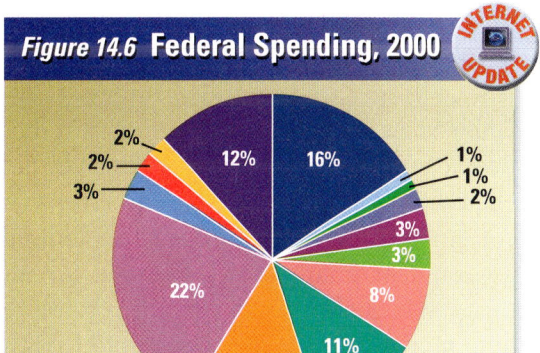

Figure 14.6 Federal Spending, 2000

- Defense
- Science, space, and technology
- Energy, natural resources, and environment
- Agriculture
- Transportation
- Education
- Health
- Medicare
- Income security
- Social Security
- Veterans benefits
- Administration of Justice
- Other
- Net interest

Note: Because of rounding, totals may be less or greater than 100 percent.
Source: Office of Management and Budget

mandatory spending *spending on certain programs that is mandated, or required, by existing law*

discretionary spending *spending category about which government planners can make choices*

The federal government spends the funds it collects from taxes and other sources on a variety of programs.
Government Analyze the categories of expenditures in the federal budget. Which categories receive the most federal funds?

▲ People who receive entitlement benefits such as Social Security, Medicare, and Medicaid include veterans, people with disabilities, and the elderly.

entitlement *social welfare program that people are "entitled to" if they meet certain eligibility requirements*

Entitlement Programs

Except for interest on the national debt, most of the mandatory spending items in the federal budget are for entitlement programs. **Entitlements** are social welfare programs that people are "entitled to" if they meet certain eligibility requirements, such as being at a certain income level or age. The federal government guarantees assistance for all those who qualify. As the number of people who qualify rises, mandatory spending rises as well. As a result, managing costs has become a major concern.

Some, but not all, entitlements are "means-tested." In other words, people with higher incomes may receive lower benefits or no benefits at all. Medicaid, for instance, is means-tested, or dependent on income. Social Security is not. A retired person who has worked and paid Social Security taxes is entitled to certain benefits. Similarly, military veterans and retired federal employees are entitled to receive pensions from the government.

Entitlements are a largely unchanging part of government spending. Once Congress has set the requirements, it cannot control how many people become eligible for each kind of benefit. Congress can change the eligibility requirements or reduce the amount of the benefit in order to try to keep costs down. Such actions, however, require a change in the law.

Social Security

Social Security is the largest category of federal spending. More than 45 million retired or disabled people and their families and survivors receive monthly benefits. The Social Security Administration became an independent agency in 1995. Before that, its spending was part of the budget for the Health and Human Services Department.

Medicare

Medicare serves about 36 million people, most of them over 65 years old. The program pays for hospital care and for the costs of physicians and medical services. It also pays health care bills for people who suffer from certain disabilities and diseases.

Medicare is funded by taxes withheld from people's paychecks. Monthly payments paid by people who make certain levels of taxable income and receive Medicare benefits also pay for the program.

Medicaid

Medicaid benefits low-income families, some people with disabilities, and elderly people in nursing homes. It is the largest source of funds for medical and health-related services for America's poorest people. The federal government shares the costs of Medicaid with state governments. The state share of the costs varies from 50 percent to 83 percent. In 1999, 27.8 million people were covered by Medicaid—about 10 percent of Americans.

Other Mandatory Spending Programs

Other means-tested entitlements benefit people and families whose incomes fall below a certain level. Requirements vary from program to program. Federal programs include food stamps, Supplemental Security Income (SSI), and child nutrition. The federal government also pays retirement benefits and insurance for federal workers, as well as veterans' pensions and unemployment insurance.

The Future of Entitlement Spending

Spending for both Social Security and Medicare has increased enormously in recent years and is expected to increase further in the next few decades. Social Security payments will rise as people in the large "baby boomer" generation, born between 1945 and 1964, start to retire. When the "baby boomers" reach 65, they will become eligible for Medicare as well.

Medicare costs have been growing rapidly, partly as a result of expensive technology, but also because people are living longer. Who will pay these costs? The following fact indicates the basic problem facing Medicare. In 1995, there were four people paying Medicare taxes for every Medicare recipient. By 2050, there will only be two people paying taxes for every recipient.

Discretionary Spending

Spending on defense accounts for about half of the federal government's discretionary spending. The remaining funds available for discretionary spending are divided among a wide variety of categories.

Defense Spending

Defense spending has dropped somewhat since the end of the cold war as a percentage of the federal budget. As you can see from the graph in Figure 14.6, defense spending consumes about 16 percent of the federal budget.

The Department of Defense spends most of the defense budget. It pays the salaries of all the men and women in the army, navy, air force, and marines, as well as the department's civilian employees. There are about 1.37 million men and women in uniform, along with about 703,000 civilian workers, working for the armed forces.

Defense spending, of course, also buys weapons, missiles, battleships, tanks, airplanes, ammunition, and all the other equipment the military needs. The defense budget also includes funds for maintaining equipment and military bases.

Other Discretionary Spending

You may be surprised at how small a portion of federal spending goes into the category that could be labeled "everything else." Here are some of the many programs that this category of federal spending pays for.

- education
- training
- scientific research
- student loans
- technology
- national parks and monuments
- law enforcement
- environmental cleanup
- housing

Medicaid *entitlement program that benefits low-income families, some people with disabilities, and elderly people in nursing homes*

▲ As the federal government reduces its size, the burden of providing public assistance programs falls more heavily on the states. How does the cartoonist portray the ability of state governments to handle this responsibility?

- land management
- transportation
- disaster aid
- foreign aid
- farm subsidies

This part of the federal budget also pays the salaries of the millions of people who work for the civilian branches of the federal government. They include members of Congress, Cabinet secretaries, park rangers, FBI agents, file clerks, geologists, CIA agents, meat inspectors, and many others.

Federal Aid to State and Local Governments

Some federal tax dollars find their way to state and local governments. In total, about $284 billion a year in federal monies is divided among the states. This is an average of about $1,000 per person.

As you have read, state and federal governments share the costs of some social programs, including Medicaid, unemployment compensation, and some of the programs that help children, families, refugees, and others. State and federal governments also share the costs of some highway construction. Additional federal money goes to the states for education, lower-income housing, mass-transit, health care, highway construction, employment training, and dozens of other programs.

Federal grants-in-aid are grants of federal money for certain closely defined purposes. States must use the federal funds only for the purpose specified and obey the federal guidelines for which aid is given. Beginning with the Reagan administration in the early 1980s, many grant-in-aid programs were converted to a block grant format. As you read in Chapter 13, block grants are lump sums of money intended to be used in a broadly defined area of public need, such as education or highways.

Section 3 Assessment

Key Terms and Main Ideas

1. How does **discretionary spending** differ from **mandatory spending**?

2. What is an **entitlement** program?

3. Why is the cost of the Social Security program expected to increase in the next decades?

4. What is the largest category of **discretionary spending**? Identify three additional examples of discretionary spending.

Applying Economic Concepts

5. *Try This* Suppose that you are running for political office. **(a)** Would you propose any new entitlement programs? If so, what would they be? **(b)** Would you propose eliminating or modifying any existing entitlement programs? Explain your answers.

6. *You Decide* Which categories of federal spending would you lower? Which would you raise? Give specific reasons for the changes you suggest.

Take It to the NET

The level and distribution of government spending are sources of continuous debate in the United States. Read several debates on government spending, and summarize your findings in a brief, well-organized essay. Use the links provided in the Social Studies area at the following Web site for help in completing this activity. **www.phschool.com**

State and Local Taxes and Spending

Objectives

After studying this section you will be able to:

1. **Explain** how states use a budget to plan their spending.
2. **Identify** where state taxes are spent.
3. **List** the major sources of state tax revenue.
4. **Describe** local government spending and sources of revenue.

Section Focus

Like the federal government, state and local governments use the revenue from taxes to pay for a variety of programs and services. In general, states spend the largest amounts on grants to local governments, education, and public welfare.

Key Terms

operating budget
capital budget
balanced budget
tax exempt
real property
personal property
tax assessor

You and your family are thinking about colleges. Which one offers the courses you want? How much does it cost? During your research, you find that colleges within your state's university system are far less expensive than private schools. The reason is that your state government is paying part of the cost of running the state colleges. In fact, higher education is one of the largest areas of state government spending.

What else do states spend money on? In this section you will look at patterns of taxing and spending by state and local governments.

State Budgets

Like families and individuals, governments must plan their spending ahead of time. The federal government has just one budget for all kinds of spending. States have two budgets: operating budgets and capital budgets.

Operating Budgets

A state's **operating budget** pays for day-to-day expenses. Those include salaries of state employees, supplies such as computers or paper, and maintenance of state facilities, from the state capitol to recreation areas and roadside parks.

Capital Budgets

A state's **capital budget** pays for major capital, or investment, spending. If the state builds a new bridge or building, the money comes from this budget. Most of these expenses are met by long-term borrowing or the sale of bonds.

operating budget *budget for day-to-day expenses*

capital budget *budget for major capital, or investment, expenditures*

▲ State colleges and universities, such as the University of Texas at Austin, receive state funding.

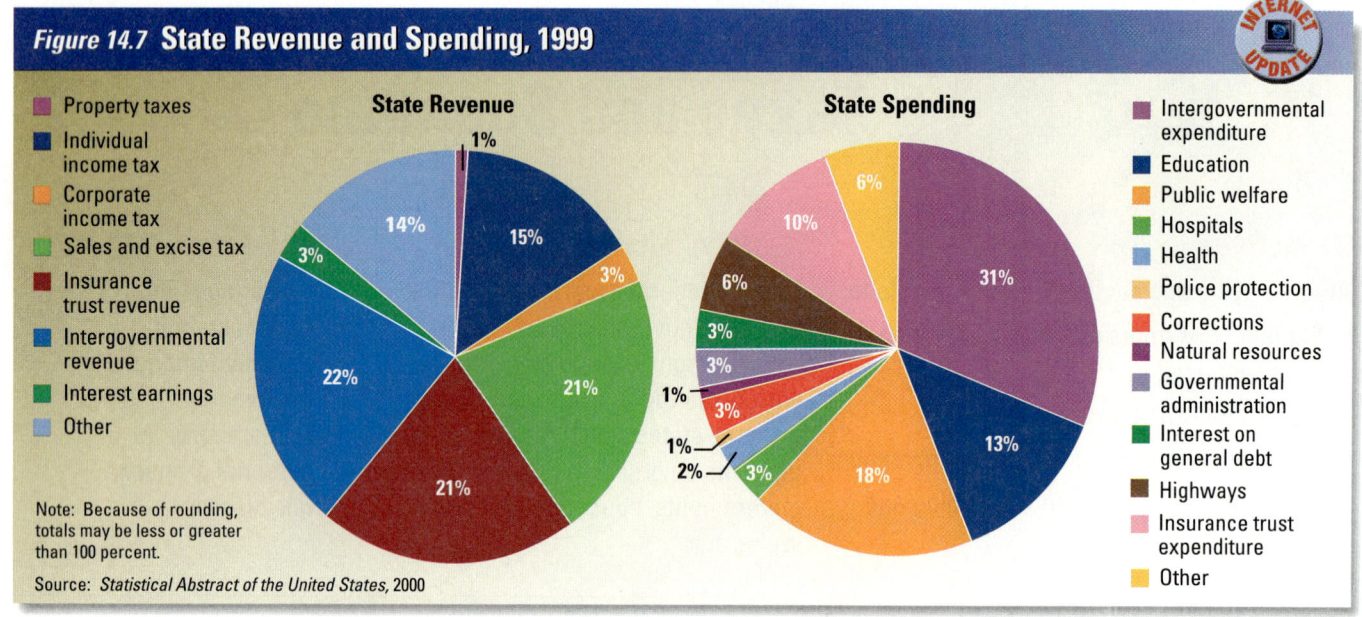

Figure 14.7 State Revenue and Spending, 1999

State Revenue

- Property taxes
- Individual income tax
- Corporate income tax
- Sales and excise tax
- Insurance trust revenue
- Intergovernmental revenue
- Interest earnings
- Other

1%, 15%, 3%, 21%, 21%, 22%, 3%, 14%

State Spending

- Intergovernmental expenditure
- Education
- Public welfare
- Hospitals
- Health
- Police protection
- Corrections
- Natural resources
- Governmental administration
- Interest on general debt
- Highways
- Insurance trust expenditure
- Other

31%, 13%, 18%, 3%, 2%, 1%, 1%, 3%, 3%, 3%, 6%, 10%, 6%

Note: Because of rounding, totals may be less or greater than 100 percent.

Source: *Statistical Abstract of the United States*, 2000

BUILDING KEY CONCEPTS

Major sources of state revenue include individual income taxes, sales and other taxes, insurance premiums, and local and federal funds ("intergovernmental revenue").
Government **What are the major categories of state government spending?**

balanced budget
budget in which revenues are equal to spending

Balancing State Budgets

In most states, the governor prepares the budget with the help of a budget agency. The legislature then discusses and eventually approves the budget.

Unlike the federal government, states have laws that require **balanced budgets**— budgets in which revenues are equal to spending. These laws, however, apply only to the operating budget, not the capital budget. That makes it easier to balance state budgets than to balance the federal budget.

Some states can borrow money or carry a deficit for several years. In states with stricter laws, however, state lawmakers may have to cut programs or raise taxes to balance the budget.

Where Are State Taxes Spent?

Spending policies differ among the fifty states. You are probably most familiar with state spending on education, highways, police protection, and state recreation areas. You can see other significant spending categories in Figure 14.7.

Education

Every state has at least one public state university. Some, such as California, have large systems with many campuses throughout the state. In many states, tax dollars also support agricultural and technical colleges, teacher's colleges, and two-year community colleges.

State governments also provide financial help to their local governments, which run elementary, middle, and high schools. Some states pay a larger share of local schools' costs than other states do. The amount of money that each state spends per student also varies. The national average is $6,251 per student per year.

Public Safety

State police are a familiar sight along the nation's highways. This police force enforces traffic laws and helps motorists in emergencies. State police also maintain crime labs that can assist local law-enforcement agencies.

State governments build and run corrections systems. These institutions house people convicted of state crimes.

Highways and Transportation

Building and maintaining highway systems is another major state expense. State crews resurface roads and repair bridges. Some money for roads comes from the federal government. In turn, states contribute money to federal and interstate highway systems.

States pay at least some of the costs of other kinds of transportation facilities, such as waterways and airports. Money for such projects may also come from federal and local government budgets.

Public Welfare

States look after the health and welfare of the public in various ways. State funds support some public hospitals and clinics. State regulators inspect water supplies and test for pollution.

As you read in Section 2, states also help pay for many of the federal programs that assist individuals, such as unemployment compensation benefits. Because states determine their own benefits, they can meet local needs better than the federal government can. For example, during a local recession, they may decide to extend the number of weeks that people can claim benefits.

Arts and Recreation

If you've hiked in a state forest or picnicked in a state park, you've enjoyed another benefit of state tax dollars. Parks and nature reserves preserve scenic and historic places for people to visit and enjoy. States also run museums and help fund music and art programs.

Administration

Besides providing services, state governments need to spend money just to keep running. Like the federal government, state governments have an executive branch (the governor's office), a legislature, and a court system. State tax revenues pay the salaries of all these and other state workers, including maintenance crews in state parks, the governor, and state court judges.

State Tax Revenue

For every dollar a state spends, it must take in a dollar in revenue. Otherwise, it cannot maintain a balanced budget. The 50 states now take in nearly $500 billion a year from taxes. Where does this money come from? Sales and individual income taxes provide the largest part of state revenues. The pie chart on the left in Figure 14.7 shows you other sources of state revenue.

Limits on State Taxation

Just as the United States Constitution limits the federal government's power to tax, it also puts limits on the states. Because trade and commerce are considered national enterprises, states cannot tax imports or exports. They also cannot tax goods sent between states.

State governments cannot tax federal property, such as military bases. Nonprofit organizations, religious groups, and charities are usually **tax exempt**; that is, they are not subject to taxes.

tax exempt *not subject to taxes*

◀ Funds for plowing state highways are included in state budgets. Would you expect these funds to be included in a state's operating budget or capital budget?

Sales Tax

As Figure 14.7 shows, sales taxes are a main source of revenue for state governments. As you read in Section 1, a sales tax is a tax on goods and services. The tax—a percentage of the purchase price—is added on at the cash register and paid by the purchaser.

All but a few of the 50 states collect sales taxes. Sales tax rates range from 3 to 8 percent. Some local governments have their own, additional, sales tax.

In every state, some categories of products are exempt from sales tax. Many states do not charge sales tax on basic needs such as food and clothing. Some do not tax prescription medicines.

Even states without a sales tax impose excise taxes that apply to specific products and activities. Some are sin taxes—taxes that are intended to discourage harmful behavior—on products like alcoholic beverages and tobacco. Other taxes apply to hotel and motel rooms, automobiles, rental cars, and insurance policies. Many states also tax gasoline. This state gasoline tax is in addition to the federal tax.

State Income Taxes

Individual income taxes are another large contributor to many states' budgets. People pay this state income tax in addition to the federal income tax. Figure 14.7 shows that state individual income taxes contribute about 14 percent of state revenue.

Some states tax incomes at a flat percentage rate (that is, as a proportional tax). Some charge a percentage of a person's federal income tax. Others have progressive rates, with a tax structure like the federal income tax. A few states tax only interest and dividends from investments, not wages and salaries.

Corporate Income Tax

Most states collect corporate income taxes from companies that do business in the state. Some states levy taxes at a fixed, flat rate on business profits. A few charge progressive rates—that is, higher tax rates for businesses with higher profits.

As you can see from Figure 14.7, corporate income taxes contribute only a small percentage of state tax revenues—about 3 percent. Nevertheless, corporate income taxes can influence a state's economy.

Low corporate taxes, along with a well-educated work force and good public services, can make it easier to attract new businesses to a state. Politicians deciding on state corporate tax rates keep this fact in mind when they determine their state's policies.

Other State Taxes

Besides the corporate income tax, businesses pay a variety of other state taxes and fees. Do you want to be a hairdresser, a carpenter, or a building contractor? If so, you will have to pay a licensing fee. A licensing fee is a kind of tax that people pay to carry on different kinds of business within a state.

Some states charge a transfer tax when documents such as stock certificates are transferred and recorded. Other states tax the value of the stock shares that corporations issue.

Many states have rich natural resources, such as gold, oil, natural gas, fish, or lumber. Some states place a tax, called a severance tax, on companies that take (or "sever") these resources from the state's land and waters.

As you read in Section 2, the federal government taxes the estate of a person who has died. States, in turn, usually charge an inheritance tax on the value of the property that goes to each heir.

Some states also tax property. That includes **real property,** such as land and buildings, or "real estate." It also includes **personal property,** such as jewelry, furniture, and boats. Some states even tax intangible property, such as bank accounts, stocks, and bonds. Today, however, most property taxes, especially on real estate, are levied by local governments.

FAST FACT

In 1999, New Hampshire legislators were faced with a dilemma: how to fund the state's education system, without placing undue hardship on low- and middle-income taxpayers. Their solution: establish an education trust fund. This fund created a uniform statewide education property tax with provisions for tax relief for certain qualified taxpayers. It also dedicated to education revenue from increases in the tobacco tax and from tobacco settlement funds, as well as from various tax increases on businesses.

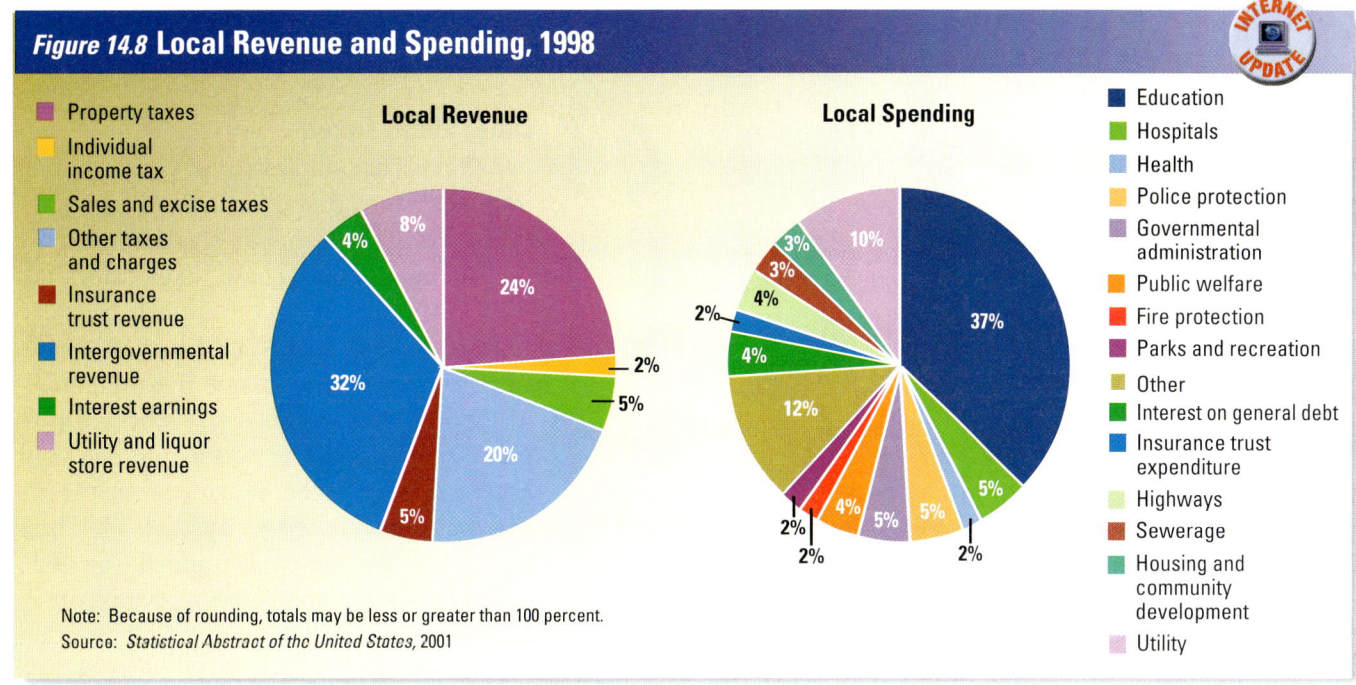

Figure 14.8 Local Revenue and Spending, 1998

Local Revenue

- Property taxes
- Individual income tax
- Sales and excise taxes
- Other taxes and charges
- Insurance trust revenue
- Intergovernmental revenue
- Interest earnings
- Utility and liquor store revenue

Local Spending

- Education
- Hospitals
- Health
- Police protection
- Governmental administration
- Public welfare
- Fire protection
- Parks and recreation
- Other
- Interest on general debt
- Insurance trust expenditure
- Highways
- Sewerage
- Housing and community development
- Utility

Note: Because of rounding, totals may be less or greater than 100 percent.
Source: *Statistical Abstract of the United States,* 2001

Major sources of local revenue include property taxes and state and federal funds ("intergovernmental revenue").
Government What are the major categories of local government spending? How do they differ from the major categories of state government spending shown on page 376?

Local Government Spending and Revenue

Your local government plays a part in many aspects of everyday life, including public grade, middle, and high schools. Local governments hire police and fire-fighters. They build roads, libraries, hospitals, and jails. They pay teachers. Even though this is the level of government closest to you, it may be the one you know the least about.

Forms of Local Government

You probably think of "local government" as a town or city. There are other types as well, including townships, counties, and special districts, such as school districts. All units of local government are created by the state government. The state gives them their powers and authority.

Today, there are more than 87,000 local government units in the United States. Together they collect more than $300 billion in tax revenues.

The Jobs of Local Government

Local governments carry major responsibilities in these areas:

- Public school systems
- Law enforcement (local police, county sheriff's departments, park police)
- Fire protection
- Public facilities such as libraries, airports, and public hospitals
- Parks and recreational facilities such as beaches, swimming pools, and zoos
- Public health (restaurant inspectors, water treatment plants, sewer systems)
- Public transportation
- Elections (voter registration, preparation of ballots, election supervision, vote counting)
- Record keeping (birth/death certificates, wills, marriage licenses, and the like)
- Social services (food stamps, child care and welfare, and similar programs)

Many of these responsibilities are reflected in the graph showing local spending (above right). In some towns and cities, separate commissions or private

▲ Local taxes pay for city and town recreation areas like this playground.

tax assessor *an official who determines the value of a property*

corporations carry out some of these jobs. You can see, though, that local governments touch our lives every day.

Property Taxes

Property taxes are levied on property owners in local communities to offset the expense of services such as street construction or maintenance. An official called a **tax assessor** determines the value of the property. Property taxes are usually figured as a fixed dollar amount per $1,000 of the assessed value. They are a main source of funding for public schools.

Other Local Taxes

Local taxes are similar to the types of taxes imposed by the states. Besides property taxes, local governments levy sales, excise, and income taxes. These taxes affect not only residents of a community but also visitors. In fact, many are designed specifically to raise revenue from nonresidents.

Suppose you've gone on a school trip to New York City. The room rate for your hotel is $140 a night. When you see the bill in the morning, however, it's $160.55! Three different taxes have been added—an 8.25 percent sales tax, a 5 percent city tax, and a $2 per room occupancy tax. Many other cities have taxes aimed at tourists and business travelers. They include sales taxes on hotel rooms and rental cars, airport taxes, and taxes on movie or theater tickets.

Some large cities collect income taxes as payroll taxes. In these cities, many workers are commuters who pay property taxes and sales taxes in the suburbs where they live. If the city did not take taxes from their paychecks, these workers would get a "free ride" on the city's services. They would be using police, street cleaning, and other services paid for only by the people who live in the city.

Section 4 Assessment

Key Terms and Main Ideas

1. Describe the difference between a state's **operating budget** and its **capital budget**.

2. What is a **balanced budget**?

3. What are the main sources of state revenue? How do they differ from the main sources of local revenue?

4. Describe the difference between **real property** and **personal property**.

Applying Economic Concepts

5. *Using the Databank* Study the bar graph showing Income Taxes per Capita on page 542 of the Databank. **(a)** Which are higher, federal income taxes or state and local income taxes? **(b)** How much are total income taxes per capita?

6. *You Decide* Turn to Figure 14.8 and study the main categories of local spending. Write a brief essay stating whether you agree with the spending priorities shown on the graph.

Take It to the NET What taxes do citizens of your state pay? How do these taxes affect you? Find out more about taxation in your state. Then describe three forms of taxation in your state. Use the links provided in the Social Studies area at the following Web site. **www.phschool.com**

The Bush Tax Cut

On June 7, 2001, President George W. Bush signed the Economic Growth and Tax Relief Reconciliation Act of 2001, called "TRA 2001" for short. This law includes major changes to the tax law that will affect most taxpayers. Although the tax cut was not as large as President Bush had sought, the Act largely fulfilled his campaign promise to reduce taxes in light of the projected federal budgetary surplus. Concerns about the slowing economy also brought more widespread support for the president's plan.

Lower Tax Brackets The new law reduces the four highest tax brackets from their 2000 levels. It also creates a new lowest tax bracket with a 10% tax rate. The Treasury mailed tax refund checks—mostly for $300—to taxpayers during the summer of 2001 in order to anticipate these tax rate reductions.

Children and Students The Bush tax bill gradually increases the tax credit for dependent children under 17 from $500 in 2000 to $1000 in 2010. The new law also makes it easier for parents to afford to send their children to school. The amount that can be saved in an Education IRA grows from $500 to $2000 a year. Students will be able to withdraw money from special tuition-saver programs without having to pay taxes. More students and their parents will be able to deduct tuition expenses and student loan interest from their taxable income.

▲ President George W. Bush signs the 2001 tax bill.

Easier Retirement Savings Taxpayers will also be able to contribute more to their retirement accounts. For example, the allowable contribution to an Individual Retirement Account (IRA) goes up from $2000 a year in 2000 to $3000 in 2002, $4000 in 2005, and $5000 in 2008. Workers over age 50 will be allowed to contribute an extra $500 a year (starting in 2002) and $1000 a year (in 2006).

Will These Changes Last? Nearly all the changes in the new tax law are phased in over several years, and then will disappear in 2011 when the law expires. This means that future Congresses and future presidents will have to decide whether to extend these provisions or return to the law as it was in 2000.

Applying Economic Ideas

1. Why did concerns about the slowing economy generate support for the president's tax cut plan? Why might it have helped the economy for the Treasury to mail out refunds in the summer of 2001 rather than waiting for people to file their taxes in early 2002?

2. What are some potential problems with having a tax cut that evaporates in 2011? Why might Congress have decided to do it this way?

Chapter Summary

A summary of major ideas in Chapter 14 appears below. See also the **Guide to the Essentials of Economics,** which provides additional review and test practice of key concepts in Chapter 14.

Section 1 *What Are Taxes? (pp. 359–363)*

The United States Constitution gives the government power to collect taxes to fund government programs. A **tax base** is a value on which a tax is calculated, such as income, property, or profits. Economists describe three different types of tax structures: **proportional, progressive,** and **regressive.** Many taxes in the United States are based on a principle of ability-to-pay. Other taxes are based on a benefits-received principle. Economists use supply and demand analysis to determine the **incidence of a tax,** or who bears the final burden of a tax.

Section 2 *Federal Taxes (pp. 365–369)*

The federal government has six major sources of **revenue,** or income. They are **individual income taxes, corporate income taxes,** social insurance payments (including **Social Security, Medicare,** and unemployment taxes), **excise taxes, estate** and **gift taxes,** and **tariffs,** or taxes on imports. Individual income taxes are paid on a pay-as-you-earn basis through payroll **withholding.** Each year, people with income must file a **tax return** and pay taxes on all **taxable income.**

Section 3 *Federal Spending (pp. 371–374)*

Much of the federal government's spending is **mandatory spending,** that is, it is required by existing law. The remainder of the budget is **discretionary spending.** Major categories of government spending include **entitlements,** such as **Social Security** and **Medicare,** defense, and interest on the national debt.

Section 4 *State and Local Taxes and Spending (pp. 375–380)*

Like the federal government, state and local governments fund their programs by levying taxes. States have two budgets, an **operating budget** and a **capital budget.** Most state and local government revenues fall into the following categories: **income tax, sales tax,** severance tax, inheritance tax, and property tax.

Key Terms

Match the following terms with the definitions listed below. You will not use all of the terms.

taxable income	balanced budget
revenue	withholding
discretionary spending	mandatory spending
progressive tax	real property

1. Income received by a government from taxes and nontax sources
2. Physical assets such as land and buildings
3. Budget category in which funds are committed to certain programs by law
4. Total income minus exemptions and deductions
5. Tax structure with a rate that increases with the amount or value being taxed
6. Amount taken out of an employee's paycheck as a prepayment on taxes

Using Graphic Organizers

7. Copy the double web map below on a separate sheet of paper. Complete the double web map by writing examples of sources of federal and state government revenue in the circles. You may add more circles as needed.

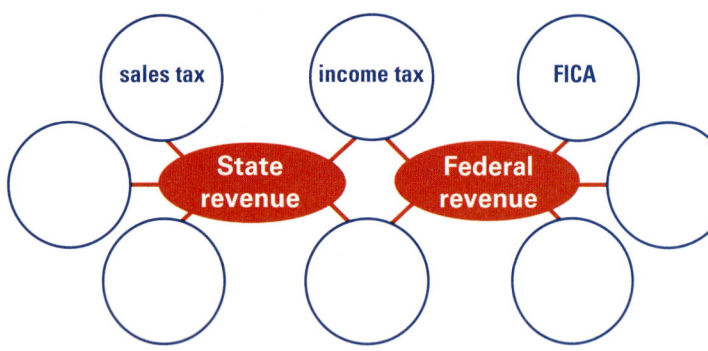

Reviewing Main Ideas

8. Why are some taxes considered to be regressive?
9. How can you determine the incidence of a tax?
10. List and describe four sources of state government revenue.
11. What are entitlement programs? Give three examples of entitlement programs and explain their purposes.

Critical Thinking

12. **Synthesizing Information** Review the powers of and limits to taxation in the United States. How does the Constitution limit federal and state powers of taxation?
13. **Predicting Consequences** Assume that you are a representative to Congress. What forms of mandatory and discretionary spending do you support? What are possible consequences of showing your support or lack of support for different forms of spending?
14. **Making Comparisons** Create a table in which you identify types of taxes at the local, state, and national levels and describe the economic importance of each.
15. **Expressing Problems Clearly** In your opinion, should a tax be applied at the same rate to all people, or should those who are wealthier be expected to pay at a higher rate? Support your opinion with concrete examples.

Problem-Solving Activity

16. Review the criteria economists use for determining a good tax. Then create a proposal for a new tax that meets those criteria. Would you be willing to pay the tax you've just proposed?

Economics Journal

Essay Writing Review your Economics Journal entry for this chapter. Write a summary of the types of taxes you pay on a regular basis, and indicate whether you think the taxes you pay are fair or not.

Skills for Life

Distinguishing Fact from Opinion Review the steps shown on page 364; then answer the following questions using the selection below.

17. Which statements in the excerpt below are facts?
18. Which statements in the excerpt below are opinions?
19. What phrases indicate that the statements are opinions?
20. Does Representative Johnson present evidence to support his opinions?
21. Has Representative Johnson supported his opinions well? Explain your answer.

Representative Sam Johnson:

"Working to Reduce Your Tax Burden"

I believe that our current tax code is economically destructive, impossibly complex, and overly intrusive. It has impeded our ability to create jobs, encourage savings and investment, and realize the American dream.

This is illustrated by the fact that our current tax code has grown from 11,000 words to over 7 million. According to West Publishing, who is an official publisher of the tax code, it takes two volumes and 1,168 pages to publish the code, plus, an additional 6,439 pages of Federal Tax Regulations that apply to income taxes. To make it easier to comply with these regulations, the IRS has created about 480 forms with an additional 280 to explain how to fill out the 480. I think this is ridiculous. That is why this system should not be changed, but replaced. . . .

Take It to the NET

Chapter 14 Self-Test As a final review activity, take the Economics Chapter 14 Self-Test in the Social Studies area at the Web site listed below, and receive immediate feedback on your answers. The test consists of 20 multiple-choice questions designed to test your understanding of the chapter content. **www.phschool.com**

Voluntary Contributions

One reason that governments tax their citizens is to pay for services that benefit the entire community, including education, public transportation, garbage collection, and fire protection. Ideally, all these public services could be provided by voluntary contributions. People would help pay for these services simply because it is the right thing to do. In reality, many people would take a "free ride" and not contribute. In this simulation, you will have a chance to look at the kind of choices citizens might make and the results of those choices. You'll see how "free riders" affect the general good.

Materials

Notebook paper
Play money
(or handmade equivalent):
one $10, three $5, and five $1 bills for each citizen-group, plus the state treasury of $500 in mixed bills

▲ In this town meeting, citizens are discussing how to pay for public education. Can it be paid for through voluntary contributions?

Preparing the Simulation

Suppose you live in a state in which the money spent on public education causes a decrease in other costs in the state budget. For every dollar contributed to education, the cost of welfare and criminal justice decrease by a total of three dollars. These budget savings are returned to citizens as tax refunds. Each citizen's refund equals the total budget savings divided by the number of citizens—regardless of the amount each citizen contributes. See the budget table for an example of how these savings would be calculated.

Step 1: Select two students from your class who will act as state treasurer and budget director. The rest should form groups of three to five students. Each group works together and makes decisions as one "citizen." One member of each citizen-group should be in charge of the group's money and record keeping.

Step 2: Each citizen-group begins the simulation with $30: one $10 bill, three $5 bills,

and five $1 bills. The state treasurer has $500 in mixed bills. He or she can also write "IOUs" for citizen tax refunds. Each citizen-group should use a sheet of notebook paper to make a contributions and refunds record, using the table on the next page as a model.

Step 3: The state budget director should use a sheet of notebook paper to make a budget worksheet using the table on the next page as a model.

Conducting the Simulation

This simulation is run in three sessions.

Session 1: Each citizen-group decides whether it wants to make a contribution to public education, and if so, how much it wants to give. Each group can choose to contribute between $0 and $10 in each session. Record your contribution on your Contributions and Refunds Record, and give the money in cash to the state treasurer.

The state budget director adds up all the first session's contributions to education. Then he or she figures the state's budget savings using the Budget Worksheet, keeping in mind that every dollar collected for education results in three dollars saved from welfare and criminal justice. The state budget director gives this information to the state treasurer, who then gives each citizen-group its refund in dollars. If no cash is available, the treasurer will issue IOUs.

Session 2: Each citizen-group again decides whether to make a contribution to public education. Even if you have received a refund, you can still contribute only $10 each day. Record your contribution on your Contributions and Refunds Record, and give the money to the treasurer.

The state budget director again adds up the total contributions, using the Budget Worksheet. He or she figures the savings, and the treasurer gives each citizen-group its refund.

Session 3: Each citizen-group decides again whether to make a contribution to education, using the same process as in earlier sessions. When refunds for this session have been calculated and given, each group adds up all the money it has in cash and IOUs. The total amount of money is the citizen-group's score.

Budget Table for a 10-Citizen State

Total Contributions	State Budget Savings	Tax Refund per Citizen
$20.00	$60.00	$6.00
$50.00	$150.00	$15.00
$80.00	$240.00	$24.00
$100.00	$300.00	$30.00

Contributions and Refunds Record

	Session 1	Session 2	Session 3
Balance at beginning of session	$	$	$
– Contribution	– $	– $	– $
+ Refund	+ $	+ $	+ $
= New balance	= $	= $	= $

Budget Worksheet

	Session 1	Session 2	Session 3
Total contributions x $3.00 = Total budget savings	$ X $3.00 $	$ X $3.00 $	$ X $3.00 $
Total budget savings ÷ Number of citizen-groups = Tax refund per citizen-group	$ ÷ ___ $	$ ÷ ___ $	$ ÷ ___ $

Simulation Analysis

Discuss these questions as a group.

1. From the state treasurer's Budget Worksheet, analyze whether all the citizen-groups were equally generous in their contributions. Did any citizens try to get a free or almost-free ride? Did this tactic pay off for them? How did that affect other groups that did make contributions?
2. Each citizen-group began with $30. How does this compare with the amount that each one has now?
3. Which session brought in the largest total amount of contributions to education?
4. **Determining Relevance** What does this experiment demonstrate about the need for governments to use taxes to pay for public services?

385

Chapter 15 Fiscal Policy

Spending more money than you earn is usually a bad idea. But what if you face an unexpected need for more cash than you have? How do you decide whether you should borrow money or not spend the money at all?

The federal government deals with this dilemma every year when it prepares its budget. Sometimes borrowing money is the best choice for the economy. Other times, borrowing money causes more problems than it solves. All debts must be repaid, sooner or later.

Economics Journal

List five items in your city or town—buildings, infrastructure, or services—that are built, run, or funded by government.

Keep It Current

Items marked with this logo are periodically updated on the Internet. Keep up-to-date with what's in the news. To get current information on fiscal policy go to
www.phschool.com

Understanding Fiscal Policy

Preview

Objectives

After studying this section you will be able to:

1. **Describe** how the government uses fiscal policy as a tool for achieving its economic goals.
2. **Explain** how the government creates the federal budget.
3. **Analyze** the impact of fiscal policy decisions on the economy.
4. **Identify** the limits of fiscal policy.

Section Focus

The federal government takes in money for the budget through taxation and borrowing. The decisions the government makes about taxing and spending can have a powerful impact on the overall economy.

Key Terms

fiscal policy
federal budget
fiscal year
Office of Management and Budget (OMB)
Congressional Budget Office (CBO)
appropriations bill
expansionary policies
contractionary policies

The word *fiscal* comes from the Latin word *fisc*, which means "basket" or "bag." Over time, the word came to be linked with a bag of money. Specifically, it meant the "bag," or pool, of money held by the government. In Chapter 14, you read about how the government collects money, primarily through taxes, and how the government spends its money on a wide variety of programs. In this section you will read about fiscal policy. **Fiscal policy** is the use of government spending and revenue collection to influence the economy.

Fiscal Policy as a Tool

As you learned in Chapter 14, the federal government takes in and spends huge amounts of money. The federal government spends about $200 million every hour, $4.8 billion every day, and about $2 *trillion* a year. The tremendous flow of cash into and out of the economy has a large impact on aggregate demand and supply in the economy.

Fiscal policies are used to achieve economic growth, full employment, and price stability. Fiscal policy decisions—how much to spend and how much to tax—are among the most important decisions the federal government makes. These decisions are made each year during the creation of the federal budget.

The Federal Budget

The **federal budget** is a written document indicating the amount of money the government expects to receive for a certain year and authorizing the amount the

fiscal policy *the use of government spending and revenue collection to influence the economy*

federal budget *a plan for the federal government's revenues and spending for the coming year*

▲ As part of its budget, the federal government spends billions of dollars each year on national defense, including items such as the F-15 fighter jet.

Figure 15.1 Creating the Federal Budget

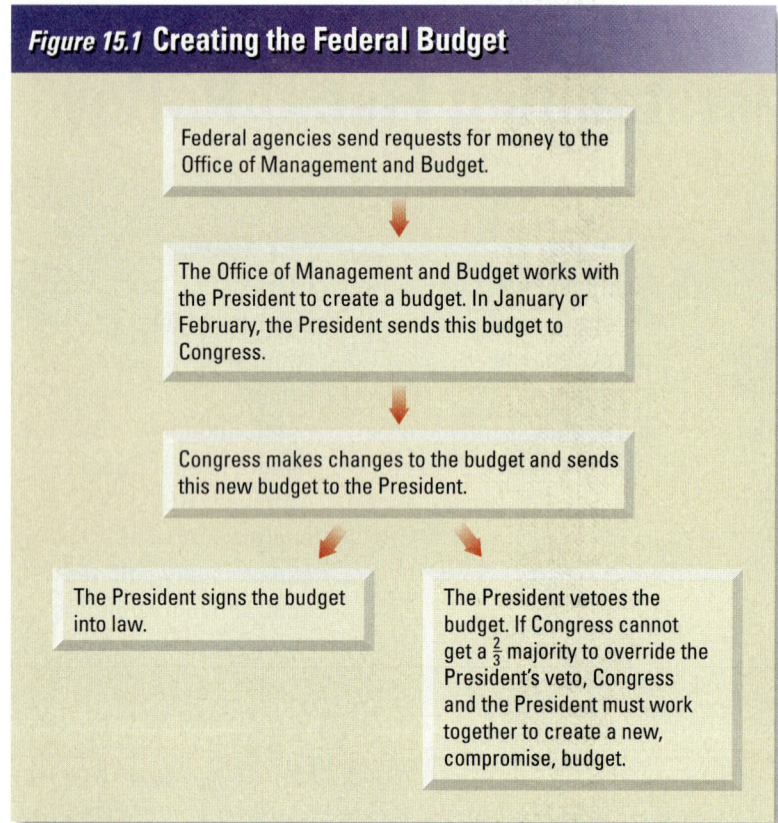

Federal agencies send requests for money to the Office of Management and Budget.

↓

The Office of Management and Budget works with the President to create a budget. In January or February, the President sends this budget to Congress.

↓

Congress makes changes to the budget and sends this new budget to the President.

The President signs the budget into law.

The President vetoes the budget. If Congress cannot get a $\frac{2}{3}$ majority to override the President's veto, Congress and the President must work together to create a new, compromise, budget.

Congress and the White House work together over the course of the year to put together a federal budget. **Government** Who takes the first step in the budget process?

fiscal year *a twelve-month period that can begin on any date*

Office of Management and Budget (OMB) *government office that manages the federal budget*

Congressional Budget Office (CBO) *government agency that provides economic data to Congress*

government can spend that year. The federal budget is just a plan to pay for the federal government's expenditures. Much like a family's budget, it lists expected income and shows exactly how the money will be spent.

The federal government prepares a new budget for each fiscal year. A **fiscal year** is a twelve-month period that is not necessarily the same as the January-to-December calendar year. The federal government uses a fiscal year that runs from October 1 through September 30.

The federal budget takes about 18 months to prepare. During this time, citizens, Congress, and the President debate the government's spending priorities. There are four basic steps in the federal budget process.

Spending Proposals

The federal budget must fund many offices and agencies in the federal government,

and Congress cannot decide all of their needs. Before the budget can be put together, each federal agency writes a detailed estimate of how much it expects to spend in the coming fiscal year.

These spending proposals are sent to a special unit of the executive branch, the **Office of Management and Budget (OMB)**. The OMB is part of the Executive Office of the President. As its name suggests, the OMB is responsible for managing the federal government's budget. Its most important job is to prepare the federal budget.

In the Executive Branch

The OMB holds several meetings to review the Federal agencies' spending proposals. Representatives from the agencies must explain their spending proposals to the OMB and convince the OMB to give them as much money as they have asked for. Usually, OMB gives each agency less than they say they need.

The OMB then works with the President's staff to combine all of the individual agency budgets into a single budget document. This document gives the President's overall spending plan for the coming fiscal year. The President presents the budget to Congress in January or February.

In Congress

The President's budget is only a starting point, and the number of changes Congress makes depends on the relationship between the President and Congress. Congress carefully considers, debates, and modifies the President's proposed budget. For help, members of Congress rely on the assistance of the **Congressional Budget Office (CBO)**. Created in 1974, the CBO gives Congress independent economic data to help with its decisions.

Much of the work done by Congress—the House of Representatives and the Senate—is done by small committees. Working at the same time in different houses of Congress, committees in the House and Senate analyze the budget and hold hearings at which agency officials and others can speak out about the budget. The

House Budget Committee and Senate Budget Committee combine their work to propose one initial budget resolution, which must be adopted by May 15 of the year. This resolution is not intended to be final, but gives initial estimates for revenue and spending to guide the legislators as they continue working on the budget.

Then, in early September, the Budget Committees for each house of Congress propose a second budget resolution that sets binding spending limits. Congress must pass this resolution by September 15, after which Congress cannot pass any new bills that would spend more money than the budget resolution allows.

Finally, the Appropriations Committees for each house submit bills to authorize specific spending. By this time, the new fiscal year is about to start and Congress faces pressure to get these **appropriations bills** adopted and submitted to the President quickly before the previous year's funding ends on September 30. If Congress cannot finish in time, it must pass short-term emergency spending legislation known as "stop-gap funding" to keep the government running. If Congress and the President cannot even agree on temporary funding, the government "shuts down" and all but the most essential federal offices will close.

In the White House

Congress sends the appropriations bills to the President, who can sign them into law. If he vetoes any of these bills, Congress must either come up with enough votes to override the veto—usually, this is impossible—or work with the President to write an appropriations bill on which both sides can agree. Once that is completed, the President signs the new budget into law.

Fiscal Policy and the Economy

Government officials who take part in the budget process debate how much should be spent on specific programs such as defense, education, and scientific research.

They also consider how much should be spent in total. The total level of government spending can be changed to help increase or decrease the output of the economy. Similarly, taxes can be raised or lowered to help increase or decrease the output of the economy.

Fiscal policies that try to increase output are known as **expansionary policies**. Fiscal policies intended to decrease output are called **contractionary policies**. By carefully choosing to follow expansionary or contractionary fiscal policies, the federal government tries to make the economy run as smoothly as possible.

Expansionary Fiscal Policies

Governments use expansionary fiscal policies to raise the level of output in the economy. That is, they use expansionary policies to encourage growth, either when the economy is in a recession or to try to prevent a recession. Recall from Chapter 12 that a recession is the part of the business

appropriations bill *a bill that sets money aside for specific spending*

expansionary policies *fiscal policies, like higher spending and tax cuts, that encourage economic growth*

contractionary policies *fiscal policies, like lower spending and higher taxes, that reduce economic growth*

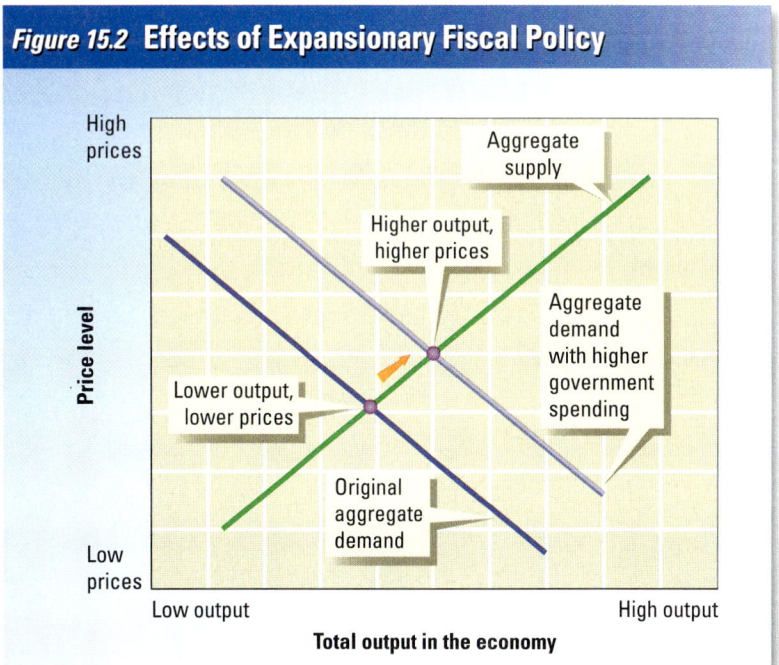

Figure 15.2 Effects of Expansionary Fiscal Policy

Aggregate supply

Higher output, higher prices

Aggregate demand with higher government spending

Lower output, lower prices

Original aggregate demand

High prices / Low prices (Price level)

Low output / High output — Total output in the economy

Expansionary fiscal policy helps the economy by increasing aggregate demand and output.
Supply and Demand How do increases in government spending affect aggregate supply?

cycle that occurs when output declines for two quarters, or three-month periods, in a row. Expansionary fiscal policies fall into either or both of two categories: increasing government spending and cutting taxes.

Increasing Government Spending

If the federal government increases its spending or buys more goods and services, it triggers a chain of events that raises output and creates jobs. Government spending increases aggregate demand, which causes prices to rise. (See Figure 15.2.) According to the law of supply, higher prices encourage suppliers of goods and services to produce more. To do this, firms will hire more workers. In short, an increase in demand will lead to lower unemployment and to an increase in output, as shown in Figure 15.3. The economy will be encouraged to expand.

Cutting Taxes

Tax cuts work much like higher government spending to encourage the economy to expand. If the federal government cuts taxes, individuals have more money to

spend, and businesses keep more of their profits. Consumers will have more money to spend on goods and services, and firms will have more money to spend on land, labor, and capital. These actions will increase demand, prices, and output.

Contractionary Fiscal Policies

At some stages in the business cycle, the government may choose contractionary fiscal policies. Contractionary fiscal policies try to decrease aggregate demand, and by decreasing demand, reduce the growth of economic output. If contractionary fiscal policies are strong enough, they may slow the growth of output to zero, or even lead to a fall in GDP.

The government sometimes tries to slow down the economy because fast-growing demand can exceed supply. When demand exceeds supply, producers must choose between raising output and raising prices. If producers cannot expand production enough, they will raise their prices, which leads to high inflation. As you read in Chapter 12, inflation is an increase in prices over time. Inflation cuts into consumers' purchasing power and discourages economic growth and stability. Fiscal policies aimed at slowing the growth of total output generally fall into either or both of two categories: decreasing government spending and raising taxes.

Decreasing Government Spending

If the federal government spends less, or buys fewer goods and services, it triggers a chain of events that may lead to slower GDP growth. A decrease in government spending leads to a decrease in aggregate demand because the government is buying less than before. Decreased demand tends to cause lower prices. According to the law of supply, lower prices encourage suppliers to cut their production and possibly fire workers. Lower production lowers the growth rate of the economy and may even reduce GDP.

BUILDING KEY CONCEPTS

The goal of expansionary fiscal policy is to add money to the economy.
Government How might cutting taxes have similar effects to those shown in the chart?

Figure 15.3 Flowchart of Effects of Expansionary Fiscal Policy

To expand the economy, the government buys more goods and services.

⬇

Companies that sell goods to the government earn profits, which they use to pay their workers and investors more and to hire new workers.

⬇

Workers and investors have more money and spend more in shops and restaurants.

⬇

Shops and restaurants buy more goods and hire more workers to meet their needs.

⬇

In the short term, government spending leads to more jobs and more output.

This chain of events is the exact opposite of what happens when the government increases spending. The government uses the same tools to try to influence the economy in both cases, but in different ways, and with very different goals.

Increasing Taxes

When the federal government raises taxes, individuals have less money to spend on goods and services or to save for the future. Firms keep less of their profits and decrease their spending on land, labor, and capital. As a result of these decreases in demand, prices tend to fall. Producers of goods and suppliers of services tend to cut production. This slows the growth of GDP.

Limits of Fiscal Policy

On paper, fiscal policies look like powerful tools that can keep the economy in perfect balance. In reality, fiscal policies can be clumsy and difficult to put into practice.

Difficulty of Changing Spending Levels

Increasing or decreasing the amount of federal spending is not an easy task. As you read in Chapter 14, many of the spending categories in the federal budget are entitlements that are fixed by law. Nearly 60 percent of the federal budget is set aside for programs such as Medicaid, Social Security, and veterans' benefits before Congress even begins the budget process. The government cannot change spending for entitlements under current law. As a result, significant changes in federal spending generally must come from the small part of the federal budget that includes discretionary spending. This gives the government less leeway for increasing or lowering spending.

Predicting the Future

Governments use fiscal policies to prevent big changes in the level of GDP. Despite the statistics, however, it is difficult to know the current state of the economy. As you read in Chapter 12, no one can predict how quickly the business cycle will move from

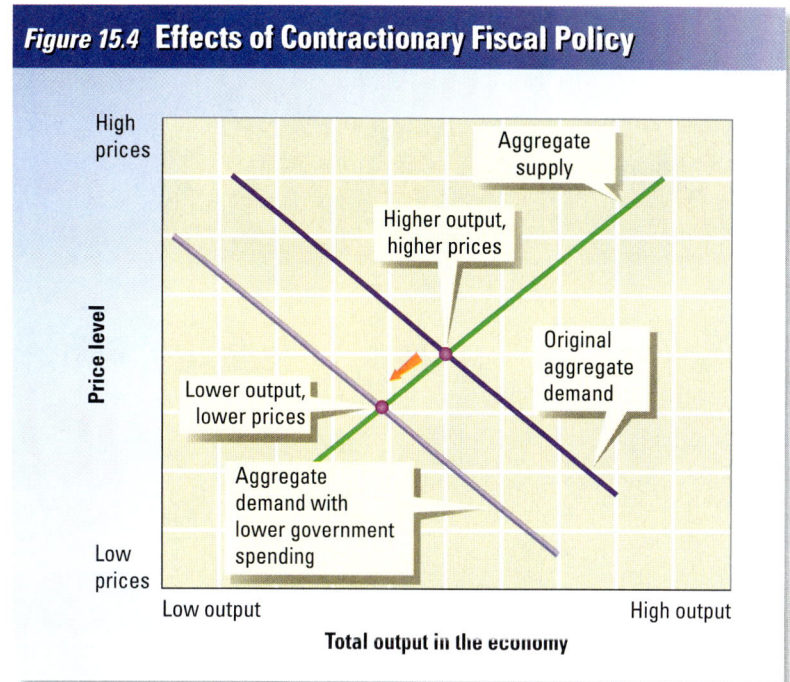

Figure 15.4 Effects of Contractionary Fiscal Policy

By cutting spending, the government can slow economic growth.
Supply and Demand How does lower government spending affect equilibrium?

one stage to the next, nor can anyone identify exactly where the economy is at any specific point in the cycle. Economists often disagree about the meaning of statistics, whether they show the economy is in good condition or ready for a recession.

Predicting future economic performance is even more difficult. As a result, lawmakers may put off making changes in fiscal policy until they know more about how the economy is performing. By then, it may be too late to act.

In addition, when lawmakers put fiscal policies in place, they base their decisions partly on the past behaviors of individuals. It is risky to assume that people will, for example, respond the same way to a tax cut in the future as they have in the past.

Delayed Results

Although changes in fiscal policy affect the economy, changes take time. Once government officials decide when and how to change fiscal policy, they have to put these changes into effect within the federal budget, which itself takes over a year to

▲ Cutting government spending is difficult because some voters will usually object to cuts that impact their interests.

money on highways in the middle of a recovery, it could lead to high inflation and a labor shortage.

Political Pressures

The President and members of Congress, who develop the federal budget and the federal government's fiscal policies, are elected officials. If they wish to be reelected, they must make decisions that benefit the people who elect them, not necessarily decisions that are good for the overall economy.

For example, government officials have an incentive to practice expansionary fiscal policies by increasing government spending and lowering taxes. These actions are usually popular with voters, although in Section 3 you will read about why some people disapprove of government spending. Government spending benefits the firms that receive government contracts and the individuals who receive direct payments from the government. Lower taxes leave more disposable income in people's pockets.

On the other hand, contractionary fiscal policies that decrease government spending or raise taxes are often unpopular. Firms and individuals that expect income from the government are not happy when the income is reduced or cut off. No one likes to pay higher taxes, unless the tax revenue is spent on a specific, highly valued good or service.

develop. Finally, they have to wait for the change in spending or taxing to affect the economy.

By the time the policy takes effect, the economy might be moving in the opposite direction. The government could propose massive public spending on highways in the middle of a recession, only to have the economy recover before construction begins. In these cases, fiscal policy would only add to the new trend, instead of correcting the original problem. If the government continued to spend lots of

Coordinating Fiscal Policy

For fiscal policies to be effective, various branches and levels of government must plan and work together. This is very difficult to do. For example, if the federal government is pursuing contractionary policies, ideally state and local governments should pursue consistent fiscal policies. Yet, state and local governments may be pursuing different goals for fiscal policy than the federal government.

Global Connections

Experimenting in Japan Japan has used expansionary fiscal policies in recent years to try to end an economic slump. When real estate prices and stock prices decreased sharply in Japan in the early 1990s, investors, businesses, and banks lost much of their wealth. Consumers and businesses spent less, and banks could not afford to lend money for new investment, so the economy suffered. The Japanese government has tried to increase demand by spending money on new roads, government-sponsored loans, and tax cuts. Between 1992 and 1999, the government passed nine major bills spending a total of $1.1 trillion, or nearly $90,000 for every man, woman, and child in Japan. After eight years of slow or negative growth, the Japanese economy appeared to be growing more quickly at the end of the decade. However, the government had to borrow heavily to pay for its programs.

Businesspeople, politicians, and economists often disagree about how well the economy is performing, and what the goals of the fiscal policy should be.

Also, different regions of the economy can experience very different conditions. California and Hawaii may have high unemployment while Nebraska and Massachusetts face rising prices and a labor shortage.

In addition, in order for the federal government's fiscal policy to be effective, it must also be coordinated with the monetary policies of the Federal Reserve. You'll read more about monetary policy in the next chapter.

Even when all of these obstacles are overcome, fiscal policy faces still another limitation. The short-term effects of fiscal policy can be different from the long-term effects. A tax cut or increased government spending will give a temporary boost to economic production and to employment. However, as the economy returns to full employment, high levels of government spending combined with market spending will lead to increased inflation as the economy overheats.

Similarly, an increase in taxes or a decrease in government spending may

◄ New community-built pools, like this one in California, have an economic impact on the local level.

"cool" the economy and lead to a recession. However, in the long run, reduced government spending will allow other types of spending to increase without risking inflation. If there is more investment spending, this could lead to higher growth in the long run. In this way, slow growth or even recession in the short term can lead to prosperity in the future.

Section 1 Assessment

Key Terms and Main Ideas

1. Explain **fiscal policy** and how it relates to the **federal budget.**

2. When does the federal government's **fiscal year** begin?

3. What role does the **Office of Management and Budget (OMB)** play in creating the federal budget?

4. What are two types of **expansionary policies?**

Applying Economic Concepts

5. *Critical Thinking* Explain how a tax cut can lead to a higher GDP in the short run.

6. *Try This* Which fiscal policy strategy do you think policymakers would use in each of these scenarios? Explain your answers. **(a)** Inflation is rising, and real GDP is up by 4 percent. **(b)** GDP is down, and the unemployment rate has increased to 10 percent.

7. *Using the Databank* The Consumer Confidence Index measures how optimistic American consumers are that the economy will do well. The graph on page 539 of the Databank measures consumer confidence in the 1990s. If you had been a policymaker in 1998, would you have recommended expansionary or contractionary fiscal policies? Explain your answer.

Take It to the NET

Creating and maintaining the federal budget is an important task. Try to manage the budget yourself, and then describe the experience in a brief paragraph. Use the links provided in the Social Studies area at the following Web site for help in completing this activity. **www.phschool.com**

Comparing Circle Graphs

A circle graph enables you to compare parts with a whole. Together, the sections of the circle add up to 100 percent. The circle graphs below show how the federal government spent its money in 1995 and 2000. The different sizes of the circles reflect the increase in spending before taking inflation into account. Use the following steps to analyze the circle graphs below.

1. **Identify the kind of information presented in the graph.** Match the colors in the circle graph to the spending categories listed in the key. **(a)** What percentage of the budget was spent on defense in 1995? **(b)** In 2000? **(c)** What program used the largest percentage of the federal budget in 2000?

2. **Look for relationships among the data.** **(a)** Which programs increased their percentages of the budget between 1995 and 2000? **(b)** Which three programs used the largest percentages of the budget in 1995? **(c)** In 2000?

3. **Use the graphs to draw conclusions.** Social Security benefits grew by 2 percent between 1995 and 2000. Based on this figure, some people might argue that government is providing more benefits to each recipient. What is another way to interpret this statistic?

Additional Practice

Locate federal budget data for any year between 1941 and 1945. Draw a circle graph showing all the programs that accounted for at least 3 percent of the budget. How does this budget differ from the 2000 budget?

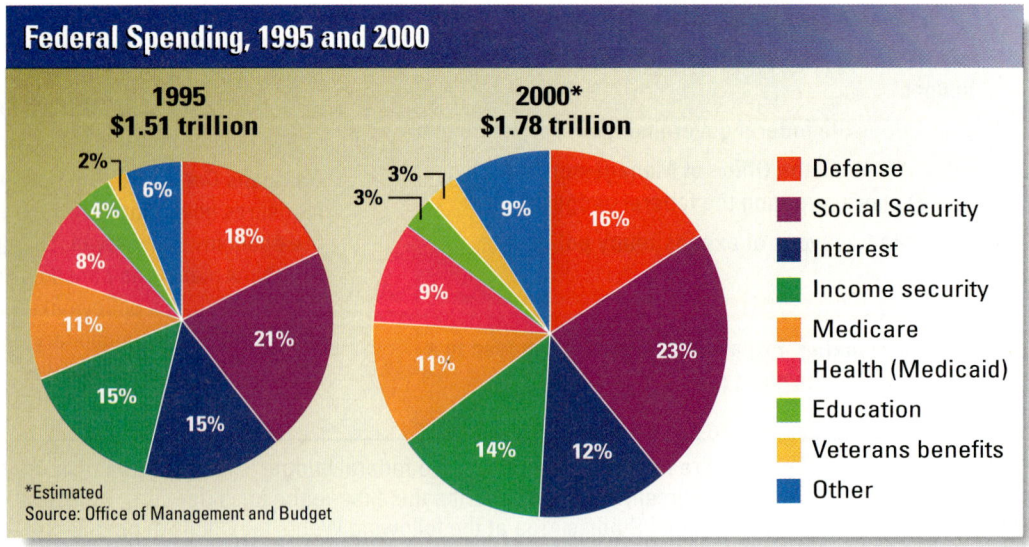

Federal Spending, 1995 and 2000

1995 $1.51 trillion

2000* $1.78 trillion

Defense
Social Security
Interest
Income security
Medicare
Health (Medicaid)
Education
Veterans benefits
Other

*Estimated
Source: Office of Management and Budget

Section 2 — Fiscal Policy Options

Preview

Objectives

After studying this section you will be able to:

1. **Compare and contrast** classical economics and Keynesian economics.
2. **Explain** the basic principles of supply-side economics.
3. **Understand** the role that fiscal policy has played in American history.

Section Focus

Fiscal policy is the use of government spending and taxes to work toward low unemployment, low inflation, and steady economic growth. Keynesian economic theories and supply-side economic theories suggest two very different ways for government to encourage growth.

Key Terms

classical economics
productive capacity
demand-side
    economics
Keynesian economics
multiplier effect
automatic stabilizer
supply-side economics
Council of Economic
    Advisers (CEA)

For thousands of years, governments have collected taxes and spent money. Until the 1930s, however, most economists believed that a government should keep its role in the economy small. These economists belonged to a school of thought called classical economics.

Classical Economics

Throughout this book, you have read about the workings of a free market economy. In a free market, people act in their own self-interest, causing prices to rise or fall so that supply and demand will always return to equilibrium. This idea that free markets regulate themselves is at the heart of a school of thought known as **classical economics**. Adam Smith, David Ricardo, and Thomas Malthus are all considered classical economists. For more than a century, classical economics dominated economic theory and government policies.

The Great Depression that began in 1929 challenged this thinking. Prices fell over several years, so demand should have increased enough to stimulate production as consumers took advantage of low prices. Instead, demand also fell as people lost their jobs and bank failures wiped out their savings. According to classical economics,

the market should have reached equilibrium, with full employment. But it didn't, and millions suffered from unemployment and other hardships. Many people were too poor to buy enough food for their families, while farmers lost their farms because corn was selling for seven cents a bushel, beef for two and a half cents a pound, and apples were five for a penny.

classical economics *the idea that free markets can regulate themselves*

▼ The economic hardships brought about by the Great Depression challenged the ideas of classical economics.

productive capacity
the maximum output that an economy can produce without big increases in inflation

demand-side economics *the idea that government spending and tax cuts help an economy by raising demand*

Keynesian economics *a form of demand-side economics that encourages government action to increase or decrease demand and output*

The Great Depression highlighted a problem with classical economics: it did not address *how long* it would take for the market to return to equilibrium. Classical economists recognized it could take some time, and looked to the "long run" for equilibrium to reestablish itself. One economist, who was not satisfied with the idea of simply waiting for the economy to recover on its own, commented: "In the long run we are all dead." That man was John Maynard Keynes (pronounced CANES).

Keynesian Economics

British economist John Maynard Keynes developed a new theory of economics to explain the Depression. Keynes presented his ideas in 1936 in a book called *The General Theory of Employment, Interest, and Money.* He wanted to develop a comprehensive explanation of economic forces. Such an explanation should, he argued, tell economists and politicians how to get out of economic crises like the Great Depression. It should also tell them how to avoid crises in the first place. In sharp contrast to classical economics, Keynes wanted to give government a tool it could use now, in the short run.

A Broader View

A key to Keynes's ideas was a broader view of a country's economy. Classical economists had always looked at the equilibrium of supply and demand for *individual products.* In contrast, Keynes focused instead on the economy *as a whole.*

Keynes looked at the productive capacity of the entire economy. **Productive capacity,** often called full-employment output, is the maximum output that an economy can sustain over a period of time without increasing inflation. Keynes attempted to answer the difficult question posed by the Great Depression: why does the actual production in an economy sometimes fall far short of its productive capacity?

Keynes argued that the Great Depression was continuing because neither consumers nor businesses had an incentive to spend enough to cause an increase in production. After all, why would a company spend money to increase production when no one had enough money to buy its products? How could unemployed consumers spend money they didn't have? The only way to end the Depression would be if someone, somewhere, started spending.

A New Role for Government

Keynes thought that the spender should be the government. In the early 1930s, only the government still had the resources to spend enough to affect the whole economy. In effect, the government could make up for the drop in private spending by buying goods and services on its own. This, Keynes argued, would encourage production and increase employment. Then, as people went back to work, they would spend their wages on more goods and services, leading to even higher levels of production. This ever-expanding cycle would carry the economy out of the depression, and the government could then step back and reduce its spending. This is known as **demand-side economics** because it involves changing demand to help the economy.

These ideas form the basis of Keynesian economics. **Keynesian economics** is basically the idea that the economy is composed of

Figure 15.5 Keynesian Economics

High output

Productive capacity

Output

Government

Consumer spending | Consumer spending

Business spending | Business spending

Low output

In a recession or depression, businesses and consumers do not demand as much as the economy can produce. Keynes argued that government spending can bring the economy up to its productive capacity.

Keynes added government spending to the classical model of demand.
Government What role did Keynes envision for government in the economy?

three sectors—individuals, business, and government—and that government actions can make up for changes in the other two. Keynesian economics proposes that by using fiscal policy the government can, and should, help the economy.

Avoiding Recessions and Depressions

Keynes argued that fiscal policy can be used to fight the two fundamental macroeconomic problems. These two opposing problems are periods of recession/depression and periods of inflation.

The federal government, Keynes argued, should keep track of the total level of spending by consumers, businesses, and government in the economy. If total spending begins to fall far below the level required to keep the economy running at full capacity, the government should watch out for the possibility of an upcoming recession or depression.

The government can respond by increasing its own spending until spending by the private sector returns to a higher level. Or, it can cut taxes, so that spending and investment by consumers and businesses increases. As you read in the previous section, raising government spending and cutting taxes are expansionary fiscal policies.

President Franklin D. Roosevelt carried out expansionary fiscal policies after his election in 1932. His New Deal put people to work building dams, planting forests, and constructing schools across the country, all paid for by the government.

Many people argue that instead of creating new jobs, such public works projects only shift employment from the private to the public sector. The taxes required to pay for them reduce demand in the private sector as much as they increase it in the public sector. In addition, work relief jobs are less productive than private sector jobs because their goal is employment, not efficient production.

Controlling Inflation

Keynes also argued that the government could use a contractionary fiscal policy to prevent inflation or reduce its severity. The government can reduce inflation either by increasing taxes or by reducing its own spending. Both of these actions decrease overall demand.

▲ During the Depression, the government's Works Progress Administration (WPA) hired artists to paint murals in public places like this California post office.

The Multiplier Effect

Fiscal policy, although difficult to control, is an extremely powerful tool. The key to its power is the **multiplier effect**. The multiplier effect in fiscal policy is the idea that every one dollar change in fiscal policy—whether it be an increase in spending or a decrease in taxes—creates a *greater than* one dollar change in the national income. In other words, the effects of changes in fiscal policy are multiplied.

Suppose the federal government finds that business investment is dropping. It fears a recession. To prevent a recession, in the next budget, the government decides to spend an extra $10 billion to stimulate the economy. How will this affect the economy?

With this government spending, demand, income, and GDP will increase by $10 billion. After all, if the government buys an extra $10 billion of goods and services, then

multiplier effect *the idea that every one dollar of government spending creates more than one dollar in economic activity*

an extra $10 billion of goods and services have been produced. However, the GDP will increase by more than $10 billion. Here's why:

The businesses that sold the $10 billion in goods and services to the government have earned an additional $10 billion. These businesses will spend their additional earnings on wages, raw materials, and investment, sending money to workers, other suppliers, and stockholders. What will the recipients do with this money? They will spend part of it, perhaps 80 percent, or $8 billion. The businesses that benefit from this second round of spending will then pass it back to households, who will again spend 80 percent of it, or $6.4 billion. The next round will add an additional $5.1 billion to the economy, and so on. When all of these rounds of spending are added up, the initial government spending of $10 billion leads to an increase of $50 billion in GDP. The multiplier effect gives fiscal policy initiatives a much bigger kick than the initial amount spent.

Automatic Stabilizers

Fiscal policy is used to achieve many economic goals. One of the most important things that fiscal policy can achieve is a more stable economy. A stable economy is one in which there are no rapid changes in the economic indicators you read about in Chapter 12. What's more, set up properly, fiscal policy can come close to stabilizing the economy *automatically*.

Figure 15.6 shows how real GDP in the United States changed each year from 1920 to 2000. Prior to World War II, there were much larger changes in GDP from year to year than after World War II. Although GDP still fluctuates, these fluctuations have not been as large as they were before World War II. Economic growth has been much more stable in the United States in the last 50 years.

Why did this happen? After the war, federal taxes and spending on transfer payments—two key tools of fiscal policy—increased sharply. Taxes and transfer payments, or transfers of cash from the government to consumers, stabilize economic growth. When national income is high, the government collects more in taxes and pays out less in transfer payments. Both of these actions take money away from consumers, and therefore reduce spending. This decrease in spending balances out the increase in spending that results from rising income in a healthy economy.

The opposite is also true. When income in the country is low, the government collects less in taxes and pays out more in transfer payments. Both actions increase the amount of money held by consumers, and thus increase spending. This increase in spending balances against the decrease in spending that results from falling income.

As the graph shows, taxes and transfer payments do not eliminate changes in the rate of growth of GDP, but they do make these changes smaller. They are known as stabilizers because they work to stabilize economic growth. It is important to note that policymakers do not have to make changes in taxes and transfer payments for them to have their stabilizing effect. Taxes

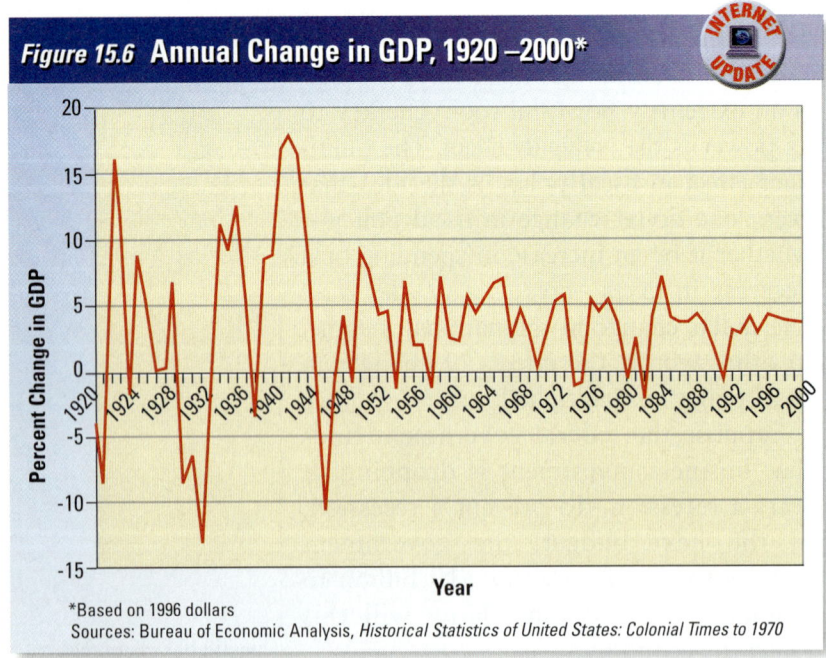

Figure 15.6 Annual Change in GDP, 1920–2000*

*Based on 1996 dollars
Sources: Bureau of Economic Analysis, *Historical Statistics of United States: Colonial Times to 1970*

BUILDING KEY CONCEPTS

The United States experienced strong economic swings before World War II.
Government How do the years after the war show the effect of automatic stabilizers on the economy?

and most transfer payments are tied to the GDP and to personal income, so they change automatically. Thus, taxes and transfer payments are known as **automatic stabilizers.**

Some stabilizers are no longer automatic. The former Aid to Families with Dependent Children, often called "welfare," lost its entitlement status in 1996 and was renamed Temporary Assistance for Needy Families (TANF). Now, the federal government gives the states a set amount of money each year to spend as they wish. However, the stabilizer effect was not completely lost. When the economy boomed in the late 1990s, state spending on TANF fell.

Supply-Side Economics

Another school of economic thought, supply-side economics, promotes a different direction for fiscal policy. **Supply-side economics** stresses the influence of taxation on the economy. Supply-siders believe that taxes have strong negative influences on economic output. While Keynesian economics uses government to change aggregate demand, supply-side economics tries to increase economic growth by increasing aggregate supply.

The Laffer Curve

Supply-side economists often use the Laffer curve, named after the economist Arthur Laffer, to illustrate the effects of taxes. The Laffer curve shows the relationship between the tax rate set by the government and the total tax revenue that the government collects. The total revenue depends on both the tax rate and the health of the economy. The Laffer curve illustrates that high tax rates may not bring in much revenue if these high tax rates cause economic activity to decrease.

Figure 15.7 depicts the Laffer curve. Suppose the government imposes a tax on the wages of workers. If the tax rate is zero, as at point a on the graph, the government will collect no revenue, although the economy will prosper from the lack of taxes. As the government raises the tax

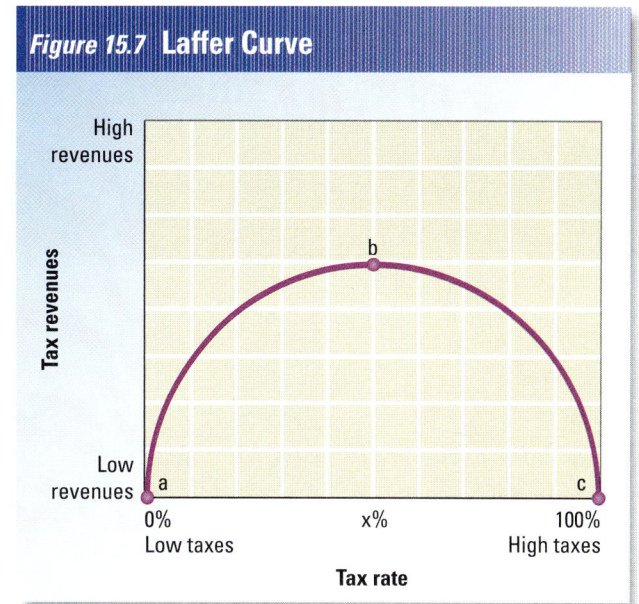

Figure 15.7 Laffer Curve

According to the Laffer curve, both a high and a low tax rate can produce the same revenues. **Incentives** **Why do higher tax rates sometimes cause revenues to fall?**

rate, it starts to collect some revenue. Follow this change in Figure 15.7 by tracing the curve from no taxes at point a to x percent taxation at point b.

To the left of point b on the curve, higher tax rates will discourage some people from working as many hours and prevent companies from investing and increasing production. The net effect of a higher tax rate and a slightly lower tax base is an increase in revenue.

To the right of point b, the decrease in workers' effort is so large that the higher tax rate *decreases* total tax revenue. In other words, high rates of taxation will eventually discourage so many people from working that tax revenues will fall sharply. In the extreme case of a 100 percent tax rate, no one would want to work! In this case, shown at point c on the curve, the government would collect no revenue.

Taxes and Output

The heart of the supply-side argument is that a tax cut increases total employment so much that the government actually collects more in taxes at the new, lower tax rate. Suppose the initial tax on labor is $3 an hour, and the typical worker works 30

automatic stabilizer *a government program that changes automatically depending on GDP and a person's income*

supply-side economics *a school of economics that believes tax cuts can help an economy by raising supply*

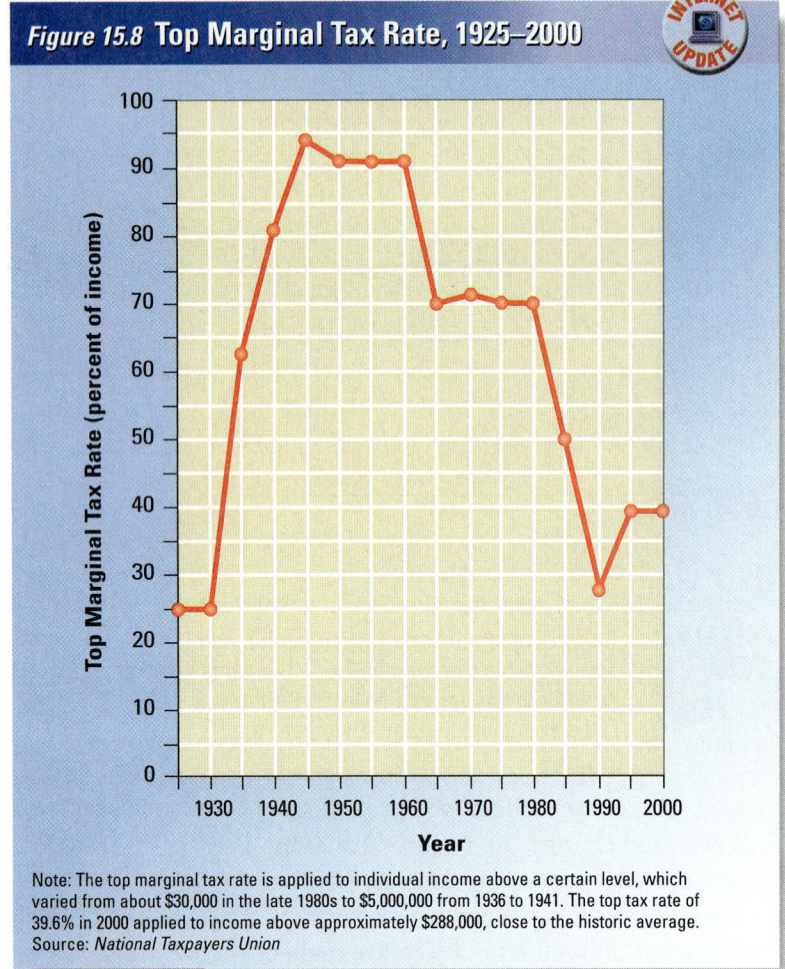

Figure 15.8 Top Marginal Tax Rate, 1925–2000

Top Marginal Tax Rate (percent of income)

Year

Note: The top marginal tax rate is applied to individual income above a certain level, which varied from about $30,000 in the late 1980s to $5,000,000 from 1936 to 1941. The top tax rate of 39.6% in 2000 applied to income above approximately $288,000, close to the historic average.
Source: *National Taxpayers Union*

Tax rates varied widely throughout the last century.
Government **When were top marginal income tax rates at their highest?**

Council of Economic Advisers (CEA) *a group of three respected economists that advise the President on economic policy*

hours per week, paying a total of $90 in taxes each week. If the government cuts the tax on labor to $2 an hour, and the worker responds by working 50 hours per week, the worker will pay $100 in taxes a week, an increase of $10. If all workers respond to the tax cut by working this much harder, the tax cut will increase total revenue.

Actual experience has proven that while a tax cut encourages some workers to work more hours, the end result is a relatively small increase in the number of hours

◀ Increasing production during World War II finally ended the high unemployment of the 1930s.

worked. In the example above, if the tax cut increased the hours worked from 30 hours to 35 hours, the worker would pay only $70 in taxes ($2 per hour times 35 hours), down from $90 ($3 per hour times 30 hours). In general, taxpayers do not react strongly enough to tax cuts to increase tax revenue.

Fiscal Policy in American History

As you recall, Keynes presented his ideas at the same time that the world economy was still engulfed in the Great Depression. President Herbert Hoover, influenced by classical economics, thought that the economy was basically sound and would return to equilibrium on its own. His popular successor, President Franklin D. Roosevelt, was much more willing to increase government spending to help lift the economy out of depression. After the Democratic party won landslide victories in the 1932 and 1934 federal elections, Roosevelt started several programs to pump money into the economy.

World War II

Keynes's theory was fully tested in the United States during World War II. As the country geared up for war, government spending increased dramatically. The government spent large sums of money to feed soldiers and equip them with everything from warplanes to rifles to medical supplies. This money was given to the private sector in exchange for goods. Just as Keynesian economics predicted, the additional demand for goods and services moved the country sharply out of the Great Depression and toward full productive capacity. After the war, Congress created the **Council of Economic Advisers (CEA)**, a group of three respected economists that could advise the President on economic policy.

The Kennedy Administration

Between 1945 and 1960, the U.S. economy was healthy and growing, despite a few minor recessions. The last recession continued into the term of President John F. Kennedy, with unemployment at 6.7 percent.

Kennedy's chief financial policy advisor was Walter Heller, a Keynesian who thought that the economy was below its productive capacity. Heller believed that unemployment would fall to 4 percent if the economy were at full capacity. He convinced Kennedy that tax cuts would stimulate demand and bring the economy closer to full productive capacity.

As Figure 15.8 shows, tax rates were extremely high in the early 1960s. The highest individual income tax rate was about 90 percent, compared to about 40 percent today. The top business rate was 52 percent, compared with 35 percent in recent years. So Kennedy proposed tax cuts, both because he agreed with Heller, and because tax cuts are popular.

A modified version of Kennedy's tax cuts was enacted in 1964, after Kennedy's assassination. At the same time, the Vietnam War raised government spending. Over the next two years, the economy grew rapidly. Consumption and the GDP increased by more than 4 percent a year. While there is no way to prove that the tax cut caused this increase, the result is what Keynesian economics had predicted.

Supply-Side Policies in the 1980s

Keynesian economics was used on many other occasions in the 1960s and 1970s to try to adjust the national economy. During the late 1970s, however, unemployment and inflation rates soared. Ronald Reagan became President in 1981 and instituted new policies based on supply-side economics. In 1981, Reagan proposed a tax cut that was put in place and reduced taxes by 25 percent over three years. Unlike Keynes, Reagan did not believe that government spending should be used to bring the economy out of a recession. After a brief but harsh recession in 1982, caused partly by the Fed's tightening of the money supply to reduce inflation, the economy recovered and flourished.

For many reasons, however, government spending continued to rise each year while Reagan was in office. During the Reagan and George H.W. Bush presidencies and the first years of Bill Clinton's first term, the federal government spent much more money than it took in. This gap caused increasing concern among economists and policymakers. In the next section, you'll read about these concerns in detail.

Section 2 Assessment

Key Terms and Main Ideas

1. What is the central idea of **classical economics**?
2. Why is full-employment output another way to describe **productive capacity**?
3. Compare and contrast **Keynesian economics** and **supply-side economics**.
4. Explain the **multiplier effect**.

Applying Economic Concepts

5. *Critical Thinking* Why can low tax rates encourage investment and increase employment and wages?
6. *Try This* Keynes suggested that building pyramids was good for the Egyptian economy. Why would Keynes have suggested this, and can you think of an analogy in our society for the building of the pyramids? Explain your answer.

Take It to the NET Write a brief essay describing the life, times, and ideas of John Maynard Keynes. Use the links provided in the Social Studies area at the following Web site for help in completing this activity. **www.phschool.com**

Profile

John Maynard Keynes
(1883–1946)

A government official, teacher, and writer, John Maynard Keynes is one of a handful of economists who have substantially affected the course of history. His revolutionary theories on supply, demand, and unemployment led to the first use of government programs to help manage the nation's economy.

Early Career and Accomplishments

Keynes graduated from the University of Cambridge with a degree in mathematics in 1905. Rising through government service, he served as Britain's economic advisor at the Versailles Conference, where the peace treaty to end World War I was drafted.

Upset over the harsh treaty, Keynes resigned from government and returned to Cambridge to teach. In 1919, he wrote *The Economic Consequences of the Peace*, which correctly predicted that the treaty's economic penalties on Germany would lead to future problems in Europe.

Keynes and the Great Depression

At the height of the Great Depression in 1936, Keynes completed his most famous book, *The General Theory of Employment, Interest and Money*. In analyzing the causes and effects of the Depression, he revolutionized thinking about government's role in a nation's economy.

Before Keynes, most economists believed that government should leave the economy alone as it passed through the low points of the business cycle. In this view, the laws of supply and demand—as they applied to employment and wages, consumption and production, and prices—would lead to economic recovery.

Keynesian Economics

Keynes claimed that in a depression, a natural recovery is impossible because the private sector cannot consume all it can produce. He argued that government should lower interest rates and taxes to encourage investment and increase spending on public projects to stimulate demand for goods and create jobs. Keynes recognized that raising spending while cutting taxes would lead to budget deficits, but he accepted that liability if it boosted employment and led to economic recovery.

Keynes's theories were controversial at the time, and remain so today, even though other economists have greatly revised and expanded upon his ideas. In the United States, politicians have followed his program of government intervention in good economic times as well as bad. This has led some critics to blame Keynesian economics for the huge federal budget deficits that the United States built up from the 1960s to the mid-1990s.

CHECK FOR UNDERSTANDING

1. Source Reading Explain the following Keynes statement: "Formerly there was no expenditure out of the proceeds of borrowing that it was thought proper for the State to incur except for war. . . . Therefore, we have not infrequently had to wait for a war to terminate a major depression."

2. Critical Thinking How would government spending programs stimulate employment, consumption, and production in the private sector of the economy?

3. Learn More Find out what involvement Keynes had with international economic institutions after World War II, and explain how these institutions now reflect Keynes's economic theories.

Section 3

Budget Deficits and the National Debt

Preview

Objectives

After studying this section you will be able to:

1. **Explain** the importance of balancing the budget.
2. **Analyze** how budget deficits add to the national debt.
3. **Summarize** the problems caused by the national debt.
4. **Identify** how a government can reduce budget deficits and the national debt.

Section Focus

Fiscal policy decisions can lead the federal government to spend more money than it brings in, causing budget deficits and a national debt. Economists, lawmakers, and citizens debate whether the benefits of government spending outweigh the costs of debt.

Key Terms

balanced budget
budget surplus
budget deficit
hyperinflation
Treasury bill
Treasury note
Treasury bond
national debt
crowding-out effect

As you have learned, the federal government uses fiscal policy—taxing and spending—to make changes in the economy. Fiscal policy is a powerful tool. It can be used to help stimulate demand, increase production, create jobs, increase GDP, avoid recessions, control inflation, and stabilize economic growth. As you'll read in this section, raising government spending can lead to yearly budget deficits that add up to an enormous debt. The costs of this debt must be measured against the benefits of higher government spending.

Balancing the Budget

The basic tool of fiscal policy is the federal budget. It is made up of two fundamental parts: revenue (taxes) and expenditures (spending programs). When the federal government's revenues equal its expenditures in any particular year, the federal government has a **balanced budget**. There is the same amount of money going into and coming out of the Treasury.

In reality, the federal budget is almost never balanced. Usually, it is either running a *surplus* or a *deficit*. A **budget surplus** occurs in any year when revenues exceed expenditures. In other words, there is more money going into the Treasury than coming out of it. A **budget deficit** occurs in any year when expenditures exceed revenues. In other words, there is more money coming out of the Treasury than going into it.

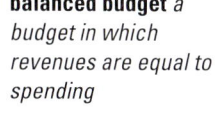

◄ Until recently the national debt, the sum of all the money owed by the federal government, seemed to be spiraling out of control.

balanced budget *a budget in which revenues are equal to spending*

budget surplus *a situation in which the government takes in more than it spends*

budget deficit *a situation in which the government spends more than it takes in*

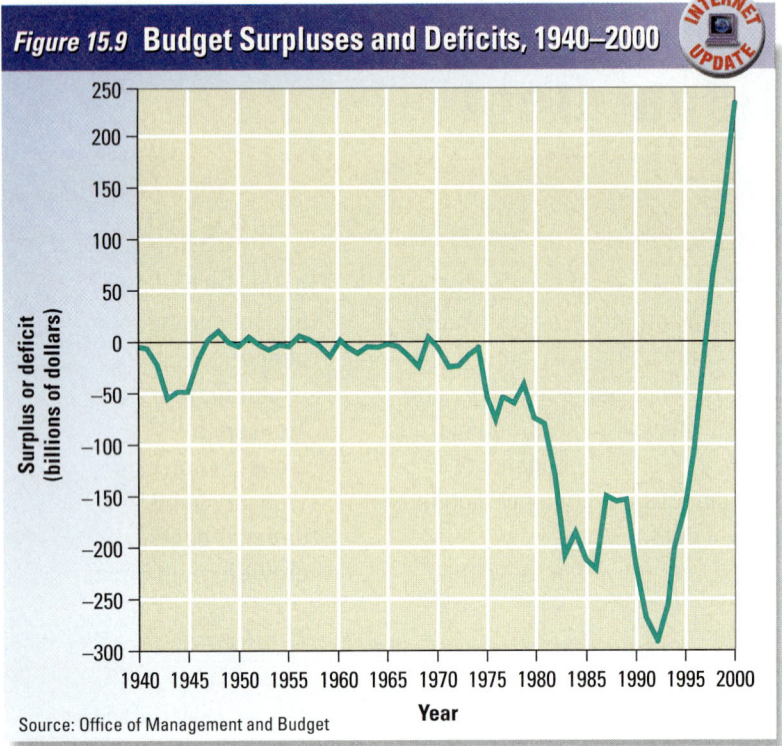

Figure 15.9 Budget Surpluses and Deficits, 1940–2000

Source: Office of Management and Budget

Budget deficits swelled in the 1980s and early 1990s. **Government** What was the dominant trend in deficits in the late 1990s?

Assume the federal government starts with a balanced budget. If the government decreases expenditures without changing anything else, it will run a budget surplus. Similarly, if it increases taxes—revenues—without changing anything else, it will run a surplus.

The same sort of analysis describes budget deficits. If the government increases expenditures without changing anything else, it will run a deficit. Similarly, if it decreases taxes without changing anything else, it will run a deficit. The deficit can grow or shrink because of forces beyond the government's control. During a recession, fewer people are working, and tax revenues fall as spending on antipoverty programs rises. Surpluses and deficits can be very large figures. The largest deficit was about $290 billion, in 1992.

Responding to Budget Deficits

When the government runs a deficit, that means it did not take in enough revenue to cover its expenses for the year. When this

hyperinflation *very high inflation*

happens, the government must find a way to pay for the extra expenditures. There are two basic actions the government can take to do so.

Creating Money

The government could create new money to pay salaries for its workers and benefits for citizens. Traditionally, governments simply printed the bills they needed. Today, the government can create money electronically by depositing money in people's bank accounts. The effect is the same. This approach works for relatively small deficits, but can cause severe problems when there are large deficits. Why?

When the government creates more money, it increases the amount of money in circulation. This increases the demand for goods and services and can increase output. But once the economy reaches full employment, output cannot increase. The increase in money will mean that there are more dollars, but the same amount of goods and services. Prices in the economy rise so that a greater amount of money will be needed to purchase the same amount of goods and services. In other words, prices go up, and the result is inflation. As you read in Chapter 13, high levels of inflation are a serious economic problem.

Covering very large deficits by printing more money can cause very high inflation, called **hyperinflation**. This happened in Germany and Russia after World War I, Brazil and Argentina in the 1980s, and Ukraine in the 1990s. If the United States experienced hyperinflation, a shirt that cost $30 in June might cost $50 in July, $80 in August, and $400 in December!

Borrowing Money

As an alternative to creating money to cover a budget deficit, the federal government can borrow money. The government commonly borrows money by selling bonds. As you read in Chapter 11, a bond is a type of loan: a promise to repay money in the future, with interest. Consumers and businesses buy bonds from the government. The government thus has the money to cover its budget deficit. In return, the purchasers of the bonds earn interest over time.

United States Savings Bonds allow millions of Americans to lend small amounts of money to the federal government for a period as brief as three months or as long as 30 years. In return, they earn interest on the bonds. Other common forms of government borrowing are **Treasury bills, Treasury notes**, and **Treasury bonds**. Treasury bills are short-term bonds that must be repaid within a year or less. Treasury notes cover periods from two to ten years. Treasury bonds may be issued for as long as 30 years.

Federal borrowing lets the government undertake more projects than it could otherwise afford. These include projects such as building airports, highways, and national parks. Wise borrowing allows the government to create more public goods and services. Federal borrowing, however, also has serious disadvantages.

The National Debt

One problem with the government borrowing money is that it creates a national debt. The **national debt** is the total amount of money the federal government owes to bondholders. Every year that there is a budget deficit, and the federal government borrows money to cover it, the national debt will grow.

The national debt is owed to investors who hold Treasury bonds, bills, and notes. If you have a federal savings bond, that bond represents money you have loaned the government. The national debt is owned by investors in the United States and around the world who have put their money and their trust in the federal government. In this way, a modest national debt is

good because it offers a safe investment for individuals and businesses.

The Difference Between Deficit and Debt

Many people are confused about the difference between the deficit and the debt. The deficit is the amount of money the government borrows for one budget, representing one fiscal year. The debt, on the other hand, is a sum of all the government borrowing up to that time, minus the borrowings that have been repaid. The debt is the total of all deficits and surpluses.

Measuring the National Debt

In dollar terms, the size of the national debt is extremely large. At the end of the twentieth century, it exceeded $5 trillion! Such large numbers can be confusing. A more useful way to evaluate the size of the debt is to look at it as a percentage of GDP.

Historically, debt as a percentage of GDP rises during wartime, when government spending increases faster than taxation, and falls during peacetime. This can be seen in the graph in Figure 15.10.

▲ In the past, governments often just printed more bills to fund government spending.

Treasury bill *a government bond that is repaid within three months to a year*

Treasury note *a government bond that is repaid within two to ten years*

Treasury bond *a government bond that can be issued for as long as 30 years*

national debt *all the money the federal government owes to bondholders*

Notice how the pattern changed in the 1980s, when the United States began to run a large debt, even though the country wasn't at war. The debt was in part a result of increases in spending during President Ronald Reagan's terms. As you read in the previous section, the Reagan administration also lowered tax rates to pull the economy out of a recession. The combined effect of higher spending and lower tax rates was several years of increased budget deficits. The government borrowed billions of dollars to cover these deficits, adding to the national debt. Meanwhile, an economic downturn in 1981–1982 reduced GDP. As a result, the ratio of debt to GDP grew very large for peacetime.

Is the Debt a Problem?

The growth of the national debt during the Reagan administration led many to focus on the problems caused by a national debt. In general, two problems can arise from a national debt.

crowding-out effect
the loss of funds for private investment due to government borrowing

Problems of a National Debt

The first problem with a national debt is that it reduces the funds available for businesses to invest. This is because in order to sell its bonds, the government must offer a high interest rate to attract buyers. Individuals and businesses, attracted by the high interest rates and the security of investing in the government, use their savings or profits to buy government bonds.

However, every dollar spent on a government bond is one fewer dollar that can be invested in private business. Less money is available for companies to expand their factories, conduct research, and develop new products, and interest rates rise. Economists call this the **crowding-out effect**, because federal borrowing "crowds out" private borrowing by making it harder for private businesses to borrow. A national debt, then, can hurt investment and slow economic growth over the long run. On the other hand, more investment in the private sector can lead to lower prices, more jobs, and overall higher standards of living.

The second problem with a high national debt is that the government must pay interest to bondholders. The more the government borrows, the more interest it has to pay. Paying the interest on the debt is sometimes called *servicing the debt*. Over time, the interest payments have become very large. At the beginning of the twenty-first century, the federal government spent about $250 billion a year servicing the debt. Moreover, there is an opportunity cost—dollars spent servicing the debt cannot be spent on something else, like defense, health care, or infrastructure.

Other Views of a National Debt

Not everyone agrees that the national debt is such a large problem. Traditional Keynesian economists believe that fiscal policy is an important tool that can be used to help achieve full productive capacity. To these analysts, the benefits of a productive economy outweigh the costs of interest on national debt.

However, a budget deficit can only be an effective tool if it is temporary. If the

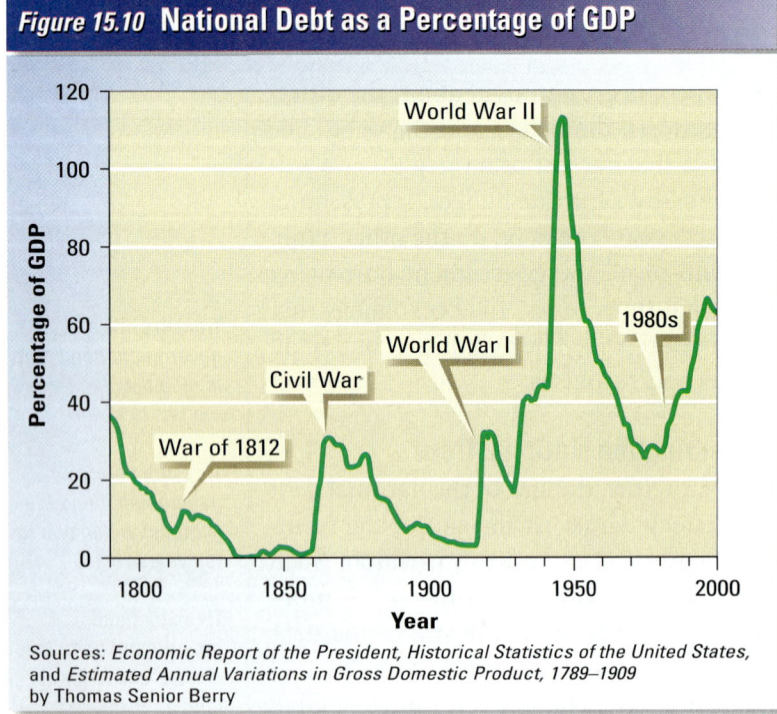

Figure 15.10 National Debt as a Percentage of GDP

Sources: *Economic Report of the President, Historical Statistics of the United States,* and *Estimated Annual Variations in Gross Domestic Product, 1789–1909* by Thomas Senior Berry

War puts special strains on government spending, and governments borrow money to pay the high costs.
Government What must governments do when the war ends?

Figure 15.11 Effects of the Budget Deficit

The federal government spends more than it takes in, and has to borrow money to cover the deficit.

Investors trust the U.S. government and loan money to the government by buying bonds.

Banks and investors have less money to lend private businesses. Private businesses must pay a higher interest rate to borrow scarce money.

Government borrowing "crowds out" private investment by taking away some funds that could have been invested in private business.

Incentives Why do lenders put their money in government bonds?

government runs large budget deficits each year, the costs of the growing debt will eventually outweigh the benefits.

Deficits, Surpluses, and the National Debt

During the 1980s and into the 1990s, annual budget deficits added substantially to the national debt. Several factors frustrated lawmakers in their attempts to control the deficits. As we have seen, much of the budget consists of entitlement spending that is politically difficult to change. Another large part of the budget consists of interest that must be paid to bondholders. Finally, specific budget cuts are often opposed by groups affected.

Efforts to Reduce Deficits

Concerns about the budget deficits of the mid-1980s caused Congress to pass the Gramm-Rudman-Hollings Act, which created automatic across-the-board cuts in federal expenditures if the deficit exceeded a certain amount. This saved lawmakers from having to make difficult decisions about individual funding cuts. The Act exempted significant portions of the budget (such as interest payments and many entitlement programs) from the cuts.

When the Supreme Court found that significant portions of the Act were unconstitutional, Congress attempted to correct the flaws. In 1990, however, lawmakers realized that the deficit was going to be much larger than expected. Because

Congress had exempted so many programs from automatic cuts, funding for non-exempt programs would be dramatically reduced.

To resolve the crisis, President George H.W. Bush and congressional leaders negotiated a new budget system that replaced Gramm-Rudman-Hollings. The 1990 Budget Enforcement Act created a "pay-as-you-go" system that requires Congress to raise enough revenue to cover increases in direct spending, so that the budget deficit cannot grow larger.

In addition, at various times citizens and politicians have suggested amending the Constitution to require a balanced budget. In 1995, a balanced budget amendment passed in the House and failed by only a single vote in the Senate. Supporters argued that the amendment would force the federal government to be more disciplined about its spending. Opponents objected that a constitutional amendment would not be flexible enough to deal with rapid changes in the economy.

End-of-Century Surpluses

The late 1990s brought a welcome reversal of fortune. For the first time in thirty years, the President and the Office of Management and Budget (OMB) were able to announce that the government was running a surplus. How did this happen? First, the new budget procedures begun

FAST FACT

Unlike the federal government, most states already require a balanced budget. However, what works well at the state level may not work for the federal government. State requirements range from strict to very weak. At least ten states can carry over budget deficits into the next year or borrow money to cover the deficit. Also, many states have a "rainy day" fund, where surplus money is stored to pay for future deficits. Neither would be allowed under a federal balanced budget amendment.

under President Bush and extended under President Clinton did help Congress control the growth of government spending. Second, tax increases by President Clinton in 1993 resulted in more federal revenue. Finally, the strong economy and low unemployment during the 1990s meant that more individuals and corporations were earning more money—and thus paying more in taxes.

The Future of Fiscal Policy

The change from deficits to surpluses in the late 1990s brought with it a vigorous debate about the best way to use the surplus. Many people argued that the extra funds should be used to strengthen Social Security. An increase in the number of retirees and a decrease in the number of working persons is expected to put a serious strain on the Social Security system. A budget surplus could be used to reduce the anticipated shortfall.

When George W. Bush was elected President in 2000, he carried through on his campaign promise for a substantial tax cut that reduced the future surplus. In addition, as the economy slowed in 2001,

estimates of the future surplus also began to fall.

Following the September 11, 2001, attacks on the World Trade Center and the Pentagon and the deepening recession, the Office of Management and Budget reported that the surplus would end and that the federal government would run a deficit until 2005. The combination of the recession and President Bush's tax cut will reduce governmental revenues, while the war on terrorism abroad and the added costs of domestic security will increase expenditures. The economic stimulus package proposed after the September 11th terrorist attacks also cuts into the surplus.

The balance of the federal budget is likely to be an issue for some time to come. As people have become more concerned about the budget and the size of the national debt, there is naturally less of a role for fiscal policy. Many economists and politicians now see Keynesian fiscal policy as a way to influence the economy only in the short term. As you will read in the next chapter, there is a second governmental economic tool—monetary policy—that has become increasingly important.

Section 3 Assessment

Key Terms and Main Ideas

1. What is a **balanced budget**?
2. How might a **budget deficit** be related to the **national debt**?
3. How does a **Treasury note** differ from a **Treasury bill**?

Applying Economic Concepts

4. *Try This* You're a lawmaker, and you get to decide what to do with this year's budget surplus. Write a brief proposal explaining whether the surplus should be used for new spending, tax cuts, or to buy back bonds and cut interest payments. Include explanations for your proposals.

5. *Math Practice* Use the data in Figure 15.9 to determine the approximate size of the largest budget deficits in each of the following decades: **(a)** 1940s **(b)** 1960s **(c)** 1970s **(d)** 1990s.

6. *Using the Databank* Study the Federal Debt and Federal Deficit graphs on page 542 of the Databank. Summarize the trends shown in the data for the period from 1980 to 1990 and the period from 1990 to 2000.

7. *Critical Thinking* Create a flowchart showing how the creation of money by the government to pay for a budget deficit can lead to inflation.

Take It to the NET

At what rate is the national debt growing or shrinking? How much was the national debt on your birthday this year? Write a summary of your findings. Use the links provided in the Social Studies area at the following Web site for help in completing this activity.
www.phschool.com

Will Social Security Survive?

Until the 1930s, paying for retirement was almost entirely up to the individual. During the 1930s, however, the Great Depression left nearly half of all senior citizens unable to support themselves. To help them, the federal government created the Social Security program in 1935.

Social Security System Here's how the program works. Workers pay a Social Security tax, which is matched by their employers. After they retire, workers receive Social Security payments for the rest of their lives.

Social Security is a "pay as you go" system. Most of the Social Security taxes paid by today's workers are used to pay benefits to today's retirees. Any surplus is put into trust funds to earn interest. In 2001, there were 3.4 workers paying taxes for every retiree receiving benefits.

Trouble Ahead Many economists are concerned about what will happen to Social Security in the future. If the system continues unchanged, experts warn that Social Security payments will exceed revenues in the year 2013. By 2032, the Social Security trust fund will be exhausted.

▲ President Franklin D. Roosevelt signed the Social Security Act into law in 1935.

Why will this system be broke by the 2030s? The reason is the "baby boom," the period between 1945 and 1964 when there was a large increase in the number of babies born. As baby boomers retire, there will only be two workers for every retiree receiving benefits. Also, life expectancies are rising, which means that Americans will collect benefits longer.

Possible Solutions In the late 1990s, the President and Congress began to focus their attention on saving Social Security. But how should it be done? Some people believe that the age of retirement should be further increased. Others believe that the government should invest Social Security reserves in the stock market. However, all agree that depriving Americans of Social Security would be disastrous.

Applying Economic Ideas

1. Do you think that paying Social Security taxes should be mandatory? Explain.

2. How do baby boomers present a challenge to the future of Social Security?

Projected Population, 2000–2050 (in thousands)

Year	Americans aged 25-64	Americans aged 65 and over
2000	142,883	34,709
2010	155,660	39,408
2020	161,999	53,220
2030	162,252	69,379
2040	171,360	75,233
2050	182,621	78,859

Source: U.S. Census Bureau

Chapter Summary

Asummary of major ideas in Chapter 15 appears below. See also the **Guide to the Essentials of Economics**, which provides additional review and test practice of key concepts in Chapter 15.

Section 1 Understanding Fiscal Policy (pp. 387–393)

The government can try to stabilize the economy through **fiscal policy**, or changing how much it taxes and spends. The tool it uses is the **federal budget**, which lists how much money the government expects to take in and how it will spend that money. **Expansionary policies** include lowering taxes and spending more to increase output. **Contractionary policies** include raising taxes and cutting spending to lower economic growth.

Section 2 Fiscal Policy Options (pp. 395–401)

The Great Depression of the 1930s seemed to disprove the idea that free markets always return to equilibrium. John Maynard Keynes argued that government spending can raise demand and help an economy recover. **Keynesian economics** drove American policy from the 1930s to the 1970s. In the 1980s, Ronald Reagan tried to increase output by putting **supply-side economics** into practice. He cut taxes to encourage people and businesses to work harder.

Section 3 Budget Deficits and the National Debt (pp. 403–408)

When the government spends more than it takes in, it runs a **budget deficit** and must create new money or borrow money to cover the difference. The government borrows money by issuing bonds. The **national debt** is all of the money the government owes to bondholders. The United States debt grew tremendously during the 1980s and early 1990s, causing problems for private businesses and leading to a public backlash against deficit spending.

Key Terms

Choose the italicized word in parentheses that best completes each sentence.

1. *(Contractionary policies/Expansionary policies)* are used to increase overall demand and GDP.
2. The theory that states that the economy regulates itself best is known as *(classical economics/Keynesian economics)*.
3. A *(Treasury note/Treasury bond)* is a long-term bond, issued sometimes for as long as 30 years.
4. *(Budget surpluses/Budget deficits)* occur when the government has money left over after paying all of its expenses for the year.
5. The maximum sustainable economic output of a society is known as its *(productive capacity/automatic stabilizer)*.
6. A government's *(fiscal year/fiscal policy)* is the use of taxing and spending to affect the overall economy.
7. The *(national debt/balanced budget)* is the total amount of money the federal government owes.

Using Graphic Organizers

8. Copy the web map below on a separate sheet of paper. Complete the diagram by filling in the primary characteristics of classical, Keynesian, and supply-side economics.

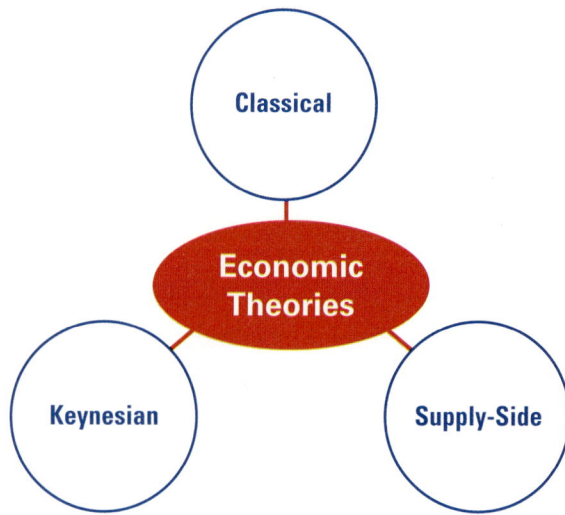

Reviewing Main Ideas

9. Describe three problems that limit fiscal policy.
10. Describe the multiplier effect in your own words.
11. Summarize the ways in which fiscal policy has affected our country since World War II.
12. How is the national debt measured?
13. What is the difference between the national debt and the budget deficit?
14. What options does the government have to respond to an annual budget deficit?

Critical Thinking

15. **Making Comparisons** What fundamental differences exist between classical economics and Keynesian economics? What events led to the popularization of Keynesian economics?
16. **Drawing Inferences** Make a list of ways in which fiscal policy affects your daily life. Which aspects of fiscal policy have the greatest effect on you?
17. **Recognizing Cause and Effect** How do automatic stabilizers affect our economy? What would our economy be like without them?
18. **Analyzing Information** Use your own words to describe the crowding-out effect. Explain why it can influence economic growth over the long run.
19. **Drawing Conclusions** What would be the benefits and drawbacks of a balanced budget amendment? Would you support such an amendment?

Problem-Solving Activity

20. Recommend your own proposal for debt reduction. Consider the examples in Section 3 when creating your proposal.

Economics Journal

Essay Writing Look at your list of items paid for by the government. Which ones do you think are essential services of government, and which do you think represent unnecessary spending, if any? In what ways has government funding helped your local economy?

Skills for Life

Comparing Circle Graphs Review the steps shown on page 394; then answer the following questions using the circle graphs below.

21. How did the percentage of federal spending on interest payments change between 1980 and 2000?
22. Which category of federal spending has seen the largest percentage decrease since 1980?
23. How have human resource outlays changed as a percentage of the federal budget?

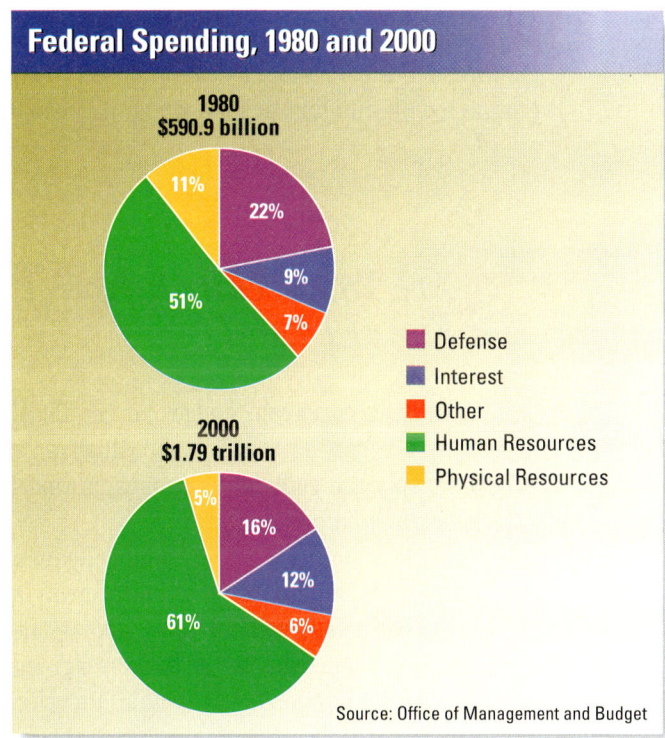

Federal Spending, 1980 and 2000

1980
$590.9 billion

11% 22% 9% 7% 51%

2000
$1.79 trillion

5% 16% 12% 6% 61%

- Defense
- Interest
- Other
- Human Resources
- Physical Resources

Source: Office of Management and Budget

Take It to the NET

Chapter 15 Self-Test As a final review activity, take the Chapter 15 Self-Test in the Social Studies area at the Web site listed below, and receive immediate feedback on your answers. The test consists of 20 multiple-choice questions designed to test your understanding of the chapter content.
www.phschool.com

DEBATING CURRENT ISSUES: *Tax Credits*

In the days before the 1999 State of the Union address, the Clinton White House proposed nearly a tax credit a day. According to *The Wall Street Journal Classroom Edition* article "Payback Time," by Jacob M. Schlesinger, Staff Reporter of *The Wall Street Journal,* each credit was "designed to ease some pocket of concern in the prosperous economy of the United States."

There was a credit for people caring for disabled relatives at home, a credit for businesses that help immigrant employees learn English, and a credit for small businesses that begin offering health insurance. For a President who promised to live by tight spending rules, tax breaks offered a way to pursue a wide-ranging social agenda. But are tax credits really effective fiscal policy?

YES | *Are Tax Credits Effective Fiscal Policy?*

MR. CLINTON'S PROPOSED budget for the fiscal year that began on Oct. 1, 1999, illustrates how sharply the political consensus on taxes has shifted over the past decade.

In 1986, Congress passed and President Reagan signed a landmark tax-reform law that swept away a raft of special breaks and lowered rates across the board. The long and bipartisan list of backers agreed that the economy, and government, would function more efficiently as a result.

But since then, President Clinton and other politicians chipped away at these reforms, using the tax code to encourage what they considered desirable behavior or to favor powerful constituencies.

President Clinton pushed to expand the earned income tax credit for the working poor, and proposed tax breaks for education. Republicans championed lower rates on capital gains to boost investment, an expansion of individual retirement accounts to lift household savings, and tax credits for families with children.

In the late 1990s, with the budget turned to surplus for the first time in decades, Republicans were calling for large, across-the-board tax cuts. While President Clinton opposed these cuts, he figured it would be easier to fight back with more limited cuts of his own rather than simply oppose tax relief. "If we're going to cut taxes, we should do it in targeted ways we can afford that serve the right ends," said Bruce Reed, head of the White House Domestic Policy Council.

Businesses that taught English to their non-English-speaking employees could earn a tax credit under a Clinton plan in the 1990s.

Clinton advisers said that, in many cases, social tax incentives made more sense than spending programs. Tax credits are designed to steer private-sector activity, and therefore appear to work more efficiently than spending programs.

Administration officials praised the earned income credit, for instance, saying it draws lower-income people into the labor force because they have to work to get the money. This would be preferable, officials said, to traditional welfare handouts that were often blamed for discouraging poor people from seeking jobs.

Moreover, providing money through tax credits doesn't require creating costly new bureaucracies or new procedures to dole out the funds.

NO Are Tax Credits Effective Fiscal Policy?

TAX-CODE TINKERING draws fire from across the political spectrum. Many conservatives consider it offensive for government to tie so many behavioral strings to a family's after-tax income. "It's the basic liberal notion of taking our money and giving it back in dribs and drabs only if we spend it on things they think are good," says Kevin Hassett, an economist at the conservative American Enterprise Institute in Washington.

Some liberals complained that the bold-sounding proposals allocated little money to serious problems, and smacked more of campaign sound bites than serious policy. They also maintained that the truly needy often get left out: The poorest third of American families already pay no income tax, and therefore would get scant benefit from this smorgasbord of new tax credits.

Meanwhile, tax experts bemoaned the continued cluttering of an already-complex tax code. Take the $1,500 Hope credit for college students, which was passed by Congress in 1997 and took effect for tax filings due in 1999. To apply for the credit, a person must fill out Form 8863, which is accompanied by two pages of instructions. The Internal Revenue Service figured the form will add an average of 91 minutes to the tax-preparation time of anyone claiming the break.

Though advocates say tax credits provide incentives to alter behavior, some economists counter that they often just give a break to taxpayers who would have done the desired deed anyway. A tax credit enacted in the late 1970s to encourage companies to hire people off welfare was widely attacked as a bust: Many firms hired people based on other qualifications, then checked to see if they could claim the credit for an employee they would have hired anyway.

Where Credits Are Due

Tax Break	Five-Year Cost
Long-term care	$5.5 billion
Energy and environment	$3.6 billion
Urban and rural development	$1 billion
Greenspace bonds	$750 million
Disabled workers	$700 million
Steel industry	$300 million
Adult literacy	$100 million
Small business health insurance	$44 million

Source: *The Wall Street Journal*

In 1999, the Clinton Administration proposed a number of new tax credits, including those listed above.

DEBATING THE ISSUE

1. Why did Clinton administration officials claim the earned income tax credit encouraged lower-income people to get a job?

2. Why do some liberals criticize tax credits?

3. **Critical Thinking** How do tax credits provide a way to "pursue a wide-ranging social agenda" at a time of tight spending rules?

4. **Reading Graphs** Use the chart to calculate the amount that tax credits for energy and the environment will cost in one year.

 Take It to the Net Visit **www.phschool.com** for additional resources relating to this debate.

Suppose you have a checkbook that allows you to write as many checks as you wish for any amount you desire. There is no need to worry about the balance in your account, and the checks will always be cashed, no matter how much you spend. Of course, no person has an account like this, but the Federal Reserve, our nation's central bank, very nearly does.

Economics Journal

Skim recent newspapers for references to policies of the Federal Reserve. List terms you don't understand. Jot down their definitions as you read this chapter.

Keep It Current

Items marked with this logo are periodically updated on the Internet. Keep up-to-date with what's in the news. To get current information on the Federal Reserve and monetary policy go to **www.phschool.com**

The Federal Reserve System

Objectives

After studying this section you will be able to:

1. **Understand** banking history in the United States.
2. **Explain** why the Federal Reserve Act of 1913 led to further reform.
3. **Explain** the structure of the Federal Reserve System.

Section Focus

To stabilize the nation's banking system, Congress created the Federal Reserve System in 1913. The Federal Reserve is owned by individual member banks. It is overseen by a small but powerful Board of Governors. As a private institution serving a public function, the Federal Reserve is a central bank relatively free from government control.

Key Terms

Board of Governors
monetary policy
Federal Reserve Districts
Federal Advisory Council (FAC)
Federal Open Market Committee (FOMC)

The American banking system is a compromise between supporters and opponents of a central bank. As a symbol of this compromise, the Federal Reserve System is the privately owned, publicly controlled central bank of the United States.

Banking History

As you read in Chapter 10, the issue of a central bank has been debated hotly since 1790, when Federalists lined up in favor of a central bank. The first bank of the United States issued a single currency. It also reviewed banking practices and helped the federal government carry out its duties and powers. Partly because of the continued debate over state versus federal powers, however, the first bank lasted only until 1811. At that time, Congress refused to extend its charter.

Congress established the Second Bank of the United States in 1816 to restore order in the monetary system. However, many people feared that a central bank placed too much power in the hands of the federal government. Political opposition toppled the Second Bank in 1836 when its charter expired.

A period of confusion followed. States chartered some banks, while the federal

government chartered and regulated others. Reserve requirements—the amount of reserves that banks are required to keep on hand— were difficult to enforce, and the nation experienced a series of serious bank runs. The Panic of 1907 finally convinced Congress to act.

The nation's banking system needed to address two issues. First, consumers and businesses needed access to increased sources of funds to encourage business expansion. Second, banks needed a source of emergency cash to prevent depositor panics that resulted in bank runs.

▲ The Federal Reserve System is headed by the Federal Reserve Board of Governors. The first Federal Reserve Board of Governors, here, was seated in 1914.

Federal Reserve Act of 1913

Congress created the National Monetary Commission (NMC) in 1908 to propose solutions to the nation's banking problems. Based on the NMC's recommendations, Congress passed the Federal Reserve Act in 1913. The resulting Federal Reserve System, now often referred to simply as "the Fed," was composed of a group of twelve independent regional banks. This central group of banks could lend to other banks in times of need.

Continued Need for Reform

Although the Federal Reserve System helped to restore confidence in the banking system beginning in 1914, it has also learned through trial and error the best ways to fulfill its responsibilities. During the Great Depression, the financial crises of 1930–1933 were exactly the kinds of problems that the NMC had hoped to avoid by creating the Federal Reserve System. The system did not work well, however, because the twelve regional banks each acted independently. Their separate actions often canceled one another out. The Governor of the Federal Reserve Bank of New York (a bank with a close relationship to Wall Street and the investment community) believed that to counteract the growing recession, the government needed to pump money into investment and help Americans get back to work. Many of the other regional governors disagreed about what kinds of action to take. They were more concerned about maintaining gold reserves and with administrative issues than with helping the economy to recover from the widespread recession. By the time Congress forced the Fed to take strong action in 1932, it was too little, too late. The financial crisis had deepened to the point that recovery became long and difficult.

A Stronger Fed

In 1935, Congress adjusted the Federal Reserve's structure so that the system could respond more effectively to future crises. These reforms created the Federal Reserve System as we know it today. The new Fed enjoys more centralized power so that the regional banks can act consistently with one another while still representing their own districts' banking concerns.

Structure of the Federal Reserve

Member banks themselves own the Federal Reserve System. Like so many American institutions, the structure of the Federal Reserve System represents compromises between centralized power and regional powers. (See Figure 16.1.)

The Board of Governors

The Federal Reserve System is overseen by the **Board of Governors** of the Federal Reserve. The Board of Governors is head-quartered in Washington, D.C. Its seven members are appointed for staggered fourteen-year terms by the President of the United States with the advice and consent of the Senate. The terms are staggered to prevent any one President from appointing a full Board of Governors and to protect board members from day-to-day political pressures. Members cannot be reappointed after serving a full term. Geographical restrictions on these appointments ensure that no one district is over-represented.

The President also appoints, from among these seven members, the chair of the Board of Governors. The Senate confirms the

Board of Governors
the seven-member board that oversees the Federal Reserve System

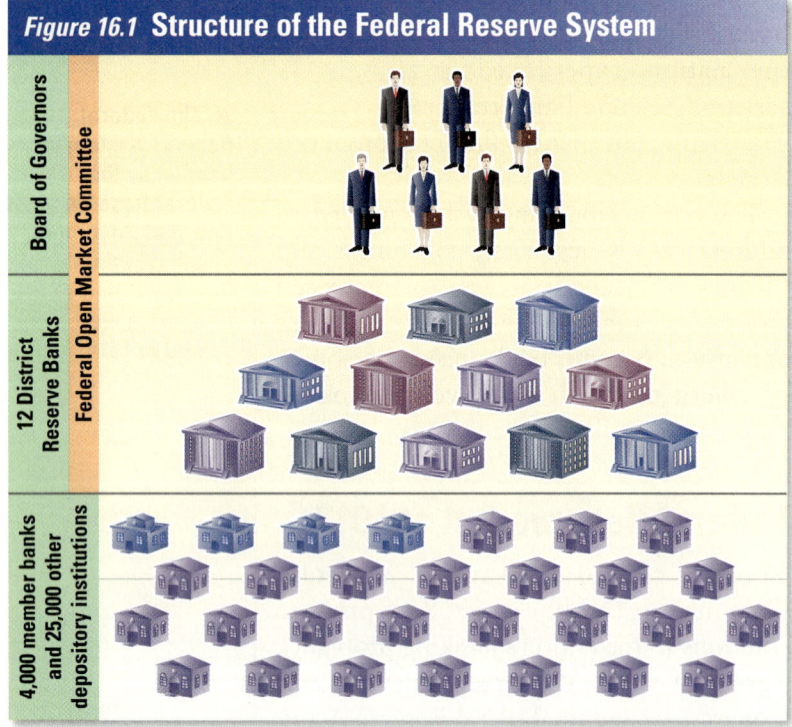

Figure 16.1 Structure of the Federal Reserve System

Board of Governors

Federal Open Market Committee — Board of Governors

12 District Reserve Banks — Federal Open Market Committee

4,000 member banks and 25,000 other depository institutions

About 40 percent of all United States banks belong to the Federal Reserve. These members hold about 75 percent of all bank deposits in the United States.
Government How does the structure of the Fed reflect a compromise between centralized power and regional powers?

Figure 16.2 Federal Reserve Districts

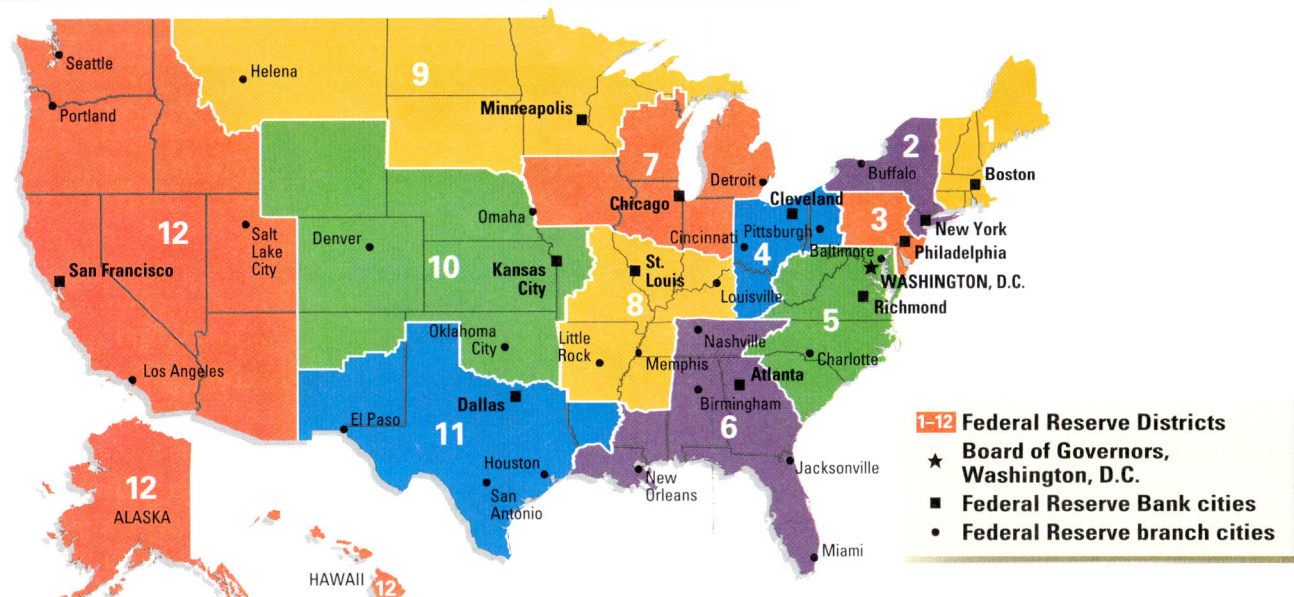

Most Federal Reserve Districts contain a variety of agricultural, manufacturing, and service industries as well as rural and urban areas.

Government How does the makeup of the Federal Reserve Districts help ensure that no single region is dominant?

appointment. Chairs serve four-year terms, which can be renewed. The chair acts as the main spokesperson for monetary policy for the country. **Monetary policy** refers to the actions the Fed takes to influence the level of real GDP and the rate of inflation in the economy.

Recent chairs of the Fed have been economists from business, academia, or government. Alan Greenspan, whose previous career was in building economic forecasting models, has been the most notable chair of the Fed in recent years. He took office in 1987, serving both Republican and Democratic administrations. (See page 424 for a profile of Greenspan.)

Twelve District Reserve Banks

The Federal Reserve Act divided the United States into twelve **Federal Reserve Districts**, as shown on Figure 16.2. One Federal Reserve Bank is located in each of the twelve districts.

Each Federal Reserve Bank monitors and reports on economic and banking conditions in its district. Each Federal Reserve District is made up of more than one state. The Federal Reserve Act aimed to establish a system in which no one region could exploit the central bank's power at another's expense.

Congress also regulated the makeup of each Bank's board of nine directors to make sure that many groups' interests would be represented. Member banks elect three bankers and three leaders in industry, commerce, or other businesses to their district boards. The remaining three directorships, appointed by the Board of Governors of the Federal Reserve, represent broad public interests. The district president is then elected from among these nine directors.

Member Banks

All nationally chartered banks are required to join the Federal Reserve System. The remaining members are state-chartered banks that join voluntarily. Since 1980, all banks have equal access to Fed services like

monetary policy the actions the Federal Reserve takes to influence the level of real GDP and the rate of inflation in the economy

Federal Reserve Districts the twelve banking districts created by the Federal Reserve Act

FAST FACT

In 1913, when the Fed was established, economic and financial power was concentrated in the East and Midwest. Notice that no Federal Reserve Bank exists in Los Angeles, now one of the largest cities in the country.

Federal Advisory Council (FAC) *the research arm of the Federal Reserve*

Federal Open Market Committee (FOMC) *Federal Reserve committee that makes key decisions about interest rates and the growth of the United States money supply*

check clearing and reserve loans, whether or not they are Fed members.

Each of the approximately 4,000 Fed member banks contributes a small amount of money to join the system. In return, they receive stock in the system. This stock earns them dividends from the Fed at a rate of up to 6 percent.

A research arm of the Fed, the **Federal Advisory Council (FAC)**, collects information about each district and reports to the Board of Governors about economic conditions within their districts. It consists of one member from each Federal Reserve District—twelve members in all. The FAC's main function is to provide feedback and advice to the Board of Governors concerning the overall financial health of each district. The FAC meets with the Board of Governors four times a year.

The fact that the banks themselves, rather than a government agency, own the Federal Reserve gives the system a high degree of political independence. This independence helps the Fed to make decisions that best suit the interests of the country as a whole.

The Federal Open Market Committee

The **Federal Open Market Committee (FOMC)** makes key decisions about interest rates and the growth of the United States money supply. The committee meets about eight times a year in private to discuss the cost and availability of credit, for business and consumers, across the country. Announcements of the FOMC's decisions can affect the financial markets, the rates for home mortgages, and many other economic institutions around the world. You will read more about the effects of monetary policy later in this chapter.

Members of the Federal Open Market Committee are drawn from the Board of Governors and the twelve district banks. All seven members of the Board of Governors sit on the FOMC. Five of the twelve district bank presidents also sit on the committee. The president of the New York Federal Reserve Bank is a permanent member. The four other district presidents serve one-year terms on a rotating basis. The Board of Governors holds a majority of the seats on the FOMC, giving them effective control over the committee's actions.

After meeting with the FOMC, the chair of the Board of Governors announces the committee's decisions to the public. The Federal Reserve Banks and financial markets spring into action as they react to Fed decisions. In the next section, you will read about how the Fed's decisions are carried out and what functions the Federal Reserve serves.

Section 1 Assessment

Key Terms and Main Ideas

1. Who serves on the **Board of Governors** of the Federal Reserve?
2. What is **monetary policy**?
3. Describe the makeup of the **Federal Reserve Districts**.
4. What does the **Federal Advisory Council (FAC)** do?
5. What is the role of the **Federal Open Market Committee (FOMC)**?

Applying Economic Concepts

6. *Critical Thinking* How does the banking system of the United States reflect a free enterprise economy?
7. *Try This* Locate your Federal Reserve District on the map on page 417. What states make up your district? What mixture of agricultural, manufacturing, and service industries does your district contain? Is it made up of both rural and urban areas?

Take It to the NET

The Federal Reserve provides businesses and individuals a basic economic report and forecast for each of the twelve Federal Reserve Districts. This economic report card is known as the "Beige Book." Locate the Federal Reserve Bank nearest you and briefly summarize the Beige Book report for your region. Use the links provided in the Social Studies area at the following Web site for help in completing this activity. **www.phschool.com**

Skills for
LIFE

Critical Thinking

Graphs and Charts

Social Studies

Technology Skills

Recognizing Bias in Writing

Bias is the particular opinion or point of view held by a writer on a specific topic. An author's bias is not always obvious at first glance. As a critical reader, you must take steps to identify whether or not a piece of writing contains bias. Any piece of writing relating to economic topics may reflect the author's point of view on a particular public policy or institution. Read the selection on the Federal Reserve Board below, and then answer the questions that follow to help you identify any bias that is reflected in the writing.

1. Identify the source. Begin your critical reading of a piece by identifying who the author is, who the audience is, and any obvious signs of bias.
(a) Who is the author of the excerpt below? (b) Is this a personal letter, diary entry, or public document? (c) Do you detect any obvious bias?

2. Look for evidence of bias. Next, search the excerpt for words or phrases that may reflect the author's bias. (a) What words does the author use to describe Mr. Greenspan and his actions? (b) Which phrases describe the author's attitude toward the Federal Reserve Board? (c) How does the author describe Humphrey-Hawkins?

3. Draw conclusions. Take any signs of bias into account when drawing conclusions about the topic. What point is the author trying to make in this article?

Additional Practice

Locate an editorial from a newspaper on a topic relating to economics, and identify any bias in the writing.

> This morning lawmakers will summon Fed Chairman Alan Greenspan over to the Hill for his mandatory semi-annual gabfest. Accountability is a useful requirement for all political figures, even mighty central bankers who stand watch over multitrillion dollar markets, so we have no trouble with the notion that Congress has the power to require Mr. Greenspan's presence and his report. We do have trouble with Humphrey-Hawkins, the law that prescribes the Chairman's testimony. Its terms assume that the Fed's job is essentially to choose between two dark scenarios. The first is growth, accompanied by inflation. The second is no growth, accompanied by no inflation. . . . We'd like to suggest that the parties involved take a deep breath here while we repeat ourselves: There are plenty of signs out there that the economy is growing without inflation.
>
> *"Phillips Think" [Editorial-Review & Outlook],* The Wall Street Journal, *February 26, 1997*

Objectives

After studying this section you will be able to:

1. **Describe** how the Federal Reserve serves the federal government.
2. **Describe** how the Federal Reserve serves banks.
3. **Describe** how the Federal Reserve regulates the banking system.
4. **Understand** the Federal Reserve's role in regulating the nation's money supply.

Section Focus

The Federal Reserve functions as the government's banker and as a banker's bank. It regulates the nation's banking system. It also monitors and regulates the nation's money supply.

Key Terms

check clearing
bank holding company
federal funds rate
discount rate
net worth

As the central bank of the United States, the twelve district banks that make up the core of the Federal Reserve System carry out several important functions. The Federal Reserve System does the following:

- provides banking and fiscal services to the federal government
- provides banking services to member and nonmember banks
- regulates the banking industry
- tracks and manages the national money supply to meet current demand and to stabilize the economy

Serving Government

The United States government has an operating budget of about $1.7 trillion. It raises about $1 trillion annually in taxes. It makes about $900 billion in transfer payments through programs such as Medicare and Social Security. For its banking needs, the federal government turns to the Federal Reserve.

Federal Government's Banker

The Federal Reserve serves as banker for the United States government. It maintains a checking account for the Treasury Department. It processes payments such as social security checks, IRS refunds, and other government payments. For example, if you receive a check from the federal government and cash it at your local bank, the Federal Reserve deducts the amount from the Treasury's account.

Government Securities Auctions

The Federal Reserve also serves as a financial agent for the Treasury Department and other government agencies. The Fed sells, transfers, and redeems government bonds, bills, and notes, or securities. It also makes interest payments on these securities.

▼ The Department of the Treasury does its banking at the Federal Reserve.

The Treasury Department periodically auctions off government bills, bonds, and notes to finance the government's activities. The funds raised from these auctions are automatically deposited into the Federal Reserve Bank of New York.

Issuing Currency

Under the Federal Reserve System, only the federal government can issue currency. The Department of the Treasury issues coins minted at the United States Mint. The district Federal Reserve Banks issue paper currency (Federal Reserve Notes), which is printed at the Bureau of Engraving and Printing. As bills become worn or torn, the Federal Reserve takes them out of circulation and replaces them with fresh ones.

Serving Banks

The Federal Reserve also provides services to banks throughout the nation. Its most visible function is in its check-clearing services. In addition, it safeguards bank reserves and lends reserves to banks that need to borrow to maintain legally required reserves.

Check Clearing

Figure 16.3 shows how checks "clear" within the Fed system. **Check clearing** is the process by which banks record whose account gives up money and whose account receives money when a customer writes a check. The Fed can clear millions of checks at any one time using high-speed equipment. Most checks clear within two days—a remarkable achievement when you consider that the Fed deals with about 20 billion checks per year.

Supervising Lending Practices

To ensure stability in the banking system, the Federal Reserve monitors bank reserves throughout the system. Each of the twelve Federal Reserve Banks sends out bank examiners to check up on lending and other financial activities of member banks.

They also study proposed bank mergers and bank holding company charters to ensure competition in the banking and financial industries. A **bank holding company** is a company that owns more than one bank. The Board of Governors approves or disapproves mergers and charters based on the findings and recommendations of the Reserve Banks.

The Federal Reserve also protects consumers by enforcing truth-in-lending laws, which require sellers to provide full and accurate information about loan terms. Under a provision called Regulation Z, millions of consumers receive information about retail credit terms, auto loans, and home mortgages every year.

Lender of Last Resort

Under normal circumstances, banks lend each other money on a day-to-day basis, using money from their reserve balances.

check clearing *the process by which banks record whose account gives up money and whose account receives money when a customer writes a check*

bank holding company *a company that owns more than one bank*

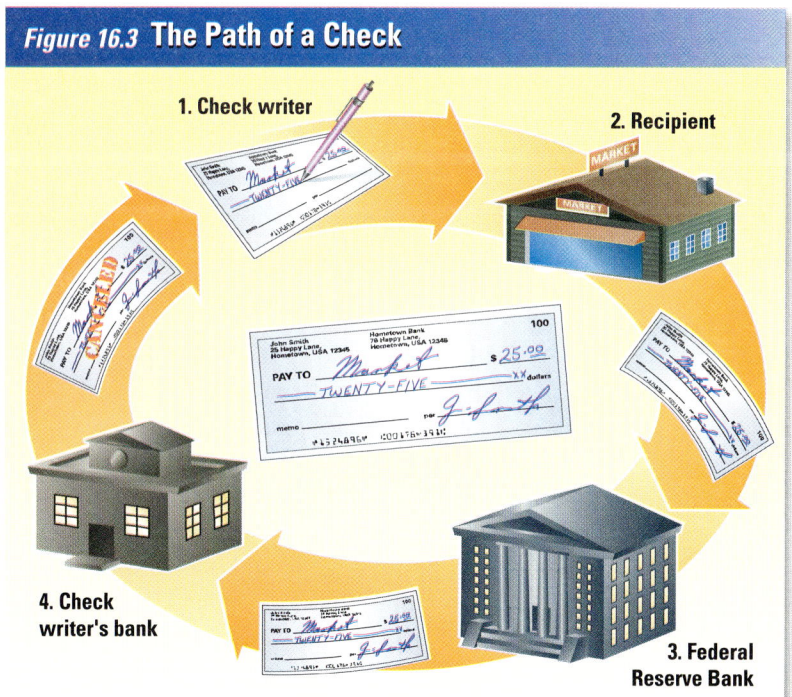

Figure 16.3 **The Path of a Check**

1. Check writer
2. Recipient
3. Federal Reserve Bank
4. Check writer's bank

After you write a check, the recipient presents it at his or her bank. The check is then sent to a Federal Reserve Bank. The reserve bank collects the necessary funds from your bank and transfers them to the recipient's bank. Your processed check is returned to you by your bank or is available for you to view on the Internet. **Economic Institutions** **In what other ways does the Fed serve banks?**

federal funds rate
interest rate banks charge each other for loans

discount rate *rate the Federal Reserve charges for loans to commercial banks*

net worth *total assets minus total liabilities*

These funds are called federal funds. The interest rate that banks charge each other for these loans is the **federal funds rate**.

Banks can also borrow from the Federal Reserve. They do so routinely and especially in financial emergencies such as severe recessions. The Federal Reserve acts as a lender of last resort, making emergency loans to commercial banks so that they can maintain required reserves. The rate the Federal Reserve charges for these loans is called the **discount rate**. You will read more about the role of the discount rate in the economy of the United States in Section 3.

Regulating the Banking System

Banks, savings and loan companies, credit unions, and bank holding companies are supervised by various state and federal authorities. The Fed coordinates all regulatory activities.

Reserves

As you read in Chapter 10, the United States banking system operates as a fractional reserve banking system. Banks hold in reserve only a fraction of their funds—just enough to meet customers' daily needs. Banks then lend their remaining reserves, charging interest to earn returns.

Each financial institution that holds deposits for customers must report daily to the Fed about its reserves and activities. The Fed uses these reserves to control how much money is in circulation at any one time. You'll read more about the Fed's role in controlling the money supply in the next section.

Bank Examinations

The Federal Reserve and other regulatory agencies also examine banks periodically to make sure that each institution is obeying laws and regulations. Examiners may make unexpected bank visits to make sure that banks are following sound lending practices.

Bank examiners can force banks to sell risky investments or to declare loans that will not be repaid as losses. If examiners find that a bank has taken excessive risks, they may classify that institution as a problem bank and force it to undergo more frequent examinations. Examiners would take the same action for banks that have low net worth. **Net worth** equals total assets minus total liabilities. In addition, any bank that goes to the Fed for emergency loans too often will be subject to financial review and close government supervision.

Regulating the Money Supply

The Federal Reserve is best known for its role in regulating the nation's money supply. You will recall from Chapter 10 that economists and the Fed watch several indicators of the money supply. M1 is simply a measure of the funds that are easily accessible or in circulation. M2 includes the funds counted in M1 as well as money market accounts and savings instruments. Economists also measure M3. M3 goes even further to include large time deposits and some government securities. The Fed's job is to consider these various measures of the money supply and compare those figures with the likely demand for money.

Factors That Affect Demand for Money

People hold money for a variety of reasons. The amount of money that firms or individuals hold depends generally on four factors:

1. cash needed on hand
2. interest rates
3. price levels in the economy
4. general level of income

People and firms need to have a certain amount of cash on hand to make economic transactions—to buy groceries, supplies, clothing, and so forth. The more of your wealth you hold as money, the easier it will be to make economic transactions.

Of course, we can't earn interest on money that we hold as cash. As interest rates rise, it becomes more expensive for individuals to hold money as cash rather than placing it in assets that pay returns, such as bonds, stocks, or savings accounts. So as interest rates rise, people and firms will generally keep their wealth in assets that pay returns. In other words, they demand less money in the form of cash. (See Figure 16.4.)

The general price level in the economy affects the demand for money, too. As price levels rise, so does the demand for cash. If your usual cost for an outing with your friends is $25 and prices rise 10 percent, you will now need $27.50 for a night out.

The final factor that influences money demand is the general level of income. On a personal level, if you take an after-school job that pays you $75 per week, you will likely carry around more cash than you did before. On a national level, as GDP or real income rises, families and firms keep more of their wealth or income in cash.

Stabilizing the Economy

The laws of supply and demand affect money, just as they affect everything else in the economy. Too much money in the economy leads to a general rise in prices, or inflation. A glut of dollars lessens their value. In inflationary times, it will take more money to purchase the same goods and services. It is the Fed's job to keep the money supply stable.

In an ideal world, in which real GDP grew smoothly and the economy stayed at

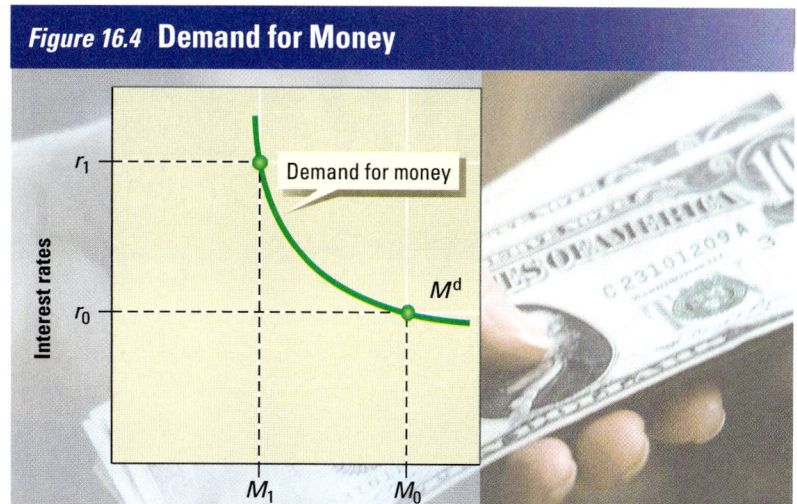

Figure 16.4 **Demand for Money**

As interest rates increase from r_0 to r_1, the quantity of money demanded falls from M_0 to M_1.
Incentives **Explain demand for money in terms of incentives**.

full employment, the Fed would increase the money supply just to match the growth in the demand for money. If the Fed could accomplish this, the country would experience very low inflation rates and, ideally, the economy would remain at full employment. As you read in Chapter 15, however, it is hard to predict economic effects.

The Fed uses its tools to stabilize the economy as best it can. In the next section, you will read about the tools that the Fed can use to help the economy function at full employment without contributing to inflation.

Section 2 Assessment

Key Terms and Main Ideas

1. What is **check clearing**?
2. What is a **bank holding company**?
3. What is the difference between the **federal funds rate** and the **discount rate**?
4. How is **net worth** calculated?

Applying Economic Concepts

5. *Try This* Create a graphic organizer showing how the Federal Reserve serves the federal government and banks.
6. *Critical Thinking* What are the advantages of having the Federal Reserve oversee the regulation of the banking system?

Take It to the NET
One of the functions of the Federal Reserve is to put currency into circulation. What recent changes have been made in the currency of the United States? Use the links provided in the Social Studies area at the following Web site for help in completing this activity.
www.phschool.com

Profile

Alan Greenspan (b. 1926)

The Federal Reserve Board (the Fed) helps to control the nation's money supply. The economist and former professional pop musician at its head may be the most powerful person in America when it comes to the nation's economy. Alan Greenspan's careful handling of the Federal Reserve won him credit for the remarkable economic boom of the 1990s and a place in the administrations of four presidents.

The Chairman of the Fed

Alan Greenspan's first term as chairman of the Federal Reserve Board began in a dramatic fashion. Soon after he took office in August 1987, the stock market crashed. Investors feared that lenders would adopt a tight-money policy, as banks had done after the last great market crash in 1929. Instead, Greenspan responded with actions that boosted the nation's money supply. The stock market quickly recovered, and the nation avoided the economic meltdown that could have followed.

Hard Times

Having grown up during the Great Depression, Greenspan knows hard economic times. As a young child he showed a gift for numbers and amazed his parents' friends with his ability to do math problems in his head. After high school, however, he decided to develop his musical talents, and enrolled at New York's Juilliard School of Music. During the 1940s, he toured with a swing band.

Soon tiring of life on the road, Alan Greenspan returned to New York City and earned bachelor's and master's degrees in economics at New York University. Moving to Columbia University to pursue a Ph.D.,

he had to quit school when he ran short of money. In 1954, he and a friend started an economic consulting firm.

The Transition to Public Life

Alan Greenspan first went to Washington, D.C., in 1974 to chair the President's Council of Economic Advisors. In 1977, he returned to New York to complete his Ph.D., but 10 years later, President Ronald Reagan recalled him to Washington to head the Federal Reserve. At the time, many people were critical of the Fed's heavy-handed role in shaping monetary policy. The previous chairman had thrown the economy into recession in the early 1980s when he raised interest rates in an effort to halt high inflation.

Although Greenspan strongly opposes inflation, he is sensitive to the loss of jobs that accompanies any major attempt to slow the growth of the money supply. Under Greenspan, interest rate adjustments were frequent but generally small in scale. He preferred to use monetary policy to make minor adjustments in the economy's course rather than to drive it in a new direction. As a result, Greenspan's terms as Fed chairman witnessed the longest period of economic growth in the nation's history.

CHECK FOR UNDERSTANDING

1. Source Reading Describe Greenspan's approach to using the powers of the Federal Reserve to influence the nation's economy.

2. Critical Thinking Explain how a sharp increase in interest rates by the Fed could slow inflation but also lead to higher unemployment and a recession.

3. Learn More Visit the Federal Reserve's Web site and summarize the most recent Fed activities that are reported there.

Monetary Policy Tools

Preview

Objectives

After studying this section you will be able to:

1. **Describe** the process of money creation.
2. **Explain** how the Federal Reserve uses reserve requirements, the discount rate, and open market operations to implement U.S. monetary policy.
3. **Understand** why some monetary policy tools are favored over others.

Section Focus

Banks create money in their day-to-day operations. The Federal Reserve uses the tools of monetary policy to control the amount of money in circulation.

Key Terms

money creation
required reserve ratio (RRR)
money multiplier formula
excess reserves
prime rate
open market operations

In early 2001, when it appeared that economic growth was slowing, the Fed began reducing interest rates. The September 11 terrorist attacks further increased the need for such changes in economic policy. By late 2001, the Fed had cut interest rates 11 times, to a 40-year low of 2%. By reducing the cost of borrowing, the Fed hoped to encourage consumers to spend more money and stimulate economic growth. In this section you will see why the Fed uses these tactics to influence economic growth.

Money Creation

The Department of the Treasury is responsible for manufacturing money. The Federal Reserve is responsible for putting dollars into circulation. How does this money get into the economy? The process is called **money creation,** and it is carried out by the Fed and by banks all around the country. Recall from Chapter 15 the multiplier effect of government spending. The multiplier effect in fiscal policy holds that every one dollar change in fiscal policy creates a change greater than one dollar in the economy. The process of money creation works in much the same way.

How Banks Create Money

Money creation does not mean the printing of money. Banks create money not by

printing it, but by simply going about their business.

For example, suppose you take out a loan of $1,000. You decide to deposit the money in a checking account. Once you have deposited the money, you now have a balance of $1,000. Since demand deposit account balances, such as your checking account, are included in M1, the money supply has now increased by $1,000. The process of money creation begins here.

Banks make money by charging interest on loans. Your bank will lend part of the $1,000 that you deposited. The amount that the bank is allowed to lend is determined by the **required reserve ratio (RRR)**—the fraction of the deposit that must be kept on reserve. This is calculated as the ratio of reserves to deposits. The RRR is the fraction of deposits that banks are required to keep in reserve. The required reserve ratio, which is established by the Federal Reserve, ensures that banks will have enough funds to supply customers' withdrawal needs.

Suppose in our example that the RRR is 0.1, or 10 percent. This means that of your $1,000 demand deposit balance, the bank is allowed to lend $900.

▲ The daily activities of banks and their customers create money printed by machines such as this one.

money creation *the process by which money enters into circulation*

required reserve ratio (RRR) *ratio of reserves to deposits required of banks by the Federal Reserve*

money multiplier formula *amount of new money that will be created with each demand deposit, calculated as 1 ÷ RRR*

Let's say the bank lends that $900 to Elaine, and she deposits it in her checking account. Elaine now has $900 she didn't have before. Elaine's $900 is now included in M1. You still have your $1,000 demand deposit account balance, on which you can write a check at any time. Thus, your initial deposit to the bank, and the subsequent loan, have caused the money supply to increase by $1,000 + $900 for a total of $1,900.

Now suppose that Elaine uses the $900 to buy Joshua's old car. Joshua deposits the $900 from Elaine into his checking account. His bank keeps 10 percent of the deposit, or $90, as required reserves. It will lend the other $810 to its customers. So, Joshua has a demand deposit balance of $900, which is included in the money supply, and the new borrower gets $810, which is also added to the money supply. This means that the money supply has now increased by $1,000 + $900 + $810 = $2,710—all because of your initial $1,000 deposit. (See Figure 16.5.)

The Money Multiplier

This process will continue until the loan amount, and hence the amount of new money that can be created, becomes very small. The amount of new money that will be created, in the end, is given by the **money multiplier formula**, which is calculated as 1 ÷ RRR. The money multiplier tells us how much the money supply will increase after an initial cash deposit to the banking system. To apply the formula, we multiply the initial deposit by the money multiplier:

Increase in money supply =

$$\text{initial cash deposit} \times \frac{1}{\text{RRR}}$$

In our example the RRR is 0.1, so the money multiplier is 1 ÷ 0.1 = 10. This means that the initial deposit of $1,000 will ultimately lead to a $10,000 increase in the money supply.

As of 1999 in the United States, banks were required to hold 3 percent reserves against demand deposit assets up to $49 million and 10 percent on all demand deposit assets exceeding $49 million.

In the real world, however, people hold some cash outside of the banking system, meaning that some funds leak out of the money multiplier process. Also, banks

In this example of money creation, the money supply increases by $2,710 after four rounds.

Money Suppose Joshua deposited only $500 of Elaine's payment into his account. How much would the money supply increase then?

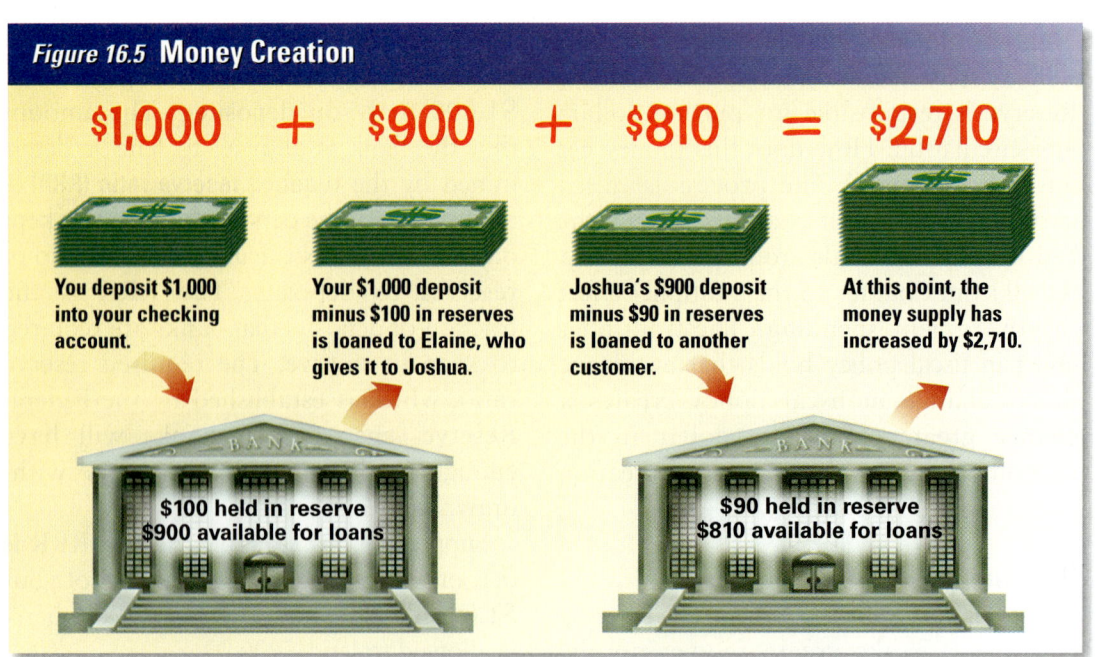

Figure 16.5 Money Creation

$1,000 + $900 + $810 = $2,710

You deposit $1,000 into your checking account.

Your $1,000 deposit minus $100 in reserves is loaned to Elaine, who gives it to Joshua.

Joshua's $900 deposit minus $90 in reserves is loaned to another customer.

At this point, the money supply has increased by $2,710.

$100 held in reserve
$900 available for loans

$90 held in reserve
$810 available for loans

sometimes hold **excess reserves**, which are reserves greater than the required amounts. These excess reserves ensure that banks will always be able to meet their customers' demands and the Fed's reserve requirements. The actual money multiplier effect in the United States is estimated to be between 2 and 3.

The Federal Reserve has three tools for adjusting the amount of money in the economy. These tools are reserve requirements, the discount rate, and open market operations.

Reserve Requirements

The simplest way for the Fed to adjust the amount of reserves in the banking system is to change the required reserve ratio. It is not, however, the tool most used by the Fed.

Reducing Reserve Requirements
A reduction of the RRR would free up reserves for banks, allowing them to make more loans. It would also increase the money multiplier. Both effects would lead to a substantial increase in the money supply.

Increasing Reserve Requirements
The process also works in reverse. Even a slight increase in the RRR would force banks to hold more money in reserves. This would cause the money supply to contract, or shrink.

Although changing reserve requirements can be an effective means of changing the money supply, the Fed does not use this tool often because it is disruptive to the banking system. Even a small increase in the RRR would force banks to call in significant numbers of loans, that is, to require the borrower to pay the entire outstanding balance of the loan. This may be difficult for the borrower. For this reason, the Fed rarely changes reserve requirements.

Discount Rate

As you read in Section 2, the discount rate is the interest rate that the Federal Reserve charges on loans to financial institutions.

Banks borrow from the Fed to maintain reserves at the required level. Changes in the discount rate affect the cost of borrowing from the Fed. In turn, changes in the discount rate can affect the prime rate. The **prime rate** is the rate of interest banks charge on short-term loans to their best customers—usually large companies with good credit ratings. Changes in the discount rate are reflected in the prime rate.

Reducing the Discount Rate
If the Fed wants to encourage banks to lend more of their reserves, it may reduce the discount rate. With a lower discount rate, banks can reduce their excess reserves by lending them out. They won't have to worry about their reserves falling too low. They can add to their reserves by borrowing from the Fed at a low rate.

These new loans will increase the money supply, just as a decrease in RRR would. The money multiplier will apply to these

excess reserves *reserves greater than the required amounts*

prime rate *rate of interest banks charge on short-term loans to their best customers*

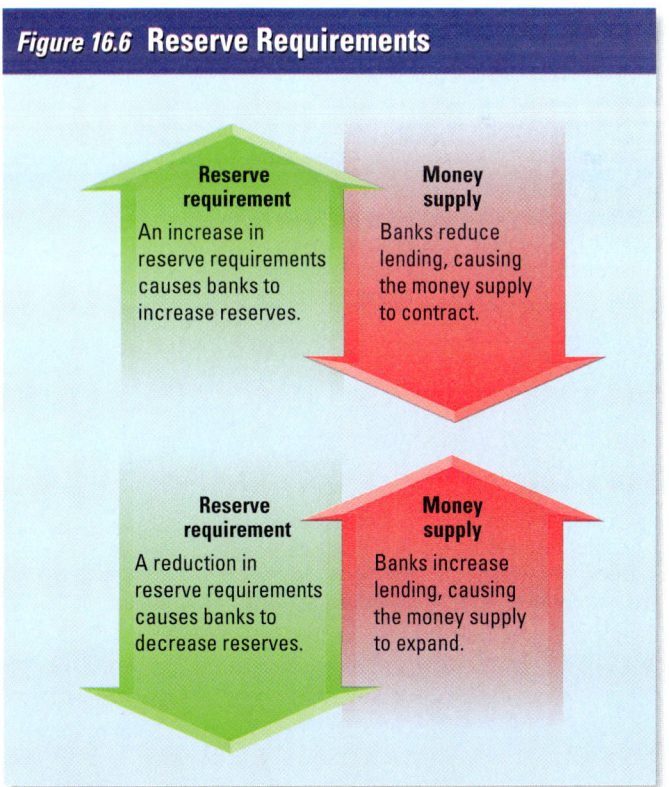

Figure 16.6 **Reserve Requirements**

Reserve requirement	**Money supply**
An increase in reserve requirements causes banks to increase reserves.	Banks reduce lending, causing the money supply to contract.
Reserve requirement	**Money supply**
A reduction in reserve requirements causes banks to decrease reserves.	Banks increase lending, causing the money supply to expand.

When the Fed increases reserve requirements, the money supply decreases. **Monetary and Fiscal Policy** **What is the effect of reducing reserve requirements? Why?**

open market operations
the buying and selling of government securities to alter the supply of money

new loans, ensuring that each dollar of reserves that is lent will create an even larger increase in the money supply.

Increasing the Discount Rate

If, on the other hand, the Federal Reserve wants to reduce the money supply, it will increase the discount rate. This will make banks less willing to borrow from the Fed. As a result, they will hold more excess reserves to keep from falling below their required levels. Banks increase their excess reserves by reducing loans. A reduction in loans, in turn, will reduce the amount of currency circulating in the economy, causing a reduction of the money supply.

If banks do not wish to borrow from the Federal Reserve, they may borrow from one another in the federal funds market. Of course, if banks find the federal funds rate too high, they may still borrow from the

Fed. In practice, however, the Fed maintains the discount rate close to the federal funds rate in order to prevent large swings in borrowed reserves.

Open Market Operations

The most important monetary policy tool is **open market operations**. Open market operations are the buying and selling of government securities to alter the supply of money. Open market operations are by far the most-used monetary policy tool.

Bond Purchases

When the Federal Open Market Committee (FOMC) chooses to increase the money supply, it orders the trading desk at the Federal Reserve Bank of New York to purchase a certain quantity of government securities on the open market.

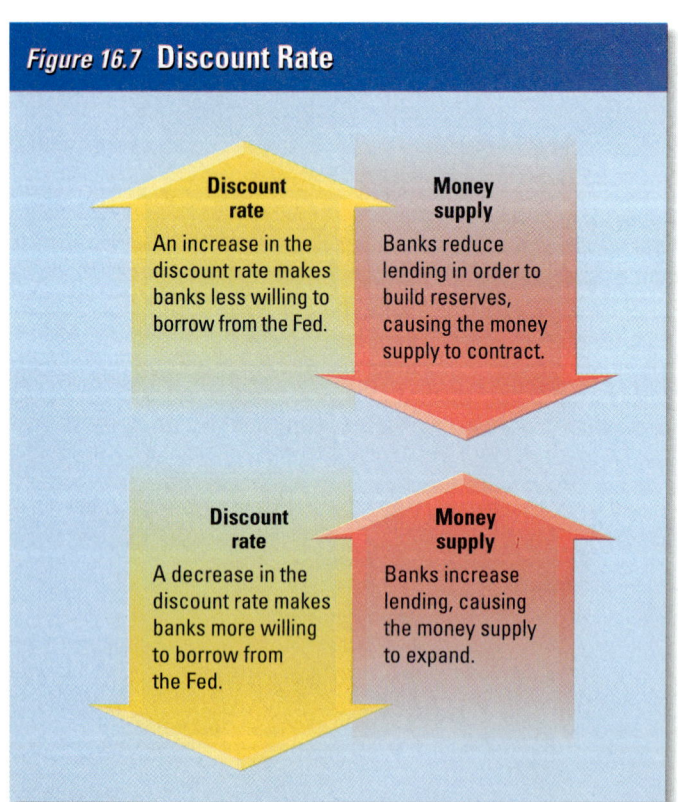

Figure 16.7 Discount Rate

Discount rate
An increase in the discount rate makes banks less willing to borrow from the Fed.

Money supply
Banks reduce lending in order to build reserves, causing the money supply to contract.

Discount rate
A decrease in the discount rate makes banks more willing to borrow from the Fed.

Money supply
Banks increase lending, causing the money supply to expand.

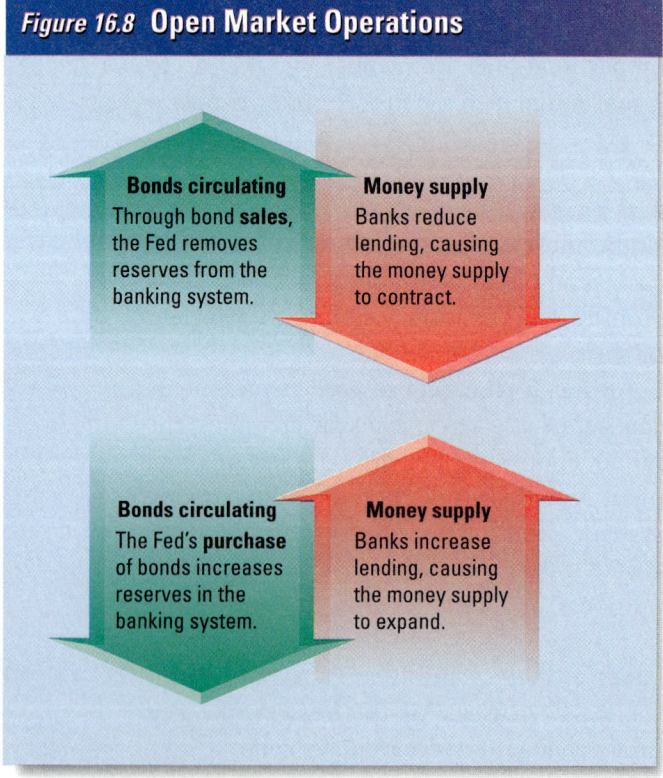

Figure 16.8 Open Market Operations

Bonds circulating
Through bond **sales**, the Fed removes reserves from the banking system.

Money supply
Banks reduce lending, causing the money supply to contract.

Bonds circulating
The Fed's **purchase** of bonds increases reserves in the banking system.

Money supply
Banks increase lending, causing the money supply to expand.

BUILDING KEY CONCEPTS

Because an increase in the discount rate makes borrowing more costly, the money supply contracts. Banks are more willing to borrow and lend money when the discount rate is low (left). Open market operations (right), however, are the most-used monetary policy tool.

Fiscal and Monetary Policy How do open market operations differ from the monetary policy tools shown in Figures 16.6 and 16.7?

The Federal Reserve Bank buys these securities with a check drawn on Federal Reserve funds. The bond seller then deposits the money from the bond sales in its bank. In this way, funds enter the banking system, setting in motion the money creation process described earlier.

Bond Sales

If the FOMC chooses to decrease the money supply, it must make an open market bond sale. In this case, the Fed sells government securities back to bond dealers, receiving from them checks drawn on their own banks. After the Fed processes these checks, the money is out of circulation. This operation reduces reserves in the banking system. Banks will reduce their outstanding loans in order to keep reserves at the required levels. The money multiplier process then works in reverse, resulting in a decline in the money supply that is greater than the value of the initial securities purchase.

Using Monetary Policy Tools

Open market operations are the most used of the Federal Reserve's monetary policy tools. They can be conducted smoothly and on an ongoing basis to meet the Fed's goals. The Fed changes the discount rate less

Global Connections

Global Monetary Policy As Europe moved toward a single currency, the European System of Central Banks (ESCB) was created to handle the European Community's monetary policy. Its job is similar to that of the Federal Reserve. The ESCB conducts monetary policy for the European Community nations, conducts foreign exchange operations, and provides banks with services such as check cashing. The ESCB's monetary policy tools include open market operations as well as reserve requirements. **How do the monetary policy tools of the ESCB resemble those of the Federal Reserve?**

frequently. It usually follows a policy of keeping the discount rate in line with other interest rates in the economy in order to prevent excess borrowing by member banks from the Fed. (See the graph "Key Interest Rates" on page 542 in the Economic Atlas and Databank.)

Today, the Fed does not change reserve requirements to conduct monetary policy. Changing reserve requirements would force banks to make drastic changes in their plans. Open market operations or changes in the discount rate do not disrupt financial institutions.

The Federal Reserve uses these monetary policy tools to adjust the money supply. Why the Fed would want to change the money supply, and the effects of monetary policy, are the subjects of the next section.

Section 3 Assessment

Key Terms and Main Ideas

1. What is **money creation**?
2. What is the **required reserve ratio (RRR)**?
3. State the **money multiplier formula**.
4. Why do banks sometimes hold **excess reserves**?
5. If the discount rate rose, would you expect the **prime rate** to rise or fall?
6. What are **open market operations**?

Applying Economic Concepts

7. *Math Practice* Suppose the RRR is 0.15. Use the money multiplier formula to determine by how much a $2,000 checking account deposit will increase the money supply.
8. *Critical Thinking* Will the money supply actually increase by the amount you calculated in Question 7? Why or why not?

Take It to the NET

The discount rate can affect the amount of money in circulation by affecting how much money banks lend to their customers. Examine the current trend in discount rate policy. Has the Fed tried to increase or decrease the money supply lately? Use the links provided in the Social Studies area at the following Web site for help in completing this activity.
www.phschool.com

Monetary Policy and Macroeconomic Stabilization

Objectives

After studying this section you will be able to:

1. **Understand** how monetary policy works.
2. **Explain** the problems of timing and policy lags in implementing monetary policy.
3. **Explain** how predictions about the length of a business cycle affect monetary policy.
4. **Describe** two distinct approaches to monetary policy.

Section Focus

The Federal Reserve uses monetary policy to try to tame business cycles. The unpredictable length of business cycles, however, makes it difficult to determine when it is wise to intervene in the economy.

Key Terms

monetarism
easy money policy
tight money policy
inside lag
outside lag

---

monetarism *the belief that the money supply is the most important factor in macroeconomic performance*

Adherents of **monetarism** believe that the money supply is the most important factor in macroeconomic performance. How, then, does monetary policy influence macroeconomic performance?

How Monetary Policy Works

Monetary policy alters the supply of money. The supply of money, in turn, affects interest rates. As you read earlier,

▶ **Keeping the economy stable requires a delicate balancing act.**

interest rates affect the level of investment and spending in the economy.

The Money Supply and Interest Rates

It is easy to see the cost of money if you are borrowing it. The cost—the price that you as borrower pay—is the interest rate. Even if you have your own money, however, the interest rate still affects you. The interest rate is also the cost of having money, because you are giving up interest by not saving or investing. Thus, the interest rate is always the cost of money.

The market for money is like any other market. If the supply is higher, the price—the interest rate—is lower. If the supply is lower, the price—the interest rate—is higher. In other words, when the money supply is low, interest rates are high. When the money supply is high, interest rates are low.

Interest Rates and Spending

Recall from Chapter 12 that interest rates are important factors of spending in the economy. Lower interest rates encourage greater investment spending by business firms. This is because a firm's cost of borrowing—or of using its own funds—decreases as the interest rate decreases.

Firms find that lower interest rates give them more opportunities for profitable investment. If a firm has to pay 15 percent interest on its loans, it may find few profitable opportunities. If interest rates fall to 8 percent, however, the firm may find that some opportunities are now profitable.

If the macroeconomy is experiencing a contraction—declining income—the Fed may want to stimulate, or expand, it. It will follow an **easy money policy**. That is, it will increase the money supply. An increased money supply will lower interest rates, thus encouraging investment spending. Such a policy may, however, encourage overborrowing and overinvestment, followed by layoffs and cutbacks.

If the economy is experiencing a rapid expansion that may cause high inflation, the Fed may introduce a **tight money policy**. That is, it will reduce the money supply. The Fed reduces the money supply to push interest rates upward. By raising interest rates, the Fed causes investment spending to decline. This brings real GDP down, too.

Even though it can only alter the money supply, the Fed has a great impact on the economy. The money supply determines the interest rate, and the interest rate determines the level of aggregate demand. Recall from Chapter 12 that aggregate demand represents the relationship between price levels and quantity demanded in the overall economy. The level of aggregate demand helps determine the level of real GDP. (See Figure 16.9.)

The Problem of Timing

Monetary policy, like fiscal policy, must be carefully timed if it is to help the macroeconomy. If policies are enacted at the wrong time, they could actually intensify the business cycle, rather than smooth it out. To see why, consider Figure 16.10.

Good Timing

Figure 16.10A shows the business cycle with a properly timed stabilization policy. The green curve, which shows greater fluctuations, is the business cycle as explained in Chapter 12. The goal of stabilization policy is to smooth out those fluctuations—

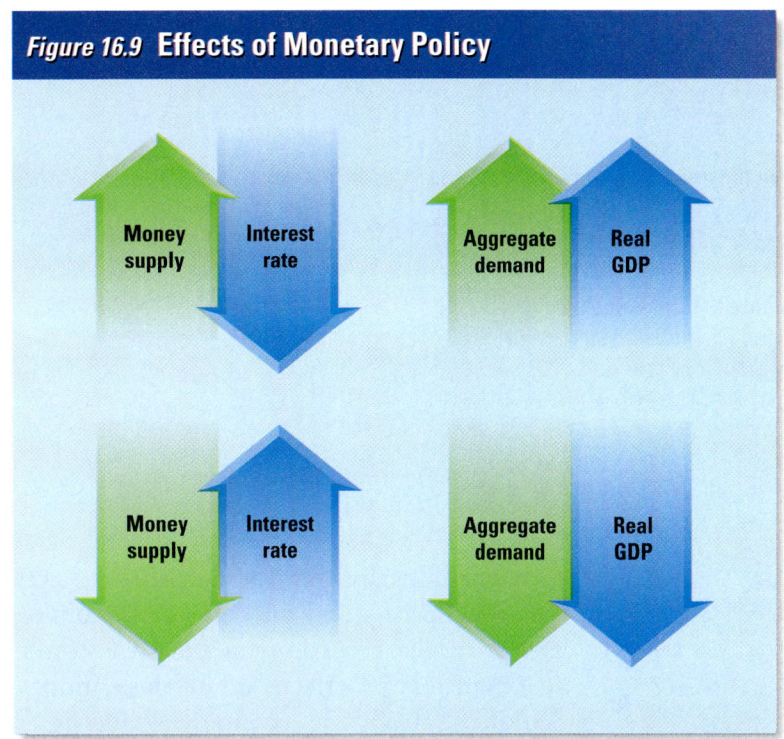

Figure 16.9 Effects of Monetary Policy

If the economy is experiencing a contraction, an easy money policy may stimulate growth. If the economy is experiencing rapid expansion that may cause high inflation, a tight money policy may help reduce the price increases.
Gross Domestic Product Explain the relationship between aggregate demand and GDP.

in other words, to make the peaks a little bit lower and the troughs not quite as deep. This will minimize inflation in the peaks and the effects of recessions in the troughs. Properly timed stabilization policy smooths out the business cycle, as shown in the red curve in Figure 16.10A.

Bad Timing

If stabilization policy is not timed properly, however, it can actually make the business cycle worse, not better. For example, suppose that policymakers are slow to recognize the contraction shown as the green line in Figure 16.10B. Perhaps because their data are inaccurate or slow to arrive, government economists simply do not realize that a contraction is occurring until the economy is deeply into it. Some period of time may pass before they recognize the contraction.

Likewise, it takes time to enact expansionary policies and have those policies

easy money policy
monetary policy that increases the money supply

tight money policy
monetary policy that reduces the money supply

The timing of monetary policy measures can intensify the business cycle.

Monetary and Fiscal Policy What are the effects of proper and improper timing?

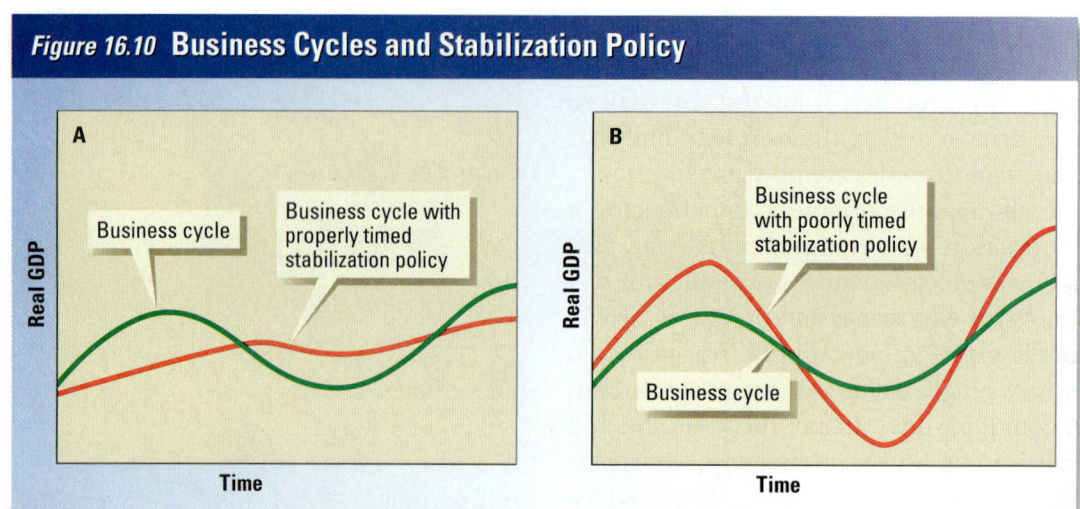

Figure 16.10 **Business Cycles and Stabilization Policy**

A

Real GDP

Business cycle

Business cycle with properly timed stabilization policy

Time

B

Real GDP

Business cycle with poorly timed stabilization policy

Business cycle

Time

take effect. By the time all of this takes place, the economy may already be coming out of the recession on its own. If the expansionary effects of a loose money policy affect the economy while it is already expanding, the result could be an even larger expansion that causes high inflation, as shown by the red line in Figure 16.10B.

Policy Lags

As you can see, there are a couple of problems in the timing of macroeconomic policy. These are called policy lags.

Inside Lags

The **inside lags** are delays in implementing policy. These lags occur for two reasons. First, it takes time to identify and recognize a problem. While economists have developed sophisticated computer models for predicting economic trends, they still cannot know for sure that the economy is headed into a new phase of the business cycle until it is already there. Statistics may conflict with one another. Hence, it can take several months or even a year to recognize a serious economic problem.

A good example of this problem occurred during a recession in the United States in 1990. Today, we date the beginning of the recession at July 1990. However, Alan Greenspan, the chair of the Board of Governors of the Federal Reserve,

testified before Congress in October 1990 that the economy had not yet slipped into recession. Looking back, however, we now know that a recession had begun months earlier. Even Greenspan, an economic expert with the staff of the Fed and other resources at his disposal, was slow to recognize that a recession had begun.

A second reason for inside lags is that once a problem has been recognized, it can take additional time to enact appropriate policy. This problem is more severe for fiscal policy than for monetary policy. Fiscal policy, which includes changes in government spending and taxation, requires actions by Congress and the President. Since Congress must debate such new plans and then get the approval of the President, it may take quite a while before a new policy is enacted.

The enactment of monetary policy, on the other hand, is streamlined. The Federal Open Market Committee meets eight times each year to discuss monetary policy—more often if necessary. Once it has decided that changes are called for, the FOMC can make open market policy or discount rate changes almost immediately.

Outside lags

Once a new policy is determined, it takes time to become effective. This time period, known as the **outside lag**, also differs for monetary and fiscal policy. For fiscal policy, the outside lag lasts as long as is required

inside lag *delay in implementing monetary policy*

outside lag *the time it takes for monetary policy to have an effect*

for new government spending or tax policies to take effect and begin to affect real GDP and the inflation rate. This time period can be relatively short, as with a tax rebate that returns government revenues to households eager for spending money. One statistical model concluded that an increase in government spending would increase GDP after just six months.

Outside lags can be much longer for monetary policy, since they primarily affect business investment plans. Firms may require months or even years to make large investment plans, especially those involving new physical capital, such as a new factory. Thus, a change in interest rates may not have its full effect on investment spending for several years. This conclusion is supported by several studies that suggest that the outside lag for monetary policy is probably rather long. More than two years may pass before the maximum impact of monetary policy is felt.

Given the longer inside lag for fiscal policy and the longer outside lag for monetary policy, it is not obvious which policy has the shorter total lag. In practice, partisan politics and budgetary pressures often prevent the President and Congress from agreeing on fiscal policy. Because of the political difficulties of implementing fiscal policy, we rely to a greater extent on the Fed to use monetary policy to soften the business cycle.

Predicting the Business Cycle

The Federal Reserve must not only react to current trends. It must also anticipate changes in the economy. How should policymakers decide when to intervene in the economy?

Monetary Policy and Inflation

You have already read that expansionary policy, if enacted at the wrong time, may push an economy into high inflation, thus reducing any beneficial impact. This is the

HEY! REMEMBER THIS GREAT CHART FROM THE NINETIES?

GOLDEN OLDIES

▲ Unprecedented economic growth led some economists to predict an end to the peaks and troughs of past business cycles. Indications of recession in the early 2000s, however, showed the economy contracting.

chief danger of using an easy money policy to get the economy out of a recession.

An inflationary economy can be tamed by a tight money policy, but the timing is again crucial. If the policy takes effect as the economy is already cooling off on its own, the tight money could turn a mild contraction into a full-blown recession.

The decision of whether to use monetary policy, then, must be based partly on our expectations of the business cycle. Some recessions are short-run phenomena that will, in the long run, disappear. Some inflationary peaks may also be expected to last for the short run and end in the long run. Given the timing problems of monetary policy, in some cases it may be wiser to allow the business cycle to correct itself rather than run the risk of an ill-timed policy change.

If a recession is expected to turn into an expansion in a short time, the best course of action may be to take a laissez-faire approach to the economy and let the economy correct itself. On the other hand, if we expect a recession to last several years, then all but the most conservative onlookers

THE WALL STREET JOURNAL.
CLASSROOM EDITION

In the News As this excerpt from a Wall Street Journal Classroom Edition *article shows, recognizing shifts in the business cycle is notoriously difficult.*

"'Nobody has a good record of predicting when a recession comes,' says Milton Friedman, the Nobel laureate economist. 'If you look at the historical record, the first quarters of most recessions have been regarded by most commentators at the time as a continuation of prosperity.'"

Figure 16.11 Fiscal and Monetary Policy Tools

	Fiscal policy tools	Monetary policy tools
Expansionary tools	1. increasing government spending 2. cutting taxes	1. open market operations: bond purchases 2. decreasing the discount rate 3. decreasing reserve requirements
Contractionary tools	1. decreasing government spending 2. raising taxes	1. open market operations: bond sales 2. increasing the discount rate 3. increasing reserve requirements

BUILDING KEY CONCEPTS

Both the federal government and the Federal Reserve can influence the nation's economy.
Fiscal and Monetary Policy How are fiscal and monetary policy similar? How do they differ?

the economy may take quite a long time to recover on its own from an inflationary peak or a recessionary trough, there is time for policymakers to guide the economy back to stable levels of output and prices.

Approaches to Monetary Policy

In practice, the lags discussed here make monetary and fiscal policy difficult to apply. Interventionist policy, a policy encouraging action, is likely to make the business cycle worse if the economy self-adjusts quickly. Laissez-faire economists who believe that the economy will self-adjust quickly will recommend against enacting new policies. Economists who believe that economies emerge slowly from recessions, however, will usually recommend enacting fiscal and monetary policies to move the process along.

The rate of adjustment may also vary over time, making policy decisions even more difficult. This debate over which approach to take with monetary policy will probably never be settled to the satisfaction of all economists.

would recommend an active policy. So the question is this: How long will a recessionary or inflationary period last?

How Quickly Does the Economy Self-Correct?

Economists disagree on the answer to this question. Their estimates for the U.S. economy range from two to six years. Since

Section 4 Assessment

Key Terms and Main Ideas

1. Why would the Federal Reserve enact an **easy money policy**?
2. Why would the Federal Reserve enact a **tight money policy**?
3. What are **inside lags**, and why do they occur?
4. Why does monetary policy have such long **outside lags**?
5. What is **monetarism**?

Applying Economic Concepts

6. *Critical Thinking* Why do business cycles make monetary policy difficult to time?
7. *Try This* With a partner, stage a debate on monetary policy. One of you will take an interventionist approach, encouraging action, the other a laissez-faire approach, discouraging action. Use information from your textbook to help craft your argument.
8. *Using the Databank* Examine the graphs on Economic Indicators in the Economic Atlas and Databank on pages 538–539. How would you describe the economic performance of the United States at the end of the twentieth century?

Take It to the NET
Summarize the most recent actions taken by the Federal Open Market Committee in a brief oral presentation. Why did the FOMC take those actions? How does the FOMC expect its actions to affect the economy? Use the links provided in the Social Studies area at the following Web site for help in completing this activity. **www.phschool.com**

Banking, Monetary Policy, and the Great Depression

In 1929, the collapse of the stock market touched off a period of economic devastation known as the Great Depression. Millions of Americans found themselves unemployed and lost their homes, farms, and life savings.

Bank Failures In late October 1929, dropping stock prices caused many panicked investors to sell their stocks, which resulted in the collapse of the stock market on October 29, 1929. Banks had invested heavily in the stock market and lost huge sums. Fearful that banks would run out of money, people rushed to their banks demanding their money. To pay back these deposits, banks had to recall loans from borrowers, but they could not do so fast enough to pay all the depositors demanding their money. Thousands of banks failed.

Emergency Action In 1933, President Franklin D. Roosevelt took emergency action and declared a bank "holiday." All banks closed temporarily to stop the banking panic.

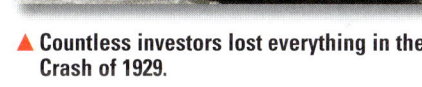

▲ Countless investors lost everything in the Crash of 1929.

Congress then passed the Banking Act of 1933, which created the Federal Deposit Insurance Corporation (FDIC) to insure deposits. This meant that even if a bank failed, deposits would be guaranteed by the federal government.

Meanwhile, banks became extremely cautious. They made fewer loans and kept enough cash on hand in case depositors all came at once to withdraw their funds. Banks began to hold substantial reserves, far in excess of those required by the Federal Reserve.

Federal Reserve Response These excess reserves concerned the Federal Reserve, which feared that banks might distribute that money, possibly causing inflation. In 1937, the Fed raised reserve requirements for the banks, thus lowering the money supply to prevent inflation. Banks responded by cutting back their loans even further to have enough cash for depositors.

This Federal Reserve policy had an unintended negative result. Banks reduced lending, which led to a recession. Since that time the Fed has learned not to make sharp increases in reserve requirements.

Applying Economic Ideas

1. Why did the Federal Reserve raise reserve requirements in 1937?

2. Were banks justified in holding excess reserves in the 1930s? Why or why not?

Chapter Summary

A summary of major ideas in Chapter 16 appears below. See also the **Guide to the Essentials of Economics,** which provides additional review and test practice of key concepts in Chapter 16.

Section 1 The Federal Reserve System (pp. 415–418)

To stabilize the nation's banking system, Congress created the Federal Reserve System. The Federal Reserve is made up of twelve **Federal Reserve Districts** and is overseen by a small but powerful **Board of Governors**. As a private institution serving a public function, the Federal Reserve is a central bank relatively free from government control.

Section 2 Federal Reserve Functions (pp. 420–423)

The Federal Reserve serves the banking needs of the government and of individual banks. It regulates the nation's banking system. It also monitors and regulates the nation's money supply.

Section 3 Monetary Policy Tools (pp. 425–429)

Money creation occurs through the day-to-day operations of banks. The Federal Reserve uses three tools of monetary policy to control the amount of money in circulation. The three tools are changing the required reserve ratio, changing the discount rate, and buying or selling bonds on the open market.

Section 4 Monetary Policy and Macroeconomic Stabilization (pp. 430–434)

The Federal Reserve enacts monetary policy to lessen the effects of business cycles. The unpredictable length of business cycles, however, makes it difficult to determine when it is wise to intervene in the economy. **Inside lags** and **outside lags** make it difficult to conduct monetary and fiscal policy.

Key Terms

Match the following definitions with the terms listed below. You will not use all of the terms.

inside lag	tight money policy
discount rate	money creation
Board of Governors	outside lag
federal funds rate	easy money policy
excess reserves	prime rate
Federal Reserve District	check clearing

1. Rate the Federal Reserve charges for loans to commercial banks
2. Process by which money enters into circulation
3. The seven-member board that oversees the Federal Reserve System
4. Monetary policy that reduces the money supply
5. Reserves greater than the required amounts
6. The process by which banks record whose account gives up money and whose account receives money when a customer writes a check
7. The time it takes for monetary policy to have an effect

Using Graphic Organizers

8. On a separate sheet of paper, copy the tree map below. Complete the tree map with the tools of monetary policy and their expected effects on the economy.

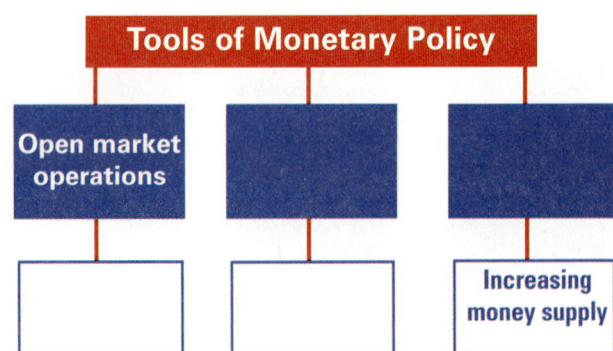

Tools of Monetary Policy

Open market operations

Increasing money supply

Reviewing Main Ideas

9. What was the reasoning behind the creation of the Federal Reserve?
10. List and describe three services the Federal Reserve offers banks.
11. Describe the money multiplier formula in your own words.
12. How do inside lags and outside lags affect monetary policy?
13. What is the difference between easy money policies and tight money polices?

Critical Thinking

14. **Analyzing Information** Review the services the Federal Reserve offers banks and the regulations it places on banks. Which service or regulation do you think is most important to the American banking system?
15. **Analyzing Information** Why are open market operations the most commonly used actions taken by the Fed? What advantages do open market operations have over other monetary policy tools?
16. **Recognizing Cause and Effect** If the Federal Reserve Board were to implement an easy money policy, what actions would it take? What would be the expected results of this policy? What conditions could lead the Fed to take such actions?

Problem-Solving Activity

17. Suppose the economy is experiencing a high rate of inflation. As chair of the Federal Reserve Board, what actions would you take to put the economy back on track?

Economics Journal

Organizing Information Review your list of terms and definitions. Use your list and other information from the chapter to create a graphic organizer summarizing the role of the Fed in the United States economy.

Skills for Life

Recognizing Bias in Writing Review the steps shown on page 419; then complete the following activity based on the passage on inflation below.

18. Who is the author of the excerpt below?
19. Is this a personal letter, diary entry, or public document?
20. What words does the author use to describe the actions of Alan Greenspan?
21. Do you detect any obvious bias?
22. What economic attitudes may have influenced the author's opinion?

"In the late 1960s, after 20 years in which the gross domestic product had grown 4% a year, inflation had remained below 2%, and the Dow Jones Industrial Average had increased fivefold, the U.S. economy began a long slide into an economic abyss. Inflation and interest rates shot up, stock prices stagnated, and by the late 1970s, few thought the U.S. economy could ever recover.

Today, many believe this same fate is once again awaiting the U.S. economy. According to the pessimists, the U.S. stock market is in a bubble that is about to burst, and inflation is about to explode. The recent dip in the stock market—prompted by more gloomy warnings from Alan Greenspan—appeared to give credence to these worrywarts. But they are wrong."

Brian S. Wesbury, chief economist at Griffin, Kubik, Stephens & Thompson, "Have No Fear, Inflation Isn't Here" [Commentary], *The Wall Street Journal Interactive Edition,* October 21, 1999

Take It to the NET

Chapter 16 Self-Test As a final review activity, take the Chapter 16 Self-Test in the Social Studies area at the Web site listed below, and receive immediate feedback on your answers. The test consists of 20 multiple-choice questions designed to test your understanding of the chapter content.
www.phschool.com

The Global Economy

These bananas were grown in Costa Rica.

Your shoes were made in Indonesia and your backpack in China. While many people take the global economy for granted, when you step back to consider the entire flow of goods, services, and money around the world, the result is mind-boggling.

- Who made your shirt, and how much were they paid for their labor?
- Which goods does the United States export, and which goods are imported?
- How does international trade affect the economy of the United States?

In this unit you'll read about why nations trade and actions nations take to restrict or increase trade. Finally, you'll look at why standards of living vary greatly from country to country and the impact of the global economy on everyone's future.

Focus Activity

Choose five items you own, and identify where they were made. Compare your list of items and countries with that of a classmate.

Chapter 17 International Trade

In today's global economy, many products that Americans use every day were produced in other countries. We drive Japanese cars, wear clothes from China, and sit on furniture from Canada. These products come by trucks and trains or arrive at United States ports aboard huge freighters like the one you see here.

Economics Journal

Check the labels on clothing, appliances, electronics, and other items that you use every day. Then make a list of the items and the countries in which they were made. What does your list suggest about the importance of international trade?

Keep It Current

Items marked with this logo are periodically updated on the Internet. Keep up-to-date with what's in the news. To get current information on international trade go to
www.phschool.com

Section 1 — Why Nations Trade

Preview

Objectives

After studying this section you will be able to:

1. **Analyze** the locations of resources and evaluate the significance of these locations.
2. **Explain** the concepts of absolute and comparative advantage and apply the concept of comparative advantage to explain why and how countries trade.
3. **Analyze** the impact of U.S. imports and exports on the United States and its trading partners.
4. **Describe** the effects of trade on employment.

Section Focus

International trade is based on resources that one country needs and another can provide. Each country in the world possesses different resources. By specializing in the production of certain goods and services, nations can use their resources more efficiently. Specialization and trade can benefit all nations.

Key Terms

absolute advantage
comparative advantage
law of comparative advantage
export
import

Have you logged on to a computer today? Ridden in a car or bus? Bought a new sweatshirt or jacket? Chances are these items all have one thing in common. They—or some of their components—were likely made outside the United States.

We know that the United States produces many products, such as jeans, machinery, and some types of computers. We don't, however, produce most of the world's video game systems or VCRs. Why? The answer lies with resources and their distribution. The unequal distribution of resources prevents countries from producing everything their citizens need and want. This is also why we trade.

Resource Distribution

As you read in Chapter 1, the resources that are used to make goods and services are called the factors of production. They include natural resources (land), human resources (labor), and capital resources.

Natural Resources

As you have read, natural resources include those materials found in nature that people use to make goods and provide services.

Natural resources include arable land (land that can be farmed), mineral deposits, oil and gas deposits, water, and raw materials like timber.

It is easy to see why a region with fertile soil, such as the central United States, is likely to have an economy based on agriculture. Similarly, you can predict that a region with large oil and natural gas reserves—such as Southwest Asia—is likely to have an economy based on income from the sale of these resources.

Natural resources, as well as climate and location, help determine what goods and services an economy produces. They are not, however, the only influences.

Human Capital

You learned in Chapter 1 that human capital is the knowledge and skills gained by a worker through education and experience. Every job requires some human capital. To be a surgeon you must learn about anatomy and acquire surgical skills. To be a taxi driver, you must know the layout of the city streets.

How do you measure the amount of human capital available in a country? One measure is the literacy rate, or percentage

▲ **Many items of clothing are traded internationally.**

Figure 17.1 Resource Distribution

	India	Peru	United Kingdom	United States
Total area (sq km)	3,287,590	1,285,220	244,820	9,629,091
Arable land (sq km)	1,664,986	38,400	60,398	1,740,202
Natural resources	Coal, iron ore, manganese, mica, bauxite, titanium ore, chromite, natural gas, diamonds, petroleum, limestone, arable land	Copper, silver, gold, petroleum, timber, fish, iron ore, coal, phosphate, potash, hydropower	Coal, petroleum, natural gas, tin, limestone, iron ore, salt, clay, chalk, gypsum, lead, silica, arable land	Coal, copper, lead, phosphates, molybdenum, uranium, bauxite, gold, iron, mercury, nickel, potash, silver, tungsten, zinc petroleum, natural gas, timber
Population	1.030 billion	27, 483,864	59,647,790	278,058,881
Labor force	441 million	9 million	30 million	143 million
Literacy rate	52%	88.7%	99%	97%
Telephones*	27 per 1,000 people	55 per 1,000 people	585 per 1,000 people	697 per 1,000 people
Airports	337	233	489	14,720

*non-cellular
Sources: *CIA World Factbook,* 2001; WorldBank

These countries each possess different natural, human, and physical resources.
Specialization How do a nation's resources determine what that nation produces?

of people over 15 who can read and write. A country with a high literacy rate is likely to have an educated, skilled work force.

Physical Capital

Physical capital includes objects made by men and women that are used to produce goods and services. Examples include factories, machinery, and computers. Physical capital also includes the public infrastructure, such as roads and bridges, that allows raw materials and finished goods to be manufactured and transported.

Economic Activity Patterns

Five major economic activities are producing, exchanging, consuming, saving, and investing. Patterns of production, distribution, and use develop as the economic activities become concentrated in urban, industrial, or agricultural areas. Geographic and human factors also influence patterns of economic activity. Ski resorts develop in the mountains, farming in the valleys, and mining where there are ore deposits. Saving and investment also follow patterns, becoming concentrated in areas of potential growth.

Unequal Resource Distribution

Each country in the world possesses different types and quantities of land, labor, and capital resources. Some of these resources are determined by nature. Others are not. A nation's culture and history affect its human and physical resources. For example, if a nation has experienced prolonged civil wars, it may not have been able to develop its resources fully.

The table in Figure 17.1 provides data on different types of resources in selected countries. You can see that the availability of resources differs greatly from country to country. For example, the United Kingdom has over twice as many airports as Peru despite its smaller land area, suggesting that the United Kingdom has more physical capital than Peru. Economists can confirm this fact with additional data. As you might expect, because countries differ in resources, they also differ in their capacities to produce different goods and services.

The Need for Trade

Specialization occurs when producers—either individuals or nations—decide to produce only certain goods and services, rather than producing all the goods and services they need. Specialization is determined by a nation's natural resources and by its human and physical capital. For example, the world's wheat is grown in regions with a cool climate. In the United States, we grow wheat, soybeans, and other crops for which we have appropriate soil and climate conditions. We cannot, however, produce diamonds or coffee.

When nations specialize in producing only certain goods, they obtain the goods they don't or can't produce through trade. For example, Costa Rica specializes in producing coffee and exports a large quantity of coffee beans. The country then uses the money it earns from coffee exports to buy products that it does not produce.

What about a nation that enjoys an abundance of resources, including a rich natural environment, a well-educated work force, and the latest technologies? It can, in theory, produce almost all that it needs by itself, without trade. If you were in charge of such a country, would you engage in large-scale trading? Or, would you decide to rely mostly on your country's own resources and be largely self-sufficient? Although self-sufficiency may sound appealing, it actually is better for countries to specialize in some products and trade for others.

Absolute and Comparative Advantage

Trading relationships benefit countries with abundant resources as well as countries with few resources. To see why, you need to look at two related concepts—absolute advantage and comparative advantage.

Absolute Advantage

A person or nation has an **absolute advantage** when it can produce more of a given product using a given amount of resources. A simple example can illustrate this idea.

Suppose that two of your friends, Carl and Kate, want to make some extra money. They decide to print designs on T-shirts and make birdhouses.

Figure 17.2 Productivity per Hour

	T-shirts per hour	Birdhouses per hour
Kate	6	2
Carl	1	1

Kate has an absolute advantage in producing both T-shirts and birdhouses.
Specialization In which good should each person specialize?

As shown in Figure 17.2, Kate can either print six T-shirts or make two birdhouses per hour. Carl can print one T-shirt or make one birdhouse per hour. In other words, Kate is more productive than Carl in making both T-shirts and birdhouses. In economic terms, Kate has an absolute advantage over Carl in producing both goods.

Suppose that each person is initially self-sufficient. Both Kate and Carl produce their own T-shirts and their own birdhouses. Because Kate enjoys an absolute advantage in both goods, should she remain self-sufficient? Or would Kate be better off if she specialized in either T-shirts or birdhouses? What should Carl produce—T-shirts, birdhouses, or both?

Countries have to face the same sorts of questions as individuals. Should a wealthy country with many resources be self-sufficient, or should it specialize in a few products and trade for the goods it doesn't produce? How does a poorer nation decide what to produce? The answer to these questions lies with the concept of comparative advantage.

Comparative Advantage

Early in the nineteenth century, British political economist David Ricardo argued that the key to determining which country should produce which goods is opportunity cost. Remember that the opportunity cost is what you give up in order to produce a certain product. The nation that has the lower opportunity cost in producing a

absolute advantage
the ability to produce more of a given product using a given amount of resources

Kate gives up three T-shirts for each birdhouse she produces. Carl gives up only one T-shirt for each birdhouse he produces.

Opportunity Costs What are Kate and Carl's opportunity costs for T-shirts and birdhouses?

Figure 17.3 Opportunity Costs for Kate and Carl

	Opportunity cost of a T-shirt	Opportunity cost of a birdhouse
Kate	$\frac{1}{3}$ birdhouse	3 T-shirts
Carl	1 birdhouse	1 T-shirt

certain good has a comparative advantage in producing that good. A country has a **comparative advantage** in the product that it can produce most efficiently given all the products it could choose to produce. It is the nation with the comparative advantage—not necessarily the absolute advantage—that should specialize in producing that good.

According to the **law of comparative advantage,** a nation is better off when it produces goods and services for which it has a comparative advantage. Each nation can then use the money it earns selling those goods to buy other goods that it cannot produce as efficiently. We can use the example of Kate and Carl to illustrate the benefits from trade that is based on comparative advantage.

The Importance of Opportunity Cost

To determine comparative advantage in the example involving Kate and Carl, you need to look at the opportunity costs of producing T-shirts and birdhouses.

- *Kate's opportunity costs* In an hour, Kate can make either six T-shirts or two birdhouses. She therefore sacrifices three T-shirts for every birdhouse she produces. In other words, the opportunity cost of a birdhouse is the three T-shirts she could have produced instead. Conversely, the opportunity cost of a T-shirt is one third of a birdhouse.
- *Carl's opportunity costs* Carl sacrifices only one T-shirt for every birdhouse. His opportunity cost for a birdhouse is the one T-shirt that he could have produced instead.

As you have read, each person should produce the good for which he or she has a

comparative advantage—that is, a lower opportunity cost than another person. Carl's opportunity cost for producing a birdhouse (one T-shirt) is lower than Kate's (three T-shirts), so it is sensible for Carl to produce birdhouses. Kate's opportunity cost for producing a T-shirt (one third of a birdhouse) is lower than Carl's (one birdhouse), so Kate should produce T-shirts.

Why is it sensible for Carl to specialize in birdhouses? Although Kate has an absolute advantage in making birdhouses, Carl has a comparative advantage in birdhouses because he has a lower opportunity cost. Remember that in order to make a birdhouse, Kate has to give up three T-shirts. In order to make a birdhouse, Carl has to give up only one T-shirt.

Benefits for Trading Partners

As you might remember from trading baseball cards or small toys when you were younger, trade usually involves bargaining. Each side tries to make the best deal it can. In a modern economy, we don't exchange goods directly—we use money. The main principle, however, remains the same: both sides agree on a price that benefits both.

When Kate wants a birdhouse, she can either produce it herself or produce some shirts and trade some of them for a birdhouse made by Carl. Suppose Kate and Carl agree to trade two T-shirts for one birdhouse. In this case, Kate will be better off producing T-shirts and trading for a birdhouse. That's because in the time she could have taken to produce her own birdhouse, Kate can produce three T-shirts. Once she pays Carl two T-shirts to get a birdhouse, she will still have one T-shirt left over. In other words, trade makes her better off by one T-shirt. (See Figure 17.4.)

When Carl wants two more T-shirts, he can either make them himself, or make some birdhouses and trade some of them for shirts made by Kate. If Kate and Carl agree to trade one birdhouse for two T-shirts, Carl will be better off producing birdhouses and trading for shirts. In the time he could have taken to produce two T-shirts for himself, he can produce two

comparative advantage *the ability to produce a product most efficiently given all the other products that could be produced*

law of comparative advantage *the idea that a nation is better off when it produces goods and services for which it has a comparative advantage*

birdhouses. Once he pays one birdhouse to Kate to get two T-shirts, he will still have one birdhouse left over. Trade makes him better off by one birdhouse.

Kate and Carl both benefit from trade. Each person specializes in the production of the good for which he or she has a comparative advantage, and then trades for the other good. The same is true with nations—both sides benefit from trade.

Comparative Advantage and International Trade

The lessons from this example of trade between two individuals apply to trade between nations. According to Ricardo, the nation that has the lower opportunity cost in producing a certain good has a comparative advantage in producing that good. Remember that comparative advantage is the ability of one nation to produce a good at a lower opportunity cost than that of another nation. It is the nation with the comparative advantage—not necessarily the absolute advantage—that should specialize in producing that good.

Suppose 2 countries, Country A and Country B, produce bananas and sugar. If Country A must sacrifice 2 tons of sugar in order to produce a ton of bananas, the opportunity cost of a ton of bananas is 2 tons of sugar. If the opportunity cost of a ton of bananas in Country B is 3 tons of sugar, Country A has a comparative advantage in producing bananas. That's because Country A's opportunity cost (2 tons of sugar) is lower than Country B's (3 tons of sugar). If Country A specializes in producing bananas, it could use the money earned from selling bananas to buy other goods and services.

The United States and Trade

The United States enjoys a comparative advantage in producing many goods and services. What, then, is its position as an

---

Figure 17.4 Benefits From Specialization and Trade for Carl and Kate

Carl			Kate		
Specialization	**Trade**	**Net Effect**	**Specialization**	**Trade**	**Net Effect**
Carl specializes, switching 2 hours from T-shirt production to birdhouse production.	Carl trades 1 birdhouse for 2 T-shirts.	Net effect is same number of T-shirts and 1 more birdhouse.	Kate specializes, switching one half-hour from birdhouse production to T-shirt production.	Kate trades 2 T-shirts for 1 birdhouse.	Net effect is the same number of birdhouses and 1 more T-shirt.

Kate and Carl both benefit from specialization and trade.

Trade What is the net effect of trade for Kate and Carl? Why are they both better off trading?

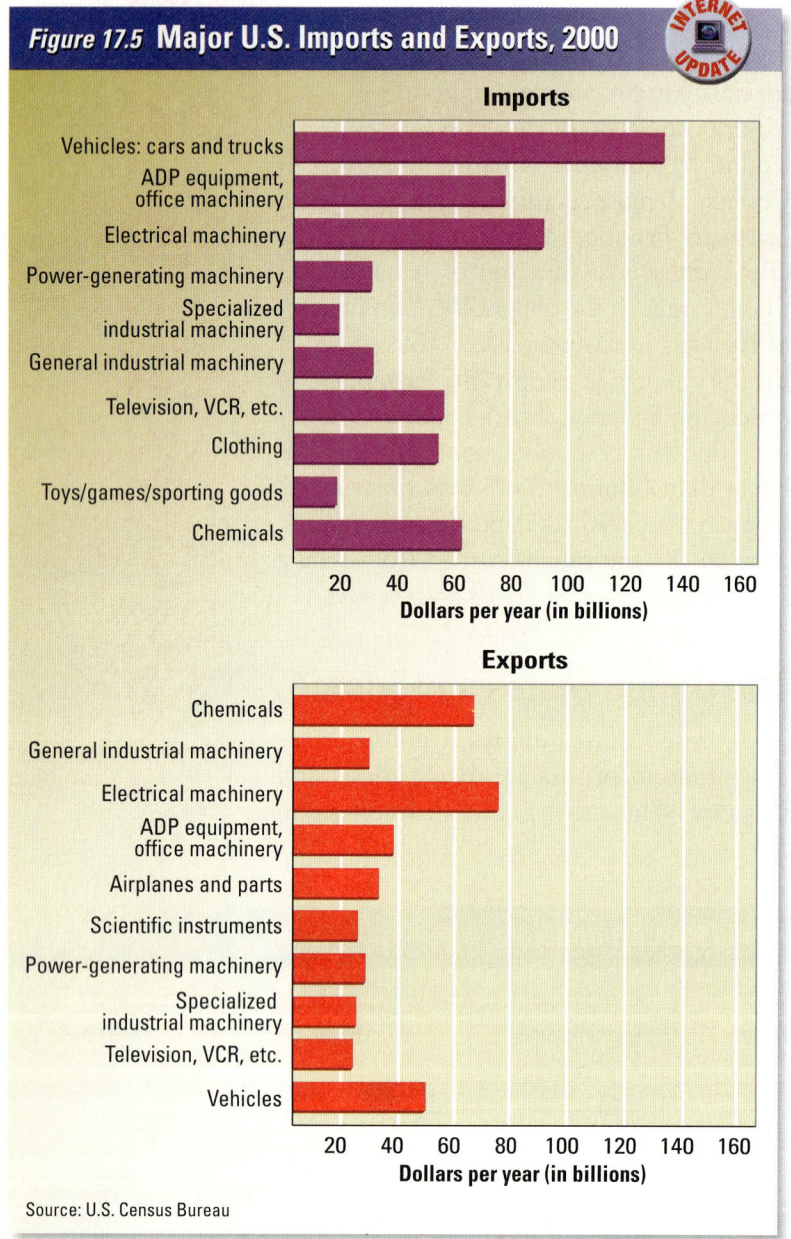

Figure 17.5 Major U.S. Imports and Exports, 2000

Imports

Vehicles: cars and trucks
ADP equipment, office machinery
Electrical machinery
Power-generating machinery
Specialized industrial machinery
General industrial machinery
Television, VCR, etc.
Clothing
Toys/games/sporting goods
Chemicals

20 40 60 80 100 120 140 160
Dollars per year (in billions)

Exports

Chemicals
General industrial machinery
Electrical machinery
ADP equipment, office machinery
Airplanes and parts
Scientific instruments
Power-generating machinery
Specialized industrial machinery
Television, VCR, etc.
Vehicles

20 40 60 80 100 120 140 160
Dollars per year (in billions)

Source: U.S. Census Bureau

BUILDING KEY CONCEPTS

The United States is both the world's largest importer and its largest exporter. **Trade** Judging from these graphs, does the United States export more than it imports or import more than it exports? Explain your answer.

export *a good that is sent to another country for sale*

import *a good that is brought in from another country for sale*

importer and exporter on the world market? In the language of international trade, an **export** is a good sent to another country for sale. An **import** is a good brought in from another country for sale.

As you can see from the map on page 545 of the Databank, the main U.S. trading partners are Canada, Mexico, Japan, and China. Trade with China has grown tremendously in recent years.

The United States as an Exporter

The United States is the world's leading exporter, followed by Germany and Japan. One reason for the success of the United States as an exporter is the wide range of its exports, from telecommunications equipment to soybeans. Another reason is that the United States has a commanding lead in manufacturing such products as computer software, medical equipment, and other advanced technology.

The United States is also in a good position to benefit from increased trade in services. Goods make up the bulk of international trade, but services are also traded on the world market. These include education, information services, computer and data processing, financial services, and medical care. Exports of services have grown rapidly over the last decade. The United States is the world's top exporter of services, so it stands to gain significantly from this trend.

The United States as an Importer

Besides being the world's largest exporter, the United States is also the world's top importer, and by a significant amount. The United States imports nearly $900 billion in goods and services, or 16.1 percent of the world's total. That amount exceeds total imports for Germany and Japan combined, the world's largest importers after the United States.

The Effects of Trade on Employment

Trade allows nations to specialize in producing a limited number of goods while consuming a greater variety of goods. However, specialization can also dramatically change a nation's employment patterns.

Specialization and Employment

To help you better understand the effects of international trade on employment, think back to the example of Kate and Carl. As you have read, Kate can make six T-shirts or two birdhouses by herself in an hour.

Suppose she hires Ari to help her build bird-houses. She later realizes that she should specialize only in T-shirts since that is where her comparative advantage lies. She no longer needs Ari to help her. Unfortunately, Ari's only skill is making birdhouses.

Ari now faces three possibilities: unemployment, retraining, or relocating to a part of the country where his skills are in demand. Ari may be able to find a training program and learn to make T-shirts or another product. He might even find himself better off than he was making birdhouses.

If Ari relocates, he may or may not be better off. How well he does depends on housing prices, the quality of his new neighborhood, the impact on his family, and a variety of other factors.

Government assistance is often available to help retrain laid-off workers for new jobs or to help them relocate to fit shifts in employment patterns. However, especially in the case of older workers or workers with families, retraining or relocation is not an easy (or sometimes not a possible) option. Some workers may become unemployed or be forced to take lower-paying jobs.

Specialization and Employment in the United States

In the United States, significant changes in employment patterns have occurred in the past two decades as a result of specialization and international trade. For example, during the 1970s, specialization, new technologies like robotics, and high productivity gave Japan a comparative advantage in producing automobiles. As a result, Japanese cars became less expensive than many comparable American-made cars. As more consumers bought Japanese cars, many American workers lost jobs in automobile-producing centers such as Detroit.

Many other shifts in employment have also taken place in the United States in recent decades as a result of world trade and other factors. The overall result has been a shift in population from the manufacturing states of the Midwest to the Sunbelt states of the South and Southwest.

▲ Workers who lose their jobs can often learn new skills.

Section 1 Assessment

Key Terms and Main Ideas

1. How do nations obtain goods and services for which they lack adequate resources?

2. Susan grows coffee in a North Dakota greenhouse under sunlamps. Growing coffee this way takes a lot of effort and money. She also grows sunflowers, which are easy to grow in the dry climate in which she lives. In which crop does she probably have a **comparative advantage?**

3. Why is a nation with abundant resources better off trading than being self-sufficient?

4. Specialization and trade can result in shifting employment patterns. **(a)** What possibilities are available to people who lose their jobs due to changes in employment patterns? **(b)** What are the advantages and disadvantages of each possibility?

Applying Economic Concepts

5. *Critical Thinking* Suppose a nation has a great deal of human capital but few natural resources. In what kinds of products might it specialize?

6. *Try This* Make a Productivity Table for yourself and a friend using the table on page 443 as a model. Choose your own goods and estimate production times. Then decide where you and your friend have a comparative advantage.

7. *Using the Databank* Turn to the map showing United States trading partners on page 545. Considering geographical location and resources, give reasons to explain why the countries shown are major U.S. trading partners.

Take It to the NET

Compare the resources available in the United States to those of two other countries. Use the links provided in the Social Studies area at the following Web site for help in completing this activity. www.phschool.com

Creating a Multimedia Presentation

Multimedia presentations communicate information in a variety of forms, both audio and visual. The preproduction, or planning, stage of a presentation requires a considerable amount of work if the production stage and final product are to go well. During the preproduction stage, the producer drafts an outline and script, decides what media to use and where, arranges interviews or photography sessions, selects images, and chooses music.

Suppose that you have been assigned to produce a multimedia presentation on how the global economy affects the lives of people in your region. Use the following steps and a copy of the preproduction topic analysis sheet below to prepare your presentation.

1. Plan your content. Select a topic for your presentation. (**a**) What possible topics might you focus on? (**b**) How could you break up your presentation into different segments? (**c**) How do these segments connect with one another?

PREPRODUCTION TOPIC ANALYSIS SHEET

Assignment: The impact of the global economy on the local community

Possible topics:
1. _____
2. _____
3. _____
My choice: _____
Sources for topic information:_____
Intended audience: _____
Information to be presented: _____
_____

Segment description and sequence:
1. _____
2. _____
3. _____
Mood:_____
Type of narration: _____
Graphics/illustrations, interviews, music
Segment #1 _____
Segment #2 _____
Segment #3 _____

---

2. Plan a script. You must decide whether to use a running commentary by a single narrator, comments by several interviewees, or a combination. (**a**) What are the advantages and disadvantages of using a single narrator? (**b**) Which script style do you feel would be most appropriate for a presentation on the local impact of the global economy, and why?

3. Make a list of images, interviews, and music. The images you choose will help viewers visualize your message. (**a**) What images would fit the content and mood of each segment? (**b**) Which people could you interview? (**c**) What pieces or types of music would best enhance the mood of your presentation?

Additional Practice

Suppose that you are planning a multimedia presentation on some aspect of life at your school. Prepare a preproduction chart like the one shown here for your presentation.

Trade Barriers and Agreements

Objectives

After studying this section you will be able to:

1. **Define** various types of trade barriers.
2. **Compare** the effects of free trade and trade barriers on economic activities.
3. **Understand** arguments in favor of protectionism.
4. **Evaluate** the benefits and costs of participation in international trade agreements.
5. **Explain** the role of multinationals in the global market.

Section Focus

The free exchange of goods can be restricted by barriers to trade, such as tariffs, quotas, and voluntary export restraints. International trade agreements and organizations work to reduce trade barriers.

Key Terms

trade barrier
import quota
voluntary export restraint (VER)
customs duty
tariff
trade war
protectionism
infant industry
international free trade agreement
World Trade Organization (WTO)
European Union (EU)
euro
free-trade zone
NAFTA

So far, our discussion of trade has assumed that international trade is not subject to government regulations. Many people, however, argue that governments should regulate trade in order to protect certain industries and jobs from foreign competition.

Trade Barriers

Most countries have some form of trade barriers that hinder free trade. A **trade barrier,** or trade restriction, is a means of preventing a foreign product or service from freely entering a nation's territory. Trade barriers take three common forms: import quotas, voluntary export restraints, and tariffs.

Import Quotas

An **import quota** is a limit on the amount of a good that can be imported. For example, the United States limits the annual amount of raw (unprocessed) cotton coming into the country from other nations. Quotas limit India and Pakistan to 908,764 kilograms of cotton, China to 621,780 kilograms, and Egypt and Sudan to 355,532 kilograms. The United States will accept no more than these

amounts of cotton from these countries. Other nations that produce cotton must also observe quotas of various amounts.

Voluntary Export Restraints

An import quota is a law. A **voluntary export restraint (VER)** is a self-imposed limitation on the number of products that are shipped to a particular country. Under a voluntary export restraint, a country voluntarily decreases its exports in an attempt to

trade barrier *a means of preventing a foreign product or service from freely entering a nation's territory*

import quota *a limit on the amount of a good that can be imported*

voluntary export restraint (VER) *a self-imposed limitation on the number of products shipped to a particular country*

◄ The cotton used to make much of the clothing Americans wear is subject to import quotas.

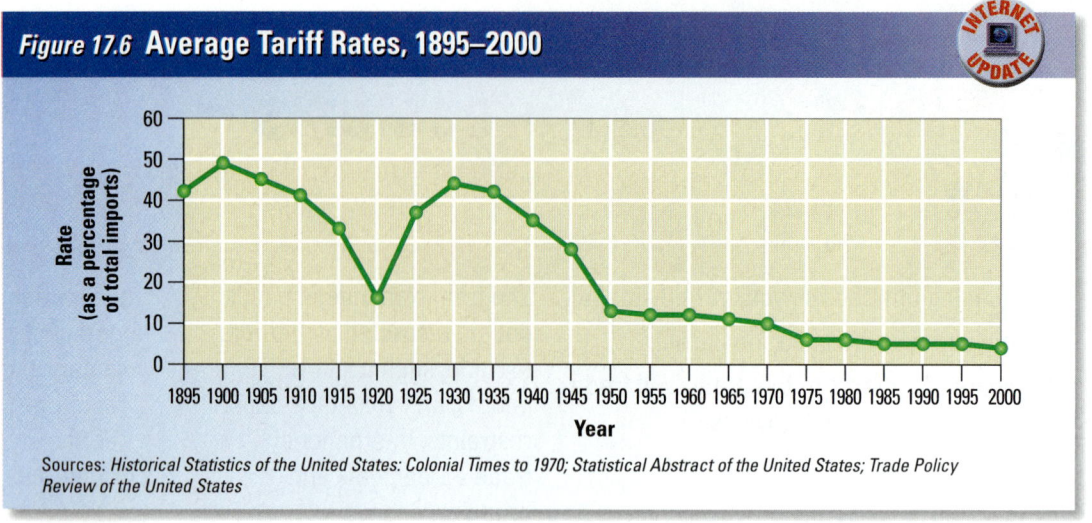

Figure 17.6 Average Tariff Rates, 1895–2000

Sources: *Historical Statistics of the United States: Colonial Times to 1970; Statistical Abstract of the United States; Trade Policy Review of the United States*

Tariffs work to safeguard American products from foreign competition.
Trade What has been the overall trend in the use of tariffs as trade barriers?

---

customs duty *a tax on certain items purchased abroad*

tariff *a tax on imported goods*

reduce the chances that the importing country will set up trade barriers.

Tariffs

If you have traveled to a foreign country, you might have had to pay a tax called a **customs duty** on certain items you purchased abroad. You might also have seen "duty free" stores at international borders and airports selling luxury items like perfume and chocolate. Countries have agreed that items purchased in these shops will be free of customs duty.

Customs duty is one kind of **tariff**, or tax on imported goods. As you read in Chapter 14, both individuals and businesses have to pay tariffs. For example, the United States collects tariffs on steel, foreign-made cars, and many other products that are brought into the country. As you can see from Figure 17.6, however, tariffs have become far less important sources of government revenue than they were in the late 1800s and early 1900s.

Other Barriers to Trade

Governments sometimes use less formal methods to limit imports. For example, sometimes a government will require foreign companies to obtain a license to sell goods in that country. High licensing fees or slow licensing processes act as informal trade barriers.

Health and safety regulations and requirements are often used by governments as subtle trade barriers. For example, suppose a nation treats the fruit it grows with an insecticide that is widely accepted in its own country. Another nation that wants to discourage imports of this product might ban any fruit treated with that insecticide. The importing nation hopes that it will be too troublesome for potential sellers to meet this condition. In this way, imports will be sharply reduced or eliminated.

Effects of Trade Barriers

Trade barriers have a number of effects, some negative and some positive. Simply put, trade barriers limit supply. You will recall that the United States limits cotton imports through import quotas. These quotas ensure that the United States manufacturers of jeans and other cotton clothing will probably not be able to meet their needs for cotton with imported cotton alone. Instead, clothing manufacturers will have to buy some cotton grown in the

United States to make up their shortfall. In this way, American cotton growers benefit from quotas on cotton.

Increased Prices for Foreign Goods

Although producers of many products may benefit from trade barriers, consumers can lose out. That's because trade barriers result in higher prices. For example, suppose the market price of an imported car is $20,000. The United States wants to use a tariff to restrict the number of imported cars coming into the country. The United States government thus places a 10 percent tariff on all foreign-auto imports. With this tariff, the price of the $20,000 imported car now rises to $22,000.

As a result of this price increase, American car makers can compete more easily in the market. American manufacturers and workers therefore benefit through increased sales. On the other hand, consumers must now pay higher prices for foreign-made cars. In addition, American manufacturers lose the economic incentive to become more efficient and produce their cars less expensively.

Trade Wars

Escalating economic conflict is another possible outcome of trade barriers. When one country restricts imports, its trading partner may impose its own restrictions against the first country. Such a cycle of increasing trade restrictions is known as a **trade war**.

Trade wars often lead to a substantial decrease in trade for both countries. As you read in Section 1, trade benefits both trading partners. Conversely, a decrease in trade hurts both trading partners. The following list describes a few of the many tariffs that have led to trade wars and that have negatively affected the United States economy.

- *Smoot-Hawley Tariff of 1930* When the United States increased its average tariff on all products to 50 percent, its trading partners retaliated with higher tariffs. The trade war that resulted decreased international trade and deepened the worldwide depression of the 1930s.

- *Chicken Tariff of 1963* The European Economic Community (or EEC, the trade organization that preceded the European Union) imposed a large tariff on frozen chickens from the United States. This tariff cut American chicken exports in half. The United States retaliated by increasing its tariffs on expensive brandies from France, potato starch from Holland, and light trucks from Germany.

- *Pasta Tariff of 1985* The United States imposed tariffs on pasta from the European Economic Community. The EEC retaliated by increasing tariffs on lemons and walnuts from the United States.

- *Beef War of 1999* The United States imposed tariffs on European clothing and specific foods, including certain cheeses, meats, and mustards, in response to a European ban on hormone-treated beef from the United States. This "Beef War" continued an ongoing trade dispute between the United States and Europe over Europe's refusal to import Caribbean bananas. (See the Global Connections on the next page.)

trade war *a cycle of increasing trade restrictions*

◀ Trade wars in the late 1990s resulted in increased prices for some imported foods such as this mustard from France.

451

protectionism *the use of trade barriers to protect a nation's industries from foreign competition*

infant industry *a new industry*

Arguments for Protectionism

Why does a country impose trade barriers? There are three main arguments that support **protectionism,** the use of trade barriers to protect industries from foreign competition. These include protecting workers' jobs, protecting infant industries, and safeguarding national security.

Protecting Jobs

One argument for protectionism is that it shelters workers in industries that would be hurt by foreign competition. For example, suppose that nations in East Asia have a comparative advantage in producing textiles. If the United States reduced existing tariffs on textile imports, domestic manufacturers may not be able to compete with East Asian imports. They would have to close their factories and lay off workers.

In an ideal world, the laid-off workers would take new jobs in other industries. In practice, however, as you read in Section 1, retraining and relocation can be difficult. Many workers do not have the skills to work in other industries, and obtaining such skills takes time and money.

In addition, industry and political leaders often do not want to shut down existing industries and lose jobs in their home regions. For example, the textile industry is heavily concentrated in the southeastern United States. Politicians and industry leaders from the Southeast might try to keep textile tariffs in place to prevent loss of jobs and business.

Protecting Infant Industries

Suppose you are learning a new skill, such as playing ping-pong. At first you find it difficult to hit the ball, but as you play more your skills improve. This process is called "learning by doing."

Similarly, new industries need time and practice to become efficient producers. Tariffs and other protectionist policies are often defended on the grounds that they protect new industries in the early stages of their development. A new industry is often called an **infant industry.**

A tariff shields a young industry from the competition of its more mature rivals. After the infant industry grows up—that is, acquires the ability to produce goods efficiently and at a competitive price—the tariff can be eliminated because the industry is able to compete.

Two main difficulties arise with protecting infant industries, however. First, a protected infant industry lacks the incentive to become more efficient and competitive. Second, once an industry is given tariff protection, it is difficult to take the protection away. In other words, the infant may never "grow up."

Safeguarding National Security

Certain industries may require protection from foreign competition because their products are essential to defending the United States. In the event of a war, the United States would need steel and other products from heavy industries. It would also need industries that provide energy and advanced technologies. For this reason, the government wants to ensure that these industries remain active in the United States.

Even supporters of free trade agree that some industries need to be protected—or at least receive government financial help—so

Global Connections

The Banana Wars Throughout much of the 1990s, the European Union and the United States were at war—a trade war, that is—and the conflict was over bananas. At the heart of the conflict was a European Union policy that favored banana imports from former European colonies in Africa and the Pacific. Much of the world's banana crop, however, is grown in Latin America and the Caribbean. To aid growers in its own hemisphere, the United States placed tariffs on a variety of items—including gourmet cheese, handbags, and cashmere clothing—imported from EU nations. These tariffs charged European exporters a fee equal to 100 percent of the good's value when it entered the United States. By the late 1990s, the trade war over bananas showed no signs of slowing, and in fact became part of a larger trade war over beef exports in 1999. **Who are the winners and losers in a trade war?**

Protecting Infant Industry

Protecting Jobs

Protecting National Security

BUILDING KEY CONCEPTS

Protectionists argue in favor of trade barriers based on protecting infant industries, jobs, and national security.
Competition How does protectionism reduce foreign competition?

that the United States will not have to depend on other nations during a crisis. Free trade supporters argue, however, that certain industries claim trade protection when in fact their products are not essential to national security at all.

International Cooperation and Agreements

Recent trends favor lowering trade barriers and increasing free trade. Many people argue that free trade is the best way to pursue comparative advantage, raise general living standards, and further international peace.

To increase free trade, a number of international free trade agreements have developed. An **international free trade agreement** results from cooperation between at least two countries to reduce trade barriers and tariffs and to trade with each other.

The Reciprocal Trade Agreement Act
The history of today's free trade movement goes back to the 1930s when the United States began to promote international trade, which had been dwindling, partly as a result of the Smoot-Hawley tariff. The Reciprocal Trade Agreements Act of 1934

gave the president the power to reduce tariffs by as much as 50 percent.

The Act also allowed Congress to grant most-favored-nation (MFN) status to U.S. trading partners. Today, MFN status is called normal trade relations status, or NTR. A country with NTR status pays the same tariffs as those paid by all NTR partners. Therefore, if the United States lowers the tariff on imported rice from 25 percent to 15 percent for one NTR nation, all other NTR nations automatically receive the reduction. (Non-NTR nations may still be taxed at the higher rate, however.)

The World Trade Organization
In 1948, GATT, the General Agreement on Tariffs and Trade, was established to reduce tariffs and expand world trade. The **World Trade Organization (WTO)** was founded in 1995 to ensure compliance with GATT, to negotiate new trade agreements, and to resolve trade disputes. Various conferences, or rounds, of tariff negotiations have advanced the goals of GATT and the WTO. For example, the Uruguay round of negotiations, completed in 1994, decreased average global tariffs by about a third. From 1930 to 1995, the average tariff in the United States dropped from about 59 percent to about 5 percent.

international free trade agreement *agreement that results from cooperation between at least two countries to reduce trade barriers and tariffs and to trade with each other*

World Trade Organization (WTO) *a worldwide organization whose goal is freer global trade and lower tariffs*

The World Trade Organization also acts as a referee, enforcing the rules agreed upon by the member countries. For example, when the banana and beef wars erupted between the United States and the European Union, the case was brought before the WTO. The WTO found in favor of the United States and allowed the United States tariffs to remain in effect.

The European Union

In recent years, many countries have formed customs unions—agreements that abolish tariffs and trade restrictions among union members, and that adopt uniform tariffs for nonmember countries. The most successful example currently is the **European Union (EU).**

The European Union as we know it today developed slowly over time. In 1957, six western European nations set up the Common Market to coordinate economic and trade policies. In the years that followed, additional European nations joined the Common Market. In 1986, member nations agreed to eliminate tariffs on one another's exports. They thereby created a single market, called the European Economic Community (EEC).

In 1993, the European Economic Community nations formed the European Union (EU). The EU has a parliament and a council in which all member nations are represented. It also has its own flag, its own anthem, and celebrates Europe Day on May 9. In early 2002, eleven member nations replaced their individual currencies with a single currency called the **euro.**

NAFTA

In other parts of the world, countries have developed **free-trade zones,** or regions where a group of countries agrees to reduce or eliminate trade barriers. **NAFTA** (the North American Free Trade Agreement) will eliminate all tariffs and other trade barriers between Canada, Mexico, and the United States by 2009. The resulting free-trade zone is the largest in the world.

NAFTA provisions include the following:

1. Tariffs on all farm products and on some 10,000 other goods are to be eliminated over 15 years.
2. Automobile tariffs are to be phased out over 10 years.
3. Special judges have authority to resolve trade disputes.
4. The agreement cannot be used to override national and state environmental, health, or safety laws.
5. Trucks are to have free access across borders and throughout the three member countries.

Before the agreement was signed, the NAFTA measure aroused a great deal of controversy in the United States. NAFTA opponents worried that American factories would relocate to Mexico, where wages were lower and government regulations, such as environmental controls, were less strict. The result would be a loss of jobs in the United States. Supporters of NAFTA claimed that the measure would instead create more jobs in the United States as a result of increased exports to Mexico and Canada.

FAST FACT

Europe and the United States account for 55 percent of world trade, 60 percent of trade in services, and 80 percent of world wealth.

▼ **NAFTA has resulted in increased trade across the Rio Grande.**

Figure 17.7 Major Trade Organization Members

EU
CARICOM
MERCOSUR
APEC
NAFTA & APEC

Many countries are members of major regional trade organizations.
Trade What is the purpose of these organizations?

The United States Senate ratified NAFTA on January 1, 1994, after a bruising Congressional battle. In 1997, the government's first study of NAFTA revealed that while some jobs had been created, an almost equal number had been eliminated. On the other hand, trade between the United States, Canada, and Mexico had increased significantly. From 1993 to 1997, United States exports to Mexico increased from $41 million to $71 million. Imports from Mexico to the United States more than doubled, from $40 million to $86 million. To the north, United States exports to Canada during that time increased by one third, from $100 million to $152 million. Imports also increased by about one third from $111 million to $168 million. Today, the United States government is working to expand the NAFTA agreement to include other countries in the Western Hemisphere.

Other Regional Trade Agreements

Throughout the world, many countries have entered into other regional trade agreements. In fact, about 100 regional trading organizations operate in the world today. The largest of these organizations include the following.

- *APEC* The Asia-Pacific Economic Cooperation includes countries that lie along the Pacific Rim, including the United States, Mexico, and Canada. These nations have signed a nonbinding agreement to reduce trade barriers among their nations.
- *MERCOSUR* The Southern Common Market is similar to the European Union

in its goals. Its members are Brazil, Argentina, Paraguay, and Uruguay.

• *CARICOM* The Caribbean Community and Common Market includes countries from South America and the Caribbean.

The Role of Multinationals

Multinational corporations (MNCs) also contribute to international trade. As you read in Chapter 8, a multinational is a large corporation that sells goods and services throughout the world. For example, an automobile company might design its cars in the United States. The same company might import parts from Asia and assemble its cars in Canada and Mexico. As a result, although you might purchase the automobile from a company based in the United States, it is not a purely domestic product.

Many goods besides cars are produced globally. Some brands of athletic shoes are

designed in the United States but are produced in East Asia. Some personal computers are designed in the United States and assembled abroad with parts and components from the United States.

The decision to build production facilities in a foreign country benefits both the multinational corporation and the host nation. By locating abroad, the corporation avoids some shipping fees and tariffs. It may also benefit from cheaper labor in much of Asia and Latin America. The host nation benefits by gaining jobs and tax revenue on the corporation's income, profits, and property.

On the other hand, host nations worry about the effect of multinationals on their countries. Multinationals in a small country with a less developed economy could gain excessive political power. In addition, host nations are concerned that multinationals could replace the host country's domestic industries and exploit their workers. In order to address these concerns, nations have instituted rules that require multinationals to export a certain percentage of their products. Host nations hope that such requirements will help protect their domestic industries.

Section 2 Assessment

Key Terms and Main Ideas

1. Describe the similarities and differences among the following barriers to free trade: **import quotas, voluntary export restraints (VERs),** and **tariffs.**

2. Explain the effects of **trade barriers** on manufacturers, workers, and consumers.

3. What are the advantages and disadvantages of protecting an **infant industry?**

4. Describe the three arguments in favor of **protectionism.**

5. Choose one of the trade organizations or agreements described in the section and explain its purpose.

Applying Economic Concepts

6. *You Decide* Suppose that you were in charge of trade policy in the United States. Would you recommend that the United States increase or decrease trade barriers on video game systems? Explain your answer.

7. *Problem Solving* Suppose that a company called NewMovies, Inc., located in Country X, has decided to produce and distribute movies. NewMovies, Inc., would like the government of Country X to impose a tariff on foreign-made movies. Why?

8. *Critical Thinking* What are the advantages of international trade agreements? What might be some disadvantages?

Take It to the NET

Several international trade agreements have been mentioned in this section, but many more exist. Describe two additional agreements. Use the links provided in the Social Studies area at the following Web site for help in completing this activity. **www.phschool.com**

Profile

Carla Anderson Hills (b. 1934)

Although a strong believer in free trade, U.S. Trade Representative Carla Anderson Hills was not afraid to use tariffs and quotas as tools to pry open foreign markets. Her approach to eliminating overseas barriers to American trade earned her the nickname "the Velvet Crowbar."

An Advocate for Free Trade

"The case for free trade does not easily fit on a bumper sticker," Carla Anderson Hills observes. Free trade, she says, results in a stronger economy with more innovation and technological development.

As U.S. Trade Representative from 1989 to 1993, Hills was charged with carrying out U.S. trade policy. She earned a reputation as a tough advocate for U.S. rights in world trade. "With less than 5 percent of the world's population, we produce more than 20 percent of the world's output," Hills asserts. "We need access to foreign markets to sell the goods we produce."

From Law to International Trade

After graduating from Stanford University, Hills earned a law degree from Yale in 1958. She joined her husband and three other attorneys to found their own law firm in 1962. In 1974, she left California to work in the Justice Department.

In 1975, President Gerald Ford named Hills Secretary of Housing and Urban Development. After Jimmy Carter became president, Hills returned to the private practice of law, where she remained until

President George Bush appointed her U.S. Trade Representative in 1989. Today her firm, Hills & Company, provides advice on trade to U.S. businesses.

The Velvet Crowbar

Hills described her negotiating approach as "a handshake wherever possible [and] a crowbar where necessary." To open the Japanese market to U.S. electronic and wood products, Hills threatened U.S. retaliation against Japanese goods. She said, "I'll never say I'm satisfied until their market is as open to our entrepreneurs as ours is to theirs."

In 1992, Hills threatened to pull the United States out of global trade talks unless the European Union agreed to cut government subsidies to its farmers. When France resisted, she slapped a 200 percent tariff on French wine and farm products.

In general, however, Hills opposes this kind of trade protection. She labels it "the worst possible policy option to deal with jobs thought to be lost to foreign competition, because in the long run it will cost more jobs by making our companies less competitive."

CHECK FOR UNDERSTANDING

1. Source Reading Explain the reasoning in the following Hills statement: "It is in our interest to persuade our trading partners to lower their barriers. That is particularly true with respect to nations of Asia and Latin America, the two fastest-growing regions in the world."

2. Critical Thinking As U.S. trade representative, why would Hills have opposed European governments who provided subsidies to European farmers?

3. Decision Making Some opponents of free trade contend that it costs American workers jobs. If you were the U.S. Trade Representative, would you try to protect American companies from foreign competition?

Measuring Trade

Objectives

After studying this section you will be able to:

1. **Analyze** how changes in exchange rates of world currencies affect international trade.
2. **Describe** the effect of various exchange rate systems.
3. **Analyze** the effects of changes in exchange rates on the balance of trade.

Section Focus

International trade is complicated by the fact that different nations have different currencies. Countries pay for imports in their own currencies and receive foreign currency for exports. If a nation imports more than it exports, or vice versa, a trade imbalance is created.

Key Terms

exchange rate
appreciation
depreciation
foreign exchange market
fixed exchange-rate system
flexible exchange-rate system
trade surplus
trade deficit
balance of trade

exchange rate the value of a foreign nation's currency in terms of the home nation's currency

Have you ever traveled to a foreign country? If so, you may have been unable to purchase goods in that country using U.S. dollars. Similarly, tourists buying goods in the United States need to exchange their home country's money for U.S. dollars. In order for foreign visitors to buy something in another country, they usually must obtain that country's currency before making any purchases.

Exchange Rates

International trade takes place whenever a good or service is produced in one country and sold in another. Trade between countries is more complex than buying and selling within the same country because of the world's many currencies and their changing values.

Foreign Exchange

If you want to buy a newspaper in Beijing, you will need to change your American dollars for Chinese renminbi. If a Mexican visitor to New York wants to buy lunch, she must change her pesos to dollars.

Changing money from one currency to another is not a simple matter of exchanging, say, one peso for one American dollar. A dollar might be worth 9 pesos—or 115 Japanese yen, or 8 Chinese renminbi.

The value of a foreign nation's currency in relation to your own currency is called the foreign exchange rate, or simply the **exchange rate**. The exchange rate enables you to convert prices in one currency to prices in another currency.

Reading an Exchange Rate Table

Exchange rates are listed on the Internet and in many major newspapers. Figure 17.8 shows a table of sample exchange rates. If you read down the first column, for example, you will see that one U.S. dollar can be exchanged for about one-and-a-half (1.478) Canadian dollars, for a bit less than one euro (0.9516), and so forth.

It is important to realize that these rates are what one U.S. dollar is worth on one particular day. Exchange rates go up and down daily.

Determing the Rate of Exchange

The following example will help you calculate exchange rates. Suppose your family is planning a trip to Mexico this summer and wants to determine the cost of staying in a

▼ **Tourists can exchange their currency for that of the country they are visiting at currency exchange outlets or centers.**

Figure 17.8 Foreign Exchange Rates

	U.S. $	Aust $	U.K. £	Canadian $	¥en	Euro	Mexican NP	Chinese renminbi
U.S. $	1	0.6489	1.599	0.6764	0.01	1.051	0.11	0.12
Australian $	1.541	1	2.465	1.042	0.01	1.62	0.17	0.19
U.K. £	0.6252	0.4057	1	0.4229	0.01	0.657	0.07	0.08
Canadian $	1.478	0.9593	2.365	1	0.01293	1.554	0.16	0.18
¥en	114.3	74.19	182.9	77.34	1	120.2	12.24	13.81
Euro	0.9516	0.6175	1.522	0.6436	0.01	1	0.1	0.11
Mexican nuevo peso	9.33	6.06	14.94	6.3	0.08	9.81	1	1.13
Chinese renminbi	8.28	5.37	13.25	5.6	0.07	8.7	9.8	1

Read down the first column of the chart to find what one U.S. dollar was worth in foreign currencies on this particular day. (Example: One U.S. dollar was worth 0.6252 British pounds.) Read across the top row to find out how much a selected foreign currency was worth in U.S. dollars. (Example: One British pound cost 1.599 U.S. dollars or about $1.60.) **Money** How much were 8.28 Chinese renminbi worth in U.S. dollars?

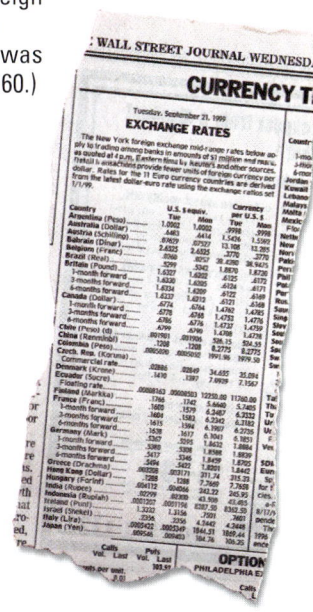

hotel. If a hotel room in Mexico costs 400 pesos per night and the exchange rate is 8.0 pesos per dollar, a hotel room will cost $50:

$$\frac{400 \text{ pesos}}{8.0 \text{ pesos per dollar}} = \$50.00$$

If your family decides to go to Mexico the following fall, however, the exchange rate will probably have changed. If by fall, the exchange rate is 8.5 pesos per dollar, the hotel room will cost only about $47 a night (assuming that the hotel still charges 400 pesos per night):

$$\frac{400 \text{ pesos}}{8.5 \text{ pesos per dollar}} = \$47.05$$

By fall, the exchange rate might, however, be only 7.5 pesos per dollar. In that case, your family would need to spend more money on your visit. The hotel room would now cost about $53 per night:

$$\frac{400 \text{ pesos}}{7.5 \text{ pesos per dollar}} = \$53.33$$

Strong and Weak Currencies

You have probably heard newscasters talk about a "strong" or "weak" dollar or a currency like the Japanese yen "rising" or "falling." What do these terms mean, and are they good news or bad news for the United States economy?

An increase in the value of a currency is called **appreciation**. When a currency appreciates, it becomes "stronger." If the exchange rate between the dollar and the yen increases from 100 yen per dollar to 110 yen per dollar, one dollar will purchase more yen. Since the dollar has increased in value, we say that the dollar has appreciated against the yen. This appreciation means that people in Japan will have to spend more yen to purchase a dollar's worth of goods from the United States.

When a nation's currency appreciates, that nation's products become more expensive in other countries. For example, a strong dollar makes American goods and services more expensive for Japanese consumers. Japan will therefore probably import fewer products from the United States. That means that total United States exports to Japan will likely decline.

On the other hand, a strong dollar means that foreign products will be less expensive for consumers in the United States. A strong dollar is therefore likely to lead consumers in the United States to purchase imported goods.

A decrease in the value of a currency is called **depreciation**. You might also hear depreciation referred to as "weakening." If the dollar exchange rate fell to 90 yen per

appreciation *an increase in the value of a currency*

depreciation *a decrease in the value of a currency*

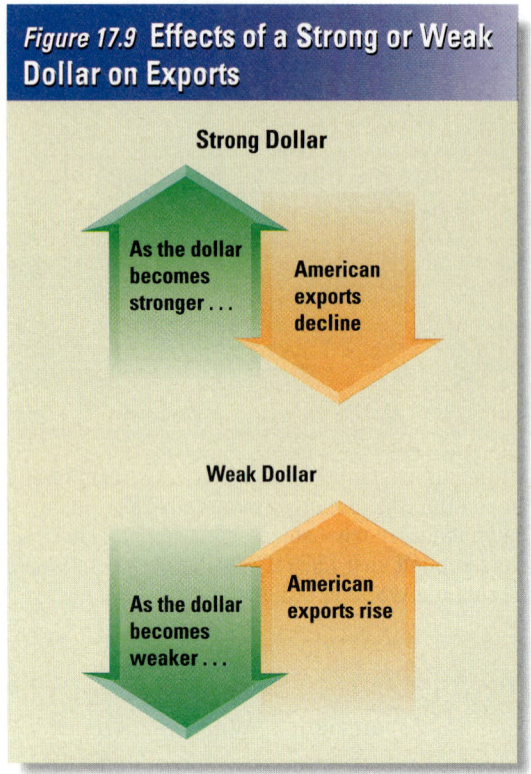

Figure 17.9 Effects of a Strong or Weak Dollar on Exports

Strong Dollar

As the dollar becomes stronger . . .

American exports decline

Weak Dollar

As the dollar becomes weaker . . .

American exports rise

A strong dollar leads to a decrease in exports. A weak dollar leads to an increase in exports. **Trade** What is the effect of a strong or weak dollar on imports?

foreign exchange market *the banks and other financial institutions that facilitate the buying and selling of foreign currencies*

dollar, you would get fewer yen for each dollar. In other words, the dollar has depreciated against the yen.

When a nation's currency depreciates, its products become cheaper to other nations. A depreciated, or weak, dollar means that foreign consumers will be able to better afford products made in the United States. As you can see from Figure 17.9, exports are likely to increase as a result of a weakened dollar. At the same time, other nations' products become more expensive for consumers in the United States, so imports are likely to decrease.

The Foreign Exchange Market

When a company in the United States sells computers in Japan, that company is paid in yen. It must, however, pay its United States workers in dollars. The company must therefore exchange its yen for dollars

in order to pay its workers. This exchange takes place on the foreign exchange market. Because each nation uses a different currency, international trade would not be possible without this market.

The **foreign exchange market** consists of about 2,000 banks and other financial institutions that facilitate the buying and selling of foreign currencies. These banks are located in various financial centers around the world, including New York, London, Paris, Singapore, Tokyo, and many other cities. Wherever they are located, the banks that make up the foreign exchange market maintain close links to one another through telephones and computers. This technology allows for the instantaneous transmission of market information and rapid financial transactions.

Exchange Rate Systems

As you read in Chapter 10, currencies varied in value from state to state in early America. In the United States today, of course, it doesn't matter whether you are in California, New York, or Texas—all prices are in dollars, and all dollars have the same value. No one asks whether your dollars came from San Francisco or Miami. Within the United States, a dollar is just a dollar.

Think how much more complicated it would be to do business if each state still had different currencies. To buy goods from a mail-order company in Indiana, for instance, you would have to find out the exchange rate between your local dollar and the Indiana dollar. Any large business in the United States would be overwhelmed by its efforts to keep track of all the exchange rates among the states. The economy would become less efficient as individuals and businesses spent time dealing with exchange rates.

You can understand from the above example how complex transactions would become if states had different exchange rates. The same ideas also apply to exchange rates among nations.

Fixed Exchange-Rate Systems

Wouldn't it be easier if all countries either used the same currency or fixed their exchange rates against one another? Then no one would have to worry about shifts in exchange rates. A currency system in which governments try to keep the values of their currencies constant against one another is called a **fixed exchange-rate system.**

In a typical fixed exchange-rate system, one country with a stable currency is at the center. Other countries fix, or "peg," their exchange rates to the currency of this central country.

Normally, the fixed exchange-rate is not just a single value, but is kept within a certain prespecified range (for example, plus or minus 2 percent). If the exchange rate moves outside of this range, governments usually step in—or intervene—to help maintain the rate.

How do governments intervene to maintain an exchange rate? Like the price of any product or service, the exchange rate relies on supply and demand. To preserve its exchange rate, a government may buy or sell foreign currency in order to affect a currency's supply and demand. It will follow this course of action until the exchange rate is back within the prespecified limits.

The Bretton Woods Conference

In 1944, as World War II was drawing to a close, representatives from 44 countries met in Bretton Woods, New Hampshire. Their purpose was to make financial arrangements for the postwar world after the expected defeat of Germany and Japan.

The Bretton Woods conference resulted in the creation of a fixed exchange-rate system for the Untied States and much of western Europe. Because the United States was the strongest economic power with the most stable currency, the U.S. dollar was at the center of the new system. Beginning in 1945, the conference participants agreed to fix their currencies to the U.S. dollar.

The Bretton Woods conference also established the International Monetary Fund (IMF) to make the new system work. Today this organization promotes international monetary cooperation, currency stabilization, and international trade. You will read more about the International Monetary Fund in Chapter 18.

Flexible Exchange-Rate Systems

Although fixed exchange-rate systems make it easier to trade, they require countries to maintain similar economic policies, including similar inflation and interest rates. By the late 1960s, changes were continually occurring in the international trading system, and worldwide trade was growing rapidly. At the same time, the war in Vietnam was causing inflation in the United States. These factors made it increasingly difficult for many countries to rely on a fixed exchange-rate system.

fixed exchange-rate system *a currency system in which governments try to keep the values of their currencies constant against one another*

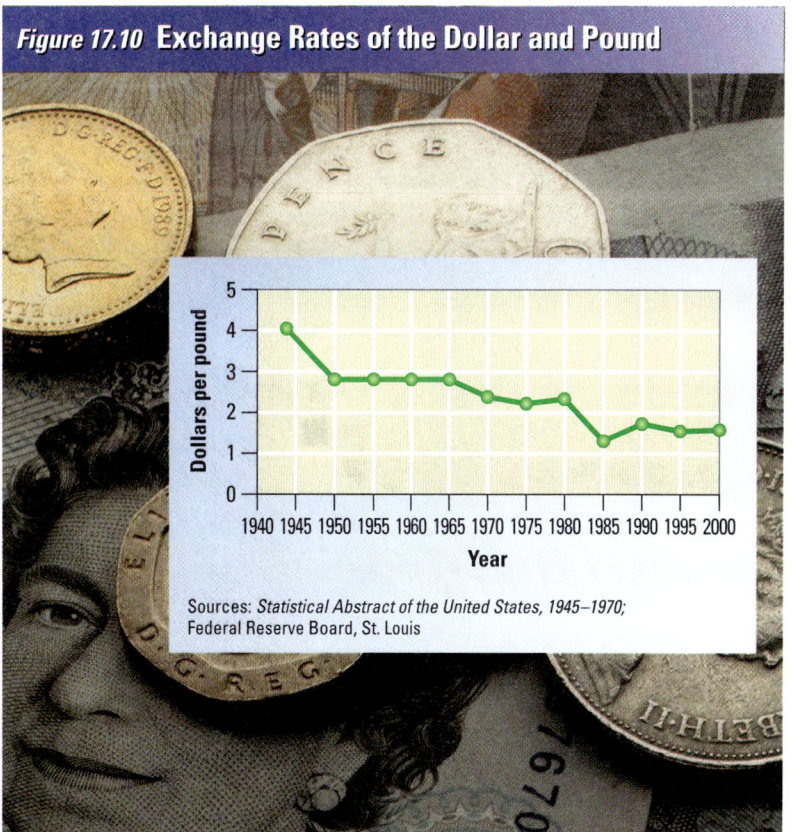

Figure 17.10 Exchange Rates of the Dollar and Pound

Sources: *Statistical Abstract of the United States, 1945–1970;* Federal Reserve Board, St. Louis

The United States and Britain shifted from a fixed rate to a flexible exchange-rate system in the early 1970s.
Money How did this shift affect exchange rates between the dollar and the pound?

flexible exchange-rate system *a currency system that allows the exchange rate to be determined by supply and demand*

trade surplus *the result of a nation exporting more than it imports*

trade deficit *the result of a nation importing more than it exports*

balance of trade *the relationship between a nation's imports and its exports*

In 1971, the West German and Dutch governments abandoned the fixed exchange-rate system. By 1973, many countries, including the United States, had adopted a system based on flexible, or floating, exchange rates.

In contrast to the fixed rate system, the **flexible exchange-rate system** allows the exchange rate to be determined by supply and demand. With a flexible exchange-rate system, exchange rates need not fall into any prespecified range.

Today, the countries of the world use a mixture of fixed and flexible exchange rates. Most major currencies, however—including the U.S. dollar and the Japanese yen—use the flexible exchange-rate system. This system accounts for the day-to-day changes in currency values that you read about earlier in this section.

When the flexible exchange-rate system was first adopted, some economists worried that changes in the exchange rate might interrupt the flow of international trade. In fact, the flexible exchange-rate system has worked reasonably well since the breakdown of the Bretton Woods fixed-rate system. World trade has grown at a rapid rate, and more nations trade today than ever before.

The Euro

Although the flexible exchange-rate system works well, some countries whose economies are closely tied together want the advantages of fixed exchange rates. One way to enjoy the advantages but avoid some of the difficulties of fixed exchange rates is to abolish individual currencies and establish a single currency.

This is just what most of the European Union countries have done. The EU has established a new currency, which twelve EU member nations have adopted. As you read in Section 2, this single currency is called the euro. Use of this common currency requires participating countries to coordinate their economic policies, but it also simplifies trade.

The Balance of Trade

When a nation exports more than it imports, it has a **trade surplus**. When a nation imports more than it exports, it creates a **trade deficit**. The relationship between a nation's imports and its exports is called its **balance of trade**.

When a large difference between a nation's imports and exports arises, it is said to have a trade imbalance. A nation that exports more goods than it imports has a positive trade balance. A nation that imports more than it exports has a negative trade balance.

Understanding the Balance of Trade

Nations seek to maintain a balance of trade with values of imports equal to values of exports. By balancing trade, a nation can protect the value of its currency on the international market. If a trade imbalance continues, with one country importing more

▲ **Most members of the European Union have phased out their individual currencies in favor of a single currency, the euro.**

than it is exporting, the value of its currency falls. For example, in the 1980s the United States imported considerably more than it exported, and the foreign exchange market was glutted with dollars. As the value of the dollar fell, the prices of imports increased and consumers paid more for the goods.

A trade imbalance can be corrected by limiting imports or increasing the number and/or quality of exports. Both of these actions affect trading partners, or course, who may retaliate by raising tariffs. Maintaining a balance of trade thus requires international cooperation and fair trade.

The United States Trade Deficit

Although the United States sells many goods abroad (supercomputers, movies, and CDs, for example), in general it buys more goods from abroad than it sells (cars, clothing, and VCRs, for example). The result is that the United States is running a large trade deficit, and has been for several decades.

The United States trade deficit has existed since the early 1970s. At that time, the Organization of Petroleum Exporting Countries (OPEC) dramatically raised the price of oil. The United States had to increase the money spent on foreign oil, thus increasing the money spent on imports. The total cost of imports to the United States then exceeded the income from exports, and a trade deficit developed. (See the United States Trading Partners map on page 545 of the Databank for the names and locations of the countries that belong to OPEC.)

As you can see from Figure 17.11, the United States suffered record trade deficits in 1986 and 1987, reaching over $150 billion in 1987. In the early 1990s, the trade deficit began to fall. By the late 1990s, however, the deficit had skyrocketed to record levels, largely as a result of increasing oil prices.

The United States trade deficit totaled over $375 billion in 2000, with the largest amounts owed to China, Japan, Canada, Germany, Mexico, Taiwan, and oil exporting countries, such as Malaysia and

Venezuela. Imported petroleum accounted for almost 25 percent of the deficit.

Reducing the Trade Deficit

You have read that trade deficit occurs when United States businesses and consumers purchase more goods and services from foreign producers than foreigners buy from the United States during the same time period. This means that Americans are spending more than they produce.

For the United States to run a trade deficit, other countries must be willing to finance the deficits by lending to the United States or buying American assets. When Americans are buying more goods abroad than they sell, extra dollars end up in the hands of foreigners. The foreigners can then use these dollars to purchase American assets. As a result of America's persistent trade deficits, people from other

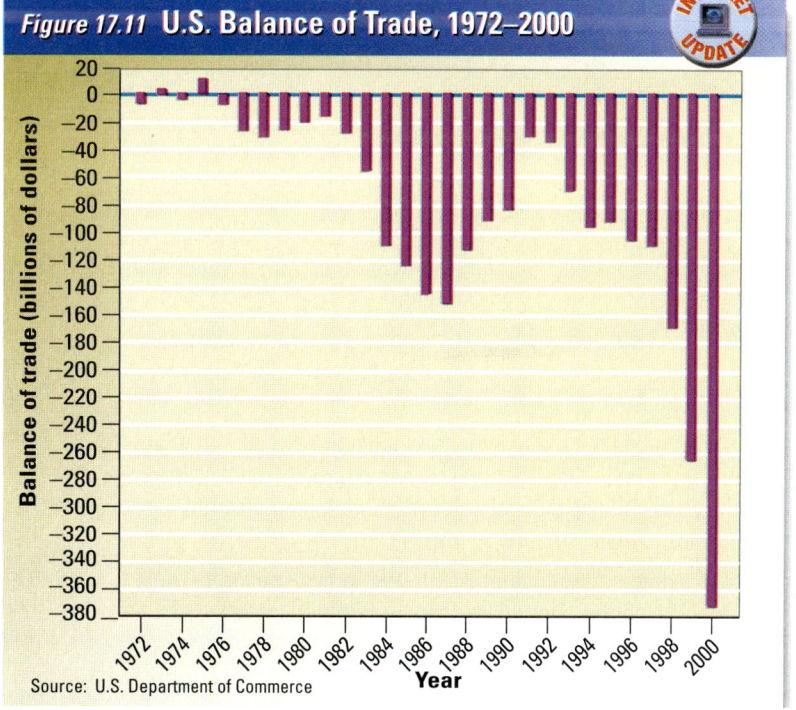

Figure 17.11 U.S. Balance of Trade, 1972–2000

Source: U.S. Department of Commerce

The United States has had a significant trade deficit since the mid-1970s.
Trade Describe the U.S. balance of trade in the 1990s.

Figure 17.12 Leading Exporters and Importers, 2000

Exporters	$ Billions	% Change 1999–2000	Importers	$ Billions	% Change 1999–2000
United States	781.1	11	United States	1257.6	19
Germany	551.5	1	Germany	502.8	6
Japan	479.2	14	Japan	379.5	22
France	298.1	-1	United Kingdom	337.0	5
United Kingdom	284.1	6	France	305.4	4
Canada	276.6	16	Canada	244.8	11
China	249.3	28	Italy	236.5	7
Italy	237.8	1	China	225.1	36
Netherlands	212.5	6	Hong Kong, China	214.2	19
Hong Kong, China	202.4	16	Netherlands	198.0	4

Note: Billions are in U.S. dollars
Source: World Trade Organization

Many of the countries listed on this chart are becoming world trade powerhouses. **Trade** Which countries are growing both as importers and exporters?

countries now own a bigger piece of the American economy. They have used the surplus dollars that they received from sales of products to Americans to purchase American land, stocks, bonds, and other assets.

Some economists worry that foreign investment might not always be available to support the trade deficit. Federal Reserve Chairman Alan Greenspan has commented that "we do not know how long net imports and U.S. external debt can rise before foreign investors become reluctant to continue to add to their portfolios of claims against the United States." The U.S. Trade Deficit Review Commission reported in 2000 that "Maintaining large and growing trade deficits is neither desirable nor likely to be sustainable for the extended future."

To reduce the trade deficit, individuals and companies could purchase fewer foreign goods or they could sell more domestic products abroad. Nationally, the country could cut back spending by adjusting its monetary or fiscal policy. Or it could appreciate the exchange rate in order to make its own goods more expensive on the world market. Some economists, however, argue that these measures are unnecessary because trade deficits correct themselves over time. Others point to the growing market for services from the United States, making the case that increased service exports will significantly reduce the trade deficit.

Section 3 Assessment

Key Terms and Main Ideas

1. Explain why you need to know the **exchange rate** when you travel to a foreign country.

2. Explain what is meant by a strong or a weak dollar. How do a strong or a weak dollar affect prices of imports and exports?

3. What is the difference between a **fixed exchange-rate system** and a **flexible exchange-rate system**? Why did the United States shift to a flexible exchange-rate system in the early 1970s?

4. What is a **trade deficit**? How would you describe the current **balance of trade** in the United States?

Applying Economic Concepts

5. *Critical Thinking* Assume you have just heard that the Canadian dollar has weakened. Is this good news or bad news for travelers from the United States visiting Canada? Explain your answer.

6. *Math Practice* Suppose you are planning to take a train between the Chinese cities of Beijing and Xian. A ticket costs 480 renminbi. Use the exchange rate table in Figure 17.8 to calculate how much money in U.S. dollars the ticket will cost.

7. *Try This* Suppose Ian buys all his groceries from a nearby store. Although he buys their groceries for many years, the store owners never buy anything from him. Should Ian be concerned about his finances? Compare this scenario to the balance of trade among countries.

Take It to the NET Find out how much your dollar can buy of a similar good (for example, a can of soda or a cup of coffee) in three different countries. Use the links provided in the Social Studies area at the following Web site for help in completing this activity. **www.phschool.com**

NAFTA: Is Free Trade a Good Idea?

In the 1980s and early 1990s, debate raged over the North American Free Trade Agreement (NAFTA). The goal of this agreement was to eliminate all trade restrictions among Mexico, Canada, and the United States. It included provisions for more than 9,000 products and services.

Pro-NAFTA Arguments Supporters of NAFTA argued it would benefit the economies of all three nations. They believed NAFTA would increase trade and promote healthy competition. They also argued that employment in some U.S. industries would increase, as the elimination of tariffs made American goods less expensive in Mexico and Canada.

Anti-NAFTA Arguments NAFTA critics argued that without tariffs, items produced in Mexico would be cheaper than American-made goods, resulting in widespread unemployment among American industrial workers. The authors of NAFTA anticipated this possibility and reduced its effects by slowly phasing out tariffs and by providing compensation to many workers who lost jobs because of NAFTA.

▲ **NAFTA has given Mexico's electronics assembly industry a boost.**

Consequences NAFTA went into effect January 1, 1994. By 1999, it was clear that NAFTA had a generally positive impact on the economies of all three trading partners. American exports of farm products, technology, and textiles to Mexico increased over pre-NAFTA levels. Canada's trade with the United States increased by 80 percent, while its trade with Mexico doubled. And although the United States did lose thousands of jobs because of increased imports, the growth in exports to Canada and Mexico resulted in thousands of newly created jobs.

Applying Economic Ideas

1. How has NAFTA benefited the economies of all three nations that signed it?

2. The table shows some of the major provisions of NAFTA. Which of these provisions benefit the United States? Which have a negative impact? Explain.

Major Provisions of NAFTA

Automobile manufacturing
- 20% Mexican tariff on U.S. cars eliminated in 1999

Agriculture
- 57% of all Canadian, U.S., and Mexican tariffs on farm products eliminated immediately
- Remaining tariffs phased out over 15 years

Clothing and Textiles
- Canadian and U.S. tariffs phased out over 10 years
- Mexican tariffs eliminated immediately

Trucking
- Mexican, Canadian, and U.S. truck drivers allowed to drive and deliver goods anywhere in North America

Banking
- U.S. banks and brokerage firms to have unlimited access to doing business in Mexico

Chapter Summary

A summary of major ideas in Chapter 17 appears below. See also the **Guide to the Essentials of Economics,** which provides additional review and test practice of key concepts in Chapter 17.

Section 1 Why Nations Trade (pp. 441–447)

Because resources are distributed unevenly throughout the world, nations specialize in producing certain goods and services, then trade to acquire the goods and services that they cannot produce. Nations, like individuals, specialize in producing goods and services based on the **law of comparative advantage:** that is, nations should specialize in producing the goods for which they have the lowest opportunity cost. As a result of specialization, both sides in the trading relationship benefit from trade.

Section 2 Trade Barriers and Agreements (pp. 449–456)

Import quotas, voluntary export restraints (VERs), and **tariffs** are three types of **trade barriers.** Their overall effect is to raise prices and protect domestic industries from foreign competition. People who favor **protectionism** argue that these measures are necessary to protect the jobs of domestic workers, shelter **infant industries,** and safeguard national security. Current trends, however, generally favor international cooperation, regional trade agreements, and an overall reduction in trade barriers.

Section 3 Measuring Trade (pp. 458–464)

After World War II, the United States and many of its trading partners used a **fixed exchange-rate system** in which exchange rates were fixed relative to the U.S. dollar. Today, most countries use a **flexible exchange-rate system** in which exchange rates shift according to market forces. As exchange rates change, currencies weaken and strengthen relative to other currencies. The difference between a nation's imports and exports is called the **balance of trade.** When a country imports more than it exports, it has a **trade deficit.** The United States has generally had a large trade deficit since the 1970s.

Key Terms

Complete each sentence by choosing the correct answer from the list of terms below. You will not use all of the terms.

comparative advantage	imports
appreciation	infant industry
exchange rate	protectionism
exports	tariff
free-trade zone	trade surplus
	depreciation

1. The ____ determines how much a foreign currency is worth in a certain nation.
2. Nations may choose to impose a ____, or tax, on imports from other countries.
3. A ____ occurs when one nation exports more goods than it imports.
4. Economists use the term ____ to refer to one nation's currency rising in value in comparison to another country's currency.
5. Goods shipped abroad for sale are ____.
6. A country has a ____ when it has the lowest opportunity cost of producing a good.
7. A young business that is shielded from foreign competition is called a(n) ____.

Using Graphic Organizers

8. On a separate sheet of paper, copy the web map below to help you organize information about trade organizations. Complete the web map by writing examples of trade organizations. Include a brief description of each organization in the blank circles.

Reviewing Main Ideas

9. How do specialization and trade benefit both trading partners?
10. Explain the concept of a flexible exchange-rate system.
11. List and describe three arguments in favor of trade barriers.
12. Why does the United States stand to benefit from increased trade in services?

Critical Thinking

13. **Analyzing Information** Suppose the United States loses its comparative advantage in producing computers. How would this loss affect employment in the United States?

14. **Drawing Conclusions** Suppose you have heard that the U.S. dollar is strong on world markets. (a) What does this news mean for imports and exports? (b) How will it affect American tourists in other countries?

15. **Recognizing Cause and Effect** Assume the United States has established a tariff on clocks. Why would the United States establish this tariff, and what are two possible effects of its enactment?

Problem-Solving Activity

16. Divide your class into small groups, each group representing a country. Have each country answer the following questions: What goods and services will you produce? With which other countries will you trade? Will tariffs and import quotas exist? Discuss the implications of your choices for the other countries in your class.

Economics Journal

Organizing Ideas Review your Economics Journal entry for Chapter 17. Then answer the following questions: Which countries do the items represent? Do the countries you have listed have any similarities, such as where they are located? What generalizations about the comparative advantages of these countries or regions can you make?

Skills for Life

Creating a Multimedia Presentation Review the steps shown on page 448; then use the chart below to help you plan your presentation. You have been asked to create a multimedia presentation on NAFTA.

17. Review the discussion of NAFTA on pages 454–455 and in the Chapter 17 Case Study on page 465. What aspects of NAFTA should you learn more about?
18. Into what segments will you divide your presentation?
19. What types of sources might you use for your presentation?
20. What sort of audio-visual aids could you use?

PREPRODUCTION TOPIC ANALYSIS SHEET

Assignment: North American Free Trade Agreement

Aspects of NAFTA to consider: _____
1. _____
2. _____
My choice: _____
Segment description and sequence:
1. _____
2. _____
3. _____
Sources of information: _____
_____
Audio-Visual Aids: _____
_____
_____

Take It to the NET

. . . .

Chapter 17 Self-Test As a final review activity, take the Chapter 17 Self-Test in the Social Studies area at the Web site listed below, and receive immediate feedback on your answers. The test consists of 20 multiple-choice questions designed to test your understanding of the chapter content.
www.phschool.com

Protectionist Policies

The laws of supply and demand apply in international trade as well as in the domestic market. Consumers and producers negotiate to find a price they can agree on. In international trade, though, there is often another player—government. Governments may put certain kinds of restrictions on particular goods in order to protect industries and workers at home. In this simulation, you will explore some effects that protectionist policies have on trade.

Materials

20 slips of paper
(one color)

10 slips of paper
(contrasting color)

10 slips of paper
(third color)

2 small boxes

notebook paper

Preparing the Simulation

In this simulation, you will role-play foreign and domestic producers who are competing to sell wool coats. Labor costs and other factors make domestic coat manufacturing more expensive. Certain government policies try to make up for this to protect domestic manufacturing. You will discover how different kinds of protectionist policies affect the workings of supply and demand.

Step 1: Your class will be divided into two equal groups: Consumers and Producers.

Step 2: The Consumers group will prepare 20 slips of colored paper that represent the prices a Consumer is willing to pay for a coat. Number these slips from $15 to $110 by fives ($15, $20, $25, and so on). Put these slips into a box.

Step 3: Meanwhile, the Producers group will prepare two sets of ten slips each (each set in a different color). These slips will represent the costs to produce a coat. One color will designate Foreign Producers. Number the Foreign Producers' slips from $10 to $50 by tens ($10, $20, etc.). The other color will designate Domestic Producers. Number the Domestic Producers' slips from $60 to $100 by tens ($60, $70, etc.). Each

▲ How might protectionist policies affect the cost of these foreign-produced coats?

amount will be used twice—two $60 slips, two $70 slips, and so on. Put all the Producer slips into a second box.

Step 4: Each member of the Consumer group will draw a slip from the Consumer box. This is the maximum price you are willing to pay for a coat. Each member of the Producer group should draw a slip from the Producer box. The color indicates whether you are a Foreign or a Domestic Producer, and the amount represents your cost to make a coat.

Conducting the Simulation

There will be three trading periods. Your goal in each trading period is to make the best deal you can—to buy below your maximum price if you are a Consumer, and to sell for more than your cost if you are a Producer.

If you are a Consumer, your score is your savings—the difference between the maximum price you were willing to pay and the price you actually paid for a coat. For example, if the price on your slip is $50, and you succeed in buying a coat for only $30, your score is $20. If you are a Producer, your score is your profit—the difference between your cost to produce the coat and the price at which you can sell it.

You do not have to buy or sell a coat in any trading period, but if you do not, your score for that round will be $0. Your teacher will keep a record of all the transactions. You should also keep a record of your own scores. The final score is the sum of all savings (Consumers) or profits (Producers).

Trading Period 1

Producers and Consumers will meet in a trading area and try to make deals. Each person can buy or sell one coat in each trading period. When you reach an agreement, report the price and your own score to the teacher. The trading period will end when no more pairs of Producers and Consumers can make a deal. Your teacher will list the prices at which coats were sold and their origins (domestic or foreign) in this trading period.

Trading Period 2

Now you will see the results of one kind of protectionist policy. The government has imposed a tariff—an import tax—of $30 on each imported coat. If you are a Foreign Producer, add $30 to your cost amount. Then trade as before. Record your transaction with your teacher.

Trading Period 3

Another government policy changes the market. Politicians from textile-manufacturing states have succeeded in banning imports of wool coats. As a result, the Foreign Producers cannot take part in this trading period. Consumers must try to buy coats from the remaining Domestic Producers. Record your transaction with your teacher.

Transactions Chart

	Trading Period 1	Trading Period 2	Trading Period 3
Number of deals made			
Number of Consumers unable to buy			
Number of Producers unable to sell			
Average price for a wool coat			
Lowest price			
Highest price			

Simulation Analysis

Use a sheet of notebook paper to create a transaction chart like the one on this page. As a class, complete the transaction chart using information that you reported to your teacher. Discuss the following questions as a group.

1. In which trading period were the largest number of coats sold?
2. In Trading Period 2, what were the effects of the tariff on the Foreign Producers? On Consumers? How did the tariff affect Domestic Producers?
3. What happened to coat prices when imports from Foreign Producers were banned in Trading Period 3? Why?
4. **Drawing Conclusions** In the real world, what would domestic coat producers probably do if imported coats were banned? Why?

The path to development is long and difficult. As nations struggle to improve their economies and their standards of living they are met with a variety of complex issues.

Economics Journal

Examine the photo on this page. What can you infer about the standard of living in this woman's country? List your ideas on a separate piece of paper.

Keep It Current

INTERNET UPDATE

Items marked with this logo are periodically updated on the Internet. Keep up-to-date with what's in the news. To get current information on economic development and transition go to **www.phschool.com**

Preview

Objectives

After studying this section you will be able to:

1. **Understand** what is meant by developed nations and less developed countries.
2. **Identify** the tools used to measure levels of development.
3. **Describe** the characteristics of developed nations and less developed countries.
4. **Understand** how levels of development are ranked.

Section Focus

Nations throughout the world exhibit varying levels of economic well-being. Many tools are used to measure a nation's level of development.

Key Terms

development
developed nation
less developed country
per capita gross domestic product (per capita GDP)
industrialization
subsistence agriculture
literacy rate
life expectancy
infant mortality rate
infrastructure
newly industrialized country (NIC)

Three billion people—half the world's population—live in extreme poverty. The United Nations estimates that 1 billion people live on less than $1 a day. Concern over these startling statistics has led to close examination of the world's economies.

Social scientists measure the economic well-being of a nation in terms of its level of development. **Development** is the process by which a nation improves the economic, political, and social well-being of its people.

Developed Nations and Less Developed Countries

Some nations enjoy a high standard of living. Wealthy nations, such as the United States, Canada, the nations of Western Europe, Australia, New Zealand, and Japan, are called developed nations. **Developed nations** are those nations with a higher average level of material well-being. Most nations, however, have low levels of material well-being. These are the **less developed countries** (LDCs). LDCs include the world's poorest countries, such as Bangladesh, Nepal, Albania, and the

nations of Central and Southern Africa. They also include nations such as Mexico, Poland, Saudi Arabia, and the former republics of the Soviet Union. The countries in this second group of nations are not the world's poorest, but they have yet to achieve the high standard of living of the world's developed nations.

It is important to remember that development refers to a nation's material well-being. It is not a judgment of the worth of a nation or its people. The level of development does not indicate cultural superiority or inferiority. Rather, the level of development indicates how well a nation is able to feed, clothe, and shelter its people. It indicates how healthy people are, how well they are educated, and how productive they are.

Measuring Development

Life expectancy, diet, access to health care, literacy, energy consumption, and many other factors are used to measure development. As you will read below, the primary measure of a country's development, however, is per capita gross domestic product (GDP).

development *the process by which a nation improves the economic, political, and social well-being of its people*

developed nation *nation with a higher average level of material well-being*

less developed country *nation with a low level of material well-being*

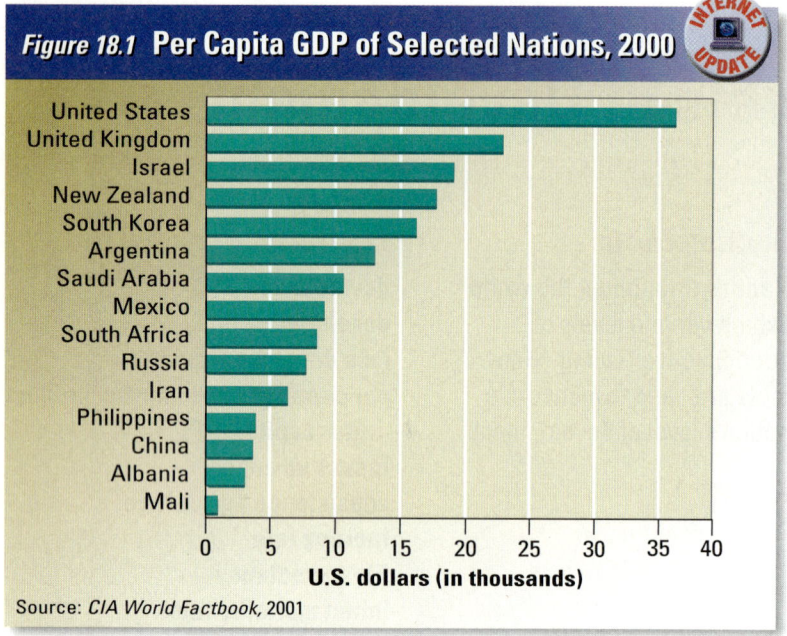

Figure 18.1 Per Capita GDP of Selected Nations, 2000

United States
United Kingdom
Israel
New Zealand
South Korea
Argentina
Saudi Arabia
Mexico
South Africa
Russia
Iran
Philippines
China
Albania
Mali

0   5   10   15   20   25   30   35   40
U.S. dollars (in thousands)

Source: *CIA World Factbook,* 2001

BUILDING KEY CONCEPTS

Per capita GDP varies greatly among nations.
Standard of Living Which nation on this graph do you think has the highest standard of living. The lowest?

per capita gross domestic product (per capita GDP) *a nation's gross domestic product (GDP) divided by its total population*

industrialization *the extensive organization of an economy for the purpose of manufacture*

subsistence agriculture *level of farming in which a person raises only enough food to feed his or her family*

Per Capita GDP

As you read in Chapter 12, gross domestic product, or GDP, is the total market value of all the final goods and services produced within an economy in a given year. It is used to measure the economic activity of a nation. GDP measures the value of production and also provides a measure of income for an economy. **Per capita gross domestic product (per capita GDP)** is a nation's GDP divided by its total population.

Development experts use per capita GDP figures because GDP alone is not adequate to compare the living standards within nations. For example, Australia and India have similar GDPs, around $390 billion for Australia and around $380 billion for India. Yet, Australia enjoys a high standard of living, while India is very poor. What accounts for this difference? The answer is population size.

Australia's $390 billion is shared by fewer than 20 million people. India's $380 billion is shared by about 1 billion people. This is why economists use per capita GDP to compare levels of development. Australia's per capita GDP is around $20,650. India's per capita GDP is around $370. (See Figure 18.2.)

These per capita figures indicate that the average Australian can more easily meet basic needs than the average Indian. The average Australian also has income left over to spend on nonessentials or to save.

Using per capita GDP to measure a nation's economic health has its limitations, however. Per capita GDP does not take into account a country's distribution of income. Within every nation, some people are wealthier than most, while others are poorer than most. In many less developed countries, the gap between rich and poor is especially wide. In some LDCs, a small, wealthy elite controls much of the wealth while most of the nation's population remains poor.

Energy Consumption

Energy consumption is another way to measure development. The amounts of fossil fuel, hydroelectricity, and nuclear energy a nation uses depends on its level of industrialization. **Industrialization** is the extensive organization of an economy for the purpose of manufacture. Industrial processes generally require large amounts of energy. For this reason, low levels of energy use tend to indicate low levels of industrial activity. High levels of energy use tend to indicate high levels of industrial activity. Because most of the developed nations of the world are highly industrialized, they are sometimes referred to as "industrialized nations."

Nations that have low levels of per capita energy consumption tend to have little industry. Most of the people in such nations are farmers working with simple tools and few machines. This is true of many LDCs, where large portions of the population engage in **subsistence agriculture.** That is, they are able to raise only enough food to feed their families.

Labor Force

What does it mean for the economy if a nation has low industrialization? It means that most of the labor force is devoted to agriculture. If most of the people are working simply to raise food for themselves, few are available to work in industry. As a result, there is little opportunity for workers to specialize. (Recall from Chapter 2 that specialization makes economies more efficient.) If individuals—or nations—are unable to produce specialized goods to sell, they are unable to generate cash income.

Consumer Goods

The quantity of consumer goods a nation produces per capita can also indicate its level of development. A large number of consumer goods in an economy means that people have enough money to meet their basic needs and still have some money left over for nonessential goods. Social scientists look to the number of large consumer goods per person to measure development. They count, for example, how many people have televisions, automobiles, refrigerators, washing machines, or telephones.

Literacy

Usually, the more a country's people attend school, the higher its level of development. This makes sense because the greater the number of people that can read and write, the more productive a population can be at both industrial and agricultural jobs.

A country's **literacy rate** is the proportion of the population over age 15 that can read and write. A well-educated nation has a high literacy rate. A low literacy rate indicates a poorly educated nation.

Life Expectancy

Life expectancy is the average expected life span of an individual. It indicates how well an economic system supports life and fends off death. A population that is well nourished and housed, as well as protected from disease, will have a long life expectancy. A population that has a poor diet and shelter and that is exposed to poor sanitation and disease will have a shorter life expectancy.

literacy rate *the proportion of the population over age 15 that can read and write*

life expectancy *the average expected life span of an individual*

BUILDING KEY CONCEPTS

Australia (left) and India (right) have very different standards of living.
Gross Domestic Product What do the photos below tell you about the population levels of Australia and India? How do their population levels affect the measurement of per capita GDP?

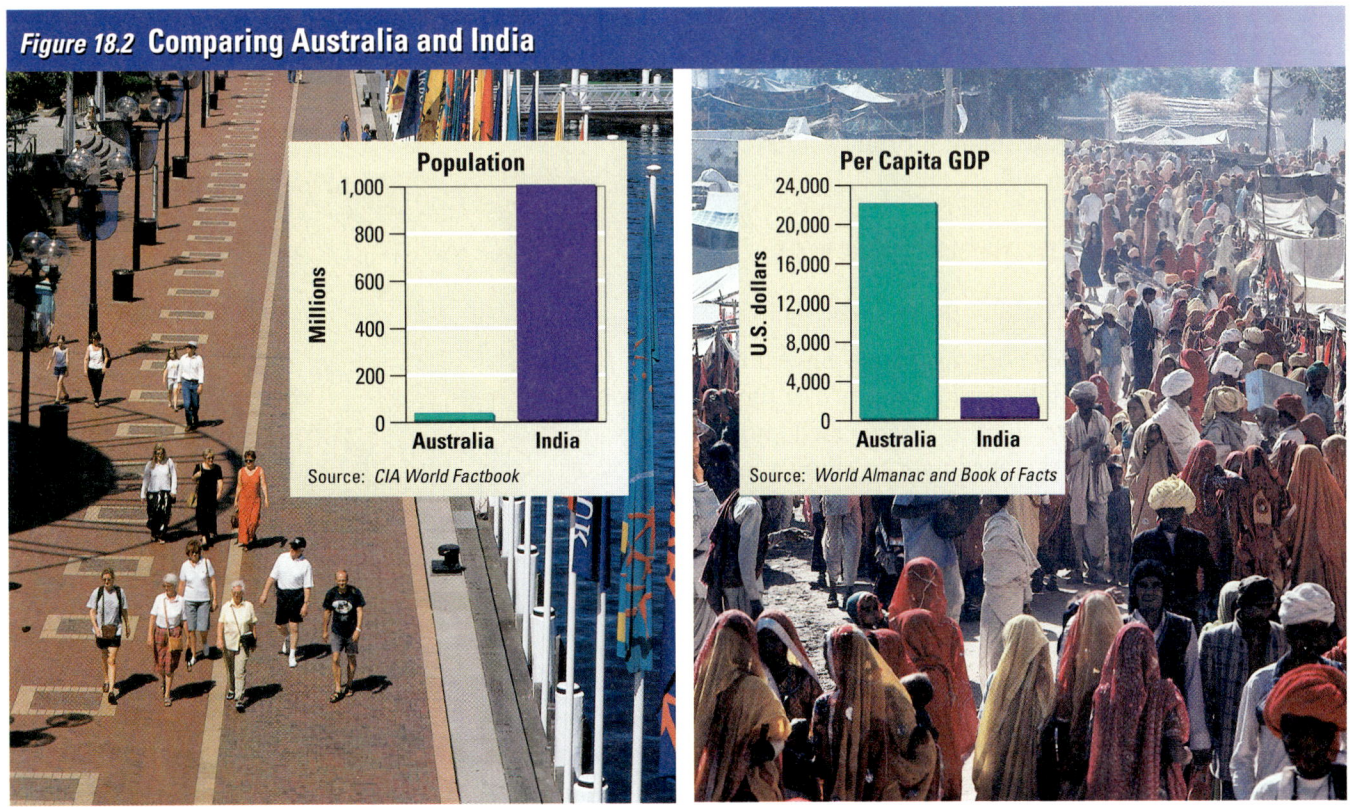

Figure 18.2 Comparing Australia and India

Population (Millions)
Source: *CIA World Factbook*

Per Capita GDP (U.S. dollars)
Source: *World Almanac and Book of Facts*

► In the developed world, the infant mortality rate is 8; in the less developed world, it is 62.

infant mortality rate *the number of deaths that occur in the first year of life per 1,000 live births*

infrastructure *the services and facilities necessary for an economy to function*

Infant Mortality Rate

Another measure of development related to nutrition and health care is a country's infant mortality rate. A country's **infant mortality rate** indicates the number of deaths that occur in the first year of life per 1,000 live births. For example, the United States has an infant mortality rate of 6.4. This means that out of every 1,000 infants born alive in a given year, 6.4 of them die before they reach their first birthdays. Like most measures of development, infant mortality rate is an average. Not all regions of a country or sectors of a population have the same infant mortality rates.

Characteristics of Developed Nations

Developed nations have high per capita GDPs, and a majority of their populations are neither very rich nor very poor. Developed nations enjoy a higher degree of economic and political freedom than do less developed countries. They also have a high degree of consumer spending. For example, in the United States, the average household has at least two television sets.

In most developed nations, agricultural output is high, but relatively few people work on farms. Use of advanced irrigation techniques, fertilizers, pesticides, seed varieties, and heavy machinery makes farmers very productive. In the United States a single farmer can feed 80 people. Compare this to many LDCs, where a single farmer can support only his or her own family.

Since only a small portion of the labor force is needed in agriculture in a developed nation, most of the labor force is available to work in industry and services. High per capita energy use in developed nations reflects a high level of industrialization. Widespread use of technology increases the productivity of the work force.

The populations of developed nations are generally very healthy. Infant mortality rates are low, while life expectancy is high. People in developed nations tend to be well educated, and literacy rates are high.

Developed nations have been urbanized for many generations. That is, most of their populations live in cities and towns and have done so for many years. A solid infrastructure has grown along with these cities and towns. **Infrastructure** is the services and facilities necessary for an economy to function. Transportation and communication systems, roads, power plants, schools, and banks are all part of a nation's infrastructure, which determines that nation's capacity to produce.

► Technology plays a huge role in agricultural productivity.

Characteristics of Less Developed Countries

Less developed countries have low per capita GDPs. Low per capita energy consumption signals their low level of industrialization. Many in the labor force work on their own farms and grow only enough food to feed themselves and their families. Unemployment rates are high, often around 20 percent. In addition, much of the labor force is underemployed. That is, some people have work, but not enough. They cannot support themselves or their families because they work less than eight hours a day.

Even if an LDC could produce consumer goods, most of the population would be unable to buy them. Subsistence-level agriculture does not provide a family with an income. It is so labor-intensive that farmers have no time for other work, even if they could find it.

The impoverished economy of an LDC has trouble educating the populace. Resources for schools are limited. In addition, children in subsistence-level economies are often needed to work on the family farm, limiting the amount of time they can spend in school.

Literacy rates in LDCs are very low. In Cambodia, for example, only 35 percent

of the people over 15 years old can read and write. Compare this figure with the United States, where the literacy rate is nearly 100 percent.

In the world's poorest countries, housing is of poor quality. Diet is, too. Along with limited access to health care, these factors lead to high infant mortality rates and short life expectancy.

There are additional characteristics common to most LDCs. In the next section, you will read about some of the difficult issues challenging less developed countries.

Levels of Development

Economic development commonly occurs in the following stages.

- *Primitive equilibrium* Economy has no formal economic organization or monetary system. It exists in equilibrium based on tradition.
- *Transition* Cultural traditions begin to crumble and people adopt new living patterns.
- *Takeoff* New industries grow and profits are reinvested.
- *Semidevelopment* Economy expands significantly and enters the international market.
- *Highly developed* Basic human needs are met easily. Economy is focused on consumer goods and public services.

Some of the more successful of the developing countries are referred to as **newly industrialized countries (NICs)**. NICs are less

newly industrialized country (NIC) *less developed country that has shown significant improvement in the measures of development*

Although income is only one measure of development, it gives a good indication of a nation's standard of living.

Income Can you see a pattern in the locations of developed nations and less developed countries?

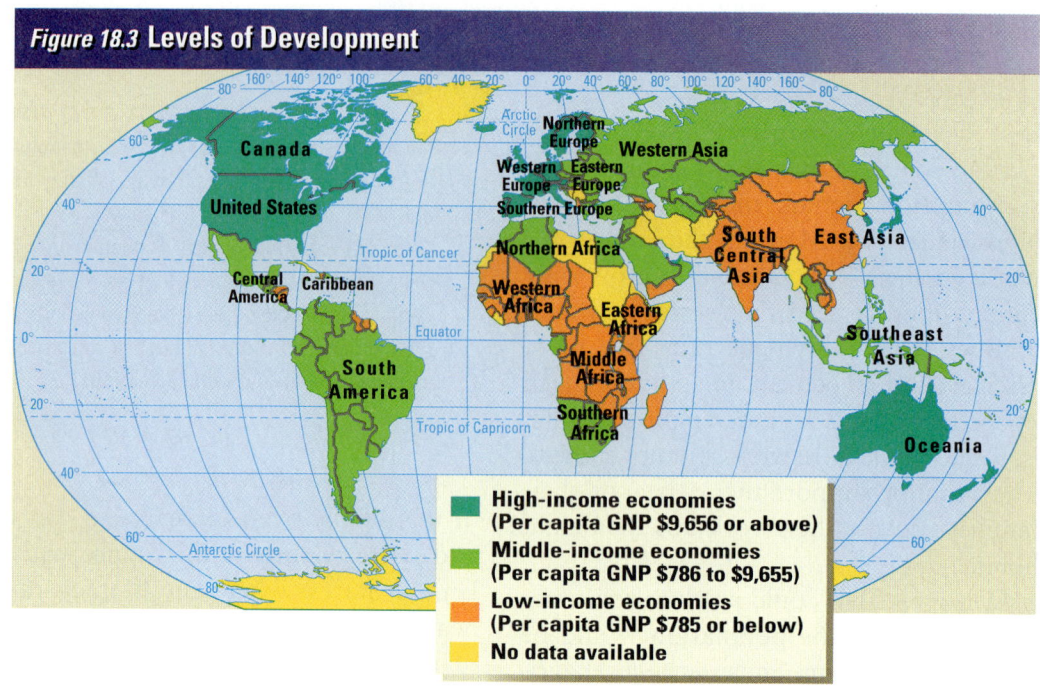

Figure 18.3 **Levels of Development**

High-income economies
(Per capita GNP $9,656 or above)

Middle-income economies
(Per capita GNP $786 to $9,655)

Low-income economies
(Per capita GNP $785 or below)

No data available

developed countries that have shown significant improvement in development. Newly industrialized countries include Mexico, Brazil, Malaysia, Thailand, Singapore, Hong Kong, South Korea, and Taiwan. The most successful of these—Singapore, Hong Kong, South Korea, and Taiwan—are known collectively as "the four Asian tigers." These countries now have incomes comparable to those of some developed nations.

The World Bank is an international organization devoted to assisting development. It uses per capita gross national product (GNP) to categorize nations as *high income, middle income,* and *low income.* High-income economies are the developed nations. Middle- and low-income economies are the less developed countries. See the map in Figure 18.3 for the distribution of these nations.

Section 1 Assessment

Key Terms and Main Ideas

1. What is **development**?
2. Why are **developed nations** sometimes referred to as industrialized nations?
3. Why is **per capita GDP** a better measure of development than GDP?
4. What role does **infrastructure** play in a nation's development?
5. List and describe three characteristics of **developed nations** and three characteristics of **less developed countries**.

Applying Economic Concepts

6. *Decision Making* Create a list of three factors used to measure a nation's development. If you were in charge of an LDC, how would you attempt to obtain higher levels of development in those three areas?

7. *Using the Databank* Turn to the charts showing the health expenditures as a percent of GDP on page 547. **(a)** Which countries spend the least percentage of GDP on health care? **(b)** How do those countries' figures compare to the amount spent in the United States?

Take It to the NET

Find out more about three countries considered to be among the least developed countries in the world. How many telephones are there per 1,000 people? What is the adult literacy rate? What percentage of the population has access to safe drinking water? Use the links provided in the Social Studies area at the following Web site for help in completing this activity. **www.phschool.com**

Profile

W. Arthur Lewis (1915–1991)

W. Arthur Lewis rose from working as a file clerk to become a world authority on economic development. Through his economic models, Lewis hoped to bring nations in Africa, Asia, and Latin America into the global marketplace and to help poor farm workers escape from poverty.

A Man of Ideas

William Arthur Lewis grew up on the island of St. Lucia, a poor British colony in the Caribbean. Leaving school at age 14, he went to work as a clerk in a government office. A few years later, he applied for a scholarship to go to college in Great Britain. He enrolled as a business student at the London School of Economics, and received a Ph.D. in 1940.

Lewis taught economics in Britain until 1958. In 1963, he accepted a position at Princeton University, where he became well respected for stressing ideas over numbers.

A Theory of Economic Development

Lewis focused his research and teaching on developing nations. In 1954, Lewis identified a "dual economy" in poor nations—a small, profitable "capitalist" sector dominated by a large, inefficient "traditional" agricultural sector. In 1955, he expanded his ideas into a book, *The Theory of Economic Growth.*

Lewis drew the path of economic development as an upside-down U. Countries grow rich by moving excess farm workers to factory jobs. On the left of the U were poor countries like Bangladesh, where growth was slow because too many people worked in the countryside. On the right were rich countries like the United States, with large manufacturing sectors and efficient farms. Growth in these wealthier countries was also slow, Lewis argued, because "the gains from diverting labour out of agriculture are almost all exploited." At the top, with the fastest-growing economies, were countries like South Korea, where the labor shifted from agriculture helped fuel manufacturing.

Lewis concluded that poor countries should move workers from farm to factory. This idea provided a model for many developing nations.

International Economic Advisor

Lewis put his ideas into practice as advisor to Ghana and as president of the Caribbean Development Bank. Britain's Queen Elizabeth II knighted him in 1963, and in 1979, Lewis was awarded a Nobel Prize in economics.

Because Lewis supported foreign investment in developing countries, critics once attacked his work as justifying capitalist exploitation. The collapse of socialism in most developing nations in the 1980s and early 1990s helped redeem his work.

CHECK FOR UNDERSTANDING

1. Source Reading Explain what Lewis meant when he said that economic growth in developed nations is slow because "the gains from diverting labour out of agriculture are almost all exploited."

2. Critical Thinking Why might Lewis's ideas have encouraged developing countries' governments to limit economic freedoms?

3. Learn More Research economic growth in an African or Asian nation and describe how closely it has followed Lewis's model for development.

Preview

Objectives

After studying this section you will be able to:

1. **Identify** the causes and effects of rapid population growth.
2. **Describe** the effects of the unequal distribution of the factors of production.
3. **Understand** the importance of human capital to development.
4. **Analyze** how political factors and debt are obstacles to development.

Section Focus

Less developed countries face a variety of complex issues. These include rapid population growth, a lack of natural resources, inadequate quantities of physical and human capital, political instability and government corruption, and debt.

Key Terms

population growth rate
natural rate of
   population increase
arable
malnutrition

---

population growth rate
the increase in a country's population in a given year, expressed as a percentage of the population figure at the start of the year

natural rate of population increase
the difference between the birth rate and the death rate

If you were an official in the government of a less developed country, you'd quickly discover that there are no easy solutions for ending decades of underdevelopment. The fortunate discovery of oil, diamonds, or some other valuable natural resource could certainly help. Natural resources, however, are but one factor in development.

► South Korea grew rapidly after the Korean War. Its capital, Seoul, became one of the world's largest cities. Today, South Korea is an industrialized nation with a lower rate of population growth.

Rapid Population Growth

One of the most pressing issues in development is the rapid population growth experienced by many less developed countries. Some economists point out that a population's quality of life depends on economic productivity, not on population density. Very dense populations can have rising living standards where free markets foster growth. Nevertheless, the already poor economies of many LDCs have trouble meeting the needs of rapidly growing populations.

Causes of Rapid Population Growth

The **population growth rate** is the increase in a country's population in a given year. It is expressed as a percentage of the population figure at the start of the year. The population growth rate takes into account the number of births, deaths, and the number of people migrating to or from a country.

When analyzing population growth in less developed countries, development experts often focus on the **natural rate of population increase**. This is the difference between the birth rate and the death rate.

Many LDCs are experiencing an increase in life expectancy. This is good news for individuals and families. However, while life expectancy has increased, birth rates have not decreased, at least not significantly.

What this means is that births are far outpacing deaths, leading to rapid population growth.

The age structure of LDCs also contributes to rapid population growth. In many LDCs, a high proportion of the population is of childbearing age. In developed nations, the largest segment of the population is older. Populations in developed nations therefore increase at a much slower rate. Figure 18.5 compares the age structure of low-income economies and high-income economies.

Consequences of Rapid Population Growth

The average population growth rate of the less developed countries is estimated to be around 1.7 percent. This may sound low to you, but at this rate the population of LDCs will double from their 1990 figure of 4.1 billion to over 8 billion by the year 2031. Compare this to the growth rate of developed nations, which is 0.5 percent. Their population won't double until 2129.

To stay at its current level of development, a country that doubles its population must also double employment opportunities, health facilities, teachers and schoolrooms, agricultural production, and industrial output. To increase its level of development, an economy must do even more. With all the obstacles less developed countries face, achieving this level of growth is a daunting task.

On the other hand, some economists argue that population growth creates larger markets; prompts improved transportation and communication to these markets, reducing the likelihood of famine; encourages economies of scale; stimulates diversified production; enlarges the pool of human ingenuity and creativity; and provides more workers to support retirees. Their research shows that per capita income rises about 35 years after the population expands.

Population growth is only one factor in development. There are additional factors that affect development, as described below. All these factors interact with each other, making both the causes of and solutions to underdevelopment difficult to identify.

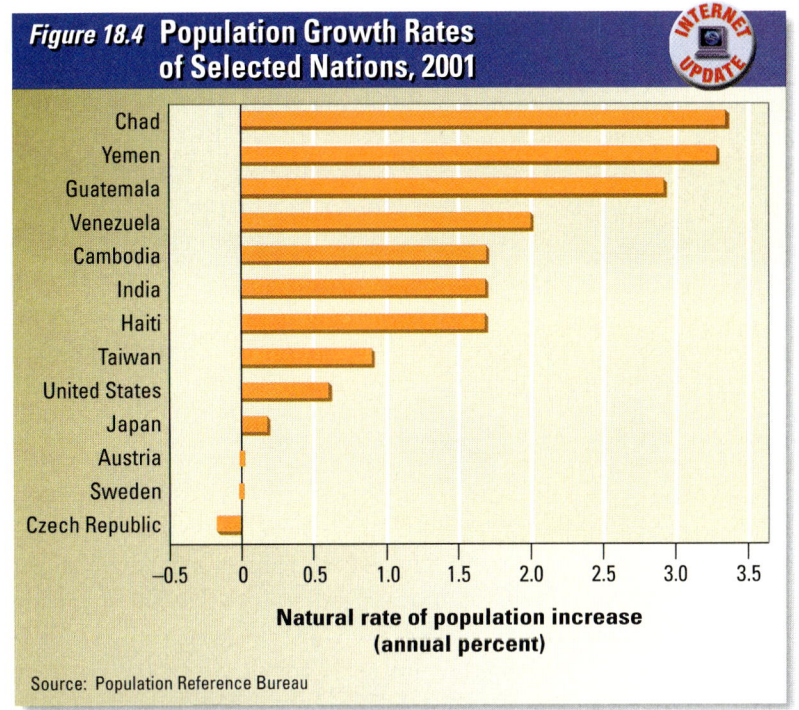

Figure 18.4 Population Growth Rates of Selected Nations, 2001

Natural rate of population increase (annual percent)

Source: Population Reference Bureau

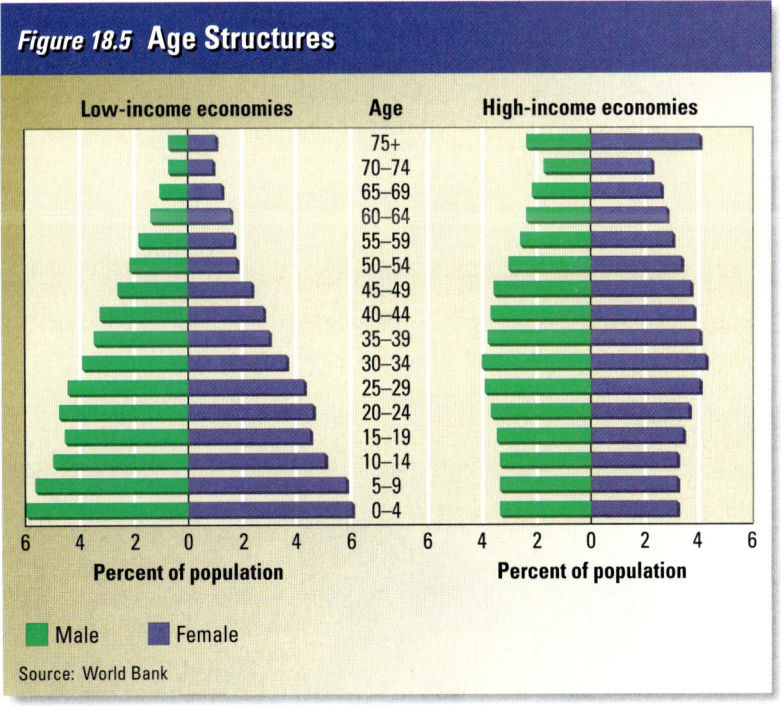

Figure 18.5 Age Structures

Low-income economies — Age — High-income economies

Percent of population

■ Male ■ Female

Source: World Bank

Rapid population growth results in a large proportion of the population being young and dependent. If the largest segment of the population is too young to work, then production does not increase along with the population.

Standard of Living What is Chad's natural rate of population increase? Describe the shapes of the age structure graphs for low-income and high-income economies. Which shape would you expect Chad's age structure to have? Why?

arable *suitable for producing crops*

Factors of Production

In parts of Africa, Asia, and Latin America, physical geography makes development more difficult. Natural resources are not spread evenly across the globe. Only about 10 percent of Earth's land is **arable**, or suitable for producing crops. Some land is more fertile than other land. Some climates are better for agriculture than others. Key mineral resources, too, are unevenly distributed across the globe. Harsh climates, uncertain rainfall, and lack of good farmland or mineral resources have contributed to the problems of some LDCs.

Sometimes the problem isn't the absence of resources. Rather, it is that the means to utilize resources are lacking in less developed countries.

Technology may help LDCs develop the resources they do have. Technology, however, is costly to develop and requires much capital. As you will read below, the formation of capital is another important issue in development.

Physical Capital

The lack of economic productivity typical of LDCs is due in part to a lack of physical capital. Physical capital, you will recall, is any human-made resource that is used to create goods and services. Without capital, industry cannot grow. Agricultural output remains low.

What's more, the resulting subsistence-level agriculture does not give individuals or households the opportunity to save. Neither does the presence of a large dependent segment of a population. A large proportion of dependents means a large number of people who don't produce and who must be supported by others. No savings means no money for purchasing capital.

Some countries turn to foreign investment to boost capital. However, as you will read below, that won't happen unless LDCs invest in human capital.

Human Capital

Human capital is the skills and knowledge gained by a worker through education and experience. Health and nutrition, as well as education and training, are important to the development of human potential. Human capital is crucial to the functioning of an economy. It is the people who develop and utilize technology, who work in agriculture, industry, and services. It is the people who manage businesses and government. When a country doesn't invest in human capital, the supply of skilled workers, industry leaders, entrepreneurs,

▼ How might increased physical and human capital help to remedy the problems shown in these photos?

Ethiopians have little more than half the per capita calorie supply of Americans.

Overgrazing has ruined this pasture land in South Africa.

government leaders, doctors, and other professionals is limited. As a result, foreign investors become discouraged because investment is profitable only if there is a skilled work force to use it.

Health and Nutrition

Proper food and nutrition are necessary not only for survival, but also for physical and mental growth and development. An individual's performance and productivity depend on the benefits of good nutrition.

Inadequate nutrition is called **malnutrition**. The populations of many less developed countries suffer chronic malnutrition. Malnourished mothers may give birth to infants with low birth weight, brain damage, and birth defects. Malnutrition in children slows or delays their physical and mental development. In adults, it can cause lethargy, heart disease, diabetes, and other health problems.

Education and Training

To be able to use technology and move beyond mere subsistence, a nation must have an educated work force. Education and training let people develop new skills and adapt to new technologies and processes. It also helps them develop new and better ways of doing things.

Many less developed countries have low literacy rates. Access to education and participation in education are limited. Adult literacy in many countries is below 40 percent. Only three out of four children in LDCs who begin primary school are still in school four years later. Throughout the world, many children are needed at home to work on the family farm, and have no time to go to school.

Improvements in literacy rates in many countries are held back by the gender gap in education. In highly developed nations, the literacy rates for men and women are nearly identical. In many LDCs, however, women's literacy lags behind that of men. The greatest difference in literacy rates between men and women exists in regions that have poor social and economic conditions for women. Some of the factors that discourage families from investing in the education of girls are the following:

- early child-bearing age
- limited job opportunities for women
- lower wages for women
- cultural factors that devalue women

malnutrition
inadequate nutrition

Medical care in LDCs often does not meet the standards of developed nations. Here in Bangladesh, there are only about 20 doctors and 5 nurses for every 100,000 people.

Figure 18.6 Education and Literacy

Country	School enrollment rate (percentage enrolled)		Literacy rate (percentage literate)	
	Female	Male	Female	Male
United States	99	91	97	97
Peru	79	81	83	94.5
Indonesia	61	68	78	89.6
Nigeria	41	49	47.3	67.3
Yemen	29	72	26	53
Chad	20	42	34.7	62.1
Niger	12	20	6.6	20.9

Sources: United Nations Development Program, *CIA World Factbook*, 2001

These Saudi Arabian women (right) are participating in a university course. Since 1960, public education has been opened to Saudi women—if they have permission from their families.
Standard of Living Examine the table. What patterns do you see in the school enrollment and literacy rates of males and females?

"Brain Drain"

Wealthy people in LDCs have the most access to education. Yet, many of the best-educated citizens leave to live and work in developed nations. The scientists, engineers, teachers, and entrepreneurs of LDCs are often attracted to the enormous opportunities developed nations can offer. This loss of educated citizens to the developed world is called "brain drain."

Political Factors

Political factors have limited and even reduced the development of many poor nations. These factors include dependence on former colonial powers, experiments with central planning, and corrupt and unstable governments.

From Colonial Dependency to Central Planning

Many LDCs are former colonies of European powers. As colonies, they had to supply their rulers with agricultural products and raw materials. In turn, they were forced to rely on their colonizers for manufactured goods. This relationship prevented the development of industry within the colonies.

After achieving independence following World War II, many of these new nations turned to central planning, rather than free enterprise, in an effort to modernize their economies quickly. They made some gains in the 1950s and 1960s. In the long run, however, central planning hindered economic growth. As you will read in Section 4, many LDCs are now making the transition to free enterprise.

Government Corruption

Corruption in the governments of many LDCs also holds back development. Leaders often make political decisions and laws to benefit themselves and their friends, not the country at large. Economic policies often benefit only the urban minority, which has greater political influence.

For example, Mobutu Sese Seko, the president of Zaire (now the Democratic Republic of Congo) from 1965 to 1997, ran a government noted for its corruption and mismanagement. Mobutu Sese Seko used his position to accumulate one of the largest personal fortunes in the world. As he plundered the nation's treasury and natural resources, Zaire's infrastructure crumbled for lack of funding. Today, the country is one of the poorest in the world, with a per capita GDP of only $98.

Political Instability

Civil wars and social unrest plague many less developed countries. El Salvador, Lebanon, Cambodia, and Rwanda, for example, suffered years of civil unrest.

In these countries, war has killed millions of people and created millions of refugees. Military leaders spend huge sums of money on weapons and warfare instead of on education, housing, health care, or other investments in development.

Debt

In the 1970s and 1980s, many less developed countries acquired loans from foreign governments and private banks to finance development. Events in the world economy, however, have hindered repayment of these loans.

In 1973, a political crisis in the Middle East prompted the oil-producing nations of the Organization of Petroleum Exporting Countries (OPEC) to reduce oil exports, and then to raise prices. The price of crude oil rose from $8 a barrel to $35 a barrel. Many LDCs, like most of the world, depend heavily on oil from OPEC. Many had to borrow yet more money to import oil. Increased debt made repayment of loans difficult, if not impossible, for many LDCs.

◄ Civil unrest in the former Yugoslavia produced scores of refugees, like these ethnic Albanians forced from Kosovo in the late 1990s. It also reduced opportunities for development in the region.

Between 1980 and 1985, the value of the U.S. dollar appreciated, or increased in value against other currencies, on the world market. Since most of their loans were based on U.S. dollars, LDCs, as a result, had further difficulty in repayment.

Between 1970 and 1984, the combined debt of LDCs increased by 1,000 percent to $700 billion. Today it exceeds $1.5 trillion. In some countries, the foreign debt is greater than the annual gross domestic product. In the next section, you will read about the ways debt repayment is being handled.

Section 2 Assessment

Key Terms and Main Ideas

1. What is **population growth rate**?
2. How does **arable** land play an important role in a nation's development?
3. How does a lack of physical capital hinder development?
4. What is the connection between human capital and foreign investment?
5. How does **malnutrition** affect human capital?
6. Why are many less developed countries carrying a large burden of debt?

Applying Economic Concepts

7. *Math Practice* The United States has a population of about 281 million and a population growth rate of about 0.97 percent. By how many people do you expect the nation's population to increase over the next year?
8. *Critical Thinking* How does the formation of physical capital relate to resource development?
9. *Decision Making* As leader of a less developed country, what measures could you undertake to limit "brain drain"?

Take It to the NET The natural environment is an important resource, both in developed nations and less developed countries. Research current environmental issues facing less developed countries and summarize your findings in one paragraph. Use the links provided in the Social Studies area at the following Web site for help in completing this activity. **www.phschool.com**

Skills for LIFE

Using the Writing Process

Good writers generally follow three steps in the writing process: prewriting, writing, and revising. During the prewriting stage, the writer decides what to write about and gathers information. In the writing stage, the writer decides the purpose of the writing, the audience, and the best form for the work. The writer then prepares a first draft. During the revising stage, the writer reviews the draft for sense, style, and errors, and shapes the work into its final form. Use the following steps to learn more about the writing process.

1. **Prewriting: Develop ideas for writing and organize your information.** Decide upon a general topic, and then brainstorm several possible areas to explore within the topic. Research these subtopics in the library or on the Internet, and list what you have found under each topic. Organize your research findings into a chart like the one below. Use the chart to answer the following questions. (**a**) What has this student chosen to research for his essay? (**b**) Why do you think he chose these three countries? (**c**) What is a likely title for his essay?

2. **Writing: Identify who will read the work and what the purpose is, and write a first draft.** (**a**) Who are the likely readers of this essay? (**b**) How should this affect the tone and style of the writing? (**c**) Would the writer be likely to use an eyewitness approach, an analytical approach, or a biographical approach? Why? (**d**) Write a topic sentence for the first draft of this essay.

3. **Revising: Review your writing to see whether it makes sense.** Ask one of your classmates to read your topic sentence and make suggestions for improving it. (**a**) What changes were suggested? (**b**) Rewrite your sentence based on any useful suggestions your classmate gave you.

Additional Practice

What problems do you foresee with using a chart to organize ideas? Can you think of an alternative way to organize your research findings?

Comparison of Three Economies		
United States' economy	**Sweden's economy**	**China's economy**
market-based economy with low level of government control	mixed economy with moderate level of government control	centrally planned economy with high level of government control
mostly white-collar work force	mostly white-collar work force	mostly blue-collar work force, strong in agriculture and manufacturing
imports much more than it exports	exports and imports balanced	exports much more than it imports
relatively low taxes	high taxes	relatively low taxes

Financing Development

Objectives

After studying this section you will be able to:

1. **Understand** the role investment plays in development.
2. **Identify** the purposes of foreign aid.
3. **Describe** the functions of various international economic institutions.

Section Focus

Less developed countries can obtain capital for economic development through investment, loans, and grants. Economic policy advice and technical help are also valuable aids to development.

Key Terms

internal financing
foreign investment
foreign direct investment (FDI)
foreign portfolio investment
World Bank
United Nations Development Program (UNDP)
International Monetary Fund (IMF)
debt rescheduling
stabilization program

Building an infrastructure, providing education and health care, and creating technology and industry all require large sums of money. Less developed countries often turn to wealthier nations for the money they need to develop their economies. Businesses, individuals, foreign governments, banks, and development organizations all contribute to the financing of international development.

Investment

As you read in Section 2, the creation of capital is crucial to development. But where does the money for purchasing capital come from? A country can use two methods to finance its economic development. It can either use internal financing or external investment. **Internal financing** is derived from the savings of the country's citizens. A developing country can also look to the developed world for investment funds. External investment originates from other countries and is called **foreign investment**.

Internal Financing

Recall from Chapter 11 the role that personal savings and investment play in capital formation. Savers deposit money in banks. Banks, in turn, lend money to firms. Firms invest in physical and human capital so they can expand. They create new products and provide new jobs. Job growth enables individuals to improve their standard of living. The economy as a whole grows.

In many less developed countries, large segments of the population do not have enough money to save. Many do not even have enough to meet their basic needs. The wealthy elite, with plenty of money to save and invest, often keep their money in foreign banks. They also often invest in foreign companies. This is because overseas savings and investments are often

internal financing
financing derived from the savings of a country's citizens

foreign investment
investment originating from other countries

▼ **In Brazil, as in most LDCs, the country's large poor population (right) has no money to save, while the tiny elite population (left) chooses to invest its money overseas.**

485

▲ LDCs often have dual economies: domestic production consisting largely of subsistence agriculture and local markets, and export production in foreign-owned multinational corporations, such as the garment factory show here. Do you think MNCs help or hurt less developed countries? Explain your reasoning.

more secure. As a result, there is often little internal financing. Most LDCs must, therefore, turn to foreign investment to finance development.

Foreign Direct Investment

There are two types of foreign investment: foreign direct investment and foreign portfolio investment. **Foreign direct investment (FDI)** is the establishment of an enterprise by a foreigner. For example, a foreign company can build a factory in an LDC, merge with an existing firm in an LDC, take over a firm in an LDC, or enter into a partnership with a firm in an LDC. Foreign direct investment often takes the form of a multinational corporation (MNC) establishing production facilities in an LDC. As you recall from previous chapters, a multinational corporation is a large corporation that produces and sells goods and services throughout the world.

MNCs are often attracted to less developed countries in their search for profit. An MNC might locate in a less developed country to take advantage of the natural resources available and the large and cheap labor force. It may also wish to introduce its products to the country.

Some economists feel that MNCs have a positive effect on LDCs. The presence of an

MNC can introduce technology, provide jobs, train the labor force, and provide the opportunity for related services and industries to develop.

Other economists argue that MNCs do little to aid less developed countries. These economists argue that most of the money earned by MNCs is not reinvested in the LDC. It goes to the foreign owners of the corporation. On the other hand, if the money were reinvested in the host LDC, critics of MNCs argue, foreign control of the economy would increase.

Supporters of MNCs point to the job opportunities these large corporations provide. But, others argue, most of the industries introduced by MNCs are capital-intensive. That is, they are highly mechanized, providing few jobs relative to the massive size of the labor pool in less developed countries.

Finally, many are concerned about the potential for unethical behavior on the part of MNCs. MNCs are attracted to the labor force of LDCs because wages in LDCs are very low compared to wages in industrialized nations. It can be argued that the cost of living in LDCs is also relatively quite low, justifying the low wages. However, critics charge MNCs with underpaying workers and using the justification that a poorly paying job is better than no job at all. In addition, in many countries, companies do not have to provide the same high standard of working conditions or environmental protection required in industrialized nations.

Foreign Portfolio Investment

Foreign portfolio investment is the entry of funds into a country when foreigners make purchases in the country's stock and bond markets. For example, an investor in the United States buys shares in a mutual fund. The mutual fund buys shares in a foreign company. That company then takes the money gained by the sale and uses it to build another plant or to pay for research and development. In other words, the funds lead indirectly to increases in production.

foreign direct investment (FDI) *the establishment of an enterprise by a foreigner*

foreign portfolio investment *the entry of funds into a country when foreigners make purchases in the country's stock and bond markets*

Foreign Aid

In Section 2, you read about development loans given to LDCs by foreign governments. Sometimes, foreign governments give, rather than loan, money and other forms of aid for development. Many developed nations provide aid to less developed countries for building schools, sanitation systems, roads, and other infrastructure. Such assistance can be motivated by humanitarian concern for the welfare of fellow human beings.

However, there are also military, political, economic, and cultural reasons for one country to extend aid to another. For example, in the early 1940s, the United States gave nearly $50 billion in food, weapons, ammunition, and other supplies to its allies in World War II. Government officials believed that this aid would help win the war. More recently, the United States has supplied large amounts of military aid to nations such as Israel, Egypt, and Taiwan.

In the years following World War II, political and economic concerns motivated American foreign aid policies. American officials noted that the Soviet Union had extended its power by establishing more Communist governments with centrally planned economies around the world. Such actions threatened both democracy and free market economic systems. Containment, or prevention of such expansion, became the cornerstone of American foreign policy.

In 1947, Secretary of State George C. Marshall unveiled a plan to help restore the war-torn countries of Europe so that they might create stable democracies and achieve economic recovery. Congress approved the plan in 1948. Over the next four years, the United States sent $13 billion in grants and loans to Western Europe. The region's economies soon recovered, and the United States gained new markets for American goods.

During the 1990s, the same logic that motivated foreign aid under the Marshall Plan prompted many countries to work together to fund the redevelopment of the war-torn Balkan nations. Figure 18.7 shows the top five recipients of aid from the United States.

International Economic Institutions

Several international institutions promote development. Among the most prominent are the World Bank, the United Nations Development Program, and the International Monetary Fund.

World Bank

The largest provider of development assistance is the **World Bank,** founded in 1940. The World Bank raises money on the financial markets and accepts contributions from the wealthier member nations.

The World Bank offers loans, advice, and other resources to more than 100 LDCs. The World Bank also coordinates with other organizations to promote development throughout the world.

United Nations Development Program

The **United Nations Development Program (UNDP)** is dedicated to the elimination of poverty through development. The UNDP

World Bank *the largest provider of development assistance*

United Nations Development Program (UNDP) *United Nations program dedicated to elimination of poverty through development*

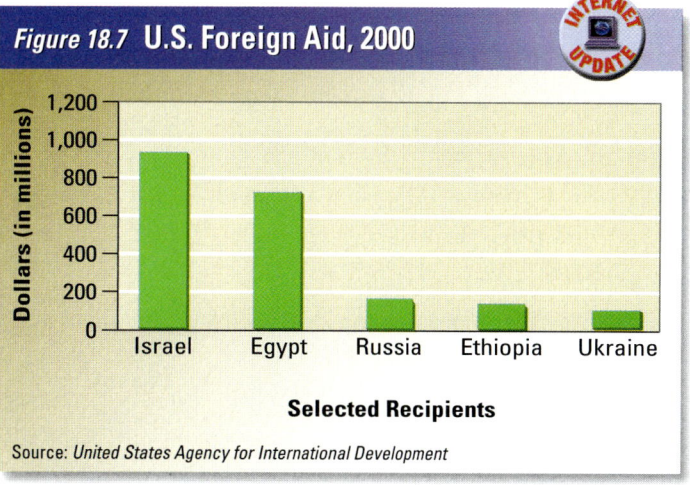

Figure 18.7 U.S. Foreign Aid, 2000

Dollars (in millions)

Selected Recipients

Source: *United States Agency for International Development*

Military, political, and humanitarian concerns motivate the United States to extend aid to certain nations.
Government **Why might it be in the interest of the United States to provide aid to Russia?**

▲ Some international institutions, like the Red Cross and the World Food Program, support development by providing disaster relief. Here, workers delivered food aid to victims of Rwanda's ethnic turmoil in the mid-1990s.

International Monetary Fund (IMF) *organization formed to stabilize international exchange rates and facilitate development*

debt rescheduling *lengthening the time of debt repayment and forgiving, or dismissing, part of the loan*

stabilization program *an agreement between a debtor nation and the IMF in which the nation agrees to revise its economic policy*

is one of the world's largest sources of grant funding for economic and social development. It devotes 90 percent of its resources to 66 low-income nations, where 90 percent of the world's poorest people live. The UNDP is funded by the voluntary contributions of United Nations member states and agencies.

International Monetary Fund

The **International Monetary Fund (IMF)** was originally developed to stabilize international exchange rates. Since its establishment in 1946, the IMF has expanded its role to facilitate development. The IMF primarily offers policy advice and technical assistance to LDCs. It also intervenes when LDCs need help in financing their international transactions.

The International Monetary Fund is often viewed as a last resort for struggling LDCs. If a less developed country has trouble repaying a debt, it may ask its lenders to reschedule the debt. **Debt rescheduling** involves lengthening the time of debt repayment and forgiving, or dismissing, part of the loan. In return, the debtor nation is expected to accept a stabilization program from the International Monetary Fund.

A **stabilization program** is an agreement between a debtor nation and the IMF. In the agreement, the nation agrees to change its economic policies to provide incentives for higher export earnings and to lower imports. By increasing exports, an LDC can earn more foreign money that can be used to pay off its debt.

Stabilization programs are sometimes controversial because they can have a negative impact on the poor in the short term. They often require the lifting of wage and price controls, causing wages to go down while prices go up. They may also include cuts in government spending on health and education services. Stabilization programs may also decrease domestic consumption of goods in order to increase exports.

Section 3 Assessment

Key Terms and Main Ideas

1. How do **internal financing** and **foreign investment** differ?
2. What is **foreign direct investment**?
3. What is **foreign portfolio investment**?
4. What are some of the ways international economic institutions help less developed countries?
5. What roles do **stabilization programs** play in **debt rescheduling**?

Applying Economic Concepts

6. *Decision Making* Your corporation is thinking about opening a factory in a less developed country. What economic factors will you consider? What ethical factors will you consider? What political factors might be important to consider?

7. *Try This* Suppose that you are the president of a less developed country. Write a speech to persuade the wealthy elite of your country to invest at home.

Take It to the NET Volunteerism and philanthropy also play a role in aiding less developed countries. Outline one potential activity that you or your class could participate in to aid development. Use the links provided in the Social Studies area at the following Web site for help in completing this activity. **www.phschool.com**

Transitions to Free Enterprise

Objectives

After studying this section you will be able to:

1. **Identify** some important steps in moving from a centrally planned economy toward a free market economy.

2. **Describe** the political and economic changes that have taken place in Russia in recent decades.

3. **Describe** the actions that China's communist government has taken to introduce free market reforms into China.

Section Focus

Making the transition from a command economy to a market economy is a difficult process. The shift requires tremendous changes on the part of the government and workers.

Key Terms

privatization
work ethic
glasnost
perestroika
light industry
special economic zones

As you read in Section 2, many less developed countries have discovered that a centrally planned economy limits development. For this reason, many communist nations are reshaping their economies. Some, like the former Soviet Union, are dismantling their centrally planned economic systems entirely and replacing them with market-based systems. Others, like China, are modifying their centrally planned economies to incorporate some free market practices.

The transition to free markets and capitalism is a huge adjustment for an economy and a nation. As you will read below, Russia has had to adjust to rapid changes in the economy and political system. China, on the other hand, is slowly introducing market reforms within its existing communist system.

Moving Toward a Market Economy

One of the key elements of a centrally planned economy is that the government, not individuals, owns and controls the factors of production. The government answers the three key economic questions of what to produce, how to produce it, and how to distribute goods and services. In contrast, in a market-based economy, the factors of production are owned by individuals. Individual buyers and sellers answer the three economic questions. One of the first steps, then, in moving from a centrally planned economy to a market economy is privatization.

Privatization

Privatization is the sale or transfer of government-owned businesses to individuals. Private ownership gives individuals, rather than the government, the right to

privatization *the sale or transfer of state-owned businesses to individuals*

▼ Hungary slowly began privatizing its economy in the 1960s. Instead of raising his flock on a collective, today this goose farmer raises geese at his own expense. He then sells the meat and feathers to a cooperative, keeping all the profits.

make decisions about what to produce and how much to produce.

There are several ways in which a government can privatize a state-owned business. First, it can simply sell the business to one owner. Another option is to sell shares in the business to interested individuals. A third method is to give every citizen a voucher or certificate that can be used to purchase shares in the businesses when they are privatized.

Simple as this may sound, privatization is a complicated process. One difficulty in privatizing is that only the profitable production facilities will continue to operate. No one will want to buy unprofitable facilities, so many people will lose their jobs. Other job opportunities will eventually appear as successful operations are expanded. However, there may be a period when total employment drops. Some people oppose privatization because it means the end of secure, lifelong government jobs with little or no competition. In a free market, jobs are not guaranteed.

Another difficulty is that there may be only one or two firms in a certain market. Even after firms are privatized, there will be little competition with so few privatized firms.

Protecting Property Rights

Even when it gives up its role as the owner and decision maker, the government still plays a vital role in ensuring the success of a new market-based economy. Legal systems under central planning do not include laws guaranteeing private property rights. A free market cannot function without such rights. As a result, the government must create new sets of laws that ensure a person's right to own and transfer property.

If property rights are uncertain, entrepreneurs will not be willing to make large

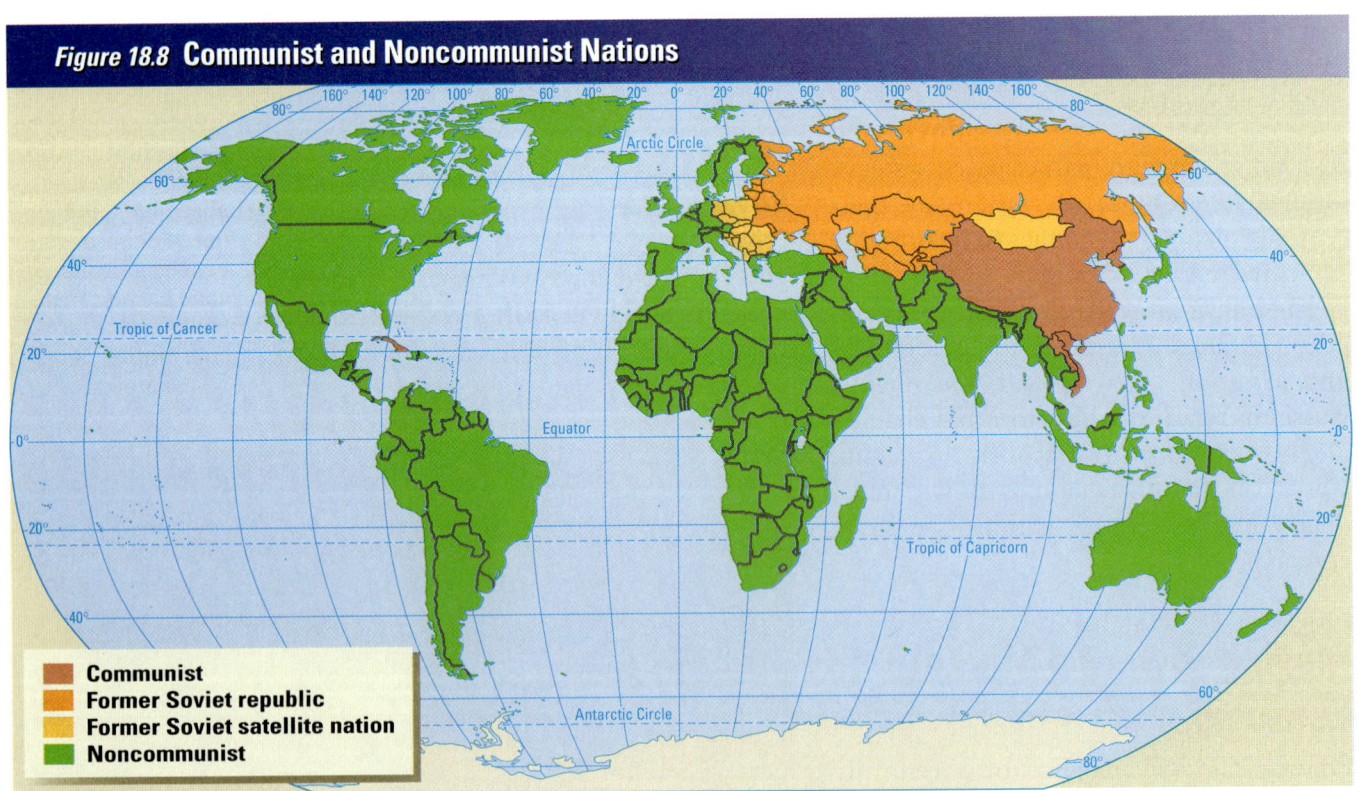

Figure 18.8 Communist and Noncommunist Nations

- Communist
- Former Soviet republic
- Former Soviet satellite nation
- Noncommunist

Beginning in the late 1980s, communism in Eastern Europe began to collapse. Countries such as East Germany, Poland, Hungary, and Czechoslovakia made profound changes in their governments and their economies.

Economic Systems *Roughly what percentage of the world remains communist?*

investments and take risks because there will be no guarantee they will benefit from successful projects. Entrepreneurs need law and order to prevent criminals from stealing the profits from legitimate enterprises. They also need a legal system that prevents the government from unduly interfering with their everyday business activities.

It will take time to develop the legal culture necessary to support a market-based economy. To have a successful market-based economy, the government must establish property rights, enforce laws, and provide a framework of regulation. Western market economies have developed the roles of government gradually over many decades. Economies making the transition to free markets need to develop these roles more rapidly.

More New Roles for Government

During privatization, government must be prepared to deal with the unrest that might develop from rising unemployment. A government could, for example, institute unemployment insurance.

The government can also play a role in helping workers make the transition from a centrally planned economy to a market economy. Workers in transition often need to learn a new **work ethic**, or system of values that gives central importance to work. In a free market, incentives, not quotas, influence people's labor.

Transition in Russia

Russia was once the dominant republic of the Soviet Union and the world's most powerful communist nation. In the latter part of the twentieth century, the lagging Soviet economy prompted economic and social reform. Change came quickly to Russia, as economic freedom led to the desire for political freedom.

Communism in Russia

As you read in Chapter 2, the Soviet Union arose out of a pair of revolutions in Russia in 1917, followed by three years of

civil war in which the Communists, led by Vladimir Lenin, won control of the government. Under the repressive control of the Communist party, central planning was introduced during the 1920s.

The Soviet government reorganized farmland into state farms and collective farms. State farm workers received wages, similar to factory workers. On the collectives, workers shared any surpluses that remained after the required quantity of products was sold and expenses were paid. Few incentives existed to encourage farmers to work hard. As a result, agricultural output remained low.

Soviet policy also emphasized the development of heavy industry. By 1940, the Soviet Union was the second-largest producer of iron and steel in Europe. The growth of heavy industry, however, came at a great opportunity cost. With so much land, labor, and capital being devoted to heavy industry, little was left over to produce consumer goods. Everyday items such as soap and shoes were in short supply.

Glasnost and Perestroika

In the late 1980s, a new leader, Mikhail Gorbachev, began a series of radical political and economic reforms. Because Gorbachev believed that economic prosperity could not happen without political freedom, he introduced *glasnost*. A policy of "openness," *glasnost* encouraged Soviet citizens to say what they wished without fear of government persecution.

▲ Entrepreneurs in the former Soviet Union had a lot to learn about free market systems.

work ethic *system of values that gives central importance to work*

glasnost *a policy of political "openness" introduced into the Soviet Union in the late 1980s*

perestroika *Soviet leader Gorbachev's plan for economic restructuring*

▼ In 1991, Communist hard-liners failed in their efforts to overthrow the democratically elected government of Boris Yeltsin. Yeltsin supporters blocked the Soviet army from the parliament building during the coup.

Gorbachev's economic reform was a plan for economic restructuring, called *perestroika*. *Perestroika* called for a gradual change from a centrally planned system to free enterprise. Gorbachev's main desire was to incorporate the use of markets and incentives into the existing structure of communism.

Under *perestroika*, the government began to allow factory managers, rather than central planners, to decide what goods to produce and how much to charge for them. It converted several factories from the production of military goods to the production of consumer goods. Many factories set goals to improve the quality of goods produced. For the first time in decades, people were allowed to start their own businesses.

Farmers were granted long-term leases on land. By making farmers their own bosses, Gorbachev hoped to increase food production.

With little experience in democracy and free enterprise, however, the transition to a market economy proved difficult. Economic reform produced some initial hardships. People lost secure government jobs, benefits, and pensions. Many people, especially the elderly, were hurt financially. Other Russians, however, quickly began to make the new system work for them, starting their own businesses. Many prospered.

Collapse of Communism

Enjoying the newfound freedoms of *glasnost* and *perestroika*, many people called for a complete end to communism and the domination of the central government. In 1991, Russians voted in their first democratic election. They chose Boris Yeltsin as president of the Russian Republic. A few months later, some officials and army officers tried unsuccessfully to restore old-style communism. The attempt backfired. One by one, the Soviet republics declared themselves independent nations. At the end of the year, Gorbachev resigned as leader, announcing the end of the Soviet Union.

Transition to the Free Market

Yeltsin came to power by promising rapid progress towards a market-based economy. Under Yeltsin's administration, there were improvements in the economy. But many hardships continued. Prices of goods in the Soviet Union were kept artificially low by the government. In 1992, Yeltsin lifted price controls. Now that prices were controlled not by the government, but by the workings of supply and demand, prices tripled.

The distribution of wealth tended to be concentrated in the urban centers such as Moscow. The uneven distribution of income led many to call for additional change. It also led to extensive corruption within the economy, including widespread organized crime.

Billions of dollars in financial aid flooded into the country from the World Bank, the International Monetary Fund, and through independent donations. However, due to mismanagement and corruption, the funds were not used efficiently.

Russia and the former Soviet republics have great potential, however. Together they comprise a market about the size of the United States, Mexico, and Canada combined, and three quarters the size of the European Union.

Transition in China

In the first half of the twentieth century, China struggled with civil war. In 1949, the supporters of communism, led by Mao Zedong, defeated the anticommunist nationalists. The Nationalist party retreated to what is now Taiwan. The communists took power in China's capital city, Beijing. Since then, China developed its own version of communism.

The Great Leap Forward

In 1958, Mao introduced an ambitious development plan called the Great Leap Forward. The Great Leap Forward was intended to turn China into a world economic power in the shortest time possible. All of the country's land was taken over by the central government. The people were organized into self-sufficient settlements called People's Communes.

These communes, sometimes with as many as 25,000 people, contained both farms and industries. Life in a People's Commune resembled life in the military. Communist party officials made all the decisions about what goods were made and who received them. The people's task was simply to work in the fields or factories. They received the same rewards no matter how much or how little they produced.

The Great Leap Forward was a huge disaster. Without incentives for workers, production fell. In the ensuing famine, about 20 million people starved to death under this development plan.

The Cultural Revolution

In the 1960s, Mao instituted a Cultural Revolution. His intention was for China to further embrace communism by destroying all traces of the past. Mao organized an army of radical young men and women, called the Red Guards, to carry out his policy. The Red Guards persecuted people in their attempt to eradicate what Mao called "the Four Olds": old ideology, old thought, old habits, and old customs. Mao succeeded only in further damaging the Chinese economy.

▲ During China's Cultural Revolution, Mao's sayings were collected and distributed in what became known as Mao's "little red book."

Transition to the Free Market

Mao died in 1976. He was succeeded by Deng Xiaoping. Deng introduced a new approach that not only shifted more power to local government, but also used the tools of the free market to improve productivity.

Deng began a program of economic reform called the Four Modernizations. The goals of the program were to improve agriculture, industry, science and technology, and defense as quickly as possible. Deng was not afraid to use free enterprise as a means of accomplishing these goals.

Deng replaced the People's Communes with the contract responsibility system. Under this arrangement, the government rented land to individual farm families. Each family then decided for themselves what to produce. The families contracted with the government to provide a certain amount of crops at a set price. Once the contract was fulfilled, they were free to sell any extra crops at markets for whatever prices they could get.

Under this system, farmers had the incentive to grow more crops. Farmers increased their production by about 8 percent. In the first eight years of the program, their incomes tripled.

Industry

As in the Soviet Union, when the communists came to power in China they had used most of the nation's resources to increase

light industry *the production of small consumer goods*

special economic zones *designated regions in China where foreign investment is encouraged, businesses can make most of their own investment and production decisions, and foreign companies are allowed to operate*

heavy industry. By the time Deng came to power, however, Chinese technology was outdated.

Deng had two goals for industry. First, he wanted people to spend more money on consumer goods. Therefore he changed the focus on production to **light industry,** or the production of small consumer goods such as clothing, appliances, and bicycles. He also wanted factories to increase production. To accomplish this, Deng gave more decision-making power to factory managers. He started a system of rewards for managers and workers who found ways to make factories more productive.

Economic Zones

In addition, Deng set up four **special economic zones** along China's east coast. In these zones, local governments are allowed to offer tax incentives to foreign investors. Businesses are allowed to make most of their own investment and production decisions. Foreign companies are allowed to operate in these zones. Deng located these first four zones near Hong Kong and Taiwan. He hoped to attract foreign investment, companies, and technology from these economic giants. The zones have proved so successful that China now has hundreds of these special economic zones.

Most of China's rapid economic growth has taken place in the special economic zones of the coastal cities. The interior regions lag far behind. The population has also shifted dramatically. About 120 million people have left the interior villages to seek their fortunes in the booming cities. Rapid urban growth has resulted in an increase in crime that the weak and sometimes corrupt police force has trouble handling.

Despite these negative effects, the economy has benefited. Since the start of Deng's reforms, China's economy has quadrupled in size. The question now at hand is whether or not China's political leaders will be able to maintain their Communist regime in the face of pressures for cultural freedom brought about by economic freedom. China's leadership continues to come under criticism for its violations of human rights and political repression.

Section 4 Assessment

Key Terms and Main Ideas

1. Identify three factors necessary for the transition to free enterprise.
2. Why is **privatization** necessary to create a free market economy?
3. What is *glasnost*?
4. What is *perestroika*?
5. Why was the Great Leap Forward such a disaster for China?
6. How does **light industry** differ from heavy industry?
7. What role do **special economic zones** play in China's transition to free enterprise?

Applying Economic Concepts

8. *Critical Thinking* What is the main difference between transition in Russia and transition in China?
9. *Problem Solving* How could China expand its economic success to the interior?

Take It to the NET

Photocopy a map of China that includes cities, provinces, and major waterways. On your map, use stars to indicate special economic zones. Why do you think these particular locations were chosen? Write a brief caption describing the location of these zones. Use the links provided in the Social Studies area at the following Web site for help in completing this activity. **www.phschool.com**

The World Bank and Economic Assistance

As World War II drew to a close, much of Europe lay in ruins, and the World Bank was created to help finance the reconstruction. Within a few years, the World Bank changed its mission from helping rebuild war-torn areas to helping developing nations achieve stable economic growth.

Function The primary function of the World Bank is to make loans to countries unable to borrow from other sources. Its loans are used for many purposes: to improve health care, to build transportation networks, and to promote economic reforms. The Bank makes about $20 billion in new loans each year.

The World Bank raises most of its money in financial markets by issuing bonds. In addition, it receives contributions from its member nations, including industrialized nations such as the United States and Japan. Even some developing nations, once borrowers from the World Bank themselves, make contributions.

▲ The World Bank helps finance highway construction in developing nations such as Colombia.

Controversy Despite its worthwhile goals, the World Bank has sometimes been a source of controversy. Some critics have argued that the United States would be better off using its money to help less fortunate American citizens. Others have criticized the Bank for not holding developing nations fully accountable for effectively carrying out projects it has funded.

Accomplishments Still, the World Bank can boast of many significant accomplishments. It has helped many developing countries improve roads, hospitals, schools, and water supplies. In addition, by strengthening the economies of less developed countries, the World Bank has helped build new markets for American goods, which in turn benefits the economy of the United States.

Applying Economic Ideas

1. How does the World Bank work to improve conditions in developing nations?

2. The table shows how the World Bank classifies selected countries according to per capita Gross Domestic Product. What factors might have led to some countries being poor for so long?

Per Capita Earnings in Selected Countries

GDP per Capita Earnings	Countries	
High income (more than $10,000)	Australia Great Britain	Japan United States
Moderate income ($5,000–10,000)	Israel New Zealand	Singapore Spain
Low income ($1,500–5,000)	Algeria Greece	Malaysia Russia
Poor income ($500–1,500)	Colombia Honduras	Nigeria Philippines
Extremely poor income (less than $500)	China Haiti	India Pakistan

Source: The World Bank

Chapter Summary

A summary of major ideas in Chapter 18 appears below. See also the **Guide to the Essentials of Economics**, which provides additional review and test practice of key concepts in Chapter 18.

Section 1 *Levels of Development* (pp. 471–476)

Nations throughout the world exhibit varying levels of economic success. The most prosperous are called **developed nations.** Nations with relatively low standards of living are called **less developed countries. Per capita gross domestic product** is the primary measure of development.

Section 2 *Issues in Development* (pp. 478–483)

Less developed countries face a wide range of issues. A high **population growth rate,** lack of natural resources, inadequate human and physical capital, political instability and corruption, and foreign debt often inhibit development.

Section 3 *Financing Development* (pp. 485–488)

Less developed countries turn to many sources to finance their development, including **internal financing, foreign investment,** and foreign aid and loans. Help also comes in the form of policy advice and technical assistance.

Section 4 *Transitions to Free Enterprise* (pp. 489–494)

Some communist and former communist nations, such as China and Russia, are making transitions to free enterprise in order to boost their lagging economies. The move to free enterprise requires **privatization** of industry and changes in the legal system.

Key Terms

Complete each sentence by choosing the correct answer from the list of terms below. You will not use all of the terms.

malnutrition	light industry
infrastructure	work ethic
industrialization	foreign direct
literacy rate	investment
internal financing	life expectancy
debt rescheduling	

1. Measuring a nation's _____ provides data on how many people in that country can read or write.
2. _____ may cause disease in adults, and may cause infants to be born with brain damage or birth defects.
3. The production of small consumer goods is referred to as _____.
4. _____ is the establishment of an enterprise in a country by a foreigner.
5. The services and facilities necessary for an economy to function are called _____.
6. A country undergoing _____ is allowed more time to pay off its loans and have a portion of its loans forgiven.
7. _____ is the extensive organization of an economy for the purpose of manufacture.
8. Economists use the term _____ to describe investment derived from the savings of a country's citizens.

Using Graphic Organizers

9. On a separate sheet of paper, copy the tree map below. Chart financing options for less developed countries by filling in each box with an example and description of a financing option.

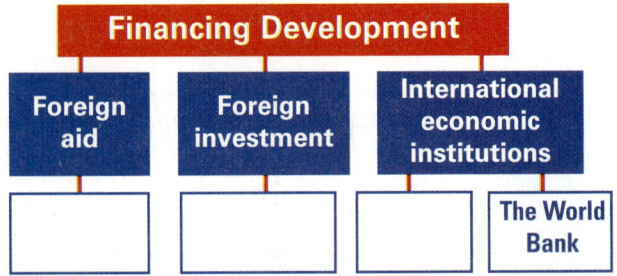

Financing Development

Foreign aid | Foreign investment | International economic institutions → The World Bank

Reviewing Main Ideas

10. List and describe three characteristics of less developed countries.

11. Which development status (developed, less developed, or newly industrialized) does each of the following characteristics describe? **(a)** low per capita GDP **(b)** many consumer goods available **(c)** shows significant improvement in the measures of economic performance **(d)** high infant mortality rate **(e)** high life expectancy

12. What issues arise when less developed countries adopt a stabilization program?

13. How did *glasnost* and *perestroika* factor in Russia's transition to a free market economy?

14. What role do special economic zones play in China's transition to a free market economy?

Critical Thinking

15. **Drawing Conclusions** In measuring development, what relationship exists between the activities of the labor force and energy consumption?

16. **Making Comparisons** Which do you believe is more important for a nation's development—physical capital or human capital? Why?

17. **Recognizing Cause and Effect** Describe four consequences faced by nations experiencing rapid population growth.

Problem-Solving Activity

18. Compare and contrast the transitions to free market economies in China and Russia. Describe three unique aspects of each country's transition. Which country do you believe will be most successful in the long run?

Economics Journal

Essay Writing Review your comments on the chapter opener photo. What comments can you add, based on your reading of the chapter? Write a brief essay to accompany the photo. Then, check an encyclopedia or other resource for information on Ghana, the country shown. Revise your essay as needed.

Skills for Life

Utilizing the Writing Process Review the steps shown on page 484; then complete the following activity based on the information below.

19. Study the chart below. **(a)** Who is involved in each of these organizations? **(b)** How could these organizations be compared?

20. You have been assigned the task of writing an essay comparing these three organizations. **(a)** What is a possible title for your essay? **(b)** Compose a topic sentence for your essay.

21. Exchange your topic sentence with a classmate. Analyze each other's topic sentences; then revise your sentence based on your classmate's input.

22. Use the information in the chart below to write a rough draft of an essay. Ask your classmate to read your draft and comment on it.

Global Economic Organizations

	World Trade Organization	G-8 Countries	International Monetary Fund
Membership characteristics	Entrance granted by vote of existing member countries	Top eight industrialized nations	Finances supported by members
Function	Establishes agreements on lowering or abolishing tariffs on a global level	Summit meetings allow members to discuss international issues	Provides monetary services and loans in attempts to stabilize global trade
Countries involved	141 as of 2001	United States, Japan, France, Germany, Italy, Great Britain, Russia, Canada	183 as of 2001

Take It to the NET

Chapter 18 Self-Test As a final review activity, take the Chapter 18 Self-Test in the Social Studies area at the Web site listed below, and receive immediate feedback on your answers. The test consists of 20 multiple-choice questions designed to test your understanding of the chapter content.
www.phschool.com

THE WALL STREET JOURNAL.

CLASSROOM EDITION

DEBATING CURRENT ISSUES: *A Strong Dollar*

In the mid-1990s, the U.S. government encouraged the dollar's rise in value compared with the Japanese yen and German mark while trying to keep inflation low and interest rates steady. The goal was to encourage stable economic growth for the United States.

In supporting this policy, Treasury Secretary Robert Rubin and Federal Reserve Chairman Alan Greenspan also in some ways were selecting winners and losers in the U.S. economy. That is the conclusion of the following excerpts from *The Wall Street Journal Classroom Edition* article "Winners and Losers" by Michael M. Phillips, Staff Reporter of *The Wall Street Journal*.

YES *Should the U.S. Government Support a Strong Dollar?*

IN MINNETONKA, MINNESOTA, executives at Insignia Systems Inc. cheered every time the dollar gained further against the yen in 1997. The company expected to turn its first profit in several years, mainly because the rising greenback had cut the cost of Japanese-made sign-printing machines that Insignia imports and resells to U.S. retailers. Insignia Systems estimated that the dollar's earlier tumble, which bottomed out at 80.63 yen in April 1995, cost the company $2 million a year.

Some companies that use imported products also benefited from the currency realignment in 1997. Rohr Inc., a San Diego aircraft-component manufacturer, realized some savings on the MD-11 engine pylons it buys in Japan. And since Boeing Co. reported that the rising dollar hadn't hurt jet sales, Rohr was shielded from the dollar's downside as well. "There's tremendous demand out there for new aircraft," said Laurence Chapman, Rohr's chief financial officer.

Some companies benefited on the interest-rate side of the economic equation, since economists believe that a stronger dollar can help check both inflation and the Fed's urge to raise interest rates.

U.S. consumers also could find lower prices for imported Japanese and European goods, although there is typically some delay before discounts appear on the shelves.

A strong dollar encourages many Americans, such as these tourists in Japan, to visit other nations where their vacation budgets will stretch further.

NO | Should the U.S. Government Support a Strong Dollar?

THE PAINS AND PROFITS of the strong dollar policy aren't evenly distributed. The negative impact goes beyond the usual complainers—U.S. auto makers have been most vocal about the rising dollar. On the pain side, there also are small commodities exporters, huge manufacturers, even service providers whose clients or competition are overseas. As the dollar climbs, these companies face the choice of cutting export prices and accepting lower profits, or passing along the price increase and losing customers.

AlliedSignal Inc., a Morristown, N.J., multinational company, ended up losing a customer in 1997, in this case a $13 million contract to supply air-bag modules to Japan's Suzuki Motor Corp. "We had a huge cost disadvantage because of the strong dollar against the yen," said Mark Greenberg, vice president for external communications.

Economists say the impact of the surge in the dollar isn't always clear right away. The industries that feel it most quickly are often those competing head-to-head with Europeans or Japanese to sell goods that are roughly indistinguishable. In 1997, Feedcom Enterprises Inc. of Seattle earned 90 percent of its revenue exporting livestock-feed hay to Japan. Weakness in the yen, however, gave North Korean and Australian hay a price edge, and during one period, Freedom's sales were down 15 percent. "It's a very price-sensitive commodity," said Ed Bitanga, Feedcom's head of international sales.

Another exchange-rate-sensitive industry is tourism, since one palm-edged beach can quickly substitute for another if prices change. In the spring of 1997, the Hawaii Visitors and Convention Bureau revised downward by 120,000 its estimate of how many Japanese would visit that year. The reason? The slow economy and the falling yen made it too expensive for many Japanese to travel to the United States.

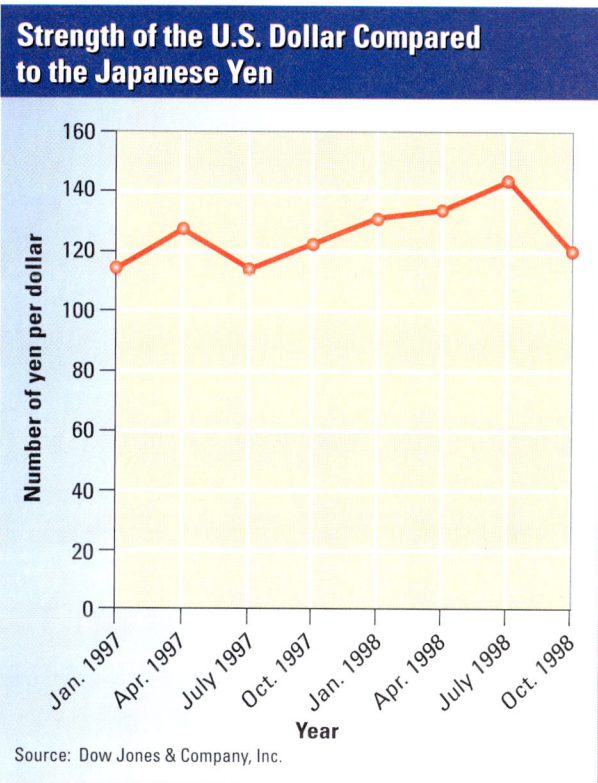

Strength of the U.S. Dollar Compared to the Japanese Yen

Source: Dow Jones & Company, Inc.

This chart shows the monthly average number of yen to one U.S. dollar. The more yen to the dollar, the weaker the yen and the stronger the dollar.

DEBATING THE ISSUE

1. What impact does the rising value of the dollar have on the cost of Japanese equipment that Insignia Systems imports and sells in the United States?

2. How did the strong dollar cause AlliedSignal to lose a contract?

3. **Critical Thinking** How can a stronger dollar help keep inflation in check?

4. **Reading Graphs** Did the dollar get weaker or stronger between April 1997 and July 1997? Did it get weaker or stronger between October 1997 and July 1998?

 Take It to the Net Visit **www.phschool.com** for additional resources relating to this debate.

Reference Section

Take It to the NET

*For **daily** updates on economic issues and personal finance matters, please visit the *Economics: Principles in Action* site in the Social Studies area at **www.phschool.com**

Keep It Current

Items marked with this logo are periodically updated on the Internet. Keep up-to-date with what's in the news. For periodic updates of the data included in the Databank, go to **www.phschool.com**

PERSONAL FINANCE HANDBOOK

GLOSSARY

SPANISH GLOSSARY

ECONOMIC ATLAS and DATABANK

INDEX

ACKNOWLEDGMENTS

Creating a Budget

A tiny drip from your bathtub faucet can send thousands of gallons of water down the drain each year. Your money can dribble away, too.

An $8 pizza, a $12 pair of sunglasses, $20 at the movies—they don't seem like much at the time. But a lifetime pattern of careless spending can be painful, even ruinous. Money problems can cause stress, wreck personal relationships, and trap people in jobs they don't like just so they can pay their bills. What a way to live your life!

Start a better way. Budget your money.

Calculate Income Versus Spending

Budgeting begins simply with writing how much money you receive and how much you spend. Try these steps:

Four Steps to Successful Budgeting

1. Make a list of your earnings like the one below right. Then calculate your total monthly income.

2. For one month, keep a record of everything you spend money on, from car payments to candy bars. You can jot down each purchase on a scrap of paper, and toss all the scraps in a shoebox. Or carry a small notebook to list items and amounts.

3. At the end of the month, organize the records of your purchases into categories such as food, clothing, entertainment, car payments, and so on. Find the total for each category.

4. On a sheet of paper or on a computer spreadsheet, make a list similar to the one on the next page. Fill in the expenditures and the amounts. Then calculate your total monthly spending.

This record of your income and spending can be very revealing. Do you have a little money left over at the end of the month? Or do you spend more than you earn? Experts recommend that you put about 10 percent of your income into savings. If you have very little left over—or worse, if you spend more than you earn—it's time to create a budget.

Living Within Your Budget

Look at your expenditures and find areas in which you can cut spending. For instance, buy a frozen pizza from the grocery store instead of ordering take-out. Get together at friends' houses instead of at the mall. Shop end-of-season clothing sales. And be careful with automatic teller machines! ATMs make it too easy to drain your bank account.

Fill in the first two columns of a chart like the one on the next page. Then in the third column, enter the reduced amounts you think you can spend. Keep cutting until you can reserve 10 percent of your earnings as savings. This is your new **budget,** a plan for saving and spending.

If you have a difficult time staying within your budget, enlist a friend or family member to review your expenditures each week to help keep you on track. Distinguish between "needs" and "wants." Try not to rationalize impulse buying. After all, you'll only be kidding yourself.

My Earnings

SOURCE	MONTHLY INCOME
Restaurant job	$392
Computer tutoring	$68
Baby-sitting	$20
TOTAL	**$480**

My Spending and Saving Plan

MONTHLY EXPENDITURE	CURRENT EXPENSES	BUDGET
Car		
Payment	$120	$120
Insurance	$42	$42
Gasoline	$27	$14
Maintenance (estimated)	$30	$30
Food		
Lunches at school	$58	$35
Snacks	$34	$20
Movies		
Theater	$28	$7
Rentals	$4	$8
Clothes		
Shoes	$16	$7
Other clothes	$39	$25
Savings for school trip	$50	$50
Magazine subscription	$5	$0
CDs	$24	$12
Gifts	$0	$35
Savings	$0	$48
Emergencies	$0	$27
TOTALS	**$477**	**$480**

Costs such as car payments are fixed.

Bike or carpool instead of driving. Savings: one tank of gas a month.

Cut out chips at lunch. Savings: $23 a month! (It's healthier, too.) Even better: Pack a lunch.

Items such as new clothes are optional expenses. Wear last year's shirt for one more season.

Borrow magazines from friends or the library. Savings: $5 a month

By cutting expenses, you can set aside money for savings, holiday gifts, and emergency needs.

Check Your Understanding

1. **Key Terms** Why is it important to create a **budget**?
2. **Review** Reread the suggested ways for saving money, and brainstorm others to add to the list.

Opening and Managing a Checking Account

If your piggy bank is bursting, consider opening a checking account.

Before banks dotted every streetcorner in America, some people stuffed their money under the mattress for safekeeping. It wasn't very safe.

Today virtually everyone has access to a bank. It's a safe place to store your money, and it offers conveniences such as check writing, electronic banking, and interest on your money.

Choosing a Bank

The most common types of bank accounts are checking and savings. If you plan to take money out of your account frequently, you probably need a checking account. Savings accounts and other savings options are discussed on page 506.

Opening a checking account is fairly easy. First you'll need some kind of identification, such as a driver's license or a pay stub. You'll also need a Social Security number. (If you don't yet have a Social Security number, you can apply on-line at the Web site of the Social Security Administration.) Finally, you'll need at least a small sum of money to deposit when you open your account.

How to Choose a Checking Account

- ❑ Do I have to keep a **minimum balance,** or amount of money, in the account to avoid fees?
- ❑ Is there a monthly fee? How much is it?
- ❑ Will I be charged check writing fees?
- ❑ How many checks can I write per month?
- ❑ Will the bank return my canceled checks each month or keep them on file?
- ❑ Will I be charged ATM fees?
- ❑ What other fees are associated with this account?

It pays to shop around for the best checking account. Although the interest that most banks pay on checking accounts ranges from little to none, other features, such as fees, vary widely. The chart above lists some of the criteria to consider when selecting a checking account.

Keeping Records

When you open an account, you'll receive a checkbook that includes sequentially numbered checks and a **check register,** a booklet in which you'll record your account transactions. You'll make your life a lot easier if you decide from the start to be a good recordkeeper. Every time you write a check, make a deposit, or use an ATM, take a few seconds to jot it down in your check register.

You won't believe how glad you'll be that you have your own records of your financial business. For example, if you earn money, the Internal Revenue Service could ask at any time to see

Journey of a Personal Check

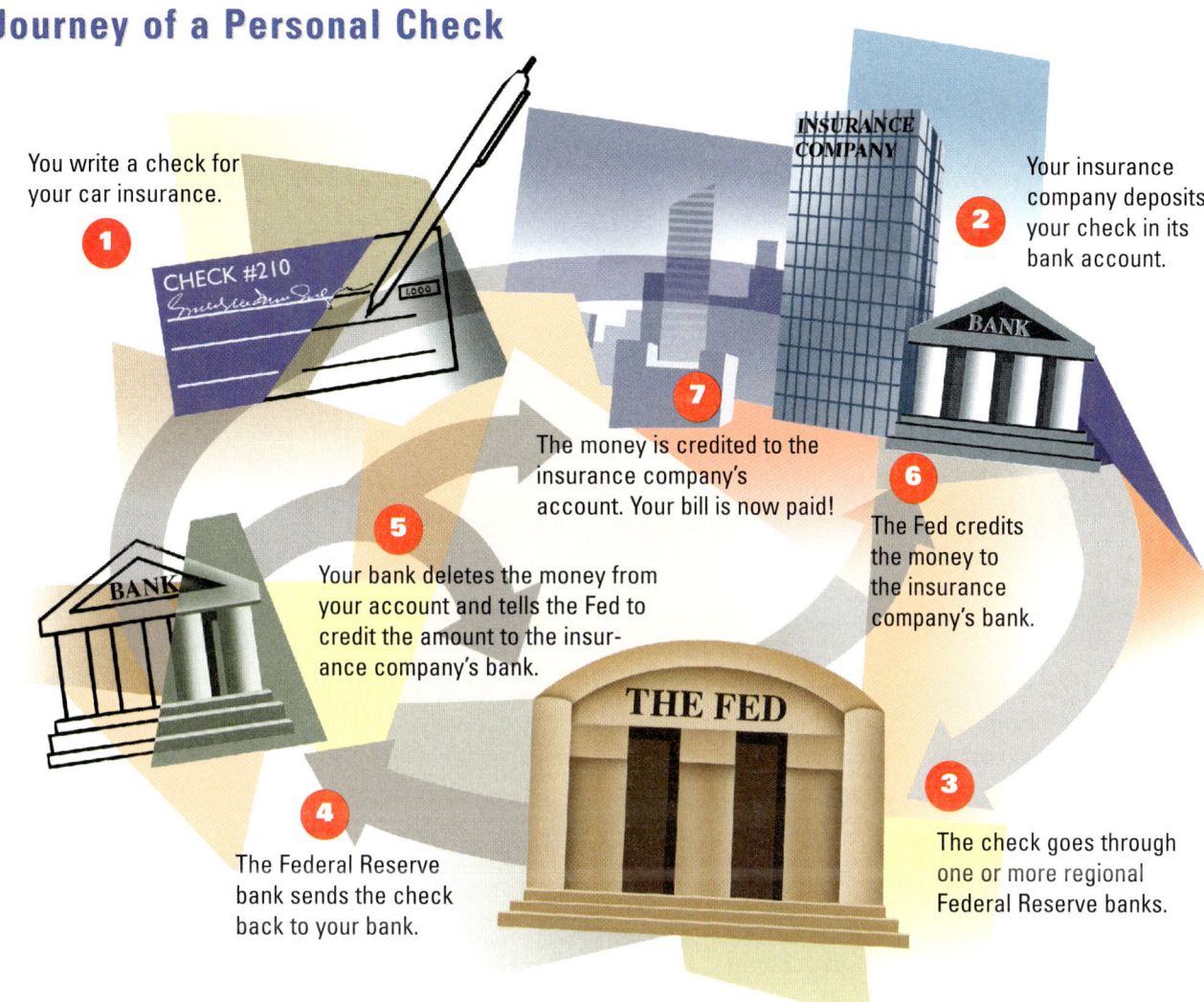

1 You write a check for your car insurance.

CHECK #210

2 Your insurance company deposits your check in its bank account.

7 The money is credited to the insurance company's account. Your bill is now paid!

6 The Fed credits the money to the insurance company's bank.

5 Your bank deletes the money from your account and tells the Fed to credit the amount to the insurance company's bank.

4 The Federal Reserve bank sends the check back to your bank.

THE FED

3 The check goes through one or more regional Federal Reserve banks.

your financial records for the past three years. Also, your bank could make a mistake. Bank records are rarely wrong, but it does happen. The ATM receipt you shoved in your wallet is your proof that you withdrew $50, not $500!

Balancing Your Checkbook

Each month you'll receive a statement, a record of your checking account activity during the last month. It lists deposits, withdrawals, ATM transactions, interest paid, and fees charged. Any checks you wrote that were cashed during the month may be returned to you in the statement, although some banks keep the originals in storage. The diagram above shows where your check goes before it is returned to you.

It's extremely important to balance your checkbook every month. That means comparing the transactions in the bank statement to your own records to make sure they agree. Most statements have a worksheet on the back to help you balance your account in a few easy steps. If you have any trouble balancing your checkbook, someone at your bank's local branch office can assist you.

Check Your Understanding

1. **Key Terms** **(a)** How is your account balance different from your **minimum balance?** **(b)** Why is it a good idea to use a **check register?**

2. **Evaluate** If you were going to open a checking account today, which criteria listed above would be most important and least important to you? Why?

Saving and Investing

It's never too early to prepare for your financial future, whether that means holiday shopping, next year's vacation, college, or retirement.

Paving the way to a sound financial future involves more than getting a job and living within a budget. Managing your money also involves saving and investing. How much you save and how much you invest depends on the lifestyle you choose for yourself in the present and the lifestyle you plan for your future.

Saving

Why do you need to save your money? While you might have enough earnings to meet your daily expenses, saving is a way to make sure you have money for special purchases and future expenses, whether planned or unplanned. The box below outlines the main types of bank or credit union accounts for saving money. The box on the next page provides questions to help you select an account.

DATE	WITHDRAWAL	DEPOSIT or INTEREST	BALANCE	
				1
				2
.12OCT94		$1.78	$1042.87	INT3
.04NOV94		$1000.00	$2042.87	CHK4
.14NOV94		$2.58	$2045.45	INT5
.12DEC94		$3.53	$2048.98	INT6
.12JAN95		$3.92	$2052.90	INT7
.14FEB95		$4.18	$2057.08	INT8
.13MAR95		$3.42	$2060.50	INT9
.12APR95		$3.81	$2064.31	INT10
.12MAY95		$3.82	$20__.13	INT11
				12
.12JUN95		$3.95	$2072.00	INT13
.12JUL95		$3.83	$20__.91	INT14
.14AUG95		$4.22	$20__.13	INT15
.12SEP95		$3.72	$2083.85	INT16
.12OCT95		$3.85	$2087.70	INT17
.13NOV95		$4.12	$2091.82	INT18
.12DEC95		$3.74	$2095.56	INT19
.12JAN96		$4.00	$2099.56	INT20
.12FEB96		$4.00	$2103.56	INT21
.12MAR96		$3.53	$2107.09	INT22
.12APR96		$3.57	$2110.66	INT23
.13MAY96		$3.58	$2114.24	INT
.12JUN96		$3.47	$2117.71	INT

Types of Accounts

Banks offer several ways for you to save your money. Each account has different features and restrictions.

Savings Accounts It's a good idea to use a **savings account** for savings that you may need to use within a short period of time. When you deposit money in a savings account, your bank or credit union will record deposits, withdrawals, fees, and any **interest** earned by your account. The interest rate is the rate of interest an account will earn on funds deposited for a full year.

Money Market Accounts A money market deposit account (MMDA) will let you save and write a limited number of checks. It usually earns higher interest than a savings account, but also usually requires a higher minimum balance and has more fees. MMDAs have a variable interest rate, which can be a benefit or a drawback depending on whether rates move up or down.

Time Deposits A **time deposit**, such as a certificate of deposit (CD), offers a guaranteed interest rate for a fixed period of time. In general, the longer the term, the higher the interest rate. Most banks will charge you a high penalty fee if you withdraw from the CD account before the term expires, or "matures." Open a CD account only if you think you won't need access to that money during the term of the CD.

How to Choose
a Savings Account

Deposits and withdrawals
- ❏ What is the minimum balance?
- ❏ When can I make my first withdrawal?
- ❏ How many deposits and withdrawals am I allowed to make each month?
- ❏ Am I limited in the dollar amount of my withdrawals?
- ❏ What are the penalties for early withdrawal?
- ❏ Can I use an automated teller machine (ATM) to make deposits and withdrawals?

Interest
- ❏ What is the interest rate?
- ❏ Is it compounded? How frequently?
- ❏ What is the minimum balance required to earn interest?
- ❏ When is the interest paid?

Fees
- ❏ What fees apply?
- ❏ What is the minimum balance needed to avoid fees?
- ❏ Do certain transactions carry penalty fees?
- ❏ What ATM fees apply?

Truth in Savings The **Truth in Savings Act** is a federal law that requires banks to provide you with certain information about the accounts they offer, including

- annual percentage yield—the amount of interest you will earn on a deposit
- interest rates
- fees and other charges that apply
- features, such as the minimum balance needed to avoid fees

Use this information to help you choose the bank and the type of account that is best for you.

Investing

Saving is a great way to plan for your future. Many experts advise saving 10 percent of your earnings annually. While keeping your money in a savings account is safe, investing your money can give your dollars the opportunity to grow. Bonds, stocks, and mutual funds are among the many investment options available to you.

Bonds A **bond** is an IOU issued by a corporation or by the government as a way for them to borrow money. When you buy a bond, you buy the right to receive a fixed amount of money at some future date as well as an annual interest payment. The face value of the bond is the fixed amount agreed upon. Corporate bonds can be risky, depending on the financial health of the firm. If the firm goes bankrupt, it won't be able to pay what it owes you. Government bonds are more secure because the government is unlikely to declare bankruptcy.

Government bonds can be purchased through your bank and are available in small denominations. Interest earned is subject to federal tax, but not state or local taxes. They are a secure investment, although the return is low compared to other types of investment.

A word about interest rates Interest rates are expressed as percentages and indicate the rate of interest an account will earn on funds deposited for a full year. Interest is compounded when it is added to your principal. In effect, compound interest is interest on interest.

Stocks A popular form of investment, **stock** represents ownership in an organization. If a firm issues and sells 10,000 shares of stock, and you purchase 1,000 of them, you own 10 percent of the firm. By purchasing a corporation's stock, you are buying the right to receive a fraction of its profit.

The two potential benefits from owning stock are dividends and capital gains. **Dividends** are portions of a corporation's profit paid to stockholders. **Capital gain** is the profit you make if you can sell your stock for more than you paid for it. Not all stocks pay dividends. Some companies reinvest their profits, rather than pay out dividends. Such "growth" stocks are attractive to investors because they expect the stock price to increase as the company grows.

Stock is available in two forms: **common stock** and **preferred stock**. Preferred stock earns dividends fixed at an annual rate, whereas any dividends earned by common stock are dependent on market fluctuations. Preferred shareholders are paid dividends before common shareholders.

Corporate stocks are bought and sold on stock markets. Most investors rely on the services of a stockbroker to purchase stock. You'll want to compare reputations, transaction fees, insurance, and services of various brokerage firms before you choose one. Many people rely on the advice of a professional financial advisor or investment advisor when choosing stock. Make sure you check an advisor's credentials.

Stocks are riskier than bonds, because stock price is based on the expectation of profit. If the firm turns out to be less profitable than expected, dividends will be smaller than expected and the market price of shares may decrease. You may find yourself selling your shares for less money than you paid for them.

Experts warn that if you get into the stock market, you should be prepared to ride the ups and downs. Sometimes you will win, and sometimes you will lose. And don't go into the stock market

On October 27, 1997, the Dow plummeted a record 554 points, leading the New York Stock Exchange to halt trading for the rest of the day.

The longest bull run—period in which stock prices rise without interruption—lasted from 1949 until 1957.

The Dow exceeded 3,000 points for the first time in 1991. By January 2000, it attained an all-time high of over 11,000 points, only to drop sharply after the September 11, 2001, terrorist attacks.

Comparing Investment Options

Type of investment	Income generated	Growth potential	Risk level
Bonds	very steady	little or none	low risk
Common stock	variable	good	high risk
Preferred stock	less variable than common stock	good	moderate risks

to make a quick profit for something crucial, like school tuition. If you do, the stock could take a tumble right at the time you need to sell it, and you could lose all of your investment.

Mutual Funds You might choose to invest your money in a **mutual fund,** which is an investment in an investment company. Investment companies sell stock in their mutual funds. Instead of producing a product or service, however, they take the money they receive for their stock and invest it in the stocks and bonds of other corporations. The mutual fund will combine the money you invest with that of other investors in order to make substantial investments in other companies.

A major benefit of investing in a mutual fund is that it provides instant diversification to your portfolio. This means that the money you invest in a mutual fund is spread out among all the different companies in which the mutual fund invests its money.

Mutual funds include stocks of varying risk levels. There are three categories of mutual funds:

- *Money market funds* are short-term, low risk investments. The money you invest will be used to make short-term loans to businesses or the government. (Do not confuse money market funds with money market deposit accounts, which are described on page 506.)
- *Bond funds* are, as the name implies, investments in bonds. They usually have higher potential yields than money market funds, but they are also riskier.
- *Stock funds,* though riskiest, offer the highest potential returns. As long-term investments, they perform better than money market funds and bond funds.

As with any investment, you must do your homework before you commit to a mutual fund. Even though a professional money manager will control your investment, mutual funds are not without risk.

Risk Versus Payout You have many options when it comes to investing your money. What you choose depends on what rate of return you'd like on your money and how much risk you are willing to accept. You also need to consider the length of your investment, the ease of making the transaction, and any tax burdens the investment may carry. In general, the safer the investment, the lower the return. High-risk investments have the potential for high returns because investors demand higher rates of return to compensate for the risk they face.

Despite stock tips, hype about hot stocks or "sure things," you should not approach investing as if you were a gambler in a casino. Informed decisions and careful planning are your best strategies for successful investment.

Check Your Understanding

1. **Key Terms (a)** What is the difference between a **bond** and a **stock**? **(b)** How does a **dividend** differ from a **capital gain**? **(c)** Explain the difference between **common stock** and **preferred stock**. **(d)** What makes a **mutual fund** an attractive investing option?

2. **Identifying Alternatives** Think about your future financial needs. Are you planning to buy a car? Do you need money for an apartment deposit or college tuition? Use the information on these pages to design a savings and investment plan that will help you reach your goals.

Financial Institutions and Services

If you have money, you're going to need the services of a bank or credit union—to save money, to manage it, and transfer it to others. If you need more money, a bank can lend it to you.

The city or town you live in probably has many banks, both large and small. Behind all that brick and chrome and glass, what are their differences? How do you choose? Begin by familiarizing yourself with the different types of banks and the various services they offer, then determine which one best suits your needs.

Types of Financial Institutions

A bank is an institution for receiving, keeping, and lending money. There are four basic types of banks:
- *commercial banks*
- *savings and loan associations*
- *savings banks*
- *credit unions*

Each offers a different range of services, although recent deregulation of the American banking industry has made them more similar than different. Whatever type of bank you choose, make sure that it is federally insured. That way, if the bank fails, you won't lose your money. Federal deposit insurance protects your deposit up to a limit of $100,000.

Banking Services

Automated teller machines (ATMs) and bank cards
A bank card and an ATM allow you 24-hour access to your accounts, although services and withdrawal amounts are limited.

Debit cards
Debit cards are used much like checks. When you make a purchase with a debit card, money is electronically deducted from your account and credited to the seller's account. Many stores let you use your ATM card as a debit card.

Credit cards
You can obtain a credit card that is directly linked to your bank account. Payments are automatically withdrawn from your bank account, making payment of your credit card bill more convenient.

Overdraft privileges
Your bank may give your checking account a small line of credit to protect you from bouncing checks.

Electronic banking
Using a computer and a modem, you can do much of your banking without entering a bank.

Direct deposit
You can move money directly from one account to another by authorizing a wire transfer.

Automatic withdrawal
You can arrange to have your regular bills, such as your car payment, deducted directly from your account.

Commercial Banks The bank that provides the most services and plays the biggest role in our economy is the **commercial bank**. Commercial banks provide checking accounts, savings accounts, and money market accounts, and they accept time deposits (CDs). Individuals as well as businesses maintain accounts at commercial banks. Commercial banks also make loans to both individuals and businesses. Many have begun to offer stock brokerage services as well.

Savings and Loans **Savings and loans associations,** as the name implies, traditionally accepted deposits from customers and specialized in offering long-term financing for homes. They were originally intended to promote savings and home ownership. Recent deregulation, however, has expanded scope of their services.

Savings Banks **Savings banks** accept deposits and specialize in low-risk investments, such as government bonds. Some of the larger ones offer some of

Wire transfers
Your employer can credit your pay directly to your account, giving you speedy access to your earnings.

Business and consumer loans
Banks can help you finance your education, automobile purchase, or other large purchase.

Investment services
You can purchase stocks through the brokerage services now offered by many of the larger commercial banks.

Safe deposit boxes
You can secure important documents and valuables by renting a safe deposit box, which is kept in the bank's vault.

How to Choose
A Bank

It can be challenging to find the right bank or credit union to suit your needs. When choosing a financial institution, be sure to get answers to the following questions:

❑ Is it conveniently located?

❑ Does it have convenient hours?

❑ Are ATMs available?

❑ What services does it offer?

❑ How high are the fees?

❑ Is it federally insured?

the same services as commercial banks, such as checking accounts.

Credit Unions **Credit unions** are nonprofit banks owned by their members, usually employees of a single organization such as a company or trade union. Their ties to industry and their tax-exempt nonprofit status enable credit unions to pay slightly higher interest rates than commercial banks. They also finance consumer loans at competitive rates.

Other Financial Institutions You may also turn to mutual fund companies, brokerage firms, and insurance subsidiaries for some financial services. Mutual fund companies and brokerage firms are useful for investing. Insurance companies can provide you with tax-deferred savings and may let you take out loans against your insurance policy. These institutions, however, do not offer a full range of banking services.

Check Your Understanding

1. **Key Terms** How does a **commercial bank** differ from a **savings and loan association?** How does a commercial bank differ from a credit union?

2. **Organizing Information** Review the chart on banking services. Rank them in order of importance to you.

Credit and Debt

Credit gives extra punch to your purchasing power; but reckless handling of credit can bury you in debt.

Seems like everyone wants to lend you money. Each year, credit-card companies bombard American consumers with alluring offers of easy money. "Congratulations—you are qualified to receive $10,000!" "You will not be turned down!" "Why postpone your dreams? Apply today."

Why do they want to lend you money? Because that's how they make money. Banks and other financial institutions lend money to both businesses and consumers. Borrowers, in return, pay fees, and those fees can be hefty. If you must borrow—for a car, for college, or for other expenses that you lack the cash to cover—learn how to borrow wisely.

Are You Credit Worthy?

Loans, credit cards, and other methods of deferred payment are known as **credit**. For a bank or other institution to extend you credit, it must be confident that you will repay all the money you borrow, plus any additional interest and fees. You, on the other hand, must understand what you're getting into before you sign on the dotted line.

Creditors, the folks who lend you money, aren't going to give you money just on your word. They are going to ask many questions about your financial past and demand evidence of your financial health to determine if you are able and willing to pay them back.

The Four Cs Creditors look for *capacity, capital, character,* and *collateral* when judging your credit worthiness. *Capacity* is your ability to repay the debt. Creditors will want to know where you work, how long you've worked there, and how much money you make. They will also want to know how much you spend.

Capital is your regular income plus the money in your savings and checking accounts.

Character is your willingness to repay your debts. Creditors will obtain a record of your past borrowing, your bill-paying habits, and your ability to live within your means. Much of this information they will obtain from an organization called a **credit bureau.** If you fail to maintain a good **credit rating,** you will find it very difficult to obtain credit. Creditors will also look for signs of stability in your life. How long have you lived at your current address? How often have you moved in the past few years? Do you own or rent your home?

Don't let the **credit card monster** consume you!

Some loans require **collateral,** which is property used to secure a loan. If you default on the loan or fail to repay it, the creditor takes ownership of the collateral. Often the item that the loan is used to purchase serves as collateral. This is usually the case with car loans and home mortgages. If you fail to keep up with your car payments, you may find yourself walking to work.

Information Creditors Can't Use The federal government has passed laws protecting consumers from being discriminated against when applying for credit. The Equal Credit Opportunity Act forbids creditors from using age, gender, marital status, race, color, religion, national origin, or public assistance income when establishing your credit worthiness. Nor can creditors discriminate against you for exercising certain rights, such as filing a billing error notice with a creditor.

Maintaining Good Credit As you begin to make purchases with loans and credit cards, credit might seem to you like free money, but it's not. When you borrow money from a financial institution, you are, in effect, renting money. Eventually you have to pay it all back, along with interest and fees, called **finance charges.** Finance charges can be quite expensive and add up rapidly. If you're not paying attention, you can quickly lose control of your debt.

Making late payments, missing payments, or borrowing more than you can pay back will damage your credit history. A poor credit history can haunt you for seven years or more. If you are irresponsible with your credit card, you're going to have a hard time financing that new car you plan to buy.

To maintain good credit, you need to develop good credit behavior. Don't overborrow or overspend, make sure you pay your bills promptly, and protect your credit cards from loss or theft. It is also crucial for you to understand the different forms of credit available to you and how their finance charges are calculated. That way, you can make sound decisions that will keep you out of financial hot water.

Types of Credit

Different forms of credit are suited to different purposes. You know that you shouldn't use your credit card to pay for a new car. And you wouldn't take out a loan to pay for dinner and a movie on Friday night. There is much more you need to know, however, about credit.

Loans Loans come in two forms: single-payment loans and installment loans. Single-payment loans are short-term loans paid off in one lump sum. Installment loans, on the other hand, are repaid at regularly scheduled intervals, or installments, usually monthly. Each installment payment is for the same amount. Each payment is applied to both the principal (the amount borrowed) and the interest (the fee for borrowing the

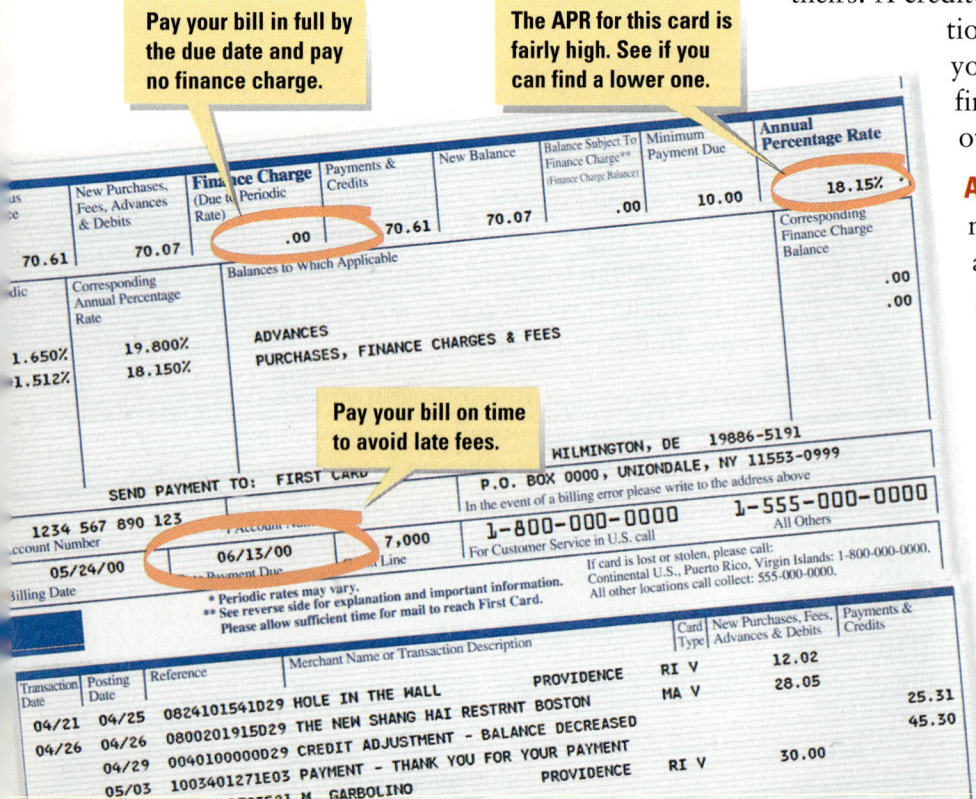

money). Although you pay the same number of dollars each month, at first, more of the payment goes toward interest than principal. An automobile loan is an example of an installment loan. (See "Buying a Car" on pages 520–521.)

Loans that require collateral are called secured loans. Loans that don't require collateral are called unsecured loans. Credit for these loans, also known as signature loans, is based on the borrower's references and credit rating. A Guaranteed Student Loan is an example of an unsecured loan.

Credit Cards One of the most popular forms of credit in the United States today is the credit card. It is a form of open-ended, or revolving, credit. A credit card lets you borrow money on an ongoing basis, up to a prearranged limit, to buy goods and services. Any amount you pay back you are able to reborrow.

Many people find credit cards more convenient than cash. You can order movie tickets, buy clothes, pay for a meal, or just about anything else

using a credit card. Bank cards such as Visa and MasterCard are the most widely accepted.

As a cardholder you receive a monthly bill and are required to pay at least some portion of the balance (the amount you owe) each month. Annual fees, interest rates, and other charges vary greatly among credit card issuers, so you should carefully compare the terms of several card offers before making any commitments. Some nonprofit organizations on the Internet offer listings of good credit card deals and guidance in applying for them.

Another form of credit is a travel and entertainment (T&E) card. It is similar to a credit card, but the borrower is required to pay the total amount owed each month. Because you pay your debt in full each month, you aren't charged interest. Usually you are required to pay an annual membership fee. American Express and Diners Club are popular travel and entertainment cards.

Finance Charges and Terms

As a borrower, you pay for the privilege of borrowing money. Interest is the primary fee for borrowing money. Just as a bank will pay you interest to use your money, you must pay your creditors to use theirs. A creditor, however, may charge you additional fees. The total dollar amount you pay to use credit is called the finance charge. It includes interest and other fees that may apply.

Annual Percentage Rate An important number for you to understand when applying for credit is the **annual percentage rate (APR)**. The APR tells you what your credit will cost. It is the finance charge expressed as an annual rate. Comparing the annual percentage rates, rather than the interest rates, offered by lenders is a good way to compare loans. Be sure you understand how your lender calculates the APR for the credit cards you are considering.

Comparing APR

EXAMPLE a $100,000, 30-year home mortgage

	Plan A	Plan B
Interest rate	7.5%	7.5%
Points	0	2.0
Other closing costs	$1,500	$1,000
APR	7.6527	7.8046

Comparing Terms on an Installment Loan

EXAMPLE a $13,500 loan with 12.5% interest

	3-year loan	5-year loan
Number of monthly payments	36	60
Amount of each payment	$451.62	$303.72
Total interest paid	$2,758.32	$4,723.20

Terms Another important factor to consider is the term, or length, of your loan. For example, if you arrange to pay for your new car in three years rather than five, your monthly payments will be higher, but in the end, you will pay less interest.

How to Choose
a Credit Card

When selecting a credit card, be sure you understand all the terms of the credit-card offer before you make a commitment.

What is the APR? You may want to choose the card with lowest APR, especially if you carry a balance on your account.

Is the APR fixed or variable? A fixed APR will stay the same. A variable APR will rise and fall as the prime rate or other economic indicator changes.

What is the periodic rate? The periodic rate is the interest rate that is applied to your account balance each billing period.

How are finance charges computed? Most creditors use your average daily balance to determine the finance charge. The average daily balance is calculated by adding up all daily balances and dividing them by the number of days in a billing period.

Is there a grace period? Many creditors will charge you no interest if you pay your bill in full before the due date.

What fees does the creditor charge? Many credit cards charge an annual membership fee, as well as fees for late payments, cash advances, or exceeding the credit limit.

Know Your Rights Credit card issuers and other lenders are required by **Truth in Lending laws** to disclose certain information. Institutions extending loans must tell you the exact finance charge on your loan. Credit card issuers must disclose monthly interest rates, the APR, and the method of finance charge calculation.

The Fair Credit Reporting Act protects you from errors on credit reports issued by credit bureaus. You are entitled to know the reason for any negative activity on your report and to have any errors corrected. Similarly, the Fair Credit Billing Act lets you dispute and correct billing information.

If you find yourself in debt and subject to debt collection, be aware that debt collectors must ensure the accuracy of the bill in question and allow you to dispute the bill if you believe it to be in error. Debt collectors may not threaten, harass, or otherwise abuse you in pursuit of the debt.

Check Your Understanding

1. **Key Terms** (a) Name two types of **credit** and explain how they are different. (b) How does **collateral** discourage borrowers from defaulting on a loan? (c) How do the Equal Credit Opportunity Act and **Truth in Lending laws** protect consumers?

2. **Analyzing Information** Analyze the credit card offers your household receives in the mail or that you see advertised. Make a chart comparing their features and finance charges. Identify and explain which credit card is the best deal.

Paying for Education

Learning how to finance your tuition is an education in itself.

By the time you finish paying for college, you may have shelled out enough money to buy a luxury car, a small yacht, or perhaps even a house. And that doesn't count the cost of graduate or professional school.

The car won't last, however, while education affects your earning power for the rest of your life. So the short-term sacrifice is generally worth the potential long-term gain. But how on Earth are you going to pay for it?

Decisions, Decisions

The hard facts about paying for college are these: even after adjusting for inflation, the average cost of tuition at public and private universities more than doubled between 1985 and 2000, while average salaries rose only 12 percent. **Tuition** is the cost of enrolling in courses. In recent years, schools have added on many other costly fees. Second, financial aid rose to meet the increased need, but mostly in terms of loans, not scholarships. How can you

achieve your educational goals without jeopardizing your financial future? Start by thinking about the type of school you want to attend. For example:

- *What school do you want to attend, and why?* Examine your goals. Can you find the educational resources you need at a less-expensive public school? The answer, often, is yes. However, if only private schools have what you're looking for, don't rule them out because of cost. Although private schools are generally more costly than public schools, private schools often can be more generous in providing financial aid.
- *How much does location matter to you?* According to the College Board, tuition costs vary considerably from region to region. Schools in the Southwest are generally less expensive than those in the East.
- *How much debt do you want to incur?* If you expect to be a freelance artist after you graduate, you might want to take on less debt than if you're planning a career as a doctor.

The costs of attending college have been rising faster than the rate of inflation. This chart, adjusted for inflation to 1999 dollars, shows how the average annual costs of attending four-year private and public colleges and universities have risen since 1980.

The ABCs of Financial Aid

Each year, millions of dollars are made available to help students pay for college. The three major types of financial aid are (a) grants and scholarships; (b) work-study programs; and (c) loans. These categories are described in the box below.

One simple equation cuts through the confusing information about financing:

Total Cost – Total Aid = What you owe

So the idea is to reduce the amount you're going to owe by applying for as many sources of aid as possible. Most students qualify for some kind of financial aid. How much you receive depends on the following criteria:

- income—yours and your parents'
- the number of college students in your family
- family assets and expenses
- the available pool of aid at the school you plan to attend
- the number of students applying for aid in a given year and their financial need compared with yours.

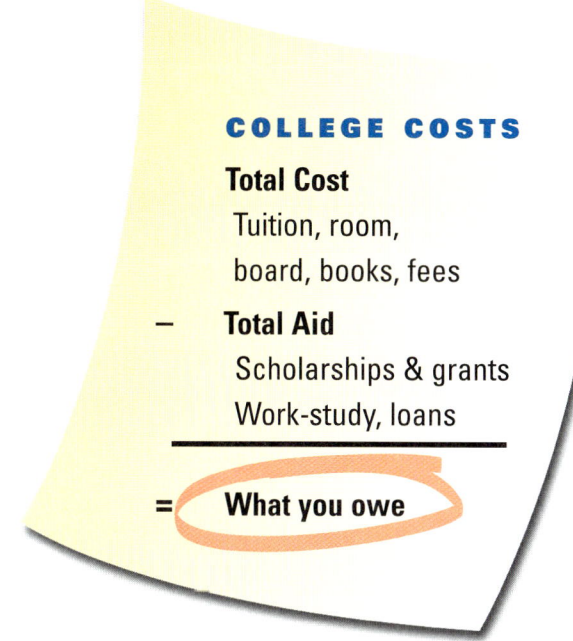

COLLEGE COSTS

Total Cost
Tuition, room, board, books, fees

– **Total Aid**
Scholarships & grants
Work-study, loans

= **What you owe**

Types of Lenders

Regardless of your income, you can qualify for some type of government loan. You might need to supplement it with a loan from your school or with a commercial loan.

Three Types of Financial Aid

Grants and Scholarships

Scholarships are often based on academic or athletic performance. But don't count yourself out if you're not valedictorian or captain of the basketball team.

All kinds of people can qualify for "free money." Federal Pell Grants and Federal Supplemental Educational Opportunity Grants are given to students with "exceptional financial need." Other grants are available to students of a certain gender or ethnic group or members of a certain club or civic organization. Companies often offer scholarships to children of their employees. If you already know what you want to major in, there are scholarships for just about every field. You can find scholarship directories in the reference section of your library, on the Web, through your guidance counselor, and through college financial aid offices.

The Reserve Officer's Training Corps (ROTC) program, offered by all branches of the armed forces, gives merit-based scholarships. These pay for tuition, fees, and books and give you a monthly living allowance in return for service in the military after you graduate.

Work-study

Many American college students work their way through school. Many colleges offer work-study programs that provide on-campus jobs for students receiving financial aid. Most work-study programs are federally funded.

Loans

Both students and parents can apply for college loans. Most college loans have a low interest rate and a generous repayment schedule.

Loans can be subsidized or unsubsidized. On a federally subsidized loan, the government pays the interest during the years you're in school, and you don't begin paying back the loan until you leave school.

The Federal Government The Department of Education offers Direct Loans and Stafford Loans for parents or students, as well as the Parent Loan for Undergraduate Students (PLUS). Each loan has different eligibility requirements, but all have a cap on the interest rate. These loans are administered by agencies that vary from state to state.

The Federal Perkins Loan provides low-interest funds to students with "exceptional financial need." The loan is administered through schools themselves.

Students who go on to take teaching jobs in certain low-income or teacher-shortage areas or who volunteer in the Americorps, Peace Corps, or VISTA programs may be eligible to have their federal loans partially repaid or even canceled.

Private Sources If money from government loans does not cover your college expenses, many other sources are available. Banks and other financial institutions offer regular commercial loans for education. These loans generally carry higher interest rates than federal loans. Trade organizations and educational institutions also provide loans, as do a variety of for-profit companies on the Web.

Pay Up! A word to the wise: Repay your student loans. Computerization and more vigorous collection efforts are resulting in more cheaters getting caught and penalized. If you run into trouble repaying your loan, call your lender, who can help you work out a manageable repayment plan.

Some loans allow you to pay just the interest for a certain period of time. Or you might get a graduated payment schedule, in which the monthly amount starts out low—when your income is relatively low—and rises later on, when presumably you can better afford to pay.

Pay off unsubsidized loans, which accrue interest while you're in school, before government **subsidized** loans, which do not.

Applying for Financial Aid

Filling out financial aid applications has gotten easier, but it still requires some time and organization.

Required Forms To qualify for any type of government financial aid, you must complete the Free Application for Federal Student Aid (FAFSA). You can obtain the form from your high school, the local library, or the U.S. Department of Education's Web site. The information you provide on the FAFSA form is used to calculate your Expected Family Contribution (EFC). The EFC is determined according to a formula established by Congress.

To receive nonfederal aid, many schools require you to fill out the PROFILE form. The College Board's financial aid

INFORMATION SOURCES

The Internet is the best thing that ever happened to students seeking financial aid. If you have or can get Internet access, you'll save yourself many hours of searching for financial aid information. In addition, you can file on-line for most scholarships and loans. Several sites have calculators that allow you to estimate your Expected Family Contribution, the amount of your aid awards, and the amount of your loan payments.

The best place for you to begin searching is Project EASI (Easy Access for Students and Institutions), the federal government's central location for aid information and on-line filing. The project, launched in the mid-1990s, is run by the federal Department of Education. Other comprehensive sources include:

- The Access Group
- College Scholarship Service (CSS), a program of the College Board
- Federal Student Aid Information Center
- SallieMae (the commonly used nickname for the acronym SLMA, or Student Loan Marketing Association; site includes a listing of major private lenders)

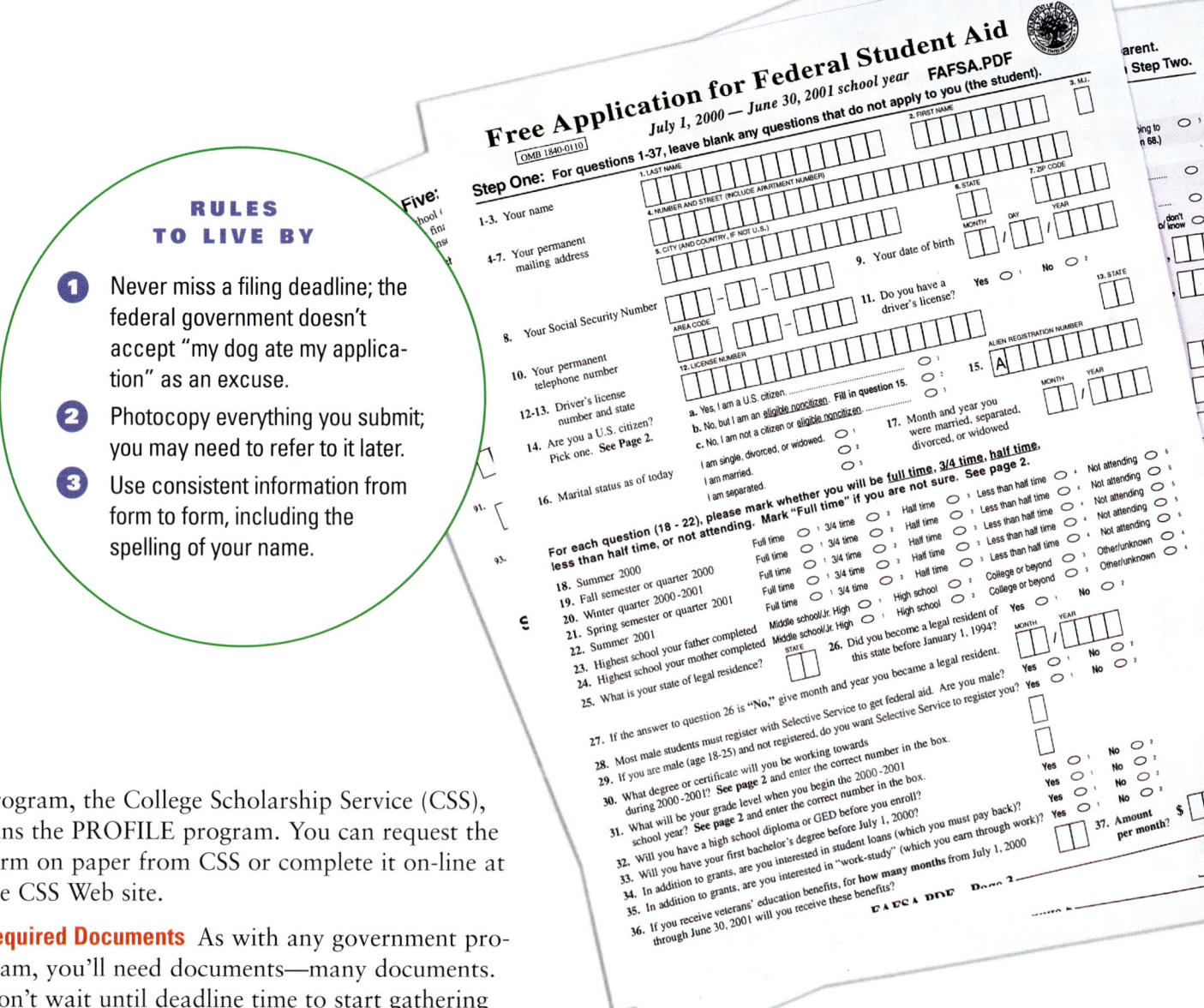

program, the College Scholarship Service (CSS), runs the PROFILE program. You can request the form on paper from CSS or complete it on-line at the CSS Web site.

Required Documents   As with any government program, you'll need documents—many documents. Don't wait until deadline time to start gathering them. They include:

- Proof of income (yours and your parents'), such as most recent tax returns, W-2 forms, and pay stubs
- Mortgage statements
- Proof of any unusual financial hardships, such as high medical expenses

Tip   If you have savings, use it to pay off any debts you may have before applying for aid. You don't get a break for having high credit card debt, but you will be expected to contribute about one third of all savings. So use your savings to pay down your debt first.

Check Your Understanding

1. **Key Terms** **(a)** What are some of the ways that students deal with skyrocketing **tuition** costs? **(b)** Why is it smart to pay off an unsubsidized loan before paying off a **subsidized** loan?

2. **Analyze** What factors might influence your own decision making about college? Explain your reasoning.

Buying a Car

Don't think of a car as a status symbol or a personal statement. The best car is the one that suits your needs—and that you can afford.

A car is one of the biggest purchases you will make. With a small investment in time and effort, you can learn what you need to make a sensible decision—and get a good deal.

Getting the Best Deal on a New Car

Most car-buying guides recommend that you identify the invoice price of the base model of the new car you want. Then request bids—in writing—from five dealers in your area, asking them how much above or below that price they will sell the car for. Save time and avoid hassling with dealers by communicating by fax if you can. Once you have received all the bids, approach the second-lowest bidder to see if he or she will beat the lowest bid.

When purchasing your car, know in advance which options you want. Don't let a dealer talk you into spending more for options than you can afford. Be especially wary of important-sounding but unnecessary add-ons such as fabric protection, paint sealant, rustproofing, and an extended warranty. An extended warranty is a service contract purchased from the dealer by the buyer. Do not confuse it with the manufacturer's warranty that comes with the car. Extended warranties are expensive and often cover repairs already covered by the manufacturer's warranty.

Financing

Before you buy your car, research the costs of auto loans at banks and other lending institutions. Compare the annual percentage rates they offer with that of the financing offered by your car dealer. Consider how much of a down payment you can afford to make. The more money you can put down, the less you have to borrow. (For more information on loans, see Credit and Debt on pages 512–515.)

Used Cars

Automobiles quickly **depreciate**, or lose their value. The new car you drive off the lot today will be worth half what you paid for it in three years. After three years, the rate of depreciation slows down. By the sixth year, it is down to 3 percent per year. You might consider buying a car that has already depreciated substantially. That way, not only will you pay a lot less for it, but it will retain its value a lot longer than a new car.

You can buy used cars from many sources: dealers, rental and leasing companies, or individuals.

To make sure the car you're buying is reliable, try to obtain all service records on the car. This way

LUXURY

you can determine how well the car has been cared for. Calculate the average annual mileage. Anything over 15,000 miles per year indicates a car that has experienced an excessive amount of wear and tear.

You should also arrange to have an independent mechanic inspect the car for you before you buy it. Look in the Yellow Pages under "Automotive Diagnostic Service" for a certified mechanic.

Dealers are required by federal law to post a Buyer's Guide on the used cars they offer for sale. The Buyer's Guide must specify whether the vehicle is being sold "as is" or with a warranty, and what percentage of the repair costs the dealer will pay.

Avoiding High-Pressure Tactics

Let's face it, a professional car dealer has much more experience in selling cars than you do in buying them. How can you avoid being pressured into spending more money than you want to?

- Be prepared. Know what you want, what you don't want, and obtain bids based on the invoice price.

PRACTICALITY

- Don't be talked into options you don't want. If the dealer doesn't have the exact car you want, have him or her try to get it from another dealer, or go to another dealer yourself.

- Don't discuss trade-ins until after you've settled on a sale price. Do not let the dealer consider the trade-in of your old car as a reduction in dealer sticker price. To "trade in" your old car is simply to sell it to the dealer. It has nothing to do with the price of the new car.

- Don't be pushed into a decision. If you're at a dealership just to look, don't let a dealer talk you into buying that day, no matter what one-day

How to Choose a Car

There are so many makes and models of cars, both new and used. How can you pick the one that's right for you? Identify your needs to help you narrow your search. Here are some questions to ask yourself:

- ❑ How many people does my car need to seat?
- ❑ How much cargo space do I need?
- ❑ What weather and road conditions will my car be subject to?
- ❑ How often will I use my car? Daily? Weekly?
- ❑ How many miles do I expect to put on my car each year?
- ❑ What do I consider acceptable gas mileage (number of miles per gallon of gasoline)?

And the most important question:

- ❑ How much can I afford to pay?

Your local library has many car-buying guides to help you choose a make and model. Check the Internet and nonprofit consumer publications for prices and evaluations of the performance, comfort, and safety of new and used cars.

specials he or she dangles before you. If you're negotiating a price and the dealer says, "Take it or leave it," don't be afraid to leave it. If you can't find a better deal elsewhere, you can always come back.

- Get it in writing. If a dealer is not willing to put all agreements in writing, walk away.

If you are feeling bullied, confused, or pressured by a dealer, just walk away. Your ability to get up and leave is the best leverage you have.

Check Your Understanding

1. **Key Terms** Why is it a wise idea to buy a car that has already **depreciated** a great deal?

2. **Analyze** **(a)** What four features would matter most to you in buying a car? List them in order, for example, a certain price range, two-door vs. four-door, or a sun roof. **(b)** What do you have to sacrifice in order to get your most-wanted feature? In other words, what is the opportunity cost of that choice?

Renting an Apartment

Home is more than a place to hang your hat. Choosing the right place to live can go a long way toward making you happy.

Renting your first apartment is an exciting prospect, but don't rush into a decision you might regret. Research your options carefully, and know your rights and responsibilities before making a commitment.

Choosing the Right Place

To locate apartments to rent, look through the real estate section of a newspaper, search the Internet, read community bulletin boards, or use the services of a realtor. Keep in mind that realtors will charge you a fee for finding you an apartment, often half a month's rent or more. Find several listings that seem attractive to you. Make appointments with the landlords or their representatives to view the apartments.

Rent and Other Costs

A good rule of thumb is to have one month's rent and utility payments equal no more than one week's take-home pay. Estimate your utility bills by asking the landlord or a previous tenant what the average monthly heating and electricity costs were for the apartment during the previous year.

Keep in mind that you will probably need a large supply of cash up front. Many landlords require in advance the first and last month's rent. Some also ask for a **security deposit**, a sum of money that you pay the landlord to ensure that you will leave the apartment in the same condition you found it in. The security deposit is usually equal to a full month's rent. After you give up the apartment, the landlord will inspect it. If you have damaged the property, the landlord will use money from your security deposit to make repairs and will return any unused portion to you. If the apartment is undamaged, you will get back your entire deposit, sometimes with interest.

Signing the Lease

Finding an apartment you like is half the battle. The other half is convincing the landlord that you'll

reno.	renovated
sngl fam.	single family
ranch	ranch-style home
br	bedrooms
eik	eat-in kitchen
d&d	dishwasher and disposal
w/d	washer and dryer
ac	air conditioned
hwf	hardwood floors
pkg	parking
wlk to T	walk to public transportation

How to Choose
an Apartment

Finding the right apartment can be difficult. Be sure to get answers to the following questions during your search.

❏ How many rooms does it have?
❏ What condition is it in?
❏ Are the door and window locks sturdy?
❏ Are there working smoke detectors?
❏ Are the walls soundproof?
❏ Does it have adequate closet space?
❏ Are there laundry facilities?
❏ What is the condition of the bathroom fixtures?
❏ Is parking available?
❏ Arc pcts allowcd?
❏ Does the neighborhood appear safe?
❏ Is it convenient to where you work or attend school?
❏ Will you have access to public transportation?
❏ How close is the nearest grocery store?
❏ What are the terms of the lease?

be a responsible tenant. Remember, you may be competing with other prospective tenants for the apartment.

You will be asked to fill out a rental application. Most applications ask you for details such as:
• The names and phone numbers of your present and previous landlords
• Your social security number
• Your employer, job position, and income
• Your bank name, address, and account numbers
• Personal references

The landlord may also perform a credit check on you—another good reason to maintain a good credit history.

If this is your first apartment rental, you'll have to rely on your personal references, rather than previous landlords, to vouch for your character. Ask responsible adults who know you well, such as a teacher, coach, employer, or clergy member, to provide you with written references.

Once you've been approved to take the apartment, you will be required to sign a **lease**, a rental agreement between landlord and tenant. Most leases require a one-year commitment and monthly rent payments. The lease also spells out rules such as whether pets are allowed, or whether a fee will be charged if your rent is late. Some landlords will let you rent month to month without a set end date other than the amount of notice previously agreed upon.

Read any lease or rental agreement carefully, and make sure you understand it before you sign. Discuss the terms with your landlord, along with any changes you'd like to make. Bear in mind that what you are signing is a **contract**, a binding legal agreement. Both you and your landlord are required to live up to its obligations.

Rights and Responsibilities Know your tenant rights. While a landlord has the right to ask for references and perform a credit check, it is against the law to discriminate against a potential tenant on the basis of race, color, national origin, religion, sex, familial status, or handicap. Contact your state's office of Housing and Urban Development for more information.

Landlords are required to provide a dwelling that is structurally safe and sanitary and that has heat, water, and electricity. Your landlord has the right to enter your apartment only to make repairs or to show it to a prospective tenant, and sometimes he must give you notice before doing so.

Rental laws vary in different locations. For example, in rent-controlled neighborhoods, landlords are limited in the amount of rent they can charge. Check with your local housing or consumer affairs office for information.

At the same time, tenants have responsibilities. As a tenant, you must pay your rent on time, keep your apartment clean and undamaged, follow the terms of your lease or rental agreement, and be considerate of your neighbors.

Check Your Understanding

1. **Key Terms** (a) What is the purpose of a **security deposit**? (b) How does a **lease** benefit both landlord and tenant?

2. **Analyze** What three factors would be most important to you when searching for an apartment? Explain your reasoning.

Buying Insurance

We hate to pay for it, but we're sometimes glad we did.

When we're young, we tend to think that nothing bad will ever happen to us. But sooner or later we usually find ourselves wanting the benefits that insurance offers.

How Insurance Works

Insurance is essentially a bet between you and your insurance company. You are betting that some type of accident will happen to you: illness or damage to your car or home. The company, on the other hand, is betting that you will not have such a problem. It bases its judgment on complicated formulas of probable risk.

Insurance Costs

In the event of an accident, you could suffer devastating financial losses. So you pay the insurance company a sum of money called a **premium**. The company then promises to pay compensation in the event of an accident. The amount the insurance company pays out could be many times what you paid in premiums.

If you remain accident-free, the company makes money. It uses part of that money to pay policyholders who do sustain some type of loss.

Most insurance policies include a **deductible,** an amount of expenses that you must pay before the insurer will cover any expenses. For example, if your car insurance policy has a $1,000 deductible, and you have an accident, you'll have to pay the first $1,000 in damages yourself, then the insurance company will pay the rest, up to a certain limit.

Coverage

Before you buy auto or home insurance, find out if the policy covers replacement cost, the amount of money needed to buy a new item to replace the lost or damaged one. Some companies only cover actual cash value (ACV), the amount that the lost or damaged item would have been worth on the market before the accident. If, for instance, your two-year-old computer is stolen, its ACV is not nearly as much as it would cost you to buy a new computer to replace the stolen one, because computers lose their value quickly.

Shop for a policy that requires the lowest possible premium while giving you the amount of coverage you need, no more and no less. But beware: Insurance policies contain complicated language and lots of fine print. Make sure you read carefully. Get estimates from several companies before you sign. Or go to a fee-only insurance advisor, an impartial expert who can help you evaluate policies and recommend the one that's right for you.

Auto Insurance

If you drive, most states require you to have your own auto insurance or to be listed as a driver on someone else's policy. If you drive a car with the owner's permission, you're usually covered.

Most insurance companies offer several types of auto insurance. Collision insurance covers damage to your vehicle regardless of who is at fault in an accident. Comprehensive insurance pays for other types of damage to your car, such as theft, broken glass, vandalism, and natural disasters. If you are at fault in an accident, liability insurance covers property damage and bodily injuries to people who are not on your policy, as well as your court costs. Other provisions pay medical costs for you and others riding in your car.

Health Insurance

Even if you're healthy, having health insurance is a good idea. Insurance plans cover a variety of health-care needs, such as hospitalization, surgeries, routine medical care, preventive care, visits to specialists, medicines, mental health care, and dental care.

The problem, however, is finding affordable care. Health insurance premiums are costly. The best rates are available through group insurance plans offered by employers and other large organizations. Purchasing an individual plan can cost hundreds of dollars a month. Health insurance companies offer a variety of plans, so you can buy the level of coverage you need to feel protected.

Dental insurance policies cover procedures and products such as fillings, crowns, extractions, bridgework, and dentures. These plans usually require deductibles and copayments.

Health insurance plans vary according to several factors:

1. The degree to which you can choose your doctors
2. The types of procedures covered
3. The amount of deductible required
4. The amount of **copayment**, which is the percentage of each visit or procedure that the patient must pay
5. Annual limits on the total amount of care covered

Property Insurance

Think for a moment about the value of your belongings: stereo, computer, television, VCR, bicycle, books, clothes, coin collection, etc. What if your apartment caught fire? What if your building were destroyed by a tornado or other natural disaster? Would you need a lot of money to replace what you own? If so, then you should insure it.

Renter's insurance is generally a type of homeowner's policy. It protects your belongings against destruction from fire, wind, lightning, explosions, and theft. It can cover your liability if someone is injured in your home. Most policies do not protect you against flood damage; you need to purchase a separate flood insurance policy for that kind of coverage. You might need to keep receipts and other records of major household items to have them covered.

Check Your Understanding

1. **Key Terms** (a) Explain the difference between a **premium,** a **deductible,** and a **copayment.** (b) Why is a policy that covers replacement cost better than one that covers actual cash value? (c) Why do you think some states require drivers to carry liability insurance but not collision insurance or comprehensive insurance?

2. **Using Graphic Organizers** Create a chart that shows the opportunity costs of buying auto insurance, health insurance, and property insurance.

Getting a Job

Finding work can seem like a full-time job in itself.

But the harder you search, the better the job you'll get. Nobody likes looking for a job. It's tedious and time consuming. You have to steel yourself for rejections and forge ahead. But remember: All you need is for one employer to say, "You're hired."

The Résumé

One of the most important tools in your job hunt is your **résumé**, a document that summarizes your employment experience, education, and other information a potential employer wants to know. Many job postings will instruct you to send in your résumé.

Reviewing résumés is the employer's first step in eliminating candidates for a job, so you'll want to make sure yours is as well-prepared as it can be.

The Cover Letter

When you send out a résumé, accompany it with a cover letter addressed to a particular individual—ideally, the hiring manager. You should mention your interest in the company and where you learned about the job opening. Your cover letter is an opportunity to highlight or add detail to points in your résumé. Keep your letter brief, however.

Heading Include your name, address, phone number, and any other contact information, such as fax number or e-mail address.

Objective Identify the type of position you seek.

Education Outline your educational achievements (degrees, diplomas, or certificates earned) .

Experience Describe your work experience and the job skills you have demonstrated.

Activities and **Other Skills** Provide any other information pertinent to the job you seek.

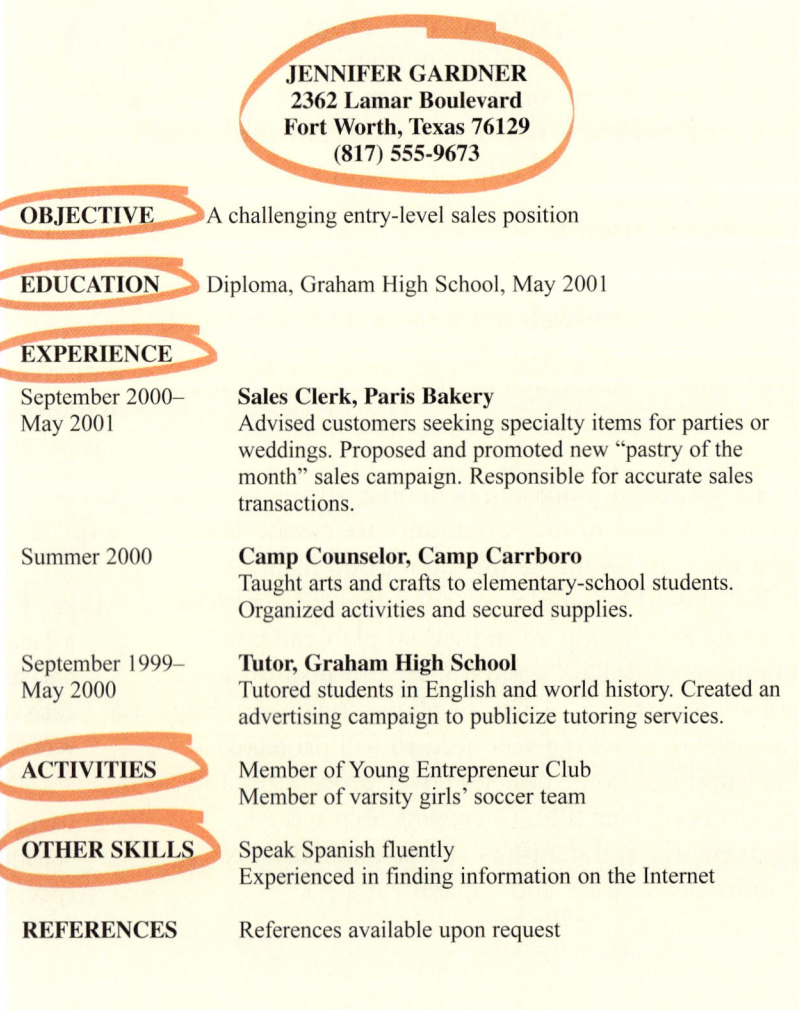

JENNIFER GARDNER
2362 Lamar Boulevard
Fort Worth, Texas 76129
(817) 555-9673

OBJECTIVE A challenging entry-level sales position

EDUCATION Diploma, Graham High School, May 2001

EXPERIENCE

September 2000–
May 2001

Sales Clerk, Paris Bakery
Advised customers seeking specialty items for parties or weddings. Proposed and promoted new "pastry of the month" sales campaign. Responsible for accurate sales transactions.

Summer 2000

Camp Counselor, Camp Carrboro
Taught arts and crafts to elementary-school students. Organized activities and secured supplies.

September 1999–
May 2000

Tutor, Graham High School
Tutored students in English and world history. Created an advertising campaign to publicize tutoring services.

ACTIVITIES Member of Young Entrepreneur Club
Member of varsity girls' soccer team

OTHER SKILLS Speak Spanish fluently
Experienced in finding information on the Internet

REFERENCES References available upon request

It's not enough to send your résumé out into the world and then sit back and wait for phone calls. Your résumé may wind up sitting in a stack of hundreds on somebody's desk. In your cover letter, mention when and how you will follow up the letter—and make sure you do.

Identifying Job Openings

The more information you have, the better your job hunt. You need to learn not only about the field you're interested in, but about the companies you're seeking a position with. Use as many information sources as you can to get the complete picture.

Networking There's a grain of truth to the adage "It's not what you know, it's who you know." Friends and family can put you in contact with people in the fields you're interested in. Talking with friends, family, and acquaintances about job leads is called networking.

Help Wanted Ads Newspapers' help wanted sections carry many advertisements for jobs. But the ads are often brief, offering few details about the job or the company. Competition for these jobs is keen, since many people turn to the help wanted ads when they are looking for a job. Respond promptly to help wanted ads, and keep a record of employers you contact.

The Internet Some Web sites let you post your résumé on-line. For example, the U.S. Department of Labor, in conjunction with state-run employment services, maintains a Web site called America's Job Bank. It offers career resources, occupational projections, job listings, and a place to post your résumé.

Employment Services Public employment services can match your qualifications with available jobs. State-run job services are free. Check the state government listing in your phone directory for the office nearest you.

Many community job centers provide job placement services, too. They may offer résumé writing tips, interview practice, testing, and job counseling. And don't forget your school guidance counselor's office for job placement and counseling.

Private employment services are also available. These businesses will charge you or your employer a

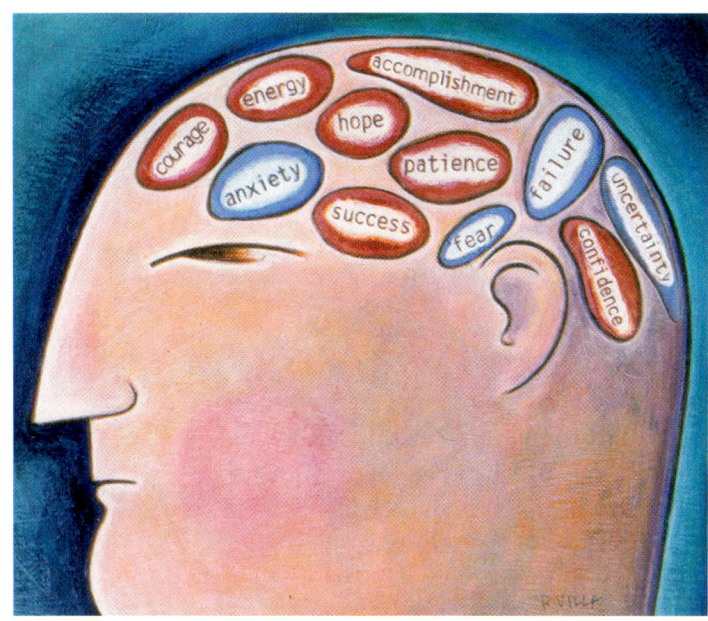

high fee for placing you in a job. Find out who will be paying the fee and what guarantees the agency offers before you sign up with them.

Interviewing

At the interview, the interviewer will talk with you to determine whether you are able and willing to do the job and whether you share the company's goals. Prepare for the interview by finding out as much about the company as you can. You'll also want to go into the interview with information about the standard salary ranges for similar positions. The employer may want to discuss salary during the interview.

Be ready to answer questions about your qualifications and goals. Also be prepared to ask questions about the position and the company. An interview can determine not only whether you're right for the job, but also whether the job is right for you.

Check Your Understanding

1. **Key Terms** To an employer, what qualities might distinguish a good **résumé** from a poor one?

2. **Formulating Questions** Plan a mock interview. Write down five questions an employer might ask you and five questions you might ask an employer.

Paying Taxes

Uncle Sam wants his share of your paycheck;
but don't give him too much.

When the Sixteenth Amendment to the Constitution took effect in 1913, the federal income tax became a fact of life. Every year of your working life you will go through the ritual of filing a federal tax return, the form(s) on which you calculate how much tax you owe. So why not decide to get organized from the start? By following a few simple guidelines, you can save time, effort, and maybe some money.

The American Tax System

Perhaps the three most dreaded letters in American English are "IRS." They stand for the **"Internal Revenue Service."**

The IRS The IRS, an agency within the Treasury Department, interprets and applies federal income tax laws passed by Congress. The agency generates tax forms and collects taxes.

The IRS will also come after you if you don't pay what you owe. In the past, the agency's aggressive pursuit of delinquent taxpayers and the surly attitude of some of its agents earned it a bad reputation. But public pressure for reform finally brought about changes in the late 1990s intended to make the IRS more helpful to citizens—most of whom are honest taxpayers.

Understanding the Tax System The current federal tax system includes a progressive tax, one in which people with the highest incomes have the highest tax rates. The system includes hundreds of tax breaks for people with special financial burdens, such as people paying for college or starting a business, or who have high medical bills. By finding out which tax deductions you qualify for and taking advantage of them, you can save hundreds of dollars a year in taxes.

People in many places have three bites taken out of their income: federal, state, and local taxes. Therefore, it is especially important to understand how to prepare for tax time.

Withholding

The federal government used to collect taxes at the end of every year. The problems were that (a) the government needed money throughout the year, not just at the end, and (b) many people weren't very good about setting aside some tax money out of every paycheck, so by tax time, they had no money to give to the tax collector.

In 1943, in need of money to finance World War II, the government introduced on a permanent basis the idea of withholding, that is, taking a certain percentage of your earnings before you get your paycheck. The amount that is withheld is shown on the **payroll withholding statement** attached to your paycheck. The money withheld goes into the federal Treasury. At the end of the year, you figure out

Form **W-4**
Department of the Treasury
Internal Revenue Service

Employee's Withholding Allowance Certificate

► For Privacy Act and Paperwork Reduction Act Notice, see page 2.

OMB No. 1545-0010

2001

1 Type or print your first name and middle initial	Last name	2 Your social security number
SUSAN A.	SMITH	123 45 6789

Home address (number and street or rural route)
111 MAIN ST.

3 ☐ Single ☐ Married ☐ Married, but withhold at higher Single rate.
Note: *If married, but legally separated, or spouse is a nonresident alien, check the Single box.*

City or town, state, and ZIP code
ANYTOWN, PA   00000

4 If your last name differs from that on your social security card, check here. **You** must call 1-800-772-1213 for a new card ►

5 Total number of allowances you are claiming (from line H above or from the worksheets on page 2 if they apply) . . | 5 | 2

6 Additional amount, if any, you want withheld from each paycheck . . . . | 6 | $

7 I claim exemption from withholding for 1999, and I certify that I meet **BOTH** of the following conditions for exemption:
• Last year I had a right to a refund of **ALL** Federal income tax withheld because I had **NO** tax liability **AND**
• This year I expect a refund of **ALL** Federal income tax withheld because I expect to have **NO** tax liability.
If you meet both conditions, write "EXEMPT" here . . . . ► | 7 |

Under penalties of perjury, I certify that I am entitled to the number of withholding allowances claimed on this certificate, or I am entitled to claim exempt status.

Employee's signature
(Form is not valid
unless you sign.) ► *Susan A. Smith*   Date ► 2/19/01

8 Employer's name and address (Employer: Complete 8 and 10 only if sending to the IRS) | 9 Office code (optional) | 10 Employer identification number
ANYTOWN PUBLIC LIBRARY

Cat. No. 10220Q

Be sure to enter your Social Security number correctly.

The worksheet on page 2 of this form will help you figure out how many deductions you can take.

Don't forget to sign and date the form!

---

the amount of tax you owe. If you had too much money withheld from your paychecks, the surplus is returned to you as a tax refund. If you did not have enough money withheld during the year, you have to pay the balance.

Too Much, Too Little Tax laws require most people to have a certain minimum percentage withheld from their paychecks. Beyond that, you choose how much to have set aside. Do you want to make sure that you won't have to pay more taxes at the end of the year? Do you want to get a big tax refund? If so, have a generous amount withheld.

The disadvantage of having a large amount withheld is that the government is holding on to your money all year and giving it back to you at the end. That's like giving the government a no-interest loan. Instead, you could put that money into savings and earn interest on it all year, then use it to pay whatever you owe at tax time. Make sure, however, that you at least have the legal minimum amount withheld, or you will be subjected to stiff penalties.

The W-4 Form To figure out how much money to have withheld from your paychecks, you must complete a Form W-4, which is shown above. When you start a new job, the employer will give you the form to complete and return. It includes worksheets to help you do the calculations required.

The W-4 form gives you the option of taking certain personal allowances that will lower the amount of tax withheld from your income. For example, you may take an exemption for yourself, your spouse, and any dependents you have. An exemption lowers the amount of your income that is taxed. The more exemptions you have, the lower your taxable income.

Estimated Taxes Under certain circumstances—if you are self-employed, for instance—you can choose not to have taxes withheld. However, you still must pay an estimated tax. Those who estimate can pay a lump sum at the beginning of the year or make quarterly estimated payments. The IRS will provide you with the forms for estimating and filing your payments.

Tax Preparation

The tax "season" runs from January to April 15. During that time, you need to fill out and file the appropriate tax forms.

The W-2 Form Some time in January or early February you should receive a Form W-2. You will get a W-2 from any employer you worked for who withheld taxes from your pay. If you don't receive this form by mid-February, contact your employer and ask about it. Employers must send out W-2s by January 31.

Save these important tax documents! The W-2s must be attached to your tax return when you file.

What you'll need to fill out your tax return

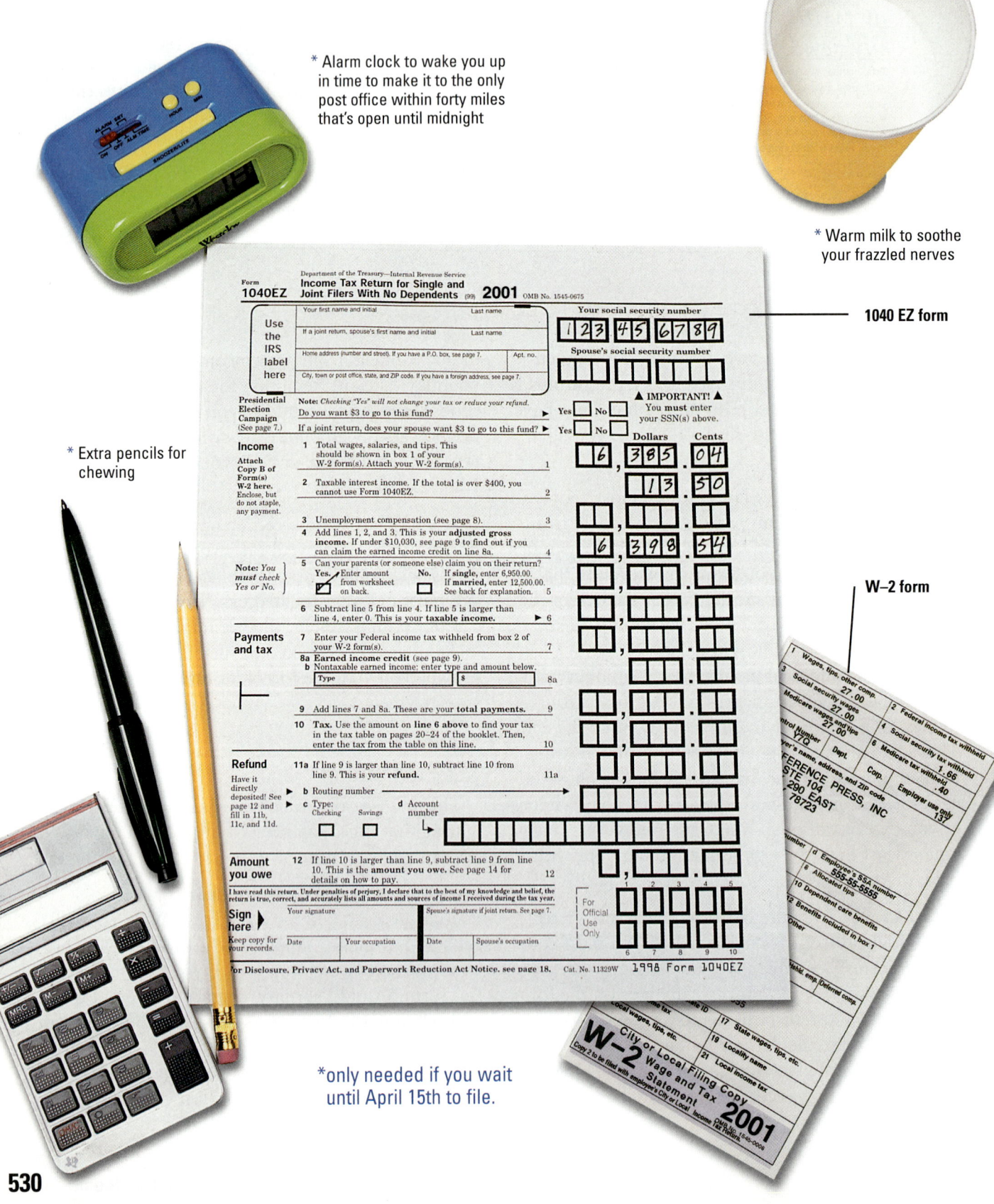

* Alarm clock to wake you up in time to make it to the only post office within forty miles that's open until midnight

* Warm milk to soothe your frazzled nerves

1040 EZ form

* Extra pencils for chewing

W–2 form

*only needed if you wait until April 15th to file.

Preparing Your Return

The Internal Revenue Service publishes dozens of tax forms that require you to provide information about your income and certain financial activities from the previous year. Then, following the directions on the forms, you calculate how much tax you owe, or how much should be refunded to you.

Federal tax forms and instruction booklets are usually available free from January through April at many post offices, public libraries, and banks. You can also quickly download dozens of forms at the IRS Web site, or receive certain forms via fax through the IRS's TaxFax Service.

Many unmarried people with no children qualify to use Form 1040EZ, which is the simplest tax form. As you can see from the sample on page 530, the 1040EZ asks you questions that you should be able to answer by looking at your W-2 and interest statements.

If you have more complicated financial circumstances, you may need to file a Form 1040A or standard Form 1040, which are more complex. Use one of these forms if you're able to claim deductions. A deduction is a provision that allows you to deduct, or subtract, money from your taxable income. The lower your taxable income, the less tax you owe. If you paid for any of the following items, they may be tax-deductible:

- *college tuition*
- *child or parental care*
- *high medical expenses*
- *a home mortgage*
- *business expenses you paid yourself*
- *business losses (if you're self-employed)*

Never put any false information on a tax form. If the IRS suspects that you've cheated on your taxes, you'll be called in for an audit, a detailed examination of your financial transactions. (Occasionally, perfectly innocent people get audited, too.) Penalties for tax fraud are severe.

What if you make an honest mistake on your tax return? If it's a simple math error, the IRS will generally catch it, inform you of it, and recalculate your tax. If you make a significant error, you may need to file an amended form as soon as possible. These mistakes generally are not considered fraudulent.

Help!

If preparing your tax return seems too daunting, don't merely guess—get help. Each form has step-by-step instructions, but they might not answer all your questions. Here are some other places to turn to:

- The Internal Revenue Service Web site is a friendly, helpful site with lots of information. Try out TaxInteractive, an on-line information service sponsored by the IRS and the American Bar Association.
- Call the IRS anytime at 1-800-829-1040. You can get help over the telephone, schedule an appointment, or take advantage of a walk-in service at certain locations and times.
- Tax-preparation services and tax accountants will fill out your tax return for you for a fee. They provide the forms, make suggestions, and answer questions. Some will file your return for you.

Ways to File   Your federal tax return usually must be postmarked by midnight on April 15. If you file late, you could be hit with substantial penalties and interest charges.

If you prepare your return on paper, you must send it to the IRS Service Center listed in the instruction booklets and at the IRS Web site. There are several ways to prepare and file your return electronically. Filing electronically will get you a faster tax refund but you usually have to pay a fee. If you owe money, you can pay by check or credit card. Call the IRS or visit its Web site for details.

Check Your Understanding

1. **Key Terms** **(a)** Why must people who earn an income file a tax return? **(b)** Who might benefit most from a progressive tax, people with a low income or people with a high income? **(c)** How do you qualify for a tax refund? **(d)** How do exemptions and deductions benefit taxpayers?

2. **Drawing Comparisons**   What are the advantages of having a large amount of money withheld for taxes? What are the advantages of having the minimum amount withheld? Which would you choose, and why?

Natural Resources

Economists use the term *land* to refer to all the natural resources used to produce goods and services. The United States enjoys an abundance of natural resources.

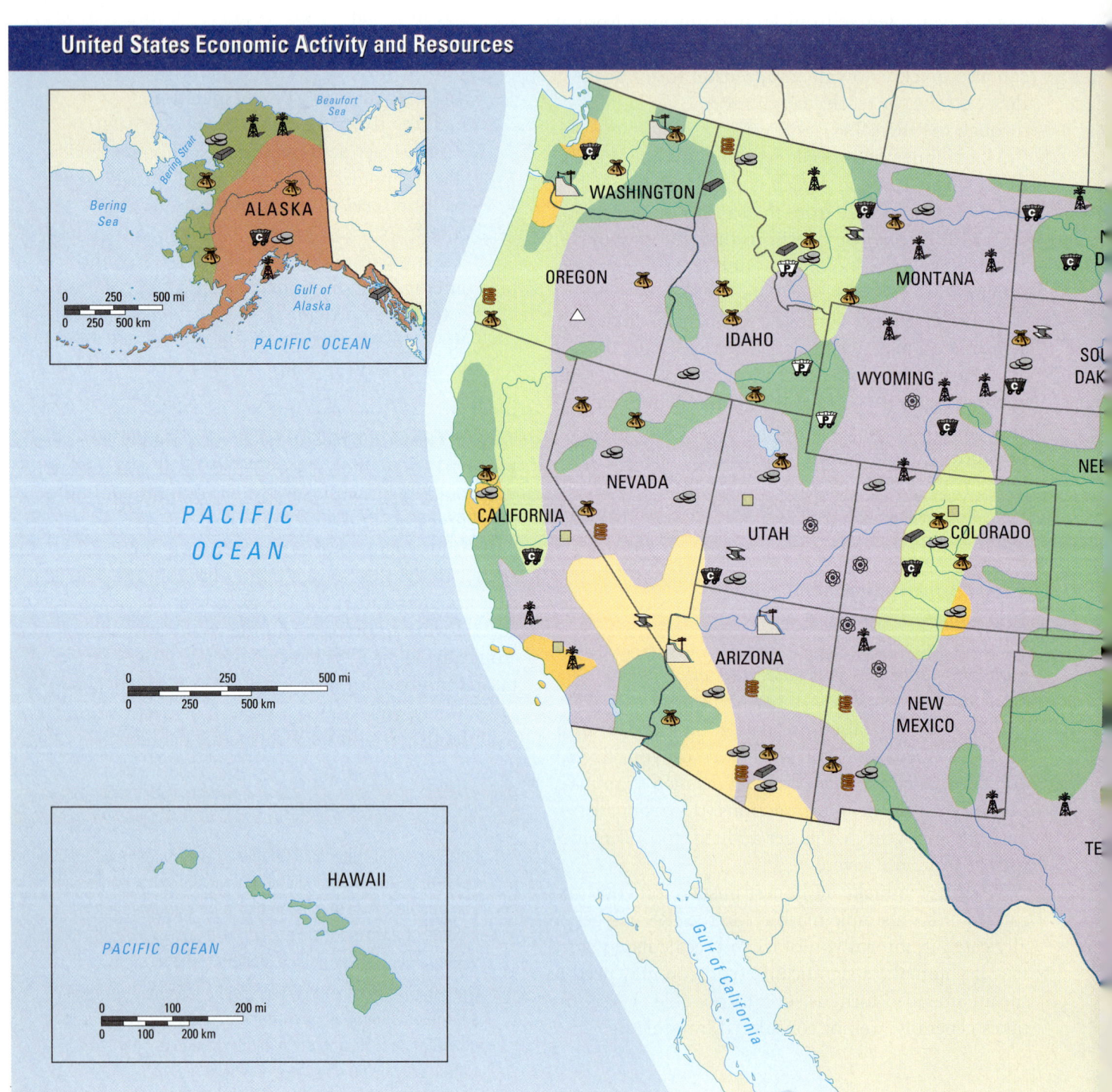

United States Economic Activity and Resources

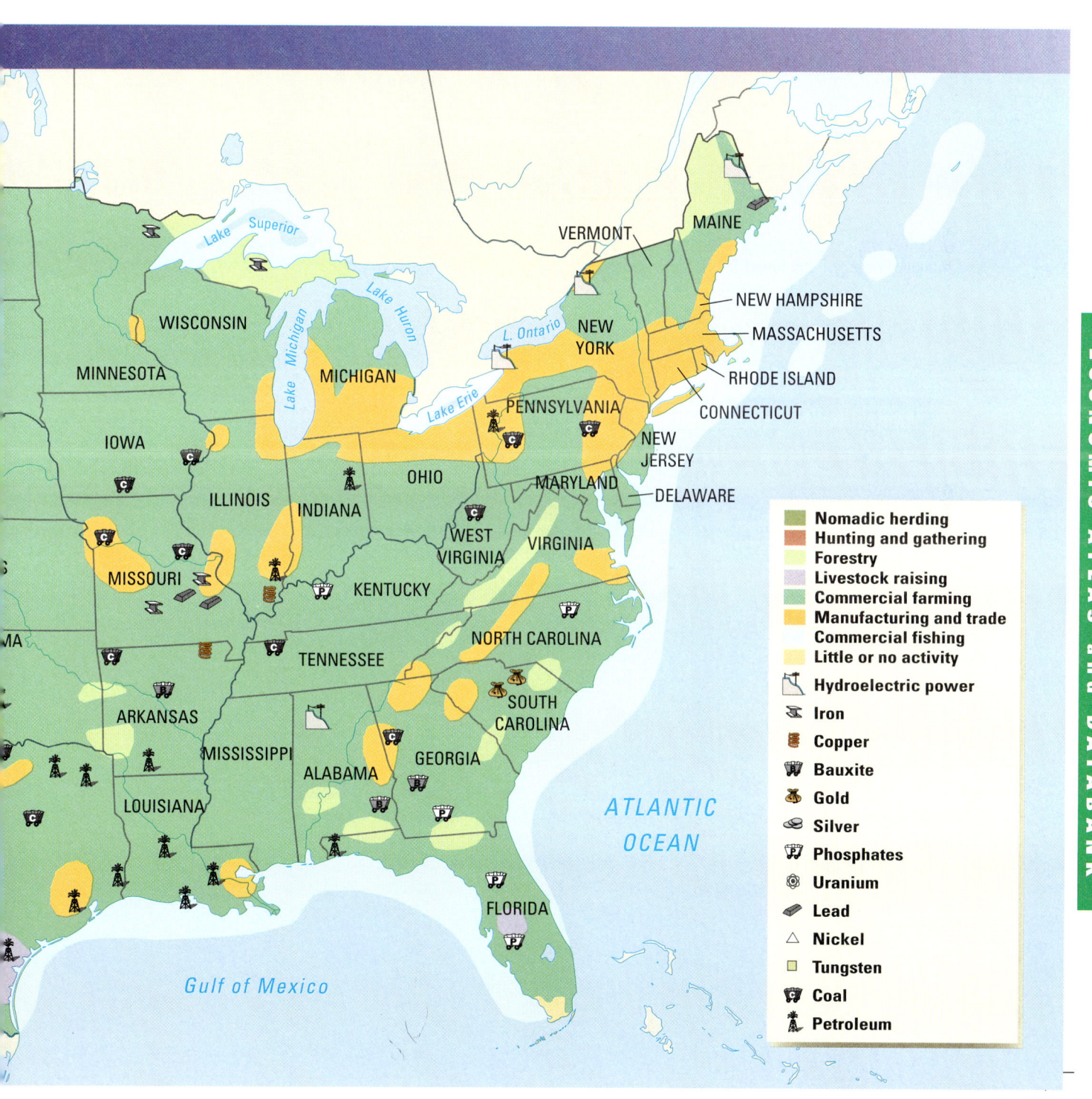

VERMONT

MAINE

NEW HAMPSHIRE

MASSACHUSETTS

RHODE ISLAND

CONNECTICUT

NEW YORK

PENNSYLVANIA

NEW JERSEY

MARYLAND

DELAWARE

Lake Superior

Lake Michigan

Lake Huron

L. Ontario

Lake Erie

WISCONSIN

MINNESOTA

MICHIGAN

IOWA

OHIO

ILLINOIS

INDIANA

WEST VIRGINIA

VIRGINIA

MISSOURI

KENTUCKY

NORTH CAROLINA

TENNESSEE

ARKANSAS

SOUTH CAROLINA

MISSISSIPPI

ALABAMA

GEORGIA

LOUISIANA

FLORIDA

ATLANTIC OCEAN

Gulf of Mexico

■	Nomadic herding
■	Hunting and gathering
■	Forestry
■	Livestock raising
■	Commercial farming
■	Manufacturing and trade
	Commercial fishing
■	Little or no activity
⚒	Hydroelectric power
⚒	Iron
⚒	Copper
⚒	Bauxite
⚒	Gold
⚒	Silver
P	Phosphates
◎	Uranium
◢	Lead
△	Nickel
▢	Tungsten
C	Coal
⚒	Petroleum

For periodic updates of the data included in the Databank, go to **www.phschool.com**

GDP of Agriculture, Forestry, Fishing, Timber-Related Manufacturing, and Mining

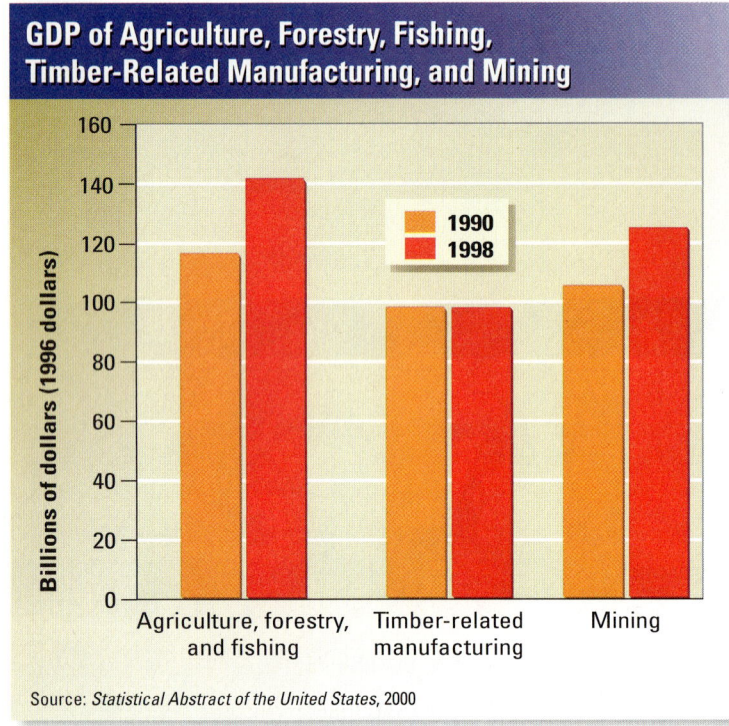

Source: *Statistical Abstract of the United States*, 2000

United States Energy Production, by Source, 1999

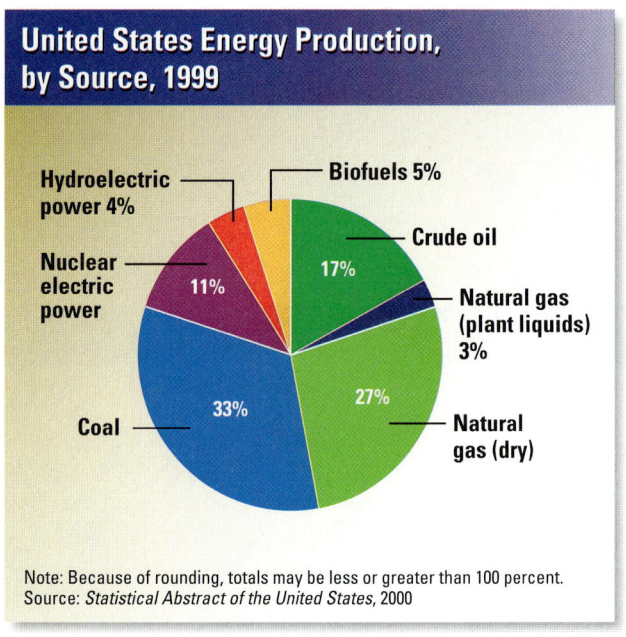

Note: Because of rounding, totals may be less or greater than 100 percent.
Source: *Statistical Abstract of the United States*, 2000

Mineral Fuels, Exports and Imports, 2000

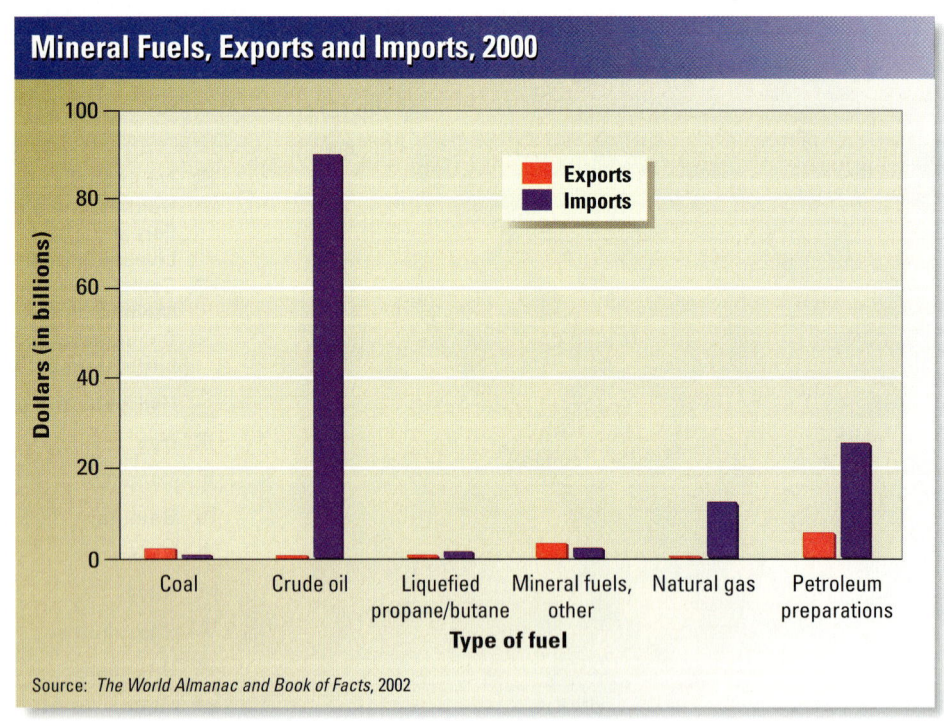

Source: *The World Almanac and Book of Facts*, 2002

534 Economic Atlas and Databank

Number of Farms

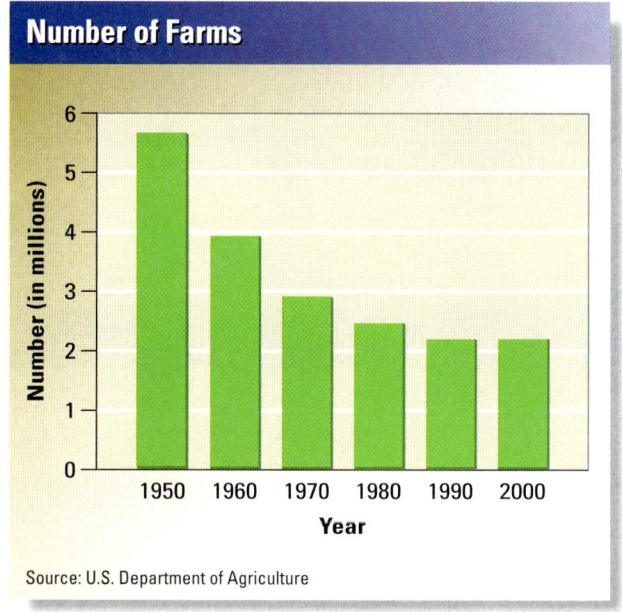

Source: U.S. Department of Agriculture

Size of Farms

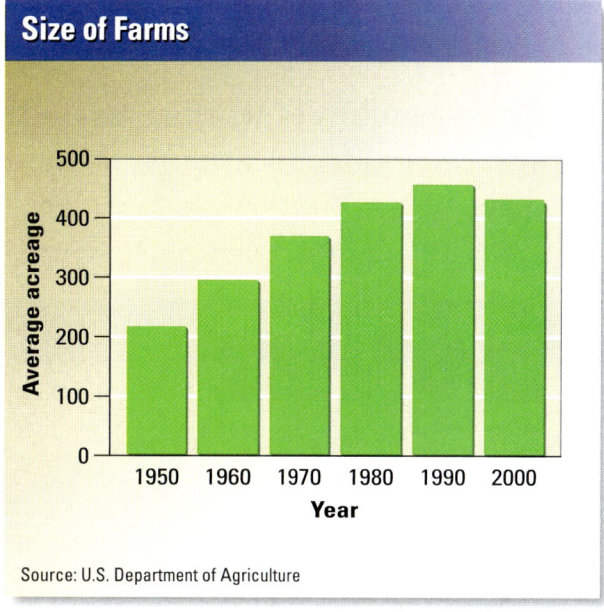

Source: U.S. Department of Agriculture

Major Agricultural Exports and Imports, 2000

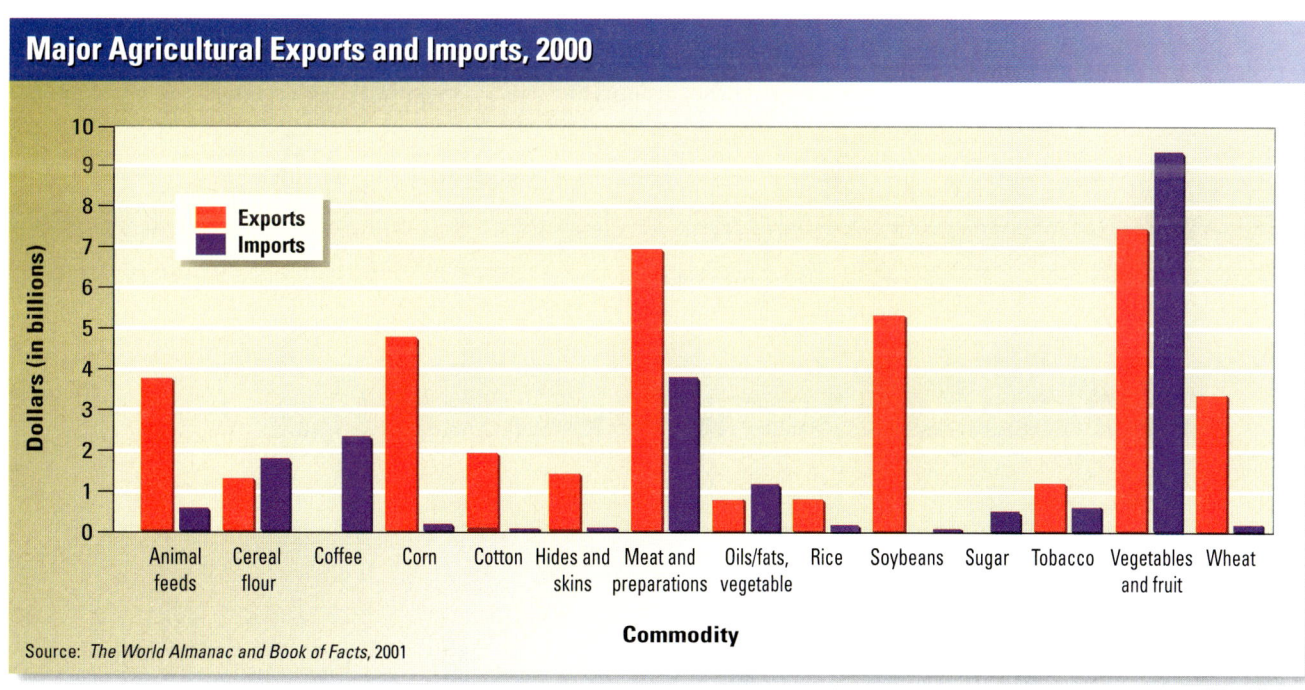

Source: *The World Almanac and Book of Facts*, 2001

ECONOMIC ATLAS and DATABANK

For periodic updates of the data included in the Databank, go to **www.phschool.com**

Americans at Work

Most full-time employees work an average of about 43 hours each week. On average, the more education a person has, the higher his or her hourly wage.

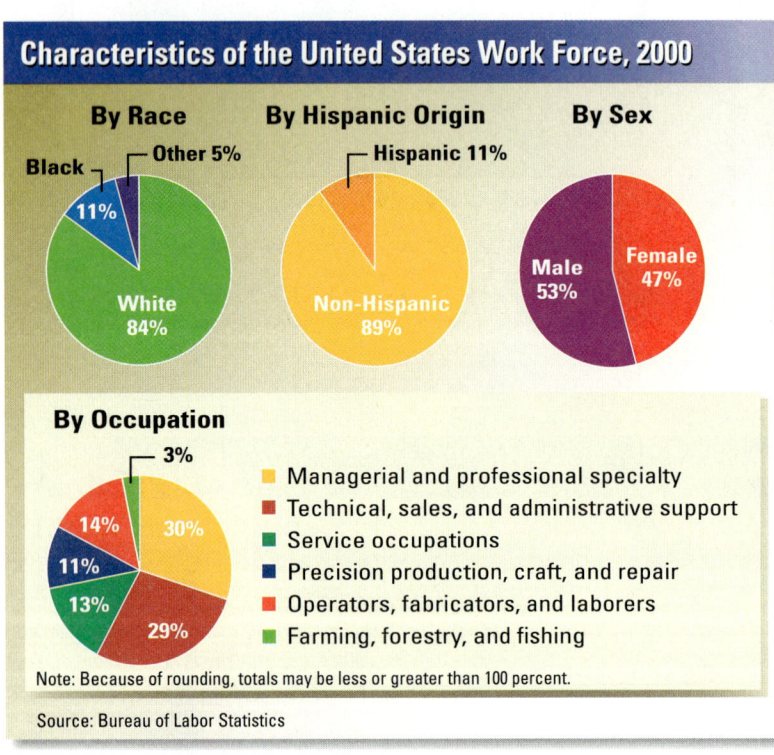

Characteristics of the United States Work Force, 2000

By Race
- Other 5%
- Black 11%
- White 84%

By Hispanic Origin
- Hispanic 11%
- Non-Hispanic 89%

By Sex
- Male 53%
- Female 47%

By Occupation
- 3%
- 30%
- 29%
- 13%
- 11%
- 14%

- Managerial and professional specialty
- Technical, sales, and administrative support
- Service occupations
- Precision production, craft, and repair
- Operators, fabricators, and laborers
- Farming, forestry, and fishing

Note: Because of rounding, totals may be less or greater than 100 percent.

Source: Bureau of Labor Statistics

Real Value of the Minimum Wage

Source: U.S. Department of Labor

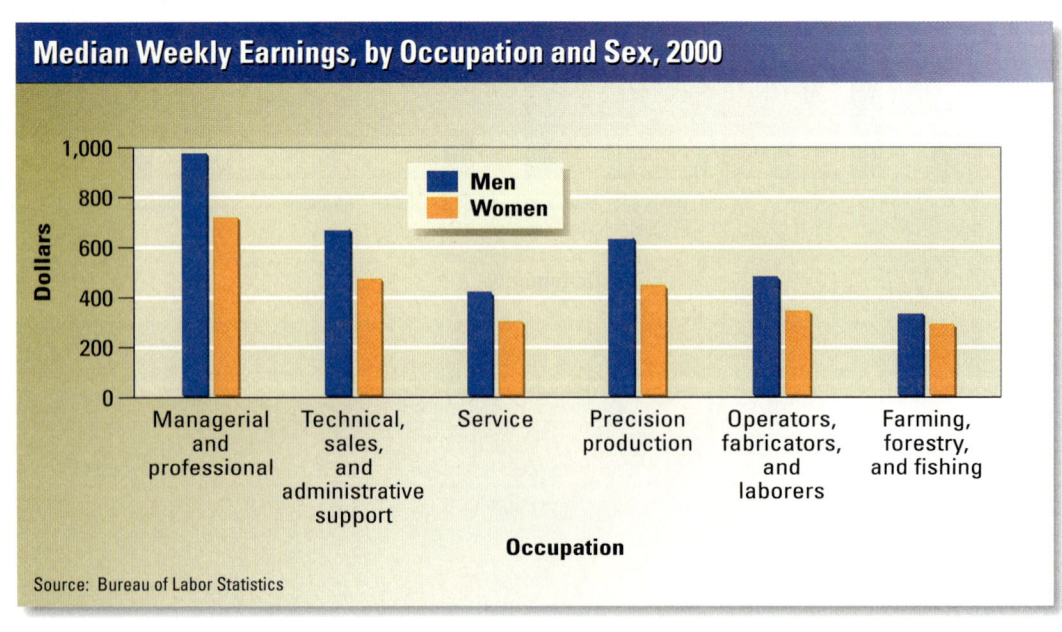

Median Weekly Earnings, by Occupation and Sex, 2000

Legend: Men, Women

Occupations: Managerial and professional; Technical, sales, and administrative support; Service; Precision production; Operators, fabricators, and laborers; Farming, forestry, and fishing

Source: Bureau of Labor Statistics

Average Real Hourly Wages, by Education Level, 1999

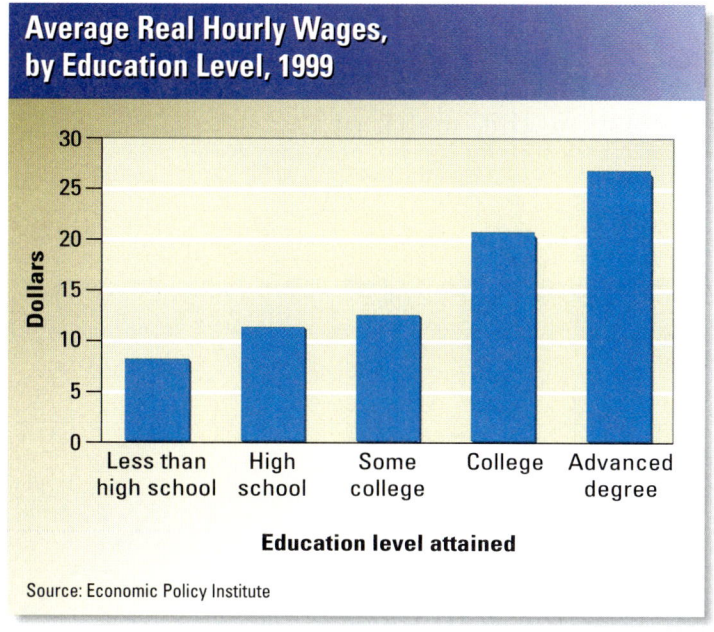

Source: Economic Policy Institute

Earnings Gap

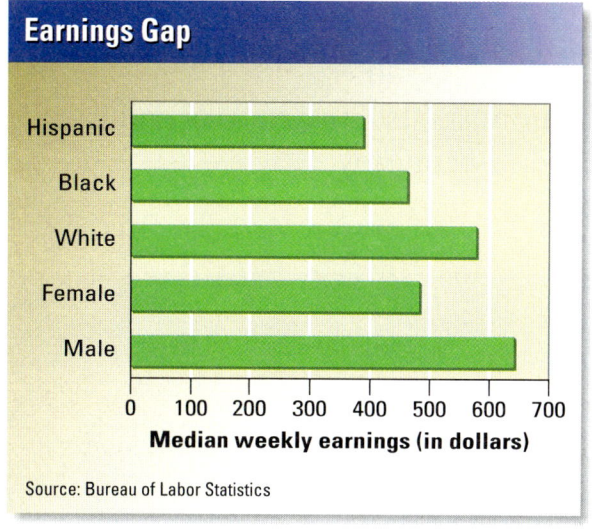

Source: Bureau of Labor Statistics

Fastest-Growing Occupations

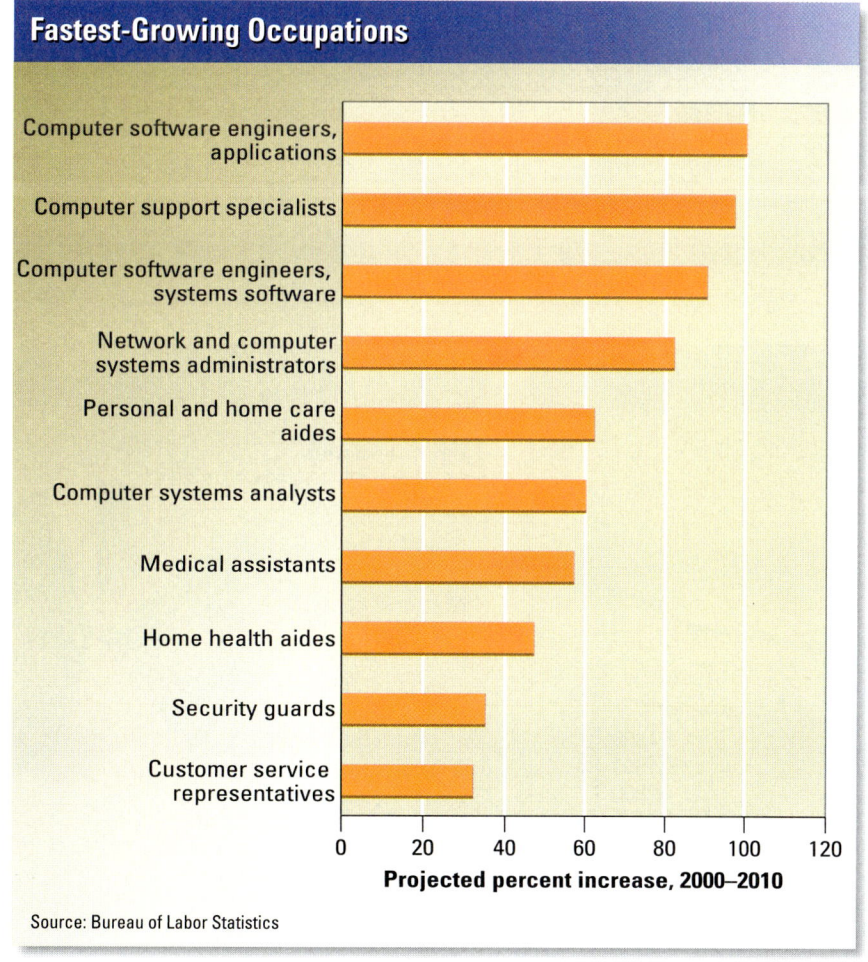

Source: Bureau of Labor Statistics

ECONOMIC ATLAS and DATABANK

Economic Indicators

Economists use a variety of indicators to determine the health of the nation's economy.

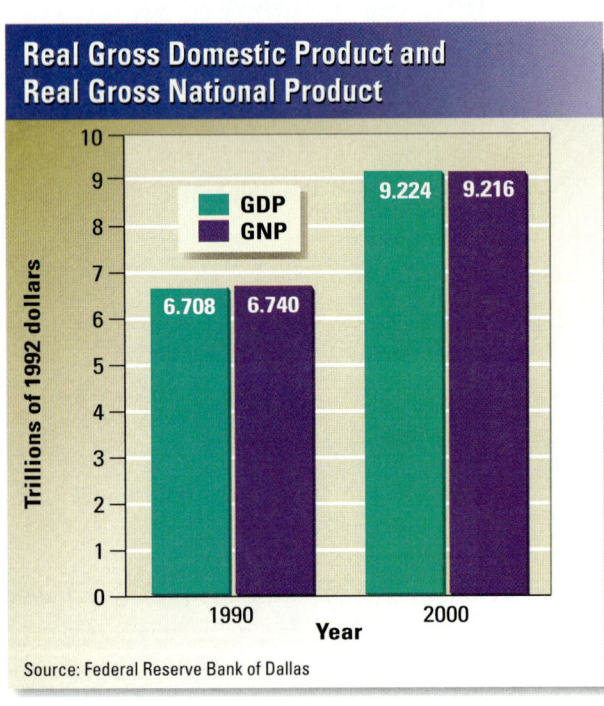

Real Gross Domestic Product and Real Gross National Product

- GDP
- GNP

1990: GDP 6.708, GNP 6.740
2000: GDP 9.224, GNP 9.216

Trillions of 1992 dollars

Year

Source: Federal Reserve Bank of Dallas

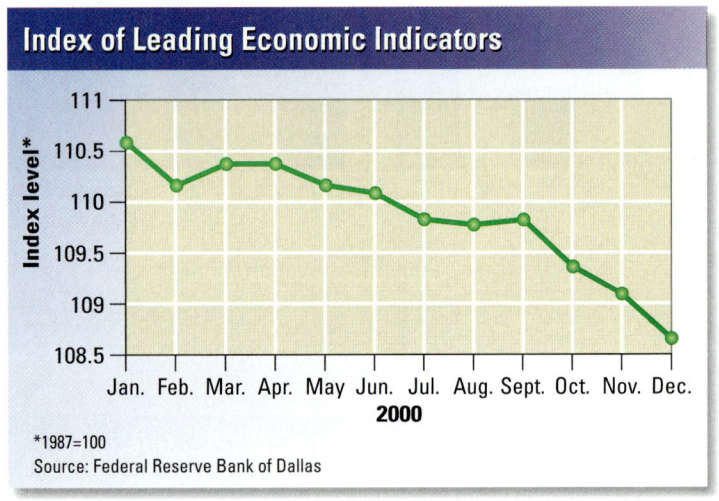

Index of Leading Economic Indicators

Index level*

Jan. Feb. Mar. Apr. May Jun. Jul. Aug. Sept. Oct. Nov. Dec.
2000

*1987=100
Source: Federal Reserve Bank of Dallas

Prentice Hall

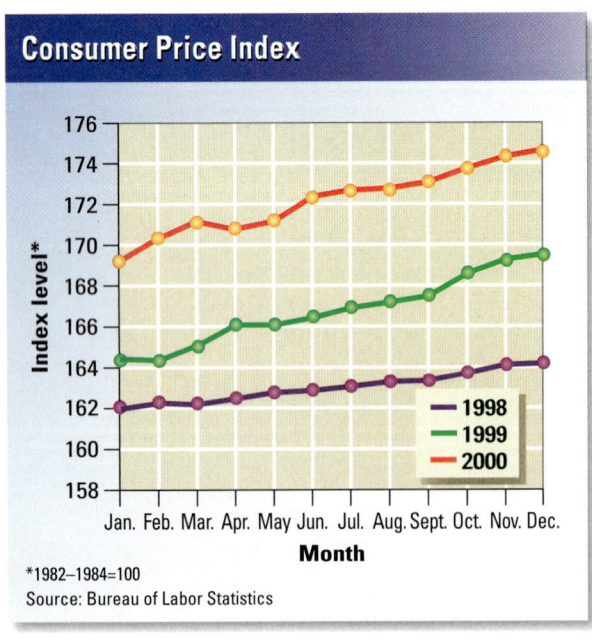

Consumer Price Index

Index level*

Jan. Feb. Mar. Apr. May Jun. Jul. Aug. Sept. Oct. Nov. Dec.
Month

- 1998
- 1999
- 2000

*1982–1984=100
Source: Bureau of Labor Statistics

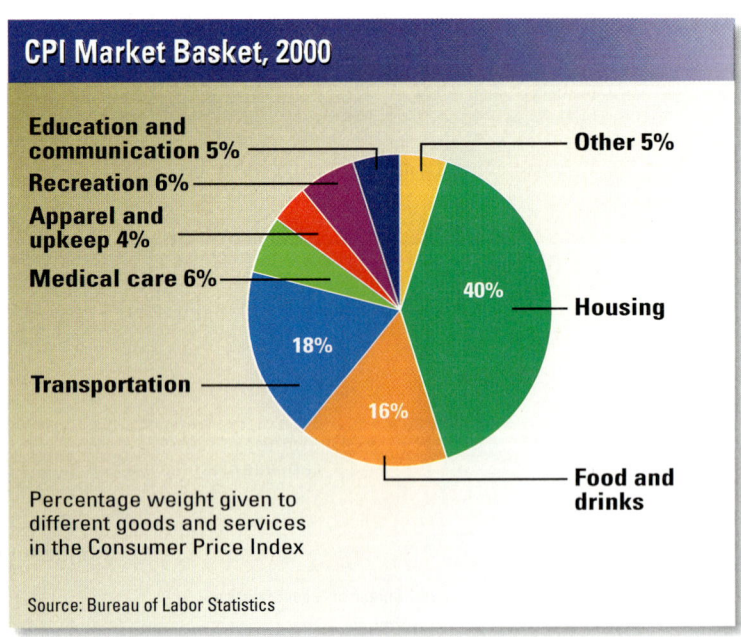

CPI Market Basket, 2000

- Education and communication 5%
- Recreation 6%
- Apparel and upkeep 4%
- Medical care 6%
- Transportation 18%
- Other 5%
- Housing 40%
- Food and drinks 16%

Percentage weight given to different goods and services in the Consumer Price Index

Source: Bureau of Labor Statistics

Retail Sales, by Type of Business, 2000

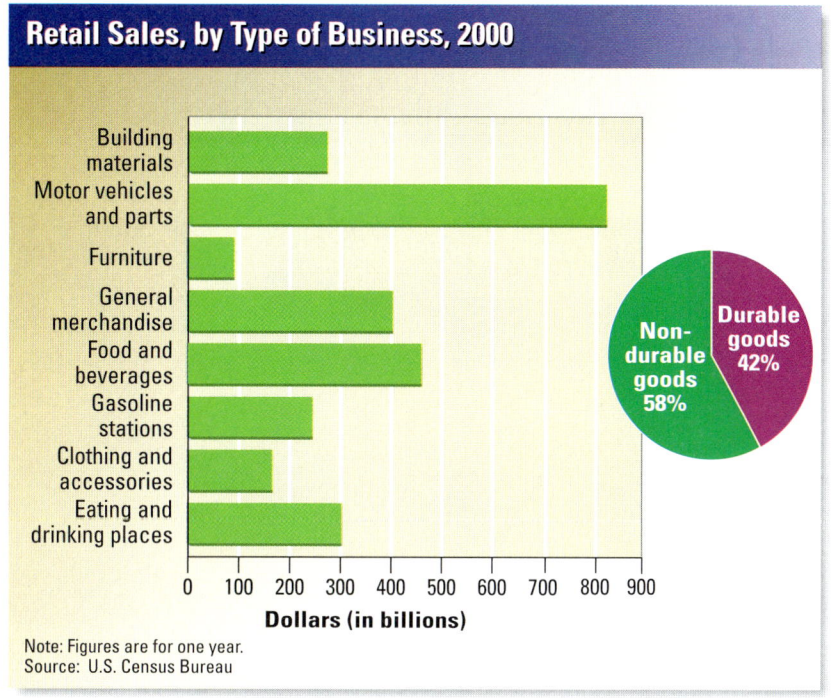

Building materials
Motor vehicles and parts
Furniture
General merchandise
Food and beverages
Gasoline stations
Clothing and accessories
Eating and drinking places

0   100   200   300   400   500   600   700   800   900

Dollars (in billions)

Non-durable goods 58%

Durable goods 42%

Note: Figures are for one year.
Source: U.S. Census Bureau

Housing Starts

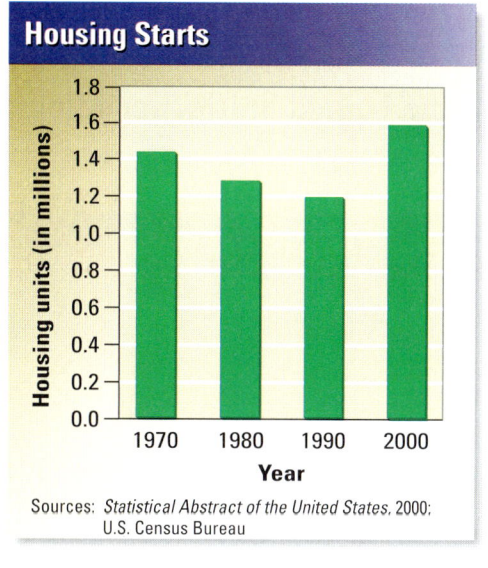

1.8
1.6
1.4
1.2
1.0
0.8
0.6
0.4
0.2
0.0

Housing units (in millions)

1970   1980   1990   2000

Year

Sources: *Statistical Abstract of the United States,* 2000;
U.S. Census Bureau

Producer Price Index

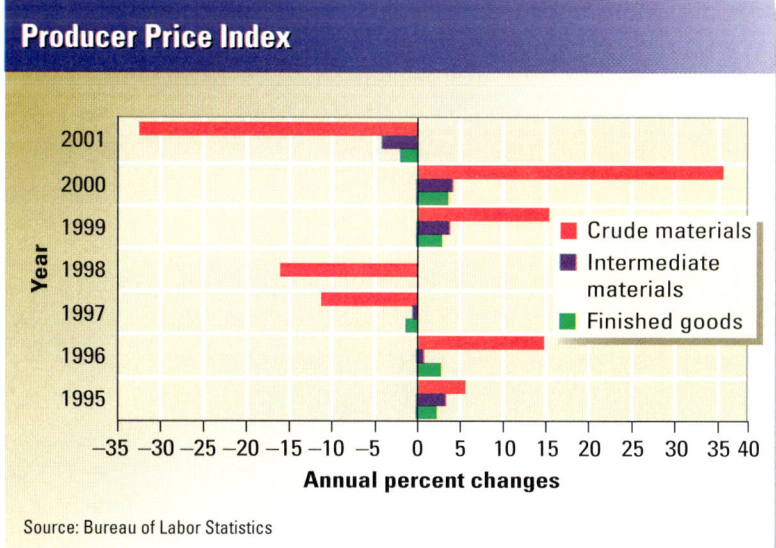

2001
2000
1999
1998
1997
1996
1995

Year

−35 −30 −25 −20 −15 −10 −5 0 5 10 15 20 25 30 35 40

Annual percent changes

- Crude materials
- Intermediate materials
- Finished goods

Source: Bureau of Labor Statistics

Consumer Confidence Index

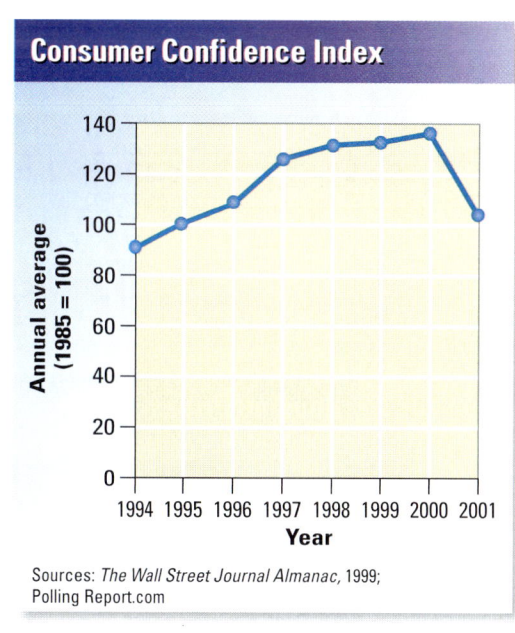

140
120
100
80
60
40
20
0

**Annual average
(1985 = 100)**

1994 1995 1996 1997 1998 1999 2000 2001

Year

Sources: *The Wall Street Journal Almanac,* 1999;
Polling Report.com

ECONOMIC ATLAS and DATABANK

For periodic updates of the data included in the Databank, go to **www.phschool.com**

The American Consumer

In the United States, spending and debt are on the rise while savings dwindle.

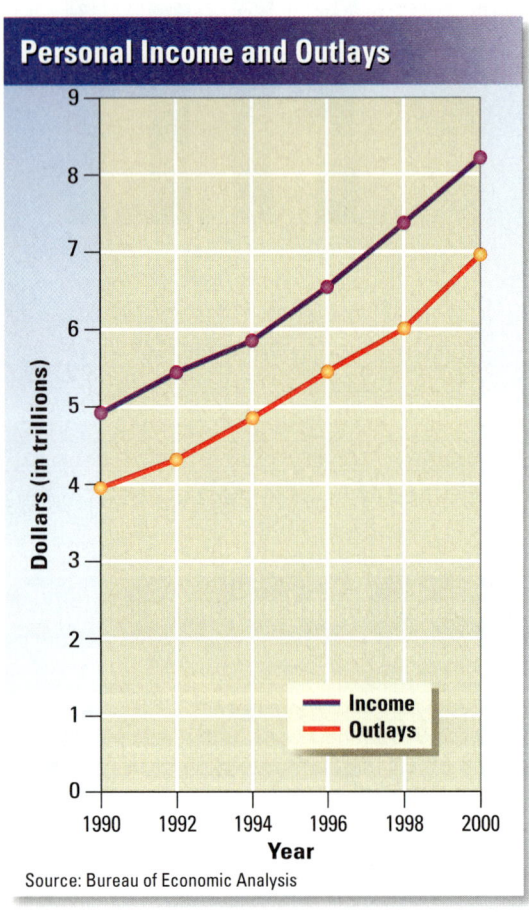

Personal Income and Outlays

Dollars (in trillions) vs Year (1990–2000)

Legend: Income, Outlays

Source: Bureau of Economic Analysis

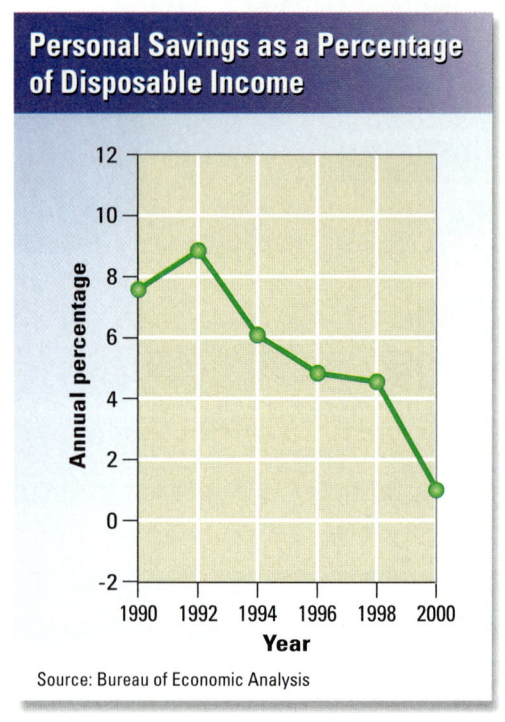

Personal Savings as a Percentage of Disposable Income

Annual percentage vs Year (1990–2000)

Source: Bureau of Economic Analysis

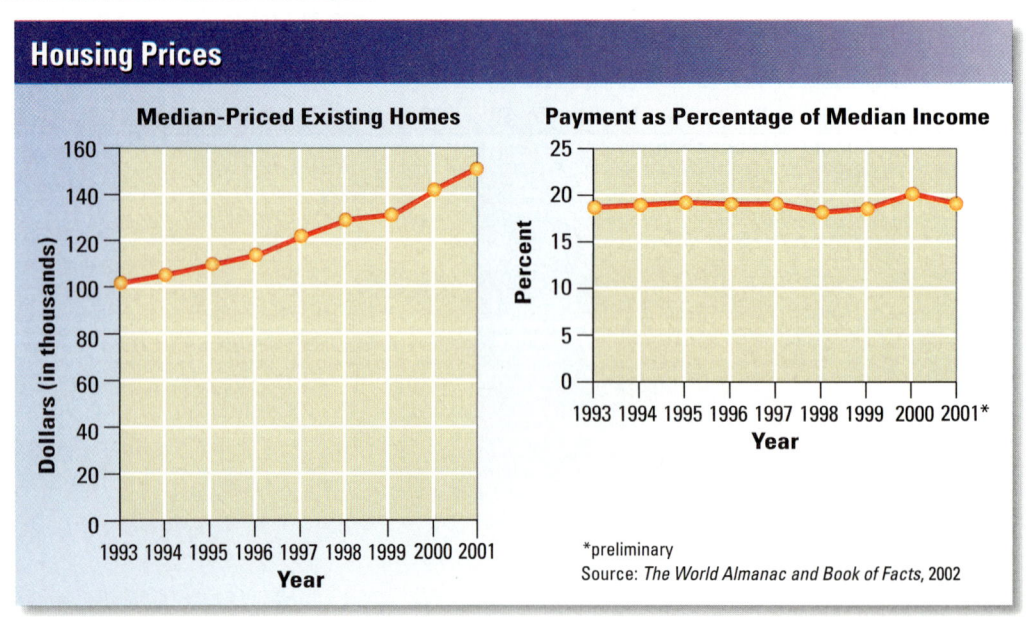

Housing Prices

Median-Priced Existing Homes

Dollars (in thousands) vs Year (1993–2001)

Payment as Percentage of Median Income

Percent vs Year (1993–2001*)

*preliminary

Source: *The World Almanac and Book of Facts*, 2002

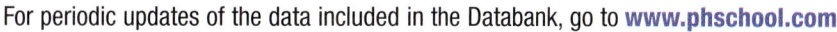 For periodic updates of the data included in the Databank, go to **www.phschool.com**

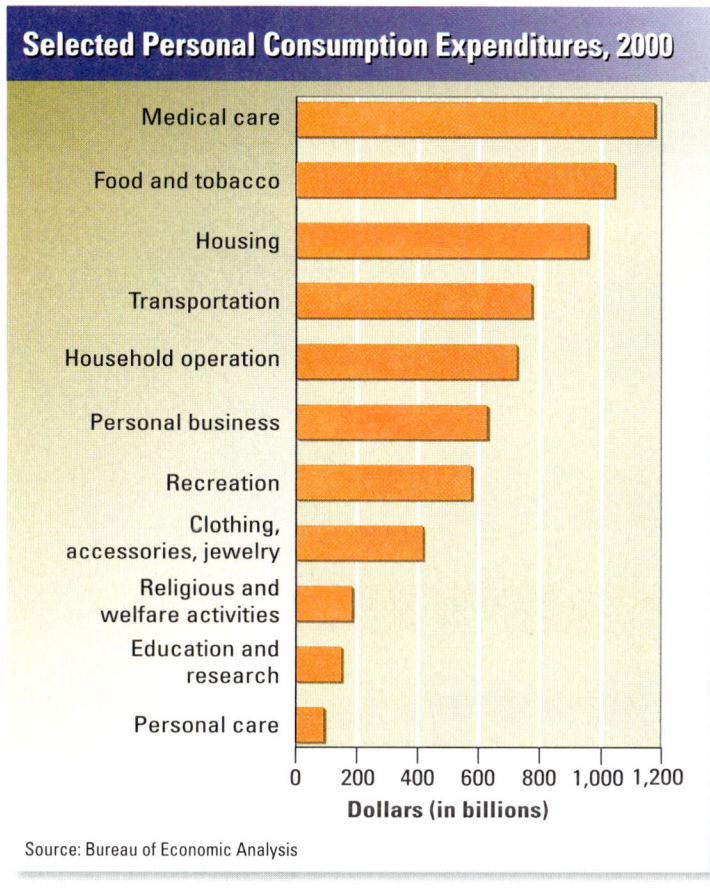

Selected Personal Consumption Expenditures, 2000

Medical care

Food and tobacco

Housing

Transportation

Household operation

Personal business

Recreation

Clothing, accessories, jewelry

Religious and welfare activities

Education and research

Personal care

Dollars (in billions)
0   200   400   600   800   1,000   1,200

Source: Bureau of Economic Analysis

Consumer Credit Debt

Dollars (in billions)
1,600
1,400
1,200
1,000
800
600
400
200
0

Year
1990 1991 1992 1993 1994 1995 1996 1997 1998 1999 2000

Source: Government Printing Office

Per Capita Energy Consumption, 1999

Rank	State	Btu (in millions)
1	Hawaii	203.7
2	New York	235.4
3	California	252.7
4	Massachusetts	254.1
5	Florida	255.0
6	Arizona	255.3
7	Connecticut	255.7
8	Rhode Island	263.5
9	Maryland	266.5
10	Vermont	277.9
11	New Hampshire	279.2
12	Colorado	284.9
13	Pennsylvania	309.8
14	New Jersey	317.9
15	North Carolina	319.8
16	Illinois	320.1
17	Missouri	323.3
18	Virginia	324.1
19	Utah	325.8
20	South Dakota	326.0
21	Michigan	328.4
22	Oregon	334.5
23	Nevada	340.1
24	Wisconsin	344.8
25	Minnesota	350.8
26	Georgia	359.3
27	Nebraska	361.3
28	New Mexico	365.0
29	Delaware	370.0
30	Tennessee	377.6
31	Ohio	384.1
32	South Carolina	384.2
33	Washington	389.3
34	Iowa	390.9
35	Kansas	395.6
36	West Virginia	407.0
37	Oklahoma	410.2
38	Idaho	414.1
39	Maine	421.9
40	Mississippi	436.5
41	Alabama	458.8
42	Indiana	460.3
43	Kentucky	462.1
44	Montana	467.1
45	Arkansas	471.8
46	Texas	573.8
47	North Dakota	577.1
48	Louisiana	826.9
49	Wyoming	879.4
50	Alaska	1,121.5

Source: U.S. Department of Energy

ECONOMIC ATLAS and DATABANK

The United States Government

The government raises and spends trillions of dollars each year.

Federal Deficit/Surplus

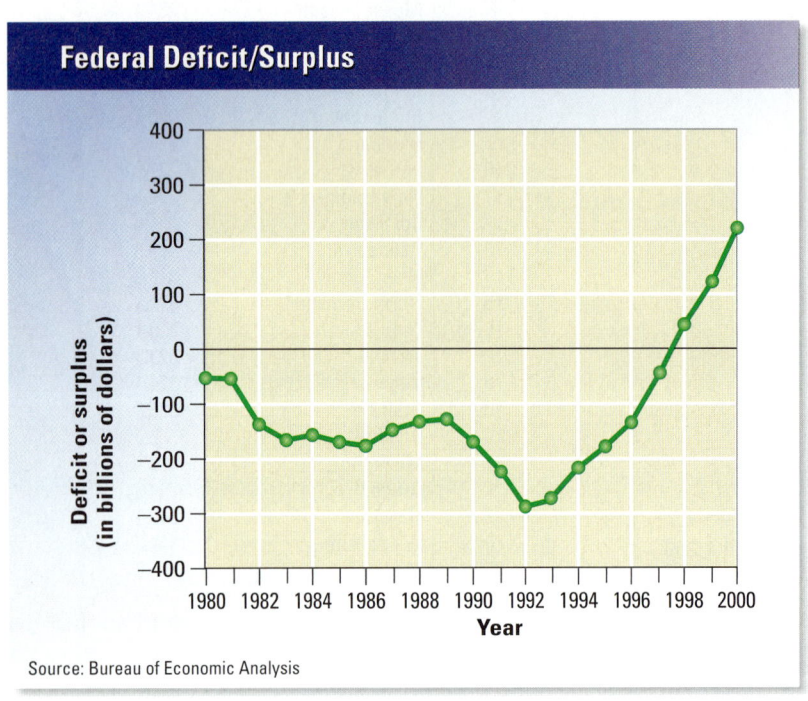

Source: Bureau of Economic Analysis

Income Taxes per Capita

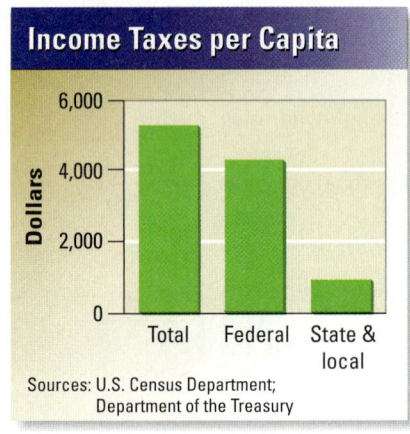

Sources: U.S. Census Department;
Department of the Treasury

Key Interest Rates

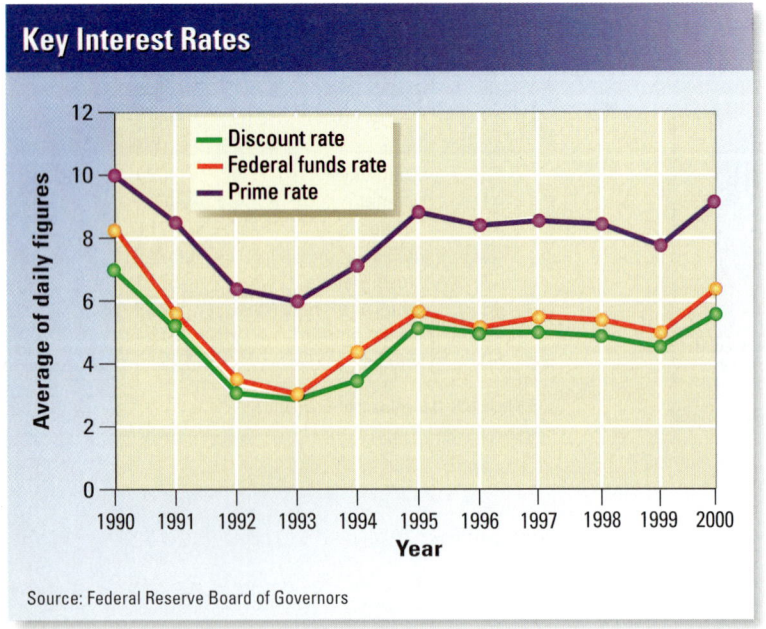

Source: Federal Reserve Board of Governors

Federal Debt

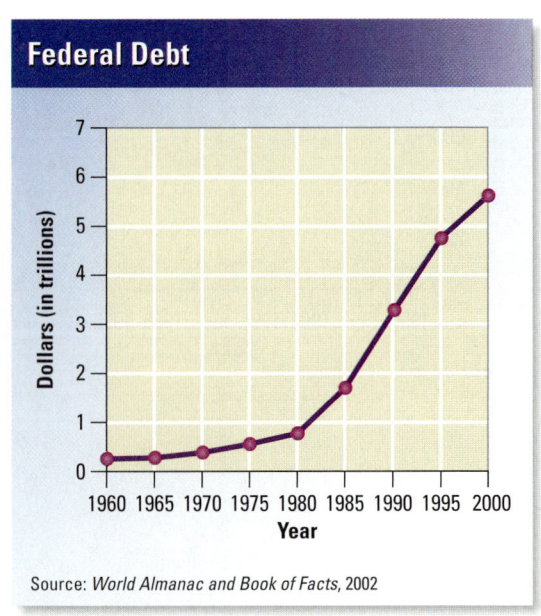

Source: *World Almanac and Book of Facts*, 2002

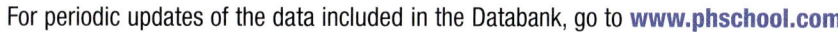

For periodic updates of the data included in the Databank, go to **www.phschool.com**

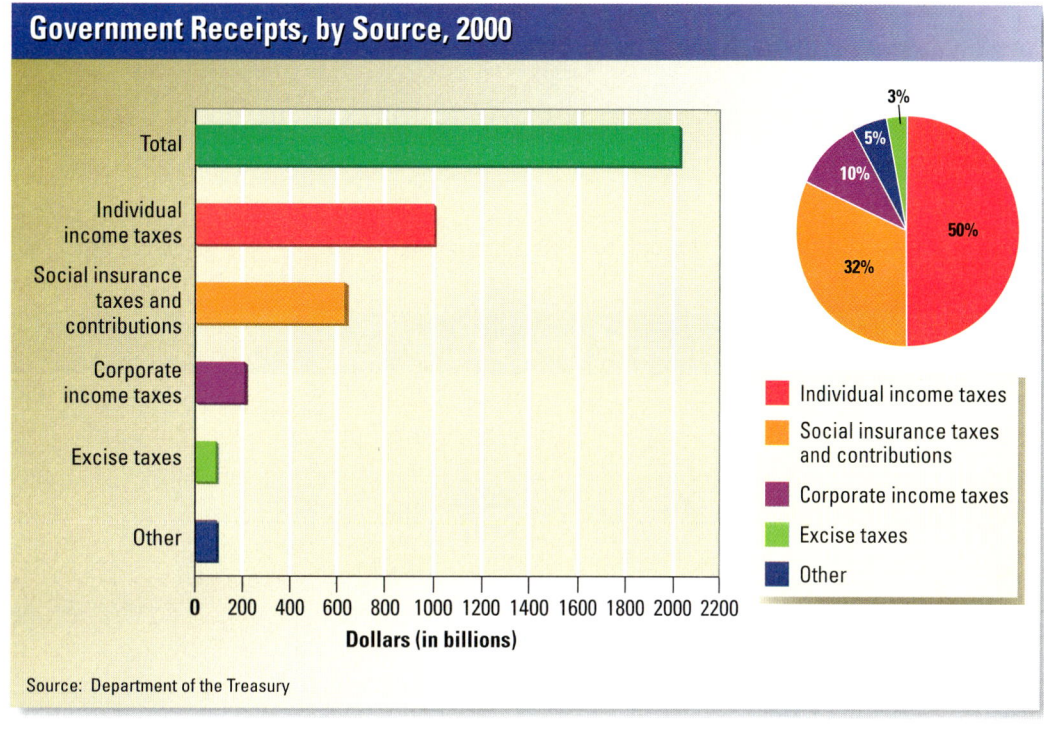

Government Receipts, by Source, 2000

Total

Individual income taxes

Social insurance taxes and contributions

Corporate income taxes

Excise taxes

Other

0 200 400 600 800 1000 1200 1400 1600 1800 2000 2200

Dollars (in billions)

50%
32%
10%
5%
3%

- Individual income taxes
- Social insurance taxes and contributions
- Corporate income taxes
- Excise taxes
- Other

Source: Department of the Treasury

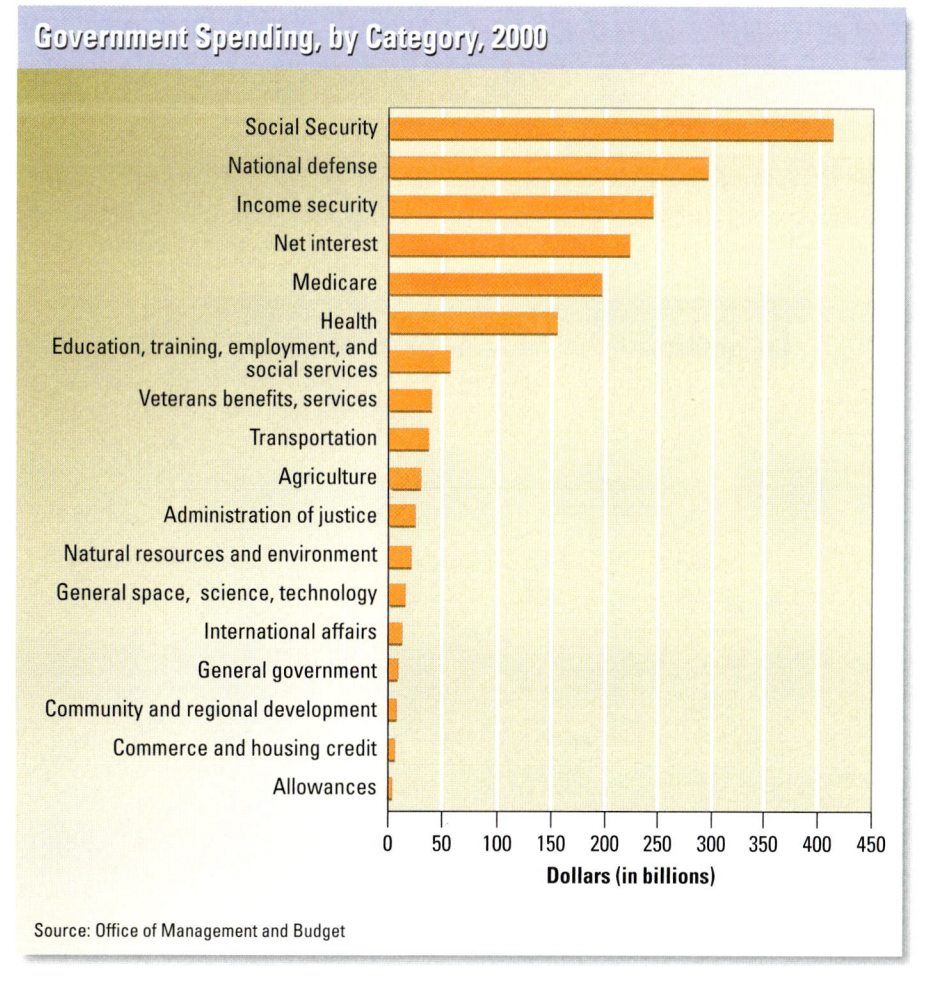

Government Spending, by Category, 2000

Social Security
National defense
Income security
Net interest
Medicare
Health
Education, training, employment, and social services
Veterans benefits, services
Transportation
Agriculture
Administration of justice
Natural resources and environment
General space, science, technology
International affairs
General government
Community and regional development
Commerce and housing credit
Allowances

0 50 100 150 200 250 300 350 400 450

Dollars (in billions)

Source: Office of Management and Budget

ECONOMIC ATLAS and DATABANK

Economic Atlas and Databank **543**

For periodic updates of the data included in the Databank, go to **www.phschool.com**

Trade

The United States is a major player in the world market. In recent years, however, it has imported more than it has exported, resulting in an annual trade deficit.

U.S. Exports and Imports, by Major Trading Partners, 2000

Dollars (in billions) — vertical axis: 0, 20, 40, 60, 80, 100, 120, 140, 160, 180, 200, 220, 240

Legend: Exports / Imports

Countries: Canada, Mexico, Japan, United Kingdom, Germany, South Korea, Taiwan, Netherlands, Singapore, France, China

Country

Source: *The World Almanac and Book of Facts*, 2001

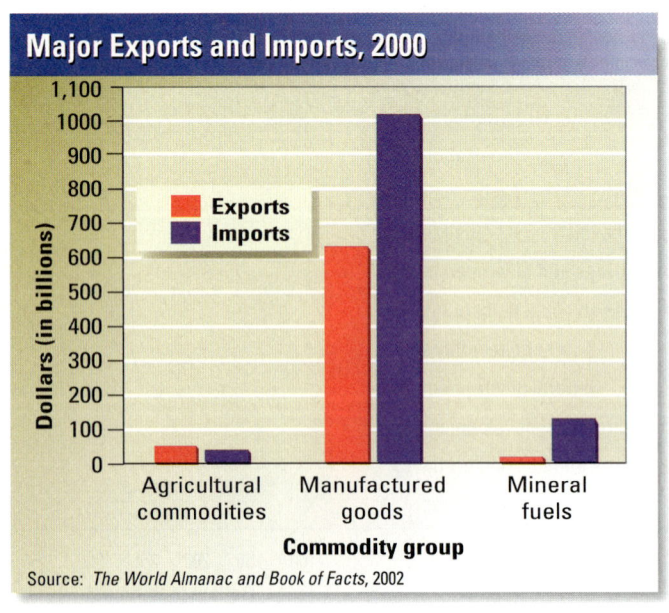

Major Exports and Imports, 2000

Dollars (in billions) — vertical axis: 0, 100, 200, 300, 400, 500, 600, 700, 800, 900, 1000, 1,100

Legend: Exports / Imports

Commodity group: Agricultural commodities, Manufactured goods, Mineral fuels

Source: *The World Almanac and Book of Facts*, 2002

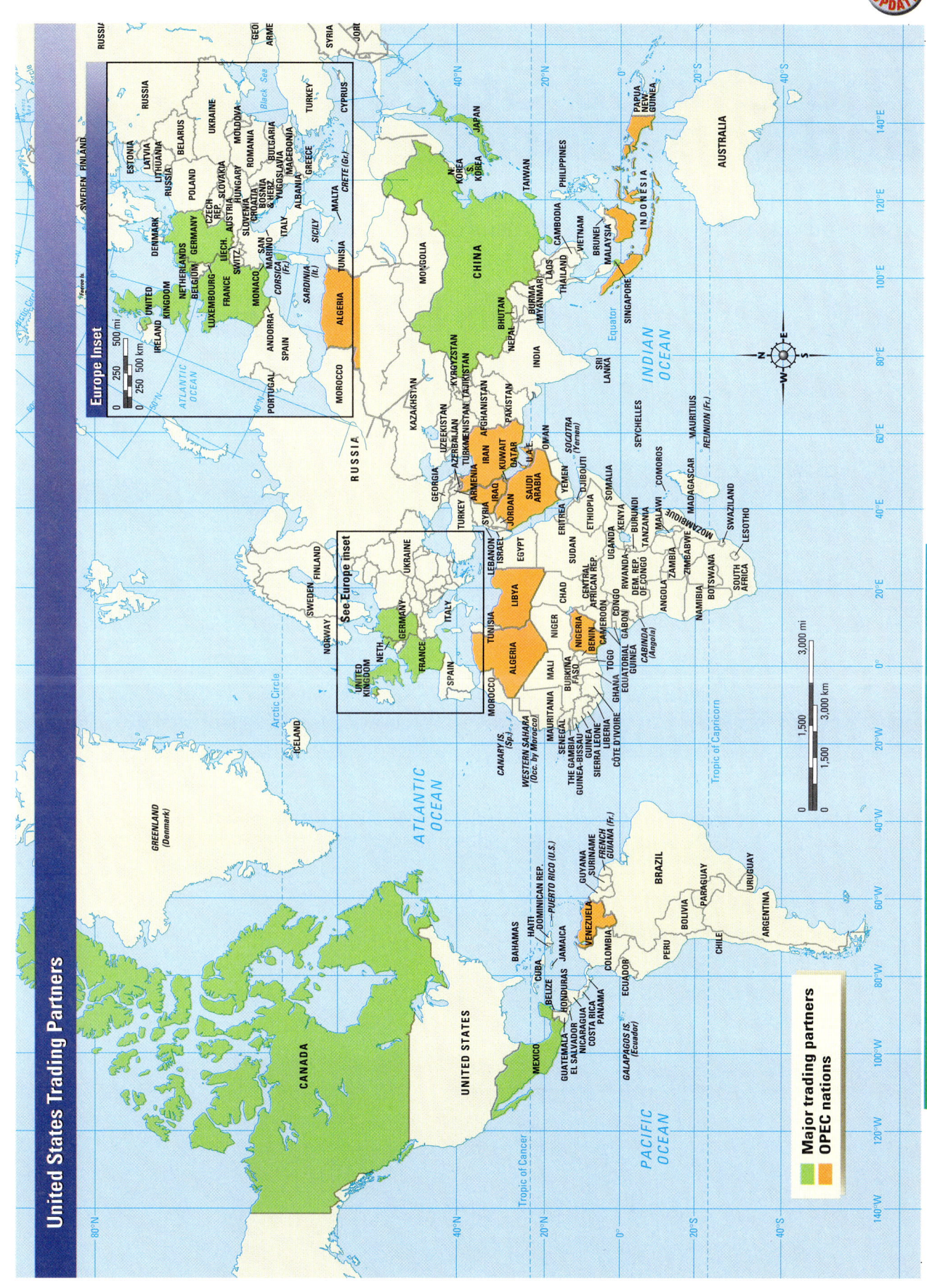

United States Trading Partners

Major trading partners
OPEC nations

Europe Inset

500 mi
250
0
500 km
250
0

See Europe inset

3,000 mi
1,500
0
3,000 km
1,500
0

ECONOMIC ATLAS and DATABANK

The United States and the World

The United States enjoys one of the highest standards of living in the world and one of the lowest tax burdens of the industrialized nations.

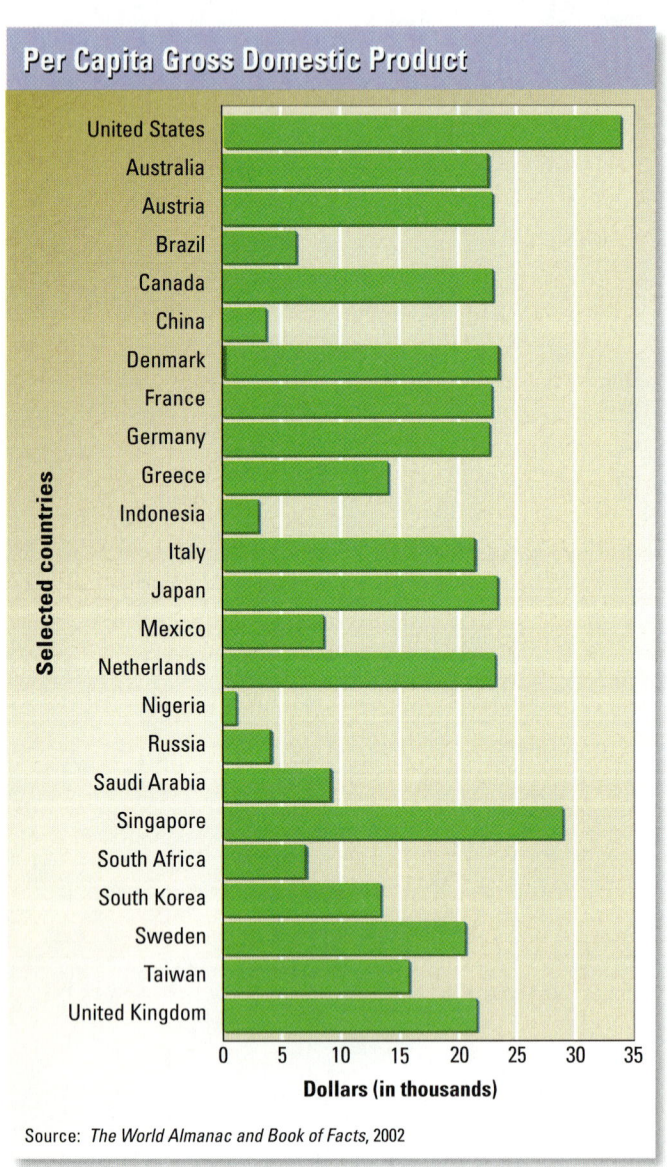

Per Capita Gross Domestic Product

Selected countries: United States, Australia, Austria, Brazil, Canada, China, Denmark, France, Germany, Greece, Indonesia, Italy, Japan, Mexico, Netherlands, Nigeria, Russia, Saudi Arabia, Singapore, South Africa, South Korea, Sweden, Taiwan, United Kingdom

Dollars (in thousands)

Source: *The World Almanac and Book of Facts*, 2002

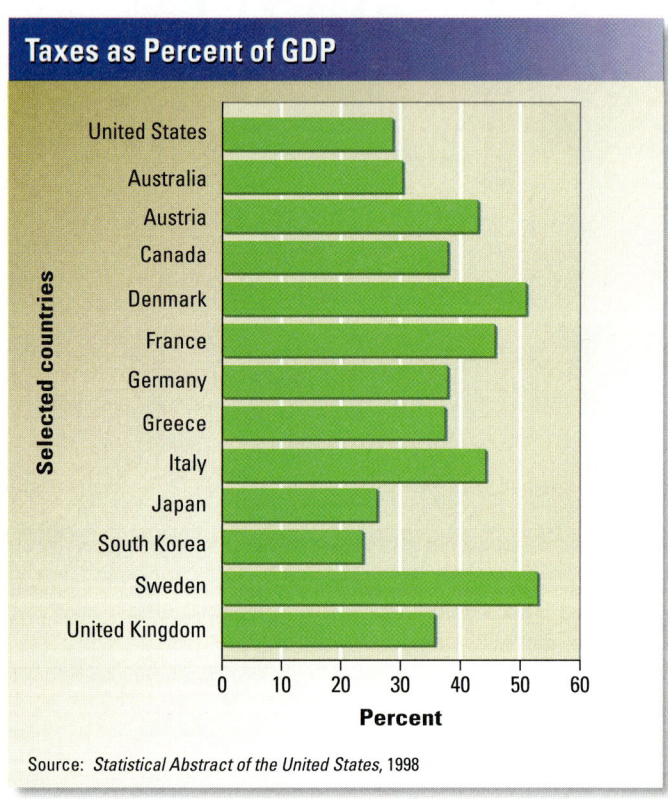

Taxes as Percent of GDP

Selected countries: United States, Australia, Austria, Canada, Denmark, France, Germany, Greece, Italy, Japan, South Korea, Sweden, United Kingdom

Percent

Source: *Statistical Abstract of the United States*, 1998

For periodic updates of the data included in the Databank, go to **www.phschool.com**

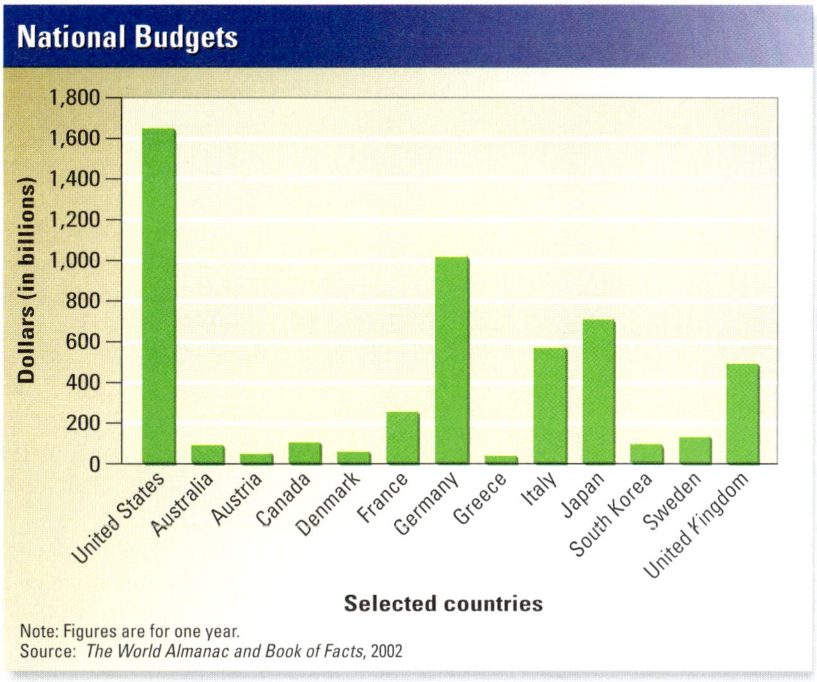
National Budgets
Dollars (in billions)
1,800
1,600
1,400
1,200
1,000
800
600
400
200
0
United States
Australia
Austria
Canada
Denmark
France
Germany
Greece
Italy
Japan
South Korea
Sweden
United Kingdom
Selected countries
Note: Figures are for one year.
Source: The World Almanac and Book of Facts, 2002

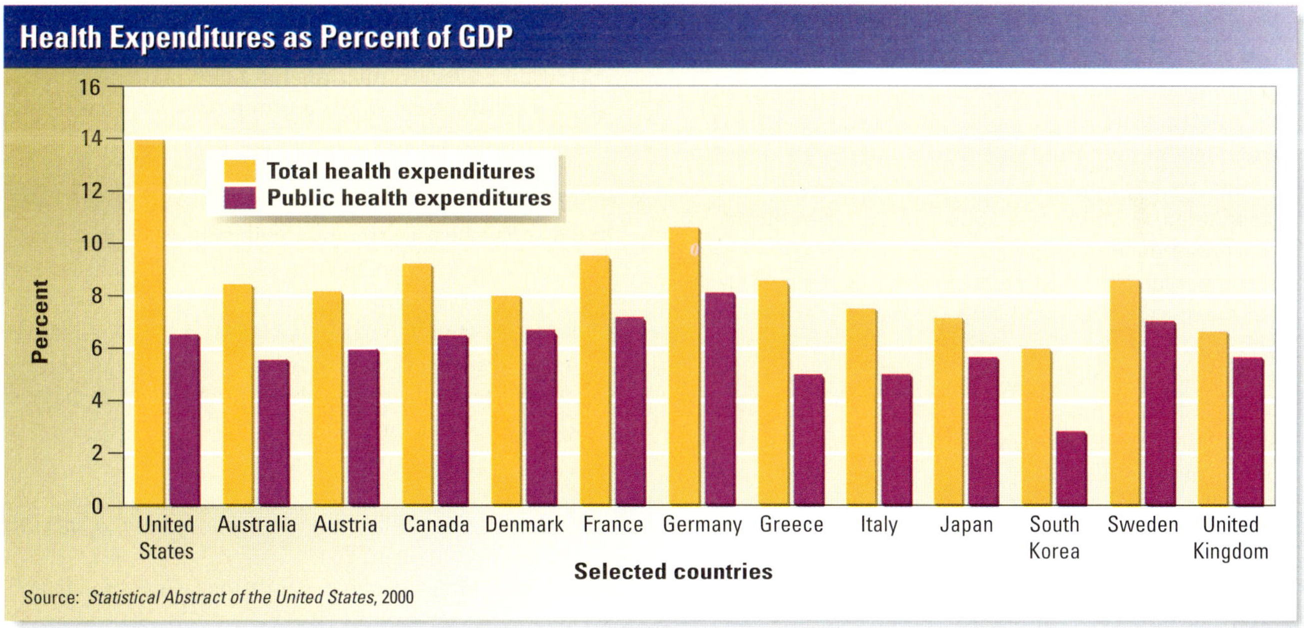
Health Expenditures as Percent of GDP
Percent
16
14
12
10
8
6
4
2
0
Total health expenditures
Public health expenditures
United States
Australia
Austria
Canada
Denmark
France
Germany
Greece
Italy
Japan
South Korea
Sweden
United Kingdom
Selected countries
Source: Statistical Abstract of the United States, 2000

ECONOMIC ATLAS and DATABANK

Glossary

A

absolute advantage the ability to produce more of a given product using a given amount of resources (p. 443)

aggregate demand the amount of goods and services in the economy that will be purchased at all possible price levels (p. 307)

aggregate supply the total amount of goods and services in the economy available at all possible price levels (p. 307)

annual percentage rate (APR) a finance charge expressed as an annual rate (p. 514)

antitrust laws laws that encourage competition in the marketplace (p. 173)

appreciation an increase in the value of a currency (p. 459)

appropriations bill a bill that sets money aside for specific spending (p. 389)

arable suitable for producing crops (p. 480)

arbitration a settlement technique in which a third party reviews the case and imposes a decision that is legally binding for both sides (p. 234)

articles of partnership a partnership agreement (p. 191)

assets money and other valuables belonging to an individual or business (p. 192)

authoritarian requiring strict obedience to an authority, such as a dictator (p. 35)

automatic stabilizer a government program that changes automatically depending on GDP and a person's income (p. 399)

B

balanced budget budget in which revenues are equal to spending (pp. 376, 403)

balance of trade the relationship between a nation's imports and exports (p. 462)

bank an institution for receiving, keeping, and lending money (p. 250)

bank holding company a company that owns more than one bank (p. 421)

bank run widespread panic in which great numbers of people try to redeem their paper money (p. 252)

barrier to entry any factor that makes it difficult for a new firm to enter a market (p. 153)

barter the direct exchange of one set of goods or services for another (p. 243)

bear market a steady drop in the stock market over a period of time (p. 290)

black market a market in which goods are sold illegally (p. 142)

block grant federal funds given to states in lump sums (p. 350)

blue-collar worker someone who works in an industrial job, often in manufacturing, and who receives wages (p. 231)

Board of Governors the seven-member board that oversees the Federal Reserve System (p. 416)

bond a formal contract to repay borrowed money with interest at fixed intervals (pp. 197, 507)

brokerage firm a business that specializes in trading stocks (p. 287)

budget a plan for saving and spending (p. 502)

budget deficit a situation in which the government spends more than it takes in (p. 403)

budget surplus a situation in which the government takes in more than it spends (p. 403)

bull market a steady rise in the stock market over a period of time (p. 290)

business association nonprofit organization that promotes collective business interests for a city, state, or other geographical area, or for a group of similar businesses (p. 204)

business cycle a period of macroeconomic expansion followed by a period of contraction (pp. 57, 310)

business franchise a semi-independent business that pays fees to a parent company in return for the exclusive right to sell a certain product or service in a given area (p. 201)

business license authorization to start a business issued by the local government (p. 186)

business organization an establishment formed to carry on commercial enterprise (p. 185)

C

call option the option to buy shares of stock at a specified time in the future (p. 288)

capital any human-made resource that is used to create other goods or services (p. 4)

capital budget budget for major capital, or investment, expenditures (p. 375)

capital deepening process of increasing the amount of capital per worker (p. 320)

capital gain the difference between a higher selling price and a lower purchase price, resulting in a financial gain for the seller (pp. 286, 508)

capital loss the difference between a lower selling price and a higher purchase price, resulting in a financial loss for the seller (p. 286)

capital market market in which money is lent for periods longer than a year (p. 283)

cartel a formal organization of producers that agree to coordinate prices and production (p. 171)

cash transfers direct payments of money to eligible poor people (p. 69)

census an official count of the population (p. 334)

central bank bank that can lend to other banks in times of need (p. 254)

centrally planned economy economic system in which the central government makes all decisions on the production and consumption of goods and services (p. 27)

certificate of incorporation license to form a corporation issued by state government (p. 197)

ceteris paribus a Latin phrase that means "all other things held constant" (p. 85)

check clearing the process by which banks record whose account gives up money and whose account receives money when a customer writes a check (p. 421)

check register a booklet used to record checking account transactions (p. 504)

classical economics the idea that free markets can regulate themselves (p. 395)

closely held corporation corporation that issues stock to only a few people, often family members (p. 196)

collateral property used to secure a loan (p. 513)

collective large farm leased from the state to groups of peasant farmers (p. 36)

collective bargaining the process in which union and company representatives meet to negotiate a new labor contract (p. 233)

collusion an agreement among firms to divide the market, set prices, or limit production (p. 171)

command economy economic system in which the central government makes all decisions on the production and consumption of goods and services (p. 27)

commercial bank a bank that provides checking accounts, savings accounts, and money market accounts and that accepts time deposits (p. 511)

commodity a product that is the same no matter who produces it, such as petroleum, notebook paper, or milk (p. 152)

commodity money objects that have value in themselves as well as for use as money (p. 246)

common stock stock whose dividends are based on market fluctuations (p. 508)

communism a political system characterized by a centrally planned economy with all economic and political power resting in the hands of the central government (p. 35)

comparative advantage the ability to produce a product most efficiently given all the other products that could be produced (p. 444)

competition the struggle among producers for the dollars of consumers; the rivalry among sellers to attract customers while lowering costs (pp. 31, 53)

complements two goods that are bought and used together (p. 88)

conglomerate business combination merging more than three businesses that make unrelated products (p. 199)

Congressional Budget Office (CBO) government agency that provides economic data to Congress (p. 388)

consumer cooperative retail outlet owned and operated by consumers (p. 203)

Consumer Price Index (CPI) a price index determined by measuring the price of a standard group of goods meant to represent the typical "market basket" of a typical urban consumer (p. 339)

consumer sovereignty the power of consumers to decide what gets produced (p. 32)

contingent employment temporary jobs or part-time jobs (p. 215)

continuum a range with no clear divisions (p. 43)

contract a binding legal agreement (p. 523)

contraction period of economic decline marked by falling real GDP (p. 310)

contractionary policies fiscal policies, like lower spending and higher taxes, that reduce economic growth (p. 389)

cooperative a business organization owned and operated by a group of individuals for their mutual benefit (p. 202)

copayment part of the cost of a medical visit or procedure that the patient must pay out of pocket (p. 525)

core inflation rate the rate of inflation excluding the effects of food and energy prices (p. 340)

corporate bond a bond that a corporation issues to raise money in order to expand its business (p. 281)

corporate income tax a tax on the value of a corporation's profits (p. 360)

corporation a legal entity owned by individual stockholders (p. 195)

cost to an economist, cost is an alternative that is given up as the result of a decision (p. 16)

cost-push theory theory that inflation occurs when producers raise prices to meet increased costs (p. 341)

Council of Economic Advisers (CEA) a group of three respected economists that could advise the President on economic policy (p. 400)

coupon rate the interest rate that a bond issuer will pay to a bondholder (p. 277)

credit any form of deferred payment (p. 512)

credit bureau organization providing information on individuals' borrowing and bill-paying habits (p. 512)

credit card a card entitling its holder to buy goods and services based on the holder's promise to pay for these goods and services (p. 261)

creditor person or institution to whom money is owed (p. 264)

credit rating an evaluation made by credit bureaus of a borrower's overall credit history (p. 512)

credit union nonprofit bank owned by its members, often members of a single organization or trade union (p. 511)

crowding-out effect the loss of funds for private investment due to government borrowing (p. 406)

currency coins and paper bills used as money (p. 245)

customs duty a tax on certain items purchased abroad (p. 450)

cyclical unemployment unemployment that rises during economic downturns and falls when the economy improves (p. 333)

D

debit card a card used to withdraw money (p. 263)

debt rescheduling lengthening the time of debt repayment and forgiving, or dismissing, part of the loan (p. 488)

deductible amount of expenses that must be paid out of pocket before an insurer will cover any expenses (p. 524)

deductions variable amounts that you can subtract, or deduct, from your gross income (p. 366)

default failure to pay back a loan (p. 261)

deflation a sustained drop in the price level (p. 343)

demand the desire to own something and the ability to pay for it (p. 79)

demand curve a graphic representation of a demand schedule (p. 82)

demand deposit the money in checking accounts (p. 258)

demand-pull theory theory that inflation occurs when demand for goods and services exceeds existing supplies (p. 341)

demand schedule a table that lists the quantity of a good a person will buy at each different price (p. 81)

demand-side economics a school of economics that believes government spending and tax cuts help an economy by raising demand (p. 396)

depreciation the loss of the value of capital equipment that results from normal wear and tear (pp. 305, 520), or, a decrease in the value of a currency (p. 459)

depression a recession that is especially long and severe (p. 311)

deregulation the removal of some government controls over a market (p. 175)

developed nation country with a higher average level of material well-being (p. 471)

development the process by which a nation improves the economic, political, and social well-being of its people (p. 471)

differentiation making a product different from other similar products (p. 167)

diminishing marginal returns a level of production in which the marginal product of labor decreases as the number of workers increases (p. 109)

discount rate rate the Federal Reserve charges for loans to commercial banks (p. 422)

discouraged worker a person who wants a job but has given up looking (p. 336)

discretionary spending spending category about which government planners can make choices (p. 371)

disequilibrium describes any price or quantity not at equilibrium; when quantity supplied is not equal to quantity demanded in a market (p. 126)

diversification spreading out investments to reduce risk (p. 273)

dividend the portion of corporate profits paid out to stockholders (pp. 198, 508)

The Dow index that shows how certain stocks have traded (p. 290)

durable goods goods that last for a relatively long time, such as refrigerators, cars, and DVD players (p. 302)

E

easy money policy monetary policy that increases the money supply (p. 431)

economic growth steady, long-term increase in real GDP (p. 310)

economics the study of how people seek to satisfy their needs and wants by making choices (p. 3)

economic system the method used by a society to produce and distribute goods and services (p. 23)

economies of scale factors that cause a producer's average cost per unit to fall as output rises (p. 157)

efficiency using resources in such a way as to maximize the production of goods and services (p. 15)

elastic describes demand that is very sensitive to a change in price (p. 90)

elasticity of demand a measure of how consumers react to a change in price (p. 90)

elasticity of supply a measure of the way quantity supplied reacts to a change in price (p. 104)

enterprise zone area where companies can locate free of certain local, state, and federal taxes and restrictions (p. 350)

entitlement social welfare program that people are "entitled" to if they meet certain eligibility requirements (p. 372)

entrepreneur ambitious leader who combines land, labor, and capital to create and market new goods or services (p. 6)

equilibrium the point at which quantity demanded and quantity supplied are equal (p. 125)

equilibrium wage the wage rate that produces neither an excess supply of workers nor an excess demand for workers in the labor market (p. 220)

equities claims of ownership in a corporation (p. 285)

estate tax a tax on the estate, or total value of the money and property, of a person who has died (p. 368)

euro a single new currency that replaces individual currencies among members of the European Union (p. 454)

European Union (EU) a regional trade organization made up of European nations (p. 454)

excess demand when quantity demanded is more than quantity supplied (p. 126)

excess reserves in banking, reserves of cash more than the required amounts (p. 427)

excess supply when quantity supplied is more than quantity demanded (p. 128)

exchange rate the value of a foreign nation's currency in terms of the home nation's currency (p. 458)

excise tax a tax on the production or sale of a good (p. 118)

expansion a period of economic growth as measured by a rise in real GDP (p. 310)

expansionary policies fiscal policies, like higher spending and tax cuts, that encourage economic growth (p. 389)

export a good that is sent to another country for sale (p. 416)

externality an economic side effect of a good or service that generates benefits or costs to someone other than the person deciding how much to produce or consume (p. 65)

F

factor market market in which firms purchase the factors of production from households (p. 29)

factor payments the income people receive for supplying factors of production: land, labor, or capital (p. 24)

factors of production land, labor, and capital; the three groups of resources that are used to make all goods and services (p. 4)

featherbedding the practice of negotiating labor contracts that keep unnecessary workers on a company's payroll (p. 225)

Federal Advisory Council (FAC) the research arm of the Federal Reserve (p. 418)

federal budget a plan for the federal government's revenues and spending for the coming year (p. 387)

Federal Deposit Insurance Corporation (FDIC) the government agency that insures customer deposits if a bank fails (p. 255)

federal funds rate interest rate banks charge each other for loans (p. 422)

Federal Open Market Committee (FOMC) Federal Reserve committee that makes key decisions about interest rates and the growth of the United States money supply (p. 418)

Federal Reserve Districts the twelve banking districts created by the Federal Reserve Act (p. 417)

Federal Reserve note the national currency we use today in the United States (p. 255)

Federal Reserve System the nation's central banking system (p. 254)

fiat money money that has value because the government has ordered that it is an acceptable means to pay debts (p. 248)

FICA taxes that fund Social Security and Medicare (p. 367)

finance charge interest accrued on, and fees charged for, some forms of credit (p. 513)

financial asset claim on the property or income of a borrower (p. 272)

financial intermediary institution that helps channel funds from savers to borrowers (p. 272)

financial system the system that allows the transfer of money between savers and borrowers (p. 272)

firm an organization that uses resources to produce a product, which it then sells (p. 29)

fiscal policy the use of government spending and revenue collection to influence the economy (p. 387)

fiscal year a twelve-month period that can begin on any date (p. 388)

fixed cost a cost that does not change, no matter how much of a good is produced (p. 111)

fixed exchange-rate system a currency system in which governments try to keep the values of their currencies constant against one another (p. 461)

fixed income income that does not increase even when prices go up (p. 343)

flexible exchange-rate system a currency system that allows the exchange rate to be determined by supply and demand (p. 462)

food stamps government-issued coupons that recipients exchange for food (p. 348)

foreign direct investment the establishment of an enterprise by a foreigner (p. 486)

foreign exchange market the banks and other financial institutions that facilitate the buying and selling of foreign currencies (p. 460)

foreign investment investment originating from other countries (p. 485)

foreign portfolio investment the entry of funds into a country when foreigners make purchases in the country's stock and bond markets (p. 486)

fractional reserve banking a banking system that keeps only a fraction of funds on hand and lends out the remainder (p. 260)

franchise the right to sell a good or service within an exclusive market (p. 159)

free contract the concept that people may decide what agreements they want to enter into (p. 53)

free enterprise an economic system characterized by private or corporate ownership of capital goods; investments that are determined by private decision rather than by state control; and determined in a free market (p. 43)

free rider someone who would not choose to pay for a certain good or service, but who would get the benefits of it anyway if it were provided as a public good (p. 63)

free-trade zone a region where a group of countries has agreed to reduce or eliminate trade barriers (p. 454)

frictional unemployment unemployment that occurs when people take time to find a job (p. 331)

fringe benefit payment other than wages or salaries (p. 188)

full employment the level of employment reached when there is no cyclical unemployment (p. 335)

futures contracts to buy or sell at a specific date in the future at a price specified today (p. 288)

G

general partnership partnership in which partners share equally in both responsibility and liability (p. 190)

gift tax a tax on money or property that one living person gives to another (p. 368)

glasnost a policy of "openness" introduced into the Soviet Union in the late 1980s (p. 491)

glass ceiling an unofficial, invisible barrier that prevents women and minorities from advancing in businesses dominated by white men (p. 224)

gold standard a monetary system in which paper money and coins are equal in value to a certain amount of gold (p. 253)

goods physical objects such as clothes or shoes (p. 3)

government monopoly a monopoly created by the government (p. 159)

Great Crash the collapse of the stock market in 1929 (p. 290)

Great Depression the severe economic decline that began in 1929 and lasted for more than a decade (p. 255)

greenback paper currency issued by the North during the Civil War (p. 253)

gross domestic product (GDP) the total value of all final goods and services produced in a particular economy; the dollar value of all final goods and services produced within a country's borders in a given year (pp. 57, 301)

gross national product (GNP) the annual income earned by U.S.-owned firms and U.S. residents (p. 305)

guns or butter a phrase that refers to the trade-off that nations face when choosing whether to produce more or less military or consumer goods (p. 8)

H

heavy industry industry that requires a large capital investment and that produces items used in other industries (p. 37)

household a person or a group of people living in the same residence (p. 29)

horizontal merger the combination of two or more firms competing in the same market with the same good or service (p. 199)

human capital the skills and knowledge gained by a worker through education and experience (p. 5)

hyperinflation inflation that is out of control; very high inflation (pp. 341, 404)

I

imperfect competition a market structure that does not meet the conditions of perfect competition (p. 153)

import a good that is brought in from another country for sale (p. 446)

import quota a limit on the amount of a good that can be imported (p. 449)

incentive an expectation that encourages people to behave in a certain way (p. 31)

incidence of a tax the final burden of a tax (p. 363)

income distribution how the nation's total income is distributed among its population (p. 348)

income effect the change in consumption resulting from a change in real income (p. 80)

increasing marginal returns a level of production in which the marginal product of labor increases as the number of workers increases (p. 109)

individual income tax a tax on a person's earnings (p. 360)

industrialization the extensive organization of an economy for the purpose of manufacturing (p. 472)

inelastic describes demand that is not very sensitive to a change in price (p. 90)

infant industry a new industry (p. 452)

infant mortality rate the number of deaths that occur in the first year of life per 1,000 live births (p. 474)

inferior good a good that consumers demand less of when their incomes increase (p. 87)

inflation a general increase in prices (p. 338)

inflation rate the percentage rate of change in price level over time (p. 340)

infrastructure the services and facilities necessary for an economy to function (p. 474)

in-kind benefits goods and services provided for free or at greatly reduced prices (p. 70)

inside lag delay in implementing monetary policy (p. 432)

interest the price paid for the use of borrowed money (p. 261), or, money earned by deposited funds (p. 506)

interest group a private organization that tries to persuade public officials to act or vote according to group members' interests (p. 54)

intermediate goods goods used in the production of final goods (p. 301)

internal financing financing derived from the savings of a country's citizens (p. 485)

Internal Revenue Service agency within the U.S. Department of the Treasury responsible for interpretation and application of federal tax law (p. 528)

international free trade agreement agreement that results from cooperation between at least two countries to reduce trade barriers and tarriffs and to trade with each other (p. 453)

International Monetary Fund (IMF) organization formed to stabilize international exchange rates and facilitate development (p. 488)

investment the act of redirecting resources from being consumed today so that they may create benefits in the future; the use of assets to earn income or profit (p. 271)

invisible hand term economists use to describe the self-regulating nature of the marketplace (p. 32)

J

junk bond a lower-rated, potentially higher-paying bond (p. 281)

K

Keynesian economics form of demand-side economics that encourages government action to increase or decrease demand and output (p. 396)

L

labor the effort that people devote to a task for which they are paid (p. 4)

labor force all nonmilitary people who are employed or unemployed (p. 211)

labor union an organization of workers that tries to improve working conditions, wages, and benefits for its members (p. 225)

laissez faire the doctrine that states that government generally should not intervene in the marketplace (p. 41)

land natural resources that are used to make goods and services (p. 4)

law of comparative advantage the idea that a nation is better off when it produces goods and services for which it has a comparative advantage (p. 444)

law of demand economic law that states that consumers buy more of a good when its price decreases and less when its price increases (p. 79)

law of increasing costs as we shift factors of production from making one good or service to another, the cost of producing the second item increases (p. 17)

law of supply tendency of suppliers to offer more of a good at a higher price (p. 101)

leading indicators key economic variables that economists use to predict a new phase of the business cycle (p. 314)

learning effect the theory that education increases productivity and results in higher wages (p. 214)

lease a rental agreement between landlord and tenant (p. 523)

legal equality the concept of giving everyone the same legal rights (p. 53)

less developed country nation with a low level of material well-being (p. 471)

liability the legally bound obligation to pay debts (p. 187)

license a government-issued right to operate a business (p. 159)

life expectancy the average expected life span of an individual (p. 473)

light industry the production of small consumer goods (p. 494)

limited liability partnership (LLP) partnership in which all partners are limited partners (p. 190)

limited partnership partnership in which only one partner is required to be a general partner (p. 190)

liquidity the ability to be used as, or directly converted to, cash (p. 258)

literacy rate the proportion of the population over age 15 that can read and write (p. 473)

Lorenz Curve the curve that illustrates income distribution (p. 349)

M

macroeconomics the study of the behavior and decision making of entire economies (p. 57)

malnutrition inadequate nutrition (p. 481)

mandatory spending spending on certain programs that is mandated, or required, by existing law (p. 371)

marginal cost the cost of producing one more unit of a good (p. 111)

marginal product of labor the change in output from hiring one additional unit of labor (p. 108)

marginal revenue the additional income from selling one more unit of a good; sometimes equal to price (p. 112)

market an arrangement that allows buyers and sellers to exchange things (p. 28)

market basket a representative collection of goods and services (p. 339)

market demand schedule a table that lists the quantity of a good all consumers in a market will buy at every different price (p. 82)

market economy economic system in which decisions on production and consumption of goods and services are based on voluntary exchange in markets (p. 27)

market failure a situation in which the market does not distribute resources efficiently (p. 64)

market power the ability of a company to change prices and output like a monopolist (p. 163)

market supply curve a graph of the quantity supplied of a good by all suppliers at different prices (p. 104)

market supply schedule a chart that lists how much of a good all suppliers will offer at different prices (p. 103)

maturity the time at which payment to a bondholder is due (p. 277)

mediation a settlement technique in which a neutral mediator meets with each side to try to find a solution that both sides will accept (p. 234)

Medicaid entitlement program that benefits low-income families, some people with disabilities, and elderly people in nursing homes (p. 373)

Medicare a national health insurance program that helps pay for health care for people over age 65 or who have certain disabilities (p. 368)

medium of exchange anything that is used to determine value during the exchange of goods and services (p. 243)

member bank bank that belongs to the Federal Reserve System (p. 254)

merger combination of two or more companies into a single firm (p. 174)

microeconomics the study of the economic behavior and decision making of small units, such as individuals, families, and businesses (p. 57)

minimum balance an amount of money required in a bank account to avoid fees (p. 504)

minimum wage a minimum price that an employer can pay a worker for an hour of labor (p. 130)

mixed economy economic system that combines the free market with limited government involvement (p. 27)

monetarism the belief that the money supply is the most important factor in macroeconomic performance (p. 430)

monetary policy the actions the Federal Reserve takes to influence the level of real GDP and the rate of inflation in the economy (p. 417)

money anything that serves as a medium of exchange, a unit of account, and a store of value (p. 243)

money creation the process by which money enters into circulation (p. 425)

money market market in which money is lent for periods less than a year (p. 283)

money market mutual fund a fund that pools money from small savers to purchase short-term government and corporate securities (p. 259)

money multiplier formula amount of new money that will be created with each demand deposit; 1 ÷ RRR (p. 426)

money supply all the money available in the United States economy (p. 258)

monopolistic competition a market structure in which many companies sell products that are similar but not identical (p. 166)

monopoly a market dominated by a single seller (p. 156)

mortgage a specific type of loan that is used to buy real estate (p. 261)

multinational corporation (MNC) large corporation that produces and sells its goods and services throughout the world (p. 199)

multiplier effect the idea that every dollar of spending creates more than one dollar in economic activity (p. 397)

municipal bond a bond issued by a state or local government or municipality to finance such improvements as highways, state buildings, libraries, parks, and schools (p. 281)

mutual fund fund that pools the savings of many individuals and invests this money in a variety of stocks, bonds and other financial assets (pp. 272, 509)

N

NAFTA agreement that will eliminate all tariffs and other trade barriers between Canada, Mexico, and the United States (p. 454)

Nasdaq American market for OTC securities (p. 288)

national bank a bank chartered, or licensed, by the national government (p. 251)

national debt all the money the federal government owes to bondholders (p. 405)

national income accounting a system that collects macroeconomic statistics on production, income, investment, and savings (p. 301)

natural monopoly a market that runs most efficiently when one large firm supplies all of the output (p. 158)

natural rate of population increase the difference between the birth rate and the death rate (p. 478)

need something like air, food, or shelter that is necessary for survival (p. 3)

net worth total assets minus total liabilities (p. 422)

newly industrialized country (NIC) less developed country that has shown significant improvement in the measures of development (p. 475)

nominal GDP gross domestic product measured in current prices (p. 304)

nondurable goods goods that last a short period of time, such as food, light bulbs, and sneakers (p. 302)

nonprice competition a way to attract customers through style, service, or location, but not a lower price (p. 167)

nonprofit organization institution that functions much like a business, but does not operate for the purpose of generating profits (p. 203)

normal good a good that consumers demand more of when their incomes increase (p. 86)

O

Office of Management and Budget (OMB) government office that manages the federal budget (p. 388)

oligopoly a market structure in which a few large firms dominate a market (p. 169)

open market operations the buying and selling of government securities to alter the supply of money (p. 428)

open opportunity the concept that everyone can compete in the marketplace (p. 53)

operating budget budget for day-to-day expenses (p. 375)

operating cost the cost of operating a facility such as a store or factory (p. 113)

opportunity cost the most desirable alternative given up as the result of a decision (p. 9)

options contracts that give investors the choice to buy or sell stock and other financial assets (p. 288)

OTC market the over-the-counter market; an electronic marketplace for stock that is not listed or traded on an organized exchange (p. 288)

outside lag the time it takes for monetary policy to have an effect (p. 432)

P

partnership a business organization owned by two or more persons who agree on a specific division of responsibilities and profits (p. 190)

par value the amount that an investor pays to purchase a bond and that will be repaid to investor at maturity (p. 278)

patent a license that gives the inventor of a new product the exclusive right to sell it for a certain period of time (p. 159)

patriotism the love of one's country; the passion that inspires a person to serve his or her country (p. 25)

payroll withholding statement document attached to a paycheck detailing the amount of money withheld (p. 528)

peak the height of an economic expansion, when real GDP stops rising (p. 310)

per capita gross domestic product (per capita GDP) a nation's gross domestic product (GDP) divided by its total population (p. 472)

perestroika Soviet leader Mikhail Gorbachev's plan for economic restructuring (p. 492)

perfect competition a market structure in which a large number of firms all produce the same product (p. 151)

personal exemption set amount that you subtract from your gross income for yourself, your spouse, and any dependents (p. 366)

personal property possessions such as jewelry, furniture, and boats (p. 378)

physical capital all human-made goods that are used to produce other goods and services; tools and buildings (p. 4)

population growth rate the increase in a country's population in a given year, expressed as a percentage of the population figure at the start of the year (p. 478)

portfolio a collection of financial assets (p. 274)

poverty rate the percentage of people who live in households with income below the official poverty line (p. 346)

poverty threshold an income level below which income is insufficient to support families or households (pp. 67, 345)

predatory pricing selling a product below cost to drive competitors out of the market (p. 173)

preferred stock stock whose dividends are based on a fixed annual rate (p. 508)

premium money paid to an insurance company for a policy (p. 524)

price ceiling a maximum price that can be legally charged for a good or service (p. 128)

price discrimination division of customers into groups based on how much they will pay for a good (p. 163)

price fixing an agreement among firms to charge one price for the same good (p. 171)

price floor a minimum price for a good or service (p. 128)

price index a measurement that shows how the average price of a standard group of goods changes over time (p. 339)

price level the average of all prices in the economy (p. 307)

price war a series of competitive price cuts that lowers the market price below the cost of production (p. 171)

primary market market for selling financial assets that can only be redeemed by the original holder (p. 283)

prime rate rate of interest banks charge on short-term loans to their best customers (p. 427)

principal the amount of money borrowed (p. 261)

private property property owned by individuals or companies, not by the government or the people as a whole (p. 41)

private property rights the concept that people have the right and priviledge to control their own possessions as they wish (p. 53)

private sector the part of the economy that involves the transactions of individuals and businesses (p. 63)

privatization the sale or transfer of state-owned businesses to individuals (p. 489)

privatize to sell to individuals state-run firms, which are then allowed to compete with one another in the marketplace (p. 43)

producer cooperative agricultural marketing cooperatives that help members sell their products (p. 203)

product market the market in which households purchase the goods and services that firms produce (p. 30)

production possibilities curve a curve that shows alternative ways to use an economy's resources (p. 13)

production possibilities frontier the line on a production possibilities graph that shows the maximum possible output for a specific economy (p. 14)

productive capacity the maximum output that an economy can produce without big increases in inflation (p. 396)

productivity value of output produced (p. 219)

professional labor labor that requires advanced skills and education (p. 221)

professional organization nonprofit organization that works to improve the image, working conditions, and skill levels of people in particular occupations (p. 203)

profit the financial gain made in a transaction (p. 29)

profit motive the force that encourages people and organizations to improve their material well-being (p. 53)

progressive tax a tax for which the percentage of income paid in taxes increases as income increases (p. 361)

property tax a tax on the value of a property (p. 360)

proportional tax a tax for which the percentage of income paid in taxes remains the same for all income levels (p. 361)

prospectus an investment report to potential investors (p. 274)

protectionism the use of trade barriers to protect a nation's industries from foreign competition (p. 452)

public disclosure laws laws requiring companies to provide full information about their products (p. 54)

public good a shared good or service for which it would be impractical to make consumers pay individually and to exclude nonpayers (p. 62)

public interest the concerns of the public as a whole (p. 54)

publicly held corporation corporation that sells stock on the open market (p. 196)

public sector the part of the economy that involves the transactions of the government (p. 63)

purchasing power the ability to purchase goods and services (p. 339)

put option the option to sell shares of stock at a specified time in the future (p. 288)

Q

quantity supplied the amount a supplier is willing and able to supply at a certain price (p. 101)

quantity theory theory that too much money in the economy causes inflation (p. 341)

R

rationing a system of allocating scarce goods and services using criteria other than price (p. 141)

real GDP gross domestic product expressed in constant, or unchanging, prices (p. 304)

real GDP per capita real gross domestic product divided by the total population (p. 319)

real property physical property such as land and buildings (p. 378)

recession a prolonged economic contraction (p. 311)

regressive tax a tax for which the percentage of income paid in taxes decreases as income increases (p. 361)

regulation government intervention in a market that affects the production of a good (p. 118)

rent control a price ceiling placed on rent (p. 129)

representative money objects that have value because the holder can exchange them for something else of value (p. 247)

required reserve ratio (RRR) ratio of reserves to deposits required of banks by the Federal Reserve (p. 425)

résumé a document summarizing an individual's employment experience, education, and other information a potential employer needs to know (p. 526)

return the money an investor receives above and beyond the sum of money initially invested (p. 274)

revenue income received by a government from taxes and nontax sources (p. 359)

right-to-work law a measure that bans mandatory union membership (p. 231)

royalty share of earnings given as payment (p. 202)

S

S & P 500 index that shows the price changes of 500 different stocks (p. 290)

safety net government programs that protect people experiencing unfavorable economic conditions (p. 26)

sales tax a tax on the dollar value of a good or service being sold (p. 360)

saving income not used for consumption (p. 320)

savings account a bank account used for depositing money that may be needed within a short period of time (p. 506)

savings and loans associations banks that accept deposits and specialize in offering long-term financing for homes (p. 511)

savings bank a bank that accepts deposits and specializes in low-risk investments (p. 511)

savings bond low-denomination bond issued by the United States government (p. 280)

savings rate the proportion of disposable income that is saved (p. 320)

scarcity limited quantities of resources to meet unlimited wants (p. 4)

screening effect the theory that the completion of college indicates to employers that a job applicant is intelligent and hard-working (p. 214)

search costs the financial and opportunity costs consumers pay when searching for a good or service (p. 136)

seasonal unemployment unemployment that occurs as a result of harvest schedules or vacations, or when industries slow or shut down for a season (p. 332)

secondary market market for reselling financial assets (p. 283)

Securities and Exchange Commission an independent agency of the government that regulates financial markets and investment companies (p. 281)

security deposit a sum of money paid to a landlord or other lessor to ensure goods are returned in the same condition as originally rented (p. 522)

self-interest one's own personal gain (p. 31)

semi-skilled labor labor that requires minimal specialized skills and education (p. 221)

service cooperative cooperative that provides a service, rather than a good (p. 203)

services actions or activities one person performs for another (p. 3)

share portion of stock (p. 285)

shortage a situation in which a good or service is unavailable (p. 4), or a situation in which the quantity demanded is greater than the quantity supplied, also known as excess demand (p. 136)

skilled labor labor that requires specialized skills and training (p. 221)

socialism a social and political philosophy based on the belief that democratic means should be used to evenly distribute wealth throughout a society (p. 35)

Social Security Old-Age, Survivors, and Disability Insurance (OASDI) (p. 367)

sole proprietorship a business owned and managed by a single individual (p. 185)

special economic zones designated regions in China where foreign investment is encouraged, businesses can make most of their own investment and production decisions, and foreign companies are allowed to operate (p. 494)

specialization the concentration of the productive efforts of individuals and firms on a limited number of activities (p. 29)

speculation the practice of making high-risk investments with borrowed money in hopes of getting a big return (p. 290)

spillover costs costs of production that affect people who have no control over how much of a good is produced (p. 144)

stabilization program an agreement between a debtor nation and the IMF in which the nation agrees to revise its economic policy (p. 488)

standard of living level of economic prosperity (p. 26)

stagflation a decline in real GDP combined with a rise in the price level (p. 311)

start-up costs the expenses a firm must pay before it can begin to produce and sell goods (p. 153)

stock a certificate of ownership in a corporation (pp. 195, 507)

stock exchange a market for buying and selling stock (p. 287)

stock split the division of a single share of stock into more than one share (p. 286)

stockbroker a person who links buyers and sellers of stock (p. 286)

store of value something that keeps its value if it is stored rather than used (p. 244)

strike an organized work stoppage intended to force an employer to address union demands (p. 229)

structural unemployment unemployment that occurs when workers' skills do not match the jobs that are available (p. 332)

subsidized loans loans for which the government pays the interest while the student is attending school (p. 518)

subsidy a government payment that supports a business or market (p. 117)

subsistence agriculture level of farming in which a person raises only enough food to feed his or her family (p. 472)

substitutes goods used in place of each other (p. 88)

substitution effect when consumers react to an increase in a good's price by consuming less of that good and more of other goods (p. 80)

supply the amount of goods available (p. 101)

supply curve a graph of the quantity supplied of a good at different prices (p. 104)

supply schedule a chart that lists how much of a good a supplier will offer at different prices (p. 103)

supply shock a sudden shortage of a good (p. 141)

supply-side economics a school of economics that believes tax cuts can help an economy by raising supply (p. 399)

surplus situation in which quantity supplied is greater than quantity demanded; also known as excess supply (p. 134)

T

tariff a tax on imported goods (pp. 369, 450)

tax a required payment to a local, state, or national government (p. 359)

taxable income income on which tax must be paid; total income minus exemptions and deductions (p. 366)

tax assessor an official who determines the value of a property (p. 380)

tax base income, property, good, or service that is subject to a tax (p. 360)

tax exempt not subject to taxes (p. 377)

tax incentive the use of taxation to encourage or discourage certain behavior (p. 369)

tax return form used to file one's income taxes (p. 366)

technological progress an increase in efficiency gained by producing more output without using more inputs (p. 322)

technology the process used to produce a good or service (p. 59)

thinking at the margin deciding whether to do or use one additional unit of some resource (p. 10)

tight money policy monetary policy that reduces the money supply (p. 431)

time deposit a deposit offering guaranteed interest for a fixed period of time (p. 506)

total cost fixed costs plus variable costs (p. 111)

total revenue the total amount of money a firm receives by selling goods or services (p. 95)

trade association nonprofit organization that promotes the interests of a particular industry (p. 204)

trade barrier a means of preventing a foreign product or service from freely entering a nation's territory (p. 449)

trade deficit the result of a country importing more than it exports (p. 462)

trade-off an alternative we sacrifice when we make a decision (p. 8)

trade surplus the result of a nation exporting more than it imports (p. 462)

trade war a cycle of increasing trade restrictions (p. 451)

traditional economy economic system that relies on habit, custom, or ritual to decide questions of production and consumption of goods and services (p. 26)

transition period of change in which an economy moves away from a centrally planned economy toward a market-based system (p. 43)

Treasury bill a government bond that is repaid within three months to a year (p. 405)

Treasury bond a government bond that can be issued for as long as 30 years (p. 405)

Treasury note a government bond that is repaid within two to ten years (p. 405)

trough the lowest point in an economic contraction, when real gross domestic product stops falling (p. 311)

trust like a cartel, an illegal grouping of companies that discourages competition (p. 173)

Truth in Savings Act federal law requiring banks to provide customers with information on accounts they offer (p. 507)

Truth in Lending laws regulations requiring institutions extending loans to disclose exact finance charges, monthly interest rates, annual percentage rates, and finance charge calculation methods (p. 515)

tuition the cost of enrolling in educational courses (p. 516)

U

underemployed working at a job for which one is overqualified, or working part-time when full-time work is desired (p. 335)

underutilization using fewer resources than an economy is capable of using (p. 15)

unemployment rate the percentage of the nation's labor force that is unemployed (p. 334)

Uniform Partnership Act (UPA) act ordering common ownership interests, profit and loss sharing, and shared management responsibilities in a partnership (p. 191)

unitary elastic describes demand whose elasticity is exactly equal to 1 (p. 91)

United Nations Development Program (UNDP) United Nations program dedicated to elimination of poverty through development (p. 487)

unit of account a means for comparing the values of goods and services (p. 244)

unskilled labor labor that requires no specialized skills, education, or training (p. 221)

V

variable a factor that can change (p. 103)

variable cost a cost that rises or falls depending on how much is produced (p. 111)

vertical merger the combination of two or more firms involved in different stages of producing the same good or service (p. 199)

voluntary exchange the concept that people may decide what and when they want to buy and sell (p. 53)

voluntary export restraint (VER) a self-imposed limitation on the number of products shipped to a particular country (p. 449)

W

wage-price spiral the process by which rising wages cause higher prices and higher prices cause higher wages (p. 342)

want an item that we desire but that is not essential to survival (p. 3)

welfare government aid to the poor (p. 68)

white-collar worker someone in a professional or clerical job who usually earns a salary (p. 232)

withholding taking tax payments out of an employee's pay before he or she receives it (p. 366)

work ethic a commitment to the value of work and purposeful activity; system of values that gives central importance to work (pp. 59, 491)

workfare a program requiring work in exchange for temporary assistance (p. 350)

World Bank the largest provider of development assistance (p. 487)

World Trade Organization (WTO) a worldwide organization whose goal is freer global trade and lower tariffs (p. 453)

Y

yield the annual rate of return on a bond if the bond were held to maturity (p. 278)

Z

zoning law law in a city or town that designates separate areas for residency and for business (p. 187)

contingent employment/empleo contingente trabajos temporales y trabajos parciales (pág. 215)

continuum/continuo extensión sin divisiones claras (pág. 43)

contract/contrato convenio legal obligatorio (pág. 523)

contraction/contracción período de depresión económica marcado por una baja real del producto interno bruto (pág. 310)

contractionary policies/políticas de austeridad políticas fiscales que disminuyen el crecimiento económico, como por ejemplo, la reducción de gastos y el aumento de impuestos (pág. 389)

cooperative/cooperativa sociedad comercial que se constituye entre productores, vendedores o consumidores, para el beneficio común de los socios (pág. 202)

copayment/copago porcentaje de cada visita o procedimiento médico que el paciente debe pagar de su propio bolsillo (pág. 525)

core inflation rate/índice de inflación básica el índice de inflación, excluidos los precios de los alimentos y la energía (pág. 340)

corporate bond/bono corporativo bono emitido por una sociedad o empresa anónima para recaudar fondos con el fin de expandir su actividad comercial (pág. 281)

corporate income tax/impuesto sobre ingresos corporativos impuesto sobre el valor de las ganancias de una corporación (pág. 360)

corporation/corporación o sociedad anónima entidad legal cuyos dueños son accionistas individuales (pág. 195)

cost/costo en términos económicos, el costo es una alternativa a la cual se renuncia como resultado de una decisión (pág. 16)

cost-push theory/teoría de costos teoría que afirma que el aumento de costos en los salarios y las materias primas provoca inflación (pág. 341)

Council of Economic Advisers (CEA)/Consejo de Asesores Económicos grupo de tres economistas distinguidos cuyo papel es asesorar al presidente en políticas económicas (pág. 400)

coupon rate/tipo de interés tasa de interés que el emisor de bonos debe pagar al tenedor de bonos (pág. 277)

credit/crédito cualquier forma de pagos diferidos (pág. 512)

credit bureau/agencia informativa sobre solvencia organismo que proporciona información sobre los hábitos de endeudamiento y pago de las personas (pág. 512)

credit card/tarjeta de crédito tarjeta con la que el portador puede comprar bienes y servicios a cambio de su promesa de pagar por ellos (pág. 261)

creditor/acreedor individuo o asociación a quien se le debe dinero (pág. 264)

credit rating/clasificación crediticia evaluación realizada por las agencias informativas sobre solvencia acerca de la historia crediticia total de un prestatario (pág. 512)

credit union/cooperativa de crédito organismos bancarios sin fines de lucro cuyos miembros son los dueños, los cuales suelen ser miembros de una organización o gremio individual (pág. 511)

crowding-out effect/efecto de desplazamiento pérdida de fondos para inversiones privadas debido a los fondos pedidos prestados por el gobierno (pág. 406)

currency/moneda monedas y billetes que se usan como dinero (pág. 245)

customs duty/derechos aduaneros impuesto que se aplica a ciertos artículos adquiridos en el extranjero (pág. 450)

cyclical unemployment/desempleo cíclico desempleo que aumenta durante períodos de contracción económica pero que disminuye cuando la economía mejora (pág. 333)

D

debit card/tarjeta de débito tarjeta que se utiliza para retirar dinero de una cuenta (pág. 263)

debt rescheduling/reajuste de los vencimientos de la deuda alargar el período de reembolso de la deuda y/o condonar o anular parte del préstamo (pág. 488)

deductible/deducible cantidad de gastos que se deben pagar en efectivo antes de que una aseguradora cubra cualquier gasto (pág. 524)

deductions/deducciones cantidad variable que una persona puede sustraer o deducir de sus ingresos brutos (pág. 366)

default/incumplimiento fallo en pagar una deuda (pág. 261)

deflation/deflación baja sostenida en el nivel general de precios (pág. 343)

demand/demanda el deseo de poseer algo y la capacidad de pagar por ello (pág. 79)

demand curve/curva de demanda representación gráfica de una tabla de demanda (pág. 82)

demand deposit/depósito a la vista dinero en una cuenta corriente (pág. 258)

demand-pull theory/teoría de la atracción de la demanda teoría que afirma que la inflación se produce por una gran demanda de productos y servicios (pág. 341)

demand schedule/tabla de demanda tabla que enumera la cantidad de un producto que una persona comprará a cada precio diferente (pág. 81)

demand-side economics/economía de demanda doctrina económica que afirma que el gasto fiscal y la reducción de impuestos ayudan a una economía mediante el aumento de la demanda (pág. 396)

depreciation/depreciación pérdida del valor de los bienes de capital debido a un desgaste normal o una devaluación de la moneda (págs. 305, 520)

depression/depresión recesión económica larga y severa (pág. 311)

deregulation/desregulación eliminación de algunas restricciones del gobierno para ciertos mercados (pág. 175)

developed nation/país desarrollado país que posee un promedio elevado de bienestar material (pág. 471)

development/desarrollo proceso por el cual una nación mejora el bienestar económico, político y social de su población (pág. 471)

differentiation/diferenciación hacer diferente un producto de otros productos semejantes (pág. 167)

diminishing marginal returns/rendimientos marginales decrecientes nivel de producción en el cual el producto de mano de obra marginal disminuye cuando el número de trabajadores se aumenta (pág. 109)

discount rate/tasa de descuento tasa que la Reserva Federal les cobra a los bancos comerciales por crédito de urgencia (pág. 422)

discouraged worker/trabajador desalentado persona que quiere un trabajo pero deja de buscarlo (pág. 336)

discretionary spending/gastos discrecionales categoría de gastos sobre los cuales pueden tomar decisiones los organismos de planificación del gobierno (pág. 371)

disequilibrium/desequilibrio describe cualquier precio o cantidad que no está equilibrada; cuando en el mercado la oferta no es igual a la demanda (pág. 126)

diversification/diversificación expansión de las inversiones con el fin de disminuir los riesgos (pág. 273)

dividend/dividendo parte de las ganancias de una empresa que les corresponde a los accionistas (págs. 198, 508)

The Dow/índice Dow Jones índice que muestra la compra y venta de ciertas acciones selectas (pág. 290)

durable goods/bienes duraderos productos que tienen un período de duración relativamente largo, como por ejemplo, los refrigeradores, los carros y los reproductores de DVD (pág. 302)

E

easy money policy/política de dinero abundante política monetaria que aumenta el medio circulante (pág. 431)

economic growth/crecimiento económico aumento sostenido y a largo plazo en el producto interno bruto (pág. 310)

economics/economía estudio de cómo los seres humanos buscan satisfacer sus necesidades y deseos mediante la toma de decisiones (pág. 3)

economic system/sistema económico método que utiliza una colectividad humana para producir y distribuir bienes y servicios (pág. 23)

economies of scale/economía de escala factores que provocan la caída de los costos medios de un productor conforme aumenta la producción (pág. 157)

efficiency/rendimiento uso eficaz de los recursos con el fin de maximizar la producción de bienes y servicios (pág. 15)

elastic/elástica describe la demanda que es muy sensible a la variación de precios (pág. 90)

elasticity of demand/elasticidad de la demanda medida de cómo reaccionan los consumidores a una variación de precio (pág. 90)

elasticity of supply/elasticidad de la oferta medida de cómo reacciona el volumen de la oferta a una variación de precio (pág. 104)

enterprise zone/zona empresarial área donde las compañías pueden operar libres de ciertos impuestos y restricciones locales, estatales y federales (pág. 350)

entitlement/derecho reglamentario programa que proporciona pagos a personas que cumplen ciertos requisitos, como por ejemplo, edad o ingresos (pág. 372)

entrepreneur/empresario líder con ambiciones que reúne factores como bienes, mano de obra y capital para crear y lanzar al mercado nuevos productos o servicios (pág. 6)

equilibrium/equilibrio económico el punto en el cual se nivelan la oferta y la demanda (pág. 125)

equilibrium wage/salario de equilibrio escala de salarios que no produce ni un número excesivo de trabajadores ni una demanda excesiva de trabajadores en el mercado laboral (pág. 220)

equities/acciones ordinarias título de propiedad en una sociedad anónima (pág. 285)

estate tax/impuesto sucesorio impuesto sobre la herencia, o valor total del dinero y la propiedad, de una persona que ha fallecido (pág. 368)

euro/euro nueva moneda que reemplaza las monedas individuales de las naciones de la Unión Europea (pág. 454)

European Union (EU)/Unión Europea (U.E.) organización mercantil regional formada por países europeos (pág. 454)

excess demand/exceso de demanda cuando el volumen de la demanda es mayor que el de la oferta (pág. 126)

excess reserves/reservas excedentes en las operaciones bancarias, reservas en efectivo mayores que las cantidades necesarias (pág. 427)

excess supply/exceso de oferta cuando el volumen de la oferta es mayor que el volumen de la demanda (pág. 128)

exchange rate/tipo de cambio valor de la moneda de un país en relación a la moneda de otros países (pág. 458)

excise tax/impuesto sobre el consumo impuesto sobre la producción o venta de un bien (pág. 118)

expansion/expansión período de desarrollo económico medido por un aumento en el producto interno bruto verdadero (pág. 310)

expansionary policies/políticas expansionistas políticas fiscales (tal como mayores gastos y reducción de impuestos) que estimulan el crecimiento económico (pág. 389)

export/artículo exportado producto que se vende a otro país (pág. 446)

externality/factor externo efecto secundario económico de un bien o servicio que genera beneficios o costos a alguien que no sea la persona que decide la cantidad de producción o de consumo (pág. 65)

F

factor market/mercado de factores mercado en el cual las compañías adquieren los factores de producción de las unidades familiares (pág. 29)

factor payments/pagos por factores los ingresos que un individuo recibe por suministrar factores de producción: bienes, mano de obra o capital (pág. 24)

factors of production/factores de producción bienes, mano de obra y capital; los tres grupos de recursos que concurren en la producción de todos los bienes y servicios (pág. 4)

featherbedding/prebendaje práctica de negociación de contratos laborales que mantienen en la planilla un número innecesario de trabajadores (pág. 227)

Federal Advisory Council (FAC)/Consejo Asesor Federal la autoridad de estudios de investigación de la Reserva Federal (pág. 418)

federal budget/presupuesto federal plan de entradas y gastos del gobierno federal para el año siguiente (pág. 387)

Federal Deposit Insurance Corporation (FDIC)/Agencia Aseguradora Federal de Depósitos agencia gubernamental que asegura los depósitos de los clientes en caso de una quiebra bancaria (pág. 255)

federal funds rate/tasa de fondos federales tasa de interés que los bancos se cobran entre sí por préstamos (pág. 422)

Federal Open Market Committee (FOMC)/Comité del Mercado Libre Federal comité de la Reserva Federal que toma decisiones clave sobre tasas de interés y el crecimiento del medio circulante de Estados Unidos (pág. 418)

Federal Reserve Districts/Distritos de la Reserva Federal los doce distritos bancarios creados por la Ley de la Reserva Federal (pág. 417)

Federal Reserve note/billetes de reserva federal dinero que actualmente circula en Estados Unidos (pág. 255)

Federal Reserve System/sistema bancario de la Reserva Federal el sistema bancario central de Estados Unidos (pág. 254)

fiat money/moneda fiduciaria dinero que posee valor porque el gobierno ha dispuesto que es un medio aceptable de pagar deudas (pág. 248)

FICA/FICA, Acta federal de contribuciones de seguros impuestos que financian el Seguro Social y *Medicare* (pág. 367)

finance charges/cargo por financiamiento interés que se acumula y derechos que se cobran por algunas formas de crédito (pág. 513)

financial asset/inmovilización financiera derecho sobre la propiedad o sobre los ingresos de un prestatario (pág. 272)

financial intermediary/intermediario financiero institución que ayuda a canalizar fondos de los ahorradores a los prestatarios (pág. 272)

financial system/sistema financiero sistema que permite el traspaso de dinero entre ahorradores y prestatarios (pág. 272)

firm/firma organización que utiliza recursos para fabricar un producto y luego venderlo (pág. 29)

fiscal policy/política fiscal normas tributarias y de gasto que aplica un gobierno con el fin de estabilizar la economía (pág. 387)

fiscal year/año fiscal período de doce meses que puede iniciarse en cualquier fecha (pág. 388)

fixed cost/costo fijo costo que no cambia sea cual sea la cantidad de producción (pág. 111)

fixed exchange-rate system/sistema de cambio fijo sistema monetario en el que un gobierno intenta mantener constante el valor de su moneda contra el de otros gobiernos (pág. 461)

fixed income/renta fija ingreso que no está sujeto a un aumento a un cuando los precios suben (pág. 343)

flexible exchange-rate system/sistema de cambio flexible sistema monetario que permite que la oferta y la demanda determinen el tipo de cambio (pág. 462)

food stamps/cupones de alimentos cupones que emite el gobierno y que se canjean por alimentos (pág. 348)

foreign direct investment/inversión extranjera directa compañía creada por extranjeros (pág. 486)

foreign exchange market/mercado de divisas bancos y otras instituciones financieras que facilitan la compra y venta de monedas extranjeras (pág. 460)

foreign investment/inversiones extranjeras inversiones provenientes de otros países (pág. 485)

foreign portfolio investment/inversión de cartera extranjera fondos que entran en un país cuando inversionistas extranjeros realizan adquisiciones en sus mercados de valores y bonos (pág. 486)

fractional reserve banking/operaciones bancarias de reserva fraccionada sistema bancario que mantiene sólo una fracción de los fondos y da prestado el resto (pág. 260)

franchise/franquicia derecho para vender un bien o un servicio dentro de un mercado exclusivo (pág. 159)

free contract/contrato libre concepto que define los acuerdos en los que quieren participar las personas (pág. 53)

free enterprise/libre empresa sistema económico que se caracteriza por la propiedad privada or corporativa sobre los bienes de capital; las inversiónes son determinadas por vías privadas y no por el gobierno; y determinada en un mercado libre (pág. 43)

free rider/aprovechador individuo que se niega a pagar por un bien o un servicio pero que toma los beneficios que éste ofrece si se le proporciona como un bien o servicio público (pág. 63)

free-trade zone/zona de libre comercio zona donde un grupo de países ha acordado disminuir las barreras comerciales entre sí (pág. 454)

frictional unemployment/desempleo friccional desempleo que surge cuando una persona busca otro trabajo (pág. 331)

fringe benefit /beneficios complementarios o extrasalariales pagos que se reciben además del sueldo o salario (pág. 188)

full employment/empleo pleno nivel de empleo que se alcanza cuando no existe el desempleo cíclico (pág. 335)

futures/futuros contratos de compra y venta en una fecha específica en el futuro a un precio específico actual (pág. 288)

G

general partnership/sociedad colectiva sociedad en la cual los socios comparten el mismo grado de responsabilidad (pág. 190)

gift tax/impuesto sobre donaciones y legados impuesto que una persona viva debe pagar sobre una donación monetaria valorada por sobre una cierta cantidad (pág. 368)

glasnost/glásnost política de apertura emprendida en la Unión Soviética a fines de la década de 1980 (pág. 491)

glass ceiling/techo de vidrio barrera invisible y oficiosa que impide que las mujeres y las minorías logren promociones o puedan superarse en organizaciones dominadas por hombres blancos (pág. 224)

gold standard/patrón oro sistema monetario en el cual billetes y monedas tienen igual valor a una cierta cantidad de oro (pág. 253)

goods/bienes objetos físicos como la ropa o los zapatos (pág. 3)

government monopoly/monopolio fiscal monopolio credo por el gobierno (pág. 159)

Great Crash/Quiebre de la Bolsa caída de la bolsa de valores en 1929 (pág. 290)

Great Depression/Gran Depresión grave crisis económica que empezó en 1929 y que duró más de una decada (pág. 255)

greenback/*greenback* papel moneda que emitió el Norte durante la Guerra Civil (pág. 253)

gross domestic product (GDP)/producto interno bruto (PIB) valor de todos los bienes y servicios finales producidos por un país dentro de su territorio en un año dado (págs. 57, 301)

gross national product (GNP)/producto nacional bruto (PNB) ingresos anuales de compañías y residentes norteamericanos (pág. 305)

guns or butter/armas o alimentos término que se refiere al dilema que enfrentan las naciones cuando deben decidir si producir una mayor o una menor cantidad de bienes militares o para el consumidor (pág. 8)

H

heavy industry/industria pesada industria que requiere grandes inversiones de capital y que produce artículos que se usan en otras industrias (pág. 37)

household/casa o unidad familiar persona o grupo de personas que viven juntos (pág. 29)

horizontal merger/fusión horizontal combinación de dos o más empresas de productos o servicios similares que compiten en el mismo mercado (pág. 199)

human capital/capital humano destrezas y conocimientos que adquiere un trabajador gracias a su educación y experiencia (pág. 5)

hyperinflation/hiperinflación inflación fuera de control (págs. 341, 404)

I

imperfect competition/competencia imperfecta estructura del mercado que no reúne las condiciones de una competencia perfecta (pág. 153)

import/artículo importado producto que se trae de otro país (pág. 446)

import quota/cuota de importación límite sobre la cantidad que se puede importar de un producto (pág. 449)

incentive/incentivo estímulo que mueve a una persona a comportarse de cierta manera (pág. 31)

incidence of a tax/incidencia de los impuestos peso final de un impuesto (pág. 363)

income distribution/distribución de ingresos la manera en que los ingresos totales de un país se distribuyen entre la población (pág. 348)

income effect/efecto de ingreso cambio en el consumo debido a un cambio en los ingresos reales (pág. 80)

increasing marginal returns/rendimiento marginal creciente nivel de producción en el que el producto de mano de obra marginal crece cuando el número de trabajadores se aumenta (pág. 109)

individual income tax/contribución individual sobre ingresos impuesto sobre los ingresos de una persona (pág. 360)

industrialization/industrialización organización extensiva de una economía para la elaboración de bienes (pág. 472)

inelastic/inelástica o fija describe la demanda que no es muy sensible a una variación de precios (pág. 90)

infant industry/industria naciente industria nueva (pág. 452)

infant mortality rate/tasa de mortalidad infantil número de muertes que ocurren en el primer año de vida por cada mil bebés nacidos vivos (pág. 474)

inferior good/bien o producto subordinado bien o producto que sufre una menor demanda cuando aumentan los ingresos de los consumidores (pág. 87)

inflation/inflación alza general de precios (pág. 338)

inflation rate/índice de inflación cambio porcentual en el nivel de precios en un período de tiempo (pág. 340)

infrastructure/infraestructura servicios e instalaciones que son necesarios para el funcionamiento de una economía (pág. 474)

in-kind benefits/beneficios en especie bienes y servicios gratis o a precios muy reducidos (pág. 70)

inside lag/demora interna retraso en la implementación de políticas monetarias (pág. 432)

interest/interés precio que se paga por el uso de dinero prestado (pág. 261), o, dinero que ganan los fondos depositados (pág. 506)

interest group/grupo de intereses agrupación privada que intenta persuadir a funcionarios públicos de que tomen medidas o voten a favor de los intereses de los miembros del grupo (pág. 54)

intermediate goods/bienes intermedios bienes utilizados en la producción de bienes finales (pág. 301)

internal financing/autofinanciación financiación que proviene de los ahorros de los ciudadanos de un país (pág. 485)

Internal Revenue Service/Servicio de Impuestos Internos organismo del Ministerio de Hacienda de Estados Unidos responsable de la interpretación y aplicación del derecho tributario federal (pág. 528)

international free trade agreement/tratado internacional de libre comercio acuerdo que resulta de la cooperación de un mínimo de dos países para eliminar barreras e impuestos comerciales en el comercio mutuo (pág. 453)

International Monetary Fund (IMF)/Fondo Monetario Internacional (F.M.I.) organismo cuyo fin es garantizar la estabilidad de los tipos de cambio internacionales y facilitar el desarrollo (pág. 488)

investment/inversión la acción de cambiar el uso de los recursos para evitar consumirlos hoy de modo que puedan crear beneficios en el futuro; el uso de activos para obtener ingresos o utilidades (pág. 271)

invisible hand/mano invisible término usado por economistas para describir la naturaleza autorreguladora del mercado (pág. 32)

J

junk bond/bono de calidad inferior bono de precio menor pero que potencialmente puede rendir un pago mayor (pág. 281)

K

Keynesian economics/economía keynesiana tipo de economía de demanda que fomenta la acción del gobierno con el fin de aumentar o disminuir la demanda y la producción (pág. 396)

L

labor/trabajo esfuerzo que se dedica a una tarea por la cual una persona es remunerada (pág. 4)

labor force/mano de obra o fuerza de trabajo todos los individuos civiles (excluyendo las fuerzas militares) que están empleados o desempleados (pág. 211)

labor union/sindicato obrero agrupación de trabajadores cuyo objetivo es mejorar las condiciones laborales, los salarios y los beneficios de sus miembros; también conocido como gremio (pág. 225)

laissez faire/política de mínima interferencia o laissez faire doctrina que afirma que, por lo general, el gobierno no debe interferir en el mercado (pág. 41)

land/tierras recursos naturales que se usan en la producción de bienes y servicios (pág. 4)

law of comparative advantage/ley de la ventaja comparativa ley que afirma que las naciones están en mejores condiciones cuando producen bienes y servicios que les significan una ventaja comparativa al ofrecerlos en el mercado (pág. 444)

law of demand/ley de la demanda ley que afirma que los consumidores compran una mayor cantidad de un pro-ducto cuando su precio disminuye y una menor cantidad cuando su precio aumenta (pág. 79)

law of increasing costs/ley de costos crecientes cuando ocurre un cambio en los factores de producción en la elaboración de un bien o un servicio a otro, esto significa el aumento del costo de producción del segundo bien o servicio (pág. 17)

law of supply/ley de la oferta tendencia de los proveedores a ofrecer una cantidad mayor de un producto a un precio más alto (pág. 101)

leading indicators/indicadores anticipados variables económicas clave que utilizan los economistas para pronosticar una fase nueva del ciclo comercial (pág. 314)

learning effect/efecto del aprendizaje teoría que afirma que la educación aumenta la productividad, lo que resulta en salarios más altos (pág. 214)

lease/arrendamiento acuerdo de renta entre un propietario y un arrendatario (pág. 523)

legal equality/igualdad legal dar a cada persona los mismos derechos legales (pág. 53)

less developed country/país menos desarrollado nación con un nivel bajo de bienestar material (pág. 471)

liability/responsabilidad (legal) obligación con fuerza legal para pagar una deuda (pág. 187)

license/permiso autorización emitida por el gobierno para conducir un negocio (pág. 159)

life expectancy/expectativa de vida promedio de vida que se espera de un individuo (pág. 473)

light industry/industria ligera producción de bienes de consumo pequeños (pág. 494)

limited liability partnership (LLP)/sociedad de responsabilidad limitada sociedad comercial en la que todos los socios son socios colectivos (pág. 190)

limited partnership/sociedad en comandita simple sociedad comercial en la que se requiere que solamente uno de los socios sea un socio colectivo (pág. 190)

liquidity/liquidez capacidad de usar o de convertir directamente en efectivo (pág. 258)

literacy rate/índice de analfabetismo porcentaje de la población que no sabe ni leer ni escribir (pág. 473)

Lorenz Curve/curva Lorenz curva gráfica que muestra ingresos totales y que ilustra la distribución del ingreso (pág. 349)

M

macroeconomics/macroeconomía estudio del comportamiento y de la toma de decisiones de economías completas (pág. 57)

malnutrition/desnutrición alimentación deficiente (pág. 481)

mandatory spending/gastos obligatorios gastos requeridos por ley para efectuarse sobre ciertos programas (pág. 371)

marginal cost/costo límite o marginal costo de producir una unidad más de un bien (pág. 111)

marginal product of labor/producto de mano de obra marginal cambio en producción que resulta al contratar una unidad adicional de mano de obra (pág. 108)

marginal revenue/ingresos marginales ingreso adicional que resulta al producir una unidad más de un bien; por lo general, es igual al precio (pág. 112)

market/mercado convenio que permite que compradores y vendedores intercambien cosas (pág. 28)

market basket/cesta de compras colección representativa de bienes y servicios (pág. 339)

market demand schedule/cuadro de la demanda del mercado tabla que enumera la cantidad de un bien que comprarán todos los consumidores de un mercado a precios diferentes (pág. 82)

market economy/economía de mercado sistema económico en el que las decisiones sobre producción y consumo de bienes y servicios se basan en intercambios voluntarios en los mercados (pág. 27)

market failure/fracaso del mercado situación en la cual el mercado no distribuye los recursos de manera eficaz (pág. 64)

market power/poder de mercado capacidad de una empresa de cambiar precios y producción como si fuera un monopolio (pág. 163)

market supply curve/curva de oferta del mercado gráfica que muestra el volumen de la oferta de todos los proveedores en todos los niveles de precios (pág. 104)

market supply schedule/cuadro de oferta del mercado tabla que enumera la cantidad de un bien que ofrecen todos los proveedores a precios diferentes (pág. 103)

maturity/vencimiento fecha en que se vence el pago a un tenedor de bonos (pág. 277)

mediation/mediación técnica de arreglo en la que un mediador neutral se reúne con cada parte en litigio para hallar una solución, sin imponérsela (pág. 234)

Medicaid/*Medicaid*** programa de derecho reglamentario que beneficia a familias de bajos ingresos, a personas discapacitadas y a personas de edad avanzada que viven en hogares de ancianos (pág. 373)

Medicare/*Medicare*** programa nacional de seguro médico que ayuda a pagar el cuidado de salud para personas mayores de 65 años o que sufren de alguna invalidez (pág. 368)

medium of exchange/medio de cambio cualquier cosa que se usa como medida de valor durante el intercambio de bienes y servicios (pág. 243)

member bank/banco afiliado banco que pertenece al Sistema de Reserva Federal (pág. 254)

merger/fusión unión de dos o más compañías en una sola empresa (pág. 174)

microeconomics/microeconomía estudio del comportamiento económico y de la toma de decisiones de unidades pequeñas, como por ejemplo, individuos, familias y negocios (pág. 57)

minimum balance/balance mínimo cantidad de dinero que se requiere en una cuenta bancaria para evitar comisión y gastos por servicio (pág. 504)

minimum wage/salario mínimo precio mínimo que puede pagar un patrón a un empleado por hora de trabajo (pág. 130)

mixed economy/economía mixta sistema económico que mezcla el sistema tradicional y el mercado libre con una participación mínima del gobierno (pág. 27)

monetarism/monetarismo creencia de que el volumen de la masa monetaria es el factor más importante en el rendimiento macroeconómico (pág. 430)

monetary policy/política monetaria medida que lleva a cabo la Reserva Federal para influir sobre el nivel del producto interno bruto real y la tasa de inflación en la economía (pág. 417)

money/dinero cualquier cosa que sirve como medio de cambio, unidad de cuenta y reserva de valor (pág. 243)

money creation/poner el dinero en circulación proceso por el cual el dinero entra en circulación (pág. 425)

money market/mercado monetario mercado en el cual se presta dinero por períodos menores de un año (pág. 283)

money market mutual fund/fondo común de inversiones fondo que atrae dinero de ahorradores pequeños para adquirir bonos del gobierno o de sociedades anónimas a corto plazo (pág. 259)

money multiplier formula/fórmula multiplicadora de dinero cantidad de dinero nuevo que se crea con cada depósito a la vista, calculada como 1 ÷ CRR (coeficiente de reservas requerido) (pág. 426)

money supply/masa monetaria todo el dinero disponible en la economía de Estados Unidos (pág. 258)

monopolistic competition/competencia monopolista estructura del mercado en la cual muchas empresas venden productos semejantes pero no idénticos (pág. 166)

monopoly/monopolio mercado controlado por un solo vendedor (pág. 156)

mortgage/hipoteca tipo específico de préstamo que se usa para comprar bienes raíces (pág. 261)

multinational corporation/corporación multinacional empresa o grupo industrial o financiero que vende sus bienes y servicios en distintas partes del mundo (pág. 199)

multiplier effect/efecto multiplicador la idea de que cada dólar invertido crea más de un dólar de actividad económica (pág. 397)

municipal bond/bono municipal bono emitido por un gobierno o una municipalidad estatal o local para financiar mejoras a carreteras, edificios, bibliotecas, parques y escuelas (pág. 281)

mutual fund/fondo mutuo fondo constituído por los ahorros de muchos inversionistas y que invierteeste dinero en una diversidad de valores y bonos (págs. 272, 509)

N

NAFTA/Tratado de Libre Comercio (T.L.C.) convenio que elimina todos los aranceles y otras barreras comerciales entre Canadá, México y Estados Unidos (pág. 454)

Nasdaq/Nasdaq (por sus siglas en inglés para National Association of Securities Dealers Automated Quotation System y American Stock Exchange Inc.) mercado que se especializa en valores de alta tecnología y energía americanos (pág. 288)

national bank/banco nacional banco registrado por el gobierno nacional (pág. 251)

national debt/deuda nacional todo el dinero que el gobierno federal les debe a los tenedores de bonos (pág. 405)

national income accounting/contabilidad del ingreso nacional sistema que reúne estadísticas macroeconómicas sobre producción, ingresos, inversiones y ahorros (pág. 301)

natural monopoly/monopolio natural mercado que opera con mucha eficacia cuando una empresa mayor suministra toda la producción (pág. 158)

natural rate of population increase/índice demográfico diferencia entre la tasa de nacimientos y la tasa de mortalidad (pág. 478)

need/necesidad algo como, por ejemplo, el aire, los alimentos o un refugio que es necesario para la supervivencia (pág. 3)

net worth/valor o activo neto activos totales menos pasivos totales (pág. 422)

newly industrialized country (NIC)/país recientemente industrializado país menos desarrollado que ha demostrado mejoras significativas en las medidas de desarrollo (pág. 475)

nominal GDP/PIB nominal producto interno bruto que se mide en precios actuales (pág. 304)

nondurable goods/bienes perecederos bienes de duración relativamente corta. Ejemplos: alimentos, bombillos de luz y zapatos tenis (pág. 302)

nonprice competition/competencia no basada en precio manera de atraer a clientes mediante estilo, servicio o ubicación, pero no a un precio menor (pág. 167)

nonprofit organization/organización sin fines de lucro empresa que funciona en forma muy parecida a una empresa comercial pero que no opera con el fin de generar ganancias (pág. 203)

normal good/producto o bien normal bien que disfruta de una mayor demanda de los consumidores cuando los ingresos de éstos aumentan (pág. 86)

O

Office of Management and Budget (OMB)/Dirección de Administración y Presupuesto agencia gubernamental que administra el presupuesto federal (pág. 388)

oligopoly/oligopolio estructura del mercado en la que unas cuantas empresas mayores controlan un mercado (pág. 169)

open market operations/operaciones de mercado abierto compra y venta de títulos del Estado con el fin de alterar el medio circulante (pág. 428)

open opportunity/oportunidad abierta concepto que define la posibilidad de que todos puedan competir en el mercado (pág. 53)

operating budget/presupuesto operativo presupuesto para los gastos diarios (pág. 375)

operating cost/gastos de operación costo de operación de una instalación como, por ejemplo, una tienda o una fábrica (pág. 113)

opportunity cost/costo de oportunidad alternativa más deseada a la que se ha renunciado como resultado de una decisión (pág. 9)

options/opciones contratos que les proporcionan a los inversionistas la opción de comprar o vender valores y otros activos financieros (pág. 288)

OTC market/mercado extrabursátil mercado electrónico para valores que no aparecen o que no se comercializan en una bolsa organizada (pág. 288)

outside lag/demora externa tiempo que tarda una política monetaria en entrar un efecto (pág. 432)

P

partnership/sociedad personal organización comercial de dos o más personas que convienen en una repartición específica de responsabilidades y ganancias (pág. 190)

par value/valor a la par cantidad que se debe pagar a un inversionista de bonos cuando el bono se vence, sin tener en cuenta el interés (pág. 278)

patent/patente derecho que concede al inventor de un producto nuevo su venta exclusiva, durante un determinado período de tiempo (pág. 159)

patriotism/patriotismo el amor por el propio país; la pasión que inspira a una persona a servir a su país (pág. 25)

payroll witholding statement/estado de cuenta de retención de nómina documento adherido al cheque de pago que indiqua la suma retenida (pág. 310)

peak/apogeo el punto más alto de una expansión económica, cuando el producto interno bruto real deja de aumentar (pág. 310)

per capita gross domestic product (per capita GDP)/producto interno bruto per cápita (PIB per cápita) el producto interno bruto de una nación dividido por su población total (pág. 472)

perestroika/perestroika plan económico puesto en marcha por el líder soviético Mikhail Gorbachev para llevar a cabo una reforma económica (pág. 492)

perfect competition/competencia perfecta estructura del mercado en la que un vasto número de empresas elaboran el mismo producto (pág. 151)

personal exemption/exención personal una suma que resta una persona de sus ingresos brutos para si mismo, su esposo, y unos dependientes (pág. 366)

personal property/bienes personales pertenencias como joyas, muebles y embarcaciones (pág. 378)

physical capital/bienes materiales todos los bienes producidos por el ser humano que se utilizan en la producción de otros bienes y servicios; herramientas y edificios (pág. 4)

population growth rate/tasa de crecimiento demográfico aumento en la población de un país en un año determinado, expresado como porcentaje de la cifra de habitantes al comienzo del año (pág. 478)

portfolio/cartera conjunto de activos financieros (pág. 274)

poverty rate/índice de pobreza porcentaje de un grupo de la población que vive en casas con ingresos por debajo del nivel de pobreza oficial (pág. 346)

poverty threshold/umbral de pobreza nivel de ingresos bajo el cual los ingresos son insuficientes para poder mantener a una familia (págs. 67, 345)

predatory pricing/precio para eliminar competidores vender un producto bajo costo para alejar a los competidores del mercado (pág. 173)

preferred stock/acciones preferentes acciones cuyos dividendos se basan en una tasa anual fija (pág. 508)

premium/prima dinero que se paga a una compañía aseguradora por una póliza (pág. 524)

price ceiling/tope de precios precio máximo que se puede pagar por un bien o un servicio (pág. 128)

price discrimination/discriminación de precios división de clientes en grupos según la cantidad de dinero que pagarán por un producto (pág. 163)

price fixing/fijación de precios convenio entre empresas para cobrar un precio por el mismo producto (pág. 171)

price floor/precio mínimo precio más bajo que se debe pagar por un bien o un servicio (pág. 128)

price index/índice de precios medida que muestra cómo cambia con el tiempo el precio promedio de un grupo estándar de bienes (pág. 339)

price level/nivel de precios promedio de todos los precios en una economía (pág. 307)

price war/guerra de precios serie de rebaja de precios que reduce el precio del mercado por debajo del costo de producción (pág. 171)

primary market/mercado primario mercado de venta de activos financieros que sólo el tenedor original puede redimir (pág. 283)

prime rate/tasa de interés preferencial tasa de interés que cobran los bancos a sus mejores clientes cuando éstos solicitan préstamos a corto plazo (pág. 427)

principal/capital o principal cantidad de dinero que se presta (pág. 261)

private property/propiedad privada la propiedad que poseen los individuos o las compañías, no el gobierno o el conjunto del pueblo (pág. 41)

private property rights/derecho a la propiedad privada concepto que define el derecho y privilegio de las personas a controlar sus posesiones como deseen (pág. 53)

private sector/sector privado parte de la economía que envuelve las transacciones de individuos y de empresas (pág. 63)

privatization/privatización venta o traspaso de empresas estatales al sector privado (pág. 489)

privatize/privatizar vender al sector privado empresas estatales, las cuales pueden competir entre sí en el mercado (pág. 43)

producer cooperative/cooperativa de producción cooperativas de comercialización agrícola que ayudan a sus miembros a vender sus productos (pág. 203)

product market/mercado de productos mercado en el cual las personas compran los bienes y servicios que producen las empresas (pág. 30)

production possibilities curve/curva de posibilidades de producción gráfica que muestra maneras alternativas para usar los recursos de una economía (pág. 13)

production possibilities frontier/límite de posibilidades de producción en una gráfica de posibilidades de producción, la línea que muestra la producción máxima posible para una economía específica (pág. 14)

productive capacity/capacidad de producción producción máxima que puede realizar una economía sin grandes alzas inflacionarias (pág. 396)

productivity/productividad valor de producción efectuada (pág. 219)

professional labor/trabajo profesional trabajo que requiere destrezas y educación avanzadas (pág. 221)

professional organization /organización profesional agrupación sin fines de lucro cuyo objetivo es mejorar la imagen, las condiciones laborales y los niveles de destrezas de individuos de un determinado oficio (pág. 203)

profit/ganancias utilidades financieras que se producen en una transacción (pág. 29)

profit motive/ánimo de lucro la fuerza que anima a las personas y organizaciones a mejorar sus condiciones materiales (pág. 53)

progressive tax/impuesto progresivo impuesto para el cual el porcentaje de ingresos que se paga en impuestos aumenta conforme lo hacen los ingresos (pág. 361)

property tax/impuesto de la propiedad impuesto sobre el valor de una propiedad (pág. 361)

proportional tax/impuesto proporcional impuesto en el que el porcentaje de ingresos que se paga es inalterable para todos los niveles de ingresos (pág. 361)

prospectus/prospecto informe de inversiones para inversionistas potenciales (pág. 274)

protectionism/proteccionismo uso de restricciones comerciales con el fin de proteger las industrias de un país de la competencia extranjera (pág. 452)

public disclosure laws/leyes de divulgación pública reglas que obligan a las empresas a proporcionar información sobre sus productos (pág. 54)

public good/bien público bien o servicio compartido que no sería práctico que los consumidores pagaran individualmente ni excluir a los que no pagan (pág. 62)

public interest/interés público inquietudes del público en general (pág. 54)

publicly held corporation/empresa pública compañía que vende valores en el mercado libre (pág. 196)

public sector/sector público parte de la economía que implica las transacciones del gobierno (pág. 63)

purchasing power/poder adquisitivo capacidad de comprar bienes y servicios (pág. 339)

put option/opción de venta opción para vender acciones en un tiempo determinado en el futuro (pág. 288)

Q

quantity supplied/volumen de oferta cantidad que un proveedor está dispuesto a, y es capaz de, producir a un precio determinado (pág. 101)

quantity theory/teoría cuantitativa del dinero teoría que afirma que demasiado dinero en la economía produce inflación (pág. 341)

R

rationing/racionamiento sistema para asignar o distribuir bienes y servicios escasos pero sin considerar los precios (pág. 141)

real GDP/PIB real producto interno bruto expresado en precios constantes o invariables (pág. 304)

real GDP per capita /PIB real per cápita producto interno bruto real dividido por la población total (pág. 319)

real property/bienes inmuebles propiedades físicas como tierras y edificios (pág. 378)

recession/recesión contracción prolongada de la economía (pág. 311)

regressive tax/impuesto regresivo impuesto para el cual el porcentaje de ingresos que se paga en impuestos disminuye conforme aumentan los ingresos (pág. 361)

regulation/regulación intervención del gobierno en un mercado que afecta la producción de un bien (pág. 118)

rent control/congelación de rentas precio máximo que se asigna a los alquileres (pág. 129)

representative money/dinero representativo artículos que poseen valor porque el tenedor puede intercambiarlos por otro objeto de valor (pág. 247)

required reserve ratio (RRR)/coeficiente de reserva requerido (CRR) coeficiente de reservas para los depósitos en los bancos requerido por la Reserva Federal (pág. 425)

résumé/resumé documento que resume la experiencia laboral, los estudios realizados y otros datos que califican a una persona, y que necesita saber un patrón potencial (pág. 526)

return/ganancia dinero que recibe un inversionista mucho más allá de la suma de dinero que invirtió inicialmente (pág. 274)

revenue/ingresos rentas públicas que recibe el gobierno por concepto de impuestos y otras fuentes exentas de impuestos (pág. 359)

right-to-work law/ley sobre libertad laboral medida que prohíbe el ingreso obligatorio a un sindicato (pág. 231)

royalty/regalía participación de ganancias dada como pago (pág. 202)

S

S & P 500/S & P 500 (por sus siglas en inglés para Standard and Poor's Corporation) índice que representa los precios de 500 valores diferentes (pág. 290)

safety net/red de asistencia: programas del gobierno que protegen a las personas que pasan por condiciones económicas adversas (pág. 26)

sales tax/impuesto sobre las ventas impuesto sobre el valor del dólar de un bien o producto en venta (pág. 360)

saving/ahorros ingresos que no se usan para el consumo (pág. 320)

savings account/cuenta de ahorros cuenta bancaria que se usa para depositar dinero que se pudiera necesitar en un tiempo relativamente corto (pág. 506)

savings and loans associations/sociedades de ahorro y préstamo bancos que aceptan depósitos y que se especializan en financiamientos a largo plazo (pág. 511)

savings bank/caja de ahorros banco que acepta depósitos y que se especializa en inversiones de bajo riesgo (pág. 511)

savings bond/bono de ahorro bono de bajo valor emitido por el gobierno de Estados Unidos (pág. 280)

savings rate/tasa de ahorros proporción de los ingresos disponibles gastados a los ingresos ahorrados (pág. 320)

scarcity/escasez cantidades limitadas de recursos para poder satisfacer necesidades ilimitadas (pág. 4)

screening effect/efecto pantalla teoría que afirma que completar los estudios universitarios les indica a los patrones que un candidato a un puesto es una persona inteligente y trabajadora (pág. 214)

search costs/costos de indagación costos financieros y de oportunidad que pagan los consumidores cuando buscan un bien o un servicio (pág. 136)

seasonal unemployment/desempleo estacional desempleo que ocurre como resultado de cosechas programadas, días festivos y vacaciones o cuando las industrias reducen sus actividades o cierran por una temporada (pág. 332)

secondary market/mercado secundario mercado para la reventa de activos financieros (pág. 283)

Securities and Exchange Commission/Comisión del Mercado de Valores organismo independiente del gobierno que regula los mercados financieros y las compañías inversionistas (pág. 281)

security deposit/depósito de garantía suma de dinero que se paga a un arrendador con el fin de asegurar que los bienes se devuelvan en las mismas condiciones que tenían al momento de arrendarse (pág. 522)

self-interest/interés propio ganancia personal propia (pág. 31)

semi-skilled labor/mano de obra semicalificada mano de obra que requiere educación y destrezas de especialización mínimas (pág. 221)

service cooperative/cooperativa de servicios cooperativa que proporciona un servicio en lugar de un bien o producto (pág. 203)

services/servicios medidas o actividades que una persona realiza para otra (pág. 3)

share/acción parte de valores o títulos (pág. 285)

shortage/insuficiencia situación en la cual un bien o un servicio no se encuentra disponible (pág. 4), o una situación en la cual el volumen de demanda es mayor que el volumen de oferta (pág. 136)

skilled labor/mano de obra calificada mano de obra que requiere educación y destrezas especializadas (pág. 221)

socialism/socialismo filosofía social y política que se basa en la creencia de que se deben utilizar medios democráticos para distribuir la riqueza uniformemente en una sociedad (pág. 35)

Social Security (OASDI)/Seguro Social Seguro de edad avanzada, sobrevivientes y invalidez (pág. 367)

sole proprietorship/negocio propio negocio que pertenece a una sola persona, la cual lo administra (pág. 185)

special economic zones/zonas económicas especiales regiones designadas en China donde se fomenta la inversión extranjera, las empresas pueden tomar la mayoría de sus propias decisiones sobre inversiones y producción y donde se permite que operen las compañías extranjeras (pág. 494)

specialization/especialización concentración de los esfuerzos productivos de individuos y de empresas en un número limitado de actividades (pág. 29)

speculation/especulación práctica de realizar inversiones de alto riesgo con dinero prestado con la esperanza de lograr grandes ganancias (pág. 290)

spillover costs/costos indirectos costos de producción que influyen sobre las personas que no tienen ningún control sobre la manera en que se produce un bien (pág. 144)

stabilization program/programa de estabilización convenio entre una nación deudora y el FMI (Fondo Monetario Internacional) por el cual la nación acuerda revisar su política económica (pág. 488)

standard of living/nivel de vida nivel de prosperidad económica (pág. 26)

stagflation/estanflación disminución del PIB real conjuntamente con un aumento del nivel de precios (pág. 311)

start-up costs/costos iniciales gastos que debe pagar una empresa antes de poder producir y vender bienes (pág. 153)

stock/valores o títulos acción que representa una parte de la participación accionaria en una sociedad anónima (págs. 195, 507)

stock exchange/bolsa de valores mercado para la compra y venta de valores (pág. 287)

stock split/división de acciones división de una acción en más de una (pág. 286)

stockbroker/corredor o agente de bolsa persona que es el vínculo entre compradores y vendedores de valores (pág. 286)

store of value/reserva de valor algo que mantiene su valor si se guarda en lugar de usarlo (pág. 244)

strike/huelga paro organizado de trabajadores cuyo objetivo es obligar a un patrón a considerar peticiones sindicales (pág. 229)

structural unemployment/desempleo estructural o endémico desempleo que ocurre cuando las destrezas que poseen los trabajadores no coinciden con los trabajos disponibles (pág. 332)

subsidized loans/préstamos subvencionados préstamos en los cuales gobierno paga el interés mientras el estudiante asiste a la escuela o la universidad (pág. 518)

subsidy/subvención ayuda económica que otorga el gobierno para auxiliar una empresa o un mercado (pág. 117)

subsistence agriculture/agricultura de subsistencia nivel de agricultura en el cual una persona produce sólo los alimentos suficientes para alimentar a su familia (pág. 472)

substitutes/substitutos productos que se usan en lugar de otros (pág. 88)

substitution effect/efecto de substitución cuando los consumidores reaccionan a un alza en el precio de un producto consumiendo una menor cantidad de ese producto y una mayor cantidad de otros productos (pág. 80)

supply/oferta la cantidad de bienes disponible (pág. 101)

supply curve/curva de la oferta gráfica del volumen de oferta de un producto en cada precio posible (pág. 104)

supply schedule/cuadro de oferta tabla que muestra una lista de la cantidad de un producto que un proveedor ofrecerá a precios diferentes (pág. 103)

supply shock/contracción de la oferta escasez repentina de un producto (pág. 141)

supply-side economics/economía de oferta doctrina económica que establece que una reducción de los impuestos puede ayudar a la economía al aumentar la oferta (pág. 399)

surplus/superávit situación en la cual el volumen de oferta es mayor que el volumen de demanda; oferta excedente (pág. 134)

T

tariff/arancel aduanero impuesto sobre los bienes importados (págs. 369, 450)

tax/impuesto pago obligatorio a un gobierno local, estatal o nacional (pág. 359)

taxable income/ingreso imponible ingresos sobre los cuales se debe pagar impuestos; ingresos totales menos las exenciones y deducciones (pág. 366)

tax assessor/tasador de impuestos oficial que evalúa propiedades (pág. 380)

tax base/base imponible ingresos, propiedad, bien o servicio sujetos a impuestos (pág. 360)

tax exempt/exento de impuestos no sujeto a pagar impuestos (pág. 377)

tax incentive/incentivo de impuesto el uso de los impuestos para alentar o desalentar ciertas acciónes específicas (pág. 369)

tax return/declaración de impuestos formulario que utiliza una persona para presentar los impuestos sobre sus ingresos (pág. 366)

technological progress/progreso tecnológico aumento que se logra en el rendimiento al producir más sin usar más recursos (pág. 322)

technology/tecnología proceso que se usa para producir un bien o un servicio (pág. 59)

thinking at the margin/pensar en el margen decidir si se debe hacer o usar una unidad adicional de algún recurso (pág. 10)

tight money policy/política de dinero escaso política monetaria que reduce el medio circulante (pág. 431)

time deposit/depósito a plazo depósito que ofrece interés garantizado durante un período de tiempo fijo (pág. 506)

total cost/costo total costos fijos más costos variables (pág. 111)

total revenue/total de ingresos cantidad total de dinero que recibe una empresa al vender bienes o servicios (pág. 95)

trade association/asociación mercantil organismo sin fines de lucro que fomenta los intereses de una industria en particular (pág. 204)

trade barrier/barrera comercial medios para evitar que un producto o servicio extranjero entre libremente al territorio de una nación (pág. 449)

trade deficit/déficit de la balanza comercial resultado de un país importar más de lo que exporta (pág. 462)

trade-off/concesión mutua alternativa que sacrificamos cuando tomamos una decisión (pág. 8)

trade surplus/superávit de la balanza comercial resultado de un país exportar más de lo que importa (pág. 462)

trade war/guerra comercial ciclo que ocurre cuando un país restringe las importaciones y su socio comercial impone sus propias restricciones (pág. 451)

traditional economy/economía tradicional sistema económico que descansa en hábitos, costumbres y normas para tomar decisiones sobre la producción y consumo de bienes y servicios (pág. 26)

transition/transición período de cambios en el cual una economía se aleja de una economía dirigida o planificada para acercarse a un sistema de mercado (pág. 43)

Treasury bill/obligación del Tesoro a corto plazo bono del gobierno pagadero entre tres meses a un año (pág. 405)

Treasury bond/bono del Tesoro a largo plazo bono del gobierno que se puede emitir hasta 30 años (pág. 405)

Treasury note/pagaré del Tesoro bono del gobierno pagadero entre dos a diez años (pág. 405)

trough/depresión punto más bajo en una contracción económica cuando el producto bruto nacional real deja de caer (pág. 311)

trust/consorcio monopolista agrupación ilegal de compañías que desalientan la competencia (pág. 173)

Truth in Savings Act/Ley de divulgación de información sobre intereses ley federal que dispone que los bancos deben divulgar a sus clientes información pertinente a las cuentas que ofrece el banco que producen intereses (pág. 507)

Truth in Lending laws/leyes de divulgación de información sobre préstamos reglamentos que disponen que las instituciones que otorgan préstamos deben divulgar cargos por financiamiento exactos, tasas de interés mensual, tasas de porcentaje annual y métodos que se utilizan en el cálculo de los cargos por financiamiento (pág. 515)

tuition/matrícula costo de la enseñanza (pág. 516)

U

underemployed/subempleado trabajar en un puesto para el cual la persona está sobrecalificada, o trabajar medio tiempo cuando se desea trabajar tiempo completo (pág. 335)

underutilization/subutilización usar menos recursos de lo que una economía puede usar (pág. 15)

unemployment rate/tasa de desempleo porcentaje de la mano de obra del país que se encuentra desempleada (pág. 334)

Uniform Partnership Act (UPA)/Ley de Uniformidad de las Sociedades Personales ley que dispone intereses comunes de participación accionaria, participación en pérdidas y ganancias y responsabilidades administrativas compartidas en una sociedad personal (pág. 191)

unitary elastic/elástica unitaria describe la demanda cuya elasticidad es exactamente igual a 1 (pág. 91)

United Nations Development Program (UNDP)/Programa de las Naciones Unidas para el Desarrollo programa de las Naciones Unidas dedicado a la eliminación de la pobreza por medio del desarrollo (pág. 487)

unit of account/unidad de cuenta medida que se usa para comparar los valores de bienes y servicios relativos entre sí (pág. 244)

unskilled labor/mano de obra no calificada trabajo que no requiere destrezas, educación o capacitación especializada (pág. 221)

V

variable/variable factor que puede cambiar (pág. 103)

variable cost/costo variable costo que sube o baja según la cantidad que se produzca (pág. 111)

vertical merger/fusión vertical unión de dos o más empresas implicadas en etapas diferentes de producción del mismo bien o servicio (pág. 199)

voluntary exchange/intercambio voluntario concepto que define la libertad de la gente para decidir qué y cuándo quieren comprar o vender (pág. 53)

voluntary export restraint (VER)/limitación voluntaria de las exportaciones limitación autoimpuesta sobre el número de productos que se envían a un determinado país (pág. 449)

wage-price spiral/espiral de salarios y precios proceso mediante el cual los salarios que aumentan pueden provocar precios más altos y, a su vez, los precios más altos fomentan salarios más altos (pág. 342)

want/deseo artículo que deseamos pero que no es indispensable para sobrevivir (pág. 3)

welfare/asistencia social auxilio económico para los necesitados que ofrece el gobierno (pág. 68)

white-collar worker/oficinista persona que tiene un trabajo de oficina y que, por lo general, recibe un sueldo (pág. 232)

withholding/retención retirar pagos del salario de un empleado antes de éste que lo reciba (pág. 366)

work ethic/ética profesional sistema de valores que da importancia principal al trabajo (págs. 59, 491)

workfare/asistencia social a cambio de trabajo programa de asistencia social temporal en el que se requiere que los recipientes realicen un trabajo de servicio público, por lo general (pág. 350)

World Bank/Banco Mundial el proveedor más grande de asistencia técnica y financiera para el desarrollo (pág. 487)

World Trade Organization (WTO)/Organización Mundial del Comercio (O.M.C.) organismo mundial cuya meta es lograr una mayor liberalización del comercio internacional y aranceles aduaneros más bajos (pág. 453)

yield/rendimiento tasa anual de ganancias de un bono si éste no se pagara hasta su vencimiento (pág. 278)

Z

zoning law/ley de zonificación ley municipal que designa áreas separadas para viviendas y para empresas (pág. 187)

Index

Note: An italicized entry with a page number preceded by a *c* indicates a chart; a *g* indicates a graph; an *m* indicates a map; and a *p* indicates a photo.

A

Aaron, Henry J., 370, *p370*
ability-to-pay principle, 362
absolute advantage, 443, *p443*
ACH. *See* Automated Clearing House.
acid rain, 66
actual cash value, 524
ACV. *See* actual cash value.
ADC. *See* Aid to Dependent Children (ADC).
advertising
  in franchises, 202
  nonprice competition and, 168
  professional organizations and, 204
  shifts in demand and, 87–88
AFDC. *See* Aid to Families with Dependent Children (AFDC).
AFL. *See* American Federation of Labor.
Africa, less developed countries in, 471
African Americans, *c224*, 344, *p344*, *c536*, *g537*
  entrepreneurs, 115
  poverty rate and, 346, *c346*, 347
  wage discrimination and, 224–226, *g225*, *g226*
aggregate demand, 307–308, *g307*, *g308*, 399
aggregate supply, 306–307, *g307*, *g308*, 313, 399
agricultural marketing cooperatives, 203
agriculture, *g534*
  arable, 480
  imports and exports, *g535*
  price supports and, 131
  in Soviet Union, 36–37, *p36*, 491
  subsistence, 472, 480
  technology and, *p474*
Aid to Dependent Children (ADC), *c68*
Aid to Families with Dependent Children (AFDC), *c68*, 69, *c69*, 399
airline industry
  deregulation of, 175, 176
  oligopolies and, 170
  targeted discounts and, 163, 164
Alabama
  energy consumption, *g541*
  natural resources, *m532–533*
Alaska
  energy consumption, *g541*
  natural resources, *m532–533*
Albania, 471, *p483*
allocation of resources, 62–66
  externalities, 65–66, *p65*
  public goods, 62–64
Amazon.com, 293
America Online, 293
American Bar Association, 204

American Federation of Labor (AFL), 229
American Management Association, 204
American Marketing Association, 204
American Medical Association, 204
American Revolution, 248
American Telephone & Telegraph (AT&T), 174, *c175*
American Tobacco Company, 174
annual percentage rate (APR), 514–515
Antifederalists, 250–251
antitrust laws, 173, *p173*
APEC. *See* Asian Pacific Economic Cooperation.
appreciation, 459
appropriations bills, 389
APR. *See* annual percentage rate.
arable land, 441, 480
arbitration, 234
Argentina, 404, *m455*, 456
Arizona
  energy consumption, *g541*
  housing costs, *g337*
  natural resources, *m532–533*
Arkansas
  energy consumption, *g541*
  Federal Reserve district, *m417*
  natural resources, *m532–533*
Articles of Confederation, 248
articles of partnership, 191
Ash, Mary Kay, 89, *p89*, 97
Asian Americans, 189, *p189*
Asian Pacific Economic Cooperation (APEC), 455, *m455*
Assessment, 20–21, 46–47, 72–73, 98–99, 122–123, 146–147, 178–179, 206–207, 236–237, 266–267, 294–295, 326–327, 352–353, 382–383, 410–411, 436–437, 466–467, 496–497
  See also Self-assessment.
assets, 192
ATF. *See* Bureau of Alcohol, Tobacco, and Firearms (ATF).
Atlanta, Georgia, *g337*, *m417*
Atlantic City, New Jersey, 97, *p97*
ATM. *See* Automated Teller Machine.
AT&T. *See* American Telephone & Telegraph (AT&T).
Australia
  balanced trade and, 462
  as developed nation, 471
  national budget of, *g547*
  per capita gross domestic product, 472, *g473*
  population, 472
Austria, *g547*
authoritarian, 35
Automated Clearing House (ACH), 264

Automated Teller Machine (ATM), 225, 263, *p263*
automatic stabilizers, 398–399
automobiles
  buying, 520–521
  inflation and, *c338*
  in Japan, 447
  labor unions in manufacturing of, *p228*
  pollution from, 118
  price changes and, 94–95, *p94*
  safety, 19, *p19*
  supply curve and, 135–136
  trade barriers and, 451
automobile insurance, 525

B

baby boomers, 87, 373
balanced budget, 376, 403, 404, 407, 408
balanced budget amendment, 407
balance of trade, 462–464, *g463*, *c464*
Balkan nations, 487
Baltimore, Maryland, *m160*, 172
Bangladesh, 471
bank holding company, 421
bank holiday, 255
banking, 257
  checking accounts, 504–505
  before Civil War, 250–252, *p250*, *p251*
  during Civil War, 253, *p253*
  deregulation of, 175, 176, *c176*, 256
  developments in American, 250–256, *c254*
  electronic, 263–264, *p263*
  Free Banking era, 252, *p252*
  Great Depression and, 255, *p255*, 435
  history, 415–416, *p415*
  reforms, 255
  regulating, 422
  role of money in, 241
  savings accounts, 259, 275, 506–510
  services, 259–262
  See also Federal Reserve System.
Banking Act (1933), 435
Bank of America, 257
Bank of the United States, first and Second, 251–252, 415
bank run, 252, *p255*
banks, 250
  economic stability of, 58
  examinations of, 422
  Federal Reserve System and, 421–422
  as financial intermediaries, 272
  foreign exchange market, 460
  loans and, 260–261
  member banks of the Federal Reserve System, 254
  mergers of, 265

INDEX

consumers of, 24–25
defined, 3
determining what to produce, 23
how to produce, 23–24
severance tax, 378
shares, 285
See also stock.
Shen Qing, 43
Sherman Antitrust Act (1890), 173, 174, *c198*
shortages, 4, 136–137, 142
shutdown, company, 113–114, *p114*
silver certificates, 248
simple interest, 261
Simulations, 48–49, 148–149, 208–209, 296–297, 328–329, 384–385, 468–469
Singapore, 476
as newly industrialized country, 475
as trading partner, *g544, m545*
sin taxes, 369, 378
site permits, 186
Sixteenth Amendment, 360, 528
skilled labor, 221
Skills Activity
analyzing tables, 84, 99
cause and effect, 132, 147
critical thinking, 132, 309, 364, 419
fact and opinion, 364, 383
flowcharts, 45, 47
graphs and charts, 12, 20, 21, 45, 84, 337, 353, 394, 411
Internet research skills, 194, 207
line graphs, 21
multimedia presentations, 448, 467
political cartoons, 155, 179
predicting consequences, 309, 327
primary sources, 61, 73
public opinion polls, 249, 267
reading stock market reports, 284, 295
recognizing bias, 419, 437
social studies, 61, 107, 155, 249, 484
statistics, 218, 237
technology, 194, 293, 448
test-taking, 107, 123
writing process, 484, 497
small business, 208–209
smart cards, 264, 268–269, *p268, g269*
Smith, Adam, 30–31, 32, 33, *p33*, 41, 143–144, 395
Smoot-Hawley Tariff (1930), 451, 453
socialism, 35
Social Security, 43, 234, 370, 372, *p372*, 373, 391, 408, 409
taxes and, 367–368
Social Security Act (1935), 334, 409, *p409*
Social Security Administration, *c68*, 69, 70, 409, *p409*
Social Studies Skills, 61, 107, 155, 249, 484
social welfare programs, 372, *p372*
societal values, 26, 27, 41
sole proprietorships
advantages of, 185–187
defined, 185
disadvantages of, 187–188
role of, 185
Solow, Robert, 323

South Africa, *p156*
South Carolina
energy consumption, *g541*
natural resources, *m532–533*
South Dakota
energy consumption, *g541*
natural resources, *m532–533*
taxes in, 360
Southern Common Market, 455, *m455*
South Korea
economic health of, *c319*
health expenditures, *g547*
multinational corporations in, 200
national budget of, *g547*
as newly industrialized country, 476
population, *p478*
as trading partner, *g544, m545*
Southwest Asia, 441
Soviet Union
centrally planned economy of, 36–37, *p36, p37*
communism in, 491
five-year plans in, 38
goods in, 142
GOSPLAN in, 141
transition to market-based economy, 489, 491–492, *p491, p492*
S & P 500. *See* Standard & Poor's 500.
space technology, 60
specialization, 28–29, *p328*
defined, 29
employment and, 446–447
marginal production of labor and, 109
resources and, 443
unemployment and, 447
specie, 248, 251
speculation, 290–291
spending
consumer expectations and, 313
discretionary, 371, *c371*, 373–374
interest rates and, 430–431
mandatory, 371–373, *c371*
spillover costs, 144
spinoffs, 70
sports marketing, 160, *m160*
SSI. *See* Supplemental Security Income.
stability, economic, 58
stabilization policy, 430–434, *g432*, 488
Stafford Loans, 518
stagflation, 311, 313
Stalin, Joseph, 38
standard of living, 58, 235, 439, *g546, g547*
defined, 26
in free market economy, 41
growth of, 58
Standard Oil Company, *c198*
Standard Oil Trust, 174
Standard & Poor's 500, 279, *c279*, 281, 290
start-up costs, 153
state government
administration of, 377
arts and recreation, 377
balanced budget, 407
budgets, 375–376
business tax, 378
corporate income tax, 378

education and, 376
federal aid to, 374, *p374*
highways and transportation and, 377, *p377*
income tax, 378
public safety and, 376–377
sales tax, 378
tax revenues, 377
Statistical Abstract of the United States, 212
statistics, analyzing, 218, 237
steel industry, *p152, p198*, 232, 317
stock, 197, 507
buying, 285–286, *p285*
defined, 195
measuring performance of, 289–290, *g289*
risks of, 286
trading of, 286–289
types of, 286
stockbroker, 286–287, *p288*, 292
stock exchanges, *p285*, 287–289
stock funds, 509
stock market
dot-coms, 293
Great Crash, 290–292
as leading indicator, 314
online reports, 284
prices, 314
reading reports, *c287*, 295
regulation of, 198
stock splits, 286
stock trading, 58
stored value card, 264, 268–269, *p268, g269*
store of value, 244–245, *c244*
strikes, labor, *p228*, 234
structural unemployment, 332–333, *p332*
students, targeted discounts and, 164
subsidies, 117
subsistence agriculture, 472, 480
substitutes, 88
availability of, 91, 93
substitution effect, 80, *c80*
Sudan, 449
sunspot theory, 310
Super Bowl, 77
supermarkets, 174
Supplemental Security Income (SSI), 373
supply
changes in, 116–120, *p116, c117, p118, p119, p120*
government influence on, 117–119
import restrictions and, 119
in labor, 220
regulations and, 118–119
subsidies and, 117–118
taxes and, 118
supply, law of
elasticity and, 104–106, *c105, p106*
market entry, 102–103
prices, 101–103, *c101*
production, 101–103, *c101*
supply curve, 104, *c104, g105*
supply schedule, 103–104, *c103, c104*
supply and demand, *m160*
affecting wages, 121
combining, 125–131
disequilibrium, 126–128, *g127*, 134–135

Acknowledgments

Team Credits The people who made up the *Economics: Principles in Action* team—representing editorial, editorial services, design services, market research, on-line services/multimedia development, product marketing, production services, and publishing processes—are listed below. Bold type denotes core team members.

Mary Ann Barton, Barbara Bertell, **Peter Brooks**, Margaret Broucek, **Todd Christy**, Lisa J. Clark, Bob Craton, Gabriela Perez Fiato, Paul Gagnon, Jonathan Gorey, **Mary Ann Gundersen**, Katharine Ingram, Tim Jones, Lynne Kalkanajian, Russ Lappa, James Lonergan, Dotti Marshall, Grace Massey, **William McAllister**, Baljit Nijjar, Elizabeth Pearson, Judi Pinkham, Emily Soltanoff, Mark Staloff, Susan Swan, Merce Wilczek, **Tracy C. Wilson**

Contributing Editors
Douglas Kinnear, Trish Taylor

Cover Design
Suzanne Schineller, Sweetlight Creative Partners, The Concept Bank
Front Cover Image, Ralph Mercer Photography

Illustration
Maps: Mapquest.com, Inc. **Charts, graphs and tables:** Precision Graphics, Inc.; J/B Woolsey and Associates; Accurate Art, Inc. **Creative art::** John Bleck 24; Doug Bowles 528; Adam Cohen 505; Jon Conrad 512; John Edwards and Associates 17; Neil Stewart 30, 42, 153, 158, 167, 169, 244, 260, 262, 273, 302, 303, 322, 342, 416, 421, 426, 445, 510; J/B Woolsey and Associates 198, 199, 278

Picture Research
Kerri Hoar, PoYee Oster, Robin Samper

Photography
Table of Contents, Page i, Ralph Mercer; **iv t**, Corel Corp.; **iv tm**, Jan Halaska/Photo Researchers; **iv bm**, Dick Luria/FPG International; **v t**, Todd Davidson/Image Bank/PNI; **v m**, Stone/Don Smetzer; **v b**, Tony Freeman/PhotoEdit; **vi t**, The Granger Collection, New York; **vi m**, Stone/Paul Chesley; **vi b**, James Marshall/The Stock Market; **vii t**, Richard Strauss/National Museum of American History, Smithsonian Institution; **vii m**, Russ Lappa; **vii b**, Stone/Brian Seed; **ix l**, A. Ramey/Stock Boston; **ix m**, AP/Wide World Photos; **ix r**, Jim Harrison/Stock Boston.

UNIT 1 Page xvi-xvii, Neal Preston/Corbis; **2 teens**, David Young-Wolff/PhotoEdit; **2 mall background**, PhotoDisc.; **4**, Jim Felt/Studio 3; **5 tl**, Garry McMichael/Photo Researchers; **5 ml**, William Taufic/The Stock Market; **5 bl**, Roger Ball/Picturesque Stock Photo; **5 m**, Stone/ Steven Peters; **5 r**, Richard Paslet/Stock Boston/PNI; **7 tl**, Ludovic/Rea/SABA Press Photos; **7 background**, Stone/Stuart McClymont; **8**, Corel Corp.; **9**, Reprinted with permission of King Features Syndicate; **12**, Chris Trotman/Duomo; **13 l**, Jeff Tinsley/Smithsonian Institution; **13 r**, The Bancroft Library, Kaiser Pictorial Collections; **14**, ©Tribune Media Services, Inc. All Rights Reserved. Reprinted with permission.; **19 background**, Stone; **19 r**, David Young-Wolff/PhotoEdit; **22**, Stone/Tim Macpherson; **25**, Bob Daemmrich/Stock Boston; **26**, Jean-Gerard Sidaner/Photo Researchers; **28 l**, Stone/Paul Chesley; **28-29**, Jan Halaska/Photo Researchers; **29 inset**, Paul Stepan/Photo Researchers; **31 t**, From *The Wall Street Journal*-Permission, Cartoon Features Syndicate; **31 b**, Bryan F. Peterson /The Stock Market; **33 tl**, Corbis/Bettmann; **33 background**, Museum der Stadt, Vienna, Austria/ET Archive, London/Superstock; **34 l**, Judi Pinkham; **34 r**, A. Keler/Corbis Sygma; **35**, B. Bisson/Corbis Sygma; **36 l**, Corbis/Bettmann; **36 m, r**, Sovfoto; **36-37**, Jeff Greenberg/dMRp/Photo Researchers; **37 t**, Shepard Sherbell/SABA Press Photos; **38**, Ricki Rosen/SABA Press Photos; **39 background**, Charles Steiners/The Image Works; **39 tr**, Stone/Steven Weinberg; **40**, Stone/Bob Handelman; **41**, David M. Grossman/Photo Researchers; **44**, John Banagan/ Image Bank; **45**, Jeff Isaac Greenberg; **48-49 background**, Prentice Hall; **48 l**, Russ Lappa; **48 r**, Thomas R. Fletcher/Stock Boston; **49 bl**, Prentice Hall; **50**, Angelo Cavalli/Image Bank; **51**, Bob Rowan; Progressive Image/Corbis; **52 tl, bl**, Russ Lappa; **52 ml**, Tony Freeman/PhotoEdit; **52 tr, br**, Tony Freeman/PhotoEdit; **53**, National Highway Traffic Safety Administration; **54**, Stone/David Young-Wolff; **56 tl**, Brooks/Glogau Photographers/Federal Reserve Board; **56 background**, Vivian Ronay/Liaison Agency;

57, Brian Orland/ East St. Louis Action Research Project/University of Illinois at Urbana-Champaign; **58 both**, Library of Congress; **59 tl**, Frank Siteman/The Picture Cube; **59 bl**, Tony Freeman/PhotoEdit; **59 tr**, Corbis Sygma; **59 br**, AP/Wide World Photos; **61**, Library of Congress; **63 background**, Stone/Baron Wolman; **63 tl**, MacDonald Photography/Index Stock Imagery; **63 bl**, Bud Freund/Index Stock Imagery; **63 tm**, Michael J. Howell/Index Stock Imagery; **63 tr**, Charles Schoffer/Index Stock Imagery; **63 br**, Stone/Frank Siteman; **64**, Nancy Simmerman/AllStock/PNI; **65 l**, PhotoDisc.; **65 r**, John Elk III/Stock Boston; **66**, Bill Horsman/Stock Boston; **68**, Russ Lappa; **69 l**, Silver Burdett Ginn; **69 r**, AP/Wide World Photos; **71 background**, Superstock; **71 tr**, AP/Wide World Photos; **74-75 background**, Russ Lappa; **74**, A. Ramey/Stock Boston.

UNIT 2 Page 76-77, Chris Trotman/Duomo; **78**, Bill Aron/PhotoEdit; **79**, Stone/Robert Torrez; **81**, Sears Roebuck & Co.; **82**, Index Stock Imagery; **84**, Stone/Ron Sherman; **85**, Jōso Azel/Aurora/PNI; **86**, Stone/Joseph Sohm; **87 t**, Dick Luria/FPG International; **87 b**, Bruce Fier/Liaison Agency; **88**, Stone/Mark Junak; **89 background**, Russ Lappa; **89 inset**, AP/Wide World Photos; **90**, Glasbergen/Rothco Cartoons; **93 l**, Bonnie Kamin/PhotoEdit; **93 r**, Sonda Dawes/The Image Works; **94 t**, Ken Giese/Superstock; **94 bl**,Volkswagen America, Inc.; **94 br**, Stone/Donald Johnston; **97 background**, Craig Hammell/The Stock Market; **97 tr**, Superstock; **100**, Stone/Andy Sacks; **101**, Telegraph Colour Library 1998/FPG International; **102 tl**, Rick Gayle/The Stock Market; **102 bl**, Dennis Hallinan/FPG International; **102 r**, Kelly-Mooney Photography/Corbis; **106 t**, Myrleen Ferguson/PhotoEdit; **106 b**, Ralph Pleasant/FPG International; **107**, Jose L. Pelaez/The Stock Market; **108**, Richard Haynes; **110**, Stone/Jeff Zaruba; **114**, Todd Gipstein/Corbis; **115 background**, Superstock; **115 tl**, Black Entertainment Television; **116 tl**, PhotoDisc.; **116 bl**, Russ Lappa; **116 the rest**, PhotoDisc.; **118**, Stone/Maurice Huser; **119**, ML Sinibaldi/The Stock Market; **120**, Stone/Mark Harwood; **121 background**, Jerry Arcieri/SABA Press Photos; **121 tr**, Darren Carroll/Duomo; **123**, Baloo/Rothco Cartoons; **124**, Stone/Charles Gupton; **125**, Phil McCarten/Photo Edit; **128**, Stone/Peter Pearson; **130**, David Young-Wolff/Photo Edit; **132**, Russ Lappa; **133**, Todd Davidson/Image Bank/PNI; **136**, Russ Lappa; **138 background**, B. Daemmrich/The Image Works; **138 tl**, B.Daemmrich/Corbis Sygma; **139**, Russ Lappa; **141**, H. Armstrong Roberts; **142**, Greg Girard/Contact Press; **143**, David McIntyre/Black Star; **143 inset**, Stone/Keren Su; **144**, Stone/Craig Wells; **145 background**, Owen Franken/Corbis; **145 tr**, Jeff Sciortino Photography; **148-149 background**, Prentice Hall; **148 l**, Russ Lappa; **148 r**, PhotoDisc.; **149 bl**, Prentice Hall; **150**, Stan Sholik/FPG Intenational; **151**, Mark Tomalty/Masterfile; **152 l**, Miro Vintoniv/Index Stock Imagery; **152 r**, Mark Tomalty/Masterfile; **155 l**, Superstock; **155 br**, ©Tribune Media Services, Inc. All Rights Reserved. Reprinted with permission.; **156**, G. Biss/Masterfile; **158**, David J. Carol/Image Bank; **159**, A. Ramey/Stock Boston; **163 l**, Stone/David Young Wolff; **163 m**, Brent Jones/Stock Boston; **163 r**, Will McIntyre/Photo Researchers; **165 tl**, Microsoft; **165 background**, Stone/Peter Poulides; **166**, Russ Lappa; **168**, L. Mulvehill/The Image Works; **171**, Stone; **172**, Stone/John Elk; **173, 174 l**, Culver Pictures; **174 r**, Brown Brothers; **175 tl**, Stone/Jon Ortner; **175 tr**, AP/Wide World Photos; **175 bm**, Corbis; **176**, AP Photo/Chris O'Meara; **177 background**, Mark Peterson/SABA Press Photos; **177 tr**, John Coletti/Stock Boston; **177 br**, Corel Corp.; **179**, United Feature Syndicate; **180-181 background**, Russ Lappa; **180**, Michael Newman/PhotoEdit.

UNIT 3 Page 182-183, Peter Vandemark/Stock Boston; **184**, Walter Bibikow/FPG International; **185**, Stone/Don Smetzer; **187**, Jose Luis Pelaez Inc./The Stock Market; **189 background**, David Young-Wolfe/PhotoEdit; **189 tl**, Courtesy of Yahoo!; **190**, Tony Freeman/PhotoEdit; **192**, The New Yorker Collection 1995 Roz Chast from cartoonbank.com. All Rights Reserved.; **193**, Stone/Bruce Ayres; **194**, Jon Feingersh; **195**, Leonard Harris/Stock Boston; **200**, Les Stone/Corbis Sygma; **201**, Index Stock Imagery; **202**, Young-Wolff/PhotoEdit; **203**, Bob Daemmrich/Stock Boston; **204 l**, The American Veterinary Medical Association for Veterinarians; **204 tm**, Better Business Bureau; **204 tr**, Lake Norman Chamber of Commerce; **204 br**, American Dental Association; **205 background**, Brian Seed; **205 both**, Courtesy of the Hitchiner Corporation; **208-209 background**, Prentice Hall; **208 l**, Russ Lappa; **208 r**, Bill Bachmann/Stock Boston; **209 bl**, Prentice Hall; **210**, Stone/Steve Smith; **213 l**, The Granger Collection, New York; **213 r**, Corbis/Bettmann; **214**, Corbis/Bettmann; **217**, Bill Pugliano/Liaison Agency; **219 background**, Richard Faverty/Liaison Agency; **219 tr**, Donald C. Johnson/The Stock Market; **219 br**, Corel Corp.; **220**, Stone/Gene Peach; **222**, Charlie Wasterman/Liaison Agency; **227**, Ed Quinn/SABA Press Photos; **228 tl**, Library of Congress; **228 background**, Culver Pictures; **232**, DILBERT reprinted by permission of United Feature Syndicate, Inc.; **234**, Russ Lappa; **235 background**, Ewing Galloway/Index Stock; **235 inset**, Farmhouse Productions/Image Bank; **238-239 background**, Russ Lappa ; **238**, J.L.Bulcao/Liaison Agency.

Text Acknowledgments
In the News
All of the In the News features include excerpts from articles that have appeared in The Wall Street Journal Classroom Edition as referenced below. Wall Street Journal Classroom Edition articles were originally published in The Wall Street Journal. All excerpts are used by permission of Dow Jones & Company. © 1997, 1998, 1999, 2000, 2001 Dow Jones & Company, Inc. All rights reserved.

Chapter 1: p. 5: from "Here's the Scoop" by Hilary Stout. May 2000, p. 8. p. 16: from "Electronic Paper" by Alec Klein, March 2000, p. 7. Chapter 2: p. 25: from "Forces of Nature." April 1999, p. 12. p. 37: from "Belarus is Tough Going for Entrepreneurs" by Mark Whitehouse. December 1998, p. 7. Chapter 3: p. 53: from "Freedom Counts" editorial, January 2001, p.23. p. 59: from "Working for Life" by Carlos Tejada, November 2000, p. 18. Chapter 4: p. 80: from "Teen Trendsetters" by Michael J. McCarthy. February 1999, p. 17. Chapter 5: p. 102: from "Making Money Isn't So Bad" editorial, March 2000, p. 14. Chapter 6: p. 135: from "Big Breakthrough" by Dean Takahashi. February 1998, p. 12. Chapter 7: p. 170: from "Playing Oligopoly" by G. Pascal Zachary. May 1999, p. 13. Chapter 8: p. 188: from "Another Path to Success" by Paulette Thomas, September 2000, p. 8. p. 192: from "Mothers and Daughters Team Up as Entrepreneurs" by Michael Selz. October 1997, p. 7. Chapter 9: p. 222: from "'Soft' Skills Sell" by Peter Vogt, November 2000, p. 11. p. 233: from "Temporary Rewards" by Timothy D. Schellhardt. March 1999, p. 6. Chapter 10: p. 252: from "Common Currency" by Lawrence Ingrassia. March 1998, p. 14. p. 260: from "Lending a Hand" by Paulette Thomas. January 1998, p. 7. Chapter 11: p. 275: from "Life on the Edge" by Bernard Wysocki, Jr. October 1999, p. 5. p. 286: from "Stash Your Cash" by Jonathan Clements. September 1998, p. 19. Chapter 12: p. 314: from "Economic ABCs: Jobs, debt and the economy" by Tristan Marby. November 1999, p. 14. p. 324: from "High and Dry" by Lee Gomes. February 1998, pp. 1, 5. Chapter 13: p. 336: from "Mind Your A's and B's" by Cheryl Matherly, November 2000, p. 10. p. 347: from "Poor Prospects" by Tony Horwitz. January 1998, p. 5. Chapter 14: p. 362: from "Tax Holiday in Texas" by Erik Siemers and Emily Nelson. November 1999, p. 19. p. 373: from "Health–Care Glossary." December 1997, p. 12. Chapter 15: p. 401: from "Payback Time" by Jacob M. Schlesinger. February 1999, p. 14. Chapter 16: p. 426: from "On the Rebound" by Fred R. Bleakly. September 1997, p. 14. p. 433: from "The Gloom Factor" by Jacob M. Schlesinger. October 1998, p. 14. Chapter 17: p. 456: from "Crossing Borders" by Joseph B. White. November 1998, pp. 1, 5. p. 463: from "Port of Last Resort" by Bernard Wysocki, Jr. December 1998, p. 1. Chapter 18: p. 481: from "Come on Down" by Joel Millman, March 2000, p. 14. p. 494: from "What's News: World Wide." October 1997, p. 3.

Debating Current Issues
The Debating Current Issues features include excerpts from articles that have appeared in The Wall Street Journal Classroom Edition as referenced below. Wall Street Journal Classroom Edition articles were originally published in The Wall Street Journal. All excerpts are used by permission of Dow Jones & Company. © 1997, 1998, 1999 Dow Jones & Company, Inc. All rights reserved.

pp. 74-75: from "Union Pacific Faces a Foe It Can't Easily Steamroller" by Marc Lifsher, The Wall Street Journal, Dec. 16, 1998, page CA1 . pp. 180-181: from "Minimum Wage: Make It a Living Wage" by Robert E. Rubin, Ronald Brown, Robert R. Reich, Joseph E. Stiglitz, and Laura D'Andrea Tyson. September 1996, p. 20. From "Minimum Wage: Don't Raise It" by Dee Dee Stanback. September 1996, p. 20. pp. 238-239: from "Trading Places: Brazilian Program Tries to Put Child Laborers Back in School" by Matt Moffett. January 1999, pp. 1 and 18. pp. 268-269: from "Future Shop" by Nicholas Bray. November 1995, p. 8. pp. 354-355: from "The Results Are In: Welfare Reform Works" by Nancy L. Johnson, The Wall Street Journal, Aug. 24, 1999, p. A18 . From "Why a Welfare Success Story May Go Back on Welfare" by Christina Duff, September 1999, p. 23. pp. 412-413: from "Payback Time" by Jacob M. Schlesinger. February 1999, p. 14. pp. 498-499: from "Winners and Losers," by Michael M. Phillips, May 1997, p. 14.